SCOTTISH QUOTATIONS

SCOTTISH QUOTATIONS

Compiled and Edited by

David Ross

Birlinn

First published in 2001 by
Birlinn Limited
8 Canongate Venture
5 New Street
Edinburgh EH8 8BH

www.birlinn.co.uk

ISBN 1 84158 099 6

British Library Cataloguing in Publication Data
A catalogue record for this book is available from the British Library

Typeset by Brinnoven, Livingston
Printed and bound by Creative Print and Design, Ebbw Vale

For Helen R. Ross

I know heaps of quotations, so I can always make a fair show of knowledge.

O. Douglas

Generally speaking, Scottish anthologies are apt to be both hackneyed and solemn.

Donald and Catherine Carswell, Preface to The Scots Week-End

To be occasionally quoted is the only fame I care for.

Alexander Smith, Dreamthorp

Do you know, I pick up favourite quotations, and store them in my mind as ready armour, offensive or defensive, amid the struggle of this turbulent existence.

Robert Burns, letter to Mrs Dunlop *(1792)*

CONTENTS

INTRODUCTION

Like loose scree on the mountains, quotations lie free on the slopes of literature and learning. Part of the great structure, they are yet individual and detachable. It is easy to pick up and carry away a few. But scree has mostly a somewhat dull uniformity, all the product of the same bedrock from which it has been broken. The bedrock of quotations is an infinitely variable matrix, holding jewels of contrasting colour, shape and density.

In the mind's dimension, a collection of Scottish quotations has a similar effect to a child's join-the-dots picture – it provides an outline of the national mind and its main predilections, from the days of William Dunbar to those of Irvine Welsh. In less modest moments it can seem that, in a collection such as this, the inner *arcanum* of the Scots nature is revealed – but if so, it is in no single place but spread in fragments throughout the book. Nor is the picture complete. Some writers are much more quotable than others; it is a matter of style and thought process, in bringing a complex content into a succinct form. The expressive sharpness and variety of Robert Burns' thoughts stand out. He is immensely quotable, as are Carlyle, Stevenson and MacDiarmid. In Carlyle's case, his quotability is currently in inverse proportion to his general readability. In contrast to that thumping earnestness, Stevenson's thought seems fluid and feminine. But both are also capable on occasion of resounding shallowness concealed by the surface shine of the words. MacDiarmid, at least in those extracts short enough to be quotations, is more consistent. The true pleasure of the quotation collector, however, is in finding a prize specimen in some unpromising or desert place. Turn almost any page of Carlyle, and you find a quotable thought. The same is not true of David Hume or James Mill. Great thinkers whose style is discursive and analytical rather than assertive or metaphorical are a challenge to the quotation hunter. Some of the best quotations come from writers considered second rate: see John Davidson. This collection also explores new ground, not only among writers of today, but among men of science – especially those who lived and wrote at a time when they were expected to have a touch of literary style as part of their overall competence.

In compiling an anthology of Scottish quotations, the editor has to frame a few ground rules, and make some definitions. A Scottish quotation can be a quotation with a Scottish theme, taken from any text by a writer of any nationality. Or it can be a quotation from a Scottish writer, on any subject under the sun. This anthology encompasses both. Far too many interesting, challenging or amusing things have been said by non-Scots about Scotland and the Scots to be ignored.

But what is a Scottish writer? If the anthologist used the selection rules of international football in making a choice, the range would be wide. From the eighteenth century onwards, the Scottish diaspora has ensured that many first- and second-generation immigrants have become literary lights in other countries. Immanuel Kant was only two generations away from his Cant forefathers in Scotland. J. K. Galbraith has written memorably of the Scots community in Canada into which he was born. One of the United States' founding fathers, John Adams, felt able to call another, Alexander Hamilton, 'the bastard brat of a Scottish peddlar'. And even within the bounds of the island of Great Britain, what are we to make of Byron (in his own words 'half a Scot by birth, And bred a whole one'), or John Stuart Mill, with his Scots father? Or John Ruskin, born in Herne Hill of expatriate Scots parents? Or Marie Stopes, born in Edinburgh of a Scots mother, but immediately removed to her father and home in England? All such figures have been excluded as not *echt*-Scottish, and hence ineligible – except if making quotable remarks on Scottish themes. Non-emigrant colonial birth is another matter. Despite his English education and *milieu*, we have used the accident of Saki's birth in India and his Scottish pedigree to claim his scintillating fragments. Another difficult area is entered where undoubted Scots have been assimilated to the very centre of 'English' cultural life. James Boswell and Thomas Campbell are prime examples. We have omitted quotations from the Londoner Boswell (though not the Edinburgh/Auchinleck one). And should Campbell's lines about the 'meteor flag of England' be included in an anthology of Scottish quotations? Why not? But we have not. We have tried to apply the national attribute of 'whunstane common sense' to the matter. Scottish viewpoints on life outside Scotland are essential elements in a collection like this. But *Ye Mariners of England* seems out of place: to retrieve the geological analogy, it is not conformable with the general theme. As a broad rule, we have collected quotations from Scottish writers on Scottish and general topics, but left lying those which focus on topics neither Scottish nor general.

Language is a further thistly question. Scotland has always had two languages – three if the general use of Latin in intellectual topics up to the eighteenth century is included. The Gaelic inheritance is rich and too little respected and known. But a quotation in translation almost invariably loses the shape and shine of the original. The only exceptions are pithy and epigrammatic thoughts, which acquire a new though perhaps different polish. Gaelic is a superb language of reflection and description, but much of its spirit dies in translation. Transliteration of thoughts which have been plucked from their living element is tedious and uninspiring to read. As a result, we have included quotations from Gaelic translations only where either an epigrammatic or emphatic quality or a strongly individual sense of personality give life to the English version; and look forward one day to a complete *Faclair nam Luaidhean*.

The last element of introduction is the compiler's point of departure. What is a quotation? In this book, it is a brief extract from a longer published work, which can stand as a piece of writing in its own right. It may frame an original or distinctive thought. It may express a common thought or feeling in an original or memorable way. It may shed light on the nature of the person who wrote it or the society from which it came. It may live anywhere on the line between profound truth and complete nonsense. It may be an especially vivid descriptive phrase, like Scott's 'sea of upturned faces'. Rarely will it contain more than one idea – the essence of an effective quotation is targeting: both its own inward concentration of sense on a single theme, and its outward deployment to precisely fit the purpose of the user. It follows that a quotation must be brief. Most importantly, it must carry a charge of its own, a positive spark, of humour, or passionate feeling, that leaps at the speed of thought to energise a receptive point within the being of the reader. Facts, descriptions or 'historical documents' are not enough. It may be interesting to know how many rivets there are in the Forth Bridge, but a mere piece of information does not create a true quotation, which must have at least a glimmering of an integral aesthetic or emotional quality.

Having made these ground rules, we have not hesitated to break them, but not very often.

This collection, the largest and most varied collection of Scottish quotations to be published, is grouped around almost seventy themes. Within each theme (except for Real Places), authors are placed in alphabetical order, after Anonymous and Traditional. To a degree, the themes have selected themselves. Many are classic fields of human thought and experience, which inevitably throw up the richest crop of quotable lines. But partly in the interest of the browser's enjoyment, and partly in the interest of avoiding an awful predictability, we have combined opposites in some sections, and tried to keep most themes as broad as possible in order to introduce as much variety as possible. The happy accidents of alphabetic proximity can be illuminating as well as fun. Adjacent quotations can sometimes strike sparks from one another. Above all, in sections like 'Land', or 'People' the variety of the quotations reflects the many-layered quality of individual observation and experience. The reader who wishes to find highly specific topics or particular authors should turn to the Indexes. The Keyword Index in particular has been compiled to help readers in the familiar predicament of trying desperately to resurrect a tantalisingly fugitive line from a single remembered word.

Quotations chart a shifting culture-scape, and there are hazards. Some much-quoted authors of earlier years now seem empty of interest and point. Words turn on their creators sometimes, and may lead them into the valley of Bathos. (William McGonagall might be expected to figure large here. But true Bathos requires an innocence of intention; and however sincere he may have been, he lost his innocence early on.) With Bathos goes Vacuity. This again could be a very large section, but splendid Vacuity is as rare as any other jewel. Another danger is that some writers of today, bright and keenly relevant as their remarks appear to be, may end up as suppliers of tomorrow's fustian. It follows from all that, that the collection will have to be revised one day. In anticipation of this, we will welcome, care of the publishers, all suggestions for addition, correction and deletion.

I am grateful to Nick Hern and Hugh Andrew for pointing me in the direction of some excellent specimens in drama and sport respectively, and to Helen R. Ross for many suggestions and contributions and her sustaining interest in the project. And finally to Janetta, Isabel and Miranda for living alongside me while the work was being done.

Actors, Acting and the Theatre

1 The theatre is a school in which much good or evil may be learned.

Joanna Baillie (1762–1851), Introductory Discourse to A Series of Plays

2 Some disquieting confessions must be made in printing at last the play of *Peter Pan*: among them is this, that I have no recollection of having written it.

J. M. Barrie (1860–1937), Introduction to the playscript of Peter Pan

3 Actors . . . tell tales of, for example, Macduff, where the company, after spending the day putting up their set, were asked by the hall-keeper, 'Well, fit film're we gettin' the night?'

Alasdair Cameron, Introduction to Scot-Free, New Scottish Plays *(1990)*

4 In 1844 a total of 96,000 people paid a penny to see the 'Bosjesmans'. They were advertised as primitive tribesmen from Africa, though they were rumoured to be Irish labourers dressed in feathers and rabbit-skins whose primitive language was Gaelic. It was also said that one of the Bosjesmans ate live rats as part of their performance. This certainly outdid another showman who merely bit off their heads and skinned them with his teeth.

Alasdair Cameron, Popular Entertainment in 19th Century Glasgow *(1990)*

5 It's a strange state of affairs when even in Scotland the use of Scots is taken by audiences as a signal to laugh.

James Campbell, Invisible Country *(1989)*

6 To an artiste, applause is like a banquet . . . Thanks for the cheese sandwich.

Billy Connolly (1942–), to a Glasgow audience, quoted in D. Campbell, Billy Connolly: The Authorised Version *(1976)*

7 I felt very sorry for her, but I thought she had given such a poor showing at the audition that I said . . . 'My dear, the best thing you can do is to get married, have a lot of children, and forget you ever wanted to go on the stage.' How wrong I was. Her name was Deborah Kerr.

Charles Landstone, theatre manager, quoted in Eric Brown, Deborah Kerr *(1977)*

8 The trial turns preceding mine had all got short shrift. Most of them were 'off' in less than a minute, and those who didn't willingly retire of their own accord were promptly hauled off by the stage manager by the aid of a long crooked stick which he unceremoniously hooked round their necks . . . Before I left, Mrs Bayliss came round and congratulated me. 'Gang hame and practise, Harry', she said.

Sir Harry Lauder (1875–1950), Roaming in the Gloaming, *on his stage debut*

9 It occurred to all of us that the club would make more money if we didn't perform, and the audience could concentrate on serious drinking for the evening.

John McGrath (1935–), on playing 'The Game's a Bogey' to a miners' club in Glenrothes

10 The imitated Scots of the stage is seldom a happy imitation.

Henry Mackenzie (1745–1831), quoted in H. W. Thomson, The Anecdotes and Egotisms of Henry Mackenzie

11 . . . when I did my fireman sketch in Scotland, a very distinguished critic, Mamie Crichton, came backstage and said it was scandalous what I was doing with the hose nozzle between my legs – I said to her, 'Och, Mamie, the precedent for phallic comedy goes right back to Aristofar-knees.' There wasn't a peep out of her after that.

Duncan Macrae (1905–1967), quoted in Ned Sherrin, Theatrical Anecdotes *(1991)*

12 . . . a meeting that Bridie was holding complained about the treatment the Scottish theatre was getting from the Scottish press. Some laconic fellow beside me said, 'Mr Bridie, it sounds to me as if it isn't criticism you want, it's praise.'
'Yes,' cried Bridie, 'praise, damn you, praise, that's what we want!'

Kenneth Roy, Conversations in a Small Country *(1989), on J. M. Bridie (Osborne Henry Mavor, 1888–1951)*

13 The theatre in Scotland has never been a powerful institution . . . The obvious explanation is that the Scot has to act his part all his life.

Wilfred Taylor, Scot Free *(1953)*

14 English players, comedians and strollers, come down to fill up our cup of sin.
> *Robert Wodrow (1679–1734), Analecta, on the Edinburgh theatre in the early 18th century*

Advice, Aphorisms and Epithets

1 Don't quote your proverb until you bring your ship into port.
> *Gaelic Proverb*

2 Three things come without seeking – jealousy, terror and love.
> *Anonymous, from Gaelic*

3 Scarce though the squirrels are, a way can be found of catching them.
> *Anonymous, 16th century,* MacGriogair à Ruadhshruth (MacGregor of Roros)

4 Though the hawk is noble,
it is often captured by guile.
> *Anonymous,* MacGriogair à Ruadhshruth

5 The earth goeth on the earth glistring
like gold,
The earth goes to the earth sooner
than it wold,
The earth builds on the earth castles
and towers,
The earth says to the earth, All shall
be ours.
> *Anonymous inscription from Melrose Abbey, noted in R. F. Mackenzie,* The Search For Scotland *(1989)*

6 Get seek your succour where ye paid blackmail.
> *Anonymous,* Jamie Telfer in the Fair Dodhead

7 The higher up the plum-tree grows,
The sweeter grow the plums;
The more the cobbler plies his trade,
The broader grow his thumbs.
> *Anonymous,* The Presbyterian Cat *(said to be a precentors' practice-verse)*

8 A good wife, a good cow, and a good razor.
> *Anonymous East Lothian farmer, describing the most valuable possessions of a farm labourer, to the Poor Law Commissioners in 1843, quoted in T. C. Smout,* A Century of the Scottish People, 1830–1950 *(1986)*

9 Times daily change and we likewise
in them;
Things out of sight do straight forgotten
die.
> *William Alexander (c.1567–1640),* Aurora

10 Ye need a cheery hert
To play the gangrel pairt.
> *J. K. Annand (1908–1993),* The Gangrel Scholars

11 Hame's hame, be it ever so hamely.
> *John Arbuthnot (1667–1735),* The Law is a Bottomless Pit

12 He lives from hand to mouth.
> *John Arbuthnot,* The History of John Bull *(1712)*

13 Poverty parts good company.
> *Joanna Baillie (1762–1851),* Poverty Parts Good Company

14 Pampered vanity is a better thing perhaps than starved pride.
> *Joanna Baillie,* The Election

15 For ilka blade o' grass
Keeps its ain drap o' dew.
> *James Ballantine (1808–1877),* Its Ain Drap o' Dew

16 A wee thing maks us think, a sma' thing maks us stare.
> *James Ballantine,* Castles in the Air

17 Creep awa', my bairnie, creep afore ye gang.
> *James Ballantine,* Creep Afore Ye Gang

18 You have been warned against letting the golden hours slip by. Yes, but some of them are golden only because we let them slip.
> *J. M. Barrie (1860–1937), rectorial address to St Andrews University (1922)*

19 Never ascribe to an opponent motives meaner than your own.
> *J. M. Barrie, rectorial address to St Andrews University*

20 Concentrate though your coat-tails be on fire.
> *J. M. Barrie,* Tommy and Grizel

21 'It's "Damn you, Jack, I'm all right," with you chaps.'
> *Sir David Bone (1874–1959),* The Brassbounder

22   . . . hypocrisy, in moderation, is oil to the wheels, a concession to society, lots of other excellent things.

  James Bridie (Osborne Henry Mavor, 1888–1951), letter to Neil Gunn, January 1932

23   Put legs to your dreams.

  Hamish Brown (1934–), The Priceless Gifts, in A. Kamm and A. Lean, A Scottish Childhood (1985)

24   High jinks go with low company

  Ivor Brown, A Word in Your Ear (1942)

25   'It's a great life if you don't weaken.'

  John Buchan (1875–1940), Mr Standfast

26   We can pay our debts to the past by putting the future in debt to ourselves.

  John Buchan, coronation address to the people of Canada, 1937

27   A fool and his money are soon parted.

  Attributed to George Buchanan (c.1506–1582)

28   Then gently scan your brother man,
  Still gentler, sister woman:'
  Tho' they may gang a kennin wrang,
  To step aside is human.

  Robert Burns (1759–1796), Address to the Unco Guid

29   Speak out, and never fash your thumb.

  Robert Burns, The Author's Earnest Cry and Prayer to the Honourable and Right Honourable The Scotch Representatives at the House of Commons

30   Nae man can tether time nor tide.

  Robert Burns, Tam o' Shanter

31   The rank is but the guinea's stamp,
  The Man's the gowd for a' that.

  Robert Burns, A Man's a Man for a' That

32   Heaven can boil the pot
  Tho' the Deil piss in the fire.

  Robert Burns, The Dean of Faculty

33   Facts are chiels that winna ding,
  And downa be disputed.

  Robert Burns, A Dream

34   Curst common sense – that imp o' hell.

  Robert Burns, The Ordination

35   Reader, attend! whether thy soul
  Soars Fancy's flights beyond the pole,
  Or darkling grubs this earthly hole
  In low pursuit;
  Know, prudent, cautious self-control
  Is Wisdom's root.

  Robert Burns, A Bard's Epitaph

36   Whistle o'er the lave o't.

  Robert Burns, Whistle o'er the Lave o't

37   Whatever is unknown is magnified.

  Calgacus (c.60 AD), quoted by Tacitus in Agricola

38   When one has been threatened with a great injustice, one accepts a smaller as a favour.

  Jane Welsh Carlyle (1801–1866), Diary, November 1855

39   Always there is a black spot in our sunshine: it is even, as I have said, the shadow of our selves.

  Thomas Carlyle (1795–1881), Sartor Resartus

40   He that has a secret should not only hide it, but hide that he has something to hide.

  Thomas Carlyle, The French Revolution

41   Nature admits no lie.

  Thomas Carlyle, Latter Day Pamphlet 5

42   Talk that does not end in any kind of action is better suppressed altogether.

  Thomas Carlyle

43   To a shower of gold, most things are penetrable.

  Thomas Carlyle

44   Captains of Industry.

  Thomas Carlyle, Past and Present

45   Organise, organise, organise.

  Thomas Chalmers (1780–1847), speech in Edinburgh, 1842, in anticipation of the Disruption of the Church of Scotland

46   You can't worry too much about the future. Life is not a rehearsal.

  Billy Connolly (1942–), Gullible's Travels

47   It is virtuous to do a sheep a good turn, but a kennan uninteresting.

  S. R. Crockett (1859–1914), The Raiders

48 In these troubled times this was better than to be the Pope's nephew.

    S. R. Crockett, The Raiders

49 If the human species fails in the course of evolution it will be because of its warlike qualities.

    Sir Frank Fraser Darling (1903–1979), Island Years

50 Timid souls are always in a hurry.

    John Davidson (1857–1909), Godfrida

51 I'll bell the cat.

    Archibald Douglas, Earl of Angus (c.1449–1514), attributed; referring to the plan to assassinate James III's favourite, Cochrane

52 And do to me as ye would be done to.

    Gavin Douglas (1475–1522), Prologue to The Aeneid

53 It's the danger of the aphorism that it states too much in trying to be small.

    George Douglas (George Douglas Brown, 1869–1902), The House with the Green Shutters

54 Burn your boats. This has ever been my system in times of stress.

    Norman Douglas (1868–1952), quoted in Paul Fussell, Abroad: British Literary Travelling Between the Wars (1980)

55 'What did you do in the Great War, granpapa?'
'I loafed, my boy.'
'That was naughty, granpapa.'
'Naughty, but nice . . .'

    Norman Douglas, Alone

56 *Know thyself*: to what depths of vain, egocentric brooding has that dictum led!

    Norman Douglas, Old Calabria

57 Externalise yourself!

    Norman Douglas, South Wind

58 No cause so vile, that some human being will not be found to defend it.

    Norman Douglas, Experiments

59 Mediocrity knows nothing higher than itself; but talent instantly recognises genius.

    Sir Arthur Conan Doyle (1859–1930)

60 He lives, who dies to win a lasting name.

    William Drummond (1585–1649), Sonnets

61 He who will not reason is a bigot, he who can-not is a fool; and he who dares not, is a slave.

    William Drummond

62 Be merry, man, and tak nocht far in mynd
The wavering of this wretchit warld of sorrow.

    William Dunbar (c.1460–c.1520), Without Glaidness Availlis no Tressour

63 Without glaidness availlis no tressour.

    William Dunbar, Without Glaidness Availlis no Tressour

64 Quho thinks he hes sufficence
Of gudis hes no indigence,
Thocht he have nowder land nor rent,
Grit micht, nor hie magnificence:
He has aneuch that is content.

    William Dunbar, Of Content

65 '. . . nothing, in my opinion, can be more unbecoming, more unfeminine, than to behold a young lady seat herself at the breakfast table with the complexion of a dairy maid and the appetite of a ploughman. Let morning walks, therefore, from henceforth have an end.'

    Susan Ferrier (1782–1854), The Inheritance

66 Don't put all your heads in one basket.

    Ian Hamilton Finlay (1925–)

67 The Trick is to Keep Breathing.

    Janice Galloway (1956–), book title

68 Gin I was guid
I wad gae mad,
But my salvation
is that I'm bad.

    Robert Garioch (Robert Garioch Sutherland, 1909–1981), The Percipient Swan, *from* Collected Poems

69 It needs smeddum to be either right coarse or right kind.

    Lewis Grassic Gibbon (James Leslie Mitchell, 1901–1935), Smeddum

70 They loved this state; it kept them warm; it saved them trouble; and they enshrined their tastes in their sayings – 'the mair dirt

the less hurt', 'the clartier the cosier' . . .
Another saying was 'Muck makes luck.'

> H. Grey Graham, The Social Life of
> Scotland in the Eighteenth Century
> (*1899*)

71 Value your cause above your skin.

> *James Guthrie, martyred Covenanter*
> *(c.1615–1661)*

72 A real leader of men is someone who is
afraid to go anywhere by himself.

> *Cliff Hanley (1922–1999), quoted in*
> *Alan Bold*, Scottish Quotations (*1985*)

73 In wealth be meik, heich not thyself;
Be glaid in wilfu povertie;
Thy power and thy warldis pelf,
Is nocht but very vanitie.

> *Robert Henryson (c.1425–c.1500)*, The
> Abbay Walk

74 Who has enough, of no more has he need.

> *Robert Henryson*, The Town Mouse and
> the Country Mouse

75 Nocht is your fairness bot ane fading
flour,
Nocht is your famous laud and high
honour
But wind inflate in other mennis ears.

> *Robert Henryson*, The Testament of
> Cresseid

76 Things past belong to memory alone;
Things future are the property of hope.

> *John Home (1724–1808)*, Lysander

77 Wherever luxury ceases to be innocent, it
also ceases to be beneficial.

> *David Hume (1711–1776)*, Of
> Refinement

78 It's a master race and it's almost run.

> *Alan Jackson (1938–)*, The Worstest
> Beast

79 For there's mony a load on shore may be
skailed at sea.

> *Violet Jacob (1863–1946)*, The Water
> Hen

80 There shall be no place in my realm where
the key shall not keep the castle and the
bracken bush the cow.

> *King James I (1394–1437), quoted*
> *in Walter Bower*, Scotichronicon
> (*1440–49*), *translated from Latin*

81 It cam wi' a lass and it shall pass wi' a lass.

> *King James V (1512–1542), attributed*
> *deathbed saying, quoted in Robert Lindsay*
> *of Pitscottie*, The Historie and Croni-
> cles of Scotland, *written in the 1570s*

82 Keep right on to the end of the road,
Keep right on to the end,
Tho' the way be long, let your heart
be strong,
Keep right on round the bend.
Tho' you're tired and weary, still journey
on,
Till you come to your happy abode –
Where all you love and are dreaming of
Will be there, at the end of the road.

> *Sir Harry Lauder (1870–1950)*, Keep
> Right On To The End Of the Road

83 Men are immortal till their work is done.

> *David Livingstone (1813–73)*, Letters

84 Experience teaches
that it doesn't.

> *Norman MacCaig (1910–1996)*, Bruce
> and That Spider – the Truth

85 The love o' economics is the mainspring
O' a' the virtues.

> *Hugh MacDiarmid (C. M. Grieve,*
> *1892–1978)*, Depth and the Chthonian
> Image

86 We are often unable to tell people what
they need to know, because they want to
know something else.

> *George Macdonald (1852–1905)*

87 Beauty and sadness always go together.

> *George Macdonald*, Within and
> Without

88 The direst foe of courage is the fear itself,
not the object of it; and the man who can
overcome his own terror is a hero and
more.

> *George Macdonald*, Sir Gibbie

89 Oh, ye canny spend a dollar when ye're
deid.

> *John Mack*, Ding Dong Dollar (*1961*)

90 Men are never so good or so bad as their
opinions.

> *Sir James Mackintosh (1765–1832)*, Ethi-
> cal Philosophy

91 No man is wiser than another –
And none knoweth much.
> *Fiona MacLeod (William Sharp,*
> *1856–1905), From the Hills of Dream*

92 Now we have mair, it is weill kend,
Nor our forbearis had to spend . . .
We waste far mair now, lik vain fulis.
> *Sir Richard Maitland (1496–1586),*
> Satire on the Age

93 Na Kindness at Court Without Siller.
> *Sir Richard Maitland,* title of poem

94 It is always a bore being ahead of one's
time.
> *Naomi Mitchison (1897–1998), Diary*
> *1940, from D. Sheridan,* Amang You
> Taking Notes: The Wartime Diaries
> of Naomi Mitchison *(1985)*

95 Seek the beginnings, learn from whence
you came,
And know the various earth of which you
are made.
> *Edwin Muir (1887–1959),* The Journey
> Back

96 . . . the Scotch method of making every
duty dismal.
> *John Muir (1838–1914),* The Story of
> My Boyhood and Youth

97 Truth will stand when a' thin's failin'.
> *Lady Nairne (1766–1845),* Caller
> Herrin'

98 His Majesty's dominions, on which the
sun never sets.
> *Christopher North (John Wilson,*
> *1785–1854),* Noctes Ambrosianae

99 'We must leave that to Providence', said
Miss Marjoribanks, with a sense of paying
a compliment to Providence in entrusting
it with such responsibility.
> *Margaret Oliphant (1828–1897),* Miss
> Marjoribanks

100 Sorrows remembered sweeten present joy.
> *Robert Pollok (1799–1827),* The Course
> of Time

101 Twa things ane shouldna be angry at: what
he can help, and what he canna help.
> *Allan Ramsay (1686–1758),* Scots
> Proverbs

102 The love of the fair is the meed of the
brave.
> *Allan Ramsay,* Farewell to Lochaber

103 Behave yoursel' before folk;
Whate'er ye do, when out o' view,
Be cautious aye before folk.
> *Alexander Rodger (1784–1846),* Behave
> Yoursel' Before Folk

104 'Tis needless to speer for the lassie
That's wooed and married and a'.
> *Alexander Ross (1699–1784),* Woo'd and
> Married and A'

105 Happy is he, the only happy man,
Who out of choice does all the good he
can.
> *Alexander Ross (fl. 18th century), quoted*
> *in J. A. Russell,* The Book of Galloway
> *(1962)*

106 I always say appearance is only sin deep.
> *Saki (H. H. Munro, 1870–1916)*

107 It's the early Christian that gets the fattest
lion.
> *Saki,* Reginald's Choir Treat

108 Haud fast to the past.
> *Dictum of Lady John Douglas Scott*
> *(1810–1900)*

109 Bluid is thicker than water.
> *Sir Walter Scott (1771–1832),* Guy Man-
> nering, *but known before*

110 They that ettle to get to the top of the
ladder will at least get up some rounds.
> *Sir Walter Scott,* The Monastery

111 Scared out of his seven senses.
> *Sir Walter Scott,* Rob Roy

112 . . . the sea of upturned faces.
> *Sir Walter Scott,* Rob Roy

113 'There's sma' sorrow at our pairtin',' as the
auld mare said to the broken cairt.
> *Sir Walter Scott,* Rob Roy

114 She's o'er the Border and awa'.
> *Sir Walter Scott,* Jock o' Hazeldean

115 Steek the awmrie, shut the kist,
Or else some gear will soon be missed.
> *Sir Walter Scott,* Donald Caird's Come
> Home Again

116 Chance will not do the work – Chance
sends the breeze;

But if the pilot slumber at the helm,
The very wind that wafts us towards
  the port
May dash us on the shelves.
> *Sir Walter Scott*, The Fortunes of Nigel

117 As cross as two sticks.
> *Sir Walter Scott*, Journal

118 Innocent mouth, miminy mouth.
> *William Bell Scott (1811–1890)*, The Witch's Ballad

119 Courage is only the overcoming of fear by faith.
> *Mary Slessor (1848–1915)*, Letter to a friend

120 Don't grow up a nervous old maid! Gird yourself for the battle outside somewhere, and keep your heart young.
> *Mary Slessor*, Letter to a friend

121 The secret of all failure is disobedience.
> *Dictum of Mary Slessor*

122 A place for everything, and everything in its place.
> *Samuel Smiles (1812–1904)*, Thrift

123 . . . a nation of shopkeepers.
> *Adam Smith (1723–1790)*, The Wealth of Nations

124 A man gazing at the stars is proverbially at the mercy of the puddles in the road.
> *Alexander Smith (1830–1867)*, Dreamthorp

125 If you wish to preserve your secret, wrap it up in frankness.
> *Alexander Smith*, Dreamthorp

126 When Jamie the Second . . . asks an old priest how he can get a gang of corrupt nobles off his back he's handed a bundle of arrows bound by a thong and told to break the bundle across his knees. 'Dinna be sae bluidy stup§id', says the king, or something regal to that effect. And the old priest loosens the thong and breaks the arrows one by one.
> *W. Gordon Smith*, Mr Jock *(1987)*

127 Some folks are wise, and some are otherwise.
> *Tobias Smollett (1721–1771)*, The Adventures of Roderick Random

128 . . . a hot-bed of genius.
> *Tobias Smollett*, The Expedition of Humphry Clinker

129 Few live exempt
From disappointment and disgrace, who
  run
Ambition's rapid course.
> *Tobias Smollett*, The Regicide

130 He who weeps for beauty gone
Stoops to pluck a flower of stone.
> *William Soutar (1898–1943)*, He Who Weeps for Beauty Gone

131 'Dark glasses hide dark thoughts,' I said.
'Is that a saying?'
'Not that I've heard. But it is one now.'
> *Muriel Spark (1918–)* The Dark Glasses

132 Vanity dies hard; in some obstinate cases it outlives the man.
> *Robert Louis Stevenson (1850–1894)*, Prince Otto

133 The cup of life's for him that drinks,
And not for him that sips.
> *Robert Louis Stevenson*, The Cup of Life

134 This is the kittle bit.
> *Robert Louis Stevenson*, Kidnapped

135 I've a grand memory for forgetting, David.
> *Robert Louis Stevenson*, Kidnapped

136 I was in no sense a hypocrite: both sides of me were in dead earnest.
> *Robert Louis Stevenson*, Dr Jekyll and Mr Hyde

137 Grand, whunstane sense.
> *Robert Louis Stevenson*, Weir of Hermiston

138 Aye gie a bit o' your cake to the wifie wha's bakin' a pie.
> *Sir D'Arcy Wentworth Thompson (1860–1948), favourite saying*

139 Better to love in the lowliest cot
Than pine in a palace alone.
> *George Whyte-Melville (1821–1878)*, Chastelar

140 When you sleep in your cloak there's no lodging to pay.
> *George Whyte-Melville*, Boots and Saddles

141 ... the auld ways are siccar, auld and siccar like the sterns.

> *Douglas Young (1913–1973)*, Sabbath i the Mearns

Angling and Poaching

1 When the twenty-four pounder leaps
   in the air
And the line flies out with a squeal;
O that is the blessedest sound upon earth:
The merry merry shriek of the reel.

> *William Black (1841–1898)*, Reel Song

2 The charm of fishing is that it is the pursuit of what is elusive but obtainable, a perpetual series of occasions for hope.

> *John Buchan (1875–1940)*, Memory-Hold-The-Door

3 The silver scalit fishes on the greit
Ourthwart clear streamis sprinkland
   for the heat,
With finnis shinand brown as synopar
And chisel tails steerand here and thar.

> *Gavin Douglas (1475–1522)*, Prologue to The Aeneid

4 Strange things happen to a lone fisherman.

> *Sir Denis Forman (1917–)*, Son of Adam

5 When the net touched the bottom of the pool, Roddie withdrew his stick and, reaching far out, the water past his knees, gave it a sharp, downward thrust. At once there was turmoil, and Finn saw the flashing silver of the salmon as it bent and heaved to clear itself of the net that ever more maddeningly enmeshed it. It took less than two minutes for Roddie to get his hands on the turmoil. Then he walked out of the pool, with the doubling salmon clasped in his hands, and up into the trees.

> *Neil Gunn (1891–1973)*, The Silver Darlings

6 'He's just a warld's wonder wi' the sweevil, a warlock wi' the worm, and wi' the flee a finisher.'

> *James Hogg (1770–1835), on 'the Major', quoted in Christopher North*, Noctes Ambrosianae

7 Just one cast more!

> *Andrew Lang (1844–1912)*, Rhymes à la Mode

8 I've crackit wi' the keeper, pockets packed
   wi' pheasants' eggs
An' a ten-pun' saumon hangin' doun in
   baith my trouser-legs.

> *G. K. Menzies*, Poaching in Excelsis

9 ... every salmon Dougie would be takin' oot o' the net he would be feeling it all over in a droll way, till I said to him, 'What are you feel-feelin' for, Dougie, the same ass if they had pockets on them? I'm sure they're all right.'

'"Oh yes," he says, "right enough, but I wass frightened they might be the laird's salmon, and I wass lookin' for the luggage label on them. There's none. It's all right; they're chust wild salmon that nobody planted."'

> *Neil Munro (1864–1930)*, The Vital Spark

10 But deep, deep the stream in,
I saw his sides a gleamin',
The King o' the Saumon, sae pleasantly
   lay he;
I thought he was sleepin',
But on further peepin',
I saw by his teeth he was lauchin' at me.

> *George Outram (1805–1856)*, The Saumon

11 Salmon, in the Highlands, is one of the mercies that is best taken with an uninquisitive appetite.

> *Alastair Phillips*, My Uncle George (1954)

12 A birr! a whirr! a salmon's on,
A goodly fish! a thumper!

> *Thomas Tod Stoddart (1810–1880)*

13 Then to the stream-side, gladly we'll hie
Where the gray trout slide silently by.

> *Thomas Tod Stoddart*, The Angler's Invitation

14 Ower at the cauld-foot,
There bides an auld troot,
No mony there be that are wiser;
It baffles a' skill
To tether his gill,
And gie the sly boy a surpriser.

> *Thomas Tod Stoddart*, The King o' the Cauld

15 Gang, Jenny, bring my fishing book,
And lay't down by my side,

That I aince mair may view the lines
And flees that were my pride.

David Wingate (1828–1892), The
Deein' Fisher

The Animal Kingdom

1 The craw killed the pussie, O,
   The craw killed the pussie, O;
   The muckle sat sat doun and grat
   In Johnnie's wee bit hoosie, O.

   Anonymous

2 Three craws sat upon a wa',
   Sat upon a wa', sat upon a wa',
   Three craws sat upon a wa',
   On a cold and frosty morning.

   Anonymous

3 There was a Presbyterian cat
   Went seeking for her prey;
   She caught a moose, within the hoose,
   Upon the Sabbath Day . . .
   Then unto execution
   Poor Baudrons she was drawn;
   And on a tree, there hanged she:
   The minister sang a psalm.

   Anonymous, The Presbyterian's Cat,
   *said to be a precentors' practice ditty but
   actually a satirical poem from the seventeenth century*

4 O, whit'll we dae wi' the herrin's heid?
   Herrin's heid, a loaf o' breid . . .
   Of a' the fish that live in the sea
   The herrin' it is the fish for me

   Traditional, The Herrin'

5 Ayont the dyke, adist the thorn,
   I heard an auld man blaw his horn,
   His beard was flesh, his neb was horn,
   And sic a beast was never born.

   *Traditional Kirkcudbrightshire riddle for
   a cockerel*

6 The auld black horse sat on his rump,
   The auld white meer lay on her wime:
   For a' that I could hup and crack,
   They wouldna rise at yokin' time.

   Traditional, The Barnyards o' Delgaty

7 A goloch is an awesome beast,
   Souple an' scaly,
   Wi' a horny heid an' a hantle o' feet,
   An' a forky tailie.

   Traditional

8 Reid-spottit jeckit
   An' polished black e'e;
   Land on my luif, an' bring
   Siller tae me.

   Traditional rhyme to the ladybird

9 Ane is ane, twa is grief,
   Three's a wedding, four's death.

   Traditional rhyme on the pyet, or magpie

10 Ding dong, ding dong,
    Fah's this that's dead?
    It's puir pussy baudrons
    O' a sehr hehd.

    Traditional rhyme, quoted in W. Gregor,
    Folklore of North-East Scotland
    (1881)

11 Then one of the executioners, pulling off
    her garters, espied her little dog, which
    was crept under her clothes, which could
    not be got furth by force, yet afterwards
    would not depart with the dead corpse, but
    came and lay between her head and her
    shoulders, which being imbrued with her
    blood was carried away and washed, as all
    things else were that had any blood was
    either burned or clean washed.

    *From the official record of Mary I's execu-
    tion, February 1587*

12 Item, it is ordainit for the destruccioun
    of wolfis that in ilk cuntré quhair ony is,
    the Scheriff or the bailzie of that cuntré
    sal gadder the cuntré folk thre tymis in
    the yeir, betuix Sanct Merkis Day and
    Lammess, for that is the tyme of the
    quhelpis . . . and he that slayis ane wolf,
    than or any othir tyme, he sal haif of ilk
    house halder of that parochine that the
    wolf is slain within, 1d.

    Act of Parliament, 1457

13 The cow – there is a thing of beauty . . .
    The eyes of a cow shine with a soft enrap-
    tured light, like moons in a misty sky . . .
    the cow lives in a deep, philosophic calm,
    she has long thoughts, and she keeps them
    to herself.

    John R. Allan, The North-East Low-
    lands of Scotland

14 . . . as a spectacle, the judging of the horses
    was supreme . . . The great beasts, shin-
    ing with health and care, pounded over
    the hollow turf, throwing back their hairy

hooves till their bright shoes caught the sunlight.he

> *John R. Allan*, The North-East Lowlands of Scotland

15 Said the whitrick to the stoat,
'I see ye've on your winter coat;
I dinna see the sense ava!
Ye're shairly no expectin' snaw?'

> *J. K. Annand (1908–1993)*, Fur Coats

16 The pawky wee sparrow will peck aff
your floor,
The bauld little robin hops in at your
door;
But the heaven-soaring lark 'mang the
cold drift will dee,
Afore he'll come cowerin' your moolins to
pree.

> *James Ballantine (1806–1877)*, Winter Promptings

17 She had the fiercie and the fleuk,
The wheezloch and the wanton yeuk;
On ilka knee she had a breuk –
What ail'd the beast to dee?

> *Patrick Birnie (fl. 1660s)*, The Auld Man's Mear's Dead

18 God's might so peopled hath the sea
With fish of divers sort,
That men therein may clearly see
Great things for their comfort.

> *Zachary Boyd (c.1585–1653)*, Zion's Flowers

19 I turned a grey stone over: a hundred forky-
tails seethed from under it like thoughts
out of an evil mind.

> *George Mackay Brown (1921–1996)*, Five Green Waves

20 Wee sleeket, cow'rin, tim'rous beastie,
O, what a panic's in thy breastie!
Thou needna start awa sae hasty
Wi' bickerin' brattle!
I wad be laith to rin and chase thee,
Wi' murderin' pattle!

> *Robert Burns (1759–1796)*, To a Mouse

21 He was a gash and faithfu' tyke
As ever lap a sheugh or dyke.
His honest, sonsie, baws'nt face
Ay gat him friends in ilka place;
His breast was white, his tousie back
Weel clad wi' coat o' glossy black;

His gawsie tail, wi' upward curl,
Hung owre his hurdies wi' a swirl.

> *Robert Burns*, The Twa Dogs

22 Ye ugly, creepin, blasted wonner,
Detested, shunn'd by saint and sinner,
How daur ye set your fit upon her –
Sae fine a lady?
Gae somewhere else, and seek your dinner
On some poor body.

> *Robert Burns*, To a Louse

23 Within the bush her cover'd nest
A little linnet fondly prest;
The dew sat chilly on her breast,
Sae early in the morning.

> *Robert Burns*, A Rosebud by my Early Walk

24 My joy, my pride, my hoggie!

> *Robert Burns*, What Shall I Do Gin my Hoggie Die?

25 Weel mounted on his grey mare, Meg,
A better never lifted leg

> *Robert Burns*, Tam o' Shanter

26 There are only two creatures I would envy –
a horse in his wild state traversing the forests of Asia, and an oyster on some of the desert shores of Europe. The one has not a wish without enjoyment; the other has neither wish nor fear.

> *Robert Burns quoted by R. W. Cromek*, Reliques of Robert Burns

27 A puddock sat by the lochan's brim,
An' he thocht there was never a puddock
like him . . .
A heron was hungry and needin' tae sup,
Sae he nabbit the puddock and gollup't
him up;
Syne runkled his feathers: 'A peer thing,'
quo' he,
'But – puddocks is nae fat they eesed tae
be.'

> *J. M. Caie (1878–1949)*, The Puddock

28 In truth, I rather take it thou hast got
By instinct wise much sense about thy lot,
And hast small care
Whether an Eden or a desert be
Thy home, so thou remain'st alive and
free
To skim the air.

> *Jane Welsh Carlyle (1801–1866)*, To A Swallow Building Under Our Eaves

29 Columba was one day in the strand of the small-fry and he trampled on a beautiful little fair Flounder and hurt her tail. The poor little Flounder cried out as loud as she could –

Thou Colum big and clumsy,
With the crooked crosswise feet,
Much didst thou to me of injust
When thou didst trample on my tail.

Columba was angry at being taunted with having crooked feet and he said –

If I am crooked-footed,
Be thou crooked-mouthed.

And he left her that way.

Alexander Carmichael (1832–1912), Carmina Gadelica

30 It was like a little old man with enormous white eyebrows, wearing a stupendous mask shaped like a beak . . . Then they saw it was a bird, very large in size, but so forlorn, old and broken that it could only flutter piteously its little flippers of wings and patiently and pathetically waggle thast strange head.
'It is the great Auk itself – we have found it!' said Anna.

S. R. Crockett (1859–1914), The Glistering Beach

31 There is noise and abandon with it all for sea-birds express their emotions with great intensity and the discordant noises blend into harmony with the deep voice of the sea. There is nothing on earth like it. One who has lain receptive by a cliff of sea-birds has known wonder.

Sir Frank Fraser Darling (1903–1979), Island Years

32 A cat is the ideal literary companion. A wife, I am sure, cannot compare except to her disadvantage. A dog is out of the question . . . Its function is that of a familiar. It is at once decorative – contemplative – philosophical, and it begets in me great calm and contentment.

William Y. Darling (1885–1962), Memoirs of a Bankrupt Bookseller, *quoted in Hamish Whyte,* The Scottish Cat (1987)

33 The curlew calls me where the salt
winds blow;
His troubled note dwells mournfully and dies.

John Davidson (1857–1909), Spring Song

34 A stag of warrant, a stag, a stag,A runnable stag, a kingly crop,Brow, bay and tray and three on top,A stag, a runnable stag.

John Davidson, A Runnable Stag

35 The fierceness of its disposition, its strength, and its agility are well-known; and although it does not seek to attack man, yet when disturbed in its lair, or hemmed in, it will spring with tiger-like ferocity on its opponent, every hair on its body bristling with rage.

Encyclopaedia Britannica, on the Scottish wildcat

36 The last of all the British great auks was caught on Stac an Armin in July of 1840 or a neighbouring year, and beaten to death by the St Kildans . . . as they thought it was a witch.

James Fisher, St Kilda, *in E. Molony,* Portraits of Islands (1951)

37 I am going tomorrow to a delightfull place, Breahead by name, belonging to Mrs Crraford, where their is ducks cocks hens bublyjocks 2 dogs 2 cats swine and which is delightful.

Marjory Fleming (1803–1811), Journals

38 O lovely O most charming pug
Thy gracefull air and heavenly mug
The beauties of his mind do shine
And every bit is shaped so fine
Your very tail is most devine . . .
His noses cast is of the romanx
He is a very pretty weomenI could not
get a rhyme for roman
And was oblidged to call it weoman.

Marjory Fleming, Poems

39 In Scotland the wren is called 'the Lady of Heaven's hen', and boys say:
Malisons, malisons mair than ten,
That harry the Lady of Heaven's hen!

Sir James G. Frazer (1854–1941), The Golden Bough

40 I kicked an Edinbro dug-luver's dug.
Leastways, I tried; my timing wes owre late,
It stopped whit it was daein on my gate an skelpit aff to find some ither mug.

Robert Garioch (Robert Garioch Sutherland, 1909–1981), Nemo Canem Impune Lacessit

41 Capers are sometimes very tame and I heard of a capercaillie cock in Rothiemurchus forest which was of a pugilistic temperament and liked nothing better than to attack a lady from the rear, aiming vicious pecks at her legs, especially if they were encased in thin silk stockings.

Seton Gordon (1886–1977), A Highland Year

42 I recall the now almost classical story of the aircraft (this was in the earlier days of flying) travelling at approximately ninety miles an hour, which was overtaken by a golden eagle flying on the same course. The pilot saw the eagle eye the aircraft with calm indifference before it slowly drew ahead of him.

Seton Gordon, A Highland Year

43 I have never yet met anyone who really believed in a pterodactyl; but every honest person believes in dragons.

Kenneth Grahame (1859–1932), Introduction to 100 Fables of Aesop

44 All along the backwater,
Through the rushes tall,
Ducks are a-dabbling,
Up tails all.

Kenneth Grahame, Duck's Ditty

45 The Soays do not bunch together into a flock and follow each other as do the blackfaced and Cheviot sheep; instead, when they are startled, they each take their individual course and it is impossible to herd them with a dog . . . my own method of controlling them was by slavish bribery.

I. F. Grant, Highland Folk Ways (1961)

46 Only the thought disturbs him –
He's noticed once or twice,
The times are somehow breeding
A nimbler race of mice.

Sir Alexander Gray (1882–1968), On a Cat Ageing

47 Today I saw about twenty Highland cattle following a cart of hay across a field. They were drawn out in a line, and with their shaggy dun coats and long horns had a soft wild beauty that held the eye . . . I do know of a man who was lucky enough to get through a fence in time from the charge of one of the timid score that I saw following the hay-cart. But the calf was only two days old and the man had gone between

it and its mother – never a wise proceeding in the case of any breed of cattle, or even, for that matter, of (what we deem) the most important mammal of all.

Neil Gunn (1891–1973), Highland Pack

48 'Pray, Lord Robertson,' said a lady to that eminent lawyer at a party, 'can you tell me what sort of a bird the bul-bul is?'
'I suppose, ma'am,' said the humorous judge, 'it is the male of the coo-coo.'

Alexander Hislop, The Book of Scottish Anecdote (1883)

49 'It's a gude sign o' a dowg, Sirs, when his face grows like his master's.'

James Hogg (1770–1835), quoted in *Christopher North*, Noctes Ambrosianae

50 Bird of the wilderness,
Blithesome and cumberless,
Sweet be thy matin o'er moorland and lea!

James Hogg, The Skylark

51 And far abune the Angus straths I saw the wild geese flee,
A lang, lang skein o' beatin' wings wi' their heids towards the sea,
And aye their cryin' voices trailed ahint them on the air

Violet Jacob (1863–1946), The Wild Geese

52 There was a snake that dwelt in Skye
Over the misty sea, oh;
He lived on nothing but gooseberry pie,
For breakfast, dinner and tea, oh!

Henry Johnstone (b.1844), The Fastidious Serpent

53 Birds are older by far than your ancestors are,
And made love and made war ere the making of Man.

Andrew Lang (1844–1912), Rhymes à la Mode

54 I'll not be a fool like the nightingale
That sits up till midnight without any ale,
Making a noise with his nose.

Eric Linklater (1899–1974), Poet's Pub

55 Whae's like us? –
Damned few,
an'
we're

aw
deid.

Douglas Lipton, Great Auk

56 Vast presences come mincing in,
Swagbellied Aphrodites, swinging
A silver slaver from each chin.
And all is milky, secret, female.

Norman MacCaig (1910–1996), Byre

57 She flowed through fences like a piece of
black wind.

Norman MacCaig, Praise of a Collie

58 The collie underneath the table
Slumps with a world-rejecting sigh.

Norman MacCaig, Crofter's Kitchen,
Evening

59 Above all, I love them because,
Pursued in water, they never
panic so much that they fail
to make stylish triangles
with their ballet dancer's
legs.

Norman MacCaig, Frogs

60 I never saw more frogs
than once at the back of Ben Dorain.
Joseph-coated, they ambled and jumped
in the sweet marsh grass
like coloured ideas.

Norman MacCaig, One of the Many
Days

61 It'll be the Bonxie, that noble Scua,
That infects a' the ither birds w' its
qualms.
In its presence even the eagle
Forbears to pounce on the lambs.

*Hugh MacDiarmid (C. M. Grieve,
1892–1978)*, The Bonxie

62 And shambles-ward nae cattle-beast e'er
passes
But I mind hoo the saft e'en o' the kine
Lichted Christ's cradle wi' their canny
shine.

Hugh MacDiarmid, Gairmscoile

63 . . . great bulls mellow to the touch,
Brood mares of marvellous approach,
and geldings
With sharp and flinty bones and silken
hair.

Hugh MacDiarmid, Cattle Show

64 The inward gates of a bird are always
open.

It does not know how to shut them.
That is the secret of its song.

Hugh MacDiarmid, On a Raised Beach

65 A bird knows nothing of gladness,
Is only a song-machine.

George Macdonald (1824–1905), A Book
of Dreams

66 Blue-burning, vaporous, to and fro
The dragon-flies like arrows go,
Or hang in moveless flight.

George Macdonald, The Child-Mother

67 And houseless slugs, white, black and red –
Snails too lazy to build a shed.

George Macdonald, Little Boy Blue

68 The myriad gnats that dance like a wall.

George Macdonald, Lessons for a Child

69 Whence do ye come, ye creatures?
Each of you
Is perfect as an angel! wings and eyes
Stupendous in their beauty – gorgeous
dyes
In feathery fields of purple and of blue.

George Macdonald, On a Midge

70 I think I almost understand
Thy owl, his muffled swiftness,
moon-round eyes, and intoned
hooting.

George MacDonald, The Sparrow

71 The only mystery about the cat is why
ever it decided to become a domesticated
animal.

Sir Compton Mackenzie (1883–1972)

72 But, hark! What is that melodious moaning we hear in the west? It is the singing of
the seals . . . Would that the present scribe
had the musical genius of Mrs Kennedy
Fraser that he might set down in due nota-
tion that merlodious moaning!

Sir Compton Mackenzie, Whisky
Galore, *parodying Alasdair Alpin Mac-
Gregor, with a sideswipe at the collector-
adaptor of* Songs of the Hebrides

73 Birds-nesting expeditions were also made
to the islands of Loch Maree, after ospreys'
eggs. There were two eyries there . . . But
alas, the birds have been extinct in that
region for at least sixty-five years.

Osgood Mackenzie (1842–1922), A Hundred Years in the Highlands

74 Holy, Holy, Holy,A wee brown bird am I:
But my breast is ruddy
For I saw Christ die.

Fiona MacLeod (William Sharp,
1856–1905), The Bird of Christ

75 One pair, joined in that brief embrace of
the insect world which seems so pathetically improbable, alighted near to me;
there was a whirring rattle of wings, and
they were swept away by a huge yellow-
banded dragonfly. He circled me, carrying
the struggling pair, and alighted on a lily-
leaf close by. He did not finish his meal, but
left, flew away, leaving them dead but still
joined, a spot of colour suddenly robbed of
meaning.

Gavin Maxwell (1914–1969), Harpoon
At a Venture, on damsel-flies

76 The eider ducks have arrived . . . they bring
with them that most evocative and haunt-
ing of all sounds of the Hebridean spring
and summer, the deep, echoing, wood-
wind crooning of the courting drakes.

Gavin Maxwell, Ring of Bright Water

77 When evening closes Nature's eye,
The glow-worm lights her little spark
To captivate her favourite fly
And tempt the rover through the dark.

James Montgomery (1771–1854), The
Glow-worm

78 Though frail as dust it meet thine eye,
He form'd this gnat who built the sky.

James Montgomery, The Gnat

79 Barely a twelvemonth after
The seven days war that put the world to
sleep,
Late in the evening the strange horses
came.

Edwin Muir (1887–1959), The Horses

80 'The Congo's no' to be compared wi'
the West o' Scotland when ye come to
insects', said Para Handy. 'There's places
here that's chust deplorable whenever the
weather's the least bit warm. Look at
Tighnabruaich!– ithey're that bad there,
they'll bite their way through corrugated
iron roofs to get at ye!'

Neil Munro (1864–1930), The Vital
Spark

81 'What kind of a canary is it?' asked the
Brodick man, jealously. 'Is it a Norwich?'
    Para Handy put up his hand as usual to
scratch his ear, and checked the act half-
way. 'No, nor a Sandwich; it's chust a plain
yellow wan.'

Neil Munro, The Vital Spark

82 He took a young pig as a pet, and it became
quite tame, and followed him about like a
dog. At first the animal shared his bed, but
when, growing up to adult swinehood, it
became unfit for such companionship, he
had it to sleep in his room, in which he
made a comfortable couch for it of his own
clothes.

Dean E. B. Ramsay (1793–1882), Remi-
niscences of Scottish Life and Charac-
ter, on Francis Garden, Lord Gardenstone
(1721–1793)

83 The mitches are troublesome but do not
ascend. I may say as the stoic did to the
gout, 'Thou art troublesome but I will
allow thee to be an evil.'

John Ramsay of Ochtertyre (1736–1814),
letter to Elizabeth Graham, October 1800

84 . . . those poor souls who claim to own a
cat, who long to recognise in bland and
narrowing eyes a look like love, are bound
to suffer.

Alastair Reid (1926–), Propinquity

85 It is indeed no small triumph to have
combined the untrammelled liberty of pri-
meval savagery with the luxury which
only a highly developed civilisation can
command.

Saki (H. H. Munro, 1870–1916), The
Square Egg, on cats

86 Puffins crowded the ledges. They wore
evening dress and carnival faces.

Alastair Scott, Native Stranger (1995)

87 A cat may look at a king –
Oh, fairly that!
But a king can swack the heid
Frae onie cat.

Alexander Scott (1920–1989), Cat and
King

88 Delightful creatures indeed. Especially
with mint sauce.

Charlotte, Lady Scott, when Sir Walter
had rhapsodised over some young lambs

89 And far up soar the wild geese, wi' weird
unyeirdly cry.
Lady John Douglas Scott (1810–1900),
The Comin' o' the Spring

90 My ewie wi' the crookit horn!
A' that kend her would hae sworn
Sic a ewie ne'er was born
Hereabouts nor far awa'.
John Skinner (1721–1807), The Ewie wi'
the Crookit Horn

91 Half doun the hill where fa's the linn,
Far frae the flaught of fowk,
I saw upon a lanely whin,
A lanely singin' gowk!
William Soutar (1898–1943) The Gowk

92 A puddock diddlin be a dub
Peer'd in to see himsel';
And smirkin' up his muckle gub,
Thocht, 'Man! I'm lookin weel.'
William Soutar, The Proud Puddock

93 A multitude of rats often disturbed his
repose by gnawing his feet and other parts
of his body, which induced him to feed
a number of cats for his protection. In a
short time these became so tame that they
would lie about him in hundreds . . . Upon
his re-turn he declared to his friends that
nothing gave him so much uneasiness as
the thoughts, that when he died his body
would be devoured by these very cats.
*Statistical Account of Scotland, Parish
of Largo, on Alexander Selkirk
(1676–1721), the model for Daniel Defoe's*
Robinson Crusoe

94 The friendly cow, all red and white,
I love with all my heart;
She gives me cream with all her might,
To eat with apple-tart.
Robert Louis Stevenson, The Cow

95 . . . a diminutive she-ass, not much bigger
than a dog, the colour of a mouse, with
a kindly eye and determined under-jaw.
There was something neat and high-bred,
a quakerish elegance, about the rogue that
hit my fancy on the spot.
Robert Louis Stevenson (1850–1894),
Travels With a Donkey

96 Who's that ringing at our door-bell?
'I'm a little black cat and I'm not very well.'
Then rub your little nose with a little
mutton fat,

And that's the best cure for a little black
cat.
*Sir D'Arcy Wentworth Thompson
(1860–1948)*, The Little Black Cat

97 The swallow sweeps
The slimy pool, to build his hanging
house.
James Thomson (1700–1748), The
Seasons

98 The stately-sailing swan
Gives out his snowy plumage to the gale.
James Thomson, The Seasons

99 So
there they go
through the wind, the rain, the snow
wild spirits
knowing what they know.
Kenneth White (1936–), A Short Introduction to White Poetics, *on wild geese*

100 My father was also very fond of the seals.
He used to play the bagpipes to them. He
would play a tune to the seals, and they
would all pop their heads out of the water,
stand up straight, listening.
Duncan Williamson (1928–), Tales of
the Seal People

101 . . . does it make for death to be
Oneself a living armoury?
Andrew Young (1885–1971), The Dead
Crab

Art and Artists

1 To be an artist is a great thing, but to be an
artist and not know it is the most glorious
plight in the world.
J. M. Barrie (1860–1937), Sentimental
Tommy

2 An artist without sentiment is a painter
without colours.
J. M. Barrie, Tommy and Grizel

3 You can't paint from a vacuum . . . if you're
being honest it comes through in your
work.
John Bellany (1942–), quoted in John
McEwen, *John Bellany (1994)*

4 I have heard Mr Millais declare that three
hours' sunshine in Scotland is worth three
months' sunshine in Cairo; and the same

authority, I believe, is responsible for the admirable aphorism that Scotland was like a wet pebble, with the colours brought out by the rain.

> *William Black (1841–1898)*, The West Highlanders

5 I bless the Academy I found in Glasgow streets. The grand indifference of the great city taught one concentration and gave one solitude.

> *Sir D. Muirhead Bone (1876–1953), quoted in Duncan Macmillan*, Scottish Art 1460–1990 *(1990)*

6 I called on Mr Donaldson, the painter, for a little . . . He said he did not like painters always choosing subjects from books. It made painting a secondary art. Let it supply itself with ideas.

> *James Boswell (1740–1795)*, Journal

7 We talked of Scotland. He said the Glasgow editions were 'très belles'. I said, 'An Academy of Painting was also established there, but it did not succeed. Our Scotland is no country for that.'
   He replied with a keen archness, 'No, to paint well it is necessary to have warm feet. It's hard to paint when your feet are cold.'

> *James Boswell*, Journal, *on a visit to Voltaire*

8 Among the Letters of Introduction that Wilkie brought to London was one to Caleb Whiteford, celebrated at that time as a wit. Whilst opening the letter and looking at the bearer, he asked his age. 'Weel, I don't exactly know', was the reply. 'What!' said Caleb, 'You come to London to wrestle with so many celebrated men, and you don't even know your own age?' This remark made so strong an impression on him at the time, that out of it he afterwards painted his 'Letter of Introduction'.

> *John Burnet*, The Art Journal, *(1860), on Sir David Wilkie (1785–1841)*

9 May the Devil fly away with the fine arts!

> *Thomas Carlyle (1795–1881)*, Latter-Day Pamphlets

10 At times it's very good, at times it's bloody awful. It's a lesser school with a few high points . . . They didn't influence anybody.

> *Timothy Clifford (1946–), quoted in* Scotland on Sunday (January 1994), *on Scottish art*

11 If you keep the original inspiration – that which fascinates you at the beginning – for a year, or a month or half an hour or for however long it takes – you might arrive at a conclusion.

> *David Donaldson (1916–1996), quoted in Bill Hare*, Contemporary Painting in Scotland *(1992)*

12 When he has made a sketch from a picture, & settled his design, He then walks about looking for a person proper to be a model for each character in his picture, & he then paints *everything from the life*.

> *Joseph Farington*, Diary, (1807), *on Sir David Wilkie (1785–1841)*

13 Carlyle, who, entirely devoid of interest in the arts, sat for everyone, seeming to look on the performance as one of the penalties of greatness.

> *William Gaunt*, The Pre-Raphaelite Tragedy *(1942), on Thomas Carlyle (1795–1881)*

14 We need to give everyone the outlook of the artist, who begins with the art of seeing – and then in time we shall follow him into the seeing of art, even the creating of it.

> *Sir Patrick Geddes (1854–1932)*, Biology and its Social Bearings

15 What more vivid evidence of the artistic destitution of the country could be found than in the long gallery at Holyrood, with its rows of well-varnished effigies of crowned heads of Scotland . . . For such a national work no native artist could be found, and in 1684 the Duke of York engaged the Dutchman Jacob de Witt.

> *H. Grey Graham*, The Social Life of Scotland in the Eighteenth Century *(1899)*

16 Jacobites too, across the water and at home, were anxious to have portraits of Mary Queen of Scots . . . which descendants of the purchasers came in time to treasure in the vain imagination that they were veritable copies from life of the unfortunate monarch, whose head was executed as ruthlessly on canvas as she herself had been at Fotheringay.

> *H. Grey Graham*, The Social Life of Scotland in the Eighteenth Century

17 . . . we stood before the great Cross of Iona, dedicated to St Martin of Tours, the friend of St Ninian. It has the easy, incomparable grace of the true Celtic Cross, strong, sure in workmanship, and at rest. You could feel the harmony behind the chisel that hewed it.

Neil Gunn (1891–1973), Off in a Boat

18 . . . to refine our taste with respect to beauties of art or nature is scarce endeavoured in any seminary of learning; a lamentable defect, considering how early in life taste is susceptible of culture, and how difficult to reform it if unhappily perverted.

Lord Kames (1696–1782), Elements of Criticism

19 I might not know what art is but I'll milk it for all it's worth.

Glasgow civic leader, paraphrased by James Kelman (1946–), in a lecture at Glasgow School of Art, 1996

20 Landseer says I was a good-looking chap twenty years ago, and he therefore asked me to sit to him, whereto I replied, 'Is thy servant a dog, that he should do this thing?' The mot is universally given to Sydney Smith, but Landseer swears he never did, nor could have asked so ugly a fellow to sit, and thinks it unfair that I should have been robbed of my joke in favour of so wealthy a joke-smith.

John Gibson Lockhart (1794–1854), Letters

21 Pictures there are that do not please
With any sweet surprise,
But gain the heart by slow degrees
Until they feast the eyes.

George Macdonald (1824–1905), The Disciple

22 If your programme is to achieve artistic success (and artistic success must be the first aim) then every object you produce must have a strong mark of individuality, beauty, and outstanding workmanship.

Charles Rennie Mackintosh (1868–1928), Lectures and Notes

23 Art's a' the go in Gleska, too; there's something aboot it every ither nicht in the papers when Lord Somebody-or-ither's no divorcin' his wife, an' takin' up the space;

and I hear there's hunders o' pictures oot in yon place at Kelvingrove.

Neil Munro (1864–1930), Erchie

24 Thon new tea room wi' the comic windows . . . The chairs is no' like ony ither chairs I ever clapped eyes on, but ye could easy guess they were chairs; and a' roond the place there's a lump o' lookin'-gless wi' purple leeks pented on it every noo and then.

Neil Munro, Erchie

25 Originality is not necessarily a mark of genius, but Mackintosh was never merely original . . . Single-handed, Mackintosh invented in one way or another almost the whole vocabulary of the modern movement.

Ian Nairn, Britain's Changing Towns *(1967)*

26 I wonder sometimes if, for the good of his soul, the Scots artist of real calibre should not choose deliberately to remain as it were beneath the salt.

Cordelia Oliver, The Visual Arts in Scotland, *in D. Glen,* Whither Scotland? *(1971)*

27 It would give me the greatest pleasure if you would take the trouble to write me at least once a year, if not oftener, and give me a little information of what is going on among the artists, for I do assure you that I have as little communication with any of them, and know almost as little about them, as if I were living on the Cape of Good Hope.

Sir Henry Raeburn (1756–1823), letter to Sir David Wilkie, in London

28 'My dear Roberts', wrote the critic in a private letter, 'you may have seen my remarks on your pictures. I hope they will make no difference to our friendship. Yours, etc.'
'My dear —,' wrote the painter in reply, 'the next time I meet you I shall pull your nose. I hope it will make no difference to our friendship. Yours, etc., D. Roberts'.

Told of David Roberts (1796–1864), in Alexander Hislop, The Book of Scottish Anecdote *(1883)*

29 To sit for one's portrait is like being present at one's own creation.

Alexander Smith (1830–1867), Dreamthorp

30 Raeburn was a born painter of portraits. He looked people shrewdly between the eyes, surprised their manners in their face, and had possessed himself of what was essential in their character before they had been many minutes in his studio.

Robert Louis Stevenson (1850–1894), Virginibus Puerisque

31 . . . that excited amateur who has to die in all of us before the artist can be born.

Robert Louis Stevenson, Memories of Fontainebleau

32 Statues and pictures and verse may be grand,
But they are not the life for which they stand.

James Thomson (1834–1882), Sunday Up the River

33 My dear Sir,
I return you my best thanks for the very handsome manner in which you have paid me for Mrs Bell's picture. You have enclosed twenty-five guineas; I return you five of them, which I have no right to accept, my price having been raised since I painted that picture.

Sir David Wilkie (1785–1841), Letter to G. J. Bell

34 . . . no art that is not intellectual can be worthy of Scotland. Bleak as are her mountains, and homely as are her people, they have yet in their habits and occupations a characteristic acuteness and feeling.Bla

Sir David Wilkie, Speech in Rome, 1827, quoted in *Allan Cunningham*, Life of Sir David Wilkie (1843)

Bad Habits

1 Ye daurna swear aboot the toon,
It is against the law,
An' if ye use profanities,
Then ye'll be putten awa'.

Traditional, *Drumdelgie*

2 It takes a wise man to handle a lie. A fool had better remain honest.

Norman Douglas (1868–1952)

3 Argument to the Scot is a vice more attractive than whisky.

Walter Elliott (1888–1958), speech to the House of Commons, 1942

4 She cried in her thin Aberdeen, What's this? Stop your Blasting and Blaspheming in here. Bruce said, I haven't sworn a damn word

Lewis Grassic Gibbon (James Leslie Mitchell, 1901–1935), Cloud Howe

5 MacDougall Brown, the postmaster, came down to the Square and preached on stealing, right godly-like, and you'd never have thought that him and his wife stayed up of a night sanding the sugar and watering the paraffin – or so folk said, but they tell such lies.

Lewis Grassic Gibbon, Cloud Howe

6 It is the restriction placed on vice by our social code which makes its pursuit so peculiarly agreeable.

Kenneth Grahame (1859–1932)

7 Herein is not only a great vanity, but a great contempt of God's good gifts, that the sweetness of men's breath, being a good gift of God, should be wilfully corrupted by this stinking smoke.

King James VI (1566–1625) A Treatise Against Tobacco

8 Everybody got intoxicated these days. Even the poor wee first-yearers were drinking too much. Mind you it was better than heroin. Or was it: at least with heroin they got an early death whereas with alcohol they were left to traverse the flagstones for a further couple of score years.

James Kelman (1946–), A Disaffection

9 . . . a lie so obvious it was another way of telling the truth.

Norman MacCaig (1910–1996), Queen of Scots

10 Oh, what a tangled web we weave,
When first we practise to deceive.

Sir Walter Scott (1771–1832)

11 A little inaccuracy sometimes saves tons of explanation.

Saki (H. H. Munro, 1870–1916), The Square Egg

12 Scandal is merely the compassionate allowance which the gay make to the humdrum. Think how many blameless lives are brightened by the indiscretions of other people.

Saki

13 We all know that Prime Ministers are
    wedded to the truth, but like other wedded
    couples, they sometimes live apart.
      Saki, The Unbearable Bassington

14 In the excitement of playing football I
    cried 'O! Christ!' for the first time. I would
    be about twelve at the time . . . I paused for
    a moment in the belief that I had commit-
    ted the unforgivable sin.Bla
      *William Soutar (1898–1943), quoted in
      Alexander Scott*, Still Life: William
      Soutar *(1958)*

15 The cruellest lies are often told in silence.
      Robert Louis Stevenson (1850–1894), Vir-
      ginibus Puerisque

16 I hate cynicism a great deal worse than
    I do the Devil; unless, perhaps, the two
    were the same thing?
      Robert Louis Stevenson, Walt Whitman

17 We called Johnny 'Mother Superior'
    because ay the length ay time he'd hud his
    habit.
      Irvine Welsh (1957–), Trainspotting

18 Thir's nivir any real dilemmas wi' junk.
    They only come when ye run oot.
      Irvine Welsh, Trainspotting

Bathos and Vacuity

1 Unmanly, shameless, worthless villain,
   Devoid o' every finer feelin',
   Who with a base affected grace,
   Applauds thy brother to his face,
   Admires his humour, shares his plack,
   And cuts his throat behind his back!
     *Anonymous Ayrshire poet, 'a very long
     way after Burns', quoted in Alexander
     Hislop*, The Book of Scottish Anecdote
     (1883)

2 Thou, Dalhousie, thou great God of War,
   Lieutenant-Colonel to the Earl of Mar.
     *Anonymous apostrophe quoted in D. B.
     Wyndham Lewis and Charles Lee*, The
     Stuffed Owl *(1930)*

3 With lips apart, with heaving heart, gazed
     Miriam on a form,
   Lovely beyond the power of death, the
     grave's polluting worm.
   A lucid air enswathed her head. How
     excellent are they

Dear God, thy ransomed ones!
On her consummate forehead lay
The moonlight of eternal peace, solemn
  and very sweet,
A snowy vesture beautiful came flowing
  o'er her feet.
    Thomas Aird (1802–1876), The Demo-
    niac: A Poem in Seven Chapters, *from*
    Blackwood's Magazine *(1830)*

4 I hope, I fear, resolved, and yet I doubt,
   I'm cold as ice, and yet I burn as fire;
   I wot not what, and yet I much desire,
   And trembling too, am desperately stout.
     William Alexander (c.1567–1640),
     Aurora

5 . . . There are, whose blood
   Impetuous rages through the turgid veins,
   Who better bear the fiery fruits of Ind
   Than the moist melon, or pale cucumber.
   Of chilly nature others fly the board
   Supplied with slaughter, and the vernal
     powers
   For cooler, kinder sustenance implore.
   Some even the generous nutriment detest
   Which, in the shell, the sleeping embryo
     rears.
     Dr John Armstrong (1709–1779), The
     Art of Preserving Health

6 Come, Scotland, tune your stock and
     horn,
   And hail with song this joyous morn,
   When on Love's eagle pinions borne,
   Harriet Beecher Stowe's come.
     James Ballantine (1808–1877), Wel-
     come to Harriet Beecher Stowe

7 But when shall Spring visit the
     mouldering urn?
   O when shall it dawn on the night of the
     grave?
     James Beattie (1735–1803), The Hermit

8 . . . the nectareous, mantling cream,
   From which, express'd by homely toil,
   The richly butyraceous oil:
   The serous parts with equal ease,
   Are formed into the lusty cheese,
   Which is, in spite of all that's rare,
   The chiefest still of Scotia's fare.
     John Bell (early 19th century)

9 Work, and wait, a sturdy liver
   Life fleetly flies!
     John Stuart Blackie (1809–1895), Hymn
     for the Young

10 Past is the race of heroes. But their fame rises on the harp; their souls ride on the wings of the wind; they hear the sound through the sighs of the storm, and rejoice in their hall of clouds! Such is Calmar. This gray stone marks his narrow house. He looks down from eddying tempests: he rolls his form in the whirlwind, and hovers on the blast of the mountain.

> *Lord Byron (1788–1824)*, The Death of Calmar and Orla, An Imitation of Macpherson's Ossian

11 Such was the sob and the mutual throb
Of the knight embracing Jane.

> *Thomas Campbell (1777–1844)*, Ritter Ban

12 To say *ach*! correctly you need generations of Scots blood behind you, and you must have been born with the peat-reek in your nostrils, and the sight of the hills as the first thing you ever clapped eyes on.

> *Ronald MacDonald Douglas (1896–1987)*, The Scots Book

13 Every Scottish heart should beat high and proud today to know that the old country is taking its place in the front of the battle-line. Every bomb dropped on Scotland is one less for London.

> The Dundee Evening Telegraph *(1940), on bombing raids on Scotland, quoted in Hugh MacDiarmid*, Lucky Poet *(1943)*

14 For tho' the Knight got but one view,
One full, intoxicating look,
It was more than his fond heart could brook:
For on the ground he fell as dead,
As he had been shot out through the head.
Now this was rather a sad o'erthrow;
I don't think I would have fallen so –

> *James Hogg (1770–1835)*, On the Origin of the Fairies

15 Loyal-hearted citizens!
Great news there's come to town;
I have not got the particulars yet,
But they'll be in the afternoon.

> *Alexander MacDonald, 'Blind Sandy', late 18th century*

16 And in this temple by the northern sea
Continually
Will surge and seethe the fire-mist of
the mind

Fettered and free,
Radiant and blind.

> *Ronald Campbell MacFie (1867–1931)*, Ode Written for the Opening of the New Buildings of Marischal College, Aberdeen

17 St Paul's Cathedral is the finest building that ever I did see,
There's no building can surpass it in the city of Dundee

> *William McGonagall (1825–1902)*, Descriptive Jottings of London

18 Alas! Lord and Lady Dalhousie are dead, and buried at last,
Which causes many people to feel a little downcast.

> *William McGonagall*, Death of Lord and Lady Dalhousie

19 Old Scotia is peerless in her magnificence: her romance is as something inenarrable ... we shall travel together in diverse airts, wandering round many a venerable ruin, listening intently to an eloquence that has grownlls mellifluous in the passing of years; we shall peep into the quivering mirrors of many a lochan to see the reflections of an ancient chivalry ...

> *Alastair Alpin MacGregor*, Wild Drumalbain *(1927)*

20 An angel by direct descent, a German by alliance,
Thou didst intone the wonder-chords which made Despair a science.
... O Sire of Song! Sonata King! Sublime and loving Master,
The sweetest soul that ever struck an octave in disaster!

> *Eric Mackay (19th century)*, Beethoven

21 Stretch the tired limbs and lay the head
Down on our own delightful bed.

> *James Montgomery (1771–1854)*, Night

22 Wallace stood on the cliff, like the newly-aroused genius of his country. His long plaid floated afar; and his glittering hair, streaming on the blast, seemed to mingle with the golden fires which shot from the heavens.

> *Jane Porter (1776–1850)*, The Scottish Chiefs

23 He wiped his iron eye and brow.

> *Sir Walter Scott (1771–1832)*, The Lady
> of the Lake

24 He took a hundred mortal wounds
As mute as fox 'mongst mangling hounds;
But when he died, his parting groan
Had more of laughter than of moan!

> *Sir Walter Scott*, Rokeby

25 She asked him but to stand beside
her grave –
She said she would be daisies – and
she thought
'Twould give her joy to feel that he
was near.

> *Alexander Smith (1830–1867)*, A Life-
> Drama

26 Trusty, dusky, vivid, true,
With eyes of gold and bramble-dew,
Steel true and blade straight
The Great Artificer
made my mate.

> *Robert Louis Stevenson (1850–1894)*, My
> Wife

Biography and Memoirs

1 Biography should be written by an acute
enemy.

> *A. J. Balfour (1848–1930), quoted in* The
> Observer, *(1927)*

2 The life of every man is a diary in which
he means to write one story, and writes
another, and his humblest hour is when he
compares the volume as it is with what he
vowed to make it.

> *J. M. Barrie (1860–1937)*, The Golden
> Book

3 Dinna speak tae me o' the guid auld days,
For wha mair than me kens better;
Wha ran barefitted in ragged claes,
In summer days and winter.

> *Mary Brooksbank (1897–1980)*, 18
> Dempster Street – The Guid Auld Bad
> Days

4 It adds a new terror to death.

> *Lord Brougham (1778–1868), on Lord
> Campbell's* Lives of the Lord Chancel-
> lors *(1845–47)*

5 . . . a well-written life is almost as rare as a
well-spent one.

> *Thomas Carlyle (1795–1881)*, Essays, *on
> Jean Paul Richter*

6 Autobiography is an attempted jail-break.

> *Stuart Hood (1915–)*, Pebbles from My
> Skull

7 My life has been an adventure, or series of
adventures, in the exploration of the mystery of Scotland's self-suppression.

> *Hugh MacDiarmid (C. M. Grieve,
> 1892–1978)*, Lucky Poet

8 The first night I appeared there certainly
was a little undue excitement amongst the
audience; and some throwing of objectionable and dangerous missiles; but on the
whole I was allowed to proceed in compara-
tive peace with my famous 'Bannockburn',
which was applauded to the echo. Next
night however – shall I ever forget it?
Never! I shall carry its memory as well as
its marks to the grave. Until that night I
never for a moment imagined that there
were so many veritable fiends in Europe,
let alone Dundee.

> *William McGonagall (1825–1902)*, Auto-
> biography *(collected, and at least partly
> written, by John Willocks, 1905)*

9 I remember when they were so numerous
and so stationed in various quarters of the
city, that if a person called *Cady*! in any of
the principal streets or lanes, he was immediately attended by one of these guides or
messengers. They exercised the functions
of Mercury in offices more confidential,
tho' less moral and honourable than that
of a messenger.

> *Henry Mackenzie (1745–1831), on Edin-
> burgh's caddies, quoted in H. W. Thomson,*
> The Anecdotes and Egotisms of Henry
> Mackenzie

10 You ask my opinion about keeping a journal. Believe me, it seldom or ever turns
to account. I once in my life thought of
some such thing, but some of my companions getting sight of one of the pages, I was
laughed out of it.

> *John Ramsay of Ochtertyre (1736–1814),
> letter to Elizabeth Graham, March 1804*

11 What a life mine has been. Half educated,
almost wholly neglected or left to myself –
5stuffing my head with most nonsensical

trash and undervalued in society for a time by most of my companions – getting forward and held. a bold and clever fellow, contrary to the opinion of all who thought me a mere dreamer – Broken-hearted for two years – My heart handsomely pieced again – but the crack will remain to my dying day – Rich and poor four or five times – Once on the verge of ruin yet opened new sources of wealth almost overflowing – onow taken in the pitch of pride and nearly winged . . . And what is to be the end of it? God knows and so ends the chatechism.

> *Sir Walter Scott (1771–1832)*, Diaries

12 The great and good do not die even in this world. Embalmed in books, their spirits walk abroad.

> *Samuel Smiles (1816–1904)*, Character

13 These deathless names by this dead
    snake defiled
    Bid memory spit upon him for their sake.

> *Algernon Swinburne (1837–1909)*, After Looking Into Carlyle's Reminiscences

Boasts, Vaunts and Challenges

1 Maydens of Englande, sore may ye morne
   For your lemmans ye haue lost at
   Bannockysborne,
   With heue a lowe.
   What, weneth the kynge of Englande
   So soone to haue wonne Scotlande?
   With rumbylow.

> *Anonymous, 14th century*

2 My hands are tied, but my tongue is free,
   And whae will this deed avow?
   Or answer by the Border law?
   Or answer to the bauld Buccleuch?

> *Anonymous*, Kinmont Willie

3 I can drink and nae be drunk,
   I can fecht and nae be slain;
   I can lie wi' another man's lass
   And aye be welcome tae my ain.

> *Traditional*, The Barnyards o' Delgaty

4 The Laird of Keppoch . . . in a winter campaign against a neighbouring laird, with whom he was at war about a possession, gave orders for rolling a snowball to lay under his head in the night; whereupon his followers murmured, saying, 'Now we

despair of victory, since our leader is become so effeminate he can't sleep without a pillow.'

> *Edmund Burt (fl. early 18th century)*, Letters from a Gentleman in the North of Scotland, *(1726–37), and often quoted of others in similar contexts*

5 . . . the chief ordered one of them to sing me a Highland song . . . in his going on, the chief (who piques himself upon his school-learning), at some particular passage, bid him cease, and cried out to me – 'There's nothing like that in Virgil or Homer!' I bowed, and told him I believed so.

> *Edmund Burt*, Letters from a Gentleman in the North of Scotland

6 I have often heard the soldiers discussing round the camp-fires as to who was the bravest man in the Grand Army. Some said Murat, and some said Lassalle, and some Ney; but for my own part, when they asked me, I merely shrugged my shoulders and smiled. It would have seemed mere conceit if I had answered that there was no man braver than Brigadier Gerard. At the same time, facts are facts, and a man knows best what his own feelings are.

> *Sir Arthur Conan Doyle (1859–1930)*, The Exploits of Brigadier Gerard

7 Long ago the Macleods of Harris and the MacDonalds of Uist, both desirous of owning St Kilda, decided that a *curach* from Harris and a *curach* from Uist should race each other across the intervening fifty miles of sea, and that the crew of the boat arriving first should have the right to claim Hirta. The long race was a close one, and the boats approached Hirta with the MacDonalds leading by a few yards. When it seemed certain that the MacLeods would be defeated . . . their leader, Colla MacLeod, chopped off his left hand at the wrist and hurled it ashore over the heads of the rival crew.

> *Seton Gordon (1888–1977)*, Afoot in the Hebrides

8 In my opinion Scotland is the great White Hope of European art.

> *William McCance (1894–1970)*, The Idea in Art, *(1930); quoted in D. Macmillan*, Scottish Art 1460–1990 *(1990)*

9 I on the other hand would sacrifice a million people any day for one immortal lyric.
   I am a scientific socialist.

   > *Hugh MacDiarmid (C. M. Grieve,
   > 1892–1978),* Scottish Scene *(see Lewis
   > Grassic Gibbon, Politics & Protest)*

10 . . . it is a common experience of mine
   to have professors and other specialists in
   this or that language or literature, or in
   subjects ranging from geology to cerebral
   localization or the physiological conditions
   of originality of thought, admit that I am
   far better read even in their own particular
   subject than they are themselves.

   > *Hugh MacDiarmid,* Lucky Poet

11 Och hey! for the splendour of tartans!
   And hey for the dirk and the targe!
   The race that was hard as the Spartans
   Shall return again to the charge.

   > *Pittendrigh MacGillivray (1856–1930),*
   > The Return

12 Each evening after dinner he sent a trum-
   peter up to his castle-tower to make the
   following proclamation: 'Ye kings, princes
   and potentates of all the earth, be it known
   unto you that Macneill of Barra has dined –
   the rest of the world may dine now.'

   > *Kenneth Macleod (1871–1955), Introduc-
   > tion to Marjory Kennedy-Fraser,* Songs
   > of the Hebrides

13 He either fears his fate too much,
   Or his deserts are small,
   That puts it not unto the touch,
   To win, or lose, it all.

   > *Marquis of Montrose (1612–1650),* To
   > His Mistress

14 Whit'll ye dae when the wee Malkies
     come,
   if they dreep doon affy the wash-hoose
     dyke,
   an pit the hems oan the stair-heid light,
   an play wee heidies oan the clean
     close-wa,
   an blooter yir windae in wi the baw,
   missis, whit'll ye dae?

   > *Stephen Mulrine (1936–),* The Coming
   > of the Wee Malkies

15 Far in the bosom of the deep,
   O'er these wild shelves my watch I keep;
   A ruddy gem of changeful light
   Bound on the dusky brow of night

   > *Sir Walter Scott (1771–1832),* Pharos

Loquitur *(written at the Bell Rock Light-
house, 1814)*

16 Come fill up my cup, come fill up my can;
   Come saddle your horses, and call out
     your men,
   Unhook the West Port, and let us gae free,
   And it's up wi' the bonnets o' Bonnie
     Dundee.

   > *Sir Walter Scott,* Bonnie Dundee

17 Prayer of the minister of the two Cumbrays, two miserable islands in the mouth
   of the Clyde: 'Oh Lord, bless and be
   gracious to the Greater and the Lesser
   Cumbrays, and in thy mercy do not forget
   the adjacent islands of Great Britain and
   Ireland.'

   > *Sir Walter Scott,* Journal, *September
   > 1827*

18 The kilt is . . . I don't know how to put
   this . . . it's an aphrodisiac. I can't tell you
   why, but it works . . . hap your hurdies with
   the passion pleats and it doesn't seem to
   matter what kind of women they are – rich,
   poor, old, young, black, white and yellow –
   they just melt, go shoogly in the legs, and,
   well, submit . . . Unconditional surrender.

   > *W. Gordon Smith,* Mr Jock *(1987)*

19 'And oh, man,' he cried in a kind of ecstasy,
   'am I no a bonny fighter?'

   > *Robert Louis Stevenson (1850–1894),*
   > Kidnapped

20 I have taken a firm resolution to conquer
   or to die and stand my ground as long as I
   have a man remaining with me.

   > *Prince Charles Edward Stewart
   > (1720–1788), letter to his father, 1745*

21 Of what is interesting in Scottish writing
   in the past twenty years or so, I have written it all.

   > *Alexander Trocchi (1925–1984), at the
   > Edinburgh International Writers' Confer-
   > ence, August 1962*

22 Scullions, hogge rubbers, kenell brakers
   and all others of the meanist sort of rascal-
   litie, to spit in your face, kicke you in the
   breach, to tred on your mushtashes, as also
   to all those that know yow to curse yow
   with all the execrations mentioned in the
   Psalmes off David . . . from thence furth
   no honest man will offer to eat drinke or

converse with yow nor any above the degre of a hangmans varlet to serve yow.

> *Sir Thomas Urquhart (1611–1660)*, His Letter to the Laird of Cromartie

23 . . . this most beautiful country, which I am proud to call my own, where there was such devoted loyalty to the family of my ancestors – for Stuart blood is in my veins, and I am now their representative.

> *Queen Victoria (1819–1901)*, Our Life in the Highlands

24 When we fell we aye got up again, and will we yet.

> *William Watson (fl. 19th century)* Come, Sit Down, My Cronie

25 The Minister said it wald dee,
the cypress buss I plantit.
But the buss grew til a tree,
naething dauntit.

It's growan, stark and heich,
derk and straucht and sinister,
kirkyairdie-like and dreich.
But whaur's the Minister?

> *Douglas Young (1913–1973)*, Last Lauch

Books and Authors

1 Now that few in England go to church, the reading of novels is probably the most effective training for emotional life – and for distinguishing between right and wrong.

> *Neal Ascherson (1932–)* The Observer

2 Walter Scott has no business to write novels, especially good ones. – It is not fair – He has fame and fortune enough as a poet, and should not be taking the bread out of other people's mouths.

> *Jane Austen (1775–1817), letter to Anna Austen, 1814*

3 John Anybody would have stood higher with the critics than Joanna Baillie.

> *Joanna Baillie (1762–1851), letter to Sir Walter Scott, c.1825*

4 It is the pleasures and not the profits, spiritual or temporal, of literature which most require to be preached in the ear of the ordinary reader.

> *A. J. Balfour (1848–1930)*, Essays and Addresses

5 There is no mood to which a man may not administer the appropriate medicine at the cost of reaching down a volume from his bookshelf.

> *A. J. Balfour*, Essays and Addresses

6 It is all very well to be able to write books, but can you waggle your ears?

> *J. M. Barrie (1860–1937), letter to H. G. Wells*

7 I remember being asked by two maiden ladies about the time I left the university, what I was to be, and when I replied brazenly, 'An Author', they flung up their hands, and one exclaimed reproachfully, 'And you an MA!'

> *J. M. Barrie*, Margaret Ogilvy

8 For several days after my first book was published, I carried it about in my pocket, and took surreptitious peeps at it to make sure that the ink had not faded.

> *J. M. Barrie, speech to the Critics' Circle, 1920*

9 They say that when the author was on the scaffold he said goodbye to the minister and the reporters, and then he saw some publishers sitting in the front row below, and to them he did not say goodbye. He said merely, 'I'll see you later'.

> *J. M. Barrie, speech to the Aldine Club, New York, 1896*

10 A man who has been able to furnish a book which has been approved by the world has established himself as a respectable character in distant society, without any danger of having that character lessened by the observation of his weaknesses.

> *James Boswell (1740–1795), Preface to* An Account of Corsica

11 He had book-making so much in his thoughts, and was so chary of what might be turned to account in that way, that he once said . . . that he made it a rule when in company never to talk of what he understood.

> *James Boswell, in a note to Langton's* Johnsoniana (1780), on Adam Smith

12 . . . copulation is a sweet and necessary act . . . it is like defecation, an exceedingly interesting process; but it is much better described in physiological textbooks than

in all the works of all the novelists ancient and modern who have ever existed.

James Bridie (Osborne Henry Mavor, 1888–1951), letter to Neil Gunn, January 1932

13   The craft of writing is in many ways a sad business; it is unlike such trades as carpentry or mason-work where having learned the rudiments, a workman can only get better with time. For the writer, the wind bloweth where it listeth.

George Mackay Brown (1922–1996)

14   Critics! appall'd I venture on the name, Those cut-throat bandits on the path of fame.

Robert Burns (1759–1796) On Critics

15   Through and through th'inspired leaves, Ye maggots, make your windings; But O, respect his lordship's taste, And spare the golden bindings!

Robert Burns, The Book Worms

16   Some books are lies frae end to end.

Robert Burns, Death and Doctor Hornbook

17   Quelle vie! Let no woman who values peace of soul ever dream of marrying an author!

Jane Welsh Carlyle (1801–1866), letter to John Sterling, 1837

18   Considering the multitude of mortals that can handle the pen in these days, and can mostly spell, and write without glaring violations of grammar, the question naturally arises: How is it, then, that no work proceeds from them, bearing any stamp of authenticity and permanence, of worth for more than one day?

Thomas Carlyle (1795–1881), Biography

19   Of the things which man can do or make here below, by far the most momentous, wonderful and worthy are the things we call Books!

Thomas Carlyle, On Heroes, Hero-Worship, and the Heroic in History

20   If a book come from the heart, it will contrive to reach other hearts; all art and authorcraft are of small amount to that.

Thomas Carlyle, On Heroes, Hero-Worship, and the Heroic in History

21   In the true Literary Man there is thus ever, acknowledged or not by the world, a sacredness: he is the light of the world; the world's Priest, – guiding it, like a sacred Pillar of Fire, in its dark pilgrimage through the waste of Time.

Thomas Carlyle, On Heroes, Hero-Worship, and the Heroic in History

22   No good Book, or good thing of any sort, shows its best face at first.

Thomas Carlyle, Novalis

23   Literary criticism is constantly attempting a very absurd thing – the explanation of a passionate utterance by utterance that is unimpassioned: it is like trying to paint a sunset in lamp-black.

John Davidson (1857–1909) Sentences and Paragraphs

24   So fat and Buddhistic and nasal that a dear friend described him as an animated adenoid.

Norman Douglas (1868–1952), quoted in R. A. Cassell, Ford Madox Ford *(1961) on Ford Madox Ford*

25   Can anything be called a book unless it forces the reader by one method or another, by contrast or sympathy, to discover himself?

Norman Douglas, Experiments

26   It is with publishers as with wives: one always wants somebody else's.

Norman Douglas, Some Limericks

27   A man should keep his little brain attic stocked with all the furniture that he is likely to use, and the rest he can put away in the lumber room of his library, where he can get it if he wants it.

Sir Arthur Conan Doyle (1859–1930), The Adventures of Sherlock Holmes

28   I cannot endure that man's writing – his vulgarity beats print.

Susan Ferrier (1782–1854) on the works of John Galt (1779–1839), quoted by James Irvine in his Introduction to The Inheritance *(1984)*

29   It is a story of crofter life near Stonehaven, but it is questionable if the author, or authoress, is correct in the description of crofter girls' underclothing of the period.

From the Fife Herald *review of* Sunset Song *by Lewis Grassic Gibbon, quoted*

in Gibbon and MacDiarmid, Scottish Scene *(1934)*

30 The only apology which this work perhaps requires is with regard to the title, for otherwise it belongs to a class of publications, of which the value is so obvious as to admit of no question.

   John Galt (1779–1839), The Bachelor's Wife

31 He also was a poet and painter – the author of t*Poems of a Painter* – which Carlyle, misreading, took to be *Poems of a Printer* and severely criticised, recommending to the supposed printer the habit of *doing* instead of *saying*.

   William Gaunt, The Pre-Raphaelite Tragedy *(1942), on William Bell Scott (1811–1890)*

32 And one book she'd thought fair daft, *Alice in Wonderland* it was, and there was no sense in it. And the second, it was *What Katy Did at School*, and she loved Katy and envied her and wished like Katy she lived at a school, not tramping back in the spleiter of a winter night to help muck the byre, with the smell of the sharn rising feuch! in her face.

   Lewis Grassic Gibbon (James Leslie Mitchell, 1901–1935), Sunset Song

33 There is not the remotest reason why the majority of modern Scottish writers should be considered Scots at all.

   Lewis Grassic Gibbon, Scottish Scene *(1934)*

34 Mr Gunn is a brilliant novelist from Scotshire who chooses his home county as the scene of his tales . . . he is the greatest loss to itself that Scottish literature has suffered in this century.

   Lewis Grassic Gibbon, Scottish Scene, *on Neil Gunn (1891–1973)*

35 Mr Eric Linklater is a lost Norseman with a tendency to go berserk amidst the unfamiliar trappings of literary civilisation.

   Lewis Grassic Gibbon, Scottish Scene

36 For Mora
   At long last, a book by her brother which will not make her blush.

   Alasdair Gray (1934–), Dedication of The Fall of Kelvin Walker

37 This slip has been inserted by mistake.

   Erratum slip in Alasdair Gray, Unlikely Stories, Mostly *(1983)*

38 Never literary attempt was more unfortunate than my *Treatise of Human Nature*. It fell *dead-born from the press*.

   David Hume (1711–1776), My Own Life

39 'I have four reasons for not writing: I am too old, too fat, too lazy, and too rich.'

   David Hume, when urged to complete his History of England, *quoted in E. Guérard*, Dictionnaire Encyclopédique

40 She read the manuscript of her first novel, *Marriage*, to her father, behind the cover of a screen that he could not see what she was reading. He told her 'It was the best book you have ever brought me.' He considered her assertion that it was written by a woman as 'nonsense', and then she confessed that it was her own work.

   From James Irvine's Introduction to The Inheritance *by Susan Ferrier (1782–1854)*

41 I told him that William Sharp had confided to a friend of mine that whenever he was preparing to write as Fiona Macleod he dressed himself entirely in woman's clothes. 'Did he?' said W.P. – 'the bitch!'

   Recorded of W. P. Ker (1855–1923) in E. V. Lucas, Reading, Writing and Remembering *(1932)*

42 Few books today are forgivable.

   R. D. Laing (1927–1989), The Politics of Experience

43 The Love of Books, the Golden Key
   That opens the Enchanted Door.

   Andrew Lang (1844–1912) Ballade of the Bookworm

44 Here stand my books, line upon line,
   They reach the roof, and, row by row,
   They speak of faded tastes of mine,
   And things I did, but do not, know.

   Andrew Lang

45 Authors and uncaptured criminals are the only people free from routine.

   Eric Linklater (1899–1974), Poet's Pub

46 . . . his amanuenses were William Laidlaw and John Ballantyne, of whom he preferred the latter when he could be at Abbotsford,

on account of the superior rapidity of his pen, and also because John kept his pen to the paper without interruption . . . whereas good Laidlaw entered with such keen zest into the interest of the story as it flowed from the author's lips, that he could not suppress exclamations of surprise and delight – 'Gude keep us a'! – 'the like o' that!' – 'eh, sirs!' – and so forth, which did not promote dispatch.

John Gibson Lockhart (1794–1854), Memoirs of the Life of Sir Walter Scott

47 Our principal writers have nearly all been fortunate in escaping regular education.

Hugh MacDiarmid (1892–1978), quoted in The Observer

48 The majority of literary critics, especially London ones, recall to me that extraordinary chirruping conversation which sounds almost human but, on investigation with an electric torch, is found to be merely a couple of hedgehogs courting beneath one's window.

Hugh MacDiarmid, Lucky Poet

49 I was a good deal affected with some very trifling passages in it; and had the name of Marmontel or Richardson been on the title page – 'tis odds I should have wept: Buta – One is ashamed to be pleased with the works of one knows not whom.

Henry Mackenzie (1745–1831), The Man of Feeling

50 With the birth of each child you lose two novels.

Candia MacWilliam (1957–), quoted in The Guardian, *(1993)*

51 He is writing a novel and his characters all want soaking in double strong disinfectant for a week.

Rhea Mitchell, wife of Lewis Grassic Gibbon (James Leslie Mitchell, 1901–1935), letter, March 1927, on his first novel, Stained Radiance

52 Men of sorrow, and acquainted with Grieve.

Edwin Muir (1887–1959), on contemporary Scottish writers, quoted in Karl Miller, Memoirs of a Modern Scotland *(1970)*

53 It is one of the hateful characteristics of a degenerate age, that the idle world will not let the worker alone, accept his offering of work, and appraise it for itself, but must insist in turning *him* inside out, and knowing all about him.

Sir James Murray (1837–1915), founder of the Oxford English Dictionary, *letter to Dr Bryce, December 1903*

54 And better had they ne'er been born, Who read to doubt, or read to scorn.

Sir Walter Scott (1771–1832), The Monastery

55 I have seen his pen gang as fast ower the paper, as ever it did ower the water when it was in the grey goose's wing.

Sir Walter Scott, The Heart of Midlothian

56 There is an ominous old proverb which says, *confess and be hanged;* and truly if an author acknowledges his own blunders, I do not know who he can expect to stand by him; whereas, let him confess nothing, and he will always find some injudicious admirers to vindicate even his faults.

Sir Walter Scott, letter to Lady Louisa Stuart, April 1813

57 To live the life of a mere author for bread is perhaps the most dreadful fate that can be encountered.

Sir Walter Scott, letter to James Bailey, 1817

58 Please return this book: I find that though many of my friends are poor arithmeticians, they are nearly all good book-keepers.

Bookmark alleged to belong to Sir Walter Scott

59 Books are a finer world within the world.

Alexander Smith (1830–1867), Dreamthorp

60 Style, after all, rather than thought, is the immortal thing in literature.

Alexander Smith, Dreamthorp

61 The skin of a man of letters is peculiarly sensitive to the bite of the critical mosquito, and he lives in a climate in which such mosquitoes swarm. He is seldom stabbed to the heart – he is often killed by pin-pricks.

Alexander Smith, Dreamthorp

62 Every person of importance ought to write his own memoirs, provided he has honesty enough to tell the truth.

  Tobias Smollett (1721–1771)

63 Books are good enough in their own way, but they are a mighty bloodless substitute for life . . . There are not many works extant, if you look the alternative all over, which are worth the price of a pound of tobacco to a man of limited means.

  Robert Louis Stevenson (1850–1894), Virginibus Puerisque

64 There is no quite good book without a good morality; but the world is wide, and so are morals.

  Robert Louis Stevenson, A Gossip on a Novel of Dumas's

65 Fiction is to the grown man what play is to the child; it is there that he changes the atmosphere and tenor of his life.

  Robert Louis Stevenson, A Gossip on Romance

66 There is but one art – to omit! O if I knew how to omit, I would ask no other knowledge.

  Robert Louis Stevenson, letter to R. A. M. Stevenson, 1883

67 I do not write for the public; I do write for money, a nobler deity; and most of all for myself, not perhaps any more noble, but both more intelligent and nearer home.

  Robert Louis Stevenson, letter to Edmund Gosse, January 1886

68 Dugald Stewart, in the true absence of mind of a philosopher, often forgot, it was alleged, to return books which he had borrowed to read. On its being said that, eminent as he was in many branches of knowledge, he confessed himself deficient in Arithmetic, a punster said, 'That, tho' very improbable, might be true; but he certainly excelled in book-keeping.'

  Recorded of Dugald Stewart (1753–1828), in H. W. Thomson, The Anecdotes and Egotisms of Henry Mackenzie *(1927)*

69 The Scots are incapable of considering their literary geniuses purely as writers or artists. They must be either an excuse for a glass or a text for the next sermon.

  George Malcolm Thomson, Caledonia

70 While Reason drew the plan, the Heart inform'd
  The moral page, and Fancy lent it grace.

  James Thomson (1700–1748), Liberty

71 Give a man a pipe he can smoke,
  Give a man a book he can read:
  And his home is bright with a calm delight,
  Though the room be poor indeed.

  James Thomson (1834–1882), Sunday Up the River

72 Write and write
  And read these stupid, worn-out books!
  That's all he does, read, write and read.

  James Thomson, In the Room

73 A blizzard of authors was sweeping through Glasgow. To get into the boozers you'd to plod through drifts of Hemingways and Mailers. Kerouacs by the dozen could be found lipping the Lanny on Glesca Green.

  Jeff Torrington (1935–), Swing Hammer Swing

74 Barbour is only the first of a long series of Scottish writers who seem not only on terms of an informal intimacy with God (or the Devil) but even to be disposed, on occasion, to argue with Him.

  Kurt Wittig, The Scottish Tradition in Literature *(1958) on John Barbour (c.1320–1395)*

75 . . . all the villanous profane and obscene books and plays . . . are got down from London by Allan Ramsay, and lent out, for an easy price, to young boys, servant women of the better sort, and gentlemen, and vice and obscenity fearfully propagated.

  Robert Wodrow (1679–1734), Analecta, *on Allan Ramsay's pioneering library*

Buildings

1 Early chosen as a religious home, both St Columba and St Cuthbert appear in the traditions of Dunkeld . . . This minster was the scene of violence to the last. When the most illustrious of its prelates, Gavin Douglas, came to take possession of his throne in 1516, he was opposed by a shower of shot from the cathedral tower and bishop's palace; and it was not until

the power of the great family to which he belonged had been gathered from Fife and Angus that he obtained access to his church, 'thanks to the intercession of St Columba', says the chronicle, without loss of life or limb.

Anonymous, The Quarterly Review, *No. 169*

2 The novelty and variety of the following designs will, we flatter ourselves, not only excuse, but justify our conduct, in communicating them to the world. We have not trod in the paths of others, nor derived aid from their labours. In the works which we have had the honour to execute, we . . . have brought about, in this country, a kind of revolution in the whole system of this useful and elegant art.

Robert (1728–1792) and James (1730–1794) Adam, The Works in Architecture of Robert and James Adam, Esqs, Volume I

3 It's grand, and you cannot expect to be baith grand and comfortable.

J. M. Barrie (1860–1937), The Little Minister

4 The oldest part of the building was invariably the stairs and stairwell . . . There was a musty vegetable dampness about these stairways – like an old gloomy cellar: earthy, mossy, feculent.

William Boyd (1952–), The New Confessions

5 . . . a jewel of great price: St Magnus Cathedral . . . Unmoving still, it voyages on, the great ark of the people of Orkney, into unknown centuries.

George Mackay Brown (1921–1996), An Orkney Tapestry

6 This mony a year I've stood the flood
   an' tide:
And tho' wi' crazy eild I'm sair forfairn,
I'll be a brig when ye're a shapeless cairn.

Robert Burns (1759–1796), The Brigs of Ayr

7 A Highland Town is composed of a few Huts for Dwellings . . . all irregularly placed, some one way, some another, and, at any Distance, look like so many heaps of Dirt.

Edmund Burt (fl. early 18th century),

Letters from a Gentleman in the North of Scotland *(1728–37)*

8 Billy remarked in 'World Tour of Scotland' that the oldest house in Glasgow, Provand's Lordship, was built in 1471 and still standing, though his Drumchapel home, built in the '50s, has since been demolished as uninhabitable. 'What did they know about building houses in 1471 that they don't know now?'

Billy Connolly (1942–), quoted by James McGowan on the Billy Connolly Website (1998)

9 . . . we find the glories of ancient Scotland jostled by taverns, workshops, and inns, rising sheer, not from green meadows or amongst tangled thickets of thorns, but out of unseemly assemblages of shops and houses, crowding up into cloister and graveyard, obliterating every trace of chapter house, refectory, dorter, even in some cases portions of the church itself.

R. C. Cram, The Ruined Abbeys of Great Britain *(1906)*

10 The typical Lewis crofter's house was built by the crofter himself . . . There was no chimney and often no window . . . only one door, used by the cattle and family alike.

J. P. Day, Public Administration in the Highlands and Islands of Scotland *(1918), quoted in T. C. Smout, A Century of the Scottish People,1830–1950 (1986)*

11 You would wonder at the change the little tenants have made in their houses and farms since they knew they are not to be removed or *raxed*, and are rid of services. These are now mostly of stone and whitened, shining like a negro's teeth through the black muir.

George Dempster, Laird of Skibo, letter to Sir Adam Ferguson, 1794

12 It is not the bulk of a fabric, the richness and quantity of the materials, the multiplicity of lines, nor the gaudiness of the finishing that give the grace or beauty or grandeur to a building: but the proportion of the parts to one another and to the whole, whether entirely plain or enriched with a few ornaments properly disposed.

James Gibbs (1682–1754), A Book of Architecture *(1728)*

13 But on the whole, the plain yet sturdy-looking little two-storied houses that one sees scattered over the crofting areas have achieved a definite local character. They fit well into their background and when, as is generally the case, they have been given a coat of dazzling lime wash, they look out, like kindly faces, from the brown hillsides.

   I. F. Grant, Highland Folk Ways *(1961)*

14 The place is, of course, technically a ruin, and internally it is literally a ruin, but it has neither the appearance nor the common characteristics of a ruin. There is no symptom of decay about its huge shell, which looks as if it might at any moment pour forth from the great doorway a troop of Border riders, with their leather jackets, their steel caps, and their faces set southward.

   Lord Ernest Hamilton, Old Days and New, *on Hermitage Castle, quoted in Hugh MacDiarmid*, Lucky Poet *(1943)*

15 'Tis but a cot roofed in with straw; a hovel
   built of clay:
   One door shuts out the snow and storm,
   one window greets the day.
   And yet I stand within this room and hold
   all thrones in scorn,
   For here, beneath this lowly thatch love's
   sweetest bard was born.

   R. G. Ingersoll (1833–1899), The Burns Cottage in Ayr

16 Whether should a ruin be in the Gothic or Grecian form? In the former, I say, because it exhibits the triumph of time over strength, a melancholy but not unpleasant thought. A Grecian ruin suggests the triumph of barbarity over taste, a gloomy and discouraging thought.

   Lord Kames (1696–1782), Elements of Criticism

17 Mr Knoxe did with our glorious Churches of Abbacies and Monasteries (which were the greatest beauties of the Kingdome) knocking all down to desolation; leaving naught to be seen of admirable edifices, but like to the ruins of Troy, Tyrus, and Theba.

   William Lithgow (c.1585–1645), Comments Upon Scotland

18 Bungalows . . . the ceilings are so low, all you can have for tea is kippers.

   Anonymous, quoted in Charles McKean, Thirties Scotland

19 All great and living architecture has been the direct expression of the needs and beliefs of man at the time of its creation, and now, if we would have good architecture created, this should still be so . . . It is absurd to think it is the duty of the modern architect to make believe he is living four, five, six hundred, or even one thousand years before.

   Charles Rennie Mackintosh (1868–1928), Lectures and Notes

20 There are many decorative features in Scottish architecture which might well be replaced by others of antiquity, but because we are Scottish and not Greek or Roman, we reject . . . I think we should be a little less cosmopolitan and rather more national in our architecture.

   Charles Rennie Mackintosh, Lectures and Notes

21 You ask how are you to judge architecture. Just as you judge painting or sculpture – form, colour, proportion, all visible qualities – and the one great invisible quality in all art, soul.

   Charles Rennie Mackintosh, Lectures and Notes

22 The castles of the chiefs were inconvenient and rude internally, though striking and picturesque in their external features. Those that I remember in their pristine condition contained very few of the comforts or conveniences of modern life . . . many thousand modern villas that are now on the outskirts of our cities are preferable houses to live in.

   Joseph Mitchell (1803–1883), Reminiscences of My Life in the Highlands

23 Abbotsford is a very strange house . . . that it should ever have been lived in is the most astonishing, staggering, saddening thing of all. It is surely the strangest and saddest monument that Scott's genius created.

   Edwin Muir (1887–1959), Scottish Journey

24 The Hebrides' only ancient church not ruinous, apart from Iona's, is the priory

church of St Clement at Rodil in south Harris . . . The south wall bears a rarity, a *sheela-na-gig*, or roughly-hewn small man holding his erect penis. The Celtic churches of Ireland have at least thirty-six of these fertility figures, but the only other in Scotland, on the west wall of Iona's nunnery, has recently disappeared. The chips knocked off this otherwise excellent Rodil specimen were caused by the countess of Dunmore, who ordered her gillie to fire his gun at it.

> *W. H. Murray*, The Islands of Western Scotland *(1973)*

25 . . . one of the most elegant structures, but one of the most unsuitable places of worship, in the Empire . . . the object of the Duchess . . . was to provide a mausoleum for the remains of her late husband, and for hers—elf, and for this purpose she spared neither her own purse, nor the feelings of her people.

> *Donald Sage (1789–1869)*, Memorabilia Domestica, *on the 'restoration' of Dornoch Cathedral by the Duchess of Sutherland*

26 In Saxon strength that abbey frowned,
With massive arches broad and round,
Built ere the art was known
By pointed aisles, and shafted stalk,
The arcades of an alleyed walk
To emulate in stone.

> *Sir Walter Scott (1771–1832)*, Marmion

27 'Ah! It's a brave kirk; nane o' yere whig-maleeries and curliewurlies and opensteek hems about it,– a solid, weel-jointed mason-wark, that will stand as lang as the warld, keep hands and gunpowther aff it.'

> *Sir Walter Scott*, Rob Roy, *on Glasgow Cathedral*

28 Standing on the ramparts of Stirling castle, the spectator cannot help noticing an unsightly excrescence of stone and lime rising on the brow of the Abbey Craig. This is the Wallace Tower.

> *Alexander Smith (1830–1867)*, A Summer in Skye

29 A monument o' strength and grace
Til the dour age o' coal and steam.

> *Sydney Goodsir Smith (1915–1975)*, The Two Brigs, *on the Forth Railway Bridge*

30 It is easy to tell which used to be the servants' bedrooms in Victorian villas in Glasgow and Edinburgh because they are the only ones with bars on the windows.

> *T. C. Smout*, A Century of the Scottish People, *1830–1950 (1986)*

31 A hoose is but a puppet-box
To keep life's images frae knocks,
But mannikins scrieve oot their sauls
Upon its craw-steps and its walls:
Whaur hae they writ them mair sublime
Than on yon gable-ends o' time?

> *Lewis Spence (1874–1955)*, The Prows o' Reekie

32 I never weary of great churches. It is my favourite kind of mountain scenery. Mankind was never so happily inspired as when it made a cathedral.

> *Robert Louis Stevenson (1850–1894)*, An Inland Voyage

33 Day by day, one new villa, one new object of offence, is added to another; all around Newington and Morningside, the dismalest structures keep springing up like mushrooms; the pleasant hills are loaded with them, each impudently squatted in its garden . . . They belong to no style of art, only to a form of business much to be regretted.

> *Robert Louis Stevenson*, Picturesque Notes on Edinburgh

34 At last I view the storied scene,
The embattled rock and valley green,
And hear, 'mid reverent Nature's hush,
The water-closet's frequent flush.

> *John Warrack, letter to* The Scotsman *on the erection of a public convenience in Princes Street Gardens, Edinburgh, December 1920*

35 Why do you propose these boxes for our people? Are they inferior people to you? Are they less useful to the community than you?

> *John Wheatley (1873–1930), on government criteria for house-building (1923)*

Robert Burns

1 There is no other poet like him. And thus, in a peculiar sense, he is not a poet at all. He had no predecessors; he has had

no disciples; and he is much too gigantic, too overflowing at too many points, to be neatly, adequately or illuminatingly categorised, labelled and filed away.

> *James Barke, Introduction to* Poems and Songs of Robert Burns *(1953)*

2 What an antithetical mind!– tenderness, roughness – delicacy, coarseness, – sentiment, sensuality – soaring and grovelling, dirt and deity – all mixed up in that one compound of inspired clay.

> *Lord Byron (1788–1824),* Journal, *1813*

3 Whose lines are mottoes of the heart, Whose truths electrify the sage.

> *Thomas Campbell (1777–1834),* On Robert Burns

4 A Burns is infinitely better educated than a Byron.

> *Thomas Carlyle (1795–1881),* Note Book

5 In a life-long crucifixion Burns summed up what the common poor man feels in widely-severed moments of exaltation, insight and desperation.

> *Catherine Carswell (1879–1946),* The Life of Robert Burns

6 The town is at present agog with the ploughman-poet, who receives adulation with native dignity, and is the very figure of his profession – strong and coarse – but has a most enthusiastic heart of LOVE.

> *Alison Cockburn (1712–1794),* Letters

7 The man's mind was not clean . . . he degraded and prostituted his intellect, and earned thereby the love and worship of a people whose distinguishing trait is fundamental lewdness . . . His life as a whole would have discredited a dustman, much less a poet . . . a superincontinent yokel with a gift for metricism.

> *T. W. Crosland,* The Unspeakable Scot *(1902)*

8 The memory of Burns – I am afraid heaven and earth have taken too good care of it to leave us anything to say . . . every man's, and boy's, and girl's head carries snatches of his songs . . . They are the property and thouse-be solace of mankind.

> *Ralph Waldo Emerson (1803–1882), address to the Boston Burns Club, 1859*

9 Someone said, if you had shaken hands with him, his hand would have burnt you.

> *William Hazlitt (1778–1830),* Lectures on the English Poets

10 We praise him, not for gifts divine, – His Muse was born of woman, – His manhood breathes in every line, – Was ever heart more human?

> *Oliver Wendell Holmes (1809–1894),* For the Burns Centennial Celebration

11 The final word on Burns must always be that he is the least rewarding of his country's major exports, neither so nourishing as porridge, or stimulating as whisky, nor so relaxing as golf.

> *Kenneth Hopkins,* English Poetry, *quoted in Hugh McDiarmid,* Lucky Poet *(1943)*

12 If you imagine a Scotch commercial traveller in a Scotch commercial hotel, leaning on the bar and calling the barmaid *Dearie*, then you will know the keynote of Burns' verse.

> *A. E. Housman (1859–1936), quoted in Jonathon Green,* Dictionary of Insulting Quotations *(1996)*

13 We went to the Cottage and took some whisky . . . Oh, the flummery of a birthplace. Cant! cant! cant! It is enough to give a spirit the guts-ache.

> *John Keats (1795–1821),* Letters

14 You don't know Burns unless you hate the Lockharts and all the estimable bourgeois and upper classes as he really did – the narrow-gutted pigeons . . . Oh, why doesn't Burns come to life again, and really salt them!

> *D. H. Lawrence (1885–1930), letter to Donald Carswell, 1927*

15 No' wan in fifty kens a wurd Burns wrote, But misapplied is a'body's property . . . Croose London Scotties wi' their braw
> shirt fronts
And a' their fancy freen's, rejoicin'
That similah gatherings in Timbuctoo,
Bagdad – and Hell, nae doot – are voicin'
Burns's sentiments o' universal love,
In pidgin English or in wild-fowl Scots,
And toastin' ane wha's nocht to them
> but an

Excuse for faitherin' Genius wi' *their* thochts.

> *Hugh MacDiarmid (1892–1978)*, A Drunk Man Looks at the Thistle

16 ... the greatest peasant – next perhaps to King David of the Jews, a peasant, a poet, a patriot and a king – whom any age had produced.

> *Charles Mackay (1814–1889)*, Forty Years' Recollections of Life, Literature, and Public Affairs

17 He indulged his sarcastic humour in talking of men, particularly if he thought them proud, or disdainful of Persons of inferior rank; his Observations were always acute and forcibly expressed. I was walking with him one day when we met a common Acquaintance not remarkable for Ability or intellectual Endowments. I observed how extremely fat he had lately grown. 'Yes,' said Burns, 'and when you have told that you have exhausted the subject of Mr — . Fatness is the only quality you can ascribe to him.'

> *Henry Mackenzie (1745–1831), quoted in H. W. Thomson*, The Anecdotes and Egotisms of Henry Mackenzie

18 Burns is a very Protestant poet. Even in remoulding old songs he never goes back in sentiment past the Reformation. His ribaldry, blasphemy, libertinism and sentimentality are all Protestant and quite narrowly so.

> *Edwin Muir (1887–1959)*, Scottish Journey

19 He has the power of making any Scotsman, whether generous or canny, sentimental or prosaic, religious or profane, more wholeheartedly himself than he could have been without assistance; and in that way perhaps more human.

> *Edwin Muir*, Essays on Literature and Society

20 ... he was always with me, for I had him by heart ... Wherever a Scotsman goes, there goes Burns. His grand, whole, catholic soul squares with the good of all; therefore we find him in everything everywhere.

> *John Muir (1838–1914)*, Thoughts on the Birthday of Robert Burns, *from L. M. Wolfe*, John of the Mountains: The Unpublished Journals of John Muir

21 To the great bard, erect a bust ...
His death deplore, accuse his fate.
And raise his name far above the great.
What call you this? Is it Insania?'
I'll coin a word, 'tis Burnomania.

> *William Peebles (fl. late 18th century)*, Burnomania

22 Burns of all poets is the most a Man.

> *Dante Gabriel Rossetti (1828–1882)*, On Burns

23 ... there must be something *terribly* wrong with the present arrangements of the universe, when these things can happen, and be thought natural. I could lie down in the dirt and cry and grovel there, I think, for a century, to save such a soul as Burns from the suffering and the contamination and the *degradation* which these same arrangements imposed on him.

> *Robert Stevenson (1772–1850), letter to William Empson, November 1837*

24 Look at Burns: that is where amourettes conduct an average good man; and a tepid marriage is only a more selfish amourette – in the long run.

> *Robert Louis Stevenson (1850–1894), letter to Trevor Hadden, June 1882)*

25 He came when poets had forgot
How rich and strange the human lot;
How warm the tints of Life; how hot
Are Love and Hate:
And what makes Truth divine, and what
Makes manhood great.

> *William Watson (1858–1935)*, The Tomb of Burns

26 I mourned with thousands, but as one
More deeply grieved, for he was gone
Whose light I hailed when first it shone,
And showed my youth
How verse may build a princely throne
On humble truth.

> *William Wordsworth (1770–1850)*, At the Grave of Burns

27 Burns has been cruelly used, both dead and alive ... It is worse than ridiculous to see the people of Dumfries coming forward with their pompous mausoleum.

> *William Wordsworth, letter to John Scott, 1816*

Childhood and Children

1 Oh, will ye never learn?
Ne'er, ne'er was sic a bairn.
Breakin' my heart, ye fidgety, fidgety,
Breakin' my heart, ye fidgety bairn.

  Anonymous, Ye Fidgety Bairn

2 'Smile na sae sweet, my bonny babes,
An' ye smile sae sweet, ye'll smile me dead.
And O, bonny babes, if ye suck sair,
Ye'll never suck by my side mair.'

  Anonymous, The Crùel Mother

3 An earthly nourrice sits and sings,
And aye she sings, 'Ba, lily wean!
Little ken I my bairn's father,
Far less the land that he staps in.'

  Anonymous, The Great Silkie of Sule
  Skerrie

4 . . . he isn't mamma's baby any more.

  Anonymous, His Sixth Birthday, *quoted
  in J. Forsyth*, Scottish National Read-
  ings *(c.1910)*

5 Ally bally, ally bally bee
Sittin' on your mammy's knee;
Greetin' for anither bawbee
To buy some Coulter's candy.

  Traditional, Coulter's Candy, *from
  Robert Coltart, Borders candy-maker*

6 Sleep an' let me to my wark –
a' thae claes to airn –
Jenny wi' the airn teeth,
Come and tak' the bairn!

  *Alexander Anderson ('Surfaceman',
  1845–1900)*, Jenny Wi' the Airn Teeth

7 They never heed a word I speak;
I try to gie a froon,
But aye I hap them up an' cry,
'O, bairnies, cuddle doon.'

  Alexander Anderson, Cuddle Doon

8 The bonnie, bonnie bairn sits poking in
  the ase,
Glowerin' in the fire wi' his wee round
  face,
Laughin' at the fuffin' lowe – what sees
  he there?
Ha! the young dreamer's biggin' castles in
  the air.

  *James Ballantine (1808–1877), quoted in
  Charles Mackay*, Poetry and Humour of
  the Scottish Language *(1882)*

9 Luis was an ugly boy, with black hair, red
face, and yellow, flabby hands, his knuck-
les pocked like a baby's and filled with dirt.
He smelt of stale tobacco, and he was too
big for his school blazer, which came in
just where his buttocks went out.

  Chaim Bermant (1929–1998), Jericho
  Sleep Alone

10 At night after we were in bed, Veronica
spoke out from her little bed and said, 'I
do not believe there is a God . . . I have
thinket it many a time, but did not like to
speak of it.' I was confounded and uneasy,
and tried her with the simple argument
that without GOD there would not be all
the things we see. 'It is HE who makes
the sun shine.' Said she: 'It shines only on
good days.' Said I: 'GOD made you.' Said
she: 'My mother bore me.'

  James Boswell (1740–1795), Journal, *19
  December 1779*

11 'Do doggies gang to heaven?' Willie
asked –
  And ah! what Solomon of modern days
can answer that.

  Robert Buchanan (1841–1901), Willie
  Baird

12 Th' expectant wee things, toddlin',
  stacher through
To meet their dad.

  Robert Burns (1759–1796), The Cottar's Saturday night

13 Lo! at the couch where infant beauty
  sleeps,
Her silent watch the mournful mother
  keeps.

  Thomas Campbell (1777–1844), The
  Pleasures of Hope

14 Stir the fire till it lowes, let the bairnie sit,
Auld Daddy Darkness is no wantit yet.

  James Ferguson (fl. 19th century), Auld
  Daddy Darkness

15 Aye maun the childer, wi' a fastin' mou',
Grumble and greet, and mak an unco
  mane.

  Robert Fergusson (1750–1774), The
  Farmer's Ingle

16 Sex was not referred to at all. Nor was it
seen . . . 'What are these dogs *doing?*' I

asked my mother. 'Just fighting', she said. Funny way to fight, I thought.

> *Sir Denis Forman (1917–)*, Son of Adam

17 You got 3d for an Irn Bru bottle, 2d for a beer bottle. At big games, the supporters wouldn't go down to the loos; they'd stay on the terracing. You learned quickly to empty the bottles, never to sample them.

> *John Gardner, Rangers fan, quoted in S. Walsh*, Voices of the Old Firm *(1996)*

18 How is it possible to make the affluent Lewis child of today understand a world in which a piece of gingerbread was an unusual and sought-for treat?

> *James Shaw Grant*, The Hub of the Universe

19 These children are happy.
It is easier for them.
They are English.

> *Alasdair Gray (1934–)*, The Fall of Kelvin Walker

20 I've a wee little loon, O! ye ne'er saw his like,
He's as duddie and towsie as ony tint tyke;
He trauchles his mother the weary day lang,
Yet she never ance thinks fat he daes can be wrang.

> *John Young Gray (1846–1934)*, My Loonie

21 Where the pools are bright and deep,
Where the grey trout lies asleep,
Up the river and over the lea,
That's the way for Billy and me.

> *James Hogg (1770–1835)*, A Boy's Song

22 He was a funny wee cunt when he was a boy. Looking back, you had to admit it.

> *James Kelman (1946–)*, Pictures

23 Because if it ever came to the choice between living and dying then christ almighty he would lay down his life and glad to do it. They were great wee weans. Great wee weans. Even if they were horrible wee weans and selfish and spoilt brats he would still have done it.

> *James Kelman*, A Disaffection

24 From the moment of birth, when the Stone Age baby confronts the twentieth-century mother, the baby is subjected to these forces of violence, called love, as its father

and mother and their parents and their parents before them, have been.

> *R. D. Laing (1927–1989)*, The Politics of Experience

25 At the age of ten I was put into the factory as a 'piecer' . . . With a part of my first week's wages I purchased Ruddiman's *Rudiments of Latin.*

> *David Livingstone (1813–1873)*

26 I love my little son, and yet when he was ill
I could not confine myself to his bedside.
I was impatient of his squalid little needs . . .
Whereas his mother sank without another care
To that dread state of nothing but life itself
And stayed day and night, till he was better, there.

> *Hugh MacDiarmid (C. M. Grieve, 1892–1978)*, The Two Parents

27 Where did you come from, baby dear?
Out of the everywhere into the here.

> *George Macdonald (1824–1905)*, At the Back of the North Wind

28 God thought about me, and so I grew.

> *George Macdonald*, At the Back of the North Wind

29 Gin they wad leave me alane!

> *Alastair Mackie (1925–)*, Adolescence

30 But what is the best way of loving? Does the man who applauds and encourages all the vices of his children, or the man who vigorously detects, and rigorously prohibits them, take the best way of loving his children?

> *James Mill (1773–1836)*, Commonplace Book

31 Wee Willie Winkie rins through the toun,
Upstairs and doun stairs in his nicht-gown,
Tirling at the window, crying at the lock:
Are a' the bairnies in their bed, it's past ten o'clock?

> *William Miller (1810–1872)*, Wee Willie Winkie

32 A wee smout of a callant.

> *David Macbeth Moir (1798–1851)*,

Mansie Wauch, The Tailor of
Dalkeith

33 The servant girls told us that 'Dandy
Doctors' clad in long black cloaks and supplied with a store of sticking-plasters of
wondrous adhesiveness, prowled at night
about the country lanes and even the town
streets, watching for children to choke
and sell. The Dandy Doctor's business
method . . . was with lightning quickness
to clap a sticking plaster on the face of a
scholar, covering mouth and nose, prevent-
ing breathing or crying for help, then pop
us under his long black cloak and carry us
to Edinburgh to be sold and sliced into
small pieces for folk to learn how we were
made.

> *John Muir (1838–1913)*, The Story of
> My Boyhood and Youth

34 There are zones of childhood through
which we pass, and we live in several of
them before we reach our school age, at
which a part of our childhood stops for
good.

> *Edwin Muir (1887–1959)*, An
> Autobiography

35 'Ah, but you canna be sure o' them at that
age,' said the Captain. 'My brother Cherlie
was merrit on a low-country woman, and
the twuns used to sit up at night and greet
in the two languages, Gaalic and Gleska,
till he had to put plugs in them.'

> *Neil Munro (1864–1930)*, The Vital
> Spark

36 *Jenny:* O, 'tis a pleasant thing to be a
bride;
Syne, whinging getts about your
ingle-side
Yelping for this or that wi' fasheous din . . .
Ae wean fa's sick, and scads itsel wi' broo,
Ane breaks his shin, another tines his
shoe;
The Deil gaes o'er Jock Webster, hame grows
hell . . .

Peggy: Yet it's a hartsome thing to be a
wife,
When round the ingle-edge young
sprouts are rife . . .
Wow, Jenny, can there greater pleasure be
Than see sic wee tots toolying at your
knee;
When a' they ettle at – their greatest

wish –
Is to be made o', an' obtain a kiss!

> *Allan Ramsay (1686–1758)*, The Gentle
> Shepherd

37 All my life I have loved a womanly woman
and admired a manly man, but I never
could stand a boily boy.

> *Lord Rosebery (1847–1929)*

38 Just at the age 'twixt boy and youth,
When thought is speech, and speech is
truth.

> *Sir Walter Scott (1771–1832)*, Marmion

39 O hush thee, my babie, thy sire was a
knight,
Thy mother a lady both lovely and bright;
The woods and the glens, from the towers
which we see,
They all are belonging, dear babie, to
thee.

> *Sir Walter Scott*, Lullaby of an Infant
> Chief

40 The tear down childhood's cheek that
flows
Is like the dew-drop on the rose;
When next the summer breeze comes by
And waves the bush, the flower is dry.

> *Sir Walter Scott*, Rokeby

41 The world is such a happy place,
That children, whether big or small,
Should always have a smiling face,
And never, never, sulk at all.

> *Gabriel Setoun (Thomas Nicoll Hepburn,*
> *b.1861)*, The World's Music

42 'Come awa, my bonnie wee Wuddles! O,
he's jist a perfect darlin'! a sweet barley-
sugar doodle o' delight! Come till his
bonnie, bonnie mother's, an' he'll get his
bonnie, bonnie, poshie an' milkie oot o'
his ain wee luggie-puggie, the dear little
dumplin's o' a darlin's. Come and his
mammy'll gie him cockie-ridey-roosey.'

> *James Smith*, Archy and Bess, *from* The
> Glasgow Weekly Mail, *December 1875,*
> *quoted in William Donaldson*, The Lan-
> guage of the People *(1989)*

43 In our play-hours we amused ourselves
with playing at ball, marbles, and especially
at 'Scotch and English', a game which represented a raid on the debatable land, or
Border between Scotland and England, in
which each party tried to rob the other
of their playthings. The little ones were

always compelled to be English, for the bigger girls thought it too degrading.

> *Mary Somerville (1780–1872), from Martha Somerville*, Personal Recollections From Early Life in Old Age of Mary Somerville *(1873)*

44 Aince upon a day my mither said to me:
Dinna cleip and dinna rype
And dinna tell a lee.

> *William Soutar (1898–1943)*, Aince Upon a Day

45 One's prime is elusive. You little girls, when you grow up, must be on the alert to recognise your prime, at whatever time of life it may occur.

> *Muriel Spark (1918–)* The Prime of Miss Jean Brodie

46 . . . all my pupils are the *crème de la crème.*

> *Muriel Spark*, The Prime of Miss Jean Brodie

47 Parents learn a lot from their children about coping with life. It is possible for parents to be corrupted or improved by their children.

> *Muriel Spark*, The Comforters

48 The funniest thing about him is the way he likes to grow –
Not at all like proper children, which is always very slow;
For he sometimes shoots up taller, like an india-rubber ball,
And he sometimes gets so little that there's none of him at all.

> *Robert Louis Stevenson (1850–1894)*, My Shadow

49 Cruel children, crying babies,
All grow up as geese and gabies,
Hated, as their age increases,
By their nephews and their nieces.

> *Robert Louis Stevenson*, Good and Bad Children

50 A child should always say what's true,
And speak when he is spoken to,
And behave mannerly at table;
At least as far as he is able.

> *Robert Louis Stevenson*, The Whole Duty of Children

51 I was the giant great and still,
That sits upon the pillow-hill

And sees before him, dale and plain,
The pleasant land of counterpane.

> *Robert Louis Stevenson*, The Land of Counterpane

52 'My children from the youngest to the eldest loves me and fears me as sinners dread death. My look is law.'

> *Lady Strange (fl. 18th century), quoted in H. G. Graham*, The Social Life of Scotland in the Eighteenth Century *(1899)*

53 The mitherless bairn creeps up to his lane bed,
Nane covers his cauld back, or haps his bare head;
His wee hackit heelies are hard as the airn,
An' lithless the lair o' the mitherless bairn.

> *William Thom (1798–1848)*, The Mitherless Bairn

54 It's almost certain that given enough scope, enough freedom, a child will go through all the past phases of humanity, from fishes to philosophers.

> *Kenneth White (1936–)*, On Scottish Ground

Commerce and Industry

1 What tho' their foundation is built on the sand,
They dash and they dare like lords o' the land,
What is readily got they mak merrily flee,
The splendid Jute Lords o' Bonnie Dundee.

> *Anonymous*, The Dundee Weekly News, *January 1856, Song*

2 'Messages run down this close'
'New-laid eggs every morning by me, Janet Stobie'

> *Glasgow street signs from Strang*, Glasgow and Its Clubs, *recorded in Alexander Hislop*, The Book of Scottish Anecdote *(1883)*

3 We cam na here to view your warks,
In hopes to be mair wise,
But only, lest we gang to hell,
It may be no surprise.

> *Robert Burns (1759–1796)*, Impromptu on Carron Ironworks

4 And call they this Improvement? – to have changed,

My native Clyde, thy once romantic shore,
Where Nature's face is banished and
   estranged,
And Heaven reflected in thy wave no
   more . . .
And for the daisied greensward, down
   thy stream
Unsightly brick-lanes smoke, and
   clanking engines gleam.

> *Thomas Campbell (1777–1844)*, Lines
> on Revisiting a Scottish River

5 Pioneering does not pay.

> *Andrew Carnegie (1835–1918), quoted in
> Burton J. Hendrick*, Life of Carnegie

6 Put all your eggs in one basket, and then
watch the basket.

> *Andrew Carnegie, quoted in Burton J.
> Hendrick*, Life of Carnegie

7 Upon the sacredness of property civilisation itself depends.

> *Andrew Carnegie*, Wealth

8 All the people in Scotland are not so void
of taste or their other senses as you incline
to think them. It is the not being able
to get good things which makes people
not have them, and if they whose business
should lead them to furnish good things,
were at more pains in supplying with good
will at all seasons and to introduce them to
some Customers, it would soon take.

> *John Cockburn of Ormiston (1685–1758),
> Letter to Charles Bell*

9 It is commonly our Scots way to do
little business but squeeze up high prices.
Whereas it would be much more real
advantage to enlarge the business, have
the profit, though small upon it, yet great
from enlarging of it, not great upon a little
but of many smalls to make a great.

> *John Cockburn of Ormiston, Letter to
> Charles Bell, December 1734*

10 When you hear of men being deprived of
their positions by sharp practice and shifti-
ness, no matter whether it be in a draper's
shop or in a gilt-edged bank, you will find
nine times out of ten there is a Scotchman
in the case.

> *T. W. Crosland*, The Unspeakable Scot
> *(1902)*

11 All schemes of Industry to be executed in
that Country are idle Dreams.

> *William Cross*, Some Considerations by
> Way of Essay Upon the Means of Civi-
> lizing the Highlands and Islands, and
> Extinguishing Jacobitism in Scotland,
> *(1748)*

12 . . . so flushed and riotous can the Scottish
mind become over a commercial prospect
that it sometimes sends native caution by
the board, and a man's really fine idea
becomes an empty balloon, to carry him
off to the limbo of vanities.

> *George Douglas (George Douglas Brown,
> 1869–1902)*, The House With the
> Green Shutters

13 I may rather term it to be a mother and
nurse for the youth and younglings of
Scotland, who are yearly sent thither in
great numbers . . . in clothing, feeding
and enriching them with the fatness of her
best things, besides 30,000 Scots families
that live incorporate in her bowels. And
certainly Poland may be termed in this
kind to be the mother of our commons,
and the first commencement of all our best
merchants' wealth

> *William Lithgow (c.1585–1645)*, Rare
> Adventures and Painful Peregrinations

14 I cannot sit still, James, and hear you abuse
the shopocracy.

> *Christopher North (John Wilson,
> 1785–1854)*, Noctes Ambrosianae

15 The propensity to truck, barter and
exchange one thing for another . . . is
common to all men, and to be found in no
other race of animals.

> *Adam Smith (1723–1790)*, The Wealth
> of Nations

16 We could probably have achieved more by
sending an aeroplane to drop £10 notes
over the area.

> *Sir Teddy Taylor, on government aid
> to Govan Shipbuilders, 1991, quoted
> in Arnold Kemp*, The Hollow Drum
> *(1993)*

17 Recession is when you tighten your belt.
Depression is when you have no belt to
tighten. When you have lost your trousers,
you are in the airline business.

> *Sir Adam Thompson*, High Risk: The
> Politics of the Air *(1990)*

18 By various means the firm acquired a considerable trade . . . as one move alone, in Scotland, some five hundred grey parrots who were set up outside licensed grocers to cry 'Drink Pattison's Whisky!'

> *Ross Wilson,* Scotch Made Easy *(1959)*

Costume

1 Their gluvis were of the raffell richt;
Their shoon were of the straitis;
Their kirtillis were of the lincum licht
Weill prest with mony plaitis.

> *Anonymous,* Christis Kirk on the Green, *sometimes ascribed to King James V (1513–1542)*

2 O laith, laith were our gude Scots lords
To wat their cork-heeled shoon,
But lang ere a' the play was play'd
They wat their hats aboon.

> *Anonymous,* Sir Patrick Spens

3 Thair meit doublet does thaim rejois:
They spread abroad thair buffit hois,
Thay taik delyt in nedill wark,
Thay gloir into thair ruffit sark . . .
Thair gluvis perfumit in thair hand
Helpis meikil thair contenance,
Et tout est à la mode de France.

> *Anonymous satire on courtiers' dress in the 1560s, from the Maitland Collection*

4 This is no my plaid,
Bonnie though the colours be.
The ground o' mine was mixed wi' blue,
I gat it frae the lad I lo'e;
He ne'er has gi'en me cause to rue,
And O! the plaid is dear to me.

> *Anonymous,* This is No My Plaid

5 She cocks a purple tammie on a stook
o yalla hair:
A jersey haps her shouthers, but she keeps
her thrapple bare,
in a what-d'ye-caa-'t – invitin ye tae tak
a second luik –
a chemie, caad a blouse, wi a snippet
gushet-neuk,
Snippit, rippit, snippit,
Rippit, snippit, rippit,
A chemie, caad a blouse, wi a snippet
gushet-neuk.

> *Anonymous,* The Station-Master's Dochter *(c.1887), from Douglas Young,* Scottish Verse 1851–1951 *(1952)*

6 The kilt, being a practical outdoor garment, failed him only once, and that occurred during a short-lived interest in bee-keeping.

> *J. M. Bannerman (1901–1969),* Bannerman: The Memoirs of Lord Bannerman of Kildonan

7 . . . though the men bene semely ynough of fygure and of shape, and fayre of face generally by kind, yet theyr own scottyshe clothynge dysfygure them full moche.

> *Bartholomew's* De Proprietatibus Rerum, *c.1250*

8 When I looked at myself in the glass last night in my Corsican dress, I could not help thinking your opinion of yourself might be yet more upraised: 'She has secured the constant affection and admiration of so fine a fellow.'

> *James Boswell (1740–1795), letter to Margaret Montgomerie*

9 For the first time I came face to face with the paraphernalia of my national costume.
  'You look grand', Oonagh said, when I tried the dress outfit on. I was not convinced. I was a city child, I felt I was being suborned by some primitive tribe.

> *William Boyd (1952–),* The New Confessions

10 Her cutty sark, o' Paisley harn,
That while a lassie she had worn,
In longitude tho' sorely scanty,
It was her best, and she was vauntie.

> *Robert Burns (1759–1796),* Tam o' Shanter

11 This dress is called the *quelt*, and for the most part, they wear the petticoat so very short that in a windy day, going up a hill, or stooping, the indecency of it is plainly discovered.

> *Edmund Burt (fl. early 18th century),* Letters from a Gentleman in the North of Scotland *(1726–37)*

12 I have been told, in Edinburgh, that the ladies distinguish their political principles, whether Whig or Tory, by the manner of wearing their plaids; that is, one of the parties reverses the old fashions, but which of them it is, I do not remember.

> *Edmund Burt,* Letters from a Gentleman in the North of Scotland

13 My muse 'gan weep, but, ere a tear was
    spilt,
    She caught Sir William Curtis in a kilt!
    . . . To see proud Albyn's tartans as a belt
    Gird the gross sirloin of a city Celt,
    She burst into a laughter so extreme
    That I awoke, and lo! it was *no* dream!

    Lord Byron (1788–1824), The Age of
    Bronze

14 The buffoon tartan pantaloon, with its
    fringed frippery (as some mongrel High-
    landers would have it), sticking wet and
    dirty to the skin, is not very easily pulled
    off, and *less so* to get on again in case of
    alarm . . . the Highlander in his native
    garb always appeared more cleanly, and
    maintained better health . . . than those
    who wore even the thick cloth pantaloon.

    *Alan Cameron of Erracht (1750–1828),
    letter to Henry Thorpe, October 1804*

15 Nay, is it not to Clothes that most men
    do reverence: to the fine frogged broad-
    cloth, nowise to the 'straddling animal
    with bandy legs' which it holds, and makes
    a Dignitary of?

    Thomas Carlyle (1795–1881), Sartor
    Resartus

16 Friends! Trust not the heart of that man
    for whom Old Clothes are not venerable.

    Thomas Carlyle, Sartor Resartus

17 The full-sized evening hoop was so mon-
    strous that people saw one half of it enter
    the room before its wearer . . . Ladies
    in walking generally carried the skirt of
    the gown over the arm and exhibited
    the petticoat; but when they entered a
    room, they always came sailing in, with
    the train sweeping full and majestically
    behind them.

    Robert Chambers (1802–1871), Tradi-
    tions of Edinburgh, *on ladies' dress of
    the 1770s*

18 And Jacob made for his wee Josie
    A tartan coat to keep him cosie.

    *Samuel Cobill (17th century), parodying
    Zachary Boyd (c.1585–1653)*

19 I think I see him . . . crisp in his mulberry-
    coloured kerseymere coat, single-breasted
    waist-coat of the same with large old-fash-
    ioned pockets; black satin breeches with
    blue steel buttons; bright morocco shoes
    with silver or blue steel buckles; white
    or quaker-grey silk stockings; a copious
    frill and ruffles; a dark brown gold-headed
    cane or a slender green silk umbrella; eve-
    rything pure and uncreased.

    Henry Thomas Cockburn (1779–1854),
    Memorials, *on the lawyer Adam Rolland
    (died 1819)*

20 Never underestimate the importance of
    haberdashery. I've got great shoes and
    great trousers . . . Try tartan shoes. The
    yellowy tartan ones are fabulous.

    *Billy Connolly (1942–), interviewed by
    Lewis Jones in the* Sunday Telegraph,
    November 1998

21 Spinal tenuity and mamillary exuberance
    have for some time been the fashion with
    the fair, but a posterior rotundity, or a bal-
    ance was wanting behind; and you may
    now tell the country lasses if they wish
    to be fashionable, they must resemble
    two blown bladdders tied together at the
    necks.

    *William Creech (1745–1815), in a letter
    to an Edinburgh newspaper*

22 . . . after that we have slayne redd deir, we
    flaye off the skyne, bey and bey, and set-
    ting of our bare foot on the insyde therof,
    for neide of cunnyge shoemakers, by your
    Grace's pardon, we play the sutters; com-
    pasinge and mesuringe so moche thereof,
    as shall retche up to our anclers, pryck-
    ynge the upper part thereof with also with
    holis, that the water may repas when it
    entres . . . so, and please your noble Grace,
    we make our shoois.

    *John Elder, letter to King Henry VIII
    (1543), quoted in Dugald Mitchell, His-
    tory of the Highlands and Gaelic Scot-
    land (1900)*

23 Braid Claith lends fock an unco heese,
    Makes many kail-worms butter-flies,
    Gies mony doctor his degrees
    For little skaith:short, you may be what
    you please
    Wi' gude Braid Claith.

    Robert Fergusson (1750–1774), Braid
    Claith

24 The shearers sweated phenomenally as
    they worked . . . Next to the skin they
    wore John Ells, the cuff of the legs visible
    between their socks and their trousers,
    the sleeves of the top half rolled up with
    their shirt sleeves. Then there was a thick

woollen shirt and tweed trousers, with hill boots, the sole rising sharply at the toe, then a tweed waistcoat and on top of that either a blue or a brown one-piece overall, full-trousered and with braces from the back to hold up the chest-piece in front. It was just after midsummer.

Sir Denis Forman (1917–), Son of Adam

25 Only in my gym-suit was I really comfortable, and as I was in the Display Team . . . I moved freely most weekdays in that amazing ensemble, which comprised a long-sleeved, high-necked garment of navy serge, buttoned throuthigh from neck to knee, worn with the school tie and baggy serge bloomers.

Amy Stewart Fraser, In Memory Long, *(1977)*

26 I know I for one would not willingly face again the miserable dread of that first lonely walk from my housemaster's front door to the school itself, with my new woollen underwear hanging down below the level of my short trousers . . . I turned and ran, but only as far as a convenient bush, where I tore off these beastly drawers and hurled them into the River Kelvin with childish curses.

George Macdonald Fraser (1926–), Introduction to The World of the Public School *(1977)*

27 The tartan tred wad gar ye lauch;
nae problem is owre teuch.
Your surname needna end in -*och*;
they'll cleik ye up the cleuch.
A puckle dollar bills will aye
preive Hiram Teufelsdrockh
A septary of Clan McKay.

Robert Garioch (Robert Garioch Sutherland, 1909–1981), Embro to the Ploy

28 Oh! to see his tartan trews,
Bonnet blue, and laigh-heeled shoes;
Philabeg aboon his knee.

Alexander Geddes (1737–1802), Lewie Gordon

29 . . . thair haill habitis sall be of grave colour, as black, russet, sad gray, sad broun, or of sergis, winsett, camlet, growgram, lytes, worsett, or siclyke, and to be schort, that the gude Word of God be thaim and thair immoderatenes be nocht sclanderit.

General Assembly of the Church of Scotland, Act regulating ministers' dress, 1575

30 . . . getting down on the floors to scrub would be an ill-like ploy, she would warrant, for the brave silk knickers that Mrs Colquhoun wore. For the Sourock's wife had never forgiven the minister's wife her bit under-things, and the way she voted at the General Election.

Lewis Grassic Gibbon (James Leslie Mitchell, 1901–1935), Cloud Howe

31 I like the thought of a Scots Republic with Scots Border Guards in saffron kilts – the thought of those kilts can awake me to joy in the middle of the night.

Lewis Grassic Gibbon, Glasgow, *in* Workers' City, *edited by Farquhar McLay (1988)*

32 The Hielan' man he wears the kilt even
     when it's snowin';
He disna ken where the wind comes frae,
     but he kens fine where it's goin'.

Joe Gordon, The Hielan' Chorus

33 But however desirous to be in fashion, every Scots lady had that essential part of national costume, the plaid, wrapped loosely about the head and body . . . These plaids were the ordinary costume of the ladies, as charac/teristic and national as the mantilla of Spain, up to the middle of the century, when at last they gave way to silk and velvet cloaks.

H. Grey Graham, The Social Life of Scotland in the Eighteenth Century *(1899)*

34 Do I like women's clothes more than their bodies? Oh, no, but I prefer their clothes to their minds. Their minds keep telling me, no thank you, don't touch, go away. Their clothes say, look at me, want me, I am exciting.

Alasdair Gray (1934–), 1982, Janine

35 Then there was Lady Saltoun who said that if the King wore the kilt at the Drawing Room, she did not know what the ladies would do, it would be shocking. And Lady Hamilton made the astute reply, 'Oh, if he's to be here so short a time, the more we see of him the better.'

Elizabeth Haldane, The Scotland of Our Fathers, *(1932)*

36 Rhynie loons wore tackety boots with a vengeance: it was a case of the more tackets the better. Arbiters of high style would

sit on the school steps comparing the shining rows of metal studs on the soles of their boots before running round the playground striking fire and thunder off the surface.

> *David Hay (1935–), Memories of a Calvinist Childhood, in W. G. Lawrence, Roots in a Northern Landscape (1996)*

37 I should rather wear a worse gown than you should appear in a shabby coat. You must get your stockings and other things mended by the person who washes your clothes; it is pitiful to think of you going about with great holes in your stockings. I hope you have got warm drawers.

> *Margaret Hogg (1790–1870), letter to her husband James in London, January 1832*

38 Art may make a suit of clothes; but nature must produce a man.

> *David Hume (1711–1776), The Epicurean*

39 ... they too crossed their legs and glanced with anxious pride at their knees. They had folded their stockings to make the most of the muscles of their legs, and they wore nothing under their kilts.

> *James Kennaway (1928–1969), The Complexion of the Colonel*

40 Sick and sore I am, worn and weary,
walking no more since my limbs are
   confined.
Cursed be the king who stretched our
   stockings,
down in the dust may his face be found.

> *John MacCodrum (c.1693–1779), Oran Mu'n Eideadh Ghaidhealach (Song to the Highland Dress), written in the period of proscription*

41 Who is so trim as a kilted laddie?

> *Alexander MacDonald (Alasdair MacMaighstir Alasdair, c.1695–1770), from Gaelic*

42 O, the pale grey breeches
cast a gloom on us this year!
A thing not seen on us before,
one we dislike to wear;
And had we all been loyal
to the king who appealed to us,
we had not been seen till Doomsday
submitting to this garment.

> *Duncan Bàn MacIntyre (1724–1812),*

Oran Dho 'N Bhriogais (Song of the Breeches), *composed in the period of proscription*

43 My kilt and tartan stockings I was
   wearing,
My claymore and my dirk and skian-dhu,
And when I sallied forth with manly
   bearing
I heard admiring whispers not a few –
'He's the best-dressed Highlander,
The best-dressed Highlander,
The best-dressed Highlander at his own
   expense.'

> *D. M. McKay (19th century), The Best-Dressed Highlander*

44 My mother's clothes came from a dress agency with a sad name, such as the Scottish Ladies' Benevolent Frock Exchange. This discreet ossuary of fashion was known as 'The Dead Women's', with a long 'o' as in womb – 'The Dead Woo-men's.'

> *Candia MacWilliam (1957–), The Many Colours of Blood, in Robert Winder, The Granta Book of the Family (1995)*

45 In fact the good old Scottish custom of making do with what you have was carried to such an extent in Aberdeenshire, the home of fine knitted stockings, that it has been said that a typical mid-century laird wore coat, breeches and stockings all knitted by his wife.

> *Stuart Maxwell and Robin Hutchison, Scottish Costume 1550–1880 (1958), on 18th-century costume*

46 When Glengarry came to Inverness, the people looked upon him with awe and respect ... he had a regiment called the 'Glengarry Fencibles', some 200 splendid fellows, who wore the Highland costume, and the little cap with a tuft of heather, since known all over the world as the 'Glengarry bonnet'.

> *Joseph Mitchell (1803–1883), Reminiscences of My Life in The Highlands*

47 Brawns to my legs there were none, as my trowsers of other years too visibly effected to show. The long yellow hair hung down, like a flax-wig, the length of my lantern-jaws, which looked, notwithstanding my yapness and stiff appetite, as if eating and they had broken up acquaintanceship. My blue jacket seemed in the sleeves to have picked a quarrel with the wrists, and had

retreated to a tait below the elbows. The haunch-buttons, on the contrary, appeared to have taken a strong liking to the shoulders, a little below which they showed their tarnished brightness. At the middle of the back the tails terminated, leaving the well-worn rear of my corduroys, like a full moon seen through a dark haze.

> *David Macbeth Moir (1798–1851)*, The Life of Mansie Wauch, Tailor of Dalkeith

48   I'm coortin' bonnie Annie noo, Rab
        Tamson's kitchie deem;
     She is five and forty, and I am seventeen,
     She clorts a muckle piece tae me, wi'
        different kinds o' jams,
     And tells me ilka nicht that she admires
        my Nicky Tams.

> *G. S. Morris*, A Pair o' Nicky Tams

49   'Wi' shanks like that ye'd better hae stuck
        to breeks.'

> *Charles Murray (1864–1941)*, Ay, Fegs

50   His waistcoat was white and his coat it
        was blue,
     A ring he put on, a sword and cock'd hat,
     And wha could refuse the Laird wi' a'
        that?

> *Lady Nairne (1766–1845)*, The Laird o'
> Cockpen

51   At last, however, she had the whole crinoline adjusted to her satisfaction, and she set it up under the green taffeta glacé. The problem now was, how to enter it. After several vain attempts she took off her pantaloons and set to in grim earnest. The obvious approach was from underneath and she tried this first. She crawled under the hem of the dress like an Indian worming into a bell-tent . . . It was hard to believe a lady had to jump into her crinoline.

> *Neil Paterson (1915–1995)*, Behold Thy
> Daughter

52   Her coats were kiltit, and did sweetly
        shaw
     Her straight bare legs that whiter were
        than snaw;
     Her cockernony snooded up fou' sleek,
     Her haffet-locks hung waving on her
        cheek.

> *Allan Ramsay (1686–1758)*, The Gentle
> Shepherd

53   His socks compelled one's attention without losing one's respect.

> *Saki (H. H. Munro, 1870–1916)*, The
> Chronicles of Clovis

54   Two long and bony arms were terminated at the elbow by triple blond ruffles, and being folded saltire-ways in front of her person, and decorated with long gloves a bright vermillion colour, presented no bad resemblance to a pair of gigantic lobsters.

> *Sir Walter Scott (1771–1832)*, The
> Antiquary

55   Let others boast of philibeg,
     Of kilt and tartan plaid,
     Whilst we the ancient trews will wear,
     In which our fathers bled.

> *Sir John Sinclair (1754–1835)*, March
> for the Rothesay and Caithness
> Fencibles

56   This tartan obsession . . . prior to Walter Scott the average clan gathering looked like a parade of tattie bags.

> *W. Gordon Smith*, Mr Jock *(1987)*

57   I am still such a country Hoyden that I could hardly find patience to be put into a condition to appear, yet I was not above six hours in the hands of the hair-dresser, who stuffed my head with as much black wool as would have made a quilted petticoat; and after all, it was the smallest head in the assembly, except my aunt's – She, to be sure, was so particular with her rumpt gown and petticoat, her scanty curls, her lappet-head, deep-triple ruffles and high stays, that every body looked at her with some surprize.

> *Tobias Smollett (1721–1771)*, The Expedition of Humphrey Clinker

58   Bluebell was what I called my grandmother's lovely blue-silk brocade going-away dress the colour of cornflowers. I have never seen anything quite so beautiful nor touched any-thing so sensuous before or since.

> *Muriel Spark (1918–)*, Curriculum
> Vitae

59   There was an old man of the Cape
     Who made himself garments of crape.
     When asked. 'Do they tear?'
     He replied, 'Here and there;
     But they're perfectly splendid for shape.'

> *Robert Louis Stevenson (1850–1894)*,

quoted in W. S. Baring-Gould, The Lure
of the Limerick *(1968)*

60 Loveliness
Needs not the foreign aid of ornament,
But is, when unadorned, adorned the
most.
   James Thomson (1700–1748), The
   Seasons

Curses, Invocations and Charms

1 Bless, O Chief of generous Chiefs,
Myself and all that is near to me,
Bless me in all my actions,
Make me safe for ever,
Make me safe for ever.
   Invocation, from Gaelic

2 May the herding of Columba
Encompass you going and returning,
Encompass you in strath and on ridge,
And on the edge of each rough region.
   Anonymous, Columba's Herding, *from
   Alexander Carmichael (1832–1912)*, Car-
   mina Gadelica

3 Lest witches should obtain the power
Of Hawkie's milk in evil hour,
She winds a red thread round the horn
And milks thro' row'n tree night and
   morn.
   Quoted by James Napier in Folk Lore
   (1879)

4 Rowan tree and red thread
Gar the witches tine their speed.
   Folk charm

5 I will pluck the yarrow fair,
That kindlier shall be my face,
That more warm shall be my lips,
That more chaste shall be my speech,
Be my speech the beams of the sun,
Be my lips the sap of the strawberry.
   The Yarrow, from Gaelic

6 I will make the charm on Monday,
In a narrow, sharp, thorny space;
Go, with the charm about you,
And let no fear be on you!
You will ascend to the tops of cliffs,
And not be thrown backwards;
You are the calm Swan's son in battle,
You will stand amidst the slaughter.
   From a Gaelic charm of invulnerability

7 O little Morag
A-climbing bens,
Descending glens,
A-climbing bens,
O little Morag,
A-climbing bens,
Tired you are
– And the calves lost.
   Fairy Song, from Gaelic

8 The curse of hell frae me sall ye bear,
Mither, mither;
The curse of hell frae me sall ye bear,
Sic counsels ye gave to me, O.
   Anonymous, Edward

9 Curs'd be the Stars which did ordain
Queen Bess a maiden-life should reign;
Married she might have brought an heir
Nor had we known a *Stuart* here.
Curs'd be the tribe who at *Whitehall*
Slew one o' the' name, and slew not all.
   *Anonymous, English anti-Stewart pas-
   quinade c.1680*

10 They'll know at Resurrection Day
To murder Saints was no sweet play.
   *Monument to the Covenanters' dead, Glas-
   gow Cathedral*

11 Curs'd be the man, the poorest wretch
in life,
The crouching vassal to a tyrant wife!
   Robert Burns (1759–1796), The Hen-
   pecked Husband

12 Flow gently, sweet Afton, amang thy
green braes,
Flow gently, I'll sing thee a song in thy
praise;
My Mary's asleep by thy murmuring
stream;
Flow gently, sweet Afton, disturb not her
dream.
   Robert Burns, Flow Gently, Sweet
   Afton

13 '. . . that d—d Sir Walter Scott, that everybody makes such a work about! . . . I wish
I had him to ferry over Loch Lomond:
I should be after sinking the boat, if I
drowned myself into the bargain; for ever
since he wrote his *Lady of the Lake*, as they
call it, everybody goes to see that filthy
hole Loch Katrine, then comes round by
Luss, and I have had only two gentlemen
to guide all this blessed season.'
   Edmund Burt (fl. early 18th century),

Letters from a Gentleman in the
North of Scotland *(1726–37), quoting a
Loch Lomond ferryman*

14 First on the head of him who did this
 deed
My curse shall light,– on him and all
 his seed:
Without one spark of intellectual fire,
Be all the sons as senseless as the sire:
If one with wit the parent brood disgrace,
Believe him bastard of a brighter race.
> *Lord Byron (1788–1824),* The Curse of
> Minerva, *on Lord Elgin (1766–1841),
> remover of the 'Elgin Marbles' from the
> Parthenon (see also Insults)*

15 Blessed be the inventor of Photography!
I set him above even the inventor of
Chloroform!
> *Janes Welsh Carlyle (1801–1866), letter
> to Mrs Stirling, 1859*

16 I curse their head and all the hairs of
their head, I curse their face, their eyes,
their mouth, their nose, their tongue, their
teeth, their shoulders, their back and their
heart . . . Before and behind, within and
without. I curse them walking and I curse
them riding. I curse them standing and I
curse them sitting . . . I dissever and part
them from the Kirk of God, and deliver
them quick to the devill of Hell.
> *Curse against those who break the laws of
> the Church, issued by Archbishop Gavin
> Dunbar of Glasgow in the early 16th cen-
> tury; quoted in George Blake,* A Scottish
> Treasure Trove *(undated)*

17 I denounce, proclaimis and declaris all and
sundry the committaris of the said saikles
murthris, slauchteris, brinying, heirchip-
pen, reiffs, thiftis and spulezies . . . and
their counsalouris and defendouris, of
thair evi gel deeds generalie CURSIT,
waryit aggregeite, and reaggregaite, with
the GREIT CURSING . . . All the malesouns and waresouns that ever gat warldlie
creature sen the begynniyng of the warlde
to this hour mot licht apon thaiPm. The
maledictioun of God, that lichtit apon
Licifer and all his fallows, that strak thaim
fra the hie hevin to the deep hell, mot
licht apon them . . . And their candillis
gangis frae your sicht, as mot their saulis
gang fra the visage of God, and thair gude
fame fra the warld, quhill thai forbeir thair
oppin synnys foirsaid, and ryse frae this

terribilll cursing, and mak satisfaction and
pennance.
> *Curse pronounced by Archbishop Gavin
> Douglas against the Border Reivers,
> c. 1625, quoted in George Macdonald
> Fraser,* The Steel Bonnets *(1971)*

18 Fra heat of body I thee now deprive,
And to thy sickness sall be na recure,
Bot in dolour thy dayis to endure.
Thy crystal ene minglit with blude I mak;
Thy voice so clear unpleasand, hoir and
 hace;
Thy lusty lire ourspred with spottis black,
And lumpis haw appearand in thy face.
> *Robert Henryson (c.1425–c.1500),* The
> Testament of Cresseid

19 Curse his new hoose, his business, his
 cigar,
His wireless set, and motor car,
Alsatian, gauntlet gloves, plus fours and
 wife,
– A'thing included in his life;
And, abune a', his herty laughter,
And, if he has yin, his hereafter.
> *Hugh MacDiarmid (C. M. Grieve,
> 1892–1978),* Thoughts on My Boss

20 O Merlin in your crystal cave
Deep in the diamond of the day.
> *Edwin Muir (1887–1959),* Merlin

21 My malison light ilka day
On them that drink and dinna pay.
> *Allan Ramsay (c.1684–1758),* Lucky
> Spence's Last Advice

22 Fyvie, Fyvie, thou's ne'er thrive ye,
As lang's in thee there's stanis three;
There's ane intil the highest tower,
There's ane intil the ladye's bower,
There's ane aneath the water yett,
And thir three stanis ye'se never get!
> *Thomas Learmonth of Ercildoun, 'The
> Rhymer' (fl. 13th century), Curse upon
> Fyvie Castle, quoted in Lauchlan
> Maclean Watt,* Scottish Life and Poetry
> *(1912)*

23 Ugie, Ugie by the sea,
Lordless shall thy landis be,
And underneath thy hearthstane
The tod shall bring her bairnis hame.
> *Thomas the Rhymer,* Curse Upon the
> Earl Marischal's Castle, *quoted in* Scot-
> tish Life and Poetry

24 Good even, good fair moon, good even
      to thee!
    I prithee, dear moon, now show to me
    The form and the features, the speech
      and degree,
    Of the man that true lover of mine shall
      be.

    Sir Walter Scott (1772–1832), The
    Heart of Midlothian

25 May William, the son of George, be as
    a leafless splintered tree, rootless, branch-
    less, sproutless. May there be no joy on
    his hearth, no wife, no brother, no son, no
    sounding harp or blazing wax.

    *John Roy Stuart (fl. 18th century), curse
    on the Duke of Cumberland after Cul-
    loden, from Gaelic*

Daily Life, Work and Business

1 O can ye sew cushions?
   Or can ye sew sheets?
   An' can ye sing ba-la-loo
   When the bairnie greets?

   Anonymous

2 O' a' the trades that I do ken,
   The beggin' is the best,
   For when a beggar's weary,
   He can aye sit doon an' rest.

   Traditional, Tae the Beggin' I Will Go

3 There was a wee cooper who lived in Fife,
   Nickety, nackety, noo noo noo,
   And he has gotten a gentle wife . . .
   She wadna bake and she wadna brew,
   Nickety, nackety, noo noo noo,
   For spoilin' o' her comely hue . . .
   She wadna card and she wadna spin,
   For shamin' o' her gentle kin.

   Anonymous, The Wee Cooper o' Fife

4 Six days shalt thou labour and do all
   That you are able;
   On the Sabbath-day wash the horses' legs
   And tiddy up the stable.

   Anonymous rhyme from the Fife Herald
   and Journal *(1903), quoted in T. C.
   Smout,* A Century of the Scottish
   People, 1830–1950 *(1986), on the
   ploughman's working week*

5 Success the ploughman's wages crown;
   Let ploughmen's wages ne'er come down,
   And plenty in Scotland aye abound,
   By labour of the ploughmen.

   John Anderson (fl. mid-19th century),
   In Praise of Ploughmen, *from J. Ord,*
   Bothy Songs and Ballads *(1930)*

6 Nothing is really work unless you would
   rather be doing something else.

   J. M. Barrie (1860–1937)

7 Oh dear me, the mill's gaen fest,
   The puir wee shifters canna get a rest:
   Shiftin' bobbins, coorse and fine,
   They fairly mak' ye work for your ten and
   nine.

   Mary Brooksbank (1897–1980), The
   Jute Mill Song

8 I'm busy too, an' skelpin' at it.

   Robert Burns (1759–1796), Epistle to
   J. Lapraik

9 *Caesar:* But surely poor folk maun be
   wretches!
     Luath: They're nae sae wretched's ane
   wad think:
       Though constantly on poortith's brink,
       They're sae accustom'd wi' the sight,
       The view o't gies them little fright.

   Robert Burns, The Twa Dogs

10 I never was cannie for hoarding o' money,
    Or claughtin' together at a', man;
    I've little to spend, and naething to lend,
    But deevil a shilling I awe, man.

    Robert Burns (1759–1796), The Ron-
    alds of the Bennals

11 . . . why should a people be branded with
    the name of idlers, in a country where
    there is generally no profitable business for
    them to do?

    Edmund Burt (fl. early 18th century),
    Letters from a Gentleman in the
    North of Scotland *(1726–37)*

12 Doon at Nether Dallachy there's neither
      watch nor knock,
    but denner time and supper time, and
      aye yoke, yoke.
    It's hingin in, aye hingin in, aa day fae
      sax tae sax,
    The deeil a meenit div ye get tae gie
      yoursel a rax.

    J. M. Caie (1878–1950), Sair Wark's
    Nae Easy

13 It is the first of all problems for a man to find out what kind of work he is to do in this Universe.

> *Thomas Carlyle (1795–1881), inaugural address, Edinburgh, 2 April 1866*

14 Work is a grand cure for all the maladies and miseries that ever beset mankind – honest work, which you intend getting done.

> *Thomas Carlyle, Inaugural address, Edinburgh*

15 A man willing to work, and unable to find work, is perhaps the saddest sight that fortune's inequality exhibits under this sun.

> *Thomas Carlyle, Chartism*

16 What worship, for example, is there not in mere washing!

> *Thomas Carlyle, Past and Present*

17 Rest is for the dead.

> *Thomas Carlyle, quoted by J. A. Froude,* Life of Carlyle: The First Forty Years

18 It's just the power of some to be a boss,
And the bally power of others to be bossed.

> *John Davidson (1857–1909),* Thirty Bob a Week

19 Business – the world's work – is the sale of lies:
Not goods, but trade-marks; and still more and more
In every branch becomes the sale of money.

> *John Davidson,* Smith

20 Work and play! Work and play!
The order of the universe.

> *John Davidson,* Piper, Play

21 'Hokey,' said the youth. 'When Ah'm in the business, Ah'll have the times!'

> *George Douglas (George Douglas Brown, 1869–1902),* The House with the Green Shutters

22 ... with thy neichbours gladly lend and borrow;
His chance tonight, it may be thine tomorow.

> *William Dunbar (c.1460–c.1520),* No Treasure without Gladness

23 In a thrifty dress of an homely guise,
All iron'd, smooth, and clean,
The factory girl, at the brief meal hour,
Is always to be seen.
And there is ever on her face
That look which seems to say,
'Industry is the noblest plan
By which to live you may.'

> *James Easson (1833–1865),* The Factory Girl

24 The couthy cracks begin when supper's owre.

> *Robert Fergusson (1750–1774),* The Farmer's Ingle

25 'I think the Scots are a lazy set of bastards, to be quite frank . . . I don't think the work ethic is very strong.'

> *Sir Monty Finniston, quoted in Kenneth Roy,* Conversations in a Small Country, *1989*

26 I'm early up, this Friday morn,
an' feelin' maist byordinar gay;
ma heid's as caller as a herrin,
I'm far owre weill to wark the day.

> *Robert Garioch (Robert Garioch Sutherland, 1909–1981),* Owre Weill

27 The workers, slaves of the ring, hurrying to and fro in obedience
to summons –
The patter of their feet like the tread of an army . . .
It is questionable indeed if the towns-people have any real personal identity at all;
If they are not really themselves part and parcel a product of Glendale & Co.

> *James Young Geddes (fl. later 19th century),* Glendale & Co *(after Walt Whitman)*

28 At the warning call of 'Gardy loo' from servants preparing to outpour the contents of stoups, pots and cans, the passengers beneath would agonisingly call out 'Haud yer hand'; but too often the shout was unheard or too late . . . the dreaded hour when the domestic abominations were flung out, when the smells (known as the 'flowers of Edinburgh') filled the air.

> *H. Grey Graham,* The Social Life of Scotland in the Eighteenth Century *(1899)*

29 Whatever the season was, 'kain' eggs and fowls must be sent to the 'big house', every egg being cautiously examined by the lady,

who measured them with rings of different sizes – those that passed the first test being reckoned twelve to the dozen; but fifteen of the second size and eighteen of the third were required to count as a dozen.

> *H. Grey Graham*, The Social Life of Scotland in the Eighteenth Century

30 A hunner funnels bleezin, reekin,
Coal and airnstane, charrin, smeekin;
Navvies, miners, keepers, fillers,
Puddlers, rollers, airn-millers;
Reestit, reekit, ragged laddies . . .
Sweitin, sweirin, fechtin, drinkin,
Change-hoose bells and gill-stowps
clinkin

> *Janet Hamilton (1795–1873)*, Oor Location

31 I refused to learn how to be poor. That's my whole story.

> *Chris Hannan (1958–)*, Elizabeth Gordon Quinn

32 Waulking, which is a process of fulling cloth, has often been described. Women get together, sit round a table, pound and pull a roll of tweed in order to shrink the tweed to a state fit for the tailor, sing rhythmically as they work and after it is finished they give the roll a quick clapping finish . . . How idyllic is the picture of a small society and its handicraft, until one learns that the essential liquid in which the cloth is stlaneeped is hot urine!

> *Frank Howes*, Folk Music of Britain and Beyond *(1969)*

33 Custom, then, is the great guide of human life.

> *David Hume (1711–1776)*, Essay on Human Understanding

34 I must go and earn this damned guinea, or I shall be sure to want it tomorrow.

> *John Hunter (1728–1793), quoted in S. R. Gloyne*, John Hunter

35 . . . a craftsman had misjudged cutting a crank by one thousandth of an inch and had thereby wasted £1,000-worth of materials. Beardmore came down, smoking a cigar, looked at the crank, and turned to the manager.
'Can we make another?'
'Yes, sir.'
'Then get the thing done.' With that he walked away, 'a very god', says Kirkwood.

> *T. C. Smout*, A Century of the Scottish People, 1830–1950, *quoting David Kirkwood*, My Life of Revolt, *on an incident in Beardmore's engineering factory in the 1900s*

36 Oh, it's nice to get up in the mornin' –
And nicer to stay in bed.

> *Sir Harry Lauder (1870–1950)*

37 Scotland has been in recent years an increasingly unprofitable sphere in which to conduct various businesses, and the alarming effect is, of course, cumulative. The way to check this trend is to inspire the people of Scotland not only with confidence and faith in their own country, but with a determination to face the facts.

> *Sir James Lithgow, in the* Daily Record, *(1932)*

38 You would not think any duty smallIf you yourself were great.

> *George Macdonald (1824–1905)*, Willie's Question

39 Ho! these are the Titans of toil and trade,
The heroes who wield no sabre;
But mightier conquests reapeth the blade
That is borne by the Lords of Labour.

> *James Macfarlan (1832–1862)*, The Lords of Labour

40 In the choosing of a line of life, it is always a sign of an erect and *manly* character to choose those employments, however poor, which are least allied to *dependence*.

> *James Mill (1773–1836)*, Commonplace Book

41 'A sale's a sublime thing,' he said, 'for if you don't like a thing you don't need to buy it.'

> *Neil Munro (1864–1930)*, The Vital Spark

42 Wha'll buy caller herrin'?
They're bonny fish and halesome fairin':
Who'll buy caller herrin'
New-drawn frae the Forth?

> *Lady Nairne (1766–1845)*, Caller Herrin'

43 'Work, eh. What a stupid way to earn a living.'

> *Ian Pattison (1950–), At the Job Centre (Rab C. Nesbitt: The Scripts, 1990)*

44 For we've established Shaving Banks
For shaving o' the lower ranks,
For which we claim their gratefu' thanks
Withouten flattery
Of you, who are but useless blanks
In life's great lottery.

> *Alexander Rodger (1784–1846), Shaving Banks, Or Matthew's Call To The Worthless, To Come And Be Shaved O' Their Siller*

45 'No-one has ever said it,' observed Lady Caroline, 'but how painfully true it is that the poor have us always with them!'

> *Saki (H. H. Munro, 1870–1916)*

46 I consider the capacity to labour as part of the happiness I have enjoyed.

> *Sir Walter Scott (1771–1832) quoted in Lockhart's* Life of Scott

47 I was not long, however, in making the grand discovery, that in order to enjoy leisure, it is absolutely necessary it should be preceded by occupation.

> *Sir Walter Scott, Introductory Epistle to* The Monastery

48 'If your honour disna ken when ye hae a gude servant, I ken when I hae a gude master.'

> *Sir Walter Scott,* Rob Roy

49 There's folk that's independent o' ither tradesmen's wark,
The women need nae barbers and the dikers need nae clerk;
But nane o' them can dae wi'oot a coat or a sark:
Na! They winna want the wark o' the weavers.

> *David Shaw (1786–1856), The Wark o' the Weavers*

50 My name is Tammie Treddlefeet,
I live in Shuttle Ha';
And I hae been a weaver lad
This twenty year and twa:
Wi' waft and warp, and shears sae sharp,
My rubbin bane, my reed and heddles,
Sae nimbly as my shuttle flees,
While up and doon I tramp my treddles.

> *David Shaw,* Tammie Treddlefeet

51 Practical wisdom is only to be learned in the school of experience.

> *Samuel Smiles (1816–1904),* Self-Help

52 It will generally be found that men who are constantly lamenting their ill-luck are only reaping the consequences of their own neglect, mismanagement, and improvidence; or lack of application.

> *Samuel Smiles,* Self-Help

53 Work is the appointed calling of man on earth; the end for which his various faculties were given; the element in which his nature is ordained to develop itself, and in which his progressive advance towards Heaven is to lie.

> *Samuel Smiles,* Self-Help

54 Our business in this world is not to succeed, but to continue to fail, in good spirits.

> *Robert Louis Stevenson (1850–1894)*

55 There is no duty we so much under-rate as the duty of being happy.

> *Robert Louis Stevenson, An Apology for Idlers*

56 Extreme *busyness*, whether at school or college, kirk or market, is a symptom of deficient vitality; and a faculty for idleness implies a catholic appetite and a strong sense of personal identity.

> *Robert Louis Stevenson, An Apology for Idlers*

57 It is not by any means certain that a man's business is the most important thing he has to do.

> *Robert Louis Stevenson*

58 Everyone lives by selling something.

> *Robert Louis Stevenson,* Beggars

59 We speak of hardships, but the true hardship is to be a dull fool, and permitted to mismanage life in our own dull and foolish manner.

> *Robert Louis Stevenson,* Travels with a Donkey

60 It is a damned thing for a man to have his all hanging by a single string . . . I cannot bear the thought of other people becoming losers by my schemes, and I have the happy disposition of always painting the worst.

> *James Watt (1736–1819), Letter to Dr Small, 1770*

61 'Ye'll need tae gie us a bung though Gav.
Ah'm fuckin brassic until this rent cheque
hits the mat the morn.'

   Irvine Welsh (1957–), Trainspotting

Death

1 This ae nighte, this ae nighte
Every nighte and alle,
Fire and fleet and candle-light;
And Christe receive thye saule.

   Anonymous, A Lyke-Wake Dirge

2 Mony an ane for him maks mane
But nane sall ken where he is gane;
Ower his white banes when they are bare,
The wind sall blaw for evermair.

   Anonymous, The Twa Corbies

3 O bonnie balms come tell me
What kind o' a daith I'll hae to dee?
Seven years a fish in the flood,
An' seven years a bird in the wood.
Seven years a tongue to the warnin' bell,
An' seven lang years in the flames o' hell.

   Anonymous, The Cruel Mother

4 I hae been to the wild wood, mother;
   mak my bed soon,
For I'm weary wi' huntin', and fain wad
   lie doon.

   Anonymous, Lord Randal

5 Ye Hielands and ye Lawlands,
O, whaur hae ye been?
They hae slain the Earl o' Moray,
And hae laid him on the green.
. . . the bonnie Earl o' Moray

Was the flower amang them a'.
O, lang may his lady
Look owre the castle Doune,
Ere she see the Earl o' Moray
Come soundin' thro' the toun.

   Anonymous, The Bonnie Earl o' Moray

6 She sought him east, she sought him west,
She sought him braid and narrow,
Syne in the cleaving of a craig
She found him droon'd in Yarrow.

   Anonymous, Willie Drowned in Yarrow

7 James Hodge continues to sell burial crapes
ready-made, and his wife's niece who lives
with him dresses dead corpses at as cheap
a rate as was formerly done by her aunt,

having been educated by her and perfected
at Edinburgh.

   *Advertisement in Glasgow, 1747, quoted
   in H. G. Graham*, The Social History
   of Scotland in the Eighteenth Century
   (1899)

8 Death is the port where all may refuge
   find,
The end of labour, entry into rest.

   William Alexander (c.1567–1640), The
   Tragedy of Darius

9 'I had the honour to set the crown on the
king's head, and now he hastens me to a
better crown than his own.'

   *Archibald, Marquis of Argyll
   (1598–1661), before his execution*

10 'This is the sweetest maiden I ever kissed,
it being the mean to finish my sin and
misery, and my inlet to glory, for which I
long.'

   *Archibald, Marquis of Argyll, attributed
   last words before his execution by the
   'Maiden'*

11 I shall die with a true heart and undaunted;
for I think no man fit to live that is not fit
to die.

   *Lord Balmerino (1688–1746), before his
   execution in London, 18 August 1746,
   quoted in* The Scots Magazine, *August
   1746*

12 To die will be an awfully big adventure.

   J. M. Barrie (1860–1937), Peter Pan

13 On this side and on that, men see their
   friends
Drop off, like leaves in autumn.

   Robert Blair (1699–1746), The Grave

14 Beyond the ever and the never,
I shall be soon.

   Horatius Bonar (1808–1889), Beyond
   the Smiling and the Weeping

15 The hangman, who was in a small room
off the hall, then came forth. He took
off his hat and made a low bow towards
the prisoner. John bowed his head towards
him. They stood looking at each other
with an awkward, uneasy attention. I inter-
fered and said, 'John, you are to have no
resentment against this poor man. He only
does his duty.'

   James Boswell (1740–1795), Journal

16 The wan moon is setting behind the
    white wave,
    And Time is setting with me, O!

>   *Robert Burns (1759–1796)*, Open the
>   Door To Me, O

17 O Death! the poor man's dearest friend –

>   *Robert Burns*, Man Was Made to
>   Mourn

18 Don't let the awkward squad fire over my
    grave.

>   *Robert Burns, quoted on his deathbed*

19 To live in hearts we leave behind
    Is not to die.

>   *Thomas Campbell (1777–1844)*, Hal-
>   lowed Ground

20 I saw a man from Liddesdale, Armstrong
    by name, hanged for horse-stealing. He
    was a strong man, grimly silent. His body
    spun and twitched horribly. I saw it before
    my eyes in the dark and in daylight for
    weeks. At last I drew the horrible figure
    on paper as exactly as I could, and thence-
    forth it ceased to haunt me.

>   *Thomas Carlyle (1795–1881)*, Letters

21 Mr Cockburn, on whom were the sweats
    of death, beg'd me to lie down with him . . .
    I strip'd instantly and was embraced in his
    cold, wet arms with such affection, dearer
    than the first embrace.

>   *Alison Cockburn (1712–1794)*, Letters
>   and A Memoir

22 He died, seated, with a bowl of milk on his
    knee, of which his ceasing to live did not
    spill a drop, a departure which it seemed,
    after the event happened, might have been
    foretold of this attenuated philosophical
    gentleman.

>   *Henry Thomas Cockburn (1779–1854)*,
>   Memorials, *on the death of Joseph Black
>   (1728–1799)*

23 God forbid that I should go to any heaven
    where there are no horses.

>   *R. B. Cunninghame Graham
>   (1852–1936)*

24 . . . they began to talk, after the Scottish
    fashion, of the funeral, before the antici-
    pated corpse.
    'Ye ken, we've got a braw new hearse
    outby, sort of Epescopalian looking, wi'
    gless a' roond, so' ye can see the kist . . .'
    The subject of the conversation took it
    cheerfully.

>   *R. B. Cunninghame Graham*, Beattock
>   for Moffat

25 In life it is your privilege to choose
    But after death you have no choice at all.

>   *John Davidson (1857–1909)*, Of the
>   Making of a Poet

26 The earth is full of graves, and mine was
    there
    Before my life began, my resting-place.

>   *John Davidson*, The Last Journey

27 To die young, is to do that soon, and in
    some fewer Days, which once thou must
    do; it is but the giving over of a Game, that
    after never so many Hazards must be lost.

>   *William Drummond (1585–1649)*, A
>   Cypresse Grove

28 Thy Death is a peece of the order of this
    All, a part of the life of this world.

>   *William Drummond*, A Cypresse Grove

29 I that in heill was and in gladnes
    Am trublit now with great seiknes,
    And feblit with infirmitie
    Timor mortis conturbat me.

>   *William Dunbar (c.1460–c.1520)*,
>   Lament for the Deth of the Makkaris

30 He taikis the campioun in the stour,
    The captane closit in the tour,
    The lady in bour full of bewtie;
    Timor Mortis Conturbat Me

>   *William Dunbar*, Lament for the Deth
>   of the Makkaris

31 Sen for the deid remeid is none,
    Best is that we for deth dispone,
    Eftir our deth that leif may we:
    Timor mortis conturbat me.

>   *William Dunbar*, Lament for the Deth
>   of the Makkaris

32 Hallowe'en, the night which marks the
    transition from autumn to winter, seems
    to have been of old the time of year when
    the souls of the departed were supposed to
    revisit their old homes in order to warm
    themselves by the fire and to comfort them-

selves with the good cheer provided for them in the kitchen or the parlour by their affectionate kinsfolk. It was, perhaps, a natural thought that the approach of winter should drive the poor, shivering, hungry ghosts from the bare fields and the leafless woodlands to the shelter of the cottage with its familiar fireside ... could the goodman and the good-wife deny to the spirits of their dead the welcome which they gave to the cows?

> *Sir James G. Frazer (1854–1941)*, The Golden Bough

33 Death is a grim creditor, and a doctor but brittle bail when the hour o' reckoning's at han'!

> *John Galt (1779–1839)*, Annals of the Parish

34 What a pity it is, mother, that you're now dead, for here's the minister come to see you.

> *John Galt*, Annals of the Parish

35 No, I'll inherit
No keening in my mountain head or sea
Nor fret for few who die before I do.

> *W. S. Graham (1918–1986)*, Many Without Elegy

36 I tremble from the edge of life, to dare
The dark and fatal leap, having no faith,
No glorious yearning for the Apocalypse;
But like a child that in the night-time cries
For light, I cry

> *David Gray (1838–1861)*, Sonnet

37 Quo Daith, the warld is mine,
I hae dug a grave and dug it deep.
For war and the pest will gar ye sleep,
Quo Daith, the warld is mine.

Quo Life, the warld is mine,
An open grave is a furrow syne,
Ye'll no keep my seed frae faain in,
Quo Life, the warld is mine.

> *Hamish Henderson (1919–)*, The Flyting o' Life and Daith

38 Of kindelie death nane suld affraied be
But sich as hope for na felicitie.

> *Alexander Hume (c.1560–1609)*, To His Sorrofull Saull, Consolatioun

39 'I am dying as fast as my enemies, if I have any, could wish, and as easily and cheerfully as my best friends could desire.'

> *David Hume (1711–1776), recorded in William Smellie*, Literary and Characteristical Lives *(1800)*

40 If suicide be supposed a crime, it is only cowardice can impel us to it. If it be no crime, both prudence and courage should engage us to rid ourselves at once of existence when it becomes a burden. It is the only way we can then be useful to society.

> *David Hume*, Essays

41 Says she, 'Guidmen I've kistit twa,
But a change o' deils is lichtsome, lass!'

> *Violet Jacob (1863–1946)*, A Change o' Deils

42 The rich man deeit, an' they buried him gran',
In linen fine his body they wrap;
But the angels tuik up the beggar man,
An' layit him doun in Abraham's lap.

> *George Macdonald (1824–1905)*, This Side an' That

43 Ane by ane they gang awa'.
The Gatherer gathers great an' sma',
Ane by ane mak's ane an' a'.

> *George Macdonald*, Ane By Ane

44 Beautiful railway bridge of the Silv'ry Tay!
Alas I am very sorry to say
That ninety lives have been taken away
On the last Sabbath day of 1879
Which will be remembered for a very long time.

> *William McGonagall (c.1825–1902)*, Beautiful Railway Bridge of the Silv'ry Tay

45 Vain are all things when death comes to your door.

> *Murdo Mackenzie (fl. 1650s)*, Diomhanas nan Diomhanas (Vanity of Vanities), *translated by William Neill*

46 Weel aff are they aneath the mools,
They never fin' the caul ava',
But in their lanely narrow beds
Do snugly doze and rot awa.

> *John MacTaggart (1791–1830)*, Raw Weather, *from* The Scottish Gallovidian Encyclopedia

47 Today, after dinner, my sentence has been announced to me, of being executed tomorrow as a criminal, at eight in the morning . . . thanks be to God, I despise death, and faithfully protest that I receive it innocent of all crime, even supposing I were in their jurisdiction.

Queen Mary I (1542–1587), letter to King Henri III of France, February 1587

48 The hangman was a distinguished and awful functionary. The official who then held the appointment was a person condemned for sheep-stealing, which was at this time a capital crime; but he received a pardon on condition he agreed to act as hangman, an office very unpopular. The former hangman . . . had died from severe treatment by a mob.

Joseph Mitchell (1803–1883), Reminiscences of My Life in the Highlands

49 Here it was arranged the customary funeral dinner should be held, and the entertainment was somewhat prolonged.

At last notice was given for the funeral party to move; but when the procession had proceeded more than a mile on the road, the undertaker came galloping up, calling,

'Gentlemen, halt, for we have forgotten the hearse.'

Joseph Mitchell, Reminiscences of My Life in the Highlands

50 So man goes to his long, long home, and mourners pass along the street, on the day when the silver cord is snapped, and the golden lamp drops broken . . . when the dust returns to the earth once more, and the spirit to God who gave it.

James Moffat (1870–1944), Translation of Ecclesiastes

51 Unfriendly friendly universe, I pack your stars into my purse, And bid you, bid you so farewell.

Edwin Muir (1887–1959), The Child Dying

52 Let children walk with nature, let them see the beautiful blending and communion of death and life, their joyous inseparable unity, as taught in woods and meadows, plains and mountains and streams of our blessed star, and they will learn that death is stingless indeed, and as beautiful as life, and that the grave has no victory, for it never fights. All is divine harmony.

John Muir (1838–1914)

53 There's nae sorrow, there John, There's neither cauld nor care, John, The day is aye fair, In the land o' the leal.

Lady Nairne (1765–1845), The Land o' the Leal

54 At a prolonged drinking bout one of the party remarked, 'What gars the Laird of Garskadden luk sae gash?'

'Ou,' says his neighbour, the Laird of Kilmardinny, 'Garskadden's been wi' his Maker these twa hours; I saw him step awa', but I dinna like to disturb gude company.'

Dean E. B. Ramsay (1793–1872), Reminiscences of Scottish Life and Character

55 Nae stroke o' fortune cloured wi' bloody claa, Nor glow'ring daith wi' sudden tempest mocked, But in his wee thatched croft he wore awa' E'en as a cruisie flickers oot unslockt.

Robert Rendall (1900–1967), The Fisherman

56 I go piecemeal. I am deaf, blind, and lame, but content, because I know God made me, and knows best how to take down His own works.

Alison Rutherford (1713–1794), Letter to the Rev. Robert Douglas, quoted in Agnes Mure Mackenzie, Scottish Pageant 1707–1802 *(1950)*

57 I have got summons already before a Superior Judge and Judiciary, and I behove to answer to my first summons, and ere your day come, I will be where few kings and great folks come.

Samuel Rutherford (1600–1661), letter from his deathbed, when summoned to appear at a charge of treason

58 Waldo is one of those people who would be enormously improved by death.

Saki (H. H. Munro, 1870–1916), Beasts and Super-Beasts

59 And, at the very idea of the general grief which must have attended his death,

the good-natured monarch cried heartily himself.

> *Sir Walter Scott (1771–1832)*, The Fortunes of Nigel

60 Like the dew on the mountain,
Like the foam on the river,
Like the bubble on the fountain,
Thou art gone, and forever.

> *Sir Walter Scott*, The Lady of the Lake

61 We slept reasonably, but on the next morning.

> *Sir Walter Scott, final entry in his* Journal

62 The SIC has taken action to end a recent insensitive practice where bereaved relations enquiring about funeral arrangements were referred to the 'Refuse' section of the council.

> Shetland Times, *quoted in Alastair Scott,* Native Stranger *(1995)*

63 A kind gudeman, and twa
Sweet bairns were round me here,
But they're a' ta'en awa',
Sin' the fa' o' the year.

> *Thomas Smibert (1810–1854)*, The Fa' o' the Year

64 As I enter up my thoughts for the day on the day following, there can be no entry for the day on which I die. Let me write it down now. 'To accept Life is to give it beauty'.

> *William Soutar (1898–1943)*, Journal, *14 May 1939*

65 There is a certain frame of mind to which a cemetery is, if not an antidote, at least an alleviation. If you are in a fit of the blues, go nowhere else.

> *Robert Louis Stevenson (1850–1894)*, Immortelles

66 Under the wide and starry sky
Dig the grave, and let me lie.
Glad did I live and gladly die,
And I laid me down with a will.

> *Robert Louis Stevenson*, Requiem

67 Cruel as death, and hungry as the grave.

> *James Thomson (1700–1748)*, The Seasons: Winter

68 There studious let me sit
And hold high converse with the mighty dead.

> *James Thomson*, Winter

69 This little life is all we must endure,
The grave's most holy peace is ever sure,
We fall asleep and never wake again.

> *James Thomson (1834–1882)*, The City of Dreadful Night

70 Though the Garden of thy Life be wholly waste, the sweet flowers withered, the fruit-trees barren, over its wall hangs ever the rich dark clusters of the Vine of Death, within easy reach of thy hand, which may pluck of them when it will.

> *James Thomson*, The City of Dreadful Night, *note.*

71 The restful rapture of the inviolate grave.

> *James Thomson*, To Our Ladies of Death

72 Our Mother feedeth thus our little life,
That we in turn may feed her with our death.

> *James Thomson*, To Our Ladies of Death

Education and Schools

1 Mr Rhind is very kind,
He goes to kirk on Sunday.
He prays to God to give him strength
To skelp the bairns on Monday.

> *Traditional, children's rhyme*

2 Knock, knock.
Who's there?
(*Refined voice*): Emma Watsonian. Who are you?
(*Demotic voice*): Humphrey Heriots.

> *Edinburgh joke noted in Arnold Kemp,* The Hollow Drum *(1993)*

3 Wherever there is access to a School, the Boys are carefully put to it; but the Parents consider Learning of any kind as of little Moment to the Girls, on which account, great Numbers of them never go to any School.

> *Contemporary comment on 18th-century schooling in the Highlands, quoted in Charles Withers,* Gaelic Scotland *(1988)*

4 . . . education . . . is a battlefield between liberality and illiberality – between cosmopoli-tanism and patriotism, between the treatment of the child as the 'heir of all the ages', and the treatment of him as job-fodder.

John Anderson (1893–1962), Education and Practicality

5 'Intern all parents', he enjoined, with reference to his theoretical child of eleven, 'and send him (or her) off to pass adolescence under the care of a deaf, offhand old centaur in a cave, and the essentials would be well looked after, supposing plenty of similar caves in the district'.

Neal Ascherson (1935–), quoted in Karl Miller (1931–), Dark Horses (1998)

6 Instinct is untaught ability.

Alexander Bain (1818–1903), Senses and Intellect

7 He would not allow Scotland to derive any credit from Lord Mansfield; for he was educated in England. 'Much', said he, 'may be made of a Scotchman, if he be *caught young*.'

James Boswell (1740–1795), Life of Samuel Johnson

8 The schoolmaster is abroad, and I trust to him, armed with his primer, more than I do the soldier in full military array, for upholding and extending the liberties of the country . . . Education makes a people easy to leaindd, but difficult to drive; easy to govern but impossible to enslave.

Lord Brougham (1778–1868), speech to the House of Commons, 1828

9 If you haven't grace, the Lord can give it to you. If you haven't learning, I'll help you to get it. But if you haven't common sense, neither I nor the Lord can give it to you.

John Brown of Haddington (1722–1787), to his students

10 . . . it was his dearest wish and prayer to have his children under his own eye till they could discern between good and evil.

Robert Burns (1759–1796), letter to Dr John Moore, August 1787, on his father, William Burnes

11 It is frightening to speculate about the next generation that is being educated to know nothing of our history and culture and can be expected to resemble the robots they are learning to manipulate . . . Who will still be able to read, let alone read anything that requires intelligence and concentration?

John Calder (1927–), letter to The Guardian, *1987*

12 Experience is the best of schoolmasters, only the school-fees are heavy.

Thomas Carlyle (1795–1881), Miscellaneous Essays

13 Of necessitie therefore we judge it, that every severall Kirk have one Schoolmaister appointed, such a one at least as is able to teach Grammar and the Latin tongue, if the town be of any reputation.

Church of Scotland, The Book of Discipline, *1621*

14 When we make laws which compel our children to go to school we assume collectively an awesome responsibility. For a period of ten years . . . our children are conscripts; and their youth does nothing to alter the seriousness of this fact.

Margaret C. Donaldson (1926–), Children's Minds

15 I do not think any civil servant can tell me my job. I may not be as intelligent. I certainly was not educated at Oxford or Cambridge – I was educated at a far better place – Glasgow.

Sir Monty Finniston (1912–), quoted in the Daily Mail, *March 1976, after being sacked as Chairman of the British Steel Corporation*

16 We have regular hours for all our occupations, first at 7 o'clock we go to the dancing and come home at 8, we then read our Bible and get our repeating and then play till ten then we get our music till 11 when we get our writing and accounts we sew from 12 till 1, after which I get my gramer and then work till five. At 7 we come and knit till 8 when we don't go to the dancing. This is an exact description.

Marjory Fleming (1803–1811), Letters

17 Afore his cless he staunds and talks
or scrieves awa wi colour'd chalks.

Robert Garioch (Robert Garioch Sutherland, 1909–1981), Garioch's Response Til George Buchanan

18 . . . monie a skelp
of triple-tonguit tawse

has gien a hyst-up and a help
towards Doctorates of Laws.

> *Robert Garioch,* Embro to the Ploy

19 A single excursion under sympathetic
and intelligent guidance to an instructive
quarry, river-ravine, or sea-shore, is worth
many books and a long course of system-
atic lectures.

> *Sir Archibald Geikie (1835–1924),* My
> First Geological Excursion

20 Perhaps all teachers should pour fine stuff
into children's ears and leave their memories to resurrect it when they find their
own thoughts inadequate.

> *Alasdair Gray (1934–),* 1982, Janine

21 The dawn of legibility in his handwriting
has revealed his utter inability to spell.

> *Attributed to Ian Hay (John Hay Beith,*
> *1876–1952)*

22 To the members of
The most responsible
The least advertised
The worst paid
And the most richly rewarded
Profession in the world.

> *Ian Hay, Dedication of* The Lighter Side
> of School Life *(1914)*

23 Their learning is like bread in a besieged
town: every man gets a little, but no man
gets a full meal.

> *Samuel Johnson (1709–1784), quoted in*
> *Boswell's* Life of Johnson, *on the Scots*

24 Nae after days are like the days
When we were at the scule.

> *Thomas Latto (b. 1818)*

25 If I had my way, indeed, I would end
all compulsory education straightaway. To
close all the schools and universities could
not have any ill – and in many ways would
almost certainly have a stimulating – effect
on the general level of intelligence and
intellectual inquiry.

> *Hugh MacDiarmid (C. M. Grieve,*
> *1892–1978),* Lucky Poet

26 . . . the schools are not on our side. They
are the agencies of the rulers. They bring
us up to do what we are told, and not to
speak back, to learn our lessons and pass

the examinations. Above all, not to ask
questions.

> *R. F. Mackenzie (1910–1987),* A Search
> for Scotland

27 Sweet time – sad time! twa bairns
at scule –
Twa bairns and but ae heart.

> *William Motherwell (1797–1835),* Jean-
> nie Morrison

28 Public opinion in a Scotch playground
was a powerful influence in controlling
behaviour.

> *John Muir (1838–1913),* The Story of
> My Boyhood and Youth

29 I want these boys and girls to acquire the
habit of looking honestly at life.

> *A. S. Neill (1883–1973),* A Dominie's
> Log

30 There is never a problem child; there is
only a problem parent.

> *A. S. Neill,* The Problem Parent

31 The born teacher is not a problem: he loves
his work, he loves children, and children
love him. But he should be pensioned off
about the early forties because, when he
arrives at the stage when play is an effort
to him, he is apt to become a pessimist
with a mechanical smile.

> *A. S. Neill,* The Problem Teacher

32 A good teacher does not draw out: he gives
out, and what he gives out is love.

> *A. S. Neill,* The Problem Teacher

33 As the rough diamond from the mine,
In breakings only shews its light,
Till polishing has made it shine;
Thus learning makes the genius bright.

> *Allan Ramsay (1686–1758),* The Gentle
> Shepherd

34 Every school needs a debating society far
more than it needs a computer.

> *Sir Malcolm Rifkind (1946–),* All Those
> in Favour . . . *in A. Kamm and A. Lean,*
> A Scottish Childhood *(1985)*

35 Good gracious, you've got to educate him
first. You can't expect a boy to be vicious
until he's been to a really good school.

> *Saki (H. H. Munro, 1870–1916)*

36 'Has he learning?'
    'Just dung donnart wi' learning.'
    Sir Walter Scott (1771–1832),
    St Ronan's Well

37 Give me a girl at an impressionable age,
    and she is mine for life.
    *Muriel Spark (1918–) The Prime of
    Miss Jean Brodie*

38 To me, education is a leading out of what is
    already there in the pupil's soul. To Miss
    Mackay it is a putting in of something that
    is not there, and that is not what I call edu-
    cation, I call it intrusion.
    *Muriel Spark, The Prime of Miss Jean
    Brodie*

39 For a brief period in the late eighteenth
    century Scotland enjoyed the largest edu-
    cational system, one of the best classical
    secondary systems, and the best univer-
    sity system in Europe, all catering for an
    unusually wide range of social classes. At
    every level Scotland in the middle and late
    eighteenth century . . . was one of the best-
    educated countries in Europe.
    *Lawrence Stone, Literacy and Educa-
    tion in England, quoted in R. D. Ander-
    son, Education and the Scottish People
    1750–1918 (1995)*

40 Delightful task! To rear the tender
    thought,
    To teach the young idea how to shoot.
    *James Thomson (1700–1748) The
    Seasons*

Epitaphs

1 Here lyes beneath thir laid-stanes
   The carcase of George Glaid-stanes,
   Wherever be his other half,
   Loe here yee's have his Epitaph.
   *Anonymous epitaph on George Gladstanes,
   Archbishop of St Andrews (d.1615)*

2 Mightier was the verse of Iain,
   Hearts to nerve, to kindle eyes,
   Than the claymore of the valiant,
   Than the counsel of the wise.
   *Epitaph on the Bard Iain Lóm, from
   Gaelic*

3 The world is a city full of streets,
   And death's a market where everyone
   meets;

But if life were a thing money could buy,
The poor could not live, and the rich
never die.
    *Epitaph in the churchyard at Abernethy,
    from Alexander Hislop, The Book of
    Scottish Anecdote (1883)*

4 Dry up your tears and weep no more
   I am not dead but gone before
   Remember me, and bear in mind
   You have not long to stay behind.
   Anonymous

5 My wife lies here conveniently
   I am at rest, and so is she.
   *Epitaph said to have been seen in Greyfri-
   ars Churchyard, Edinburgh*

6 John Carnegie lies here,
   Descended from Adam and Eve
   If any can boast of a pedigree higher
   He will willingly give them leave.
   Anonymous

7 Content he was with portion small
   Keeped shop in Wigtown, and that's all.
   *Wigtown epitaph, from Stephen Bone,
   Albion: An Artist's Britain (1939)*

8 Poor
   White.
   *Epitaph in a graveyard by Loch Fyne,
   quoted in George Blake, Scottish Treasure Trove (undated)*

9 Halt, curious passenger, come here and
   read,
   Our souls triumph with Christ our
   glorious Heid.
   In self-defence we murdered here do lie
   To witness 'gainst the nation's perjury.
   *Inscription at the field of Aird's Moss,
   where Richard Cameron and other mem-
   bers of the Cameronian sect were killed,
   July 22, 1680*

10 Here lys
    James Stewart
    He sall rys.
    *Epitaph from the church wall at Dowally,
    Perthshire (undated)*

11 Here lies Durham
    But Durham lies not here.
    *Proposed epitaph for Mr Durham of
    Largo, noted for his exaggerations*

12 Gow an' time are even now;
Gow beat time, now Time beats Gow.
*Anonymous epitaph on Neil Gow, violinist
(1727–1807)*

13 A faithful holy minister here lies hid
One of a thousand, Mr Peter Kid,
Firm as a stone, but of a heart contrite
A wrestling, praying, weeping Israelite.
*Epitaph of Rev. Peter Kid, Carluke
Churchyard*

14 Ah, me, I grovel and am dust,
And to the grave descend I must,
O painted piece of human clay,
Now, be not proud of thy short stay.
*Epitaph of Peter Lowe (1550–1612), first
master of Glasgow Trades Hospital, in
Glasgow Cathedral*

15 Scotland bore me, England adopted me,
France taught me, Germany holds me.
*From the Latin epitaph on the tomb of
Duns Scotus (c.1265–1308), in Cologne,
Germany*

16 Lament him, Mauchline husbands a',
He aften did assist ye;
For had ye staid hale weeks awa',
Your wives they ne'er had missed ye.

Ye Mauchline bairns, as on ye press
To school in bands together,
O tread ye lightly on his grass –
Perhaps he was your father!
*Robert Burns (1759–1796), Epitaph for
a Wag in Mauchline*

17 Here lie Willie Michie's banes,
O Satan, when ye tak him,
Gie him the schulin o' your weans,
For clever deils he'll mak them!
*Robert Burns, Epitaph for William
Michie*

18 Here lies Boghead among the dead
In hopes to get salvation;
But if such as he in heav'n may be,
Then welcome – hail! damnation.
*Robert Burns, Epitaph on James Grieve,
Laird of Boghead, Tarbolton*

19 Below thir stanes lie Jamie's banes,
O Death, it's my opinion,
Thou'll ne'er take such a bleth'rin' bitch
Into thy dark dominion.
*Robert Burns, Epitaph on a Noisy
Polemic (James Humphrey, a Mauchline
mason)*

20 He who set the flame
of his native genius
under the cumbering whin
of the untilled field
lit a fire in the Mearns
that illumines Scotland,
clearing her sullen soil
for a richer yield.
*Helen B. Cruickshank (1886–1975),
Spring in the Mearns, for Lewis Grassic
Gibbon, 23 February 1935*

21 Lay me here where I may see
Teviot round his meadows flowing,
And about and over me
Winds and clouds forever going.
*Thomas Davidson (1838–1870), And
There Will I Be Buried*

22 Sen she is deid, I speak of her no more.
*Robert Henryson (c.1425–c.1500), The
Testament of Cresseid*

23 Here lie I, Martin Elginbrodde:
Hae mercy o' my soul, O God,
As I wad do, gin I were God
And ye were Martin Elginbrodde.
*George Macdonald (1824–1905), David
Elginbrod*

24 I do my best to leave aboon
The grave's lang, lanely hame,
A poor man's richest legacy,
And that's an honest name.
*Epitaph of Alexander Maclagan, Bal-
moral, 1871, quoted in J. Grant, The
Scottish National Dictionary (1934)*

25 Here lies of sense bereft –
But sense he never had.
Here lies, by feeling left –
But that is just as bad.
Here lies, reduced to dirt –
That's what he always was.
George Outram (1805–1856), Here Lies

26 In manly words he stated solemn truth.
*Alexander Pennecuik (fl. 18th century),
The Faithful Shepherd, on Thomas
Paterson, 1726*

27 Here lies the worst of kings and the most
wretched of men in the whole kingdom.
*King Robert III (c.1340–1406), self-pro-
nounced epitaph, from Walter Bower,
Scotichronicon, translated from Latin*

28 . . . to his native Thrums
He would return, even as the cuckoo

comes,
Only with summer; and, like that lone
    bird, rest
An egg of wisdom in some broody nest
Of twittering culture. Then to the south
With *Courage!* echoing in the ears of
    youth.

> *William Soutar (1898–1943)*,
> Impromptu Epitaph for Barrie

29 In peace and war he suffer'd overmuch:
    War stole away his strength, and peace his
    crutch.

> *William Soutar*, Epitaph for a Disabled
> Ex-Serviceman

30 This be the verse you grave for me:
    Here he lies where he longed to be,
    Home is the sailor, home from sea,
    And the hunter home from the hill.

> *Robert Louis Stevenson (1850–1894)*,
> Requiem

Fame and Fortune

1 Lo, one who loved true honour more than
    fame.

> *William Alexander (c.1567–1640)*,
> Doomsday

2 Fame is rot: daughters are the thing.

> *J. M. Barrie (1860–1937)* Dear Brutus

3 Ne'er mind how Fortune waft and warp;
    She's but a bitch.

> *Robert Burns (1759–1796)*, Second Epis-
> tle to J. Lapraik

4 Fortune! if thou'll but gie me still
    Hale breeks, a scone, and whisky-gill,
    An' rowth o' rhyme to rave at will,
    Tak' a' the rest.

> *Robert Burns*, Scotch Drink

5 We have not the love of greatness, but the
    love of the love of greatness.

> *Thomas Carlyle (1795–1881)*, Essays

6 In all times and places the Hero has been
    worshipped. It will ever be so. We all love
    great men.

> *Thomas Carlyle*, On Heroes, Hero-Wor-
> ship, and the Heroic in History

7 Sir, there is something incompatible be-
    tween greatness and the provostship of a
    Scottish burgh.

> *John Davidson (1857–1909)*, The
> Career of Ninian Jamieson

8 Fame is a revenue payable only to our
    ghosts; and to deny ourselves all present sat-
    isfaction, or to expose ourselves to so much
    hazard for this, were as great madness as
    to starve ourselves or fight desperately for
    food to be laid on our tombs after our
    death.

> *Sir George Mackenzie (1636–1691)*,
> Essay on Preferring Solitude

9 Who grasped at earthly fame
    Grasped wind.

> *Robert Pollok (1798–1827)*, The Course
> of Time

10 Sound, sound the trumpet, sound the fife,
    Loud the glorious truth proclaim:
    One crowded hour of glorious life
    Is worth an age without a name.

> *Sir Walter Scott (1771–1832)*, Sound,
> Sound the Trumpet

11 Fortune has often been blamed for her
    blind-ness; but Fortune is not so blind as
    men are.

> *Samuel Smiles (1816–1904)*, Self-Help

12 If it is for fame that men do brave actions,
    they are only silly fellows after all.

> *Robert Louis Stevenson (1850–1894)*,
> The English Admirals

Family, Society and Social Life

1 'O hold your hand, Lord William,' she
        said,
    'For your strokes they are wondrous sair;
    True lovers I can get many an ane,
    But a father I can never get mair.'

> *Anonymous*, The Douglas Tragedy

2 'Ye maun gang to your father, Janet,
    Ye maun gang to him sune;
    Ye maun gang to your father, Janet,
    In case that his days are dune.'

> *Anonymous*, Fair Janet

3 'And what will ye leave to your bairns
        and your wife,
    Edward, Edward?
    And what will ye leave to your bairns

and your wife,
When ye gang owre the sea, O?'
'The warld's room – let them beg
    through life,
Mither, mither;
The warld's room – let them beg through
    life,
For them never mair will I see, O.'

Anonymous, Edward

4 The sone of ane prince beand distitut of
vert is no gentil man; ande in opposit,
ane sone of ane mechanyc plebien, beand
verteous, he is ane gentil man . . . Quhen
the corrupit flesche is consumit fra the
banis, no man can put defferens betuix ane
prince and ane beggar.

Anonymous, The Complaynt of Scotland *(1549)*

5 In a wee bit croft ayont the hill,
Abune the neuk frae Sprottie's mill,
Tryin' a' his life the time to kill,
Lived Geordie MacIntyre.
He had a wife, as sweir's himsel',
And a dochter as black as Old Nick in
    Hell

Anonymous, The Muckin' o' Geordie's
Byre

6 Greatest horror – dream I am married –
wake up shrieking.

*Sir J. M. Barrie (1860–1937), quoted in
A. Birkin*, J. M. Barrie and the Lost
Boys *(1979)*

7 Ye see yon birkie ca'd a lord,
Wha struts, and stares, and a' that?
Though hundreds worship at his word,
He's but a coof for a' that.

Robert Burns (1759–1796), A Man's a
Man For a' That

8 I have had many foes, but none like
    thee . . .
Even on such a basis hast thou built
A monument, whose cement hath been
    guilt!
The moral Clytemnestra of thy lord,
And hew'd down, with an unsuspected
    sword,
Fame, peace, and hope – and all
the better life,
Which, but for this cold treason of
    thy heart,
Might still have risen from the grave

of strife,
And found a nobler duty than to part.

Lord Byron (1788–1824), Lines on
Hearing that Lady Byron Was Ill

9 This is the curious abyss that divides
the closest kin, that the tender curiosity
appropriate to lovers is inappropriate, here,
where the bond is involuntary, so that the
most important things stay undiscovered.

Angela Carter, Sugar Daddy, *in Robert
Winder*, The Granta Book of the
Family *(1995)*

10 One of the great delusions of Scottish society is the widespread belief that Scotland
is a tolerant and welcoming country and
that racism is a problem confined to England's green and unpleasant land.

Stuart Cosgrove, Hampden Babylon
(1991)

11 Many a man who thinks to found a home
discovers that he has merely opened a
tavern for his friends.

Norman Douglas (1868–1952), South
Wind

12 To run a household and cook an omelette
or a stew is what every boy ought to
learn from his mother – supposing modern
mothers to be still capable of such things.

Norman Douglas, Looking Back

13 'I' my granfather's time, as I have heard
him tell, ilka maister o' a faamily had his
ain sate in his ain hoose; aye, an' sat wi' his
hat on his heed afore the best in the land;
an' had his ain dish, an' wus aye helpit first,
an' keepit up his authority as a man should
do. Paurents were paurents then – bairns
daurdna set up their gabs afore them as
they dae noo.'

Susan Ferrier (1782–1854), Marriage

14 There is no sense among the Scots that a
working class man who has taken a degree
has got above himself – there is no upper
limit to Scottish aspiration.

Iain Finlayson, The Scots *(1987)*

15 There is a core of opinion that the Scottish aristocracy are utterly futile, that their
role in modern Scotland is non-existent,
and that they have degenerated into wimps
and drunks.

Iain Finlayson, The Scots

16 The awe and dread with which the untutored savage contemplates his mother-in-law are amongst the most familiar facts of anthropology.

Sir James Frazer (1854–1941), The Golden Bough

17 'A sair blow to the widow, Andra's death; he was a good man to her.'

No-one answering him, he qualified what he had said by adding: 'Aye, sort of mid-dlin',' and glanced round warily to see if he had overstepped the bounds by the too indiscriminating nature of his praise.

R. B. Cunninghame Graham (1852–1936), Scottish Stories

18 Lying asleep turning
Round in the quay-lit dark
It was my father standing
As real as life. I smelt
The quay's tar and the ropes.
I think he wanted to speak,
But the dream had no sound.
I think I must have loved him.

W. S. Graham (1918–1986), To Alexander Graham

19 I can make a lord, but only God Almighty can make a gentleman.

King James VI (1566–1625)

20 In circumstances roughly similar to this one, in certain tribes of chimpanzees, individuals bare their arses to each other, a method of pacifying the aggressor. But this wasn't the place to display arses. This was family.

James Kelman (1946–), A Disaffection

21 Sometimes yew felt like dropping deid, just to escape the company.

James Kelman, The Good Times

22 The thing about a house without a woman, her mother often said, was just that it lacked a woman's touch always emphasising her own touch. Holding the jam she had just made admiringly up against the light, whisking the invisible dust off her highly polished dresser.

Jessie Kesson (1916–1994), Where the Apple Ripens

23 Marriage is a ghastly public confession of a strictly private intention.

Ian Hay (John Hay Beith, 1876–1952)

24 Poor mother, she thought, she's had five children and she's as barren as Rannoch Moor. What did she know of life with her church committees and her Madeira cakes and her husband who was more Calvinistic than Calvin himself?

Joan Lingard (1932–), The Prevailing Wind

25 And the atmosphere warm with that lovely heat,
The warmth of tenderness and loving souls, the smiling anxiety,
That rules a house where a child is about to be born.

Hugh MacDiarmid (C. M. Grieve, 1898–1972), Lo! A Child is Born

26 Wi' every effort to be fair
And nae undue antagonism
I canna but say that my sweethheart's mither
Is a moolie besom, a moolie besom,
Naething but a moolie besom!

Hugh MacDiarmid, A Moolie Besom

27 Women do not find it difficult nowadays to behave like men, but they often find it extremely difficult to behave like gentlemen.

Compton Mackenzie (1883–1972) Literature in My Time

28 You waitit for me to be born
I wait for you to dee.

Alastair Mackie (1925–), For My Father

29 We hardly conceive of our parents as human.

Alasdair Maclean, Night Falls on Ardnamurchan *(1989)*

30 . . . 'middle class', that is people with ideas above their station.

Edwin Muir (1887–1959), Scottish Journey

31 My parents were wonderful, always there with a ready compromise. My sister wanted a cat for a pet, I wanted a dog. They bought a cat and taught it to bark.

Chic Murray (1919–1985), quoted in A. Yule, The Chic Murray Bumper Fun Book *(1991)*

32 Up starts a *carle*, and gains good,
And thence comes a' our gentle blood.

Allan Ramsay (1686–1758), Scots Proverbs

33 Marriage is one long conversation, chequered by disputes.

> *Robert Louis Stevenson (1850–1894)*

34 Matrimony . . . no more than a sort of friendship recognised by the police.

> *Robert Louis Stevenson*

35 She thought that her relatives were so boring. They hung onto the mundane for grim life; it was a glum adhesive binding them together.

> *Irvine Welsh (1957–)*, Trainspotting

36 See our street?
You were middle-class if you wore your dentures in mid-week.

> *Gordon Williams*, See Scotland? *in I. Archer and T. Royle*, We'll Support You Evermore *(1976)*

Fantasy, Visions And Magic

1 The door of the Fionn is always open.

> *Traditional saying, quoted in Hugh Mac-Diarmid (C. M. Grieve, 1892–1978),* The Islands of Scotland

2 . . . through the opened heaven, not by a parting of the natural elements but by the sight of his spiritual vision, like blessed Jacob the patriarch . . . he had seen angels ascending and descending, and in their hands was borne to heaven a holy soul, as if in a globe of fire.
Then immediately awakening the shepherds, he described the wonderful vision just as he had seen it, prophesying further to them that it was the soul of a most holy bishop or some other great person.

> *Anonymous monk of Lindisfarne (c.700),* Life of St Cuthbert, *describing the young Cuthbert's vision of the death of St Aidan, August 651*

3 It fell about the Martinmas
When nights are lang and mirk,
The carline wife's three sons cam' hame,
And their hats were o' the birk.
It neither grew in syke nor ditch,
Nor yet in any sheugh;
But in the howe o' Paradise
That birk grew fair eneuch.

> *Anonymous,* The Wife of Usher's Well

4 The cock doth craw, the day doth daw,
The channerin' worm doth chide

> The Wife of Usher's Well

5 Wae's me, wae's me,
The acorn's not yet
Fa'n from the tree,
That's to make the wood,
That's to make the cradle,
That's to rock the bairn,
That's to grow a man,
That's to lay me.

> *Anonymous,* The Wandering Spectre

6 My mouth it is full cold, Margaret,
It has the smell now of the ground;
And if I kiss thy comely mouth,
Thy days of life will not be lang.

> *Anonymous,* Clerk Saunders

7 Then up and crew the milk white cock,
And up and crew the grey,
Her lover vanished in the air,
And she gaed weeping away.

> Clerk Saunders

8 Harp and carp, Thomas', she said,
Harp and carp along wi' me.'

> *Anonymous,* Thomas the Rhymer

9 'And see ye not that bonnie road
That winds about the ferny brae?
That is the road to fair Elfland,
Where thou and I this night maun gae.'

> Thomas the Rhymer

10 For forty days and forty nichts
He wade thro' red blude to the knee,
He saw neither sun nor mune,
But he heard the roarin' o' the sea.

> Thomas the Rhymer

11 She cam' tripping adown the stair,
And a' her maids before her;
As soon as they saw her weel-faur'd face,
The cast the glamourie owre her.

> *Anonymous,* Johnnie Faa

12 'I saw the new moon late yestreen,
Wi' the auld moon in her arm;
And if we gang to sea, master,
I fear we'll come to harm.'

> *Anonymous,* Sir Patrick Spens

13 'But I hae dreamed a dreary dream,
Beyond the Isle of Skye:
I saw a dead man win a fight,
And I think that man was I.'

> *Anonymous,* The Battle of Otterbourne

14 Pew, pew,
   My mimmie me slew,
   My daddy me chew,
   My sister gathered my banes,
   And put them between two milk-white
      stanes,
   And I grew and grew
   To a milk-white Doo,
   And I took to my wings and away I flew.

    Traditional, The Milk-white Doo

15 Touching this Agnis Tompson, she is the
   onlye woman, who by the diuels perswasion should haue entended and put in hand
   the Kings Maiesties death in this manner.
     She confessed that she tooke a blacke
   Toade, and did hang the same vp by the
   heeles, three days, and collected and gathered the venome as it dropped and fell
   from it in an Oister shell, and the kept
   the same venome close couered, vntill she
   should obtaine any parte or peece of foul
   linnen cloth, that had appertained to the
   Kings Maiestie . . .

    Anonymous, Newes from Scotland
    (1599), on the Earl of Bothwell's attempt
    to bewitch King James VI

16 Gin ye ca' me imp or elf,
   I rede ye look well to yourself;
   Gin ye ca' me fairy,
   I'll work ye muckle tarry;
   Gin guid neibour ye ca' me,
   Then guid neibour I will be.
   But gin ye ca' me seelie wicht,
   I'll be your friend both day and nicht.

    Traditional, from Chambers' Popular
    Rhymes

17 There cam a wind oot of the North,
   A sharp wind and a snell,
   And a dead sleep cam over me,
   And frae my horse I fell.
   The Queen of the Fairies she was there,
   and took me to hersel',
   And never would I tire, Janet,
   In fairyland to dwell.
   But aye at every seven years,
   They pay the teind to hell,
   and though the Queen mak's muckle
     o' me,
   I dout 'twill be mysel'.

    Traditional, from Chambers' Popular
    Rhymes

18 When the first baby laughed for the first
   time, his laugh broke into a million pieces,
and they all went skipping about. That was
the beginning of fairies.

    J. M. Barrie (1860–1937), The Little
    White Bird

19 The shore was cold with mermaids and
   angels.

    George Mackay Brown (1921–1996),
    Beachcomber

20 In 1682 he was married to Isabel Weir, the
   ceremony being performed by Alexander
   Peden, who made the strangest, weirdest
   wedding address ever heard in Scotland.
   'Isabel,' he said, 'you have got a good man,
   but you will not enjoy him long. Prize his
   company, and keep linen by you to be his
   winding sheet, for you will need of it when
   you are not looking for it, and it will be a
   bloody one.'

    James Barr, The Scottish Covenanters
    (1947) on John Brown, a Covenanter shot
    on Claverhouse's order, 1 May 1685

21 Oh! Drumossie, thy bleak moor shall, ere
   many generations have passed, be stained
   with the best blood of the Highlands.

    The Brahan Seer (Coinneach Odhar, fl.
    16th–17th centuries), prediction of the
    Battle of Culloden, quoted in A. Macken-
    zie, The Prophecies of the Brahan Seer
    (1977 ed.)

22 Coffins stood round, like open presses,
   That shaw'd the dead in their last dresses;
   And (by some devilish cantraip sleight)
   Each in its cauld hand held a light.

    Robert Burns (1759–1796), Tam o'
    Shanter

23 1612. In the month of March and April
   fell furth prodigious works and rare accidents. A cow brought forth fourteen great
   dog whelps instead of calves . . . One of
   the Earl of Argyle's servants being sick,
   vomited two toads and a serpent, and so
   convalesced: but vomited after a number
   of little toads.

    David Calderwood (1575–1650), Histo-
    rie of the Kirk of Scotland

24 In harvest, there was a struggle to escape
   being the last done with the shearing, and
   when tillage in common existed, instances
   were known of a ridge being unshorn (no
   person would enter it) because of it being
   behind the rest. The fear entertained was
   that having the 'famine of the farm' (*gort*

a bhaile), in the shape of an imaginary old woman (*cailleach*) to feed till next harvest.

> *J. G. Campbell, minister of Tiree, quoted by Sir James Frazer (1854–1941) in* The Golden Bough

25 Yit scho wanderit and yeid by to ane
        elriche well,
    Scho met thar, as I wene,
    Ane ask rydand on a snaill,
    And cryit, 'Ourtane fallow, haill!'
    And raid ane inch behind the taill,
    Till it wes neir evin.

> *William Dunbar (c.1460–c.1520)*, The Ballad of Kynd Kittok

26 So in Scotland witches used to raise
    the wind by dipping a rag in water
    and beating it thrice on a stone, saying:
    '*I knok this rag upon this stane*
    To raise the wind in the divellis name,
    It sall not lye till I please againe.'

> *Sir James G. Frazer (1854–1941)*, The Golden Bough

27 Whenever you enter a fairy dwelling you should always remember to stick a piece of steel, such a knife, a needle, or a fish-hook, in the door; for then the elves will not be able to shut the door until you come out again. So, too, when you have shot a deer and are bringing it home at night, be sure to thrust a knife into the carcase, for that keeps the fairies from laying their weight on it.

> *Sir James G. Frazer*, The Golden Bough

28 . . . a strange dream came to her as they plodded up through the ancient hills.
      For out of the night ahead of them came running a man, father didn't see him or heed to him, though old Bob in the dream that was Chris's snorted and shied. And as he came he wrung his hands, he was mad and singing, a foreign creature, black-bearded, half-naked he was; and he cried in the Greek *The ships of Pytheas! The ships of Pytheas!* and went by into the smore of the sleet-storm on the Grampian hills.

> *Lewis Grassic Gibbon (James Leslie Mitchell, 1901–1935)*, Sunset Song

29 When we wold go in the liknes of an cat,
        we say thryse ower,
    I sall goe in till ane catt,
    With sorrow, and sych, and a blak shot!

And I shall goe in the Divellis nam,
Ay quhill I com home again!

> *Isabel Goudie, at her trial for witchcraft, 1662, quoted in Hamish Whyte,* The Scottish Cat *(1987)*

30 In 1845 it could seriously be written in the new *Statistical Account* that a late Principal of Aberdeen University had contributed 'by his benevolent exertions in an eminent degree to the expulsion of fairies from the Highland Hills'.

> *I. F. Grant,* Highland Folk Ways *(1961)*

31 The Second Sight is an unwelcome gift. To whoever has it, visions come not of his own seeking, and their significance is almost invariably tragic

> *I. F. Grant,* Highland Folk Ways

32 The most remarkable thing I discovered in Adamnan's remarkable record is this pre-occupation with light as the manifestation or symbol of goodness. The miracles are the light in legendary form. And many of them – particularly those relating to pre-vision or 'second sight' – may not be so legendary as all that.

> *Neil Gunn (1891–1973)*, Off in a Boat, *on Adamnan's* Life of St Columba

33 Syne our a muir, with thornis thick and
        sharp,
    Weepand alane a wilsum way he went.

> *Robert Henryson (c.1425–c.1500)*, Orpheus and Eurydice

34 O doulie place and groundless deep
        dungeoun,
    Furnace of fire, with stink intolerable,
    Pit of despair, without remissioun.

> *Robert Henryson*, Orpheus and Eurydice

35 Late, late in a gloamin' when all was still,
    When the fringe was red on the westlin'
        hill,
    The wood was sere, the moon i' the wane,
    The reek o' the cot hung over the plain,
    Like a little wee cloud in the world its
        lane;
    When the ingle glowed wi' an eiry leme –
    Late, late in the gloaming Kilmeny came
        hame!

> *James Hogg (1770–1835)*, Kilmeny

36 Kilmeny look'd up wi' a lovely grace,
    But nae smile was seen on Kilmeny's face;
    As still was her look, and as still was

her e'e,
As the stillness that lay on the emerant
lea.

James Hogg, Kilmeny

37 A murmuring sough is on the wood,
And the witching star is red as blood.
And in the cleft of heaven I scan
The giant form of a naked man;
His eye is like the burning brand,
And he holds a sword in his right hand.

James Hogg, A Witch's Chant

38 O there are doings here below
That mortal ne'er should ken;
For there are things in this fair world
Beyond the reach o' men!

James Hogg, May of the Moril Glen

39 And underneath the wheele saw I there
An ugly pit as deep as ony hell,
That to behold thereon I quoke for fear;
Bot o thing heard I, that who there-in fell
Come no more up again tidings to tell.

King James I (1394–1437), The Kingis
Quair

40 The usewall Method for a curious Person
to get a transient Sight of this otherwise
invisible Crew of Subterraneans . . . is to
put his left Foot under the Wizard's right
Foot, and the Seer's Hand is put on the
Inquirer's Head, who is to look over the
Wizard's right Shoulder . . . then will he
see a Multitude of Wights, like furious
hardie Men, flocking to him haistily from
all Quarters, as thick as Atoms in the Air.

Robert Kirk (c.1641–1692), The Secret
Commonwealth of Elves, Faunes and
Fairies

41 Far thair appeared unto him in the nor-
east ane gritt fir upoun the sea, moveing
in sundrie pairtes, quhill at the last it
appeared to him upoun the cittie of Sanct
Andros, and lighted upon the castle thairof, and brak in sunder.

Robert Lindsay of Pitscottie (c.1532–1580),
Historie and Cronicles of Scotland, *on
a portent seen by George Wishart just
before his execution by burning in 1546*

42 'Captane, God forgive yon man that lyis so
glorious on yon wall head; but within few
days he sall ly as shamfull as he lyis glorious now.'

Robert Lindsay of Pitscottie, Historie and
Cronicles of Scotland, *quoting George*

*Wishart's prediction of the fate of Cardi-
nal Beaton (1546)*

43 At Hallowe'en, when fairy sprites
Perform their mystic gambols,
When ilka witch her neebour greets
On their nocturnal rambles;
When elves at midnight hour are seen,
Near hollow caverns sportin'.
Then lads and lasses oft convene
Wi' hopes to ken their fortune
By freets that night.

Janet Little (1759–1813), Hallowe'en

44 Across the silent stream
Where the dream-shadows go,
From the dim blue Hill of Dream
I have heard the West Wind blow.

*Fiona MacLeod (William Sharp,
1856–1905)*, From the Hills of Dream

45 I have no playmate but the tide
The seaweed loves with dark brown eyes:
The night waves have the stars for play,
For me but sighs.

Fiona MacLeod, The Moon-Child

46 How beautiful they are,
The lordly ones
Who dwell in the hills,
In the hollow hills.

Fiona MacLeod, Fairy Chorus

47 On this stone – the old Druidic Stone of
Destiny, sacred among the Gael before
Christ was born – Columba crowned Aidan
King of Argyll . . . It now lies in Westmin-
ster Abbey . . . If ever the Stone of Destiny
be moved again, that writing on the wall
will be the signature of a falling dynasty.

Fiona MacLeod, Iona

48 I said to him I was only a wandering
shade,
My ancestors waiting, unborn, in the
waves,
In the land beyond.

Kenneth Macleod (1871–1955), Songs of
the Isles

49 According to a tale in the old Irish life of
Columba, it was revealed to the saint that
a human sacrifice would be necessary for
his mission . . . Oran, one of the twelve
brethren who accompanied him to Iona,
offered himself and was buried alive. On
the third day, Columba caused the grave
to be opened, whereupon Oran opened
his eyes and said, 'There is no such great

wonder in death, nor is hell what it has been described.' Such heresy was not pleasing to the saint's ear and his reply, 'Earth, earth on Oran's eyes, lest he further blab,' has passed into a proverb.

F. Marian McNeill (1885–1973), Iona

50 The devil, clad in a black gown, with a black hat upon his head, preached unto a great number of them out of the pulpit . . . Now after that the devil had ended his admonitions, he came down out of the pulpit, and causedack all the company come kiss his arse: which they said was cold like ice; his body hard like iron, as they thought who handled him; his face was terrible.

Sir James Melville (1535–1617), Memoirs of His Own Life, *on a black mass*

51 . . . future Tennants will arise.
Like those who raised me to the skies,
Some giant measure to devise,
That even steam,
With all its powers,will in men's eyes
A trifle seem.

John Mitchell (fl. 19th century), The St Rollox Lum's Address To His Brethren

52 Out of this ugliness may come,
Some day, so beautiful a flower,
That men will wonder at that hour,
Remembering smoke and flowerless slum,
And ask . . .
'But why were all the poets so dumb?'

William Montgomerie (1904–), Glasgow Street

53 'Last night I dreamed a ghastly dream,
Before the dirl o' day.
A twining worm cam out the wast,
Its back was like the slae.

'It ganted wide as deid men gant,
Turned three times on its tail,
And wrapped itsel the warld around
Til ilka rock did wail.'

Edwin Muir (1887–1959), Ballad of the Flood

54 . . . the mouth of the night is the choice hour of the *Sluagh*, the Host of the Dead, whose feet never touch on earth as they go drifting on the wind till the Day of Burning; of the *Fuath*, the Spirit of Terror, that 'frightens folk out of the husk of their hearts'; of the Washer, who sits at the ford with herself in the twilight; of the slim green-coated ones, the water horse . . . the

light that is shadowless, colourless, softer than moonlight, is ever the light of their liking.

Amy Murray, Father Allan's Island (1936)

55 Though thy land is not large this day among thy brothers, yet it is thou shalt be king. From thee shall ever descend the kings of this land.

Saint Patrick (fl. 5th century), quoted in a 10th-century Life, *prophecy made to Fergus Mòr Mac Erc, King of Dalriada (from Gaelic)*

56 There's nae sorrow there, John,
There's neither cauld nor care, John,
The day is aye fair
In the land o' the leal.

Lady Nairne (1766–1845), The Land o' The Leal

57 It is an impressive feature of extant, or very recently extant, Highland folklore, that one can constantly glimpse, beneath all the borrowings and accretions that have taken place down the centuries, traces of that much older, much more powerful Celtic world, where the gods and goddesses walked side by side with mankind, with goodwill or hostility, as the case might be, and where the day to day life of the people was moulded and controlled by hidden forces, the powers of which remain today as pale shadows.

Anne Ross, The Folklore of the Scottish Highlands (1976)

58 And, dancing on each chimney top,
I saw a thousand darling imps
Keeping time with skip and hop.
And on the provost's brave ridge-tile,
On the provost's grand ridge-tile,
The Blackamooor first to master me
I saw, I saw that winsome smile,
The mouth that did my heart beguile,
And spoke the great Word over me,
In the land beyond the sea.

William Bell Scott (1811–1890), The Witch's Ballad

59 Each one in her wame shall hide
Her hairy mouse, her wary mouse,
Fed on madwort and agramie, –
Wear amber beads between her breasts,
And blind-worm's skin about her knee.

William Bell Scott, The Witch's Ballad

60   We swing ungirded hips,
       And lightened are our eyes,
       The rain is on our lips,
       We do not run for prize.
       We know not whom we trust
       Nor whitherward we fare,
       But we run because we must
       Through the great wide air.
              C. H. Sorley (1895–1915), The Song of
              the Ungirt Runners

61   But nane will ken whaur I hae been
       Atween the glimmer and the grey;
       Nor hear the clapper o' the mune,
       Ding up the nicht, ding doun the day.

       . . . thru the flicherin' floichan-drift
       A beast cam doun the hill.

       It steppit like a stallion,
       Wha's heid hauds up a horn,
       And weel the men o' Scotland kent
       It was the unicorn.
              William Soutar (1898–1943), Birthday

62   Yon castel braw, ma bonny bit hinny,
       It is the Scottis Glamourie;
       There's a spell intil't and a well intil't
       And the sang o' a siller bell intil't,
       But the braes abune it are dowf and
              whinny,
       And the bracken buries the lea.
              Lewis Spence (1874–1955), The Stown
              Bairn

63   For there was Janet comin' doun the
       clachan – her or her likeness, nane could
       tell – wi' her neck thrawn, an' her heid on
       ae side, like a body that has been hangit,
       an' a girn on her face like an unstreakit
       corp.
              Robert Louis Stevenson (1850–1894),
              Thrawn Janet

64   . . . when a' o' a sudden, he heard a laigh,
       uncanny steer up-stairs; a foot gaed to an'
       fro in the chalmer whaur the corp was
       hangin'; syne the door was opened, though
       he minded weel that he had lockit it; an'
       syne there was a step upon the landin', an'
       it seemed to him as if the corp was lookin'
       ower the rail and doun on him whaur he
       stood.
              Robert Louis Stevenson, Thrawn Janet

65   As I pushed the pedals down, it was as
       if I had suddenly cycled into an alter-
       native town, a place existing parallel to
       Montrose and yet fundamentally different.

This town, this Montrose, was charged
with gold, streamed with light. Everything
glowed. Even the douce grey concrete
lamp-posts were surrounded by radiance . . .
I knew the joy and sorrow of things, the littleness and hugeness of our briefness and
immortality.
       Raymond Vettese (1950–), The Seeds of
       Poetry, *from W. G. Lawrence*, Roots in
       a Northern Landscape *(1996)*

Festivals

1   A guid New Year to ane and a'
      And mony may ye see;
      And during a' the year to come,
      Happy may ye be.
             Anonymous, A Guid New Year

2   Now we hae gotten't in aboot,
      An' a' oor thingies ticht,
      We gather roun' the festive board
      To spend a jolly night.
             Anonymous, The Hairst o' Rettie

3   Rise up, guidwife, and shake yir featers;
      Dinna think that we are beggars,
      We're only bairnies come to play
      So up and gie's our Hogmanay.
             Children's Hogmanay rhyme

4   Tonight is the hard night of Hogmanay,
      I am come with a lamb to sell –
      The old fellow yonder sternly said
      He would strike my ear against a rock.
      The woman, better of speech, said
      That I should be let in;
      For my food and for my drink,
      A morsel due and something with it.
             *Traditional, from Gaelic, quoted in
             A. Carmichael*, Carmina Gadelica
             (1928)

5   So that's the way o' it! Yuletide's comin'!
      Haverin' hypocrites, hear them talk:
      Peace and goodwill to men and women,
      But thraw the neck o' the bubbly-jock.
             W. D. Cocker (1882–1970), The Bubbly-
             Jock

6   Here's to the year that's awa'!
      We'll drink it in strong and in sma'!
             John Dunlop (1755–1820), Here's to the
             Year That's Awa'

7   When merry Yule-day comes, I trow,
      You'll scantlins find a hungry mou';

Sma' are our cares, our stamacks fou
O gusty gear.

> *Robert Fergusson (1750–1774),* The
> Daft Days

8   I remember, I remember
Nothing further after that,
But I wakened in the morning
On an alien lobby mat,
And I felt not unpersuaded
(though my reasons were not clear),
That I'd spent a merry Christmas,
And a prosperous New Year.

> *George Fletcher,* Glasgow University
> Magazine, *1905–6, quoted in F. Marian
> McNeill (1885–1973),* The Scots Cellar

9   All that is desired is (1) to get some useful
publicity; (2) make money; and (3) jack up
a little the general illusion that the Scots
are really a cultured people with an interest in the arts. In short it is just another
lousy racket.

> *Hugh MacDiarmid (C. M. Grieve,
> 1872–1978),* The Company I've Kept,
> *on the Edinburgh Festival*

10 When the last big bottle's empty, and
        the dawn creeps grey and cold,
And the last clan-tartan's folded, and
        the last damned lie is told;
When they totter down the footpath in a
        braw unbroken line,
To the peril of the passers and the tune of
        'Auld Lang Syne',
You can tell the folk at breakfast
        as they watch the fearsome sicht,
They've only been assisting at a braw
        Scots Nicht!

> *Will H. Ogilvie (1869–1963),* A Braw
> Scots Nicht

11 Fell kebbucks, three year auld, an' mitey,
Wi' horns o hilan' ackavity,
Drive thro' the streets, wi' unca stear,
To bid some chiel A gude new year.

> *E. Picken,* Poems Etc. *(1788), quoted in
> J. Grant,* The Scottish National Dic-
> tionary *(1934)*

12 *Magrit:* Are ye gaun oot the night . . . at
the bells?
Andy: Aye. We're first fittin ma mother, and
then we're gaun tae a party in Partick . . .
Dolly: That's whit ah like aboot this time
o' the year, ye meet people ye've never met
before.
Magrit: Aye . . . an usually ye hope ye never
meet them again.

> *Tony Roper,* The Steamie *(1987)*

Food and Drink

1   Food today, and feud tomorrow.
> *Gaelic saying, on the tradition of
> hospitality*

2   O gude ale comes and gude ale goes,
Gude ale gars me sell my hose,
Sell my hose and pawn my shoon,
Gude ale hauds my heart aboon.
> *Anonymous*

3   There's cauld kail in Aberdeen.
An' custocks in Strathbogie,
Whaur ilka man may hae his lass,
But I maun hae my cogie.
For I maun hae my cogie, sirs,
I canna want my cogie;
I wadna gie my three-girr'd cog
For a' the wives in Bogie.
> *Anonymous*

4   Moderation, sir, aye. Moderation is my
rule. Nine or ten is reasonable refresh-
ment, but after that it's apt to degenerate
into drinking.
> *Anonymous*

5   Says I to him, 'Will ye hae a hauf?'
Says he, 'Man, that's ma hobby.'
> *Anonymous,* For We're Nae Awa' Tae
> Bide Awa'

6   For if you feed your good man well
He'll love you all your life, oh!
And then to all the world he'll tell
There ne'er was such a wife, oh!
> *Anonymous,* The Quaker's Wife

7   . . . it is no exaggeration to conclude that
before Winter there will not be one sound
Potatoe in all the Highlands and Islands . . .
nearly half a million of the population in
these districts have before them the prospect of absolute want.
> *Contemporary comment on the 1846*

Potato Famine, from the Scottish Records Office, quoted in Charles Withers, Gaelic Scotland *(1988)*

8 'Jock!' cried a farmer's wife to the cow-herd, 'come awa' in to your parritch, or the flees 'll be droonin' themselves in your milk bowl.'

'Nae fear o' that,' replied Jock, 'they could wade through it.'

'Ye rogue!' she cried, 'd'ye mean to say I dinna gie ye eneuch milk?'

'Oh, aye,' said Jock. 'There's eneuch milk, for a' the parritch that's in it.'

Traditional

9 We live only by the death of others. Of course the vegetarians have an answer; but how valid is it? Who knows what agonies the cabbage suffers as the reticulations of its heart are shredded down to recreate a classical economist?

John R. Allan, Farmer's Boy

10 In dinner talk it is perhaps allowable to fling any faggot rather than let the fire go out.

J. M. Barrie (1860–1937)

11 'Tell me, have you eaten that or are you going to?'

J. M. Barrie, to Bernard Shaw, quoted in C. Fadiman, The Little, Brown Book of Anecdotes *(1985) on seeing Shaw's vegetarian food at a dinner party*

12 Sam'l, like the others, helped himself. What he did was to take potatoes from the pot with his fingers, peel off their coats, and then dip them into the butter. Lisbeth would have liked to provide knives and forks, but she knew that beyond a certain point T'nowhead was master in his own house.

J. M. Barrie, The Courting of T'nowhead's Bell

13 'You will take something, Mr Cortachy?'
'No, I thank you, madam.'
'A little ginger wine?'
'It agrees ill with me.'
'Then a little wh-wh-whisky?'
'You are ower kind.'
'Then may I?'
'I am not heeding.'
'Perhaps, though, you don't take?'
'I can take it or want it.'
'Is that enough?'

'It will do perfectly.'
'Shall I fill it up?'
'As you please, ma'am.'

J. M. Barrie, Sentimental Tommy

14 What harm in drinking can there be,
Since punch and life so well agree?

Thomas Blacklock (1721–1791), On Punch

15 At dinner, Dr Johnson ate several plate-fulls of Scotch broth with barley and peas in it, and seemed very fond of the dish. I said, 'You never ate it before?' Johnson: 'No, sir, but I don't care how soon I eat it again.'

James Boswell (1740–1795), Journal of a Tour to the Hebrides

16 I did not get drunk; I was, however, intox-icated, and very ill next day . . . The drunken manners of this country are very bad.

James Boswell, Letter to the Rev. Mr Temple, August 1775

17 'I'll take a rum.'
'Rum it shall be, Mr Todd.'
'I thought this was a temperance hotel?' I said.
'Oh, aye, it is. That way we get no trouble frae the polis.'

William Boyd (1952–), The New Confessions

18 'Dish or no dish,' rejoined the Caledonian, 'there's a deal o' fine confused feedin' about it, let me tell you.'

John Brown (1810–1882), Horae Subse-civae, *on haggis*

19 Some hae meat and canna eat,
And some hae nane that want it;
But we hae meat, and we can eat,
And sae the Lord be thankit.

The 'Selkirk Grace', *attributed to Robert Burns (1759–1796)*

20 See Social-life and Glee sit down
All joyous and unthinking,
Till, quite transmogrified, they've grown
Debauchery and Drinking.

Robert Burns, An Address to the Unco Guid

21 Go fetch to me a pint o' wine,
And fill it in a silver tassie;

That I may drink before I go,
A service to my bonnie lassie.

> *Robert Burns*, The Silver Tassie

22 We are na fou, we're nae that fou,
But just a drappie in our e'e.

> *Robert Burns*, O Willie Brew'd a Peck
> o' Maut

23 Fast by an ingle, bleezin' finely,
Wi' reamin' swats that drank divinely . . .
The night drave on wi' sangs and clatter,
And aye the ale was growing better.

> *Robert Burns*, Tam o' Shanter

24 We'll tak' a richt gude-willie waught
For Auld Lang Syne.

> *Robert Burns*, Auld Lang Syne

25 Food fills the wame, and keeps us livin';
But, oiled by thee,
The wheels o' life gang down-hill
    scrievin',
Wi' rattlin' glee.

> *Robert Burns*, Scotch Drink

26 Freedom an' whisky gang thegither.

> *Robert Burns*, The Author's Earnest
> Cry and Prayer to the Right Honour-
> able and Honourable, the Scotch Rep-
> resentatives in the House of Commons

27 Fair fa' your honest, sonsie face,
Great chieftain o' the pudding-race.

> *Robert Burns*, Address to a Haggis

28 While thro' your pores the dews distil
Like amber bead.

> *Robert Burns*, Address to a Haggis

29 His knife see rustic Labour dight,
An' cut you up wi' ready sleight,
Trenching your gushing entrails bright,
Like ony ditch;
And then, O what a glorious sight,
Warm-reekin', rich!

> *Robert Burns*, Address to a Haggis

30 Inspiring bold John Barleycorn!
What dangers thou canst make us scorn:
Wi tippeny, we fear nae evil,
Wi usquabae, we'll face the devil!

> *Robert Burns*, Tam o' Shanter

31 Gudewife, count the lawin,
An' bring a cogie mair.

> *Robert Burns*, Gudewife, Count the
> Lawin

32 Gude forgie me, I gat myself sae notouri-
ously bitchify'd the day after kail-time that
I can hardly stotter but and ben.

> *Robert Burns*, Letter to William Nicol,
> 1st June 1787 – or I believe the 39th o'
> May rather

33 The cook was too filthy an object to be
described; only another English gentleman whispered me and said, he believed,
if the fellow was to be thrown against the
wall, he would stick to it.

> *Edmund Burt (fl. early 18th century)*,
> Letters from a Gentleman in the
> North of Scotland *(1728–37)*, *on an
> Edinburgh eating house*

34 Few go away sober at any time, and for the
greatest part of his guests, in the conclusion, they cannot go at all.

> *Edmund Burt*, Letters from a Gentle-
> man in the North of Scotland, *on
> Forbes of Culloden*

35 I have here the cursedest parish that ever
God put breath into; for after all my preaching they will go into a change-house after
sermon, and the first thing they'll get is a
mickle capfull of hot ale, and they will say,
I wish we had the minister in the midst of
it.

> *Robert Calder, quoted in* Scots Presbyte-
> rian Eloquence Displayed

36 Liquid madness.

> *Thomas Carlyle (1795–1881)*, On
> Chartism

37 Men that can have communication in nothing else can sympathetically eat together,
can still rise into some glow of brotherhood over food and wine.

> *Thomas Carlyle*

38 The pot still has passed into tradition as
the 'ewie wi' the crookit horn', and in
the *port-a-beul* song comes the line 'all
the sheep have milk but the ewe with the
crooked horn has a gallon'.

> *Hugh Cheape and I. F. Grant*, Periods in
> Highland History *(1987)*

39 Nip-pint, Nip-pint –
Mustn't-get-drunk, mustn't-get-drunk.
Nip-pint, Nip-pint –
Tae pot wi' it a', tae pot wi' it a'.

> *Robin Cockburn*, The Galliard

40 Advocaat: the alcoholic's omelette.

    Billy Connolly (1942–), Gullible's Travels

41 . . . the *Suilven* is a floating extension of Ullapool's chip-strewn littoral: no herring on the menu, no mackerel, no salmon, no trout, no prawns, nothing that remotely reflects the products of the region.

    Derek Cooper (1925–), The Road to Mingulay

42 There is no finer breakfast than flounders fried in oatmeal with a little salt butter, as ever they came out of the water, with their tails jerking 'flip-flop' in the frizzle of the pan.

    S. R. Crockett (1859–1914), The Raiders

43 Douglas Young, the Scottish poet and scholar, used to maintain that whisky was invented by the Irish as an embrocation for sick mules, and that once it was brought to Scotland its use was perverted from external animal application to internal human consumption.

    David Daiches (1912–1999), Scotch Whisky *(1969)*

44 The proper drinking of Scotch whisky is more than indulgence; it is a toast to civilisation, a tribute to the continuity of culture, a manifesto of man's determination to use the resources of nature to refresh mind and body and enjoy to the full the senses with which he has been endowed.

    David Daiches, Scotch Whisky

45 . . . the grossly overrated potato, that marvel of insipidity.

    Norman Douglas (1868–1952), Together

46 Than culit thai thair mouthis with confortable drinkis;
And carpit full cummerlik with cop going round.

    William Dunbar (c.1460–c.1520), The Tretis of the Twa Mariit Wemen and the Wedo

47 A double Scotch is about the size of a small Scotch before the War, and a single Scotch is nothing more than a dirty glass.

    Lord Dundee (1902–)

48 Let us praise the humble fish,
Though not all that one could wish,

'Tis an inexpensive dish –
Pisces Benedicite.

    Walter Elliot (1888–1958), Sestette to Fish

49 The cure for which there is no disease.

    John Ferguson (fl. 19th century), on whisky

50 Whan big as burns the gutters rin,
Gin ye hae catcht a droukit skin,
To Luckie Middlemist's loup in,
And sit fu' snug
O'er oysters and a dram o' gin,
Or haddock lug

    Robert Fergusson (1750–1774), Auld Reekie

51 Auld Reekie's sons blyth faces wear;
September's merry month is near,
That brings in Neptune's caller chere,
New oysters fresh;
The halesomest and nicest gear
Of fish or flesh.

    Robert Fergusson, Caller Oysters

52 A wee soup drink dis unco weel
To had the heart aboon.

    Robert Fergusson, Poems

53 For rabbits young and for rabbits old,
For rabbits hot and for rabbits cold,
For rabbits tender and for rabbits tough,
Our thanks we render – but we've had enough.

    Impromptu grace given by Robert Fergusson at St Salvator's College Hall, St Andrews

54 What renders his death Particularly distressing, is, that Lady Maclaughlan is of opinion it was entirely owing to eating Raw oysters, and damp feet. This ought to be a warning to all Young people to take care of Wet feet, and Especially eating Raw oysters, which are certainly Highly dangerous, particularly where there is any Tendency to Gout.

    Susan Ferrier (1782–1854), Marriage

55 Playing his part, Falkland sampled it with nose and tongue, and commended it as a fine malt, well aged and not too strongly reminiscent of the peat. But in truth he thought it rather dry and bodiless . . . In

matters of this sort he had always played up to Tobin as one did to a woman.

James Allan Ford (1920–), A Judge of Men

56 'It's an awful thing the drink!' exclaimed a clergyman, when the barber, who was visibly affected, had drawn blood from his face for the third time.

'Aye,' replied the tonsorial artist with a wicked leer in his eye, 'it maks the skin tender.'

Robert Ford, Thistledown *(1901)*

57 . . . decent ladies coming home with red faces, cosy and cosh, from a posset-masking.

John Galt (1779–1839), Annals of the Parish

58 And they'd broth, it was good, and the oatcakes better; and then boiled beef and potatoes and turnip; and then rice pudding with prunes; and then some tea.

Lewis Grassic Gibbon (James Leslie Mitchell, 1901–1935), Sunset Song

59 High tea in Aberdeen is like no other meal on earth. It is the meal of the day, the meal par excellence, and the tired come home to it ravenous . . . Tea is drunk with the meal, and the order of it is this: first, one eats a plateful of sausage and eggs and mashed potatoes; then a second plateful to keep down the first. Eating, one assists the second plateful to its final home by mouthfuls of oatcake spread with butter. Then you eat oatcake with cheese. Then there are scones. Then cookies. Then it is really time to begin on tea – tea and bread and butter and crumpets and toasted rolls and cakes. Then some Dundee cake. Then, about half past seven, someone shakes you out of the coma into which you have fallen and asks you persuasively if you wouldn't like another cup of tea and just *one* more egg and sausage.

Lewis Grassic Gibbon, Scottish Scene *(1934)*

60 . . . when days of refinement came, old topers mourned over these departed times when 'there were fewer glasses and more bottles'.

H. Grey Graham, The Social Life of Scotland in the Eighteenth Century *(1899)*

61 Except in a real old-fashioned Scotch house, where no dish was attempted that was not national, the various abominations served up in corner dishes under French names were merely libels upon housekeeping.

Elizabeth Grant (1797–1885), Memoirs of a Highland Lady

62 Single malts must be drunk with circumspection. Contrary to the old joke about the Highlander liking two things to be naked, one of them whisky, malts are best drunk with a little water to bring out the aroma and flavour.

Neil Gunn (1891–1973), Whisky and Scotland

63 Oh, the dreadfu' curse o' drinkin'!
Men are ill, but to my thinkin',
Lookin' through the drucken fock,
There's a Jenny for ilk Jock.

Janet Hamilton (1795–1873), Oor Location

64 Claret wyn is helesum til all complexioun, nocht ower poignant or ower sweit, bot delytable of hew and gust . . . Sik wynis confortis the stomak and helpis to the natural heit and to the guid digestioun, and kepis the stomak fra al corruptioun.

Sir Gilbert Hay (c.1419–1460), Buke of the Governance of Princes

65 They drank the water clear,
Instead of wine, but yet they made good cheer.

Robert Henryson (c.1425–c.1500), The Town Mouse and the Country Mouse

66 A mouthful or two satisfied both that the experiment was a failure, but each was ashamed to yield first. At last Black, stealing a look at his friend, ventured to say, 'Dinna ye think they're a little green?'

'Confoundedly green!' emphatically replied Ferguson; 'tak' 'em awa'; tak' 'em awa'!'

Alexander Hislop, The Book of Scottish Anecdote *(1883), on Joseph Black (1728–1799) and Adam Ferguson (1723–1816) trying snail soup*

67 Gie me the real Glenleevit . . . and I weel believe that I could mak drinkable toddy out o' sea-water . . . If a body could just find out the exac proportion o' quantity that ought to be drank every day, and keep to that, FrI verily trow that he micht leeve for

ever, without dying at a', and that doctors and kirkyards would go out o' fashion.

James Hogg (1770–1835), in Christopher North (John Wilson,1785–1854), Noctes Ambrosianae

68 . . . for what's better than a haggis?

James Hogg, in Christopher North, Noctes Ambrosianae

69 A month without an R in it has nae richt being in the year.

James Hogg, in Christopher North, Noctes Ambrosianae

70 We'll bring down the red deer, we'll
    bring down the black steer,
 The lamb from the bracken, and doe
    from the glen;
 The salt sea we'll harry, and bring
    to our Charlie
 The cream from the bothy, and curd from
    the pen.

James Hogg, Come O'er the Stream, Charlie

71 Irn Bru . . . the wee boy's Drambuie.

Jack House (1906–1991), The Heart of Glasgow

72 In good company you need not ask who is the master of the feast. The man who sits in the lowest place, and who is always industrious in helping everyone, is certainly the man.

David Hume (1711–1776), Essays

73 Cookery, the Science to which I intend to addict the remaining years of my Life . . . for Beef and Cabbage (a charming dish) and old Mutton, old Claret, no body excels me.

David Hume, letter to Sir Gilbert Elliot, October 1769

74 He was a bold man who first swallowed an oyster.

Attributed to King James VI (1566–1625)

75 This is smart stuff.

John Keats (1795–1821), on first tasting whisky

76 But he does have a packet of potato crisps which he can stuff between two slices of margarined bread. A piece on crisps. Aye beautiful. Crunchy and munchy. And a cup of good strong coffee.

James Kelman (1946–), A Disaffection

77 The Scotch do not drink . . . During the whole of two or three pleasant weeks spent lecturing in Scotland, I never on any occasion saw whisky made use of as a beverage. I have seen people take it, of course, as a medicine, or as a precaution, or as a wise offset against a rather treacherous climate; but as a beverage, never.

Stephen Leacock (1869–1944), My Discovery of England

78 How beit we want the spices and
    the winis,
 Or uther strange fructis delicious,
 We have als gude, and more needfull for
    us.

Sir David Lindsay (c.1490–1555), The Dreme of the Realme of Scotland

79 'He's dead now, but he lived to a great age. I mind him saying once – he was fou' at the time – "Man, I've only got one vice, but it's given me more pleasure than all my virtues."'

Eric Linklater (1899–1974), Magnus Merriman

80 O English Food! How I adore looking
    forward
 to you, Scotch trifle at the North
    British Hotel,
 Princes Street, Edinburgh. Yes, it is
    good, very good,
 the best in Scotland.

George Macbeth (1935–), An Ode to English Food

81 If it was raining, it was 'We'll have a dram to keep out the wet'; if it was cold, 'We'll have a dram to keep out the cold'; and if it was a fine day why then, 'We'll drink its health.'

J. A. MacCulloch, The Misty Isle of Skye (1905)

82 The majority of Glasgow pubs are for connoisseurs of the morose, for those who relish the element of degradation in all boozing . . . It is the old story of those who prefer hard-centre chocolates to soft, storm to sunshilacne, sour to sweet. True Scots always prefer the former of these opposites.

Hugh MacDiarmid (C. M. Grieve, 1892–1978), The Dour Drinkers of Glasgow

83 The fermenters of barley have come,
the singed distillers with their tubes,
who amassed a fortune by plundering
   drunkards ...
These are the worthless creatures ...
who rule in the Highlands of Scotland.

   Iain Mac a'Ghobhainn (19th century),
   Oran Luchd an Spors (Song for
   Sportsmen)

84 *John:* I tell you what, when I'm dead will
you pour a bottle of the Talisker over my
dead body?
Alex: Certainly, certainly, you won't mind
if I pass it through the kidneys first.

   John McGrath (1935–), The Cheviot,
   The Stag and the Black, Black Oil

85 ... both in a river and in a dish
I hate that ubiquitous blasted fish.

   *Flight Lieutenant James MacGregor,
   with a Commander, RN*, Ode to a
   Salmon, *from A. Silcock*, Verse and
   Worse *(1952)*

86 I think broth is always better the second
day, but I don't like my chips back-het.

   William McIlvanney (1936–), Growing
   Up in the West, *from K. Miller*, Memoirs of a Modern Scotland

87 Mountain Dew, *clear* as a Scot's
   understanding,
Pure as his conscience wherever he goes,
Warm as his heart to the friends he has
   chosen,
Strong as his arm when he fights with his
   foes!

   Charles Mackay (1814–1889), Poetry
   and Humour of the Scottish Language

88 Love makes the world go round? Not at all.
Whisky makes it go round twice as fast.

   Compton Mackenzie (1883–1972),
   Whisky Galore

89 You are offered a piece of bread and butter
that feels like a damp handkerchief and
sometimes, when cucumber is added to it,
like a wet one.

   Compton Mackenzie, Vestal Fire

90 The cry of *Caller Laverocks* was always
heard in severe winters ... The lark was
never much used for the table in Scotland,
tho' at the time to which I allude people
whose scruples against eating the poor
songsters did not prevent them, bought
theGho larks from the women who sold

them, generally the wives of Newhaven
fishers.

   *Henry Mackenzie (1745–1831), quoted in
   H. W. Thomson*, The Anecdotes and
   Egotisms of Henry Mackenzie

91 When I came to my friend's house of a
morning, I used to be asked if I had my
morning draught yet? I am now asked if
I have had my tea? And in lieu of the big
quaigh with strong ale and toast, and after
a dram of good wholesome Scots spirits,
there is now the tea-kettle put to the fire,
the tea table and silver and china equipage
brought in, and marmalade and cream.

   *William Mackintosh of Borlum
   (1662–1743)*, Essay on Ways and
   Means of Enclosing

92 ... it is a thoroughly democratic dish,
equally available and equally honoured in
castle, farm and croft. Finally, the use
of the paunch of the animal as the receptacle of the ingredients gives the touch of
romantic barbarism so dear to the Scottish
heart.

   F. Marian McNeill (1885–1973), The
   Scots Kitchen, *on haggis*

93 In Kinross, the browst which the gudewife
of Lochrin produced from a peck of malt
is thus commemorated:

Twenty pints o' strong ale,
twenty pints o' sma',
twenty pints o' hinky-pinky,
twenty pints o' ploughman's drinkie,
twenty pints o' splitter-splatter,
twenty pints was waur nor water.

   F. Marian McNeill, The Scots Cellar

94 Just a wee deoch an doruis,
Just a wee drop, that's a';
Just a wee deoch an doruis,
Afore ye gang awa'.
There's a wee wifie waitin'
In a wee but-and-ben;
But if ye can say 'It's a braw bricht
   moonlicht nicht,'
It's a' richt, ye ken.

   R. F. Morrison, A Wee Deoch an
   Doruis *(1911)*

95 Scotland, the best place in the world to
take an appetite.

   H. V. Morton (1892–1979), In Search of
   Scotland

96 Our diet was a curious one . . . a great
number of luxuries which we did not know
to be luxuries, such as plovers' eggs, trout,
crab and lobster. I ate so much crab and
lobster as a boy that I have not been able to
enjoy them since.

> *Edwin Muir (1887–1959)*,
> Autobiography

97 I have never tasted a gannet, but Francis
Watt once declared it can be served up as
fish, fowl or flesh, and you would hesitate
to decide which you were eating.

> *Augustus Muir,* Heather Track and
> High Road *(1944)*

98 'That's the thing that angers me aboot
an egg,' continued the Captain. 'It never
makes ye gled to see it on the table; ye
know at once the thing's a mere put-by
because your wife or Jum could not be
bothered makin' something tasty.'
'We'll hae to get the hens to put their
heids together and invent a new kind o'
fancy egg for sailors', said Sunny Jim.

> *Neil Munro (1864–1930)*, The Vital
> Spark

99 'There's not mich that iss wholesomer than
a good herrin',' said Para Handy. 'It's a
fush that's chust sublime.'

> *Neil Munro,* The Vital Spark

100 . . . though we're a' fearfu' fond o' oor parritch in Scotland, and some men mak' a
brag o' takin' them every mornin' just as
if they were a cauld bath, we're gey gled to
skip them at a holiday and just be daein' wi'
ham and eggs.

> *Neil Munro,* Erchie

101 'The honestest thing I ever saw said aboot
tea was in a grocer's window in Inverness –
'Our Unapproachable: 2s6d.'

> *Neil Munro,* Jimmy Swan, the Joy
> Traveller

102 . . . the Cummers' Feast. This was a supper,
where each gentleman brought a pint of
wine to be drunk by him and his wife . . .
There was an eating posset in the middle of
the table, with dried fruits and sweetmeats
at the sides. When they had finished their
supper, the meat was removed, and in a
moment everybody flies to the sweetmeats
to pocket them. Upon which a scramble
ensued, chairs overturned, and everything
on the table, wrassalling and pulling at one

another with the utmost noise. When all
was quieted, they went to the stoups (for
there was no bottles) of which the women
had a good share. For though it was a disgrace to be seen drunk, yet it was none to
be a little intoxicate in good company.

> *Elizabeth Mure of Caldwell, recording
> her uncle's early 18th-century memories,
> quoted in Agnes Mure Mackenzie,* Scot-
> tish Pageant, 1707–1802 *(1950)*

103 Fat say ye till a dram?

> *Charles Murray (1864–1941),* Docken
> Afore his Peers

104 He found that learnin', fame,
Gas, philanthropy, and steam,
Logic, loyalty, gude name,
Were a' mere shams;
That the source o' joy below,
An' the antidote to woe,
An' the only proper go,
Was drinkin' drams.

> *George Outram (1805–1856),* Drinkin'
> Drams

105 Good claret best keeps out the cauld,
And drives away the winter soon,
It makes a man baith gash and bauld,
And heaves his saul beyond the moon.

> *Allan Ramsay (1686–1758),* To the Phiz,
> an Ode

106 They have need of a canny cook that have
but one egg for dinner.

> *Allan Ramsay,* Scots Proverbs

107 'Oh!' said the minister, 'nae doubt there's
a hantle o' miscellawneous eating aboot a
pig.'

> *Dean E. B. Ramsay (1793–1872),*
> Reminiscences of Scottish Life and
> Character

108 Of this Mr Paul it was recorded that, on
being asked if he considered porter a wholesome beverage, he replied, 'Oh, yes, if you
don't take above a dozen.'

> *Dean E. B. Ramsay,* Reminiscences of
> Scottish Life and Character

109 The Frenchman offended the old Scottish
peeress by some highly disparaging
remarks on Scottish dishes . . . All she
would answer was, 'Weel, weel, some fowk

like parritch, and some fowk like paddocks.'

> *Dean E. B. Ramsay*, Reminiscences of
> Scottish Life and Character

110 To give us a more than ordinary treat tea
was prepared for breakfast. She put about
a pound of tea into a tolerably large-sized
pot, with nearly a gallon of 'burn' water,
and seasoned the whole as she would any
other stew, with a reasonable proportion
of butter, pepper, and salt!

> *Donald Sage (1789–1869)*, Memorabilia
> Domestica, *on Kildonan, Sutherland, in*
> *1802*

111 The boy flew at the oranges with the enthusiasm of a ferret finding the rabbit family
at home after a long day of fruitless subter-
ranean research.

> *Saki (H. H. Munro, 1870–1916)*, The
> Toys of Peace

112 The cook was a good cook, as cooks go;
and as good cooks go, she went.

> *Saki*, Reginald

113 'There's nothing in Christianity or Buddhism that quite matches the sympathetic
unselfish-ness of an oyster.'

> *Saki*, The Chronicles of Clovis

114 That Scotland is, pretty near at least, the
most drunken nation on the face of the
earth is a fact never quite capable of
denial.

> The Scotsman, *Editorial, May 1850*

115 'Lord, for what we are about to receive
Help us to be truly thankful – Aimen –
Wumman, ye've pit ingans in't again.'

> *Tom Scott (1918–1985)*, Auld Sanct
> Aundrians

116 A glass of wine is a glorious creature, and
it reconciles poor humanity to itself: and
that is what few things can do.

> *Sir Walter Scott (1771–1832)*

117 I wish for a sheep's head and whisky toddy
against all the French cookery and cham-
pagne in the world.

> *Sir Walter Scott*, Journal, *November*
> *1826*

118 . . . an overdose of the creature.

> *Sir Walter Scott*, Guy Mannering

119 . . . when they were seated under the
sooty rafters of Lucky Macleary's only
apartment, thickly tapestried with cob-
webs, their hostess appeared with a large
pewter measuring-pot containing at least
three English quarts, familiarly denomi-
nated a 'Tappit Hen'.

> *Sir Walter Scott*, Waverley

120 And there will be fadges and brochen,
Wi' fouth o' good gabbocks o' skate,
Powsowdie, and drammock and crowdie,
An' caller nowtfeet in a plate.
An' there will be partans and buckies,
And whitin's and speldin's enew,
And singit sheep's heid, and a haggis,
And scadlips to sup till ye spue.

> *Attributed to Francis Sempill*
> *(c.1616–1682)*, The Wedding of
> Maggie and Jock

121 The water from the granite is cold. To
drink it at the source makes the throat
tingle. The sting of life is in its touch.

> *Nan Shepherd (1893–1981)*, The Living
> Mountain

122 A coggie o' yill and a pickle aitmeal,
And a dainty wee drappie o' whisky,
Was our forefathers' dose to swill
    down their brose,
And keep them aye cheery and frisky.

> *Andrew Sherrifs (fl. 18th century), quoted*
> *in D. K. Cameron*, The Ballad and the
> Plough *(1978)*

123 We each day dig our graves with our
teeth.

> *Samuel Smiles (1816–1904)*, Duty

124 The sauce-bottles are filled with old
    blood
above the off-white linen.

> *Iain Crichton Smith (1928–1998)*, By
> the Sea

125 Tattie-scones, and the mealy-dot,
And a whack o' crumpy-crowdie;
And aye a bit pickle in the pat
For onie orra body.

> *William Soutar (1898–1943)*, Hamely
> Fare

126 Whisky can't be a remedy, you know. It
only makes you feel better.

> *William Soutar*, Symposium

127 You boiled the kettle, and just before it
came to the boil you half-filled the teapot

to warm it. When the kettle came to the boil, you kept it simmering while you threw out the water in the teapot and then put in a level spoonful of tea for each person, and one for the pot. Up to four spoonfuls of tea from that sweetly odorous tea-caddy would make the perfect pot. The caddy-spoon was a special shape, like a small silver shovel. You never took the kettle to the teapot; always the pot to the kettle, where you filled it, but never to the brim.

You let it stand, or 'draw', for three minutes.

Muriel Spark (1918–), Curriculum Vitae

128 At last the supreme moment comes, and the fowl in a lordly dish is carried in. On the cover being raised, there is something so forlorn and miserable about the aspect of the animal that we both roar with laughter . . . 'That fowl', says Brough to the landlady, 'is of a breed I know. I knew the cut of its jib whenever it was put down. That was the grandmother of the cock that frightened Peter.'

. . . 'Na-na, it's not so old', says the landlady, 'but it eats hard.'

Robert Louis Stevenson (1850–1894) Letters, *on a meal on Iona*

129 . . . drunk as owls.

Robert Louis Stevenson, Treasure Island

130 Fifteen men on a dead man's chest –
Yo-ho-ho, and a bottle of rum!
Drink and the devil had done for the rest –
Yo-ho-ho, and a bottle of rum!

Robert Louis Stevenson, Treasure Island

131 A dense black substance, inimical to life.

Robert Louis Stevenson, quoted in Iain Finlayson, The Scots *(1987), on 'black bun'*

132 The king o' drinks, as I conceive it,
Talisker, Isla, or Glenlivet!

Robert Louis Stevenson, The Scotsman's Return from Abroad

133 Each true-hearted Scotsman, by nature jocose,
Can cheerfully dine on a dishfu' o' brose,
And the grace be a wish to get plenty of those;

And it's O for the kail brose o' Scotland,
And O for the Scottish kail brose.

Alexander Watson, quoted in Charles Mackay, Poetry and Humour of the Scottish Language *(1882)*

Friends and Enemies

1 I would give him a night's quarters though he had a man's head under his arm.

Gaelic proverbial phrase

2 Friends are lost by calling often; and by calling seldom.

Anonymous

3 And may I ever have a friend,
In whom I safely may depend,
To crack a joke, or tell a tale,
Or share a pint of napppy ale.

Anonymous, The Frugal Wish

4 There is no treasure which may be compared
Unto a faithful friend.

Anonymous, Roxburghe Ballads

5 He pursues us with malignant fidelity.

A. J. Balfour (1848–1930), quoted in Winston Churchill, Great Contemporaries *(1937), on an undesired associate*

6 For much better it is
To bide a friend's anger than a foe's kiss.

Alexander Barclay (c.1475–1552), The Mirrour of Good Manners

7 It fluttered and vexed me that a man I disliked so much should be so lucky.

James Boswell (1740–1795), Journal, July 1781, *on Sir Adam Fergusson's obtaining a public office*

8 'O,' interrupted Mr Bruce, coolly, 'I shall not poison him. But I may bribe his servant to tie a rope across his staircase, on some dark night, and then, as I dare say the miserly wretch never allows himself a candle to go up and down stairs, he may get a tumble, and break his neck.'

This idea set him into a fit of laughter quite merry to behold.

Fanny Burney 1752–1840), on James Bruce of Kinnaird (1730–1794), discoverer of the source of the Nile, quoted in C. F. Beckingham, Introduction *to* Trav-

els to Discover the Source of the Nile
(1964)

9 ... Souter Johnnie,
His ancient, trusty, drouthy crony

> *Robert Burns (1759–1796),* Tam o'
> Shanter

10 I do not hate him nearly as much as I fear I
ought to.

> *Thomas Carlyle (1795–1881), quoted in
> Froude's* Life, *on the Bishop of Oxford*

11 No enemy
Is half so fatal as a friend estranged.

> *John Davidson (1857–1909),* Godfrida

12 To find a friend one must close one eye. To
keep him – two.

> *Norman Douglas (1868–1952),* Almanac

13 One may dislike individuals; to dislike an
entire nation is a feat of which only fools
are capable.

> *Norman Douglas,* Experiments

14 I like to taste my friends but not to eat
them.

> *Norman Douglas,* A Plea for Better
> Manners

15 Here's to the friends we can trust
When storms of adversity blaw;
May they live in our songs and be nearest
our hearts,
Nor depart like the year that's awa'.

> *John Dunlop (1755–1820),* The Year
> That's Awa'

16 'Here am I, who have written on all sorts
of subjects calculated to arouse hostility,
moral, political, and religious; and yet I
have no enemies, except indeed, all the
Whigs, all the Tories, and all the Christians.'

> *David Hume (1711–1776), quoted in
> Lord Brougham's* Men of Letters and
> Science in the Reign of George III

17 I leave my friend, Mr John Home of
Kilduff, 12 dozen of my old claret at his
choice, and a single bottle of that other
liquor called port. I also leave him 6 dozen
of port, provided that he attests under his
hand, signed John *Hume*, that he has himself finished the bottle in two sittings. By
this concession he will terminate the only

two differences that ever came between us
on temporal matters.

> *David Hume,* Last Will and Testament

18 'Fare ye a' weel, ye bitches!'

> *Lord Kames (1696–1782), valediction to
> his fellow judges of the Court of Session,
> quoted in John Kay,* Original Portraits
> *(1877)*

19 My experience has led me to observe that
there are two things which are peculiarly
fatal to friendship, and these are great intimacy and pecuniary obligations.

> *James Mill (1773–1836), letter to Jeremy
> Bentham, 1814*

20 'Let them alone', said a lunatic in the lucid
fit, to a soldier who had told him, when
asked why he carried a sword, that it was
to kill his enemies – 'Let them alone, and
they will all die of themselves.'

> *Hugh Miller (1820–56),* The Testi-
> mony of the Rocks

21 I do not know him quite so well
As he knows me.

> *R. F. Murray (1863–1893),* Adventure
> of a Poet

22 *North:* 'This world's friendships, James –'
Shepherd: 'Are as cheap as crockery, and as
easily broken by a fa'. They seldom can
bide a clash, without fleein' into flinders.'

> *James Hogg (1770–1835), quoted in
> Christopher North (John Wilson,
> 1785–1854),* Noctes Ambrosianae, *1830*

23 Friends given by God in mercy and in
love;
My counsellors, my comforters, and
guides.

> *Robert Pollok (1798–1827),* The Course
> of Time

24 The chain of friendship, however bright,
does not stand the attrition of close
contact.

> *Sir Walter Scott (1771–1832),* Journal,
> February 1826

25 Should auld acquaintance be forgot, and
never thought upon?

> *Francis Sempill (c.1616–1685),* Auld
> Lang Syne, *from James Watson's* Choice
> Collection of Scots Poems *(1711)*

26 So long as we are loved by others I should say that we are almost indispensable; and no man is useless while he has a friend.

> *Robert Louis Stevenson (1850–1894)*

27 . . . the dearest friends are the
    auldest friends,
And the young are just on trial.

> *Robert Louis Stevenson*, It's an Ower-
> come Sooth

28 When I came into Scotland I knew well enough what I was to expect from my enemies, but I little foresaw what I meet with from my friends.

> *Prince Charles Edward Stewart*
> *(1720–1788), letter, quoted in Blaikie*,
> Itinerary of Prince Charles Stuart
> *(1897)*

29 Foes in the forum in the field were friends,
By social danger bound.

> *James Thomson (1700–1748)*, Liberty

Heraldry

1 And that the nobillis of Scotland suld be the mair mindfull of the foirsaid League, to the King of Scottis armes (quhilkis wes at that tyme ane reid Lyoun rampand in ane field of gold) wes eikit ane double tressour, with contrair lilleis, including about the Lyoun in all pointis: to signifie that the said Lyoun wes then armit, keipt, and defendit with the lilleis, richis, and freindschip of that nobill and most puissant kingdom of France.

> *Habbakkuk Bisset (fl. early 17th century)*,
> Rolment of Courtis *(c.1620), on the sup-*
> *posed source of the double tressour on the*
> *Scottish royal standard*

2 This awfull beist full terrible of cheir,
Persing of luk, and stout of countenance,
Right strong of corpes, of fassoun fair
    but feir . . .
In field of gold he stude full myghtely
With floure-de-lucis sirculit lustely.

> *William Dunbar (c.1460–c.1520)*, The
> Marriage of the Thrissil and the Rose,
> *on the Scottish lion*

Highlands, Lowlands and Borders

1 Speak well of the Hielands, but live in the laigh.

> *Traditional proverb*

2 Ye Highlands and ye Lowlands,
O whaur hae ye been?
They hae slain the earl o' Moray
And laid him on the green.

> *Anonymous*, The Bonnie Earl o' Moray

3 Their notions of virtue and vice, are very different, from the more Civiliz'd part of Mankind; they think it the most sublime virtue, to Pay a servile, and Abject Obedience to the Commands of their Superiors, altho' in Opposition to their Sovereign and the Laws of the Kingdom

> *Contemporary comment on the Highland-*
> *ers, 1724, quoted in Charles Withers*,
> Gaelic Scotland *(1988)*

4 I have been greatly disgusted with the appearance of the brave highlanders. They strike me as stupid, dirty, ignorant and barbarous. Their mode of life is not different from that of African negroes. Their huts are floorless except for earth; and they all live together in them like pigs; there are no chimneys, hardly a window; no conveniences of life of any sort.

> *Henry Brooks Adams (1838–1918), letter*
> *to C. F. Adams, 1863*

5 Our worst enemies are our own kin in the east. They accepted the domination of the Saxon. Got the superiority complex in so doing, and no-one looks so disdainfully now on the west-coaster as the east-coaster who has lost, or almost lost, his Gaelic . . . a pure case of the fox that lost its tail.

> *John Bannerman (1870–1938), letter to*
> *his son John M. Bannerman (1901–1969),*
> *quoted in* Bannerman: The Memoirs of
> Lord Bannerman of Kildonan

6 Converse with men makes sharp the
    glittering wit,
But God to man doth speak in solitude.

> *John Stuart Blackie (1809–1895)*, High-
> land Solitude

7 Highland people, so agreeable, even so decorative, do not live where they do just that the visitor may be catered for and amused.

> *George Blake (1893–1961)*, The Heart
> of Scotland

8 The Lowland Scot differs from the rest of mankind in that he has no Unconscious Mind. He is aware and critical of all the

levels of his consciousness, even when he is asleep or tipsy.

James Bridie (Osborne Henry Mavor, 1888–1951), One Way of Living

9   My heart's in the Highlands,
    My heart is not here;
    My heart's in the Highlands,
    A-chasing the deer.

    Robert Burns (1759–1796), My Heart's in the Highlands

10 The Highlanders are exceedingly proud to be thought an unmixed people, and are apt to upbraid the English with being a composition of all nations; but, for my own part, I think a little mixture in that sense would do themselves no manner of harm.

    Edmund Burt (fl. early 18th century), Letters from a Gentleman in the North of Scotland *(1726–37)*

11 . . . a Highland woman, who, begging a charity of a Lowland laird's lady, was asked several questions, and, among the rest, how many husbands she had had? To which she answered, three. And being further questioned, if her husbands had been kind to her, she said the first two were honest men, and very careful of their family, for they both 'died for the law'– that is, were hanged for theft. 'Well, but as to the last?' 'Hout!' says she, 'a fulthy peast! He dy'd at hame, lik an auld dug, on a puckle o' strae.'

    Edmund Burt, Letters from a Gentleman in the North of Scotland

12 As the Lowlanders call their part of the country the land of cakes, so the natives of the hills say they inhabit a land of milk and honey.

    Edmund Burt, Letters from a Gentleman in the North of Scotland

13 He who first met the Highlands swelling blue,
    Will love each peak that shows a kindred hue,
    Hail in each crag a friend's familiar face,
    And clasp the mountain in his mind's embrace.

    Lord Byron (1788–1824), The Highlands Swelling Blue

14 Oh for the crags that are wild and majestic!

The steep frowning glories of dark Loch na Garr.

    Lord Byron, Lachin y Gair

15 Their heads, their necks, their legs and thighs
    Are influenced by the skies;
    Without a clout to interrupt them.

    William Cleland (1661–1689), on the Highlanders

16 Nowhere will you find people of robuster physique, higher spirited, or longer lived, more active in old age and later in reaching it, than among the Highlanders; and that in spite of their entire dependence on cheese, flesh, and milk, like the Scythians.

    Sir Thomas Craig, De Unione Regnorum Britanniae *(1603–5)*

17 In Lowland families, children as a rule have not been encouraged to speak their minds in the presence of their elders . . . Even in later life, when they have established themselves in their own villages and towns, they feel the glances of appraisal following them and hear the whispers of 'Mphm, that'll be Sandy Thomson's Jimmie.'

    Ian Finlay, Scotland *(1945)*

18 They are not, to put it as tactfully as possible, the most immediately lovable folk in the United Kingdom.

    George Macdonald Fraser, The Steel Bonnets, *on the Borderers*

19 There is said to be a tradition among the Borderers that when a male child was christened, his right hand should be excluded from the ceremony, so that in time of feud he would be better equipped to strike 'unhallowed' blows upon his family's enemies.

    George Macdonald Fraser, The Steel Bonnets

20 As for the Highlands, I shortly comprehend them all in two sorts of people: the one, that dwelleth in our mainland, that are barbarous for the most part, and yet mixed with some show of civility: the other, that dwelleth in the Isles, and are utterly barbarians

    King James VI (1566–1625), Basilikon Doron

21 This advantage of conversing freely with their superiors, the peasantry of no other

European country enjoyed; and the consequence was that in 1745 the Scottish Highlanders of all descriptions had more of the polish of mind and sentiment which constitutes real civilisation than in general the inhabitants of any other country we know of, not even excepting Iceland . . . These facts indicate a very high degree of intellectual refinement, entirely independent of the fashion of their lower garments, from the sight of which, and the sound of a language which they did not understand, their neighbours were fully satisfied of their *barbarity*, and enquired no further.

> *Robert Jamieson (c.1780–1844), Introduction to Burt's* Letters from a Gentleman in the North of Scotland *(1818 edition)*

22 Could we analyse the soul of a Highland crofter, it would disclose a spiritual being quite unique in our matter-of-fact civilisation.

> *W. R. Lawson*, The Poetry and Prose of the Crofter Question, *from* National Review *(1885)*

23 . . . among the Highlanders generally, to rob was thought at least as honourable an employment as to cultivate the soil.

> *Lord Macaulay (1800–1859),* History of England

24 . . . what actuates me in regard to these islands is sheer love of every inch and particle of the soil which is the natural base of our national life – a regard in which these islands are as the wayward tendrils of a swe.etheart's hair.

> *Hugh MacDiarmid (C. M. Grieve, 1892–1978),* The Scottish Islands

25 We cannot however but testify our surprise, that in an age in which the study of antiquity is so much in fashion . . . this language alone, which is the depository of the manners, customs and notions of the earliest inhabitants of this island . . . this people and this language should be alone persecuted and intolerated.

> *Alexander MacDonald (Alasdair Mac Mhaighstir Alasdair, c.1695–c.1770),* Ais-Eiridh na Sean-Chanoin Albannaich (Resurrection of the Ancient Scottish Speech)

26 My blessing with the foxes dwell,
For that they hunt the sheep so well!

Ill fa' the sheep, a grey-faced nation
That swept our hills with desolation.

> *Duncan Bàn MacIntyre (1724–1812),* Oran nam Balgairean (Song to the Foxes)

27 . . . the light of the peat-fire flame,
The light that hill-folks yearn for.

> *Kenneth Macleod (1871–1955),* By the Light of the Peat-Fire Flame

28 Bowed with sadness many a Gael
bred up in the Land of Mists,
smothers now in urban streets
from city stour and reek of coal.

> *Mary Macpherson (1821–1898),* Soraidh leis an Nollaig ùir (Farewell to the New Christmas)

29 Join a Highland regiment, my boy. The kilt is an unrivalled garment for fornication and diarrhoea.

> *John Masters (1914–1983),* Bugles and a Tiger

30 When a man gives out much, he must absorb much; and it is good to live with the gods for a bit; that is why some folk made pilgrimage to the Western Isles of Scotland.

> *Jessie Matthay,* Life of Tobias Matthay

31 Bishop Knox . . . expressed his doubts as to the wisdom of rooting out one pestiferous clan in order to 'plant in another little better'. 'Garring ane devil dang anither', was the expressive phrase.

> *Dugald Mitchell,* History of the Highlands and Gaelic Scotland *(1900), referring to Andrew Knox, Bishop of Argyll and the Isles in the early 17th century*

32 No two sets of people could be more tempera-mentally incompatible.

> *Edwin Muir (1887–1959),* Scottish Journey, *on Highlanders and Lowlanders*

33 A hunter's fate is all I would be craving,
A shepherd's plaiding, and a beggar's pay,
If I might earn them where the heather, waving,
Gives fragrance to the day.

> *Neil Munro (1864–1930),* The Heather

34 And the droll thing was, for a' they misca'd Gleska, and grat aboot Clachnacudden, ye

couldna get yin o' them to gang back to Clachnacudden if ye pyed the train ticket and guaranteed a pension o' a pound a week.

Neil Munro, Erchie

35 Many readers may be surprised to know that in the golden age of the thirteenth to sixteenth centuries, the entire Hebrides and Highland coast formed one Atlantic principality, self-supporting, powerful, and independent, whose ambasssadors treated direct with the kings of Scotland, England and Europe.

W. H. Murray, The Islands of Western Scotland *(1973)*

36 Ithaca, Cyprus and Rhodes
Are names to the Muses dear;
But sweeter still doth Icolmkill
Fall on a Scotsman's ear.

Alexander Nicolson (1827–1893), Isle of My Heart

37 I sought for merit wherever it was to be found, and it is my boast that I was the first minister who looked for it and found it in the mountains of the north. I called it forth and drew into your service a hardy and intrepid race of men, who when left by your jealousy became prey to the artifice of your enemies, and had gone nigh to have overturned the state in the war before the last.

William Pitt, Earl of Chatham (1708–1778), Speech to the House of Commons, 1766

38 For what are the bens and glens
but manifold qualities,
Immeasurable complexities of soul?
What are these islands but a song sung by
island voices?

Kathleen Raine (1908–), The Ancient Speech, *from* Eileann Chanaidh

39 And whether the blood be Highland
or Lowland or no';
And whether the hue be white or
black as the sloe;
Of kith and of kin we're one, be it
right, be it wrong,
If only the heart beat true to the lilt of
the song.

Sir Hugh S. Roberton (1874–1952), Air Fa La La La

40 There's nought in the Highlands but
syboes and leeks,
And lang-leggit callants gaun wanting the
breeks.

Sir Walter Scott (1771–1832), David Gellatley's Song from Waverley

41 Ye ken Highlander and Lowlander, and Border-men, are a' ae man's bairns when you are over the Scots dyke.

Sir Walter Scott, The Two Drovers

42 I started as a Highlander and I suppose I am now much more a Lowlander. I suspect, however, that these old distinctions are now becoming much less meaningful. I am Scots – proud of it, and very glad to be able to live in and enjoy my own country – all of it.

John Smith (1936–1994), leader of the Labour Party

43 In the highlands, in the country places,
Where the old men have rosy faces,
And the young fair maidens
Quiet eyes.

Robert Louis Stevenson (1850–1894), In the Highlands

44 The fact remains: in spite of the difference of blood and language, the Lowlander finds himself the sentimental countryman of the Highlander.

Robert Louis Stevenson, Memories and Portraits

45 But from his compatriot in the south the Lowlander stands consciously apart . . his ear continues to remark the English speech; and even though his tongue acquire the Southern knack, he will still have a strong Scotch accent of the mind.

Robert Louis Stevenson, Memories and Portraits

46 . . . the dear, dear Highlands . . . There is a great peculiarity about the Highlands and the Highlanders; and they are such a chivalrous, fine, active people.

Queen Victoria (1819–1901), Our Life in the Highlands

47 Though he is largely unaware of it, the staunch Lowlander carries on his back a Gaelic biological and linguistic heritage.

Kurt Wittig, The Scottish Tradition in Literature *(1958)*

48 Now they are gone it seems they
    never mattered,
much, to the world, those proud and
    violent races,
clansmen and chiefs whose empassioned
    greed and blindness
made desolate these lonely lovely places.

    Douglas Young (1913–1973), For the
    Old Highlands

History

1 Napoleon was an emperor:
He ruled by land and sea;
He was King of France and Germany
But he ne'er ruled Polmadie.

    Anonymous, Johnnie Lad

2 Pray get yir facts right, or dinne try to
rewrite 'History', a Big Subject! Which is
always a Bitch!

    *Anonymous, pencilled marginal comment
    in a sports history book in the Edinburgh
    Central Library*

3 I am always fascinated when people talk
about the forging of a nation. Most nations
are forgeries, perpetrated in the last century or so.

    Neal Ascherson (1932–), The Observer,
    1985

4 The Scottish versions of history seem to
oscillate between extolling the virtues of
passive suffering and glorifying moments
of volcanic, almost involuntary violence.
Where are the episodes in which the
Scottish people, by holding together and
labouring patiently and wisely, achieved
something?

    Neal Ascherson, Games With Shadows

5 History does not repeat itself. Historians
repeat each other.

    A. J. Balfour (1848–1930)

6 Progress is a goddess who, up to now, has
looked after her children well . . . It is
difficult to picture this goddess of plenty
as other than some huge computer-figure,
that will give our children what they desire
easily and endlessly – food, sex, excitement – a synthetic goddess, vast and bland

as Buddha, but without love or tenderness
or compassion.

    George Mackay Brown (1921–1996), An
    Orkney Tapestry

7 What is the history of Scotland? In the
first place, it is the history of a very poor
nation.

    John Buchan (1875–1940), The Scots
    Tongue

8 As for the present I am occupiit in writing
of our historie, being assurit to content
few and to displease monie thar throw. As
to the end of it yf ye gett it not or this
wynter be passit lippen not for it . . . the
rest of my occupation is with the gout.

    *George Buchanan (1506–1582), letter,
    August 1577*

9 Happy the people whose annals are blank
in the history books.

    Thomas Carlyle (1795–1881)

10 No great man lives in vain. The history of
the world is but the biographies of great
men.

    Thomas Carlyle, On Heroes, Hero-Wor-
    ship and the Heroic in History

11 History, as it lies at the root of all science,
is also the first distinct product of man's
spiritual nature; his earliest expression of
what can be called Thought.

    Thomas Carlyle, On History

12 We have tested the faith of the Scots in
adverse times – a faithful nation, a people
most worthy of friendship and renown,
tried in manhood, whom we cannot honour
enough nor praise worthily. Nor is the
league between us written in parchment of
sheepskin, but rather in the flesh and skin
of men, traced not in ink but in blood shed
in many places.

    *Alain Chartier, Chancellor of Bayeux,
    Speech made in a French diplomatic mis-
    sion to King James I, 1427 (original in
    Latin)*

13 Myths about a nation's history should be
treated with considerable caution at the
best of times: if they also incorporate
an unjustified – and wholly unhistorical –
sense of national grievance, they should
be handled with especial care . . . the
Scots have a strong and pervasive sense of

history, yet all too often they prefer the romantic myth to the complicated truth.

> *Tam Dalyell (1932–)*, Devolution: The End of Britain?

14　The Scots are beset by Scottish history; they cherish it, but have no use for it.

> *Iain Finlayson*, The Scots (1987)

15　One of Scotland's misfortunes is that she was not conquered by the Roman cohorts who bequeathed to Western Europe their basic civilisation.

> *Arnold Fleming*, The Medieval Scots Scholar in France *(1952)*

16　There is a tendency to regard the high midnight of the Border Reiver as a stirring, gallant episode in British history. It was not like that; it was as cruel and horrible in its way as Biafra or Vietnam.

> *George Macdonald Fraser*, The Steel Bonnets *(1971)*

17　In short, our history may be summed up in this one sentence – that while the Scotsman has often led the age, Scotland has no less often lagged in it.

> *Sir Patrick Geddes (1854–1932)*, Scottish University Needs and Aims

18　The cold sober truth is that the history of Scotland is the most romantic, the most incredible, of any country in Europe. Whenever a venture appeared to be a forlorn hope, a lost cause, there were the Scots battling for it. Whenever it was possible for the Scots to stand in their own material light, they did so with fanatic zeal.

> *Neil Gunn (1891–1973)*, The Man Who Came Back

19　Great Julius, that tribute gat of a'
His winning was in Scotland bot full sma'.

> *'Blind Harry' (fl. 1490s)*, Wallace

20　If you should bid me count the lies of Hector's History, I might as well assay to sum the stars or waves of sea.

> *John Leland on Hector Boece's* Scotorum Historiae, *quoted in A. H. Williamson*, Scottish National Consciousness in the Age of James VI *(1979)*

21　So lang as the King is young, greit men reignis at thair awin libertie, oppressand al men, as thay, without doubt, will be punisched thairaftir.

> *Robert Lindsay of Pitscottie (c.1500–c.1565)*, Historie and Cronicles of Scotland

22　Be this, the post cam out of Linlithgow, schowing the king good tidings, that the queen was deliverit. The king inquired whedder it was a man or woman. The messenger said it was ane fair dochter. He answered and said, 'Fairwell, it cam with ane lass and it will pass with ane lass.'

> *Robert Lindsay of Pitscottie*, Historie and Cronicles of Scotland, *on the birth of Queen Mary I*

23　And history leans by a dark entry
with words from his mouth
that say *Pity me, pity me*
but never forgive.

> *Norman MacCaig (1910–1996)*, Old Edinburgh

24　. . . the visit gave me what I'd never had before, a feeling for the past *in which I had ancestors*. It gave me the beginnings of a sense of history in which I belonged almost as in the present.

> *Norman MacCaig*, A Month That Changed Things, *from A. Kamm and A. Lean*, A Scottish Childhood *(1985)*, *on his first visit to Scalpay*

25　A King has not the same unconditional possession of his kingdom as you have of your coat . . . It is the free people who first give power to the King, and his power depends on the whole people. Fergus, the first King of Scots, had no other law, and so it is everywhere.

> *John Major (1469–1550)*, Historia Majoris Britanniae, *translated from Latin*

26　. . . entered low down among the ordure of the privy, that was all of hard stone and none window nor issue thereupon save a little square hole even at the side of the bottom of the privy, that at the making thereof of old time was left open to cleanse and ferme the said privy, by which the said King might well have escaped, but he made to let stop it well three days afore . . . because that when he played there at the paume the balls that he played with often ran in at that foul hole.

> *John Shirley, transcribed account (in the*

1440s) of an ironic aspect of the assassination of King James I

27 Jenny Geddes and her stool are precious articles of our national belief not to be given up without danger of sapping the foundations of society in our beloved Scotland.

> *David Masson, Professor of Rhetoric at Edinburgh University, quoted in C. P. Finlayson,* The Symposium Academicum, *in G. Donaldson,* Four Centuries: Edinburgh University Life *(1983)*

28 I cannot look back over much more than twenty years of the past; and yet in that comparatively brief space, I see the stream of tradition rapidly lessening as it flows onward, and displaying, like those rivers of Africa which lose themselves in the burning sands of the desert, a broader and more powerful volume as I trace it towards its source.

> *Hugh Miller (1802–1856),* Notes and Legends of the North of Scotland

29 There is an obscurity which hangs over the beginnings of all history – a kind of impalpable fog – which the writer can hardly avoid transferring from the first openings of his subject to the first pages of his book.

> *Hugh Miller,* Notes and Legends of the North of Scotland

30 We were a family, a tribe, a people.

> *Edwin Muir (1887–1959),* Scotland *(1941)*

31 But Knox and Melville clapped their
    preaching palms
And huddled all the harvest gold away,
Hoodicrow Peden in the blighted corn
Hacked with his rusty beak the starving
    haulms.
Out of that desolation we were born.

> *Edwin Muir,* Scotland, *(1941)*

32 The normal development of a nation is founded solidly on its past. The development of Scotland during the last three centuries has been bought at the expense of shedding one bit of its past after another until almost the only thing that remains now is a sentimental legend.

> *Edwin Muir,* Scottish Journey

33 It is a sobering thought, and one conducive to a proper sense of historical perspective, that before the first savages set foot upon the soil of Scotland the first urban, and in that sense civilised community, had been flourishing at Jericho for more than a thousand years.

> *Stuart Piggott,* The Prehistoric Peoples of Scotland *(1962)*

34 . . . the eternal Scots problem, the integration of Scottish historical experience into a civilised nation.

> *Tom Scott (1918–1995), note on the title of his poem* Fergus

35 The sentimentality that encumbers Scottish history has done very little to give us any sensible pride in tradition.

> *George Scott-Moncrieff (1910–),* The Stones of Scotland *(1938)*

36 History's easy. Dead easy. Very dead and very easy.

> *W. Gordon Smith,* Mr Jock *(1987)*

37 Before his arrival, Scotland's history had been purely vegetable.

> *George Malcolm Thomson,* A Short History of Scotland *(1930), on the first man in Scotland*

38 It is plain that the agreement set out in the articles was not an Act of either the English or the Scottish Parliament, still less of the Parliament of Great Britain. There was no 'Act of Union'. The agreement was an international treaty between Anne, Queen of Scots, and Anne, Queen of England, on terms negotiated by commissioners appointed by the two Queens, signed by them on July 22, 1706, and presented to the Queens.

> *David M. Walker,* A Legal History of Scotland, Volume 5 *(1998)*

39 Scottish historiography has been for too long bogged down in a preoccupation with the myriad aspects of the Labour movement and associated areas of working-class history, to the exclusion of wider themes left virtually untouched. Short of an actual census of head-lice among the children of handloom weavers in the nineteenth century, no detail of proletarian experience has been left unexplored.

> *Gerald Warner,* The Scottish Tory Party *(1988)*

Home

1 Hame's hame, be it never sae hamely.
    *John Arbuthnot (1667–1735), The Law
    is a Bottomless Pit*

2 'Working-class Tenements'. Inspiring name!
    These are inhabited by the majority of the
    Scottish people: more than half the popu-
    lation, in fact, are in one – and two-room
    tenements – a state of things unparalleled
    in Europe or America, in fact, in the his-
    tory of civilisation.
    *Sir Patrick Geddes (1854–1932), Cities
    in Evolution*

3 Of a' roads to happiness ever were tried,
    There's nane half so sure as ane's ain
    fireside.
    *Elizabeth Hamilton (1785–1816), My
    Ain Fireside*

4 O, we're a' noddin', nid nid noddin',
    O, we're a' noddin at our house at hame.
    *Adapted by L. J. Nicolson (19th century),
    We're A' Noddin'*

Hopes, Fears and Disappointments

1 Heave awa', chaps! I'm no' dead yet.
    *Inscription above Paisley Close, High
    Street, Edinburgh, commemorating the
    rescue of a boy from a collapsed building
    there*

2 The best-laid plans o' mice and men,
    Gang aft agley,
    And leave us nocht but grief and pain,
    For promised joy.
    Robert Burns (1759–1796), To a Mouse

3 But, och, I backwards cast my e'e
    On prospects drear!
    And forward, though I canna see,
    I guess, and fear.
    Robert Burns, To a Mouse

4 Hope springs exulting on triumphant
    wing.
    *Robert Burns, The Cottar's Saturday
    Night*

5 Then let us pray that come it may
    (An' come it will for a' that)
    That Sense and Worth o'er a' the earth
    Shall bear the gree and a' that!

For a' that, and a' that,
It's comin' yet, for a' that,
That man to man, the world o'er,
Shall brothers be for a' that.
    *Robert Burns, A Man's a Man For a'
    That*

6 All, all forsook the friendless guilty mind,
    But Hope, the charmer, still remain'd
    behind.
    *Thomas Campbell (1777–1844), The
    Pleasures of Hope*

7 I'm braaly hoopfil at wir communities
    could be on de aidge o a time o economic
    growth an excitin new developments at wir
    never kent afore. But dis'll only happen if
    we hae an awaarness o wir ain identity an
    a confidence i wir ain abilities. An forbye
    dat, we maun hae mair say in decisions
    aboot wir ain future.
    *John Goodlad, Vice-chairman of the Shet-
    land Movement, Shetland Times, 1991*

8 I am a young man, and gif I haif litill, I
    haif als littil to fear. I have my sword undis-
    honorit, and that is aneuch to me: yit gif
    evir God send me a fortune, I hoip to use
    it weill.
    *James Henderson (fl. early 17th century),
    Scots mercenary, letter sent from The
    Hague, September 1608*

9 Most happy state, that never tak'st
    Revenge . . .
    Nor know'st Hope's sweet disease, that
    charms our sense,
    Nor its sad cure, dear-bought Experience.
    *Sir Robert Kerr (fl. early 17th century),
    In Praise of a Solitary Life*

10 I thank God for preserving my life where
    so many have fallen, and enabling me to do
    something which I trust will turn out for
    the true and permanent welfare of Africa.
    *David Livingstone (1813–1873), letter to
    his parents and sisters, March 1856*

11 Nothing now my heart can fire
    But regret and desire.
    Queen Mary I (1542–1587)

12 My pleasure shall consist . . . in establish-
    ing to myself that name in the world for
    wisdom and knowledge which was the dar-
    ling object even of my infant years to think
    I should one day attain.
    James Mill (1773–1836), quoted in

Alexander Bain, James Mill:
A Biography *(1882)*

13 Let them bestow on ev'ry Airth a limb;
Open all my Veins, that I may swim
To Thee, my Saviour, in that Crimson
Lake;
Then place my pur-boil'd Head upon a
Stake;
Scatter my Ashes, throw them in the Air;
Lord (since Thou know'st where all
these Atoms are)
I'm hopeful, once Thou'll recollect
my Dust,
And confident Thou'lt raise me with the
Just.

Marquis of Montrose (1612–1650), His
Metrical Prayer, *composed on the eve of
his execution*

14 In God's wilderness lies the hope of the
world.

John Muir (1838–1914), quoted in John
of the Mountains: The Unpublished
Journals of John Muir *(1938)*

15 I was inordinately ambitious, I suppose, to
be *fully stretched* . . . inordinately ambitious
to be of service.

Lord Reith (1889–1971), Lord Reith
Looks Back, *BBC Television, 1967*

16 Dreams come true
Surely mine is nearly due
Four apartments and a view
and an inside toilet too . . .
Me and John will get a new
House in Drumchapel where Dreams
come true.

Tony Roper, Dreams Come True I, *from*
The Steamie *(1987)*

17 The sickening pang of hope deferr'd.

Sir Walter Scott (1771–1832), The Lady
of the Lake

18 No hope of gilded spurs today.

Sir Walter Scott, Marmion

19 And thus Hope me deceiv'd, as she
deceiveth all.

Sir Walter Scott, Harold the Dauntless

20 Hope is like the sun, which, as we journey
towards it, casts the shadow of our burden
behind us.

Samuel Smiles (1816–1904), Self-Help

21 When we have discovered a continent, or
crossed a chain of mountains, it is only to
find another ocean or another plain upon
the further side.

Robert Louis Stevenson (1850–1894), Virginibus Puerisque

22 But I strode on austere;
No hope could have no fear.

James Thomson (1834–1882), The City
of Dreadful Night

Human Nature

1 And muckle thocht our gudewife to
hersell,
But never a word she spak.

Anonymous, Get Up and Bar the Door

2 It's pride puts a' the country doun,
Sae tak' your auld cloak about ye.

Anonymous, Tak' Your Auld Cloak
About Ye

3 Faculty meeting and dinner at Fortune's . . .
A little intoxicated. About nine went out to
street. Met fine wench; with her to room
in Blackfriars Wynd, and twice. Back and
coffee and whist.

James Boswell (1740–1795), Journals

4 If happiness hae not her seat
An' centre in the breast,
We may be wise, or rich, or great,
But never can be blest.

Robert Burns (1759–1796), Epistle to
Davie

5 Good lord, what is man? for as simple
as he looks,
Do but try to develop his hooks
and his crooks!
With his depths and his shallows, his
good and his evil;
All in all he's a problem must puzzle the
devil.

Robert Burns, Inscribed to the Hon.
C. J. Fox

6 But human bodies are sic fools,
For a' their colleges and schools,
That when nae real ills perplex them,
They mak enow themsels to vex them.

Robert Burns, The Twa Dogs

7　In the human breast,
　　Two master-passions cannot co-exist.
　　　　Thomas Campbell (1777–1844),
　　　　Theodric

8　The greatest of faults, I should say, is to be
　　conscious of none.
　　　　Thomas Carlyle (1795–1881), On
　　　　Heroes, Hero-Worship, and the
　　　　Heroic in History

9　Up the Noran water,
　　The country folk are kind;
　　And wha the bairnie's daddy is
　　They dinna muckle mind.
　　　　Helen B. Cruickshank (1886–1975), Shy
　　　　Geordie

10　The heart of man is made to reconcile
　　contradictions.
　　　　David Hume (1711–1776), Essays

11　The great men sayis that their distress
　　Comis for the peoples wickedness;
　　The people sayis for the transgressioun
　　Of great men, and their oppressioun
　　Bot nane will their awin sin confess.
　　　　Sir Richard Maitland (1496–1586), How
　　　　Suld Our Commonweill Endure

12　'It will be time to sharp the maiden for
　　shearing o' craigs and thrapples. I hope to
　　see the auld rusty lass linking at a bluidy
　　hairst again.'
　　　　Sir Walter Scott (1771–1832), Rob Roy

13　Good humour and generosity carry the
　　day with the popular heart all the world
　　over.
　　　　Alexander Smith (1830–1867),
　　　　Dreamthorp

14　The conscience has morbid sensibilities; it
　　must be employed but not indulged, like
　　the imagination or the stomach.
　　　　Robert Louis Stevenson (1850–1894),
　　　　Ethical Studies

15　... the year
　　they hauled the old woman out on
　　　to the dung-heap,
　　to demonstrate how knowledgeable they
　　　were in Scripture,
　　for the birds of the air had nests
　　　(and the sheep had folds)
　　though she had no place in which to lay
　　　her head.
　　　　Derick Thomson (Ruaraidh MacThomais,
　　　　1921–), Strathnaver

16　... We canna bide sae crouse,
　　but aye maun pursue whait we aye
　　　hae socht,
　　that vision o perfection, yon crystal
　　　dancer
　　birlin i the sunlicht.
　　　　Raymond Vettese (1950–), The Crystal
　　　　Dancer

17　For everything created
　　In the bounds of earth and sky
　　Hath such longing to be mated,
　　It must couple or must die.
　　　　G. J. Whyte-Melville (1821–1878), Like
　　　　to Like

Humour

1　I have never had to try to get my act
　　across to a non-English-speaking audience,
　　except at the Glasgow Empire.
　　　　Arthur Askey (1900–1982)

2　A great deal of what is called Scottish
　　sentiment *is* funny. To anybody who
　　knows the people who indulge in it, Wal-
　　lacethebruceism, Charlieoverthewaterism,
　　Puirrabbieburnsism, Bonniebonniebank-
　　sism, Myainfolkism and Laymedoonan-
　　deeism, those not very various forms
　　of Scottish Sentiment, are very comical
　　indeed.
　　　　James Bridie (Osborne Henry Mavor,
　　　　1888–1951), A Small Stir

3　Without humour, you cannot run a sweetie-
　　shop, let alone a nation.
　　　　John Buchan (1875–1940) Castle Gay

4　True humour springs not more from the
　　head than from the heart; it is not con-
　　tempt, its essence is love; it issues not in
　　laughter, but in still smiles, which lie far
　　deeper. It is a sort of inverse sublimity,
　　exalting as it were, into our affections what
　　is below us, while sublimity draws down
　　into our affections what is above us.
　　　　Thomas Carlyle (1795–1881), Essays

5　Among other good qualities, the Scots
　　have been distinguished for humour – not
　　for venomous wit, but for kindly, genial
　　humour, which half-loves what it laughs
　　at – and this alone shows clearly enough
　　that those to whom it belongs have not

looked too exclusively on the gloomy side of the world.

J. A. Froude (1818–1894), rectorial address to Edinburgh University

6 . . . jocosity that was just a kittle to hear.

John Galt (1779–1839), Annals of the Parish

7 'Give me the letter. But before I open it, let me know how he received mine . . . Did he not kiss the seal? Did he not in trembling ecstasy press it to his throbbing bosom? Tell me, tell me all, I conjure you.'

'He did not kiss a bit of it that I saw, Ma'am,' returned Jenny. 'He only took it out of my hand, and said Pshaw.'

Eliza Hamilton (1758–1816), Memoirs of Modern Philosophers

8 What do you mean, funny? Funny-peculiar or funny ha-ha?

Ian Hay (Ian Hay Beith, 1876–1952) The Housemaster

9 The Scot – agree or disagree, as you wish – is very much what I choose to call a secret humorist. He quietly creates his wit and jokes as if they were an unpermitted diversion, frowned on by the authorities.

Gordon Irving, The Wit of the Scots *(1969)*

10 Och aye, laddie, it's a hard life. But mind ye, there's no' much use in bein' daft if ye're no' tae be weel peyed for't.

Attributed to Sir Harry Lauder (1870–1950)

11 It is a peculiar element in Scotch humour, as appreciated by Scotchmen, that the harder it is to see, the better it is esteemed. If it is obvious it is of less account.

Stephen Leacock (1869–1944), Humour

12 No jokes of any kind are understood here, I have not made one for two months and if I feel one coming I shall bite my tongue.

James Clerk Maxwell (1831–1879), elected to the Chair of Mathematics at Marischal College, Aberdeen, in 1856

13 Humour is a flash of eternity bursting through time.

A. W. Petrie (c.1853–1937), The Clincher, *March 1898*

14 'The country's looking very green, but after all, that's what it's there for,' he remarked to his wife two days later.

'That's very modern, and I dare say very clever, but I'm afraid it's wasted on me,' she observed coldly.

Saki (H. H. Munro, 1870–1916), The Jesting of Arlington Stringham

15 It requires a surgical operation to get a joke well into a Scotch understanding. Their only idea of wit, which prevails occasionally in the north and . . . is so infinitely distressing to people of good taste, is laughinll g immoderately at stated intervals.

Sydney Smith (1771–1845), quoted in Lady Holland, Memoir of the Rev. Sydney Smith *(1855)*

16 There is nothing very funny about Scotland.

Wilfred Taylor, Scot Free *(1953)*

Insults

1 'I wiss ye were on yon tree,'
Quo' the fause knicht upon the road.
'An' a gude ladder under me,'
Quo' the wee boy, and still he stude.

Anonymous, The Fause Knicht Upon the Road

2 This is the savage pimp without dispute
First bought his mother for a prostitute;
Of all the miscreants ever went to hell,
this villain rampant bears away the bell.

Anonymous, on the first Duke of Lauderdale (1616–1682), Secretary for Scotland

3 Open your doors, you devils, and prepare
A room that's warm for honest Lady Stair.

Anonymous, Upon the Long-wished for and Tymely Death of the Right Honourable the Lady Stair, *from James Maidment,* A Book of Scottish Pasquils *(1868). Margaret Ross, wife of the first Viscount Stair, was believed to be a witch.*

4 Stair's neck, mynd, wife, sons, grandson, and the rest,
Are wry, false, witch, pets, parricid, possest.

Anonymous, Satyre on the Familie of Stairs, *early 18th century*

5 Your testicles, some say, did tripartite,
To satiate the lecherous female kind,
Left two before, and placed one stone
    behind . . .
Hence your unparalleled amorous deeds,
Your frequent unions, and the obvious
    itch
Is in your privie members when you
    preach.

> *Mr Finnie*, Epithalamium on the
> Match Betwixt Mr Williamson and
> Mrs Jean Straiton, *20 May 1700. The
> Rev. David Williamson was celebrated for
> having married seven wives in succession*

6 Sir James Stewart, thou'lt hing in a string,
Sir James Stewart, knave and rogue
    thou art,
For thou ne'er had a true heart
To God or King,
Sir James Stewart, thou'lt hing in a string.

> *Anonymous Jacobite verse on Sir James
> Stewart (died 1713), Lord Advocate*

7 Auld Satan cleekit him by the spaul
And stappit him in the dub o' Hell.
The foulest fiend there doughtna bide
    him,
The damned they wadna fry beside him,
Till the bluidy Duke cam trysting thither,
And the ae fat butcher fried the ither.

> *Anonymous, from Cromek's* Select Scot-
> tish Songs *(1810), on Sir John Murray
> of Broughton, the turncoat Jacobite, and
> the Duke of Cumberland*

8 Here continueth to stink
The memory of the Duke of Cumberland
Who with unparalleled barbarity,
And inflexible hardness of heart,
In spite of all motives to lenity
That policy or humanity could suggest,
Endeavoured to ruin Scotland
By all the ways a Tyrant could invent.

> *Anonymous Jacobite 'epitaph' of 1746,
> quoted in R. Forbes,* The Lyon in
> Mourning *(1748)*

9 O Bute, if instead of contempt and
    of odium,
You wish to obtain universal eulogium,
From your breast to your gullet transfer
    the blue string,
Our hearts are all yours from the very
    first swing.

> *Anonymous pasquinade against Lord Bute
> (1713–1792), Prime Minister; quoted in
> Alan Lloyd,* The Wickedest Age

10 'A great deal rests on this gentleman's credibility. He is a Jew and may be an atheist.
We are honest Scots. What faith can we
put in this "gentleman's" words?'

> *Advocate for the defence in the murder
> trial of the trades unionist Alfred French
> (1912), quoted in Peter Slowe,* Manny
> Shinwell *(1993), referring to Emmanuel
> Shinwell, a key witness*

11 Here continueth to rot
The body of Francis Charteris,
Who, with an Inflexible Constancy and
Inimitable Uniformity of Life
Persisted
In spite of Age and Infirmities
In the practice of Every Human Vice,
Excepting Prodigality and Hypocrisy:
His insatiable Avarice exempted him
    from the first,
His matchless Impudence from the
    second.

> *John Arbuthnot (1667–1735),* Success

12 Reporter, at Barrie's front door: 'Sir James
Barrie, I presume?'
    Sir James Barrie: 'You do.' (closes door)

> *Sir J. M. Barrie (1860–1937), quoted in
> C. Fadiman,* The Little, Brown Book
> of Anecdotes *(1985)*

13 A Glasgow carter asked a pompous-look-
ing gent to hold his horse for him. 'My
man,' said the pompous gent, 'do you realise that I'm a bailie?'
    'Even if you are,' said the carter, 'surely
you widnae steal my horse?'

> *Colm Brogan,* The Glasgow Story
> *(1952)*

14 Wha called ye partan-face, my bonnie
man?

> *John Buchan (1875–1940),* Prester John

15 Bright ran thy line, o Galloway,
Thro' many a far-fam'd sire;
So ran the far fam'd Roman way,
So ended in a mire.

> *Robert Burns (1759–1796),* On the Earl
> of Galloway

16 That there is falsehood in his looks
I must and will deny:
They tell their master is a knave,
And sure they do not lie.

> *Robert Burns,* On Hearing It Asserted
> Falsehood Is Expressed in the Rev. Dr
> Babington's Very Looks

17 Of lordly acquaintance you boast,
And the Dukes that you dined with
yestreen;
Why, an insect's an insect at most,
Tho' it crawl on the curl of a Queen!

 Robert Burns, The Toadeater

18 Sic a reptile was Wat, sic a miscreant slave,
That the worms ev'n damned him when
laid in his grave;
'In his flesh there's a famine,' a starved
reptile cries,
'And his heart is rank poison!' another
replies.

 Robert Burns, Epitaph for Mr Walter
Riddell

19 She tauld thee weel thou wast a skellum,
A blethering, blustering, drunken blellum.

 Robert Burns, Tam o' Shanter

20 . . . Jeffrey! pertest of the train
Whom Scotland pampers with her fiery
grain!
Whatever blessing wait a genuine Scot,
In double portion swells thy glorious lot;
For thee Edina culls her evening sweets,
And showers her odours on thy candid
sheets,
Whose hue and fragrance to thy work
adhere –
This scents its pages, and that gilds its
rear.

 Lord Byron (1788–1824), English Bards
and Scotch Reviewers, *on Francis Jeffrey, of the* Edinburgh Review

21 What a pity it is that I shall be beyond
the Bosphorus before the next number has
passed the Tweed! But I yet hope to light
my pipe with it in Persia.
 My northern friends have accused me,
with justice, of personality towards their
great literary anthropophagus, Jeffrey; but
what else was to be done with him and
his dirty pack, who feed by 'lying and slan-
dering', and slake their thirst with 'evil
speaking'?

 *Lord Byron, Postscript to the second edition
of* English Bards and Scotch Reviewers

22 The Gothic monarch and the Pictish peer
Arms gave the first his right, the
last had none,
But basely stole what less barbarians won.
So, when the lion quits his fell repast,
Next prowls the wolf, the filthy jackal last.

 Lord Byron, The Curse of Minerva, *on

Alaric, king of the Goths, and Thomas
Bruce, Lord Elgin (1766–1841), who
removed the 'Elgin Marbles' from the Par-
thenon in Athens*

23 They sent me word that I was like the first
puff of a haggis, hottest at the first.

 *Sir Robert Carey, Warden of the English
March, of a message from the Armstrongs,
1601*

24 . . . a cursed old Jew, not worth his weight
in cold bacon.

 *Thomas Carlyle (1795–1881), on Ben-
jamin Disraeli, recorded in Moneypenny
and Buckle,* The Life of Benjamin
D'Israeli, Lord Beaconsfield

25 . . . sitting in a sewer, and adding to it.

 *Thomas Carlyle, on Algernon Charles
Swinburne*

26 Thirty million, mostly fools.

 *Thomas Carlyle, attributed, when asked
the population of England*

27 Last time I saw a mouth like yours, pal,
Lester Piggott was sitting behind it.

 *Billy Connolly (1942–), quoted in
D. Campbell,* Billy Connolly: The
Authorised Version *(1976), to a heckler*

28 But a Scotchman certainly does make
one feel that underneath his greasy and
obviously imperfect civilisation the hairy
simian sits and gibbers.

 T. W. Crosland, The Unspeakable Scot
(1902)

29 He has all the qualifications for a great Liberal Prime Minister. He wears spats and
he has a beautiful set of false teeth.

 *R. B. Cunninghame Graham
(1852–1936), on Sir Henry Campbell-
Bannerman (1836–1908)*

30 It seldom pays to be rude. It never pays to
be only half-rude.

 Norman Douglas (1868–1952)

31 The Anglo-Saxon is hard to wake up, being
phlegmatic and self-righteous to such a
degree that the only thing which will really
wake him up is brute force.

 Norman Douglas, How About Europe?

32 Ruskin. Good God! He's not a man: he's
    an emetic.
        Norman Douglas, South Wind, *on John
        Ruskin*

33 Thae tarmegantis, with tag and atter,
    Full loud in Ersche began to clatter,
    And rowp lyk revin and ruke.
    The devil sa devit was with thair yell,
    That in the depest pot of hell
    He smorit thame with smuke.
        William Dunbar (c.1460–c.1520), The
        Daunce of the Sevin Deidly Sinnis

34 I have ane wallidrag, ane worm, ane
        auld wobat carle.
    A wastit wolroun, nae worth but wordis
        to clatter;
    Ane bumbart, ane drone bee, ane
        bag full of flewme,
    Ane skabbit skarth, ane scorpioun, ane
        scutard behind.
        William Dunbar, The Tretis of the Twa
        Mariit Wemen and the Wedo

35 He dois as dotit dog that damys
        on all bussis,
    And liftis his leg apone loft, thoght he
        nought list pische.
        William Dunbar, The Tretis of the Twa
        Mariit Wemen and the Wedo

36 Mandrag, mymmerkin, maid maister
        but in mows,
    Thrys scheild trumpir with ane threid
        bair goun,
    Say Deo mercy, or I cry the doun.
    – Quod Kennedy to Dunbar
    Iersche brybour bard, vyle beggar with
        thy brattis
    Cuntbittin crawdoun Kennedy, coward
        of kynd . . .
    Thy trechour tung hes tane ane heland
        strynd –
    Ane lawland ers wald mak a bettir noyis.
    – Quod Dunbar to Kennedy
        William Dunbar, The Flyting of
        Dunbar and Kennedie

37 Mr Coleridge was in bad health;– the par-
    ticular reason is not given; but the careful
    reader will form his own conclusions . . .
    Upon the whole, we look upon this publica-
    tion as one of the most notable pieces of
    impertinence of which the press has lately
    been guilty.
        The Edinburgh Review, *anonymous
        review of* Kubla Khan *(1816)*

38 A man does well to rid himself of a turd.
        *King Edward I of England (1239–1307),
        on leaving Scotland after the Battle of
        Falkirk, 1298*

39 One day, sitting opposite Charlemagne at
    a meal, that jester cruelly asked: 'What is
    there betwixt *Sottum* and *Scottum*?' Quick
    came the reply of John: 'The breadth of
    this table, Sire.'
        Arnold Fleming, The Medieval Scots
        Scholar in France *(1952), on John Scotus
        (c.810–c.877)*

40 Today I pronounced a word which should
    never come out of a ladys lips it was that I
    called John an Impudent Bitch.
        Marjory Fleming (1803–1811), Journals

41 The bleatings of a sheep.
        *John Fraser, Professor of Celtic at Oxford
        University, on the Gaelic translations
        of Kenneth Macleod (1871–1955), quoted
        in John M. Bannerman*, Bannerman:
        The Memoirs of Lord Bannerman of
        Kildonan

42 Weill, gin they arena deid, it's time they
    were.
        *Robert Garioch (Robert Garioch
        Sutherland,1909–1981)*, Elegy

43 Union Street has as much warmth in its
    face as a dowager duchess asked to contrib-
    ute to the Red International Relief.
        *Lewis Grassic Gibbon (James Leslie
        Mitchell, 1901–1935), on Aberdeen*

44 We don't get God saying, 'Poor little gay
    men, we'll have to open the church hall
    and let them have their own little gay
    church and their own gay minister.' God
    says, 'To death with them.'
        Pastor Jack Glass, quoted in Steve Bruce,
        No Pope of Rome *(1985)*

45 A very weak fellow, I'm afraid, and, like
    the feather pillow, bears the marks of the
    last person who has sat on him!
        *Earl Haig (1861–1928), Letter to his wife,
        on Lord Derby*

46 Among ourselves, the Scotch, as a nation,
    are particularly disagreeable. They hate
    every appearance of comfort themselves,
    and refuse it to others. Their climate, their
    religion, and their habits are equally averse
    to pleasure. Their manners are either dis-
    tinguished by a fawning sycophance (to

gain their own ends, and conceal their natural defects), that makes one sick; or by a morose, unbending callousness, that makes one shudder.

William Hazlitt (1778–1830), Essays

47 'Ye're nut on, laddie. Ye're on tae nothin' . . . A gutless wonder like you, that hasn't got the gumption of a louse.'

Archie Hind (1928–), The Dear Green Place

48 'You are, sir, a presumptuous, self-conceited pedagogue . . . a mildew, a canker-worm in the bosom of the Reformed Church.'

James Hogg (1770–1835), The Private Memoirs and Confessions of a Justified Sinner

49 The Barbarians who inhabit the banks of the Thames.

David Hume (1711–1766), letter to Sir Gilbert Elliot, October 1769, on the inhabitants of London

50 Mr James MacPherson – I received your foolish and impudent letter. Any violence offered me I shall do my best to repel; and what I cannot do for myself, the law shall do for me . . . I thought your book an imposture; I think it an imposture still . . . what I hear of your morals, inclines me to pay regard not to what you shall say, but to what you shall prove.

Samuel Johnson (1709–1784), letter in reply to a challenge from James Macpherson (1736–1796), author of Fragments of Ancient Poetry

51 Jean Hamilton . . . fell out on me publiklye that I could no spell nor pronounce and then told that I was Kings Advocat and had sold the King as Judas had sold his Master, that their was a Judas heir, that I had killed earle of Montrose . . . that tho I pretended to denye the world I had it fast in my airmes.

Archibald Johnston of Warriston (1611–1663), Diary, June 1656

52 There was very little amusement in the room but a Scotchman to hate . . . At Taylor's, too, there was a Scotchman – not quite so bad for he was as clean as he could get himself.

John Keats (1795–1821), letter quoted in Catherine and Donald Carswell, The Scots Week-End (1936)

53 Though thou're like Judas, an apostate black,
In the resemblance thou dost one thing lack;
When he had gotten his ill-purchased pelf,
He went away and wisely hanged himself:
This thou may do at last, but yet I doubt
If thou hast any bowels to gush out.

Charles Lamb (1775–1834), Epigram on Sir James Mackintosh (1765–1832)

54 . . . lyke ane boisteous bull, ye run and ryde
Ryatouslie lyke ane rude rubiatoure
Ay fukkand lyke ane furious fornicatour.

Sir David Lindsay (c.1486–1555), Answer to the King's Flyting, to King James V

55 *Diligence:* Swyith, begger bogill, haist the away! art over pert to spill our play.
Pauper: I will not gif for all your play worth an sowis fart.

Sir David Lindsay, Ane Satyre of the Thrie Estaitis

56 It is a better and wiser thing to be a starved apothecary than a starved poet: so back to the shop Mr John, back to 'plasters, pills and ointment boxes'.

John Gibson Lockhart (1794–1854), Edinburgh Review, on John Keats's Endymion

57 Servile and impertinent, shallow and pedantic, a bigot and a sot, bloated with family pride, and eternally blustering about the dignity of a born gentleman, yet stooping to be a talebearer, an eavesdropper, a common butt in the taverns of London.

Lord Macaulay (1800–1859), on James Boswell (1740–1795)

58 Ablachs, and scrats, and dorbels o' a' kinds
Aye'd drob me wi' their puir eel-dronin' minds,
Wee drochlin' craturs drutling their bit thochts
The dorty bodies! Feech! Nae Sassunach drings
'll daunton me.

Hugh MacDiarmid (C. M. Grieve, 1872–1978), Gairmscoile (on some contemporary versifiers)

59 In spite of all their kind some elements of worth

With difficulty persist here and there on earth.

> Hugh MacDiarmid, Another Epitaph on an Army of Mercenaries

60 Nearly all the prominent people in Scottish public life today . . . remind me of the oxpeckers, an African genus of starlings. These birds are parasitic on the large mammals whose bodies they search for ticks and other vermin . . . So strikingly prehensile are their claws that Millais relates that when 'a dead bird that had grown stiff was thrown on the back and sides of an ox, so that the feet touched the animal's hide, the claws held fast at once, and could not easily be withdrawn'. That is precisely the relationship of most of these people (all dead – born dead, in fact) to Scottish life.

> Hugh MacDiarmid, Lucky Poet (*1943*)

61 . . . a leader of the white-mouse faction of the Anglo-Scottish *literati* and a paladin in mental fight with the presence of a Larry the Lamb.

> Hugh MacDiarmid, Lucky Poet, *referring to Edwin Muir (1887–1959)*

62 . . . the whole gang of high mucky-mucks, famous fatheads, old wives of both sexes, stuffed shirts, hollow men with headpieces stuffed with straw, bird-wits, lookers-under-beds, trained seals, creeping Jesuses, Scots Wha Ha'evers, village idiots, policemen, leaders of white-mouse factions and noted connoisseurs of bread and butter . . . and all the touts and toadies and lickspittles of the English Ascendancy, and their infernal womenfolk.

> Hugh MacDiarmid, Lucky Poet

63 High falutin' nonsense,
Spiritual masturbation of the worst description.

> Hugh MacDiarmid, Two Scottish Boys, *on the work of Fiona Macleod (William Sharpe, 1856–1905)*

64 Calf-fighter Campbell . . .
there's an operation to do first
– To remove the haemorrhoids you call your poems
. . . the goose,
or bustard rather, that, when its foe comes nigh.
Cocks up its shitepoke and with that lets fly.

> Hugh MacDiarmid, quoted in Edwin

Morgan, Crossing the Border, *on the South African poet Roy Campbell*

65 Here's your likeness again:
a wisp-headed scowler,
without hat or wig,
without headpiece or crest,
you're plucked bald and bare;
with mange at your elbows
and the scratch marks of itch at your arse.

> Duncan Bàn MacIntyre (*1724–1812*), Oran do'n Taillear (Song for the Tailor)

66 . . . You have adopted the rule and course
That Judas, your own brother, followed;
great is the scandal to your country
that such a brute did grow in it . . .
You have talked unsparingly of Scotland,
and had better have kept silent;
Were you to come near the Rough Bounds,
woe to one in your case.

> Duncan Bàn MacIntyre, Oran Iain Faochag (Song to John Wilkes)

67 How could he compose a song
lacking skill and native wit?
. . . in the splutter of talk he produces,
There lives no man who understands his Gaelic.

> Duncan Bàn MacIntyre, Aoir Uisdean (Lampoon on Hugh)

68 A jocular anecdote of old blind Mr Stewart (of Appin). The boy who was reading to him from the Book of Job mispronounced the word *camels*. 'If he had so many Cawmells in his household,' said Mr Stewart, 'I do not wonder at his misthriving.'

> Henry Mackenzie (*1745–1831*), in H. W. Thomson, The Anecdotes and Egotisms of Henry Mackenzie

69 The laird's nae what you would call very intelligent. There's naething in him except what he puts in with a spoon.

> Noted in R. F. Mackenzie, A Search For Scotland (*1989*)

70 Of course, with the kind of people who call Mrs Kennedy-Fraser's travesties of Gaelic songs 'faithful reproductions of the spirit of the original', I have no dispute. They are harmless as long as ignorance and crass-

ness are considered failings in criticism of poetry.

　　Sorley MacLean (1911–1996), Criticism and Prose Writings

71　Ya knee-crept, Jesus-crept, swatchin' little fucker, ah'll cut the bliddy scrotum aff ye! Ah'll knacker and gut ye, ah'll eviscerate ye! Ya hure-spun, bastrified, conscrapulated young prick, ah'll do twenty years for mincin' you . . . ya parish-eyed, perishin' bastart.

　　Roddy MacMillan, The Bevellers *(1973)*

72　You think he's twistit. Ye want tae have seen his oul' man.

　　Roddy MacMillan, The Bevellers

73　Boswell was praising the English highly, and saying they were a fine, open people. 'Oh —,' said Macpherson, 'an open people! their mouths, indeed, are open to gluttony to fill their belly, but I know of no other opennness they have.'

　　James Macpherson (1734–1796), quoted in Charles Rogers, Boswelliana *(1874)*

74　The fattest hog in Epicurus' sty.

　　William Mason, An Heroic Epistle to Sir William Chambers, *on David Hume (1711–1776)*

75　Glasgow has been a great home for the people of Inverness, who used to come down with the hayseed in their boots and the heather sticking out of their ears.

　　James Maxton (1885–1946), speech in the House of Commons, 1934, attacking the MP for Inverness

76　In the furor which followed Boswell's *Life of Johnson*, he was asked what he now thought of Boswell. He replied, 'Before I read his Book I thought he was a Gentleman who had the misfortune to be mad: I now think he is a madman who has the misfortune not to be a Gentleman.'

　　Lord Monboddo (1714–1799), quoted in E. L. Cloyd, James Burnett, Lord Monboddo *(1972)*

77　Polwart, ye peip like a mouse among thornes,
　　No cunning ye keip; Polwart, ye peip;
　　Ye luik lyk a sheip and ye had twa hornes

　　Alexander Montgomerie (c.1545–1611), The Flyting of Montgomerie and Patrick Hume of Polwarth

78　Bewar what thou speikes, little foull earthe taid,
　　With thy Canigait breikis, bewar what thou speiks,
　　Or ther sall be weit cheikes for the last that thou made
　　. . . And we mell thou sall yell, little cultron cuist.

　　Montgomerie to Polwarth, The Flyting of Montgomerie and Polwarth

79　Kaily lippis, kis my hippis, in grippis thou's behint
　　. . . Jock Blunt, thrawin frunt, kis the cunt of ane kow.
　　Purspeiller, hen steiller, cat keiller, now I know thee.
　　Rubiatour, fornicatour by natour, foul fa' thee.

　　Polwarth to Montgomerie, The Flyting of Montgomerie and Polwarth

80　He comes out of the shop
　　with the latest fashion from France
　　and the fine clothes worn on his person
　　yesterday with no little satisfaction
　　are tossed into a corner.

　　Roderick Morison (c.1656–c.1714), Oran do Mhacleòid Dhùn Bheagan (Song for Macleod of Dunvegan), *translated by William Matheson*

81　Jemmy . . . in recording the noble growlings of the Great Bear, thought not of his own Scotch snivel.

　　Christopher North (John Wilson, 1785–1854), Noctes Ambrosianae, *on James Boswell (1740–1795)*

82　For thee, James Boswell, may the hand of Fate
　　Arrest thy goose-quill and confine thy prate! . . .
　　To live in solitude, oh! be thy luck
　　A chattering magpie on the Isle of Muck.

　　Peter Pindar (John Wolcott, 1738–1819), Bozzy and Piozzi

83　I was present in a large company at dinner, when Bruce was talking away. Someone asked him what musical instruments were used in Abyssinia. Bruce hesitated, not being prepared for the question, and at last said, 'I think I saw one *lyre* there.' George Selwyn whispered his next man, 'Yes, and there is one less since he left the country.'

　　John Pinkerton, Walpoliana, *on James Bruce (1730–1794)*

84 When Carlyle's thunder had been followed
by his wife's sparkle, their sardonic host
said in a half-soliloquy which was intended
to be audible: 'As soon as that man's tongue
stops, that woman's begins!'

> *Recorded of Samuel Rogers in Francis
> Espinasse*, Literary Recollections and
> Sketches *(1893)*

85 His breath's like a burst lavy, ye could strip
paint wi' it.

> *Tony Roper*, The Steamie *(1987)*

86 . . . it appeared that Johnson no sooner saw
Smith than he attacked him for some point
of his famous letter on the death of Hume.
'What did Johnson say?' was the universal
enquiry. 'Why, he said,' replied Smith,
with the deepest impression of resentment,
'he said, *you lie!*' 'And what did you reply?'
'I said, *you* are the son of a —.' On such
terms did these two great moralists meet
and part.

> *Sir Walter Scott (1771–1832), in* The
> Life of Samuel Johnson, LLD, *edited
> by J. W. Croker, on the meeting in Glas-
> gow between Adam Smith and Samuel
> Johnson*

87 The Right Honourable Gentleman is
indebted to his memory for his jests, and
to his imagination for his facts.

> *Richard Brinsley Sheridan (1751–1816),
> Speech to the House of Commons, on
> Henry Dundas (1742–1811)*

88 [Palmerston's] manner when speaking is
like a man washing his hands; the Scotch
members don't know what he is doing.

> *Sydney Smith (1771–1845), quoted in
> Lady Holland,* A Memoir

89 I am heartily tired of this Land of Indifference and Phlegm, where the finer
Sensations of the Soul are not felt, and
Felicity is held to consist in stupefying
Port and overgrown Buttocks of Beef,
where Genius is lost, and Taste altogether
extinguished.

> *Tobias Smollett (1721–1771), letter to
> Alexander Carlyle, March 1754, on
> England*

90 The grating scribbler! whose untuned
    Essays
Mix the Scotch Thistle with the English
    Bays;
By either Phoebus preordained to ill,

The hand prescribing, or the flattering
    quill,
Who doubly plagues, and boasts two Arts
to kill.

> *J. M. Smythe,* One Epistle to Mr Alex-
> ander Pope, *on the doctor-poet John
> Arbuthnot (1667–1735)*

91 Sin a' oor wit is in oor wame
Wha'll flyte us for a lack o' lair;
Oor guts maun glorify your name
Sin a' oor wit is in oor wame.

> *William Soutar (1898–1943),* From Any
> Burns Club to Scotland

92 . . . up to his death three years earlier she
had been living with Lord Alfred Douglas,
the fatal lover of Oscar Wilde, an arrange-
ment which I imagine would satisfy any
woman's craving for birth controlith . . .
I was young and pretty; she had totally
succumbed to the law of gravity without
attempting to do a thing about it . . . I used
to think it a pity that her mother rather
than she had not thought of birth control.

> *Muriel Spark (1918–),* Curriculum
> Vitae, *on Marie Stopes*

93 He is cauld kail in Aberdeen (or should
we say St Andrews?) preaching against hot
haggis; the coldest of cold water prelect-
ing on the ardour of whisky. His voice is
pitched to the pious tuning of the Pharisee
who thanked God he was not as this Publican . . . He swims serene in a sea of moral
platitudes.

> *James Thomson (1834–1882),* The Lib-
> eral *(1879), on a life of Burns by Princi-
> pal Shairp of St Andrews University*

94 There is a certain class of clever Scotsmen,
who complete their education at the University of Oxford, with results not very
creditable to themselves, or to the country of their origin . . . possessed with an
innate flunkeyism which leads them, not
merely to bow down to and humbly accept
Anglian ideas and Anglicising influences;
but also with these, a desire to belittle the
country which gave them birth, and to
sneer at Scottish ways.

> *T. D. Wanliss, in* The Thistle *(December
> 1912), attacking Professor J. H. Millar
> of Edinburgh University, quoted in H. J.
> Hanham,* Scottish Nationalism *(1969)*

95 Dr Taylor, the oculist, was one evening
supping at William Earl of Dumfries's, at

Edinburgh. He harangued with his usual fluency and impudence, and boasted that he knew the thoughts of everybody by looking at their eyes. The first Lady Dumfries, who was hurt with his behaviour, asked him with a smile of contempt, 'Pray, sir, do you know what I am thinking?'

'Yes, madam,' said he.

'Then', replied the countess, 'it's very safe, for I am sure you will not repeat it.'

> *Alexander Webster (–1784), quoted in*
> *Charles Rodgers, Boswelliana (1874)*

96 Fuck off, ya plukey-faced wee hing-oot.

> *Irvine Welsh (1957–), Trainspotting*

97 Ah don't hate the English. They're just wankers. We're colonised by wankers . . . We're ruled by effete arseholes. What does that make us? The lowest of the fuckin low . . . the most wretched, servile, miserable, patheti a' ooc trash that was ever shat intae creation. Ah don't hate the English. They just git oan wi the shite thuv goat. Ah hate the Scots.

> *Irvine Welsh, Trainspotting*

98 People say that the Souness revolution was responsible for the rise in Rangers support but I think it's more to do with the Government Care in the Community policies, which threw these unfortunates on to the streets.

> *Irvine Welsh, interview on ErinWeb,*
> *1997*

99 . . . the most scandalously cringing of reptiles.

> *John Wilkes (1727–1797), in* The
> North Briton, *on the Scots, quoted in*
> Agnes Mure Mackenzie, *Scottish Pageant 1707–1802 (1950)*

100 It is of Inglis natioune
The common kind conditioune
Of Trewis the wertu to forget,
And rekles of gud Faith to be.

> *Andrew of Wyntoun (c.1350–c.1424),*
> Orygynalle Cronykil of Scotland

Journalism and News

1 The printing-press is either the greatest blessing or the greatest curse of modern times, one sometimes forgets which.

> *J. M. Barrie (1860–1937),* Sentimental
> Tommy

2 Considerable value was placed on what were known as 'human stories', which by definition concerned animals.

> *James Cameron (1911–1985),* Point of
> Departure, *on writing for the* Sunday
> Post

3 Journalism is not and never has been a profession; it is a trade or calling . . . we are at our best craftsmen.

> *James Cameron,* Point of Departure

4 The Press is the Fourth Estate of the realm.

> *Thomas Carlyle (1795–1881),* On
> Heroes, Hero-Worship, and the
> Heroic in History

5 . . . journalism suits the Scot as it is a profession into which you can crawl without enquiry as to your qualifications, and because it is a profession in which the most middling talents will take you a long way.

> *T. W. Crosland,* The Unspeakable Scot
> (1902)

6 The tyrant on the throne
Is the morning and evening press.

> *John Davidson (1857–1909),* Fleet
> Street Eclogues

7 Would you find that news in the *Mearns Chief?* – you wouldn't, so you knew it couldn't be true . . . Ay, the *Mearns Chief* was aye up-to-date, and showed you a photo of Mrs MacTavish winning the haggis at a Hogmanay dance.

> *Lewis Grassic Gibbon (James Leslie*
> *Mitchell, 1901–1935),* Cloud Howe

8 It's all lies and trash anyway.

> *Arran ferryman, on seeing the daily news-*
> *papers falling into the water, 1947, quoted*
> *in Alastair Hetherington,* News, News-
> papers and Television

9 No news is better than evil news.

> *King James VI (1566–1625), quoted in*
> Loseley Manuscripts

10 Donald Cameron had no qualifications for any profession except the ability to drive a moderately crooked furrow and to direct the fire of a six-gun battery of eighteen-pounder guns, and so he resolved to try his fortune as a journalist.

> *A. G. Macdonell (1895–1941),* England,
> Their England

11 He joined the *Daily Record* as Art Editor –
a position, he recalls, which had extremely
little to do with art, and almost nothing to
do with editing.

> *Magnus Magnusson and others*, The Glo-
> rious Privilege *(1957), on Sir Alastair
> Dunnett*

12 It is the natural, nay, we may confidently
say, the necessary effect of a free press, so
to harmonise together the tone of the government and the sentiments of the people,
that no jarring opposition between them
can ever arise.

> *James Mill (1773–1836)*, The Liberty
> of the Press

13 'The old woman's gone.'
'What old woman?'
'The Old Woman Herself.'
'What, Herself?'
'The Old Woman at the Steering.'
'Och, has she gone at last?'
    So that's the way it came to Father Allan's
Island – the news of the death of the Queen
of Great Britain and Ireland.

> *Amy Murray*, Father Allan's Island
> *(1936) (rendering into English of a Gaelic
> conversation)*

14 As far as I'm concerned, Scotland will be
reborn when the last minister is strangled
with the last copy of the *Sunday Post*.

> *Tom Nairn (1932–)*, The Three
> Dreams of Scottish Nationalism, *in
> K. Miller*, Memoirs of a Modern Scot-
> land *(1970)*

15 We cultivate literature on a little oatmeal.

> *Sydney Smith (1771–1845), proposed
> motto for the* Edinburgh Review, *but
> 'too near the truth to be admitted' (Lady
> Holland,* Memoir*)*

16 As a journalist, I rely on two qualifications,
a congenital laziness, and a poor memory.

> *Wilfred Taylor,* Scot Free *(1953)*

Lamentations

1 I am washing the shrouds of the fair men
Who are going out but shall never
    come in;

The death-dirge of the ready-handed men
Who shall go out, seek peril, and fall.

> Song of the River Sprite Nigheag, *from
> Gaelic*

2 When Alysandyr our King was dede
That Scotland led in luf and le,
Away was sons of ale and brede,
Of wine and wax, of gamyn and gle;
Our gold was changyd into lead.
Christ born into Virginitie
Succour Scotland and remede
That stad is in perplexytie.

> *Anonymous, 13th century, on the death of
> Alexander III*

3 Oh, how dolorous, bitter and dark that
unlooked-for day, how mournful and disastrous, how pregnant with tears, calamity,
and grief, forecasting such a time of unrest
and dule. Truly it might be said, 'Woe to
the folk of Scotland, for here is the beginning of all sorrow.'

> *Anonymous,* Liber Pluscardensis *(14th
> century), on the death of Alexander III*

4 It is for our sin that widespread ruin
    now enters in.
The evil we do – alas! that the world
    should love it so.

> *Anonymous,* Poem on the Cause of the
> Plague *(1349), quoted in T. O. Clancy,*
> The Triumph Tree *(1998), from Latin*

5 Half owre, half owre to Aberdour
'Tis fifty fathoms deep,
And there lies gude Sir Patrick Spens,
Wi' the Scots lords at his feet.

> *Anonymous,* Sir Patrick Spens

6 'Ohone, alas, for I was the youngest,
And aye my weird it was the hardest.'

> *Anonymous,* Cospatrick

7 O there is nane in Galloway,
There's nane at a' for me.
I ne'er lo'ed a lad but ane,
And he's drooned in the sea.

> *Anonymous,* The Lawlands o' Holland

8 'Yestreen the Queen had four Maries,
The night she'll hae but three:
There was Marie Seton, and Marie
    Beaton,
And Marie Carmichael, and me . . .
'O, little did my mither ken,
The day she cradled me,

The lands I was to travel in;
The death I was to dee.'

Anonymous, The Queen's Marie

9 To seek het water beneith cauld ice,
   Surely it is a great folie –
   I have asked grace at a graceless face,
   But there is nane for my men and me!

Anonymous, Johnie Armstrong

10 Hame cam' his gude horse,
   But never cam' he.

   Down ran his auld mither,
   Greetin' fu' sair;
   Out ran his bonny bride,
   Reaving her hair:
   My meadow lies green,
   And my corn is unshorn,
   My barn is to bigg,
   And my babe is unborn.

Anonymous, Bonny George Campbell

11 O Helen fair, beyond compare!
   I'll mak' a garland o' thy hair,
   Shall bind my heart for evermair,
   Until the day I dee!

Helen of Kirkconnel

12 I took his body on my back,
   And whiles I gaed, and whiles I sat;
   I digg'd a grave, and laid him in,
   And happ'd him with the sod sae green.

Anonymous, The Lament of the Border
Widow, *traditionally for Piers Cockburn,
hanged by James V in 1529*

13 I sit here alone by the level roadway,
   Trying to meet in with a fugitive
   Coming from Ben Cruachan of the Mist,
   One who will give me news of Clan
      Gregor,
   Or word of where they have gone.

Anonymous (16th century), Clan Gregor
Outlawed (Clann Ghriogair Air
Fogradh)

14 But the broken heart kens nae second
      Spring again,
   Though the waefu' may cease frae their
      greetin'.

Anonymous, Loch Lomond *(19th century), sometimes attributed to Lady John
Scott (1810–1900)*

15 Happy the craw
   That biggs in the Trotten shaw,

And drinks o' the Water o' Dye –
For nae mair may I.

Anonymous

16 The energies of our system will decay;
   the glory of the sun will be dimmed,
   and the earth, tideless and inert, will no
   longer tolerate the race which has for a
   moment disturbed its solitude. Man will
   go down into the pit and all his thoughts
   will perish.

A. J. Balfour (1848–1930), The Foundations of Belief

17 Seventeen years of warding valour,
   In the sovereignty of Alban,
   After slaughtering Cruithneach, after
      embittering Galls,
   He dies on the banks of the Earn.
   It was bad with Alban then,
   Long ere another like him shall come.

St Berchan, Prophecy *(1094), from
Latin, on the death of King Kenneth
MacAlpin*

18 But twice unhappier is he, I lairn,
   That feedis in his hairt a mad desire,
   And follows on a woman throw the fire,
   Led by a blind and teachit by a bairn.

Mark Alexander Boyd (1563–1601),
Cupid and Venus

19 In all the earth like unto me is none,
   Farre from all living I heere lye alone,
   Where I entombed in melancholy sink,
   Choak'd, suffocat, with excremental stink.

Zachary Boyd (c.1585–1653), History of
Jonah

20 Ah, Kingdom of Scotland, I think that
   your days are now shorter than they were,
   and your nights longer, since you have lost
   that princess who was your light.

Pierre de Brantome (c.1530–1614),
Dames Illustres, *on Queen Mary I*

21 Farewell, ye dungeons dark and strong,
   The wretch's destinie!
   McPherson's time will not be long
   On yonder gallows tree.

Robert Burns (1759–1796), McPherson's Farewell

22 But oh! what crowds in ev'ry land,
   All wretched and forlorn,

Through weary life this lesson learn,
That man was made to mourn.
Robert Burns, Man Was Made To
Mourn

23 Few, few shall part where many meet!
The snow shall be their winding-sheet,
And every turf beneath their feet
Shall be a soldier's sepulchre!
Thomas Campbell (1777–1844),
Hohenlinden

24 I've seen the smiling of Fortune
beguiling,
I've felt all its favours and found its decay.
Alison Cockburn (1712–1794), The Flowers of the Forest

25 Now they are moaning on ilka green
loaning,
The flowers o' the Forest are a' wede away.
Jane Elliott (1727–1805), The Flowers
o' the Forest

26 And aye the owercome o' his lilt
Was 'Wae's me for Prince Charlie!'
William Glen (1789–1826), Wae's Me
for Prince Charlie

27 'Twas not a life:
'Twas but a piece of childhood thrown
away!
*David Gray (1838–1861), letter to
Arthur Sutherland (1861) on his own life*

28 They're wearin' by, the guid auld lives
O' leal and thrifty men an' wives;
They're wearin' ooot, the guid auld
creeds,
That met a simple people's needs.
*Hugh Haliburton (John Logie Robertson,
1846–1922), On the Decadence Of
the Scots Language, Manners and
Customs*

29 'My ae fald friend when I was hardest stad!
My hope, my heal, thou wast in
maist honour!
. . . Though I began and took the
war on hand.
I vow to God, that has the warld in wauld,
Thy deid sall be to Southeron full dear
sauld.'
'Blind Harry' (fl. 1490s), Wallace
(Lament for the Graham)

30 Alas, Scotland, to whom sall thou
complain:
Alas, fra pain who sall thee now restrain!,

thy help is fastlie brought to ground,
Thy best chieftain in braith bandis is
bound.
'Blind Harry', Wallace

31 A man is born, a man dies,
And in between are miseries.
J. F. Hendry (1912–), Tir-nan-Og

32 'Ochane! is my breist with stormy
stoundis stad,
Wrappit in woe, ane wretch full of wane.'
Robert Henryson (c.1425–c.1500), The
Testament of Cresseid

33 Woe to the realm that has owre young a
king.
Sir David Lindsay (1490–1555), Complaynt of the Common Weill of
Scotland

34 Lourd on my hert as winter lies
The state that Scotland's in the day.
*Hugh MacDiarmid (C. M. Grieve,
1892–1978)*, Lourd on my Hert

35 Alas! How easily things go wrong!
A sigh too deep or a kiss too long,
And then comes a mist and a weeping rain,
And life is never the same again.
George Macdonald (1824–1905),
Phantastes

36 It is this that has left me afflicted,
That today I am telling your virtues,
And you will not come to hear my tale.
Duncan Bàn MacIntyre (1724–1812),
Cumha Chailean Ghlinn Iubhair
(Lament for Colin of Glenure)

37 . . . deer have extended ranges, while
men have been hunted within a narrower
and still narrower circle. The strong have
fainted in the race for life; the old have
been left to die.
Donald MacLeod (fl. 19th century),
Gloomy Memories (1857), on the Highland Clearances

38 The scene of wretchedness which we witnessed as we entered on the estate of
Col. Gordon was deplorable, nay heartrending . . . I never witnessed such
countenances – starvation on many faces –
the children with their melancholy looks,
big-looking knees, shrivelled legs, hollow
eyes, swollen-like bellies – God help them,
I never did witness such wretchedness.
Norman MacLeod (1812–1872), Memo-

rials, *quoted in James Hunter*, The Making of the Crofting Community *(1976), on the potato famine of 1847*

39 He fell as the moon in a storm; as the sun from the midst of his course, when clouds rise from the waste of the waves, when the blackness of the storm inwraps the rocks of Ardannidir. I, like an ancient oak on Morven, I moulder alone in my place. The blast has lopped my branches away; and I tremble at the wings of the north. Prince of warriors, Oscur my son! Shall I see thee no more.

    James Macpherson (1736–1796), Fragments of Ancient Poetry

40 I sit on a knoll
All sorrowful and sad,
And I look on the grey sea
In mistiness clad,
And I brood on strange chances
That drifted me here,
Where Scarba and Jura
And Islay lie near.

    Mary MacLeod (c.1615–c.1705), A Song of Exile, *translated from Gaelic*

41 The heroes of the Clan of Conn are dead,
How bitter to our heart is the grief
  for them.
We shall not live long after them . . .
Now that they have gone under the clay
  and are hidden,
To be left after them is a lasting
  sorrow . . .
It is time for the ollamh to go after them,
Now that there will be no presents to the
  poets.

    Cathal MacMhuirich (fl. early 17th century), Elegy on Four Men of Clanranald, *from Gaelic*

42 In this new yeir I see but weir,
Nae cause to sing;
In this new yeir I see but weir,
Nae cause there is to sing.

    Sir Richard Maitland (1496–1586), On the New Yeir 1560

43 It was then we had a King and Court and
  Country of our ain,
But Scotland can never be Old Scotland
  again.

    David Macbeth Moir (1798–1851), Old Scotland's Lament

44 Anis on a day I seemed a seemly sicht.
Thou wants the wight that never said
  thee nay:
Adieu for ay! This is a lang gude nicht!

    Alexander Montgomerie (c.1545–c.1611), A Lang Gudenicht

45 I'll sing thine obsequies with trumpet
  sounds,
And write thine epitaph in blood and
  wounds.

    Marquis of Montrose (1612–1650), Lines on the Execution of King Charles I

46 Sometimes we think of the nations
  lying asleep,
Curled blindly in impenetrable sorrow.

    Edwin Muir (1887–1959), The Horses

47 Here's a health and here's a heartbreak,
  for it's hame, my dear, no more
To the green glens, the fine glens, we
  knew.

    Neil Munro (1864–1930), John O' Lorn

48 Mony a hert will brak in twa,
Should he ne'er come back again . . .
Sweet's the laverock's note, and lang,
Lilting wildly up the glen,
But aye to me he sings ae sang,
Will ye no' come back again?
. . . Better lo'ed ye canna be:
Will ye no' come back again?

    Lady Nairne (1766–1845), Will Ye No' Come Back Again?

49 Woe be to them who choose for a clan
Four-footed people.

    Alexander Nicolson (1827–1893), Skye

50 Fair weill, my lady bricht,
And my remembrance rycht;
Fair weill and haif gud nycht:
I say no moir.

    Alexander Scott (c.1520–c.1590), A Lament

51 Oh and alas, right sad was our case,
We were now all prisoners ta'en.
Our hearts were sair, our purse was bare,
And far we were from hame.

    John Scott (fl. early 18th century), Reminiscences

52 But woe awaits a country when
She sees the tears of bearded men.

    Sir Walter Scott (1771–1832), Marmion

53 This morn is merry June, I trow,
    The rose is budding fain,
    But she shall bloom in winter's snow,
    Ere we two meet again.

    Sir Walter Scott, Rokeby

54 He is gone on the mountain,
    He is lost to the forest,
    Like a summer-dried fountain,
    When our need was the sorest . . .
    Fleet foot on the correi,
    Sage counsel in cumber,
    Red hand in the foray,
    How sound is thy slumber!
    Like the dew on the mountain,
    Like the foam on the river,
    Like the bubble on the fountain
    Thou art gone, and forever.

    Sir Walter Scott, Coronach, *from* The
    Lady of the Lake

55 Our harvests not in the ordinary months,
    many shearing in November and Decem-
    ber, yea, some in January and February;
    many contracting their Deaths and losing
    the Use of Hands and Feet sharing and
    working amongst it in Frost and Snow;
    and after all some of it standing still and
    rotting upon the ground, and much of it
    little use to Man or Beast. When Meal was
    sold in Markets, I have seen Women clap-
    ping their Hands and tearing the clothes
    off their Heads, crying, 'How shall we go
    home and see our children die in Hunger?
    They have got no meat these two days, and
    we have nothing to give them.'

    . . . the living were wearied in the bury-
    ing of the Dead.

    Patrick Walker, Biographia Presbyteri-
    ana, *on the famine years of the late 17th
    century*

The Land

1 Beloved land of the East,
   Alba of marvels . . .
   O that I might not leave the Land
       of the East,
   But that I go with my beloved.

   Anonymous, The Song of Deirdre, *from
   Gaelic, the Glenmasan Manuscript (1238)*

2 I wondered not, when I was told
   The venal Scot his country sold:

   I rather very much admire
   How he could ever find a buyer.

   Anonymous, quoted in Nicholson, Select
   Collection of Poems (1780)

3 Frae Kenmore to Ben More
   The land is a' the Marquis's;
   The mossy howes, the heathery knowes
   And ilka bonny park is his

   Anonymous, The Highland Crofter

4 John Bull, otherwise a good-natured man,
   was very hard-hearted to his sister Peg,
   chiefly from an aversion he had conceived
   in his infancy. While he flourished, kept
   a warm house, and drove a plentiful trade,
   poor Peg was forced to go hawking and
   peddling about the streets, and when she
   could not get bread for her family, she was
   forced to hire them out at journey-work to
   her neighbours. Yet in these poor circumstances she still preserved the air and mien
   of a gentlewoman, a certain decent pride,
   that extorted respect from the haughtiest
   of her neighbours; when she cam into any
   full assembly, she would not yield the *pas*
   to the best of them. If one asked her, 'Are
   you related to John Bull?' 'Yes,' says she,
   'he has the honour to be my brother.'

   *John Arbuthnot (1667–1735), a conceit
   on Scots–English relations, from* The
   Famous History of John Bull *(1712)*

5 Scotland rises as the border of the world.

   Ludovico Ariosto (1474–1533), Orlando
   Furioso *(translated from Italian)*

6 The old proverb says *piscinata Scotia* (Scotland rich in fish).

   *Don Pedro de Ayala, Spanish ambassador
   to James IV, official report, July 1498*

7 Ownership in land exists for the sake of
   the people; not the people for the sake of
   the ownership.

   John Stuart Blackie (1809–1895), The
   Scottish Highlanders and the Land
   Laws

8 Then come and scour the Bens with me,
       ye jolly stalkers all,
   With lawyers to defend your rights, and
       gillies at your call!
   Those crofter carles may cross the sea,
       but we are masters here,

And say to all, both great and small, *Let none disturb the deer.*
> *John Stuart Blackie*, The Scottish High-
> landers and the Land Laws

9 . . . land of the omnipotent No.
> *Alan Bold (1943–)*, A Memory of Death

10 Scotland the wee.
> *Tom Buchan (1931–1995)*, Scotland the
> Wee

11 . . . the lang Scots miles,
The mosses, waters, slaps and styles,
That lie between us and our hame.
> *Robert Burns (1759–1796)*, Tam o'
> Shanter

12 And well I know within that bastard land
Hath wisdom's goddess never held
command . . .
Whose thistle well betrays the niggard
earth,
Emblem of all to whom the land gives
birth:
Each genial influence nurtured to resist:
A land of meanness, sophistry, and mist.
> *Lord Byron (1788–1824)*, The Curse of
> Minerva

13 They burned the rest of them; and this
crofter's was the last. He pleaded hard to
be left in the house till his wife was well.
The factor did not heed him, but ordered
the house to be burned over him. The
crofter was in the house, determined not
to quit until the fire compelled him. The
factor told us the plan we were to take –
namely, to cut the rafters and then set fire
to the thatch. This we did, but I shall never
forget the sight. The man, seeing it was
now no use to persist, wrapt his wife in
the blankets and brought her out. For two
nights did that woman sleep in a sheep-cot,
and on the third night she gave birth to a
son.
> *J. Campbell, letter in the* Inverness
> Courier, *quoted by Joseph Mitchell
> (1803–1883) in* Reminiscences of My
> Life in the Highlands

14 Listening to the oral tradition of the wind.
> *Myles Campbell (1944–)*, An Clamhan
> (The Buzzard)

15 Our fathers fought, so runs the glorious
tale,
To save you, country mine, from tyrants
rash,

And now their bones and you are up
for sale,
The smartest bidder buys for ready cash.
> *J. R. Christie*, My Native Land

16 There is no land in which a man may
live more pleasantly and delicately than in
Scotland.
> *Sir Thomas Craig*, De Unione Regnum
> Britanniae (1603–5)

17 But these I saw while you to butts were
striding
Guided by servile ghillies to your sport.
*Fast-rooted bracken where the corn once
ripened;*
Roofless and ruined homesteads by the score.
> *Helen B. Cruickshank (1886–1975),*
> Shooting Guest, Nonconformist

18 Hame, hame, hame, hame, fain wad I be!
Hame, hame, hame, hame to my ain
countrie!
> *Allan Cunningham (1784–1842)*, Hame,
> Hame, Hame

19 . . . ownership is really custodianship.
> *Sir Frank Fraser Darling (1903–1979),*
> Island Farm

20 First Younger Sister to the Frozen Zone,
Battered by Parent Nature's constant
Frown,
Adept to Hardships, and cut out for Toil;
The best worst Climate and the worst best
Soil.
> *Daniel Defoe (1660–1731)*, Caledonia

21 Scotland was a country to reckon with
as long as she was not incorporated
with England; but, as M. Voltaire said,
a poor country, neighbour to a rich one,
becomes venal at last; and such is Scotland's misfortune.
> *Denis Diderot (1713–1784),*
> L'Encyclopédie, Paris (1751–52)

22 The lowest and vilest alleys of London
do not present a more dreadful record of
sin than does the smiling and beautiful
countryside.
> *Sir Arthur Conan Doyle (1859–1930),*
> The Adventures of Sherlock Holmes:
> The Copper Beeches

23 Did not strong connections draw me else-
where, I believe Scotland would be the

country I should choose to end my days
in.

Benjamin Franklin (1706–1790)

24 It must be owned that man, in much of
his struggle with the world around him,
has fought blindly for his own ultimate
interest. His contest, successful for the
moment, has too often led to sure and sad
disaster. Stripping forests from hill and
mountain, he has gained his immediate
object in the possession of their abundant
stores of timber; but he has laid open the
slopes to be parched by drought, or swept
bare by rain.

Sir Archibald Geikie (1835–1924), Geo-
graphical Evolution

25 . . . and a darkness down on the land he
loved better than his soul or God.

*Lewis Grassic Gibbon (James Leslie
Mitchell, 1901–1935),* Sunset Song

26 And then John Guthrie cried *Get up!* and
swung the horses down the bout, and the
hungry snarl changed to a deep, clogged
growling as the corn was driven on to the
teeth by the swinging reaper flails, and
down the bout, steady and fine, sped the
reaper.

Lewis Grassic Gibbon, Sunset Song

27 Sea and sky and the folk who wrought
and fought and were learnèd, teaching and
saying and praying, they lasted but as a
breath, a mist of fog in the hills, but the
land was forever, it moved and changed
below you, but was forever, you were close
to it and it to you, not at a bleak remove it
held you and hurted you.

Lewis Grassic Gibbon, Sunset Song

28 What a fine and heartsome smell has rank
cow-dung as the childe with the graip
hurls it steady heap upon heap from the
rear of his gurling cart.

*Lewis Grassic Gibbon, quoted in D. K.
Cameron,* The Cornkister Days *(1984)*

29 This is my country
The land that begat me,
These windy spaces
Are surely my own.

Sir Alexander Gray (1882–1967),
Scotland

30 My name is Norval; on the Grampian
hills
My father feeds his flocks.

John Home (1724–1808), Douglas

31 And oh! What grand's the smell ye'll get
Frae the neep-fields by the sea!

Violet Jacob (1863–1946), The Neep-
Fields by the Sea

32 Once you get the hang of it, and appre-
hend the type, it is a most beautiful and
admirable little country – fit, for distinction etc., to make up a trio with Italy and
Greece.

*Henry James (1843–1916), letter to Alice
James, 1878*

33 I am not sure whether Scotland (especially
the West Coast) is not the finest country
in the world, and her people, notwithstanding their awkwardness, the greatest race.

*Benjamin Jowett (1817–1893), letter to
Lady Stanley of Alderley (1890)*

34 . . . in Scotland I felt as if in a second home,
and that I was received as a son, and never
repudiated . . . The chief national characteristics of the Scots are constancy and an
unwearied perseverance. These qualities
have made that dreary and barren land a
home of prosperity, a flourishing paradise.

Lajos Kossuth (1802–1894)

35 So this is your Scotland. It is rather nice,
but dampish and Northern and one shrinks
a trifle under one's skin. For these countries, one should be amphibian.

*D. H. Lawrence (1885–1930), letter to
Dorothy Brett, 1926*

36 Scotland's an attitude of mind.

Maurice Lindsay (1918–), Speaking of
Scotland

37 Scotland small? Our multiform, our
infinite Scotland *small?*
Only as a patch of hillside may be
a cliché corner
To a fool who cries 'Nothing but heather!'

*Hugh MacDiarmid (C. M. Grieve,
1892–1978),* Scotland Small?

38 We are the men
Who own your glen
Though you won't see us there –
In Edinburgh clubs

And Guildford pubs
We insist how much we care.

> John McGrath (1935–), The Cheviot,
> the Stag and the Black, Black Oil

39 So – picture it, if you will, right there at
the top of the glen, beautiful vista – the
Crammem Inn, High-Rise Motorcroft –
all finished in natural, washable, plastic
granitette. Right next door, the 'Frying
Scotsman' All Night Chipperama – with
a wee ethnic bit, Fingal's Café – serving
seaweed suppers in the basket and draught
Drambuie.

> John McGrath, The Cheviot, the Stag
> and the Black, Black Oil

40 Before a Duke came or any of his people
Or a royal George from Hanover's realm,
The low-lying isle, with its many
    shielings
Belonged as a dwelling to the Children of
    the Gael.

> John MacLean of Balemartin, Tiree
> (1866), from Gaelic, quoted in Hugh
> Cheape and I. F. Grant, Periods in High-
> land History (1987)

41 And heavy on the slumber of the
    moorland
The hardship and poverty of the
    thousands
of crofters and the lowly of the lands.

> Sorley Maclean (1911–1996), The
> Cuillin

42 I was present at the pulling down and burning of the house of William Chisholm,
Badinloskin, in which was lying his wife's
mother, an old bed-ridden woman of nearly
100 years of age, none of the family being
present. I informed the persons about to
set fire to the house of this circumstance,
and prevailed upon them to wait until Mr
Sellar came. On his arrival, I told him of
the poor old woman being in a condition
unfit for removal, when he replied, Damn
her, the old witch, she has lived too long –
let her burn.

> Donald MacLeod (c.1814–1857), Gloomy
> Memories

43 It's the far Cuillins that are puttin'
    love on me,
As step I wi' the sunlight for my load . . .
Sure, by Tummel and Loch Rannoch and
    Lochaber I will go,
By heather tracks wi' heaven in their

wiles . . .
It's the blue Islands that are pullin'
    me away,
Their laughter puts the leap upon the
    lame

> Kenneth Macleod (1871–1955), The
> Road to the Isles, Written for the Boys
> in France, 1914

44 In this village
people travel only once
and the stones that made walls
become cairns.

> Aonghas MacNeacail (1942–), glen
> remote

45 The place commanded us by God,
where we can't travel moor or strand,
and every bit of fat or value
they have grabbed with Land Law from
    us.

> Mary Macpherson (1821–1898), Bro-
> snachadh nan Gaidheal (Incitement of
> the Gaels), translated by William Neill

46 It is a stone land, a land hard of bone,
of lean muscle and atrophied membrane
ridged over ribs.
This is a pterodactyl land.

> Donald Macrae (1921–), The Pterodac-
> tyl and Powhatan's Daughter

47 This is a difficult country, and our home.

> Edwin Muir (1892–1978), The Difficult
> Land

48 One of the best places to look at gneiss is
the west coast of Coll, where the hills grip
the beaches in strong pink talons, dividing
them into coves. Here different kinds of
gneiss alternate. The colour is fresh, the
grain either compact or coarsely crystal-
line. The rock sparkles. You might feel a
momentary awe at its age, but will at once
understand why geologists feel affection
for rock so easy on the eye, and call it the
Old Boy.

> W. H. Murray, The Islands of Western
> Scotland (1973)

49 These prodigious wonders in one Coun-
trey are admirable, but these are not half of
them. Loughness never freezes; in Lough
Lommond are fishes without fins: and 2dly
the Waters thereof rage in great waves

without wind in calm weather: and thridly and lastly, therein is a floating island.

> The Observator's New Trip to Scotland (*1708*)

50 *Macduff*: Stands Scotland where it did?
Ross: Alas, poor country,
Almost afraid to know itself, It cannot
Be called our Mother, but our Grave;
   wherre nothing
But who knows nothing, is once seen to smile.

> *William Shakespeare (1564–1616)*,
> Macbeth

51 Scotland is bounded on the South by England, on the East by the rising sun, on the North by the arory-bory-Alice and on the West by Eternity.

> *Nan Shepherd (1893–1981)*, Quarry Wood

52 This is the land God gave to Andy Stewart –

> *Iain Crichton Smith (1928–1998)*, The White Air of March

53 The earth eats everything there is.

> *Iain Crichton Smith*, The Earth Eats Everything

54 When shall I see Scotland again? Never shall I forget the happy days I passed there, amidst odious smells, barbarian sounds, bad suppers, excellent hearts, and most enlightened and cultivated understanding.

> *Sydney Smith (1771–1845), quoted in* Memoir *by Lady Holland*

55 That garret of the earth – that knuckle-end of England – that land of Calvin, oatcakes, and sulphur.

> *Sydney Smith, quoted in* Memoir *by Lady Holland*

56 Son, I've travelled the world, and Scotland is the only country where six and half a dozen are never the same thing.

> *W. Gordon Smith*, Mr Jock (*1987*)

57 ... in truth well named the country of lost causes.

> *William Soutar (1898–1943)*, Journal, *July 1942*

58 Blows the wind today, and the sun and the rain are flying,
Blows the wind on the moors today and now,

Where about the graves of the martyrs the whaups are crying,
My heart remembers how!

> *Robert Louis Stevenson (1850–1894)*,
> Blows the Wind Today

59 If you measure the richness, in terms of content and future, of all the countries of the world that contributed towards the civilisation we now know, Scotland would be way ahead of anywhere except maybe Jerusalem.

> *Norman Stone, quoted in Iain Finlayson*,
> The Scots (*1987*)

60 ... Caledonia, in romantic view,
Her airy mountains, from the waving main
Invested with a keen diffusive sky,
Breathing the soul acute.

> *James Thomson (1700–1748)*, The Seasons

61 Scotland is the country above all others that I have seen, in which a man of imagination may carve out his own pleasures; there are so many *inhabited* solitudes.

> *Dorothy Wordsworth (1771–1855)*, Recollections of a Tour Made in Scotland

The Law

1 Up the Lawnmarket
And doun the West Bow,
Up the lang ladder,
And doun the pickle tow.

> *Traditional Edinburgh rhyme*

2 Art and part.

> (*An accessory after the act): Scots law phrase quoted by Sir Walter Scott (1771–1832) in* Tales of a Grandfather

3 Law is a Bottomless Pit.

> *John Arbuthnot (1667–1735), title of a pamphlet, 1712*

4 To speak well, when I despise both the cause and the judges, is difficult; but I believe I shall do so wonderfully. I look forward with aversion to the little dull labours of the Court of Session.

> *James Boswell (1740–1795), letter to Mr Temple, June 1775*

5 Let them bring me prisoners, and I'll find
   them law.

   *Lord Braxfield (1722–1799), Tory judge
   of the Court of Session*

6 Muckle he made o' that – he was hanget.

   *Lord Braxfield, in a political trial, in
   sotto-voce reply to the comment that
   Jesus Christ too was a reformer, quoted
   by Lord Cockburn in* Memorials of His
   Time *(1856)*

7 Ye're a verra clever chiel', man, but ye'll be
   nane the waur o' a hanging.

   *Lord Braxfield, to a defendant, quoted by
   J. G. Lockhart,* Memoirs of the Life of
   Sir Walter Scott *(1837–8)*

8 A fig for those by law protected!
   Liberty's a glorious feast!
   Courts for cowards were erected,
   Churches built to please the priest.

   Robert Burns (1759–1796), The Jolly
   Beggars

9 At Edinburgh the old judges always had
   wine and biscuits on the bench when the
   business was clearly to be protracted . . .
   Black bottles of strong port were set down
   beside them on the bench with glasses, car-
   affes of watderer, tumblers and biscuits;
   and this without the slightest attempt at
   concealment.

   Henry Thomas Cockburn (1779–1854),
   Memorials

10 We find that the prisoner killit not the particular man aforesaid, yet that *neverthelesse*
   he is deserving of hanging.

   S. R. Crockett (1859–1914), Raiderland,
   on a Galloway jury

11 I knew a very wise man . . . he believed that
   if a man were permitted to make all the
   ballads, he need not care who should make
   the laws of a nation.

   Andrew Fletcher of Saltoun (1653–1716),
   An Account of a Conversation Concerning a Right Regulation of Gov-
   ernments for the Common Good of
   Mankind

12 When Lord Meadowbank was yet Mr
   Maconochie, he one day approached his
   facetious professional brother, John Clerk
   of Eldin, and after telling him he had
   prospects of being raised to the bench,
   asked him to suggest what name he should
   adopt.

   'Lord Preserve Us,' said Clerk, and moved
   on.

   Robert Ford, Thistledown *(1901)*

13 God help the people who have such
   judges.

   *Charles James Fox (1749–1806), on the
   Court of Session in the 1790s*

14 There was a characteristic touch of Scots
   kindliness and sympathy with poverty in
   the law of the time, exempting from the
   category of thief, with its consequent penalty, a man who, being in utmost necessity
   and with no other means to supply it,
   took meat from another. No man could be
   charged with theft for as much meat as he
   could carry on his back.

   H. Grey Graham, The Social Life of
   Scotland in the Eighteenth Century
   (1899)

15 Great public satisfaction was felt when a
   well-known offender sat upon a cuck-stool,
   with neck and hand in the pillory, having
   his ears nailed to the same, or, with still
   further refinement of cruelty, stood with
   his ear nailed until he summoned resolution to 'tear away his lug with the gristle'.

   H. Grey Graham, The Social Life of
   Scotland in the Eighteenth Century

16 . . . when a poor man was found guilty
   by his master, the proprietor of Ballindal-
   loch, and put into the pit until the gallows
   was prepared, he drew a short sword and
   declared he would kill the first man that
   put a hand on him, his wife remonstrated
   and prevailed on him with the argument,
   'Come up quietly and be hanged, and do
   not anger the laird.'

   Hall's Travels in Scotland, *quoted in
   Graham,* The Social Life of Scotland
   in the Eighteenth Century

17 The law knows it can either say 'It's against
   the law to go on strike', and jail the lot
   of us; or it can say 'But then there will
   be no-one left to build ships', and leave
   us alone. What decision the law takes
   depends on how much the country needs
   what you've got.

   Chris Hannan (1958–), Elizabeth
   Gordon Quinn

18 That's checkmate to you, Matthew.

> *Attributed to Lord Kames (1696–1782),*
> *pronouncing the death sentence in 1780 on*
> *Matthew Hay, with whom he had played*
> *an unfinished chess game. But Joseph Reed*
> *and Frederick Pottle, editors of Boswell's*
> Journals, *have ascertained it was said to*
> *the defendant's counsel and not to Hay.*

19 Justice may nocht have dominatioun,
But where Peace makis habitatioun.

> *Sir David Lindsay (c.1490–1555),* The
> Dreme of the Realme of Scotland

20 I, Donald of Donalds, sitting in Dundonald, give to Mackay a right to Kilmahunaig from today till tomorrow, and from that forever.

> *Charter from the Lord of the Isles, 15th*
> *century, quoted in Agnes Mure Mackenzie,*
> Scottish Pageant 55 BC–AD 1513, *from*
> *Gaelic*

21 A Judge has sentenced himself to a
    suicide's grave?
– The nearest to a just sentence any judge
    ever gave.

> *Hugh MacDiarmid (C. M. Grieve,*
> *1892–1978),* A Judge Commits Suicide

22 In just about every case I've investigated, I've wanted to implicate as many people as I could, including myself. My ideal dock would accommodate the population of the world. We would all give our evidence, tell our sad stories and then there would be a mass acquittal and we would all go away and try again.

> *William McIlvanney (1936–),* Strange
> Loyalties

23 When ane of them sustenis wrang,
We cry for justice' heid, and hang;
But when our neichbours we owr-gang
We lawbour justice to delay.

> *Sir Richard Maitland (1496–1586),*
> Satire on the Age

24 Never give your reasons; for your judgement will probably be right, but your reasons almost certainly will be wrong.

> *Lord Mansfield (1705–1793),* Advice to
> Judges

25 On one occasion an old woman, accused of being a witch, was brought before him. She was also charged with walking through the air. The judge listened attentively to all the evidence and then dismissed the accused woman. 'My opinion', he said, 'is that this good woman should be suffered to return home, and whether she shall do this, walking on the ground or riding through the air, must be left entirely to her own pleasure, for there is nothing contrary to the laws of England in either.'

> *Lord Mansfield, quoted in Daniel George,*
> A Book of Anecdotes

26 I remember . . . that when a Justice of Peace court was sitting in my native town, may years ago, a dark cloud came suddenly over the sun; and that a man who had been lounging on the street below, ran into the Court-room to see who it was that, by swearing a false oath, had occasioned the obscuration.

> *Hugh Miller (1820–1856),* Notes and
> Legends of the North of Scotland

27 Laws were made to be broken.

> *Christopher North (John Wilson,*
> *1785–1854),* Noctes Ambrosianae

28 An advocate complaining to his friend, an eminent legal functionary of the last century, that his claims to a judgeship had been overlooked, added acrimoniously, 'and I can tell you they might have got a *waur,*' to which the only answer was a grave '*Whaur?*'

> *Dean E. B. Ramsay (1793–1872),*
> Reminiscences of Scottish Life and
> Character

29 . . . that bastard verdict, *Not proven.* I hate that Caledonian *medium quid.* One who is not proven guilty is innocent in the eye of law.

> *Sir Walter Scott (1771–1832),* Journal,
> *(1827)*

30 No laws, however stringent, can make the idle industrious, the thriftless provident, or the drunken sober.

> *Samuel Smiles (1816–1904)* Self-Help

31 . . . you are a most notorious offender. You stand convicted of sickness, hunger, wretchedness, and want.

> *Tobias Smollett (1721–1771),* The Expedition of Humphrey Clinker

32 'And what would the clan think if there
was a Campbell shot, and naebody hanged,
and their own chief the Justice-General?'

> *Robert Louis Stevenson (1850–1894),*
> Kidnapped

33 I have been the means, under God, of hanging a great number, but never just such a
disjaskit rascal as yourself.

> *Robert Louis Stevenson*, Weir of
> Hermiston

34 Here enter not Attorneys, Barristers,
Nor bridle-champing law-Practitioners:
Clerks, Commissaries, Scribes nor
   Pharisees,
Wilful disturbers of the People's ease:
Judges, destroyers, with an unjust breath,
Of honest men, like dogs, ev'n unto death.
Your salary is at the gibbet-foot:
Go drink there

> *Sir Thomas Urquhart (1611–1660),*
> *Translation from Rabelais,* Gargantua
> and Pantagruel

Love

1 Follow love, and it will flee:
Flee it, and it follows ye.

> *Anonymous*

2 It is a pity I was not with the Black-haired
Lad on the brow of the hill under the rain-
storms, in a small hollow of the wilds or in
some secret place; and I'll not take a greybeard while you come to my mind.

> *Anonymous, from Gaelic, translated by*
> *Kenneth Jackson*

3 The white bloom of the blackthorn, she;
The small sweet raspberry blossom, she;
More fair the shy, rare glance of her eye
Than the world's wealth to me.

> *Anonymous, from Gaelic*

4 My heart is heich abufe,
My body is full of bliss,
For I am set in lufe,
As weil as I wald wiss.

> *Anonymous*, My Heart is Heich Abufe

5 Ane lad may luve ane lady of estate
Ane lord ane lass: luve has no uthir law.
Wha can undo that is predestinate?

> *Anonymous*

6 I lean'd my back unto an aik,
I thought it was a trusty tree;
But first it bow'd, and syne it brak,
Sae my true love did lightly me.

O waly, waly! but love be bonnie
A little time, while it is new;
But when 'tis auld, it waxeth cauld,
And fades away like morning dew.

> *Anonymous*, O Waly, Waly

7 And wow! but they were lovers dear,
And lov'd fu' constantlie;
But ay the mair when they fell out,
The sairer was their plea.

> *Anonymous*, Young Benjie

8 'O Annie, Annie,' loud he cried,
'O Annie, Annie, bide!'
But aye the mair he cried 'Annie,'
The braider grew the tide.

> *Anonymous*, The Lass of Lochroyan

9 Why weep ye by the tide, ladye,
Why weep ye by the tide?
I'll wed ye to my youngest son,
And ye shall be his bride.
And ye shall be his bride, ladye,
Sae comely to be seen:
But aye she loot the tear doon fa'
For Jock o' Hazeldean.

> *Anonymous*, Jock o' Hazeldean

10 They sought her baith by bower and ha',
The lady was na seen;
She's owre the border and awa
Wi' Jock o' Hazeldean.

> Jock o' Hazeldean

11 Willie's rare, and Willie's fair;
And Willie's wondrous bonny:
And Willie hecht to marry me,
Gin e'er he married ony.

> *Anonymous*, Willie's Rare

12 And fain wad I marry Marion,
Gin Marion wad marry me.

> *Anonymous*, The Ewe-Bughts

13 Of all thir maidens mild as meid
Was nane say gymp as Gillie;
... Though a' her kin suld hae bin deid,
Sche wuld hae bot sweit Willie.

> *Anonymous*, Christis Kirk on the
> Green, *sometimes ascribed to King James*
> *V (1512–1542)*

14 He grew canty and she grew fain,
But little did her auld minny ken
What thir slee twa togither were sayn
   Anonymous, The Gaberlunzie Man

15 For harmis of bodie, handis and heid
The pottingar will purge the painis:
But all the membris are at feid
Quhair that the law of luve remainis.
   Anonymous, from the Bannatyne manu-
   scripts (collected 1568)

16 Tho' his richt e'e doth skellie, an' his left
   leg doth limp ill,
He's won the heart and got the hand of
   Kate Dalrymple.
   Anonymous, Kate Dalrymple

17 Kissed yestreen, and kissed yestreen,
Up the Gallowgate, down the Green:
I've woo'd wi' lords, and woo'd wi' lairds
I've mool'd wi' carles, and mell'd wi'
   cairds,
But the ae best kiss that e'er I had
Was the ane I gat frae the yellow-hair'd
   lad.
   Anonymous

18 My beloved sall ha'e this he'rt tae break,
Reid, reid wine and the barley cake,
A he'rt tae break, and a mou' tae kiss,
Tho' he be nae mine, as I am his.
   Marion Angus (1866–1946), Mary's
   Song

19 Gif she to my desire wad listen,
I wadna caa the king my cuisin.
   J. K. Annand (1908–1993), My Weird
   Is Comforted

20 There is no worldly pleasure here below
Which by experience doth not folly prove;
But among all the follies that I know,
The sweetest folly in the world is love
   Sir Robert Aytoun (1570–1638), On
   Love

21 Yea, I have died for love, as others do;
But praised be God, it was in such a sort
That I revived within an hour or two.
   Sir Robert Aytoun, On Love

22 If I ever really love it will be like Mary
Queen of Scots, who said of her Bothwell
that she could follow him round the world
in her nighty.
   J. M. Barrie (1860–1937), What Every
   Woman Knows

23 Convuls'd in Love's tumultuous throes
We feel the aphrodisian spasm;
Tir'd nature must at last repose,
Then wit and wisdom fill the chasm.
   James Boswell (1740–1795), Epitha-
   lamium on Dr J. and Mrs T.

24 . . . a certain delicious Passion, which in
spite of acid Disappointment, gin-horse
Prudence and bookworm Philosophy, I
hold to be the first of human joys, our dearest pleasure here below . . . Thus with me
began Love and Poesy.
   Robert Burns (1759–1796), letter to Dr
   John Moore, 1787

25 She is a winsome wee thing,
She is a handsome wee thing,
She is a lo'esome wee thing,
This dear wee wife o' mine.
   Robert Burns, My Wife's a Winsome
   Wee Thing

26 Bonnie wee thing, cannie wee thing,
Lovely wee thing, wert thou mine,
I would hold thee in my bosom,
Lest my jewel I should tine.
   Robert Burns, Bonnie Wee Thing

27 My luve is like a red, red rose,
That's newly sprung in June;
My luve is like a melody,
That's sweetly play'd in tune.

But fair thou art, my bonie lass,
So deep in luve am I;
And I will luve thee still, my dear,
Till a' the seas gang dry.
Till all the seas gang dry, my dear,
And the rocks melt wi' the sun,
And I will love thee still, my dear,
While the sands o' life shall run.
   Robert Burns, My Luve is Like a Red,
   Red Rose

28 Ilka lassie has her laddie,
Nane, they say, ha'e I:
Yet a' the lads they smile at me,
When comin' through the rye.
   Robert Burns, Comin' Through the
   Rye

29 It is the wish'd, the trysted hour.
   Robert Burns, Mary Morison

30 Tho' this was fair, and that was braw,
And yon the toast of a' the town,

I sigh'd, and said amang them a',
'Ye are na Mary Morison.'
  Robert Burns, Mary Morison

31 The wild woods grow, and rivers row,
And mony a hill between,
But day and night my fancy's flight
Is ever with my Jean.
  Robert Burns, O' A' the Airts the Wind
  Can Blaw

32 I'll meet thee on the lea-rig,
My ain kind dearie, O.
  Robert Burns, My Ain Kind Dearie

33 My love she's but a lassie yet;
My love she's but a lassie yet:
We'll let her stand a year or twa:
She'll nae be half sae saucy yet.
  Robert Burns, My Love She's But a
  Lassie Yet

34 And ilka bird sang o' his love,
And fondly sae did I o' mine.
Wi' lightsome heart I pu'd a rose
Fu' sweet upon its thorny tree:
But my fause lover staw my rose,
But oh! he left the thorn wi' me.
  Robert Burns, Ye Banks and Braes o'
  Bonnie Doon

35 But steal me a blink o' your bonnie
  black e'e,
Yet look as if ye werena lookin' at me . . .
O whistle and I'll come to you, my lad.
  Robert Burns, O Whistle and I'll Come
  to You

36 Had we never lov'd sae kindly,
– Had we never lov'd sae blindly,
Never met – or never parted,
We had ne'er been broken-hearted.
  Robert Burns, Parting Song to Clarinda

37 It ne'er was wealth, it ne'er was wealth,
That coft contentment, peace or pleasure;
The bands and bliss o' mutual love,
O! that's the chiefest warld's treasure.
  Robert Burns, The Lads o' Gala Water

38 When I roved a young Highlander
  o'er the dark heath,
And climbed thy steep summit, oh
  Morven of snow!
To gaze on the torrent that thunder'd
  beneath,
Or the mist of the tempest that gather'd
  below,
Untutor'd by science, a stranger to fear,
And rude as the rocks where my
  infancy grew,
No feeling, save one, to my bosom
  was dear:
Need I say, my sweet Mary, 't was centred
in you?
  Lord Byron (1788–1824), When I
  Roved a Young Highlander

39 Lord Ullin reached the fatal shore,
His wrath was changed to wailing . . .
One lovely hand she stretched for aid,
And one was round her lover.
  Thomas Campbell (1777–1844), Lord
  Ullin's Daughter

40 For Godsake write the instant this reaches
you, if you have not done before. I shall
learn no lesson, settle no occupation, till I
have your Letter. Wretch! You cannot conceive what anxiety I am in about you.
  Jane Welsh Carlyle (1801–1866), letter to
  Thomas Carlyle, May 1824

41 My daddy is a cankered carle,
He'll no twine with his gear;
But let them say or let them do,
It's a' ane to me:
For he's low doun – he's in the broom,
That's waiting for me.
  James Carnegie (fl. 18th century), It's A'
  Ane To Me (1765)

42 Her brow is like the snaw-drift,
Her neck is like the swan;
Her face it is the fairest
That e'er the sun shone on.
That e'er the sun shone on,
And dark blue is her e'e:
And for bonnie Annie Laurie
I'd lay me doun and dee.
  William Douglas (fl. c.1700), Annie
  Laurie

43 The flow'rs did smile, like those upon
  her face,
And as their aspen stalks those fingers
  band,
That she might read my case,
A hyacinth I wish'd me in her hand.
  William Drummond (1585–1649), Like
  the Idalian Queen

44 Lassie wi' the yellow coatie,
Will ye wed a muirlan' Jockie?
  James Duff (fl. early 19th century),
  Lassie Wi' the Yellow Coatie

45 'Had you spoken as well for yourself, I
    might have answered differently.'

    Mary Erskine, refusing an offer of mar-
    riage made on behalf of a shy friend by
    Alexander Webster (?–1784), quoted in
    Charles Rodger, Boswelliana *(1874). She*
    and Webster subsequently married.

46 So it was she knew she liked him, loved
    him as they said in the soppy English
    books, you were shamed and a fool to say
    that in Scotland.

    Lewis Grassic Gibbon (James Leslie
    Mitchell, 1901–1935), Sunset Song

47 A nice wee lass, a bonnie wee lass,
    Is bonnie wee Jeannie McColl;
    I gave her ma mither's engagement ring
    And a bonnie wee tartan shawl.
    I met her at a waddin'
    In the Co-operative Hall,
    I was the best man,
    And she was the belle o' the ball.

    Joe Gordon, Bonnie Wee Jeannie
    McColl

48 If doughty deeds my lady please,
    Right soon I'll mount my steed . . .
    Then tell me how to woo thee, Love,
    O tell me how to woo thee!

    Robert Graham of Gartmore
    (c.1735–1797), O Tell Me How to Woo
    Thee

49 Busk ye, busk ye, my bonnie bride,
    Busk ye, busk ye, my winsome marrow.

    William Hamilton (1704–1754), Busk
    Ye, Busk Ye

50 Flooer o the gean,
    yere aefauld white she wore yestreen.
    Wi gentle glances aye she socht me.
    Dwell her thochts whaur dwalt her een?

    George Campbell Hay (1915–1984),
    Flooer o the Gean

51 'At lufis lair gif thou will lear,
    Tak there ane a b c:
    Be heynd, courtass, and fair of feir,
    Wyse, hardy and free.'

    Robert Henryson (c.1425–c.1500),
    Robene and Makyne

52 Give me the highest joy
    That the heart o' man can frame:

My bonnie, bonnie lassie,
When the kye come hame.

    James Hogg (1770–1835), When the
    Kye Come Hame

53 But O, her artless smile's mair sweet,
    Than hinny or than marmalete.

    James Hogg, My Love She's But a
    Lassie Yet

54 O love, love, love!
    Love is like a dizziness
    It winna let a poor body
    Gang about his biziness.

    James Hogg

55 I'll woo her as the lion woos his brides.

    John Home (1724–1808), Douglas

56 So ferre I falling into lufis dance,
    That sodeynly my wit, my contenance,
    My hert, my will, my nature and my
       mynd,
    Was changit clene rycht in ane other kind.

    King James I (1394–1437), The Kingis
    Quair

57 I have watched thy heart, dear Mary,
    And its goodness was the wile.
    That has made thee mine for ever,
    Bonny Mary of Argyle.

    C. Jefferys, Bonny Mary of Argyle

58 She fairly won my fancy, and stole away
       my heart,
    Drivin' intae Glesca on the soor milk cart.

    Thomas Johnstone (fl. late 19th century),
    The Soor Milk Cart

59 I love a lassie, a bonnie, bonnie lassie;
    She's as pure as the lily in the dell.
    She's as sweet as the heather,
    The bonny purple heather,
    Mary, my Scotch bluebell.

    Sir Harry Lauder (1870–1950), Mary,
    My Scotch Bluebell

60 O sair did we greet, and mickle did we
       say;
    We took but ae kiss, and we tore ourselves
       away.

    Lady Anne Lindsay (1750–1826), Auld
    Robin Gray

61 *Leeze, or leeze me on . . . to be satisfied with,*
    to be pleased or delighted with. A Gaelic
    periphrase for 'I love.' The Highlanders

do not say, 'I love you,' but 'love is on me
for you.'

    Charles Mackay (1814–1889), The
    Poetry and Humour of the Scottish
    Language

62 His very foot has music in't
    When he comes up the stair.

      W. J. Mickle (1734–1788), The Mari-
      ner's Wife

63 Art ye on sleip, quod she. O fye for shame!
    Haf ye nocht tauld that luifaris takis no
    rest?

      Alexander Montgomerie (c.1545–c.1610),
      A Dream

64 The fire that's blawn on Beltane een
    May weel be black gin Yule;
    But blacker faa awaits the heart
    Where first fond love grows cool.

      William Motherwell (1797–1835), Jean-
      nie Morrison

65 'If you're goin' to speak aboot love, be
    dacent and speak aboot it in the Gaalic. But
    we're no talkin' aboot love: we're talkin'
    aboot my merrage.'

      Neil Munro (1864–1930), The Vital
      Spark

66 The sodger frae the wars returns,
    The sailor frae the main;
    But I hae parted frae my love,
    Never to meet again.

      *Captain Ogilvie of Inverquharity (fl. 18th
      century)*, It Was A' For Our Rightful'
      King

67 'Why, he's an authority, he knows as much
    as anybody alive about the life of the her-
    ring. Man', she said, angry at the sceptical
    look which still lingered on the Minister's
    face, 'don't you see he is the most romantic,
    the only romantic, man I have ever met!'

      Neil Paterson (1915–1995), Behold Thy
      Daughter

68 Ye're a bonny lad, and I'm a lassie free,
    Ye're welcomer to tak' me than to let me
    be.

      Allan Ramsay (1686–1758)

69 My Peggy is a young thing,
    And I'm nae very auld.

      Allan Ramsay, The Waukin' o' the
      Fauld

70 The Yellow-haired Laddie sat doon on
      yon brae,
    Cried – Milk the ewes, Lassie! Let nane
      o' them gae!
    And ay she milked, and aye she sang –
    The Yellow-haired Laddie shall be my
      gudeman!

      Allan Ramsay, The Yellow-Haired
      Laddie

71 While hard and fast I held her in my grips,
    My very saul came lowping to my lips.

      Allan Ramsay

72 'But gin ye'll just come hame wi' me,
    An' lea'e the carle, your father,
    Ye'se get my breeks to keep in trim,
    Mysel', an' a' thegither.'

    'Deed, lad,' quo' she, 'Your offer's fair,
    I really think I'll tak' it,
    Sae gang awa', get out the mare,
    We'll baith slip on the back o't.'

      Alexander Rodger (1784–1846), My
      Auld Breeks

73 Love is ane fervent fire
    Kendillit without desire;
    Short pleasure, lang displeasure,
    Repentence is the hire.

      Alexander Scott (c.1520–c.1590), A
      Rondel of Luve

74 Whatten ane glaikit fule am I
    To slay myself with melancholy,
    Sen weill I ken I may nocht get her?

      Alexander Scott, To Luve Unluvit

75 Oppressit hairt, indure
    In dolour and distress,
    Wappit without recure
    In wo remediless.
    Sen sche is merciless
    And causis all thy smert
    Quhilk suld thy dolour dress,
    Indure, oppressit hairt.

      Alexander Scott, Oppressit Hairt,
      Indure

76 Love swells like the Solway, but ebbs like
    its tide.

      Sir Walter Scott (1771–1832),
      Lochinvar

77 She look'd down to blush, and she look'd
      up to sigh,
    With a smile on her lips and a tear in her
      eye.

      Sir Walter Scott, Lochinvar

78   Love rules the court, the camp, the grove,
     And men below and saints above;
     For love is heaven, and heaven is love.
          Sir Walter Scott, The Lay of the Last
          Minstrel

79   It is best to be off wi' the old love
     Before ye be on wi' the new.
          Sir Walter Scott, The Bride of
          Lammermoor

80   For love, they say, gives one an air,
     And ev'n improves the mind.
          John Skinner (1721–1807), John of
          Badenyon

81   Thy fatal shafts unerring move,
     I bow before thine altar, Love.
          Tobias Smollett (1721–1771), The Adven-
          tures of Roderick Random

82   A' thru the nicht we spak nae word
     Nor sinder'd bane frae bane:
     A' thru the nicht I heard her hert
     Gang soundin' wi' my ain.
          William Soutar (1898–1943), The Tryst

83   I will make you brooches and toys for
          your delight
     Of bird-song at morning and star-shine at
          night.
          Robert Louis Stevenson (1850–1894),
          Romance

84   Absences are a good influence in love, and
     keep it bright and delicate.
          Robert Louis Stevenson, Virginibus
          Puerisque

85   I will twine thee a bow'r
     By the clear siller fountain,
     An' I'll cover it o'er
     Wi' the flowers o' the mountain.
          Robert Tannahill (1774–1810), The
          Braes o' Balquhidder, *adapted by Francis
          McPeake (20th century) as* Wild Moun-
          tain Thyme

86   We always believe our first love is our last,
     and our last love our first.
          George Whyte-Melville (1821–1878)

Men and Women

1   Though all the wood under the heaven
          that growis
     Were crafty pennis convenient to write . . .
     All the men were writtaris that ever
          took life
     Could not not write the false dissaitful
          despite
     And wicketness contenit in a wife.
          Anonymous

2   We lighted down to bait our steed,
     And out there came a lady sheen;

     Wi' four and twenty at her back
     A' comely clad in glisterin' green;
     Tho' the King of Scotland had been there,
     The warst o' them might ha' been his
          queen.
          Anonymous, The Wee Wee Man

3   He has sent to the wood
     For whins and hawthorn,
     An' he has ta'en that gay lady,
     An' there he did her burn.
          Anonymous, The Laily Worm and the
          Machrel o' the Sea

4   When Aberdeen and Ayr are baith ae
          toun,
     And Tweed sall turn and rinnis into
          Tay . . .
     When Paradise is quit of heavenly hue,
     She whom I luve sall steadfast be and true.
          Anonymous

5   'Gif ye'll not wed a tocherless wife,
     A wife will ne'er wed ye.'
          Anonymous, Lord Thomas and Fair
          Annet

6   'Now stay for me, dear Annet,' he said,
     'Now stay, my dear,' he cried;
     Then strake the dagger untill his heart,
     And fell dead by her side.
          Anonymous, Lord Thomas and Fair
          Annet

7   'A bed, a bed,' Clerk Saunders said,
     'A bed for you and me.'
     'Fye na, fye na,' said may Margaret,
     'Till anes we married be.'
          Anonymous, Clerk Saunders

8   'I'll wager, I'll wager, I'll wager wi' you
     Five hundred merks and ten,
     That a maid shanna gae to the bonny
          broom
     And a maiden return again.'
          Anonymous, The Broomfield Hill

9   'Come doun to me, ye lady gay,
     Come doun, come doun to me;

Thos night sall ye lig within my arms,
Tomorrow my bride sall be.'

'I winna come doun, ye fals Gordon,
I winna come doun to thee
I winna forsake my ain dear lord,
That is sae far frae me.'

Anonymous, Edom o' Gordon

10 It's narrow, narrow, mak your bed,
And learn to lie your lane;
For I'm gaun far owre the sea, Fair Annie,
A braw bride to bring hame.
Wi' her I will get gowd and gear,
Wi' you I ne'er gat nane.

Anonymous, Fair Annie

11 Word is to the kitchen gane,
And word is to the ha'.
And word is to the noble room
Amang the ladies a',
That Marie Hamilton's brought to bed,
And the bonny babe's miss'd and awa'.

Anonymous, The Queen's Marie

12 Then up sho gat ane meikle rung
And the gudeman made to the door;
Quoth he, 'Dame, I sall hauld my tongue,
For, an we fecht, I'll get the waur.'

Anonymous, The Wife of
Auchtermuchty

13 They say in Fife
That next to nae wife,
The best thing is a gude wife.

Traditional male saying

14 Bell, my wife, she lo'es nae strife,
But she would guide me if she can;
And to maintain an easy life,
I aft maun yield, though I'm gudeman.
I think the warld is a' gane wrang
When ilka wife her man wad rule.

Anonymous, Tak' Your Auld Cloak
About Ye

15 Mealie was his sark,
Mealie was his siller,
Mealie was the kiss,
That I gat frae the miller.

Anonymous

16 Roseberry to his lady says,
'My hinnie and my succour,
O shall we dae the thing ye ken.
Or shall we hae our supper?'

Wi' modest face, sae fu' o' grace
replies the bonnie lady,

'My lord, ye may do as ye please:
But supper is na ready.'

*Anonymous, 18th century, though the orig-
inal is ancient Greek*

17 Waiting at the sheiling O, Mhairi Bhan
Mo Chridh;
Looking from the sheiling, O, far away
to sea:
Homeward come the bonnie boats,
Mhairi Bhan Mo Chridh,
And homeward come the bonnie lads, sing
hey and ho and hee, O!

Traditional Hebridean song, from Gaelic

18 But the plooman laddie's my delight,
The ploooman laddie loe's me;
When a' the lave gang tae their bed,
The plooman comes an' sees me.

Anonymous, farm song, 18th century

19 The ploughman lad's a jolly lad,
He spends his money free,
And when he meets a bonny lass,
He taks her on his knee.

Anonymous, bothy song, 19th century

20 The weaker sex, to piety more prone.

Sir William Alexander (c.1567–1640),
Doomsday

21 The women are courteous in the extreme.
I mention this because they are really
honest, though very bold. They are absolute mistresses of their houses and even
of their husbands, in all things concerning the administration of their property,
income as well as expenditure. They are
very graceful and handsome women.

Do Pedro de Ayala (fl. 15th century),
Spanish Ambassador to James IV, Report
to the King of Spain, July 1498

22 Can spirit from the tomb, or fiend from
Hell,
More hateful, more malignant be than
man?
Than villainous man?

Joanna Baillie (1762–1851), Orra

23 Oh neighbours, what had I ado for to
marry!
My wife she drinks posset and wine o'
Canary,
And ca's me a niggardly, throw-gabbit
cairly.
O gin my wife wad drink hooly and fairly,

Hooly and fairly, hooly and fairly,
O gin my wife wad drink holy and fairly.

Joanna Baillie, Hooly and Fairly

24 . . . the great leaven that breaks through
all Scots bawdry. It is never sneering or sly
or sexy or prurient or titillating. It is lusty
like a good broad female buttock.

James Barke, Introduction to The Merry
Muses of Caledonia *(1982)*

25 You see, dear, it is not true that woman was
made from man's rib; she was really made
from his funny bone.

J. M. Barrie (1860–1937), What Every
Woman Knows

26 Every man who is high up loves to think
he has done it himself; and the wife smiles,
and lets it go at that.

J. M. Barrie, What Every Woman
Knows

27 Dio has a pleasant story which shows that
the Empress found some intellectual diversion in the island. In conversation with
the wife of a Caledonian named Argentocoxus, after the treaty had been concluded,
Julia had joked with her about the sexual
customs of her people, referring to their
women's freedom in having intercourse
with men. The Caledonian woman showed
a biting humour in her reply: 'We fulfil the
demands of nature in a much better way
than you Roman women. We have intercourse openly with the best men – you
allow yourselves to be seduced in secret by
the worst of men.'

Anthony Birley, Septimius Severus:
The African Emperor *(1971)*, *quoting
the Roman historian Dio Cassius
(c.150–c.235) on Severus' invasion of
AD 208–9*

28 Wisdom hath no sex.

John Stuart Blackie (1809–1895), The
Wise Men of Greece

29 At supper my wife and I had a dispute
about some trifle. She did not yield readily enough and my passion rose to a pitch
I could not quite command. I started up
and threw an egg in the fire and some beer
after it . . . My wife soon made up our difference. But I begged of her to be more
attentive again.

James Boswell (1740–1795), Journal

30 Dr Johnson was curious to know where
she slept. I asked one of the guides, who
questioned her in Erse. She answered with
a tone of emotion, saying (as he told us),
she was afraid we wanted to go to bed with
her. This *coquetry*, or whatever it might be
called, of so wretched a being was truly
ludicrous. Dr Johnson and I afterwards
were merry on it.

James Boswell, Journal of a Tour to the
Hebrides

31 'Ye stupid auld bitch . . . I beg your pardon,
mem, I mistook ye for my wife.'

Lord Braxfield (1722–1799), *attributed
to his partner at whist*

32 Lissy, I am looking out for a wife, and I
thought you just the person that would
suit me. Let me have your answer, aff or
on, the morn, and nae mair about it.

*Lord Braxfield's proposal to his second wife,
recorded in John Kay*, Original Portraits
(1877)

33 He can lie on his back, a posture long
sustained by no other uncarapaced animal
except in death . . . He is badly constructed
for locomotion by road or by tree. The
slowest fish swims faster. He is adapted primarily for rest.

*J. M. Bridie (Osborne Henry Mavor,
1888–1951)*, Tedious and Brief, *on
homo sapiens*

34 She's fair and fause that causes my smart

Robert Burns (1759–1796), She's Fair
and Fause

35 What can a young lassie, what shall a
young lassie,
What can a young lassie do wi' an auld
man?

Robert Burns, What Can a Young
Lassie Do Wi' an Auld Man?

36 O gie the lass her fairin, lad,
O gie the lass her fairin,
An' something else she'll gie to you
That's waly worth the wearin.

Robert Burns, Gie the Lass Her Fairin

37 Every man proper for a member of this
Society, must have a frank, honest, open
heart; above anything dirty or mean; and

must be a professed lover of one or more of the female sex.

> *Robert Burns and Others*, Rules of the Tarbolton Bachelors' Club

38 Auld Nature swears, the lovely dears
Her noblest work she classes, O;
Her prentice han' she tried on man,
An' then she made the lasses, O.

> *Robert Burns*, Green Grow the Rashes, O

39 O wha my babie-clouts will buy,
O wha will tent me when I cry;
Wha will kiss me where I lie?
The rantin' dog the daddie o't.

> *Robert Burns*, The Rantin' Dog the Daddie O't.

40 . . . our hame
Where sits our sulky, sullen dame,
Gathering her brows like gathering storm,
Nursing her wrath to keep it warm.

> *Robert Burns*, Tam o' Shanter

41 Ah, gentle dames! it gars me greet,
To think how mony counsels sweet,
How mony lengthen'd, sage advices,
The husband frae the wife despises!

> *Robert Burns*, Tam o' Shanter

42 The Landlady and Tam grew gracious,
Wi' secret favours, sweet and precious.

> *Robert Burns*, Tam o'Shanter

43 A souple jade she was and strang.

> *Robert Burns*, Tam o' Shanter

44 She's gane, like Alexander,
To spread her conquests farther.

> *Robert Burns*, Saw Ye Bonnie Lesley

45 While quacks of State must each produce his plan,
And even children lisp the Rights of Man,
Amid this mighty fuss just let me mention,
The Rights of Woman merit some attention.

> *Robert Burns*, The Rights of Woman

46 As father Adam first was fool'd
(A case that's still too common);
Here lies a man a woman rul'd –
The Devil rul'd the woman.

> *Robert Burns*, Epitaph on a Hen-pecked Squire

47 Gin a body meet a body
Comin through the rye,

Gin a body kiss a body,
Need a body cry?

> *Robert Burns*, Comin Through The Rye

48 Mony a body meets a body
They darena weel avow;
Many a body fucks a body,
Ye wadna think it true.

> *Robert Burns*, Comin Through the Rye, *bawdy version*

49 Now we maun totter down, John,
And hand in hand we'll go,
And sleep thegither at the foot,
John Anderson my jo!

> *Robert Burns*, John Anderson, My Jo

50 Fra my tap-knot to my tae, John,
I'm like the new fa'n snow:
And it's a' for your convenience,
John Anderson, my Jo.

> *Robert Burns*, John Anderson, My Jo, *bawdy version*

51 I've seen the day ye buttered my brose,
And cuddled me late and early, O!
But Downa-do's come o'er me now,
And oh I feel it sairly.

> *Robert Burns*, The Deuk's Dang O'er My Daddie

52 Wantonness for evermair,
Wantonness has been my ruin.
Yet for a' my dool and care,
It's wantonness for evermair.

> *Robert Burns*, Wantonness for Evermair

53 O what a peacemaker is a guid weel-willy pintle! It is the mediator, the guarantee, the umpire, the bond of union, the solemn league and covenant, the plenipotentiary, the Aaron's rod, the Jacob's staff, the prophet Elisha's pot of oil, the Ahasuerus' sceptre, the sword of mercy, the philosopher's stone, the Horn of Plenty, and Tree of Life between Man and Woman.

> *Robert Burns*, letter to Robert Ainslie, *1788*

54 . . . in spite of the honestest efforts to annihilate my *I-ity*, or merge it in what the world doubtless considers my better half; I still find myself as self-subsisting and alas! Self-seeking Me . . . 'I too am here.'

> *Jane Welsh Carlyle (1801–1866), letter to John Sterling, June 1835*

55 Can you keep the bee from ranging,
    Or the ringdove's neck from changing?
    No ! nor fettered Love from dying
    In the knot there's no untying.

    Thomas Campbell (1777–1844), Song

56 Clever men are good; but they are not the
    best.

    Thomas Carlyle (1795–1881), Goethe

57 The barrenest of all mortals is the
    sentimentalist.

    Thomas Carlyle, Characteristics

58 What is man? A foolish baby;
    Vainly strives, and fights, and frets;
    Demanding all, deserving nothing,
    One small grave is what he gets.

    Thomas Carlyle, Cui Bono

59 Thus does society naturally divide itself
    into four classes: Noblemen, Gentlemen,
    Gigmen, and Men.

    Thomas Carlyle, Essays

60 . . . all women know talent when they share
    a bed with it.

    Catherine Carswell (1879–1946), Lying
    Awake: An Unfinished Autobiography
    and Other Papers

61 It wasn't a woman who betrayed Jesus with
    a kiss.

    Catherine Carswell, The Savage
    Pilgrimage

62 Infidelity . . . a fearful blindness of the
    soul.

    Thomas Chalmers (1780–1847)

63 The Almighty made all things very good
    without doubt, but he left some mighty
    queer kinks in woman. But then the whole
    affair of her creation was an afterthought.

    S. R. Crockett (1859–1914),

64 The souls of men that pave their hell-
       ward path
    With women's souls lose immortality.

    John Davidson (1857–1909), Smith

65 There is not a maid, wife or widow, whose
    fancy any man, if he set himself to it,
    could not conquer; nor any man whom any
    woman could not subdue if she chose.

    John Davidson, A Romantic Farce

66 Men, even the good ones, are kittle cattle;
    God didn't give them much sense, and it's
    the woman's job to make the best of them.

    O. Douglas (Anna Buchan, 1877–1948),
    Jane's Parlour

67 Ay, when that caribald carl wald climb on
       my wame,
    Then am I dangerus and dain and dour
       of my will;
    Yet let I never that larbar my leggis gae
       between,
    To fyle my flesh, na fumyll me, without
       a fee great.

    William Dunbar (c.1460–c.1520), The
    Tretis of the Twa Mariit Wemen and
    the Wedo

68 Now I am a wedow, I wise and weill am
       at ese;
    I weip as I were woful, but wel is me for
       ever;
    . . . My clokis thai ar caerfull in colour of
       sabill,
    But courtly and right curyus my corse is
       ther undir.

    William Dunbar, The Tretis of the Twa
    Mariit Wemen and the Wedo

69 Man thinks more, woman feels more. He
    discovers more but remembers less; she is
    more receptive and less forgetful.

    Sir Patrick Geddes (1854–1932), The
    Evolution of Sex *(with J. Arthur
    Thomson)*

70 *Four of a family's fine; there'll be no more.*
    And father thundered at her, that way he
    had. *Fine? We'll have what God in His mercy
    may send to us, woman. See you to that.*

    He wouldn't do anything against God's
    will, would father, and sure as anything
    God followed up Alec with the twins.

    *Lewis Grassic Gibbon (James Leslie
    Mitchell, 1901–1935)*, Sunset Song

71 As houses were incommodious and hos-
    pitality was exuberant, it was usual for
    two gentlemen or two ladies, however
    unknown to each other they might be, to
    sleep together, lying overwhelmed with
    the burden of from six to ten pair of Scots
    blankets.

    H. Grey Graham, The Social Life of
    Scotland in the Eighteenth Century
    (1899)

72 Alas, my son, you little know
The sorrows that from wedlock flow,
Farewell to every day of ease,
When you have got a wife to please.

Janet Graham (c.1724–1805), The Wayward Wife

73 Lie over to me from the wall or else
Get up and clean the grate.

W. S. Graham (1918–86), Baldy Bane

74 She vow'd, she swore, she would be mine,
She said she lo'ed me best of ony;
But oh! the fickle, faithless quean,
She's ta'en the carle, and left her Johnnie.

Elizabeth Grant (1745–1814), Roy's
Wife of Aldivalloch

75 Donnchadh Bàn Mac an t-Saoir, commonly known as Duncan Bàn MacIntyre,
wrote a song to his fair young Mhàiri after
their marriage saying that he had put his
net into the clear fresh water, drawn it
ashore and landed from it a sea-trout as
shining as a swan on the sea. Then one
morning Donnchadh Bàn (who could neither read nor write) lay in bed in their
heather-thatched cabin in Glen Orchy,
composing.

It was raining, rain came in, drip, drip,
drip on to the bed. Not to be interrupted
in the inexorability of composition, the
inexorability of the poem (perhaps it was
his 'Misty Corrie'), Donnchadh Bàn called
'Out with you and put some heather on,
fair young Mhàiri. It's raining.'

Or so it is said.

Geoffrey Grigson (1905–1985), The Private Art: A Poetry Notebook

76 A curious treachery there was in women;
not so much treachery as a ruthlessness.
They would lie, and deceive, and be treacherous to the utmost degree, in order to get
their desire. As if their desire was something more than themselves and knew no
law.

Neil Gunn (1891–1973), The Serpent

77 . . . the experience of a laird of ancient
title who had it pointed out to him that
his ganekeeper resembled him so closely
they might almost be brothers. Intrigued,
he summoned the man and asked him if

his mother had ever been in service at the
Big House.

'No, my lord,' said the gamekeeper, 'but
my father was your mother's butler for a
while.'

Cliff Hanley (1922–1999), The Scots

78 Wumman's beauty gies man true content.

George Campbell Hay (1915–1984),
Flooer o the Gean

79 The Big Boy took me into a lonely corner
of the Field and told me the awful things
that fathers and mothers did together. It
was several years before I discovered that
he was quite wrong.

Jack House (1906–1991), Pavement in
the Sun

80 What better school for manners than the
company of virtuous women?

David Hume (1711–1776), Essays

81 . . . as I took a particular pleasure in
the company of modest women, I had no
reason to be displeased with the reception
I got from them.

David Hume, My Own Life

82 Women, destined by nature to be obedient, ought to be disciplined early to bear
wrongs without murmuring. This is a hard
lesson; and yet it is necessary even for their
own sake.

Lord Kames (1696–1782), Loose Hints
Upon Education

83 For men were just a perfect nuisance –
wasn't that so, now? My goodness me! No
wonder women always aged much quicker
than their menfolk, considering all they
had to put up with, one way or another.
A man could go on being a man till he
dropped into his grave, but a woman had
to call a halt, some time or other.

*Jessie Kesson (Jessie Grant McDonald,
1915–1994)*, A Glitter of Mica

84 To promote a Woman to beare rule, supe-
rioritie, dominion, or empire above any
Realme, Nation or Citie, is repugnant to
Nature; contumelie to God, a thing most
contrary to his revealed will and approved
ordinance; and finallie it is the subversion
of good Order, of all equitie and justice.

John Knox (1505–1572), The First Blast
of the Trumpet Against the Monstrous Regiment of Women

85 I found myself necessitated to prove by experience the certain truth of that maxim, that neither reason nor force can hinder a woman from vengeance, when she is impelled there by love.

> *Margaret Lambrun (fl. 1587), caught attempting to assassinate Queen Elizabeth I of England, from* Biographies of Distinguished Women, *edited by Sarah Hale, 1876*

86 I gang like a ghaist, and I carena to spin;
I daurna think on Jamie, for that wad
  be a sin;
But I'll do my best a gude wife aye to be,
For auld Robin Gray he is kind unto me.

> *Lady Anne Lindsay (1750–1826),* Auld Robin Gray

87 Oh I am wild-eyed, unkempt, hellbent,
  a harridan.
My sharp tongue will shrivel any man.

> *Liz Lochhead (1947–),* Harridan

88 Oh, we spill the beans and we swill
  our gin,
and discover we're Sisters Under
  The Skin.

> *Liz Lochhead,* True Confessions

89 'But when eer ye meet a pretty maid,
And two miles from a town, sir,
You may lay her doon,' she said,
'And never mind her gown, sir.'

> *Agnes Lyle (fl. early 19th century),* The Baffled Knight

90 Scottish women of any historical importance or interest are curiously rare . . . A long list of famous Englishwomen is easy to compile; it is impossible to draw up any corresponding list of Scotswomen.

> *Hugh MacDiarmid (C. M. Grieve, 1892–1978),* Elspeth Buchan, *in* Scottish Eccentrics

91 I must say here that the race of true Scotswomen, iron women, hardy, indomitable, humorous, gay, shrewd women with an amazing sense of values, seems to be facing extinction too in today's Scotland.

> *Hugh MacDiarmid,* Lucky Poet

92 And you sall hae my breists like stars,
My limb like willow wands,
And on my lips ye'll heed nae mair,
And in my hair forget,

The seed o' a' the men that in
My virgin womb ha'e met.

> *Hugh MacDiarmid,* A Drunk Man Looks at the Thistle

93 Mind you, we weemen folk will only be helpit when we help oorsels. Men and men's Government are only daidlin' and dandlin' wi' the business sae faur as the real guid o' the masses are concerned, and that will never be richtly mended till weemen get the pooer they are noo sae sairly needin'.

> *'Jean MacFarlane',* The Weekly News, *January 1906*

94 'Buffers like yon would stop the Flying Scotsman going full tilt at Longniddry,' Binnie said. 'Fine I'd like a wee sit-out with her.'

> *Bruce Marshall (1899–1987),* Teacup Terrace

95 The women of this country ought to be educated or to have the option of being educated at the same institutions as the men . . . Till this is done, our nation is unjust to half its members and exists spiritually, intellec shtually, and in every other respect at but half its possible strength.

> *David Masson,* Macmillan's Magazine *(1867), quoted in C. P. Finlayson,* The Symposium Academicum, *in G. Donaldson,* Four Centuries: Edinburgh University Life *(1983)*

96 For there's nae luck aboot the hoose,
There's nae luck at a';
There's little pleasure in the hoose,
When our gudeman's awa'.

> *W. J. Mickle (1734–1788),* The Mariner's Wife

97 The indignant husband explained the reason for his wrath: had he not good cause for stabbing a wife who was unfaithful to him? If he expected the cummers of Aberlady to sympathise, and denounce the erring woman, he got a drop, for one of them stepped forward and retorted, 'Losh, if that be the trouble, you might as well stick us a' in Aberlady.'

> *Augustus Muir,* Heather Track and High Road *(1944)*

98 If a celestial journalist, notebook in hand, had asked her what kind of woman she

was, she would have replied, with some surprise, that she was a minister's sister.

> *Willa Muir (1890–1970)*, Imagined Corners

99 'I couldna afford a wife,' the Tar always maintained. 'They're all too grand for the like of me.'

'Och ay! but you might look aboot you and find a wee, no' awfu' bonny wan,' said Para Handy.

'If she was blin' or the like o' that, you would have a better chance of gettin' her,' chimed in Dougie.

> *Neil Munro (1864–1930)*, The Vital Spark

100 She's a classy girl, though, at least all her tattoos are spelt right.

> *Chic Murray (1919–1985)*

101 Scotland has or had a peculiar faculty in the production of womankind – womankind not of genius, but *character* – mighty in the grand and ancient vocation of life.

> *Margaret Oliphant (1828–1897)*, Scottish National Character

102 Mr —, in the Kyle,
Ca'd me a common —:
But if he hadna tried himsel',
He wadna be so sure.

> *Isobel Pagan (1741–1821)*, Lines on Mr —

103 But the thing nae man can bide,
An' he be human,
Is that mim-moothed snivellin' fule,
A fushionless woman.

> *Dorothy Margaret Paulin (b.1904–)*, Said the Spaewife

104 The Scarlet Whore, indeed, they snarl at,
But like right well a whore in scarlet.

> *Allan Ramsay (1686–1758)*, Epistle to Mr H. S. at London, *November 1738*

105 Let dorty dames say Na!
As lang as e'er they please,
Seem caulder than the snaw
While inwardly they bleeze.

> *Allan Ramsay*, Polwarth on the Green

106 'Is't a laddie or a lassie?' said the gardener. 'A laddie,' said the maid. 'Weel,' says he, 'I'm glad o' that, for there's ower many women in the world.' 'Hech, man,' said Jess, 'div ye no ken there's aye maist sawn o' the best crap?'

> *Dean E. B. Ramsay (1793–1872)*, Reminiscences of Scottish Life and Character

107 Women are the best opposite sex that men have got.

> *Jimmy Reid (1932–)*, The Glasgow Herald, *March 1981*

108 Frae flesher Rab that lived in Crieff,
A bonnie lassie wanted to buy some beef;
He took her in his arms, and doun they did fa',
And the wind blew the bonnie lassie's plaidie awa' . . .
What will the auld folks, the auld folks say ava'?
I canna say the wind blew my plaidie awa'!

> *'Blind Rob' (early 19th century)*, The Wind Blew the Bonnie Lassie's Plaidie Awa'

109 You get up at the crack of dawn
Get everybody's breakfast on
Make the weans get out of bed
Get them dressed and get them fed
Turn them oot the best you can
Then dae the same thing for your man
You don't even get a cup
Of tea before you tidy up.

> *Tony Roper*, Isn't it Wonderful to Be a Woman, *from* The Steamie (1987)

110 They would have all men bound and thrall
To them, and they for to be free.

> *Alexander Scott (c.1520–c.1590)*, Of Womankind

111 O woman! in our hours of ease
Uncertain, coy and hard to please . . .
When pain and anguish wring the brow,
A ministering angel thou!

> *Sir Walter Scott (1771–1832)*, Marmion

112 Woman's faith and woman's trust,
Write the characters in dust.

> *Sir Walter Scott*, The Betrothed

113 I no great Adam and you no bright Eve.

> *Iain Crichton Smith (1929–1998)*, At the Firth of Lorne

114 Tell me, pet, were you angry at me for allowing you to do what you did – was it

very bad of me. We should, I suppose, have waited till we were married.

> *Madeleine Smith (1834–1928), letter to Pierre Emile L'Angelier, June 1856 (She was acquitted of poisoning him, 'Not Proven' in 1857)*

115 My mother asked a somewhat rhetorical question: how do you keep men happy? 'You have to feed 'em at both ends,' replied my grandmother.

> *Muriel Spark (1918–),* Curriculum Vitae

116 The brooding boy and sighing maid, Wholly fain and half afraid.

> *Robert Louis Stevenson (1850–1894),* Underwoods

117 O for ten Edinburgh minutes, six pence between us, and the ever-glorious Lothian Road, or dear, mysterious Leith Walk.

> *Robert Louis Stevenson, letter to Charles Baxter*

118 Marriage is one long conversation, chequered by disputes.

> *Robert Louis Stevenson,* Memories and Portraits

119 In marriage, a man becomes slack and selfish, and undergoes fatty degeneration of his moral being.

> *Robert Louis Stevenson,* Virginibus Puerisque

120 To marry is to domesticate the Recording Angel.

> *Robert Louis Stevenson,* Virginibus Puerisque

121 She oped the door, she loot him in: He cuist aside his dreepin' plaidie: 'Blaw your warst, ye wind and rain, Since Maggie, now, I'm in aside ye.'

> *Robert Tannahill (1774–1810),* Oh! Are Ye Sleepin', Maggie?

122 'What, what!' quo' MAG, 'must it thus be my doom To spend my prime in maidhood's joyless state, And waste away my sprightly body's bloom In spouseless solitude without a mate? . . .'

> *William Tennant (1784–1848),* Anster Fair

123 He saw her charming, but he saw not half The charms her downcast modesty concealed.

> *James Thomson (1700–1748),* The Seasons

124 She was so good, and he was so bad, A very pretty time they had!

> *James Thomson (1834–1882),* Virtue and Vice

125 . . . they derive none of their beauty from paint. Indeed, neither their colour nor their complexion stand in need of it, for I know not where they will find their equals in either.

> *Edward Topham (b.1751),* Letters from Edinburgh, *on Scottish women*

126 My mother said always look under the bed Before you blow the candle out, To see if there's a man about: I always do, but you can make a bet, It's never been my luck to find a man there yet.

> *Nellie Wallace (b.1870)*

127 God, give us the grace to hate our unemancipated state, and to wipe from Scotland's face her intellectual disgrace.

> *Nannie K. Wells,* A Prayer *(c.1939)*

128 He worried about her, however; thinking that anyone who would sleep with him would sleep with anybody.

> *Irvine Welsh (1957–),* Trainspotting

129 Bad luck tae the lad that'll coort twa lassies, May he never prosper or grow fat That'll wear twa faces under his hat!

> *Betsy White, recorded by Hamish Henderson in* Tocher, *Vol. 2 (1973–74)*

The Mind and Medicine

1 Did he die a natural death, or was the doctor sent for?

> *Annandale saying, quoted in Charles Rodgers,* Familiar Illustrations of Scottish Life *(1866)*

2 Up the close and doun the stair, But an' ben wi' Burke an' Hare.

Burke's the butcher, Hare's the thief,
Knox the boy that buys the beef.

Anonymous, 19th century, The West
Point Murders

3   'Why, Madam,' said he, 'do you know
there are upwards of thirty yard of bowels
squeezed under that girdle of your daughter's? Go home and cut it; let Nature have
fair play, and you will have no need of my
advice.'

*Dr John Abernethy (1764–1831), quoted
in George McIlwain,* Memoirs of John
Abernethy

4   Sour Melancholy, night and day provokes
Her own eternal wound.

*Dr John Armstrong (1709–1779), lines
contributed to the first canto of James
Thomson's* The Castle of Indolence

5   With us, the man of no complaint
demands
The warm ablution just enough to keep
The body sacred from indecent soil.
Still to be pure, even did it not conduce
(As much it does) to health, were
greatly worth
Your daily pains.

Dr John Armstrong, The Art of Preserving Health

6   I find I'm haunted with a busie mind . . .
O what a wandring thing's the Mind!
What contrares are there combin'd?

John Barclay (late 17th century)

7   'What are ye gaun to get frae her?'
'A big cup o' Greegory's Mixtur' wi'
a Queen Anne Pooder in it.'
'Will ye tak' that?'
'I'll get naething else to eat till I dae.'

J. J. Bell (1871–1934), Wee McGreegor

8   Any really good doctor ought to be able to
tell before a patient has fairly sat down, a
good deal of what is the matter with him
or her.

Joseph Bell (1837–1911), quoted in Joseph
Bell: An Appreciation by an Old
Friend *(1913)*

9   Trust the Unconscious. And that, I
suppose, is
How to get rid of hallucinoses
And pseudopathomorphic

psychosomaticoses
And lie on a perpetual bed of roses.

*J. M. Bridie (Osborne Henry Mavor,
1888–1951),* Tedious and Brief

10   There is a temptation for any creature
who seems to be doing the work of the
Almighty to imagine he is a god. This is
particularly so in medicine, and an almost
unavoidable error in the hospital physician
or surgeon. He is surrounded by respect-
ful and even adoring acolytes, and he holds
the power of life and death over helpless
persons . . . If he is to avoid madness, he
must stand aside from the business from
time to time, and deride hidmself and his
colleagues.

J. M. Bridie, Tedious and Brief

11   I learned how to talk to people and
improved somewhat my technique in
lying.

J. M. Bridie, One Way of Living, *on
being in general medical practice*

12   They didn't like the idea of a woman
doctor. Why? They feared the loss of something – delicacy? – modesty? – Women
should be protected from the harsh things,
the sordid facts of life. What facts? Sex?
What was modesty? Can real modesty be
harmed by knowledge?

Elizabeth Bryson, Look Back in Wonder
(1967)

13   My curse upon your venom'd stang,
That shoots my tortur'd gooms alang,
An' thro' my lug gies mony a twang.

Robert Burns (1754–1796), Address to
the Toothache

14   I am more and more persuaded that there
is no complete misery in the world that
does not emanate from the bowels.

*Jane Welsh Carlyle (1801–1866), letter to
Eliza Stoddart (1834)*

15   . . . medical men all over the world having
merely entered into a tacit agreement to
call all sorts of maladies people are liable
to, in cold weather, by one name; so
that one sort of treatment may serve for
all, and their practice thereby be greatly
simplified.

*Jane Welsh Carlyle, letter to John Welsh
(1837)*

16 The uttered part of a man's life, let us always repeat, bears to the unuttered, unconscious part a small unknown proportion.

Thomas Carlyle (1795–1881), Essays, *on Walter Scott*

17 Published in 1305, the *Lilium Medicinae* was very soon afterwards translated into Gaelic and several copies of the translation exist. One of these, belonging to the Beaton medical family in Skye, was said to be . . . so valuable that when the doctor crossed an arm of the sea the book was sent round by land.

Hugh Cheape and I. F. Grant, Periods in Highland History *(1987)*

18 One of his pills, known as *Pilulae Magistri Michaelis Scoti*, is noted by a thirteenth-century copyist as effective to relieve headache, purge the humours wonderfully, produce joyfulness, brighten the intellect, improve the vision, sharpen hearing, preserve youth and retard baldness. These pills were composed of aloes, rhubarb, nine fruits and flowers made into a confection, and might fairly be described as excellent after-dinner pills.

John D. Comrie, History of Scottish Medicine, Vol. 1 *(1927)*, *on Michael Scott (c.1175–c.1230) as physician*

19 At a time when personal peculiarity was widely affected by Edinburgh people, Wood specially distinguished himself by going to see his patients accompanied by a pet sheep and raven.

John D. Comrie, History of Scottish Medicine, Vol. 2, *on Alexander 'Lang Sandy' Wood (1725–1807)*

20 An old Scotch physician . . . used to say, as we were entering the patient's room together, 'Weel, Mr Cooper, we ha' only twa things to keep in meend, and they'll searve us for here and herea'ter; one is always to have the fear of the Laird before our ees: that'll do for herea'ter; and the t'other is to keep your booels open, and that will do for here.'

Sir Astley Cooper (1768–1841), Lectures on Surgery

21 Minds are like parachutes. They only function when they are open.

Attributed to Sir James Dewar (1842–1923)

22 Mechanics, not microbes, are the menace to civilisation.

Norman Douglas (1868–1952), The Norman Douglas Limerick Book

23 Give me the trifles of life, and keep the rest. A man's health depends on trifles; and happiness on health.

Norman Douglas, Alone

24 Whenever patients come to I,
I physics, bleeds and sweats 'em;
If after that they choose to die,
What's that to me! – I *letts* 'em.

Thomas, Lord Erskine (1750–1823), Epigram on Dr John Lettsom

25 In 1590 a Scotch witch of the name of Agnes Sampson was convicted of curing a certain Robert Kers of a disease 'laid upon him by a westland warlock when he was at Dumfries, whilk sickness she took upon herself, and kept the same with great groaning and torment till the morn, at whilk time there was a great din heard in the house'. The noise was made by the witch in her efforts to shift the disease, by means of clothes, from herself to a cat or dog. Unfortunately the attempt partly miscarried. The disease missed the animal and hit Alexander Douglas of Dalkeith, who dwined and died of it, while the original patient . . . was made whole.

Sir James G. Frazer (1854–1941), The Golden Bough

26 . . . off to the asylum they hurled the daftie, he went with a nurse's mutch on his head and he put his head out of the back of the waggon and said *Cockadoodledo!* to some school bairns the waggon passed on the road and they all ran home and were fell frightened.

Lewis Grassic Gibbon (James Leslie Mitchell, 1901–1935), Sunset Song

27 These 'slaters', alias millipedes, alias woodlice, were in constant request . . . we may see from a prescription by the great Dr Pitcairn to heal the scurvy: 'Take 2 lbs of shavings of sarfa cut and sliced, boil in 3 gallons of wort, put barm in it, one half pound of crude antimony, with 4 ounces sharp-leaved docks, barrel it, then put in dried rosemary with the juice of 400 or 500 sclaters squeezed through linen into

the barrel. When it is 20 days bottled drink it.'

> *H. Grey Graham*, The Social Life of Scotland in the Eighteenth Century *(1899)*

28 I wish I had the voice of Homer
To sing of rectal carcinoma,
Which kills a lot more chaps, in fact,
Than were bumped off when Troy was sacked.

> *J. B. S. Haldane (1892–1964),* Cancer's a Funny Thing

29 I've never met a healthy person who worried much about his health, or a good person who worried about his soul.

> *J. B. S. Haldane*

30 'If this that you tell me be true,' said I, 'then is it as true that I have two souls, which take possession of my bodily frame by turns, the one being all unconscious of what the other performs . . .'

> *James Hogg (1770–1835),* The Private Memoirs and Confessions of a Justified Sinner

31 The stomach is the distinguishing point between an animal and a vegetable; for we do not know any vegetable that has a stomach, nor any animal without one.

> *John Hunter (1728–1793),* Principles of Surgery

32 There is no seventh sense of the mystic kind . . . But if there is not a distinct magnetic sense, I say it is a very great wonder that there is not.

> *Lord Kelvin (1824–1907), presidential address to the Birmingham and Midland Institute*

33 The fumes rose hotly from the new-tarred surface. 'Best cure in the world for whooping-cough,' her mother always said. 'Nonsense,' her father had countered, for he had no faith in miracles. You went when your time came. Tar or no tar.

> *Jessie Kesson (Jessie Grant Macdonald, 1916–1994),* Where the Apple Ripens

34 We are born into a world where alienation awaits us.

> *R. D. Laing (1927–1989),* The Politics of Experience

35 Madness need not be all breakdown. It may also be breakthrough.

> *R. D. Laing,* The Politics of Experience

36 As the chill snow is friendly to the earth,
And pain and loss are friendly to the soul,
Shielding it from the black heart-killing frost;
So madness is but one of God's pale winters.

> *George Macdonald (1824–1905),* A Story of the Sea-Shore

37 Dr Porterfield, a celebrated physician in my younger days, being asked by an acquaintance who wished to save a fee what he should take, answered, 'Take advice.'

> *Henry Mackenzie (1745–1831), quoted in H. W. Thomson,* The Anecdotes and Egotisms of Henry Mackenzie

38 I remember Adam Smith's saying that half the people standing one day at the Cross of Edinburgh were mad without knowing it.

> *Henry Mackenzie,* The Anecdotes and Egotisms of Henry Mackenzie

39 . . . having done some weird and wonderful work to my inside which has enabled me to live seven years longer, probably, than the majority of people thought I deserved.

> *James Maxton (1885–1946), on Glasgow Royal Infirmary, in a medical students' charity magazine, 1933*

40 . . . John Hunter once saying to Lord Holland, 'If you wish to see a great man you have one standing before you. I consider myself a greater man than Sir Isaac Newton.' Explained then why: that discoveries which lengthen life and alleviate suffering are of infinitely more importance to mankind than anything relating to the stars, etc.

> *Thomas Moore,* Diary, *1825*

41 A girl on her arrival was asked whether she had had the smallpox.
'Yes, mem, I've had the sma'pox, the nirls, the blabs, the scaw, the kinkhost and the fever, the branks and the worm.'

> *Dean E. B. Ramsay (1793–1872),* Reminiscences of Scottish Life and Character

42 If (my mind) is indeed what the *Treatise of Human Nature* makes it, I find I have been

only in an enchanted castle, imposed on by spectres and apparitions.

Thomas Reid (1710–1796), An Inquiry into the Human Mind, *on the philosophy of David Hume*

43 Happening on Dawson of Penn in the Athenaeum, he asked how I was. Ill; a serious disease. His medical interest and sympathy were aroused; what was the disease. Accidie, *'Accidie?'* he queried, his encyclopaedic medical knowledge rumbling in his brain. He had to admit he had never heard of it.

Lord Reith (1889–1971), Into the Wind

44 I wrote to my wife, 'I have seen something very promising indeed in my new mosquitoes' and I scribbled the following unfinished verses in one of my *In Exile* notebooks, in pencil:

This day designing God
Hath put into my hand
a wondrous thing. And God
Be praised. At His command
I have found thy secret deeds,
O million-murdering Death.

Sir Ronald Ross (1857–1932), Memoirs

45 I was sadly worried by the black dog this morning, that vile palpitation of the heart – that *tremor cordis* – that hysterical passion which forces unbidden sighs and tears, and falls upon a contented life like a drop of ink on white paper, which is not the less a stain because it carries no meaning.

Sir Walter Scott, Journal *(March 1828)*, *quoted in J. G. Lockhart*, The Life of Sir Waler Scott

46 I think for my part one-half of the nation is mad – and the other not very sound.

Tobias Smollett (1721–1771), The Adventures of Sir Launcelot Greaves

47 A seasonable fit of illness is an excellent medicine for the turbulence of passion.

Tobias Smollett, The Adventures of Peregrine Pickle

48 The pills are good for nothing; I might as well swallow snowballs to cool my reins.

Tobias Smollett, Humphrey Clinker

49 Sic a hoast hae I got:
Sic a hoast hae I got:
I dout my days are on the trot.

William Soutar (1898–1943), Sic a Hoast

50 Every man has a sane spot somewhere.

Robert Louis Stevenson (1850–1894), The Wrecker *(with Lloyd Osbourne)*

51 I keep my health better in these wild mountains than I used to do in the Campagna Felice, and sleep sounder lying on the ground than I used to do in the palaces of Rome.

Prince Charles Edward Stewart (1720–1788), letter to his father from Perth, September 1745

52 . . . a fine excuse for the airing of his expensive dental repair-work (expensive for the molar-howker, that is, for Rudge had probably extracted his co-operation on a 'you-fix-my-mouth-cheap-or-I'll-fix-your-mouth-expensive' deal).

Jeff Torrington (1935–), Swing Hammer Swing

53 In 1817 James Mill was beginning to plan the *Analysis of the Human Mind*, which he published in 1829. 'If I had time to write a book,' he says, 'I would make the human mind as plain as the road from Charing Cross to St Paul's.'

Graham Wallas, The Life of Francis Place *(1951)*

54 Ah'm no sick yet, but it's in the fuckin post, that's fir sure.

Irvine Welsh (1957–), Trainspotting

55 Here ah am in the junky's limbo; too sick tae sleep, too tired tae stay awake. A twilight zone ay the senses where nothing's real except the crushing, omnipresent misery n pain in your mind n body.

Irvine Welsh, Trainspotting

Moments

1 On the meadow and the mountains
Calmly shine the winter stars,
But across the glistening lowlands
Slant the moonbeams' silver bars:
In the silence and the darkness,
Darkness growing still more deep,

Listen to the little children
Praying God their souls to keep.

> *Mary C. H. Alexander*, Now I Lay Me Down To Sleep

2 But it is the other window I turn to, with a pain at my heart, and pride and fondness too, the square foot of glass where Jess sat in her chair and looked down the brae.

> *Sir J. M. Barrie (1860–1937)*, A Window in Thrums

3 I said to Davies, 'Don't tell him where I come from.'– 'From Scotland', cried Davies, roguishly. 'Mr Johnson', said I, 'I do indeed come from Scotland, but I cannot help it.' . . . 'That, Sir, is what I find a very great number of your countrymen cannot help.'

> *James Boswell (1740–1795)*, Life of Johnson

4 She was a little woman of mild and genteel appearance, mighty soft and well-bred. To see Mr Samuel Johnson salute Miss Flora Macdonald was a wonderful romantic scene to me . . . To see Mr Samuel Johnson lying in Prince Charles's bed, in the Isle of Skye, in the house of Miss Flora Macdonald, struck me with such a group of ideas as it is not easy for words to describe as the mind perceives them.

> *James Boswell*, Journal of a Tour to the Hebrides

5 . . . the smell of neeps after rain. Surely that exquisite aroma is essential Scotland: it has the sharp tang of so many Scottish things; of whisky, especially, and smoked fish, of pine-woods and of peat.

> *Ivor Brown (1891–1974)*, A Word in Your Ear

6 I was, at that moment, in possession of what had for many years been the principal object of my ambition and wishes: indifference, which, from the usual infirmity of human nature, follows, at least for a time, complete enjoyment, had taken place of it. The marsh and fountains, upon comparison with the rise of many of our rivers, became now a trifling object in my sight. I remembered that majestic scene in my own country, where the Tweed, Clyde and Annan rise in one hill . . .

> *James Bruce (1730–1794)*, Travels and Discoveries of the Source of the Nile, *thoughts at the source of the Nile*

7 In some village the name of which I have forgotten, we drew up at an inn, and Raymond addressed the assembled rustics on the virtues of total abstinence. It was the most perfect parody conceivable of a temperance speech, and it completely solemnised his hearers. Then he ordered beer all round.

> *John Buchan (1875–1940)*, These for Remembrance *(1919)*, *on Raymond Asquith*

8 Kings may be blest, but Tam was glorious, O'er a' the ills o' life victorious.

> *Robert Burns (1759–1796)*, Tam o' Shanter

9 That night, a child might understand, The deil had business on his hand.

> *Robert Burns*, Tam o' Shanter

10 And, in an instant, all was dark.

> *Robert Burns*, Tam o' Shanter

11 I like the evening in India, the one magic moment when the sun balances on the rim of the world, and the hush descends, and ten thousand civil servants drift homeward on a river of bicycles, brooding on the Lord Krishna and the cost of living.

> *James Cameron (1911–1985)*, What A Way To Run the Tribe

12 There was silence deep as death; And the boldest held his breath.

> *Thomas Campbell (1771–1844)*, The Battle of the Baltic

13 . . . my fellow-passenger in the railway, took it it into his head to smile visibly when I laid off my white broadbrim, and suddenly produced out of my pocket my grey Glengarryrom . . . I looked straight into his smiling face and eyes, a look which I suppose enquired of him, 'Miserable ninth part of the fraction of a tailor, art thou sure that thou hast a right to smile at me?' The smile instantly died into another expression of emotion.

> *Thomas Carlyle (1795–1881)*, Letters, *to his wife*

14 Mill had borrowed that first volume of my poor *French Revolution* . . . I learned from Mill this fact: that my poor Manuscript, all except some four tattered leaves, was *annihilated!* He had left it out (too carelessly); it had been taken for waste-paper: and so five months of as tough labour as

I could remember of, were as good as vanished, gone like a whiff of smoke.

Thomas Carlyle, letter to his brother John

15 It was on March 10, 1876, over a line extended between two rooms in a building at No 5 Exeter Place, Boston, that the first complete sentence was ever spoken by Bell and heard by Watson, who recorded it in his notebook at the time. It consisted of these words: 'Mr Watson, come here; I want you.' Thus the telephone was born.

J. J. Carty, in Smithsonian Report *(1922), on Alexander Graham Bell (1847–1922)*

16 Buttered toast and tea,
The yellow licht o' the lamp,
An' the cat on the clootie rug
Afore the fire.

Helen B. Cruickshank (1886–1975), Background

17 No man dared to speak. They gazed with blanched faces at the House with the Green Shutters, sitting dark there and terrible, beneath the radiant arch of dawn.

George Douglas (George Douglas Brown,1869–1902), The House with the Green Shutters

18 ... the awe-inspiring mid-day hush.

Norman Douglas (1868–1952), Siren Land

19 Night like a drunkard reels
Beyond the hills.

William Drummond of Hawthornden (1585–1649), Summons to Love

20 ... the schools skailed, and all the children came shouting to the market.

John Galt (1779–1839), The Provost

21 To stand and not to think, receptive to the influences of earth and sky, scent and sound and silence, is easy and natural. But something then comes seeping in, sometimes very slight, so slight that it scarcely seems to come at all; and yet, *if the pause be held*, there supervenes a delicacy of tension, a certain strangeness within oneself and going out through the far reaches of the world; and the burden of the day's care slowly falls away like the leaf.

Neil Gunn (1891–1973), in Saltire Review

22 He lookit on her ugly leper face,
The whilk before was white as lily flour,
Wringand his hands.

Robert Henryson (c.1425–c.1500), The Testament of Cresseid

23 It was perhaps not before time that I asked myself what that man had to do with my life, what I had to do with his, and what we were doing stranded together on an island in one of the almost forgotten corners of the world.

Lucy Irvine, Castaway *1983*

24 Wan water from the border hills,
Dear voice from the old years,
Thy distant music lulls and stills
And moves to quiet tears.

Andrew Lang (1844–1912), Twilight on Tweed

25 This Abbott tuik in hand to fly with wingis ... and to that effect he causit maik ane pair of wingis of fedderis, quhilk beand fassinit upoun him, he flew off the castel wall of Striveling; bot schortlie he fell to the grund and braik his thie-bane; bot the wyte thairof he ascryvit to that thair wes sum hen fedderis in the wingis, quhilk yernit and covet the middin and not the skyis.

John Leslie, History of Scotland, *translated by Father Dalrymple (1596), on Damian's attempt to fly at Stirling, around 1510*

26 Suddenly, from out of doors, there came a single, prolonged, piercing wail, such as a banshee might be imagined to utter. It ceased abruptly and was not repeated.

'What's that?' called out Maskull, disengaging himself impatiently from Krag. Krag rocked with laughter. 'A Scottish spirit, trying to reproduce the bagpipes of its earthly life – in honour of our departure.'

David Lindsay (1878–1945), A Voyage to Arcturus

27 This was the state of affairs when Swanson and Macaulay came round the corner of the mill, and forgot their own dissension before the unusual spectacle of a Member of Parliament, naked among the branches of a tree, while thirty or forty elderly

women, of sober habit and good repute in the village, stood below and howled abuse.

Eric Linklater (1899–1974), Laxdale Hall

28 I will not feel, I will not
feel, until
I have to.

Norman MacCaig (1910–1996), Visiting Hour

29 I was suddenly aware of some flowers, of the way the *existence* of some tall flowers was *blazing* in them . . . I knew at that moment I was doing what I – what we are all – in the world for. A sort of χ*pietas* I had towards the whole world of life and its wonder.

Fionn MacColla (Thomas Macdonald, 1906–1975), Too Long in This Condition (*This satori overtook MacColla in Montrose. See also Raymond Vettese, Fantasies & Visions.*)

30 The lightning and the thunder
They go and they come;
But the stars and the stillness
Are always at home.

George Macdonald (1824–1905), The Lightning and the Thunder

31 The west is broken into bars
Of orange, gold, and gray
Gone is the sun, come are the stars,
And night infolds the day.

George Macdonald, Songs of the Summer Nights

32 He wanted a book out of the Advocates' Library, of which the learned antiquarian Goodall, author of the first Vindication of Queen Mary, was then Acting Librarian. He was sitting in his elbow-chair so fast asleep, that neither David nor a friend who accompanied him could wake Goodall by any of the usual means. At last David said, 'I think I have a method of waking him,' and bawled into his ear, 'Queen Mary was a strumpet and a murtherer.' – 'It's a damned lie,' said Goodall, starting out of his sleep, and David obtained the book he sought.

Henry Mackenzie (1745–1831), quoted in H. W. Thomson, The Anecdotes and Egotisms of Henry Mackenzie, *on David Hume*

33 Mr Andro boir doun and utterit the commissioun as from the michtie God, calling the King bot Goddis sillie vassal, and taiking him be the sleive . . . 'I maun tell yow, thair is twa kingis and twa kingdomis in Scotland. Tfaihair is Christ Jesus the King, and His kingdom the kirk, quhais subject King James the saxt is, and of quhais kingdom nocht a king, nor a lord, nor heid, bot a member.'

James Melville (1556–1614), diary, on the confrontation in 1592 between Andrew Melville and King James VI

34 While two gentlemen were passing the scene of these improvements in the mail coach, one remarked to the other on the cruelty of dispossessing so suddenly the old inhabitants, and so sacrilegiously cutting down the old timber about the castle. 'I suppose', says his fellow-traveller, 'you have been reading that scurrilous print, the *Inverness Journal*, edited by Mackintosh of Raigmore.' To which the other gentleman replied, 'That he begged to intimate to him that he *was* Mackintosh of Raigmore.' 'Then sir,' says his neighbour, 'I am Mr Skirving, the person who laid out the improvements.'

Joseph Mitchell (1803–1883), Reminiscences of My Life in the Highlands

35 In the hush of the night-time I hear them
go by,
The horses of memory thundering
through
With flashing white fetlocks all wet with
the dew.

Will H. Ogilvie (1869–1963), The Hoofs of the Horses

36 Her mother did fret, and her father did
fume,
And the bridegroom stood dangling his
bonnet and plume.

Sir Walter Scott (1771–1832), Young Lochinvar

37 But answer came there none.

Sir Walter Scott, The Bride of Triermain

38 But with the morning cool repentance
came.

Sir Walter Scott, Rob Roy

39 For all stood bare: and in the room
Fitz-James alone wore cap and plume . . .

And Snowdoun's Knight is Scotland's
King.

   Sir Walter Scott, The Lady of the Lake

40   With disk like battle-target red
     He rushes to his burning bed,
     Dyes the wide wave with bloody light,
     Then sinks at once – and all is night.

        Sir Walter Scott, Rokeby

41   O'er the astonish'd throng
     Was silence, awful, deep, and long.

        Sir Walter Scott, The Lord of the Isles

42   'Our riches will soon be equal,' said the
     beggar, looking out upon the strife of the
     waters – 'they are sae already, for I hae nae
     land, and you would give your fair bounds
     and barony for a square yard of rock that
     would be dry for twal hours.'

        Sir Walter Scott, The Antiquary

43   A beam, cool as a butler,
     Steps from the lighthouse.

        Burns Singer (1928–1964), Peterhead in
        May

44   We twain have met like the ships upon
        the sea,
     Who hold an hour's converse, so short,
        so sweet;
     One little hour! and then, away they
        speed
     On lonely paths, through mist, and
        cloud, and foam,
     To meet no more.

        Alexander Smith (1830–1867), A Life
        Drama

45   I am a child again, barefooted, jerseyed,
     bare-kneed, the daisies are growing, the
     daffodils are a blaze of yellow. The smoke
     of the village chimneys is rising into the
     sky. There is a vague desultory hammering,
     dogs are barking, there are cows munch-
     ing clothes on the line.

        Iain Crichton Smith (1928–1998), As I
        Remember, *on childhood on Lewis*

46   The gaslight flichtered on the stair,
     The streaman cobbles black wi rain.

        Sydney Goodsir Smith (1915–1975), The
        Moment

47   This is the day of change
     And this the hour . . .

Life lifts a hand to turn his hour-glass
round.

   William Soutar (1898–1943), The Turn
   of the Year

48   Between the clicking of the clock
     A star dies and a star is born.

        William Soutar, The Moment

49   My tea is nearly ready and the sun has
        left the sky;
     It's time to take the window to see Leerie
        going by;
     For every night at tea-time and before you
        take your seat,
     With lantern and with ladder he comes
        posting up the street.

        Robert Louis Stevenson (1850–1894),
        The Lamplighter

50   Sighed and looked unutterable things.

        James Thomson (1700–1748), The
        Seasons

51   A sunbeam like an angel's sword
     Shivers upon a spire.

        Alexander Thomson (1830–1867),
        Glasgow

52   He stood there in a strait, with everything
     against him; whither to turn he knew not.
     He had come to announce to his mother
     that his father and brother had been slain,
     and he found his mother, whom he loved
     most dearly, at the point of death. Whom
     to lament first he knew not.

        Turgot (c.1060–c.1115), The Life of St
        Margaret, Queen of Scotland , *on
        Edgar's arrival at Queen Margaret's
        deathbed, 1093*

53   And mist like hair hangs over
     One barren breast and me,
     Who climb, a desperate lover,
     With hand and knee.

        Andrew Young (1885–1971), The Paps of
        Jura

54   And with wren, finch and tit
     And all the silent birds that sit
     In this snow-travelled wood
     I warm myself at my own blood.

        Andrew Young, A Heap of Faggots

Monsters

1 The side was steep, and the bottom deep;
  From bank to bank the water pouring;
  The bonny grey mare she swat for fear,
  For she heard the water-kelpie roaring.

  Anonymous, Annan Water

2 'What wae hae ye sic a sma' sma' neck?'
  'Aih-h-h!– late – and wee-e-e moul.'
  'What way hae ye sic a muckle, muckle
  heid?'
  'Muckle wit, muckle wit.'
  'What do you come for?'
  'For *you*.'

  Anonymous, An Old Wife Sat at her
  Reel

3 A visitor viewing Loch Ness
  Met the Monster, who left him a mess;
  They returned his entrails
  By the regular mails
  And the rest of the stuff by express.

  Anonymous limerick

4 Mester Stoorworm, the largest, and the
  first, and the greatest of all sea serpents. It
  was that beast which, in the Good Book,
  is called the Leviathan, and if it had been
  measured in our day, its tail would have
  touched Iceland, while its snout rested at
  John-o'-Groat's Head.

  Elizabeth Grierson, Mester Stoorworm,
  from a traditional story, in G. Jarvie,
  Scottish Folk and Fairy Tales *(1992)*

5 Morag, harbinger of death,
  Giant swimmer in deep-green Morar,
  The loch that has no bottom . . .
  There it is that Morag the monster lives.

  Alleged 'old lay', quoted in E. M. Camp-
  bell, The Search for Morag *(1972)*

6 The monster, which was lying in the river
  bed . . . perceiving the surface of the
  water disturbed by the swimmer, suddenly
  comes up and moves towards the man as he
  swam in midstream, and with a great roar
  rushes on him with open mouth, while
  all who were there, barbarians as well as
  Brethren, were greatly terror-struck. The
  blessed man seeing it, after making the salutary sign of the Cross in the empty air
  with his holy hand upraised, and invoking
  the name of God, commanded the fero-
  cious monster saying 'Go thou no further;
  nor touch the man: go back at once.' Then,
  on hearing this word of the Saint, the monster was terrified, and fled away.

  Saint Adamnan (679–704), Life of
  St Columba, *translated by Wentworth*
  Huyshe

7 As we looked towards the castle, the little
  girl pointed out a black thing in the
  water and asked if it was a rock, but the
  object began to move and soon set off
  at a high speed to Lochend. We left the
  car and climbed down to the water's edge.
  A V-shaped wash was clearly seen, and a
  whole foaming wake, like that caused by a
  motor boat.

  Lady Maud Baillie

8 The Great Grey Man of Ben Macdhui, or
  Ferlas Mor as he is called in the Gaelic,
  is Scotland's Abominable Snowman . . .
  he has been seen by responsible people
  who have reputations to lose, most of them
  expert mountaineers accustomed to hills at
  night and not given to imagining things.

  Alastair Borthwick, Always a Little
  Further

9 Ghost, kelpie, wraith,
  And all the trumpery of vulgar faith.

  Thomas Campbell (1777–1844), The Pil-
  grim of Glencoe

10 It lay motionless on the water, a long oval
  shape, a distinct mahogany colour and on
  the left flank a huge dark blotch could be
  seen, like the dapple on a cow . . . I knew
  at once that I was looking at the extraordinary humped back of some huge living
  creature.

  Tim Dinsdale, The Loch Ness Monster
  (1961)

11 In this tyme, thair wes ane monstrous
  fische in Loch Fyne, havand greit ein in
  the heid thairof, and at sumtymis wald
  stand abune the watir as heich as the mast
  of ane schippe.

  The Diurnal of Occurrents, *July 1570*

12 . . . the monsters which inhabited the three
  large and deep Highland lochs, Ness, Shiel
  and Morar, were so well known by the old
  Gaelic-speaking people that they had distinctive names. The Loch Ness Monster
  was spoken of as *An Niseag*, the Loch Shiel

Monster as *An Seileag*, and the Loch Morar
Monster as *A' Mhorag*.

> *Seton Gordon (1886–1977)*, A Highland
> Year

13 . . . with the greatest readiness and simplicity, just took haud o' the side an' wide
gown, an' in sight of a' present, held it
aside as high as the preacher's knee, and
behold, there was a pair of cloven feet!

> *James Hogg (1770–1835)*, The Private
> Memoirs and Confessions of a Justified
> Sinner

14 Just below the surface, I then made out
a shape. It was thick in the middle and
tapered towards the extremities. It was a
sort of blackish-grey in colour . . . It was
simply an elongated shape of large size
moving purposefully to and fro at the edge
of deep water.

> *F. W. Holiday*, The Great Orm of Loch
> Ness *(1968)*

15 . . . the animal, upon the whole was
between four and five feet long, as near
as he could judge . . . it had a head, arms
and body down to the middle like a human
being, only that the arms were short in
proportion to the body which appeared to
be about the thickness of that of a young
lad, and tapering gradually to the point of
the tail . . . for the first time he saw its
face, every feature of which he could see
distinctly marked, and which, to him, had
all the appearance of the face of a human
being, with very hollow eyes.

> *John McIsaac, deposition to the sheriff-sub-
> stitute at Campbeltown, October 29, 1811,
> on his observing a merman on the Kintyre
> shore*

16 My stalker, John Stuart at Achnacarry, has
seen it twice and both times at sunrise
in summer, when there was not a ripple
on the water. The creature was basking
on the surface; he saw only the head and
hind-quarters, proving its back was hollow,
which is not the shape of any fish, or of a
seal. Its head resembled that of a horse.

> *Earl of Malmesbury, Memoirs (1857), on
> a monster in Loch Arkaig*

17 Downward we drift through shadow and
   light,
Under yon rock the eddies sleep,
Calm and silent, dark and deep.
The Kelpy has risen from the fathomless
pool,
He has lighted his candle of death and of
dool.

> *Sir Walter Scott (1771–1832)*, On
> Tweed River

18 It's all humbug.

> *Professor Peter Tait (1831–1901)*

Mottoes and Slogans

A selection of the more memorable or picturesque. Some clans and families have
used a variety of mottoes and slogans.

1 Sure and stedfast.

> *Boys' Brigade motto, taken by Sir Wil-
> liam Smith (1854–1914), from the Bible
> (Hebrews 6:19)*

2 I bide my time.

> *Campbell of Loudon*

3 Nec tamen consumebatur
(And yet it shall not burn away).

> *Church of Scotland*

4 Thou shalt want ere I want.

> *Cranstoun*

5 I dare.

> *Dalziel*

6 Gang warily.

> *Drummond*

7 Bydand to the last.

> *Gordon*

8 I distribute cheerfullie.

> *George Heriot's School*

9 We'll put it to a venture.

> *Johnston of Coubister*

10 They say. What say they? Let them say.

> *Keith*

11 I mak siccar.

> *Kirkpatrick*

12 Nec parcas nec spernas
(Neither spare nor dispose).

> *Lamont*

13 Grip fast.

> *Leslie*

14 Corda serrata fero
(I bear a locked heart).
   Lockhart

15 E'en do, and spare nocht.
   MacGregor

16 Touch not the cat bot a glove.
   MacIntosh, MacPherson (Clan Chattan)

17 Buaidh no bàs
(Victory or death).
   MacDougall, also used by MacNeil

18 Bàs no beatha
(Death or Life).
   MacLean

19 Timor omnis abesto
(Let fear be far from all).
   Macnab

20 Even the hare tramples on the fallen lion.

21 Trampled upon, she giveth out greater
fragrance.

22 In my end is my beginning.
   Mottoes used by Queen Mary I

23 Furth Fortune and fill the fetters.
   Murray of Atholl

24 Garg 'n uair dhuis gear
(Fierce when roused).
   Robertson

25 Nemo me impune lacessit
(No-one attacks me with impunity).
   Kingdom of Scotland

26 Feight.
   Sinclair

27 Ready, aye ready.
   Thirlestane

28 What I have I hold.

29 What is thine shall be mine.

Mountains and Climbers

1 On Tintock-tap there is a mist,
And in that mist there is a kist,
And in the kist there is a caup,
And in the caup there is a drap,
Tak up the cup, drink aff the drap,
And set it doun on Tintock-tap.
   Traditional rhyme on Tinto Hill

2 There's Cairnsmore of Fleet,
And there's Cairnsmore of Dee;
But Cairnsmore of Carsphairn
Is the highest o' the three.
   Traditional Galloway rhyme

3 Oh, the Gallowa' hills are covered
   wi' broom,
Wi' heather bells, in bonnie bloom;
Wi' heather bells an' rivers a',
An' I'll gang oot ower the hills to
   Gallowa'.
   Traditional, The Gallowa' Hills

4 For tonight I leave from Euston
And leave the world behind;
Who has the hills as lover
Will find them wondrous kind.
   *Anonymous, written on the door of Ryvoan
   Bothy, quoted in H. Brown,* Poems of the
   Scottish Hills *(1982)*

5 What hills are like the Ochil Hills?
There's nane sae green tho' grander.
What rills are like the Ochil rills?
Nane, nane on earth that wander.
   *Anonymous, based on Hugh Haliburton,
   quoted in H. Brown,* Poems of the Scot-
   tish Hills *(1982)*

6 'I am patient, young man,' Munro bagger
   said,
'For I have enjoyed a long life through;
It is not the ones left that are keeping
   me going,
But the new ones they are making me do.'
   Anonymous, The Old Munro Bagger,
   *recorded in the Shenaval Bothy Book, and
   quoted in H. Brown,* Poems of the Scottish Hills *(1982)*

7 For wale o aa the manly sports
Climbin bears the gree.
   J. K. Annand (1908–1993)

8 By the time you have topped a hundred
Munros (the incurable stage usually), you
will know Scotland – and yourself – in a
fuller, richer way.
   Hamish Brown (1934–), The Munros:
   A Personal View, *in D. Bennet,* The
   Munros *(1985)*

9 Mountaineering lays one alongside the
bones of mother earth. One meets her on
equal terms and matches one's skill and

endurance against something that has no care for human life.

> *John Buchan (1875–1940)*, Memory-Hold-the-Door

10 Blythe hae I been on yon hill.

> *Robert Burns (1759–1796)*, Blythe Hae I Been on Yon Hill

11 There is not much variety in it, but gloomy spaces, different rocks, and heath high and low. To cast one's eye from an eminence towards a group of them, they appear still one above the other, fainter and fainter according to aerial perspective, and the whole of a dismal brown drawing upon a dirty purple, and most of all disagreeable when the heath is in bloom.

> *Edmund Burt (fl. early 18th century)*, Letters from a Gentleman in the North of Scotland *(1726–37)*

12 Thus you creep slowly on . . . continually hoping the next ridge before you will be the summit of the highest, and so often deceived in that hope, as almost to despair of ever reaching the top.

> *Edmund Burt*, Letters From a Gentleman in the North of Scotland

13 Once a week the sun shines, and then the mountain peaks are revealed in all the inexpressible tints of blue; and there is blueness which is azure, mother-of-pearl, foggy or indigo, clouded like vapours, a hint or mere reminder of something beautifully blue . . . I tell you, unknown and divine virtues arose within me at the sight of this unbounded blueness.

> *Karel Capek (1890–1938)*, Letters from England

14 It is the finest mental and physical tonic a man can take. Whether it be the grim determination of desperate struggles with difficult rocks, or with ice, or whether it be the sight of range after range of splendid peaks basking in the sunshine, or of mists half hiding the black precipices, or the changing fairy colours of a sunrise, or the subtle curves of the wind-blown snow, all these are good for one.

> *Norman Collie (1859–1942)*, Climbing in the Himalaya and Other Mountain Ranges

15 The Highlands of Scotland contain mountain form of the finest and most subtle kind.

> *Norman Collie*, Climbing in the Himalaya and Other Mountain Ranges

16 The individuality of the Cuillin is . . . most of all the mountain mystery that wraps them round: not the mystery of clearness such as is seen in the Alps and Himalaya . . . but in the secret beauty born of the mists, the rain, and the sunshine, in a quiet and untroubled land, no longer troubled by the more rude and violent manifestations of the active power of Nature.

> *Norman Collie*, Scottish Mountaineering Club Journal

17 The high grasslands on a summer day have an idyllic quality. They are remote and quiet. They are green and kind to the eye. They are ease to the feet. The flowers have great variety and a new beauty, and the very pebbles among which they grow have a sparkle and show of colour . . . Take a little tent and remain in the quietness for a few days. It is magnificent to rise in the morning in such a place.

> *Sir Frank Fraser Darling (1903–1979)*, The Highlands and Islands *(with J. Morton Boyd)*

18 When he some heaps of hills hath overwent,
Begins to think on rest, his journey spent,
Till, mounting some tall mountain he do find
More heights before him than he left behind.

> *William Drummond (1585–1649)*, Flowers of Sion

19 Near the otter's track on the snows of Foinne Bheinn a ptarmigan rose on white wings and disappeared over the ridge into the corrie. Alas, before we could reach the hilltop the mist swept in on the northwest wind. Fog-crystals in beautiful fern-shape grew from the rocks; the frozen moisture fell as delicate spicules of ice. Here, at three thousand feet above the sea, the frost was sufficient to freeze the water vapour in the air.

> *Seton Gordon (1886–1977)*, A Highland Year

20 'Look, the peaks of Arran.' I saw a low dark smudge against a pale patch of clear sky

but was not much impressed. On a clear day in central Scotland you can see Arran from any high place West of Tinto.

Alasdair Gray (1934–), 1982, Janine

21 ... the Mountains are extatic & ought to be visited in pilgrimage once a year. None but these monstrous creatures of God know how to join so much beauty with so much horror.

Thomas Gray (1716–1771), Letters

22 Watch Ben Laoghal play with its four granite peaks on the legendary stuff of history, or is it of the mind? ... Once going down towards bleak Kildonan, I unthinkingly glanced over my shoulder and saw them crowned with snow. I have never forgotten the unearthly fright I got then.

Neil Gunn (1891–1973), Caithness and Sutherland, in A. McCleery, Landscape and Light (1987)

23 ... this frieze of mountains, filed on the blue air. Stac Polly, Cul Beag, Cul Mor, Suilven, Canisp – a frieze and a litany.

Norman MacCaig (1910–1996)

24 Wagnerian Devil wrote the Coigach score;
And God was Mozart when he wrote Cul Mor.

Norman MacCaig, Musical Moment in Assynt

25 I have often seen a little hill in Harris collapse to half its size when a cow appeared on the top of it ... I think it is part of patriotism to stare at the hill till there's a cow on it.

Norman MacCaig, Living in Scotland, from Scottish Field (September 1957)

26 The North face of Liathach lives in the mind like a vision. From the deeps of Coire na Caime, which is the Crooked Corrie, sheer cliffs rise up to spurs and pinnacles and jagged teeth. Its grandeur draws back the heart.

Hugh MacDiarmid (C. M. Grieve, 1892–1978), Lucky Poet

27 Those two bad shepherds, hunched above their sheep.

Naomi Mitchison (1897–1998), Buachaille Etive Mor and Buachaille Etive Beag

28 There is hardly any bad luck in the mountains, only good.

Gwen Moffat, Two Star Red

29 Ben Nevis looms the laird of a'.

Charles Murray (1864–1941), Bennachie

30 Between us and the mountains of Mamore lay the Leven valley; its bottom invisible to us, its breadth nearly five miles. Across this great gap there suddenly travelled a broad wave of light, which seemed to break like a roller on the crest of our reef, and then stream in a wide shimmering curtain across Glencoe. The wave was followed by another, and yet another. It was the aurora borealis.

W. H. Murray, Undiscovered Scotland

31 ... there was conveyed into the mind by the hills and stars themselves and through part agency of the senses this knowledge that the night hush of earth is expectant: as though our universe were a live being, not a dead thing.

W. H. Murray, Undiscovered Scotland

32 A mystic twilight, like that of an old chapel at vespers, pervaded these highest slopes of Buachaille. We stood at the everlasting gates, and as so often happens at the end of a great climb, a profound stillness came upon my mind, and paradoxically the silence was song and the diversity of things vanished. The mountains and the world and I were one. But that was not all: a strange and powerful feeling that something as yet unknown was also within my grasp, was trembling into vision.

W. H. Murray, Mountaineering in Scotland

33 The Old Man of Hoy ... Height for height it is considerably more spectacular than the final 450 feet of any Alpine peak of my knowledge.

Tom Patey (1932–1970), One Man's Mountains

34 At the top of the pedestal was a large ledge, the essence of comfort had I not shared it with a young fulmar petrel. When molested these birds have a characteristic and unpleasant trait – they eject a foul-smelling odour into the face and eyes of any intruder, leaving a pungent odour on

skin and clothing which no amount of scrubbing or deodorant can remove.

Tom Patey, One Man's Mountains

35 'How do you know this rope is safe, Hamish?'

'I don't,' he replied in his abstract way.

'Well, how are we to find out whether it's safe, if you can't tell us from up there?'

MacInnes was the model of patience. 'Try climbing up the rope,' he remarked, encouragingly. 'I'll be most surprised if it comes away.'

Tom Patey, One Man's Mountains

36 The rock is like porridge – in consistency though not quality, for porridge is part of our national heritage and a feast fit for a king. This was not.

Tom Patey, One Man's Mountains

37 I shall always remember that as the noisiest climb I ever had. There was a foot or more of loose rock which had been shattered by the lightning and frost of ages. This formed the edges of the pinnacle and had to be thrust down as we climbed up. The noise was appalling: the very rock of the pinnacle itself seemed to be vibrating with indignation at our rude onslaught.

Lawrence Pilkington, Scottish Mountaineering Club Journal, *April 1939, recalling the first ascent of the Inaccessible Pinnacle, Skye, August 1880*

38 The rocky summits, split and rent,
Formed turret, dome or battlement,
Or seemed fantastically set
With cupola or minaret.

Sir Walter Scott (1771–1832), The Lady of the Lake

39 'The Hielan' hills, the Hielan' hills – I never see them but they gar me grew.'

Sir Walter Scott, Rob Roy

40 All are aspects of one entity, the living mountain. The disintegrating rock, the nurturing rain, the quickening sun, the seed, the root, the bird – all are one. Eagle and alpine veronica are part of the mountain's wholeness.

Nan Shepherd (1893–1981), The Living Mountain

41 Yet often the mountain gives itself most completely when I have no destination, when I reach nowhere in particular, but have gone out merely to be with the mountain as one visits a friend, with no intention but to be with him.

Nan Shepherd, The Living Mountain

42 That awful loneliness
Received our souls as air receives the smoke.

Nan Shepherd, Above Loch Avon

43 You cannot feel comfortable at Loch Coruisk, and the discomfort rises in a great degree from the feeling that you are outside of everything – that the thunder-smitten peaks have a life with which you cannot intermeddle. The dumb monsters sadden and perplex.

Alexander Smith (1830–1867), A Summer in Skye

44 The Quirang is frozen terror and superstition.

Alexander Smith, A Summer in Skye

45 The truth is, if you're to gae up Benledi, you maun mak up your mind to do'd. It's no to be trifled wi' . . . Yon that ye thocht was the head yestreen is the third ridge fae the tap only.

'Tammy Trampalot', The People's Journal, *September 1854*

46 'Tell me,' I said, 'where could I buy two pints of foaming shandy in shining tankards?'

'Sligachan,' replied Ling.

'How far?'

'Ten miles.'

'Say it in hours.'

'Six hours.'

This 'free men of the hills' stuff has its tragic moments.

J. E. B. Wright, Mountain Days in the Isle of Skye *(1934)*

47 It was towards evening when by a steep but safe passage I outwitted the mountain's formidable defences, reaching the curious top that makes it resemble a cockatoo and gives it the name Stack Polly.

Andrew Young (1881–1975), A Retrospect of Flowers

48 Above all was Suilven, throwing its dark shadow, a mountain huger than itself.

Andrew Young, A Retrospect of Flowers

Music, Song and Dance

1   O sing to me the auld Scotch sangs
     In the braid Scottish tongue,
     The sangs my father loved to hear,
     The sangs my mother sung.
          Traditional, The Auld Scotch Sangs

2   An first he played da notes o noy,
     An dan he played da notes o joy.
     An dan he played da god gabber reel,
     Da meicht ha made a sick hert hale.
          Anonymous, King Orfeo (*A Shetland Ballad*)

3   There's some come here for to see
          me hang,
     And some to buy my fiddle:
     But ere I see it amang them fa',
     I'll brak it doon the middle.
          Anonymous, Macpherson's Rant

4   Oh, he'll gang the hie road and I'll
          gang the low,
     But I'll be in Heaven afore him;
     For my bed is prepared in the mossy
          graveyard,
     'Mang the hazels o' green Inverarnan.
     The thistle shall bloom, and the King
          hae his ain,
     An' fond lovers meet in the gloamin',
     An' I an' my true love will yet meet again,
     Far abune the bonnie banks o' Loch
          Lomond.
          Anonymous, Loch Lomond (*18th century*), *quoted in J. K. Annand*, A Scots Handsel (*1980*)

5   O, ye'll tak the high road, and I'll tak
          the low road,
     And I'll be in Scotland afore ye;
     But me and my true love will never meet
          again,
     By the bonny, bonny banks o' Loch
          Lomond.
          Anonymous, Loch Lomond (*19th century*), *sometimes ascribed to Lady John Scott (1810–1900)*

6   The high, high notes o' *Bangor's* tune
     Are very hard to raise;
     And trying hard to reach them gars
     The lassies burst their stays.
          Anonymous, said to be a precentor's rehearsal verse

7   I wish I were a brewer's horse,
     Three quarters of the year

I'd turn my head where tail should be,
And drink up all the beer.
     Anonymous, said to be a precentor's rehearsal verse

8   She's my beauteous *nighean ruadh*,
     My joy and sorrow too,
     And although she is untrue,
     Well, I cannot live without her,
     For my heart's a boat in tow.
          Sir Harold Boulton (1859–1935), Loch Tay Boat Song

9   I asked the piper, 'How long does it take to learn to play a pibroch?'
          He answered, 'It takes seven years to learn to play the pipes, and seven years to learn to play a pibroch. And then you need the poetry.'
          George Bruce (1909–), radio interview with Pipe Major Robert U. Brown

10   Blast upon blast they blew,
     Each clad in tartan new,
     Bonnet and blackcock feather:
     And every Piper was fou' –
     Twenty Pipers together!
          Robert Buchanan (1845–1901), The Wedding of Shon Maclean

11   Yestreen, when to the trembling string
     The dance gaed thro' the lichted ha'.
          Robert Burns (1759–1796), Mary Morison

12   Chords that vibrate sweetest pleasure,
     Thrill the deepest notes of woe.
          Robert Burns, Sweet Sensibility

13   I am a fiddler to my trade,
     An' a' the tunes that e'er I played,
     The sweetest still to wife or maid
     Was whistle o'er the lave o't.
          Robert Burns, The Jolly Beggars

14   There's threesome reels, there's foursome
          reels,
     There's hornpipes and strathspeys, man,
     But the ae best dance e'er cam to the land
     Was the deil's awa wi' th' Exciseman.
          Robert Burns, The Deil's Awa Wi' Th' Exciseman

15   Nae cotillion, brent new frae France,
     But hornpipes, jigs, strathspeys, and reels
     Put life and mettle in their heels.
          Robert Burns, Tam o' Shanter

16 There sat Auld Nick, in shape o' beast . . .
    He screw'd the pipes, and gart them skirl,
    Till roof and rafters a' did dirl.
      Robert Burns, Tam o' Shanter

17 They reel'd, they set, they crossed, they
      cleekit,
    Til ilka carlin swat and reekit,
    And coost her duddies on the wark
    And linkit at it in her sark!
      Robert Burns, Tam o' Shanter

18 Those who think that composing a Scotch
    song is a trifling business – let them try.
      Robert Burns, Letter to James Hoy, *1787*

19 Hark to the pibroch's pleasing note!
    Hark to the swelling nuptial song!
    In joyous strains the voices float,
    And still the choral peal prolong.
      Lord Byron (1788–1824), Oscar of Alva

20 It is thought by many, indeed, that Scot-
    land has not only reached the level of
    Ireland, but in science and skill of music
    has far surpassed it, so that men now seek
    that land as the true fountain-head of the
    art.
      Giraldus Cambrensis (c.1146–c.1223),
      Topographia Hiberniae, *from Latin*

21 Her fingers witched the chords they
      passed along,
    And her lips seemed to kiss the soul in
      song.
      Thomas Campbell (1777–1844),
      Theodric

22 . . . here the music has remained a specta-
    cle, as in the earliest times.
      Karel Capek (1890–1938), Letters from
      England

23 Such a set of ugly creatures as the Chorus
    I never did see! I grew so sorry for them,
    reflecting perhaps that each had a life of
    her own; that perhaps 'somebody loved
    that pig'; that, if I had any tears in me at
    the moment, I would have cried for them
    all packed there like herrings in a barrel,
    into one mass of sound.
      Jane Welsh Carlyle (1801–1866), *on a per-
      formance of* The Messiah

24 One day after my piano-playing, and after
    various songs by other Scottish ladies, they
    brought in a kind of accordion and my host-
    ess (who was regarded locally as a great

musician) began with the utmost gravity
to play on it the most atrocious tunes.
      Frederic Chopin (1810–1849), *on the
      Duchess of Hamilton, quoted in T. Rat-
      cliffe Barnett*, Scottish Pilgrimage in
      the Land of Lost Content *(1949)*

25 Jocky, whose manly high-boned cheeks
      to crown,
    With freckles spotted, flamed the golden
      down,
    With meikle art could on the bagpipes
      play
    E'en from the rising to the setting day:
    Sawney as long without remorse could
      bawl
    Home's madrigals and ditties from Fingal.
      Charles Churchill (1731–1764), Proph-
      ecy of Famine

26 Scotch songs are not 'pretty' . . . They
    were not meant to be merely ornamental;
    they were the growth of simple taste, of
    true feeling, often of intense passion. Love,
    joy and patriotism are their inspiration.
      Eliza Cook, Eliza Cook's Journal *(1852)*,
      quoted in D. Gifford and D. McMillan, A
      History of Scottish Women's Writing
      (1997)

27 On Scotia's plains, in days of yore,
    When lads and lasses tartan wore,
    Saft Music rang on ilka shore
    In hamely weid:
    But harmony is now no more,
    And music dead.
      Robert Fergusson (1750–1774), Elegy on
      the Death of Scots Music

28 'It's impossible the bagpipe could frighten
    any body,' said Miss Jackie in a high
    voice: 'nobody with common sense could
    be frightened at a bagpipe.'
      Mrs Douglas here mildly interposed, and
    soothed down the offended pride of the
    Highlanders, by attributing Lady Juliana's
    agitation entirely to surprise. The word
    operated like a charm; all were ready to
    admit, that it was a surprising thing when
    heard for the first time.
      Susan Ferrier (1782–1854), Marriage

29 They made the people break and burn
    their pipes and fiddles. If there was a fool-
    ish man here and there who demurred, the
    good ministers and the good elders them-
    selves broke and burned their instruments,
    saying 'Better is the small fire that warms

on the little day of peace, than the big fire that burns on the great day of wrath.'

Sir Archibald Geikie (1835–1924), Scottish Reminiscences

30 But then Chae cried *Strip the Willow*, and they all lined up, and the melodeon played bonnily in Chae's hands, and Long Rob's fiddle bow was darting and glimmering, and in two minutes, in the whirl and go of *Strip the Willow*, there wasn't a cold soul in Blawearie barn.

Lewis Grassic Gibbon (James Leslie Mitchell, 1901–1935), Sunset Song

31 . . . it came on Chris how strange was the sadness of Scotland's singing, made for the sadness of the land and sky in dark autumn evenings, the crying of men and women of the land who'd seen their lives and loves sink away in the years, things wept for beside the sheep-buchts, remembered at night and in twilight.

Lewis Grassic Gibbon, Sunset Song

32 Now the skill of this piper was not rated too highly locally, and he had scarcely taken his pipes from their box and walked on to the platform when one of the audience with more vigour than taste, yelled at the top of his voice, 'Sit doon, ye useless cratur.' At once the chairman was on his feet and called out in stern and disapproving tones, 'Who called the piper a useless cratur?' Came the answer instantly, 'Who called the useless cratur a piper?'

Recalled by Seton Gordon (1886–1977), in A Highland Year

33 I have heard the story that MacCrimmon would write down a tune on the wet sand as the tide began to ebb, and would expect his pupils to be able to play it before the flood tide once more flowed over the sand and washed away the marks.

Seton Gordon, A Highland Year

34 Lady Anne Lindsay heard her own ballad 'Auld Robin Gray' sung to the accompaniment of the harp, and applauded by companies who were unaware that the bright blushing girl in the corner had written it.

H. Grey Graham, The Social Life of Scotland in the Eighteenth Century *(1899)*

35 He heard a heavenly melody and sound, Passing all instrumentis musical, Causit be the rolling of the spheris round.

Robert Henryson (c.1425–c.1500), Orpheus and Eurydice

36 Of sic music to write I do but dote, Therefore of this matter a straw I lay, For in my life I couth never sing a note.

Robert Henryson, Orpheus and Eurydice

37 These songs had floated down on the stream of oral tradition, from generation to generation, and were regarded as a precious treasure belonging to the country; but when Mr Scott's work appeared their arcanum was laid open, and a deadening blow was inflicted on our rural literature.

James Hogg (1770–1835), On the Changes in the Habits, Amusements and Condition of the Scotch Peasantry, *referring to Scott's* Minstrelsy of the Scottish Border

38 Cam' ye by Atholl, lad wi' the philabeg, Down by the Tummel or banks o' the Gary? Saw ye the lads, wi' their bonnets and white cockades Leaving their mountains to follow Prince Charlie?

James Hogg, Cam' Ye By Atholl?

39 A person doesn't make a life singing Scottish traditional music on a basis of charm . . . Everything she most deeply feels and believes in – about death and country and love and womanhood – comes out in these songs. The songs aren't pictures. They're rocks. They're the mountain itself.

Garrison Keillor, on the singing of Jean Redpath (1936–)

40 The way a seated jazz musician gets him or herself and the instrument prepared, these wee glimmers of a smile to the fellow musicians, the friends and acquaintances in the audience, but also taking great care not to confront directly the stares from members of the ordinary people – otherwise enter irony: the kind that leads to a lack of overall control.

James Kelman (1946–), A Disaffection

41 One thing he had learned this afternoon:
    playing the pipes was not a substitute for
    sex!

    James Kelman, A Disaffection *(the refer-*
    ence is to domestic water pipes)

42 They were made for singing and no for
    reading, but ye hae broken the charm now,
    and they'll never be sung mair. And the
    warst thing o' a'– they're neither richt
    spelled nor richt setten doun.

    Margaret Laidlaw (1730–1813), mother
    of James Hogg, to Sir Walter Scott, on his
    transcriptions of traditional songs

43 It was said that this was the manner in
    which the overture, *The Hebrides*, took its
    rise: Mendelssohn's sisters asked him to
    tell them something about the Hebrides.
    'It cannot be told, only played,' he said.
    No sooner spoken than he seated himself
    at the piano and played the theme which
    afterwards grew into the overture.

    W. A. Lampadius, Life of Mendelssohn,
    quoted in F. Marian McNeill, An Iona
    Anthology, *(1971)*

44 There are two kinds of artists left: those
    who endorse Pepsi, and those who simply
    won't.

    Annie Lennox, quoted in The Guardian,
    November 1990

45 I should not have omitted to mention that
    a certain rapturous yelp, which every now
    and then escapes the male dancers in the
    height of their glee, seems to give new
    spirit to their movements.

    John Lettice, English visitor in 1792,
    quoted in Agnes Mure Mackenzie, Scot-
    tish Pageant 1707–1802 *(1950)*

46 And then, as the music went on, they found
    they were dancing in the proper patterns,
    for they had partners who had come from
    nowhere, who led them first to the right
    and then to the left, up the middle and
    down the sides, bowing and knocking their
    heels in the air.

    Eric Linklater (1899–1974), The
    Dancers

47 I will try to follow you on the last day
       of the world,
    And pray I may see you all standing
       shoulder to shoulder
    With Patrick Mor Macrimmon and
    Duncan Ban Macrimmon in the centre . . .

    And you playing: 'Farewell to Scotland,
       and the rest of the earth.'

    Hugh MacDiarmid (C .M. Grieve,
    1892–1978)

48 Instinct right, reflection wrong,
    When you get a man to sing a song.

    Father Allan MacDonald, quoted in Amy
    Murray, Father Allan's Island *(1936)*

49 The God-imprisoned harmonies
    That out in gracious motions go.

    George Macdonald (1824–1905), Organ
    Songs

50 On one occasion, as Iain and another
    apprentice were playing the same tune
    alternately, Macrimmon asked the other
    lad why he did not play like Iain Dall. The
    lad replied, 'By Saint Mary, I'd do so if my
    fingers had not been after the skate,' allud-
    ing to the sticky state of his fingers after
    having eaten some of that fish . . . And
    this has become a proverbial taunt which
    northern pipers to this day hurl at their
    inferior brethren from the south.

    Osgood Mackenzie (1842–1922), A Hun-
    dred Years in the Highlands

51 I am convinced that Scottish Gaelic song
    is the chief artistic glory of the Scots, and
    of all people of Celtic speech, and one of
    the great artistic glories of Europe.

    Sorley Maclean (1911–1996), Old Songs
    and New Poetry, *in K. Miller*, Memoirs
    of a Modern Scotland *(1970)*

52 Ye sing like the shuilfie in the slae.

    Robert Maclellan (1907–), Sang

53 Dance to your shadow when it's good to
       be living, lad,
    Dance to your shadow when there's
       nothing better near you.

    Kenneth Macleod (1871–1955), Dance to
    Your Shadow

54 'Stand abeigh, ye foolish forward folk, and
    gi'e her ladyship's goon room for the reel!'

    Ronald Macrailt, Hoolachan *(1923)*,
    quoted in J. Grant, The Scottish
    National Dictionary *(1934)*

55 Translated into music, Iona is Debussy,
    Eigg is Wagner.

    Jessie Matthay, Life of Tobias Matthay
    (1858–1945)

56 I luvit singing and playing on instrumentis passing weil, and wald gladlie spend tyme quhair the exercise thairof wes within the College; for two or thrie of our condiscipulis playit feloun weil on the virginalis, and ane uther on the lute and githorn. Our Regent had also the pinaldis in his chalmer . . . It wes the greit mercie of my God that keipit me from anie greit progres in singing and playing on instrumentis, for gif I had atteininiet to anie resonabil messour thairin, I had nevir done gude uthirwayis, in respect of my amorous dispositioun.

James Melville (1556–1614), Diary

57 The chapel . . . is now roofless, grass and ivy grow there; and at the broken altar Mary was crowned Queen of Scotland . . . I believe I found today in that old chapel the beginning of my Scottish Symphony.

Felix Mendelssohn-Bartholdy (1809–1847), Letters, *quoted in Maurice Lindsay*, The Eye is Delighted

58 . . . that patchwork of blasphemy, absurdity, and gross obscenity, which the zeal of an early Reformer spawned under the captivating title of *Ane Compendious Booke of Godlie and Spirituall Songs* is neither comprehended under the description of song as we are now in quest of, nor do its miserable and profane parodies reflect any trace whatsoever of the stately ancient narative ballad.

William Motherwell (1797–1835), Introduction to Minstrelsy Ancient and Modern

59 'You don't need tickets for a Furnace baal so long as you ken the man at the door and talk the Gaalic at him.'

Neil Munro (1864–1930), The Vital Spark

60 'And good pipers iss difficult nooadays to get; there's not many in it. You'll maybe get a kind of a plain piper going aboot the streets of Gleska noo and then, but they're like the herrin', and the turnips, and rhubarb, and things like that – you don't get them fresh in Gleska'.

Neil Munro, The Vital Spark

61 'Do ye hear that?' said he. '"Dark Lochnagar": I used ance to could nearly play't on the mooth harmonium.'

Neil Munro, Erchie

62 He filled the bag at a breath and swung a lover's arm round about it. To those who know not the pipes, the feel of the bag in the oxter is a gaiety lost. The sweet round curve is like a girl's waist; it is friendly and warm in the crook of the elbow and against a man's side, and to press it is to bring laughing or tears.

Neil Munro, The Lost Pibroch

63 He was whistlin' to the porridge that were hott'rin' on the fire,
He was whistlin' ower the travise to the baillie in the byre;
Nae a blackbird nor a mavis, that hae pipin' for their trade,
Was a marrow to the whistle that the wee herd made.

Charles Murray (1864–1941), The Whistle

64 There grows a bonnie brier bush in our kail-yard,
And white are the blossoms o't in our kail-yard.

Carolina Oliphant, Lady Nairne (1766–1845), There Grows a Bonnie Brier Bush

65 Experts have been puzzled by a new kind of bagpipe music played by Pipe Major Iain Macleod. Now it turns out the tapes were recorded backwards. More than 1,000 records went out without anyone realising the mistake. And 400 were sold without complaint.

Report in The Observer, *1967*

66 Put no faith in aught that bears the name of music while you are in Scotland . . . I was asked to a private concert; I suffered the infliction of several airs with exemplary patience.

Amedée Pichot, French consul in Edinburgh, 1822, quoted in Catherine and Donald Carswell, The Scots Week-End *(1936)*

67 He touched his harp and nations heard, entranced,
As some vast river of unfailing source,
Rapid, exhaustless, deep, his numbers flowed,
And opened new fountains in the human heart.

Robert Pollok (1798–1827), The Course of Time

68 Come along, come along,
Let us foot it out together,
Come along, come along,
Be it fair or stormy weather,
With the hills of home before us,
And the purple of the heather,
Let us sing in happy chorus,
Come along, come along.

> *Sir Hugh S. Roberton (1874–1952),* The
> Uist Tramping Song, *from the Gaelic of
> Archibald MacDonald*

69 Westering home, and a song in the air,
Light in the eye, and it's goodbye to care.

> *Sir Hugh S. Roberton,* Westering Home

70 The whole was so uncouth and extraordinary; the impression which this wild music made on me contrasted so strongly with that which it made upon the inhabitants of the country, that I am convinced we should look upon this strange composition not as essentially belonging to music, but to history.

> *B. F. St-Fond (1741–1819),* Travels in
> England and Scotland

71 The bigots of the iron time
Had called his harmless art a crime.
A wandering harper, scorned and poor,
He begged his bread from door to door.

> *Sir Walter Scott (1771–1832),* The Lay
> of the Last Minstrel

72 Hearken, my minstrels! Which of ye all
Touched his harp with that dying fall,
So sweet, so soft, so faint,
It seemed an angel's whispered call
To an expiring saint?

> *Sir Walter Scott,* The Bride of
> Triermain

73 I'm a piper to my trade,
My name is Rob the Ranter:
The lassies loup as they were daft,
When I blaw up my chanter.

> *Francis Sempill (c.1616–1685),* Maggie
> Lauder

74 Meg up and walloped ower the green,
For brawly could she frisk it.

> *Francis Sempill,* Maggie Lauder

75 . . . the dank euphonies of the Glasgow
Orpheus Choir.

> *Alan Sharp,* A Dream of Perfection, *in
> I. Archer and T. Royle,* We'll Support
> You Evermore *(1976)*

76 The reel should be played crisp and birly
like a weel-gaun wheelie.

> *Scott Skinner (James Skinner,
> 1843–1927)*

77 First the heel and then the toe,
That's the way the polkas go;
First the toe and then the heel,
That's the way to dance a reel;
Quick about and then away,
Lightly dance the glad Strathspey;
Jump a jump and jump it big,
That's the way to dance a jig.

> *Alexander Stewart ('Nether Lochaber')*

78 Singing is sweet, but be sure of this,
Lips only sing when they cannot kiss.

> *James Thomson (1834–1882),* Sunday
> Up the River

79 Were you to hear a Scots lady repeat the verses of any of the true original songs, and afterwards to sing them to the notes, you would find such an affinity to the tone of her voice in speaking, that the notes would appear only the accents of the language made exquisitely sweet and musical.

> *Edward Topham (b.1751),* Letters from
> Edinburgh *(1776)*

Nature

1 The men of Angus do not understand a nature-lover's ecstasies. They have been growing potatoes so long that the Golden Wonder has entered into their souls.

> *John R. Allan,* Summer in Scotland
> *(1938)*

2 O Nature! A' thy shows an' forms
To feeling, pensive hearts hae charms!

> *Robert Burns (1759–1796),* Epistle to
> William Simpson

3 Ye banks and braes o' bonnie Doon,
How can ye bloom sae fresh and fair?

> *Robert Burns,* Ye Banks and Braes o'
> Bonnie Doon

4 In Scotland, I have eaten nettles, I have slept in nettle sheets, and I have dined off a nettle tablecloth. The young and tender nettle is an excellent potherb. The stalks of the old nettle are as good as flax for making cloth. I have heard my mother say

that she thought nettle cloth more durable than any other species of linen.

Thomas Campbell (1777–1844), Letters from the South

5 Nature, which is the time-vesture of God, and reveals Him to the wise, hides Him from the foolish.

Thomas Carlyle (1795–1881), Sartor Resartus

6 Gane but were the winter cauld,
And gane were but the snaw,
I could sleep in the wild woods
Where the primroses blaw.

Allan Cunningham (1784–1842)

7 There is an extraordinary feeling of joy in being among the birches when the leaves are opening from the bud.

Sir Frank Fraser Darling (1903–1979), with J. Morton Boyd, The Highlands and Islands

8 The daisy did onbreid her crownell small,
And every flour unlappit in the dale.

Gavin Douglas (1475–1522), Prologue to the Aeneid

9 One birch in particular I have in mind. It is a tree perhaps fifty years old, its stem, with almost pure white bark, straight and graceful, its branches pendulous and often shaken by the wind, for it grows on a hillside without shelter. Sometimes I have looked long on that tree and have seen it as it were dissolve in thought and assume a new and delicate beauty not of this world.

Seton Gordon (1886–1977), A Highland Year

10 The muirlan' burnie, purple-fringed
Wi' hinny-scented heather,
Whaur gowden king-cups blink aneath
The brecken's waving feather.

Janet Hamilton (1795–1873), Auld Mither Scotland

11 But the better all the works of nature are understood, the more they will be ever admired.

James Hogg (1770–1835), The Private Memoirs and Confessions of a Justified Sinner

12 There's gowd in the breast of the primrose pale,
An' siller in every blossom;
There's riches galore in the breeze of the vale,
And health in the wild wind's bosom.

James Hogg, There's Gowd in the Breast

13 Dame Nature's petticoat is not so easily lifted as that of the Princess Obrea.

James Hutton (1726–1797), letter to Sir Joseph Banks, Winter 1772, referring to an alleged escapade of Banks on Tahiti

14 What a lovely, lovely moon. And it's in the constituency too.

Alan Jackson (1938–), Young Politician

15 Ever since I have been enquiring into the works of nature, I have always admired and loved the simplicity of her ways.

George Martine, Medical Essays and Observations, *(1747)*

16 Let them popple, let them pirl,
Plish-plash and plunk and plop and ploot,
In quakin' quaw or fish-currie,
I ken a' they're aboot.

Hugh MacDiarmid (C. M. Grieve, 1892–1978), Water Music

17 My earliest impressions are of an almost tropical luxuriance of nature – of great forests, of honey-scented heather hills, and moorlands infinitely rich in little-appreciated beauties of flowering, of animal and insect life, of subtle relationships of water and light, and of a multitude of rivers, each with its own distinct music.

Hugh MacDiarmid, The Thistle Rises

18 The rose of all the world is not for me.
I want for my part
Only the little white rose of Scotland
That smells sharp and sweet – and breaks the heart.

Hugh MacDiarmid, The Little White Rose

19 Bountiful Primroses,
With outspread heart that needs the rough leaves' care.

George Macdonald (1824–1905), Wild Flowers

20 That one year – in 1868 – I got 99 and a half brace of grouse off the crofters' hill ground, 60 brace off Isle Ewe . . . and my total in that year was 1,314 grouse, 33 black game, 49 partridge, 110 golden plover, 35 wild ducks, 53 snipe, 91 blue rock pigeons, 184 hares, without mentioning geese, teal,

ptarmigan and roe, etc . . . Now so many of these good birds and beasts are either quite extinct or on the verge of becoming so . . .

> *Osgood Mackenzie (1842–1922)*, A Hundred Years in the Highlands

21 The whins are blythesome on the knowe wi candles bleezan clear.

> *A. D. Mackie (1904–)*, A New Spring

22 The curled young bracken unsheath their green claws.

> *Fiona Macleod (William Sharp, 1856–1905)*

23 Until a man has seen good machair, like that of Berneray, or of the Monach Isles, or of Tiree, he may find it hard to realise that although the crofters call it 'gress' it grows not grass but flowers.

> *W. H. Murray*, The Islands of Western Scotland (1973)

24 Crimson dockens, snowy daisies, with
    their rounded breasts of gold;
Tangled tufts of purple heather, thistles,
    buttercups and bells.

> *J. Hume Nisbet (1849–1921)*, A Forenoon Effect, Borderland

25 . . . a noble tree is in some measure a matter of public concern.

> *John Ramsay of Ochtertyre (1736–1814)*, quoted in Agnes Mure Mackenzie, Scottish Pageant 1707–1802 (1950)

26 And what saw ye there
At the bush aboon Traquair?
Or what did you hear that was worth
    your heed?
I heard the cushat croon
Thro' the gowden afternoon,
And the Quair burn singin' doun to the
    Vale o' Tweed.

> *J. C. Shairp (1819–1885)*, The Bush Aboon Traquair

27 . . . the day kept up its enchantment as I walked up the bridle-path – the birk-stems were white, the birk leaves brown and gold, and the waters of the Tilt gold and tawny in the sunlight:
Sweet the laverock's note and lang –
Lilting wildly up the glen –

it is always this stretch of Glen Tilt that comes to mind.

> *Janet Adam Smith (1905–)*, Mountain Holidays

28 Here I can blow a garden with my breath,
And in my hand a forest lies asleep.

> *Muriel Stuart (1900–1991)*, The Seed Shop

29 Anyone who aspires to being made a mummy, need only arrange to be buried in a bog.

> *Andrew Young (1885–1971)*, A Retrospect of Flowers

30 *Primula Scotica* might be an even better emblem for Scotland. It is not common everywhere like the Thistle; it is confined to Scotland, growing nowhere else.

> *Andrew Young*, A Retrospect of Flowers

The People

1 Saint Peter said to God, in ane sport
    word –
'Can ye nocht mak a Hielandman of
    this horse turd?'
God turned owre the horse turd with
    his pykit staff,
And up start a Hielandman as black as ony
    draff.

> *Anonymous*, How the First Hielandman was Made

2 A fond fule, fariar,
A cairtar, a cariar,
A libber, and a lyar,
And riddill revar . . .
Ane auld monk, a lechour,
A drunkin drechour,
A double-toungit counsalour . . .

> *Anonymous*, Colkelbie Sow

3 God send the land deliverance
Frae every reiving, riding Scot;
We'll sune hae neither cow nor ewe,
We'll sune hae neither staig nor stot.

> *Anonymous*, The Death of Parcy Reed

4 . . . there are no finer Gentlemen in the World, than that Nation can justly boast of; but then they are such as have travelled, and are indebted to other Countries for those Accomplishments that render them

so esteemed, their own affording only Pedantry, Poverty, Brutality, and Hypocrisy.

Anonymous, Scotland Characterised,
1701

5 See how they press to cross the Tweed,
And strain their limbs with eager speed!
While Scotland from her fertile shore
Cries, On my sons, return no more.
Hither they haste with willing mind,
Nor cast one longing look behind.

*Anonymous English pasquinade, 18th
century*

6 We're either in or oot wi' folk,
We're a' ae oo, we're a' ae oo.

Anonymous, 19th century, We're A' Ae
Oo

7 The Campbells are comin' o ho, o ho,
The Campbells are comin' o ho, o ho:
The Campbells are comin', from bonnie
    Loch Leven;
The Campbells are comin' o ho, o ho.

Anonymous, The Campbells are Comin'

8 The Campbells are comin,' I ken by
    the smell;
And when they get here we'll all send
    them tae Hell.

Anonymous, children's burlesque

9 . . . the Scots are not industrious, and the
people are poor. They spend all their time
in wars, and when there is no war they
fight with one another.

*Don Pedro de Ayala, Spanish ambassador
to James IV, official report, July 1498*

10 Nowhere beats the heart so kindly
As beneath the tartan plaid.

W. E. Aytoun (1830–1865), Charles
Edward at Versailles

11 Chopin hated the English, and of the
Scots he said that they were ugly but good-
natured . . . 'They are kind, but so boring
that the Lord preserve them.'

T. Ratcliffe Barnett, Scottish Pilgrimage in the Land of Lost Content *(1949)*

12 As Dr Johnson never said, Is there any
Scotsman without charm?

*J. M. Barrie (1860–1937), address to
Edinburgh University*

13 His Lordship may compel us to be equal
upstairs, but there will never be equality
in the servants' hall.

J. M. Barrie, The Admirable Crichton

14 Among other remarkable feats they could
allegedly live immersed in swamps with
only their heads above water, for many
days at a time, and they could subsist on
special iron rations – 'a small portion about
the size of a bean, of this special food, prevents them from feeling either hunger or
thirst.'

Anthony Birley, Septimius Severus: The
African Emperor *(1971), on Roman com-
mentators' views of the Maeatae and Cale-
donii, tribal groups of the late 2nd century*

15 The two classes that mek ahl the mischief
of the kintry are weemen and meenisters.

William Black (1841–1898), Highland
Cousins

16 Trust yow no Skott.

*Andrew Boord, 1536, English agent, letter
to Thomas Cromwell*

17 *James Boswell:* I do indeed come from Scotland, but I cannot help it.
Samuel Johnson: That, Sir, I find, is what
a very great many of your countrymen
cannot help.

James Boswell (1740–1785), The Life of
Samuel Johnson

18 We take a pleasure, a malicious pleasure,
I am afraid, in pricking bubbles; and,
though we are very sentimental ourselves,
we like to pour cold water on other people's sentiment.

John Buchan (1875–1940), Some Scottish Characteristics, *in W. A. Craigie,*
The Scots Tongue

19 Really, we are getting horribly like our
neighbours.

John Buchan, The Scots Tongue

20 The truth is that we are at bottom the
most sentimental and emotional people on
earth.

John Buchan, The Scots Tongue

21 For a' that, and a' that,
It's comin yet for a' that,
That Man to Man, the world o'er,
Shall brothers be, for a' that.

Robert Burns (1759–1796), A Man's a
Man for a' That

22 From scenes like these, old Scotia's
   grandeur springs,
That makes her lov'd at home, rever'd
   abroad:
Princes and lords are but the breath
   of kings:
An honest man's the noblest work o' God.

   Robert Burns, The Cottar's Saturday
   Night

23 How dreary a thing it is that a community should have to dismiss the choice
   of its children from its own bosom, and
   how happy is the condition of that . . .
   state which under a strong and free government . . . has resources enough to keep
   its most active and adventurous citizens at
   work on national objects, and neither lends
   its children to the stranger nor calls a foreign force into its own soil. There is little
   satisfaction in stranger laurels.

   John Hill Burton, The Scot Abroad
   (1864)

24 Then thousand schemes of petulance
   and pride
Despatch her scheming children far
   and wide:
Some east, some west, some everywhere
   but north,
In quest of lawless gain they issue forth.

   Lord Byron (1788–1824), The Curse of
   Minerva

25 Who hath not glow'd above the page
   where fame
Hath fix'd high Caledon's unconquer'd
   name;
The mountain-land which spurned the
   Roman chain,
And baffled back the fiery-crested Dane,
Whose bright claymore and hardihood
   of hand
No foe could tame – no tyrant could
   command?
The race is gone, but still their children
   breathe,
And glory crowns them with redoubled
   wreath.

   Lord Byron, Address Intended to be
   Recited at the Caledonian Meeting
   (May 1814)

26 For body-killing tyrants cannot kill
The public soul . . .

and slaughtered men
Fight fiercer in their orphans o'er again.

   Thomas Campbell (1777–1844), Lines
   on Poland

27 Had *Cain* been *Scot*, God would have
   changed his doom,
Not forc'd him wander, but confin'd him
   home.

   J. Cleveland, Poems, *1647*

28 'You don't get the old characters now,'
   said a man who was patently already a
   'character'.

   Derek Cooper (1925–), The Road to
   Mingulay

29 Turloch O' Neill ruled Tyrone in general
   with satisfaction to the Government. But
   as dowry with his wife Agnes Campbell,
   daughter of the fourth Earl of Argyll, he
   got two thousand Hebridean Scots, and
   the enlistment of these professional fight-
   ers aroused suspicion. 'One Scot', it was
   said, 'was worth two of the Irish.'

   Edmund Curtis, A History of Ireland
   (1936)

30 Society, the mud wherein we stand
Up to the eyes.

   John Davidson (1857–1909), Smith

31 I thought of pre-commercial Scotland, a
   land of brigands and bigots.

   Norman Douglas (1868–1952), Siren
   Land

32 Many a single county in Scotland has produced more men of original genius than
   tracts twice as large in the more favoured
   climates of Europe.

   Norman Douglas, Siren Land

33 'A *Scozzeze*. What kind of animal is that?'
'A person who thinks ahead.'

   Norman Douglas, Alone

34 The men o' the North are a' gone gyte,
A' gone gyte thegither, o,
The derricks rise tae the northern skies,
And the past is gane forever, o.

   Sheila Douglas, The Men o' the North,
   quoted in Gordon Wright, Favourite
   Scots Lyrics *(1973)*

35 They plume themselves on their skill in
   dialectic subtleties.

   *Desiderius Erasmus (c.1466–1536), on
   Scottish scholars*

36 If the Scots knew enough to go indoors when it rained, they would never get any exercise.

　　Simeon Ford (1855–1933), My Trip to Scotland

37 Some maintain that the people of the Picts were called *Picti* either from their beauty, the graceful stature of their body, or their embroidered garments . . . or that perhaps other people called them *Picti* in derision, by antiphrasis, because they were so shabby.

　　John of Fordun (fl. 14th century), Scoti-chronicon, *from Latin*

38 . . . it is supposed, not without a considerable degree of probability, that the invasion of Severus is connected with the most shining period of the British history or fable. Fingal . . . is said to have commanded the Caledonians in that memorable juncture, to have eluded the power of Severus, and to have obtained a signal victory on the banks of the Carun, in which the son of *the King of the World,* Caracalla fled from his arms along the fields of his pride. Something of a doubtful mist hangs over these Highland traditions . . .

　　Edward Gibbon (1737–1794), The Decline and Fall of the Roman Empire, Book 1, *on the invasion of Septimius Severus,* AD *208–9, and the Ossianic legend*

39 . . . if we could, with safety, indulge the pleasing supposition, that Fingal lived, and that Ossian sung, the striking contrast of the situation and manners of the contending nations might amuse a philosophic mind. The parallel would be little to the advantage of the more civilised people . . . if, in a word, we contemplated the untutored Caledonians, glowing with the warm virtues of nature, and the degenerate Romans, polluted with the mean vices of wealth and slavery.

　　Edward Gibbon, The Decline and Fall of the Roman Empire, Book 1

40 And you couldn't but laugh at the joke of the gent.

　　Lewis Grassic Gibbon (James Leslie Mitchell, 1901–1935), Cloud Howe

41 . . . a set of bloody freebooters, with more hair on their thievish faces than clothes to cover their nakedness.

　　Gildas (c.493–570), De Excidio et Conquestu Britanniae, *on the Picts (from Latin)*

42 . . . there emerged from the coracles that had carried them across the sea valleys, the foul hordes of Scots and Picts like dark throngs of worms.

　　Gildas, De Excidio et Conquestu Britanniae

43 Man alone seems to be the only creature who has arrived to the natural size in this poor soil; every part of the country presents the same dismal landscape, no grove nor brook lend music to cheer the stranger, or to make the inhabitants forget their poverty; yet with all these disadvantages to call him down to humility, a Scotchman is one of the proudest things alive.

　　Oliver Goldsmith (1728–1774), letter to Robert Bryanton (September 1753)

44 This is certainly a fine country to grow old in. I could not spare a look to the young people, so much was I engrossed in contemplating their grandmothers.

　　Ann Grant (1755–1838), Letters from the Mountains

45 The truth is, we are a nation of arselickers, though we disguise it with surfaces: a surface of generous, openhanded manliness, a surface of dour practical integrity, a surface of futile maudlin defiance.

　　Alasdair Gray (1934–), 1982, Janine

46 The secret of it is that we are a peasant and proletarian people and have never had courtly airs to strait-jacket us . . . our practicability is of people with a living to make, a daily job to do, and no fine airs to impose on anybody.

　　John Grierson (1898–1972), John Grierson's Scotland

47 There is an incurable nosiness in the national character.

　　Cliff Hanley (1922–1999), The Scots

48 'I hope you in Oxford don't think we hate you?' John Stuart Blackie asked Benjamin

Jowett in 1866. 'We don't think about you,' was the reply.

> *Christopher Harvie (1944–)*, Scotland and Nationalism, *from Abbott and Campbell*, Benjamin Jowett, *1897*

49 We know they can remedy their poverty when they set about it. No-one is sorry for them.

> *William Hazlitt*, Essays

50 Between the Peerage, the Houses of Chiefs and Chieftains, the Baronage, the Gentlemen or lesser Lairds, and Tacksmen it has been calculated that at the time of the Union there were (in a population of about a million) over ten thousand houses, each as proud and as nobly descended as any of the great Continental *noblesses*. Allowing for the expansion of even the near circle of these houses and lines of chieftains, it follows that about one in each twenty-four people were actually members of a titled or chiefly house, and that about one half of the Scottish nation consciously regarded themselves as members of the aristocracy. Such a proportion is unknown in any other nation, and the moral and social effect on the Scottish nation has been incalculable.

> *Sir Thomas Innes of Learney, Lyon King of Arms (1893–1971)*, Tartans of the Clans and Families of Scotland

51 Permit me to begin with paying a just tribute to Scotch sincerity wherever I find it. I own, I am not apt to confide in the professions of gentlemen of that country; and when they smile, I feel an involuntary emotion to guard myself against mischief.

> *'Junius'*, Letters *(1770)*

52 A glance at their history or literature . . . reveals what lies under the slow accent, the respectability and the solid flesh. Under the cake lies Bonny Dundee.

> *James Kennaway (1928–1968)*, Household Ghosts

53 I have been trying all my life to like Scotchmen, and am obliged to desist from the experiment in despair.

> *Charles Lamb (1775–1834)*, Imperfect Sympathies, *in* Essays of Elia

54 For I marvel greatlie, I you assure, Considderand the people and the ground,

That riches suld nocht in this realm redound.

> *Sir David Lindsay (c.1490–1555)*, The Dreme of the Realme of Scotland

55 Our gentyl men are all degenerate; Liberalitie and Lawtie, both, are loste; And cowardice with Lordis is laureate; And knichtlie curage turnit in brag and boast

> *Sir David Lindsay*, The Complaint of the Commoun Weill of Scotland

56 . . . they contracted ideas and habits, quite incompatible with the customs of regular society and civilized life, adding greatly to those defects which characterize persons living in a loose and unreformed state of society.

> *James Loch (1780–1855), architect of the Sutherland Clearances, on the natives of Sutherland, quoted in Ian Grimble*, The Trial of Patrick Sellar *(1962)*

57 'We arra peepul' is the strange, defiant cry heard from some of Scotland's football terraces in the late twentieth century. But which people? A foreign visitor might well be confused.

> *Michael Lynch*, Scotland, A New History *(1991)*

58 Scotsmen take all they can get, and a little more if they can.

> *Lord Advocate Maitland*

59 We do not like the confiding, the intimate, the ingratiating, the hail-fellow-well-met, but prefer the unapproachable, the hardbitten, the recalcitrant, the sinister, the malignant, the sarcastic, the saturnine, the cross-grained and the cankered, and the howling wilderness to the amenities of civilisation, the irascible to the affable, the prickly to the smooth. We have no damned fellow-feeling at all, and look at ourselves and others with the eye of a Toulouse-Lautrec appraising an obscene old toe-rag doing the double-split.

> *Hugh MacDiarmid (1892–1978)*, The Dour Drinkers of Glasgow

60 . . . a' the dour provincial thocht That merks the Scottish breed.

> *Hugh MacDiarmid*, A Drunk Man Looks at the Thistle

61 A people one of whose proverbs
is the remarkable sentence:
'Every force evolves a form.'

    Hugh MacDiarmid, Island Funeral

62 . . . a small family in the congregation of
Europe.

    Moray MacLaren, The Scots *(1930)*

63 . . . though no news came
Of their destruction's night
to reach the world agony of grief,
the fall of the Asturians in their glory,
their lot was the lot of all poor people,
hardship, want and injury,
ever since the humble of every land
were deceived by ruling class, State
   and Civil Law,
and by every prostitute
who sold their soul for that price
that the bitches of the world have earned.

    Sorley Maclean (1911–1996), The
    Cuillin

64 In Scotland, everybody represses you, if
you but propose to step out of the beaten
track.

    *James Mill (1773–1836), quoted in Alex-
ander Bain,* James Mill: A Biography
(1881)

65 Far frae my hame I wander, but still my
   thoughts return
To my ain folk ower yonder, in the
   sheiling by the burn . . .
And it's oh! but I'm longing for my ain
   folk,
Though they be but lowly, poor and plain
   folk.

    Wilfrid Mills, My Ain Folk

66 Folk wha say their say and speir their
   speir,
Gedder birns o' bairns and gey muckle
   gear,
And gang their ain gait wi' a lach or a spit
   or a sweir.

    John C. Milne (1897–1962), Fut Like
    Folk? *on the people of Buchan*

67 The people's will moves slowly, as the ice
Of glaciers, blind to whither and from
   whence;
They cannot see an end, but know the
   way.

    William Montgomerie (1904–), The
    Castle on the Hill

68 An old pot seething with dissatisfaction
which fortunately can be relied on never
to come to the boil.

    Edwin Morgan (1920–), Crossing the
    Border

69 Our fathers all were poor,
Poorer our fathers' fathers;
Beyond, we dare not look.

    Edwin Muir (1887–1959), The Fathers

70 The Scots have always been an unhappy
people; their history is a varying record of
heroism, treachery, persistent bloodshed,
perpetual feuds, and long-winded and san-
guine arguments.

    Edwin Muir, Scottish Journey

71 In all companies it gives me pleasure to
declare that the English, as a people, are
very little inferior to the Scots.

    *Christopher North (John Wilson,
1785–1854),* Noctes Ambrosianae

72 'Athenians, indeed! where is your theatre?
who among you has written a comedy?
where is your Attic salt? which of you
can tell who was Jupiter's great-grand-
father? . . . you know nothing that the
Athenians thought worth knowing, and
dare not show your faces before the civilised world in the practice of any one art in
which they were excellent.'

    Thomas Love Peacock (1785–1866),
    Crotchet Castle

73 Such Mediocrity was ne'er on view,
Bolster'd by tireless Scottish Ballyhoo –
Nay! In two Qualities they stand
   supreme;
Their Self-advertisement and Self-esteem.

    Anthony Powell (fl. 18th century),
    Caledonia

74 . . . thanks to Normanized nobles, the
schism between Gael and Lowlander, Flodden and the English raids, religious debates
and wranglings, emigration, Londonism,
and the eruption of crude industrialism,
the Scots have never had a real chance to
develop themselves or their own country.

    William Power, Scotland and the Scots
    (1934)

75 Proud as a Scot.

    François Rabelais (c.1494–c.1553), Gar-
    gantua and Pantagruel

76 Walking into town, I saw, in a radiant
    raincoat,
    the woman from the fish-shop. 'What
    a day it is!'
    cried I, like a sunstruck madman.
    And what did she have to say for it?
    Her brow grew bleak, her ancestors raged
    in their graves
    as she spoke with their ancient misery:
    'We'll pay for it, we'll pay for it, we'll pay
    for it.'

    Alastair Reid (1926–), Weathering

77 . . . that plateau of uncomfortable, grunt-
    punctuated silence which Borderers seem
    to inhabit most of the time.

    *Alastair Reid, Borderlines, in K. Miller,
    Memoirs of a Modern Scotland (1970)*

78 The perfervid Scot (Proefervidum in-
    genium Scotorum).

    André Rivet (fl. 16th century)

79 Where are the folk like the folk o' the
    West?
    Canty, and couthy, and kindly, the best.

    *Sir Hugh S. Roberton (1874–1952),
    Westering Home*

80 It is beginning to be hinted that we are a
    nation of amateurs.

    *Lord Rosebery (1847–1929), Rectorial
    address to Glasgow University*

81 O! We're a' John Tamson's bairns,
    We're a' John Tamson's bairns;
    There ne'er will be peace till the
    warld again
    Has learned to sing wi' micht an' main,
    We're John Tamson's bairns.

    *Joseph Roy (b.1841), We're A' John Tam-
    son's Bairns*

82 We're a' sae feared to speak our mind,
    As if a word our life wad bind.

    *William Sanderson, Scottish Life and
    Character (1919)*

83 Laziness was not in the biology of a people
    who succeeded in clawing an existence
    from nature's harshness, and who, when
    they went abroad, became the dynamic
    forces of the New World.

    Alastair Scott, Native Stranger (1995)

84 Who o'er the herd would wish to reign,
    Fantastic, fickle, fierce, and vain?

. . . Thou many-headed monster-thing,
O who would wish to be thy king?

    Sir Walter Scott (1771–1832), The Lady
    of the Lake

85 I have heard higher sentiments from the
    lips of poor, uneducated men and women . . .
    than I ever yet met with out of the Bible.

    *Sir Walter Scott, quoted by J. G. Lockhart
    in* The Life of Sir Walter Scott

86 The Celt . . .
    From out the sunrise, evermore has felt,
    Like a religion, ties and dues of blood.

    Alexander Smith (1830–1867), Torquil
    and Oona

87 With equanimity we accept the fact that
    possession of a Scottish birth certificate
    guarantees us a place in the front of the
    queue for death certificates.

    W. Gordon Smith, Mr Jock (1987)

88 Who knows now what it was like to be fed
    only on three meals of potatoes a day? Or
    to experience as a child the rigours of the
    Scottish sabbath, where the highlight was
    a visit to the cemetery?

    T. C. Smout, A Century of the Scottish
    People *(1986)*

89 For the Lord has pity on the bairns
    Wha belang to Caledonie.
    Her likely lads are wurlin weans
    And cudna be onie ither,
    Sic a toom howe is in the breist
    O' their sair forjaskit mither.

    William Soutar (1898–1943), Second
    Childhood

90 . . . the peasantry in the southern districts
    can all read and are generally more or
    less skilful in writing and arithmetic, and
    under the disguise of their uncouth appear-
    ance they possess a laudable zeal for
    knowledge.

    Second Statistical Account of Scotland,
    1826

91 One cannot but be conscious of an under-
    lying melancholy in Scotswomen. This
    melancholy is particularly attractive in
    the ballroom, where it gives a singular
    piquancy to the enthusiasm and earnest-
    ness they put into their national dances.

    Stendhal (Henri Beyle, 1783–1842)

92 Each has his own tree of ancestors, but at the top of all sits Probably Arboreal.
  Robert Louis Stevenson (1850–1894), Memories and Portraits

93 Scotland is indefinable; it has no unity except on the map. Two languages, many dialects, innumerable forms of piety, and countless local patriotisms and prejudices, part us among ourselves more widely than the extreme east and west of that great continent of America.
  Robert Louis Stevenson, In the Valley: The Scot Abroad

94 A little society is necessary to show a man his failings.
  Robert Louis Stevenson, Ethical Studies

95 We Scots need the English because otherwise we would have slaughtered each other in a kind of ghastly turned-inwards energy, which is after all the history of Scotland, pre-unification.
  Norman Stone, The Sunday Times, *February 1992*

96 There are some people who think they sufficiently acquit themselves, and entertain their company, with relating facts of no consequence . . . this I have observed more frequently among the Scots than any other nation, who are very careful not to omit the minutest circumstances of time or place; which kind of discourse, if it were not a little relieved by the uncouth terms and phrases, as well as accent and gesture peculiar to that country, would be hardly tolerable.
  Jonathan Swift (1667–1745), Hints Towards an Essay on Conversation

97 Scotsmen are metaphysical and emotional, they are sceptical and mystical, they are romantic and ironic, they are cruel and tender, and full of mirth and despair.
  Rachel Annand Taylor (1876–1900), Dunbar

98 Why do you softly, richly speak Rhythm so sweetly scanned?
  Poverty hath the Gaelic and Greek In my land.
  Rachel Annand Taylor (1876–1900), The Princess of Scotland

99 The most accomplished nation in Europe, the nation to which, if any one country is endowed with a superior partition of sense, I should be inclined to give the preference in that particular.
  Horace Walpole (1717–1797)

100 The stamp-peyin self-employed ur truly the lowest form ay vermin oan god's earth.
  Irvine Welsh (1957–), Trainspotting

101 It is never difficult to distinguish between a Scotsman with a grievance and a ray of sunshine.
  P. G. Wodehouse (1881–1975), quoted in Richard Usborne, Wodehouse at Work *(1961)*

102 The Scotch are great charmers, and sing through their noses like musical tea-kettles.
  Virginia Woolf (1882–1941), Letters

103 One factor that has made the Scots 'a peculiar people' is the Covenanting phase of the seventeenth century . . . largely responsible for the specific aboulia, lack of will-power, and disseminated sclerosis of the Scottish nation today.
  Douglas Young (1913–1973), Scotland

Persons and Personalities

Real and Imaginary

1 'I'll gie thee Rozie o' the Cleugh,
  I'm sure she'll please thee weel eneuch.'
  'Up wi' her on the bare bane dyke,
  She'll be rotten or I'll be ripe.'
  Anonymous, Hey, Wully Wine

2 The doughty Douglas on a steed
  Rode all his men beforn;
  His armour glitter'd as did a glede,
  Bolder bairn was never born.
  Anonymous, Chevy Chase

3 She kept a stir in tower and trench,
  That brawling, boisterous Scottish wench;
  Came I early, came I late:
  I found Agnes at the gate.
  Anonymous lines on 'Black Agnes', Countess of Dunbar, ascribed to the Earl of Salisbury in 1338

4 Up wi' the souters o' Selkirk,
  And down wi' the Earl of Home.
  Traditional Selkirk song

5 Oh, ma name it's wee Jock Elliot,
And wha daur meddle wi' me?

Anonymous, Jock Elliot

6 He is weil kend, John of the Syde,
A greater thief did never ride.

*Anonymous lines on John Armstrong of
Liddesdale, quoted in George Macdonald
Fraser, The Steel Bonnets (1971)*

7 Doe ye not know quho layes in this
corner?
It's a Scots Ambassador extraordinar . . .
Ladyes I request you, keep from the Wall,
Or the Scots Ambassador will occupey
you all.

Anonymous, Pasquil on the Earl of
Rothes, *from James Maidment*, A Book
of Scottish Pasquils *(1868). It was
Rothes (1600–c.1640) who, when accused
of dissolute behaviour as King's Commis-
sioner, said he had the King's reputation
to maintain.*

8 *John Steuarte:* Say no Treuth
Johne, Lord Traquair: A Lyer Honor
Aquyred

*Anagrams coined on the name of John
Stewart, Earl of Traquair, in 1640*

9 Thou soncie auld carle, the world hes
not thy like,
For ladies fa' in love with thee, tho' thou
be ane auld tyke.

*Anonymous, lines on the marriage in 1700
of Viscount Tarbat to the much younger
Countess of Wemyss, from James Maidment,* A Book of Scottish Pasquils

10 Oh! John Carnagie in Dunlappie,
Thou hes a wife both blythe and sappie,
A bottle that is both white and nappie;
Thou sits, and with thy little cappie,
Thou drinks, and never leaves a drappie,
Until thou sleepest like a tappie,
O! Were I John, I would be happie.

*Anonymous, Lynes to John Carnagie
(early 18th century), from James Maidment,* A Book of Scottish Pasquils

11 He was a hedge unto his friends,
A heckle to his foes.

Anonymous, from Rob Roy *in Chambers'*
Scottish Ballads, *on Robin Og MacGregor, son of Rob Roy*

12 Four Scotsmen by the name of Adams
Who keep their coaches and their
madams,

Quoth John, in sulky mood, to Thomas,
Have stolen the very river from us.

*Anonymous London comment on the
Thames-side buildings of the Adams
brothers*

13 His first appearance was somewhat appalling to persons of low animal spirits.

Anonymous, The Edinburgh Annual
Register *(1811), on John Leyden
(1775–1811), poet and physician, quoted
in H. W. Thomson,* The Anecdotes and
Egotisms of Henry Mackenzie *(1927)*

14 'I looked to see a muckle fat faggot, but the
child's a decent-like body, and can walk
on his legs as well as the best o' 'em.'

*Anonymous citizen of Edinburgh, on the
visit of George IV, 1822*

15 If the Lord Chancellor knew only a little
law, he would know a little of everything.

Anonymous, quoted in G. W. E. Russell,
Collections and Recollections, *on Lord
Brougham (1778–1868)*

16 It is really very generous of Mr Thomson
to consent to live at all.

*A contemporary critic on James Thomson
(1834–1882), poet of voluptuous death,
quoted in notes to Douglas Young,* Scottish Verse 1851–1951 *(1952)*

17 O, I'm a weaver, a Calton weaver;
I'm a rash and a roving blade.

Anonymous, The Calton Weaver

18 Don't try to dodge me if ye can,
For I'm neither Jesus Christ not Douglas
Fairbanks,
I'm the Means Test Man.

Anonymous, The Means Test Man
(1929)

19 There was a man lived in the moon,
Lived in the moon, lived in the moon;
There was a man lived in the moon,
And his name was Aiken Drum.
And he played upon a ladle, a ladle, a
ladle;
He played upon a ladle, and his name was
Aiken Drum.

Traditional children's song

20 I am a very promising young man.

*Robert Adam (1728–1792), letter to his
family, 1756*

21 . . . the Saint, sitting in his little hut, which rested on a wooden floor, hearing the shout, says: 'The man who is shouting beyond the strait is not a man of refined sentiment, for today he will upset my inkhorn.' And Diormit, his attendant, hearing this word, standing for a little while in front of the gate, awaited the arrival of the troublesome guest that he might guard the ink-horn. But for some cause or other he soon went thence; and after he had gone the troublesome guest arrived, and in eager haste to kiss the Saint upset the ink-horn, overturned by the skirt of his garment.

> *Saint Adamnan (679–704)*, The Life of Saint Columba, *translated from Latin by Wentworth Huyshe*

22 O Wallace, peerless lover of thy land,
We need thee still, thy moulding brain and hand!

> *Francis Lauderdale Adams*, Lines Written for the Wallace Monument at Ballarat, Australia

23 That other, round the flanks so slight of form,
Is Michael Scott, who verily knew well
The lightsome play of every magic fraud.

> *Dante Alighieri (1265–1321)*, Inferno, *from Italian*

24 Queens should be cold and wise,
And she loved little things.

> *Marion Angus (1866–1946)*, Alas! Poor Queen, *on Mary I*

25 A distracted man, a distracted subject, in a distracted time.

> *Archibald, Marquis of Argyll (c.1606–1661), on himself, quoted in* G. Donaldson, The Faith of the Scots *(1990)*

26 John Bull.

> *Synonym for the Englishman, first used in print by John Arbuthnot (1667–1735)*, The History of John Bull *(1712)*

27 He is courageous, even more than a king should be . . . He is not a good captain because he begins to fight before he has begun his orders.

> *Don Pedro de Ayala, Spanish ambassador to Scotland, on King James IV, July 1498*

28 There was glory on his forehead,
There was lustre in his eye,

And he never walked to battle,
More proudly than to die.

> *W. E. Aytoun (1830–1865)*, The Execution of Montrose

29 Fhairshon had a son
Who married Noah's daughter,
And nearly spoil'd ta Flood,
By trinking up ta water.
Which he would have done,
I at least pelieve it,
Had ta mixture peen
Only half Glenlivet.

> *W. E. Aytoun*, The Massacre of the MacPherson

30 If he were a horse, nobody would buy him: with that eye, no one could answer for his temper.

> *Walter Bagehot (1826–1877)*, Biographical Studies, *on Lord Brougham (1778–1868)*

31 . . . such was the wisdom and authoritie of that old, little, crooked souldier, that all, with ane incredible sumission, from the beginning to the end, gave over themselves to be guided by him, as if he had been Great Solyman.

> *Robert Baillie (1599–1662)*, Letters and Journals, *on Alexander Leslie*

32 My father had a strong dislike for marriages of necessity, common enough at one time in Scotland. He was called to officiate at one of these, and arrived with reluctance and disgust half an hour late. 'You are very late, Mr Baird,' said the bridegroom. 'Yes, about six months too late,' replied Mr Baird.

> *John Logie Baird (1888–1946)*, Sermons, Soap and Television

33 I never forgive but I always forget.

> *A. J. Balfour (1848–1930), quoted in Robert Blake*, The Conservative Party *(1970)*

34 Oh, blithe be the auld gaberlunzie-man,
Wi' his wallet o' wit he fills the lan',
He's a warm Scotch heart, and a braid Scotch tongue,
And kens a' the auld sangs that ever were sung!

> *James Ballantine (1808–1877)*, The Auld Gaberlunzie-Man

35 All men luffit him for his bounté,
For he was of full fair affeir,

Wys, curteis and deboneir,
Large and luffand als was he.

> *John Barbour (c.1320–1395)*, The Brus,
> *on Sir James Douglas*

36 McConnachie . . . the name I give to the
unruly half of myself: the writing half. We
are complement and supplement. I am the
half that is dour and practical and canny . . .
he prefers to fly around on one wing.

> *J. M. Barrie (1860–1937), rectorial
> address to the University of St Andrews,
> 1922*

37 Oh the gladness of her gladness when
she's glad,
And the sadness of her sadness when
she's sad:
But the gladness of her gladness,
And the sadness of her sadness,
Are as nothing . . .
To the badness of her badness when she's
bad.

> *J. M. Barrie*, Rosalind

38 David Hume ate a swinging great dinner,
And grew every day fatter and fatter;
And yet the huge bulk of a sinner
Said there was neither spirit nor matter.

> *James Beattie (1735–1803)*, On the
> Author of The Treatise of Human
> Nature

39 And now his look was most demurely sad;
And now he laughed aloud, yet none
knew why.
The neighbours stared and sighed, yet
blessed the lad:
Some deemed him wondrous wise, and
some believed him mad.

> *James Beattie*, The Minstrel

40 One of the most perfect creatures that ever
was seen . . . she has given so great an
expectation of her that it is not possible
to hope for more from any princess of the
earth.

> *Jean de Beaugué, French soldier-diplomat,
> on the young Queen Mary I, 1548, quoted
> in Agnes Mure Mackenzie*, Scottish Pag-
> eant 1513–1625 (1948)

41 With the publication of his Private Papers
in 1952, he committed suicide twenty-five
years after his death.

> *Lord Beaverbrook (1879–1964)*, Men
> and Power, *on Earl Haig (1861–1928)*

42 At the bishop's request the king sat down
and began to be merry; but Aidan on the
contrary grew so sad that he began to shed
tears. His chaplain asked him in his own
language, which the king and his servants
did not understand, why he wept. Aidan
replied, 'I know that the king will not live
long; for I have never before seen a humble
king.' Not very long after, as I have related,
the bishop's foreboding was borne out by
the king's death.

> *St Bede (c.673–735)*, Ecclesiastical
> History of the English People, *on
> St Aidan (d.651) and Oswald, King of
> Northumbria*

43 Alban was brimful from his day,
His was the fair long reign . . .
With fruits on slender trees,
With ale, with music, with fellowship,
With corn, with milk, with active kine,
With pride, with success, with elegance.

> *St Berchan*, Prophecy (1094), *on King
> Constantine (d.952), from Latin*

44 The red one was fair yellow tall,
Pleasant was the youth to me,
Brimful was Alban east and west
During the reign of Dearg the Fierce.

> *St Berchan*, Prophecy, *on Macbeth
> (c.1005–1057), King of Scots*

45 No woman bore or will bring forth
in the east
A king whose rule will be greater
over Alban;
And there shall not be born forever,
One who had more fortune or greatness.

> *St Berchan*, Prophecy, *on King
> Malcolm III (c.1031–1093)*

46 Dr Campbell, looking once into a pamphlet at a bookseller's shop, liked it so well
as to purchase it; and it was not till he
had read it half-way through that he discovered it to be of his own composition.

> Biographica Britannica, *on the author
> John Campbell (1708–1775)*

47 He appeared to take it for granted that
all nature, animate and inanimate, was in
a conspiracy to maim, injure and destroy
him, John; and that he, John, was therefore
justified in taking his revenge beforehand,
whenever he got the chance.

> *William Black (1841–1898)*, Highland
> Cousins

48 An ugly, cross-made, splay-footed, shape-less, little dumpling of a fellow.

> Blackwood's Magazine *on Lord Macaulay (1800–1859)*

49 One of these intelligent eccentrics of whom Scotland has the manufacturing secret.

> *William Bolitho*, Murder for Profit *(1926), on Dr Robert Knox (1791–1862), the anatomist*

50 The wanderer, forgetting his assumed sex, that his clothes might not be wet, held them up a great deal too high. Kingsburgh mentioned this to him, observing it might make a discovery . . . He was very awkward in female dress. His size was so large, and his strides so great.

> *James Boswell (1740–1795)*, Journal, *on Prince Charles Edward Stewart*

51 Am I not fortunate in having something about me that interests most people at first sight in my favour?

> *James Boswell, letter to Mr Temple, June 1779*

52 I have some fixed principles; but my existence is chiefly conditioned by the powers of fancy and sensation.

> *James Boswell*, Journal, *on himself*

53 For he lifted his hand not only against the King of England and his accomplices, but also against all the kingdom of Scotland itself, save for a few well-wishers of his own, who in the face of those who then opposed them were as a single drop to the waves of the sea . . . for the art of war and the valour of his body, Robert then had no peer in any clime of the world.

> *Walter Bower (d. 1449)*, Scotichronicon, *on Robert I, quoted in Agnes Mure Mac-kenzie*, Scottish Pageant 55 BC–AD 1513 *(1946)*

54 My first act on entering this world was to kill my mother.

> *William Boyd (1952–), opening line of* The New Confessions

55 Being dressed (as I have seen her) in the barbaric fashion of the savages of her country, she seemed in a mortal body and a rude and barbaric dress, a true goddess.

> *Pierre de Brantome (c.1530–1614)*, Dames Illustres, *on Queen Mary I*

56 I have heard the greatest understandings of the age giving forth their efforts in its most eloquent tongues, but I should, without hesitation, prefer, for mere intellectual gratification, to be once more allowed the privilege which I in those days enjoyed of being present while the first philosopher of his age was the historian of his own discoveries.

> *Lord Brougham (1778–1868), on Joseph Black (1728–1799)*

57 Wonderful man! I long to get drunk with him.

> *Lord Byron (1788–1824), on Sir Walter Scott, quoted in Rupert Christiansen,* Romantic Affinities *(1985)*

58 His behaviour under all that barbarous usage was as great and firm to the last, looking on all that was done to him with a noble scorn, as the fury of his enemies was black and universally detested.

> *Gilbert Burnet (1643–1715)*, History of His Own Time, *on the death of Montrose*

59 He was the coldest friend and the violentest enemy that I ever had.

> *Gilbert Burnet,* History of His Own Time, *on the Duke of Lauderdale (1616–1682)*

60 A little upright, pert, tart, tripping wight, And still his precious self his dear delight.

> *Robert Burns (1759–1796)*, The Poet's Progress

61 To see her is to love her
And love her but for ever;
For nature made her what she is,
And never made anither!

> *Robert Burns*, Bonnie Leslie

62 Mally's meek, Mally's sweet,
Mally's modest and discreet;
Mally's rare, Mally's fair,
Mally's every way complete.

> *Robert Burns*, Mally's Meek, Mally's Sweet

63 . . . a fine fat fodgel wight,
O' stature short, but genius bright.

> *Robert Burns*, On the Late Captain Grose's Peregrinations Through Scotland

64 Searching auld wives' barrels,
Ochon, the day!
That clarty barm should stain my laurels;

But – what'll ye say?
These movin' things ca'd wives and weans
Wad move the very hearts o' stanes!

> Robert Burns, On Being Appointed to
> an Excise Division

65 Whoe'er thou art, O reader, know
That Death has murdered Johnny!
And here his body lies fu' low,
For saul he ne'er had ony.

> Robert Burns, On Wee Johnny (*John
> Wilson, printer of the first edition of his
> Poems*)

66 The fient a pride, nae pride had he,
Nor sauce, nor state that I could see,
Mair than an honest ploughman.

> Robert Burns, On Meeting With Lord
> Daer

67 She's bow-hough'd, she's hen-shinned,
Ae limpin' leg a hand-breed shorter;
She's twisted right, she's twisted left,
To balance fair in ilka quarter.

> Robert Burns, Willie Wastle

68 It was very good of God to let Carlyle
and Mrs Carlyle marry one another and so
make only two people miserable instead of
four.

> Samuel Butler (*1835–1902*)

69 A coward brood, which mangle as they
prey,
By hellish instinct, all that cross their
way;
Aged or young, the living or the dead
No mercy find – these harpies must be
fed.

> Lord Byron (*1788–1824*), English Bards
> and Scotch Reviewers, *on the* Edin-
> burgh Review

70 But I am half a Scot by birth, and bred
A whole one.

> Lord Byron, Don Juan

71 Forgive me, Sire, for cheating your intent
That I, who should command a regiment,
Do amble amiably here, O God,
One of the neat ones in your awkward
squad.

> Norman Cameron (*1905–1953*), Forgive
> Me, Sire

72 He was the only person ever to have been
expelled from the Communist Party for
being a Scottish Nationalist, and from

the Scottish National Party for being a
communist.

> James Campbell, Invisible Country
> (*1984*), on Hugh MacDiarmid
> (*1892–1978*)

73 Celestial peace was pictured in her look.

> Thomas Campbell (*1777–1844*),
> Theodric

74 At three, it is claimed, he asked, on looking
at blood from his cut forehead, 'Is it oxy-
haemoglobin or carboxyhaemoglobin?'

> John Carey, The Faber Book of Science
> (*1995*), on J. B. S. Haldane (*1892–1964*)

75 If you awakened him from his reverie,
and made him attend to the subject of
the conversation, he immediately began a
harangue, and never stopped till he told
you all he knew about it, and with the
utmost philosophical ingenuity.

> Alexander Carlyle (*1722–1805*), quoted in
> R. B. Haldane, Adam Smith, *on Adam
> Smith* (*1723–1790*)

76 Never did I see such apparatus got ready
for thinking, and so little thought.

> Thomas Carlyle (*1795–1881*), Essays (*on
> Samuel Taylor Coleridge, 1772–1834*)

77 Poor Lamb! Poor England! when such a
despicable abortion is named genius.

> Thomas Carlyle, on Charles Lamb
> (*1775–1834*)

78 Let me have my own way exactly in everything, and a sunnier and pleasanter
creature does not exist.

> Ascribed to Thomas Carlyle in
> conversation

79 I like to tell people when they ask 'Are you
an native born?' 'No sir, I am a Scotchman,' and I feel as proud as I am sure ever
Roman did when it was their boast to say,
'I am a Roman citizen.'

> Andrew Carnegie (*1835–1918*),
> Autobiography

80 Hero of 1,000 blunders and one success.

> Verdict on Henry Bell (*1767–1830*),
> inventor and engineer, quoted in Robert
> Chambers, Scottish Biographical
> Dictionary

81 We know that he has, more than any other
man, the gift of compressing the largest

amount of words into the smallest amount of thought.

Winston Churchill (1874–1965), speech in the House of Commons, 1933, on Ramsay Macdonald (1866–1937)

82 ... by marrying a Rothschild, being Prime Minister, and winning the Derby, he demonstrated that it was possible to improve one's financial status and run the empire without neglecting the study of form.

Claud Cockburn (1904–1981), Aspects of English History, *on Lord Rosebery*

83 There was a singular race of excellent Scotch old ladies. They were a delightful set; strong-headed, warm-hearted and high-spirited; the fire of their temper not always latent; merry even in solitude; very resolute; indifferent about the modes and habits of the modern world

Henry Thomas Cockburn (1779–1854), Memorials

84 Nobody could sit down like the Lady of Inverleith. She would sail like a ship from Tarshish gorgeous in velvet or rustling in silk, and done up in all the accompaniments of fan, ear-rings and finger-rings, falling sleeves, scent bottle, embroidered bag, hoop and train – all superb, yet all in the purest taste; and managing all this seemingly heavy rigging with as much ease as a full-blown swan does its plumage, she would take possession of the centre of a large sofa, and at the same moment, without the slightest visible exertion, would cover the whole of it with her bravery.

Henry Thomas Cockburn, Memorials

85 Dr Joseph Black was a striking and beautiful person; tall, very thin, and cadaverously pale; his hair carefully powdered, though there was little of it except what was collected into a long thin queue; his eyes dark, clear and large, like deep pools of pure water.

Henry Thomas Cockburn, Memorials

86 ... his two coats, each buttoned only by the upper button, flowed open below, and exposed the whole of his curious and venerable figure. His gait and air were noble, his gestures slow, his look full of dignity and composed fire. He looked like a philosopher from Lapland. I never heard of him dining out, except at his relation's, Joseph Black's, where his son, Sir Adam

(the friend of Scott) used to say 'It was delightful to see the two rioting over a boiled turnip.'

Henry Thomas Cockburn, Memorials, *on Adam Ferguson*

87 His name was a tower. His voice a thunderbolt. Many of his opponents will now rail, & many of his own party chatter, who were dumb before him.

Henry Thomas Cockburn, letter to Mrs Rutherford, June 1847, on Thomas Chalmers (1780–1847)

88 Silly, snobbish, lecherous, tipsy . . . he needed Johnson as a ivy needs an oak.

Cyril Connolly, The Evening Colonnade *(1990), on James Boswell*

89 She is a little, quiet, feminine woman, who you would think might shrink from grappling with the horrors of a tragedy, and whom it would be possible to mistake for the maiden sister of the curate, bent only on her homely duties.

J. Fenimore Cooper (1759–1851), England, With Sketches of Life in the Metropolis, *on Joanna Baillie (1762–1851)*

90 Thinking of Helensburgh, J. G. Frazer
Revises flayings and human sacrifice;
Abo of the Celtic Twilight, St Andrew Lang
Posts him a ten-page note on totemism
And a coloured fairy book.

Robert Crawford (1959–), Scotland in the 1890s

91 James Murray combs the dialect from his beard
And files slips for his massive *Dictionary.*

Robert Crawford, Scotland in the 1890s

92 An hour after the appointed time, in stalked Pollochok, dressed in his full Highland attire.

'I am little used to wait thus for any man,' exclaimed the chafed chieftain, 'especially when such game is afoot as we are boune after.'

'What sort of game are ye after, Mackintosh?' said Pollochok.

'The wolf, sir, did not my messenger instruct you?'

'Ou, aye, that's true,' said Pollochok, with a good-humoured smile. 'But an' that be a',' continued he, groping with his right hand among the ample folds of his plaid, 'there's the wolf's head . . . As I came through the slochk, by east the hill there, I foregathered wi' the beast. My long dog there turned him. I buckled wi' him, and dirkit him, and syne whittled his craig, and brought awa' his countenance, for fear he might come alive again, for they are very precarious creatures.'

> *Sir Thomas Dick-Lauder (1774–1848),* The Great Floods of 1829

93 '*He was a great fellow my friend Will,*' he rang out in that deep voice of his. '*The thumbmark of his Maker was wet in the clay of him.*' Man, it made a quiver go down my spine.

> *George Douglas (George Douglas Brown, 1869–1902),* The House With the Green Shutters

94 It has long been an object of wonder to us how this resourceful lady appears to be the sheet-anchor of many a foreigner's knowledge of Scottish Church history.

> *J. D. Douglas,* Light in the North *(1964), on Jenny Geddes*

95 So fat and Buddhistic and nasal that a dear friend described him as an animated adenoid.

> *Norman Douglas (1868–1952), quoted in R. A. Cassell,* Ford Madox Ford *(1961), on Ford Madox Ford (1873–1939)*

96 It is most certainly to you that I owe Sherlock Holmes . . . I do not think his analytical work is in the least an exaggeration of some effects which I have seen you produce in the out-patient ward.

> *Sir Arthur Conan Doyle (1859–1930), Letter to Joseph Bell, May 1892*

97 The Wardraipper of Venus boure,
To giff a doublett he is als doure,
As it war off ane futt syd frog:
Madame, ye hev a dangerouss Dog!

> *William Dunbar (c.1460–c.1520), Of James Dog, Kepar of the Quenis Wardrop*

98 He is nae Dog; he is a Lam.

> *William Dunbar, Of the Same James, When He Had Pleasit Him*

99 It was Watt who told King George III that he dealt in an article of which kings were said to be fond – Power.

> *Ralph Waldo Emerson (1803–1882), Let-*

ters and Social Aims, *on James Watt (1736–1819)*

100 He had a wonderful intellectual power, an astonishing knowledge of everything, an unconquerable magnanimity, and the most abundant generosity.

> *Desiderius Erasmus (c.1466–1536), on King James IV*

101 The king of Scots was skilled in warfare and in inflicting damage on the enemies he fought; but he was too much in the habit of seeking new advice . . . He never had much affection for those of his own country whose right it was to counsel him.

> *Jordan Fantosme (fl. 12th century),* Chronicle, *quoted in D. D. R. Owen,* William The Lion *(1997), on King William I (1143–1214)*

102 Yonder's the tomb o' wise Mackenzie fam'd,
Whase laws rebellious bigotry reclaim'd,
Freed the hail land frae covenanting fools,
Wha erst ha'e fash'd us wi' unnumbered dools.

> *Robert Fergusson (1750–1774),* The Ghaists: A Kirkyard Eclogue *, on Sir George Mackenzie (1636–1691)*

103 Near some lamp-post, wi dowy face,
Wi' heavy een, and sour grimace,
Stands she that beauty lang had kend
Whoredom her trade, and vice her end.

> *Robert Fergusson,* Auld Reekie

104 A young Australian, after meeting Cameron of Lochiel, thought that Boat of Garten and Mull of Kintyre must be clan chiefs too.

> *Iain Finlayson,* The Scots *(1987)*

105 When Montaigne was made Gentleman-of-the-Bedchamber to Henry II of France, he met Mary as a favourite daughter-in-law of that King, who enjoyed his company. This caused Buchanan to exclaim:

'Look at him! He can talk with monarchy as an equal! That is the result of a well-born soul, a well-filled purse is my opinion. Such lads should have no means, like myself, for egotism will ruin the most promising career ever launched from any college. All he wishes to do is to draw himself as a painter does his portrait with a crayon. He cares nought for worldly prospects, nor fame; never desires his works to be read, or quoted, after he is dead; thinks learning nothing to be proud of, and the clever to be foolish, laws are merely a convention, and habit a timid convenience. His one desire is to be Master of the Art of Life. What is the rising generation coming to?'

> Arnold Fleming, The Medieval Scots Scholar in France *(1952), on George Buchanan (c.1506–1582)*

106 At the Council of Constance in 1414, a Dr Gray attended as Ambassador of Scotland. He had taken his degree at the Sorbonne, so was well qualified. As the offspring of a nun, he suffered a formidable handicap, but he was a man of such sterling character that four Popes granted him absolution, dispensation and rehabilitation.

> Arnold Fleming, The Medieval Scots Scholar in France

107 I am very strong and robust and not of the delicate sex nor of the fair but of the deficient in look. People who are deficient in looks can make up for it by virtue.

> Marjory Fleming *(1803–1811),* Journals

108 I love in Isa's bed to lie
O such a joy and luxury
The boton of the bed I sleep
And with great care I myself keep
Oft I embrace her feet of lillys
But she has goton all the pillies.

> Marjory Fleming, Journals

109 ... he thought rather to be with the foremost than with the hindermost.

> Jean Froissart *(c.1333–c.1404),* Chroniques, *on Sir James Douglas (c.1286–1330), from French*

110 He was a ... sort of Field Marshal Sir Douglas Haig turned inside out ... After a lifetime of excesses – confronted by temptation, he always followed his own favorite suggestion, 'Why not, my dear?' – he apparently couldn't die, even at the age of 84, and had to put himself down with an overdose of pills.

> Paul Fussell, Abroad: British Literary Traveling Between the Wars *(1980), on Norman Douglas (1868–1952)*

111 He was a man of no smeddum in discourse.

> John Galt *(1779–1839),* The Provost

112 Sometimes even with the very beggars I found a jocose saying as well received as a bawbee, although naturally I dinna think I was ever what could be called a funny man, but only just as ye would say a thought ajee in that way.

> John Galt, The Provost

113 He was now fifty-eight, had tufted eyebrows that went up at the corners like those of Mephistopheles, had lost his hair and wore a wig about which he was sensitive, and had a genial partiality for the wine of his native land.

> William Gaunt, The Pre-Raphaelite Tragedy *(1942), on William Bell Scott (1811–1890)*

114 He had sufficient conscience to bother him, but not sufficient to keep him straight.

> David Lloyd George *(1863–1945), recorded by A. J. Sylvester, 1938, on Ramsay Macdonald (1866–1937)*

115 A one-eyed fellow in blinkers.

> David Lloyd George, quoted in A. J. Sylvester, Life With Lloyd George, *on Lord Rosebery (1847–1929)*

116 And the funny thing about the creature was that she believed none spoke ill of her, for if she heard a bit hint of such, dropped sly-like, she'd redden up like a stalk of rhubarb in a dung patch.

> Lewis Grassic Gibbon *(James Leslie Mitchell, 1901–1935),* Sunset Song

117 And because she just couldn't thole him at all, he made her want to go change her vest, Chris smiled at him and was extra polite.

> Lewis Grassic Gibbon, Cloud Howe

118 She'd reddish hair, and high, skeugh nose, and a hand that skelped her way through life; and if ever a soul had seen her at rest when the dark was done and the day was come he'd died of the shock and never let on.

> Lewis Grassic Gibbon, Smeddum

119 I am a jingo patriot of planet earth: 'humanity, right or wrong!'

> Lewis Grassic Gibbon, Scottish Scene

120 ... by some slight accident he was missing from the battle of Flodden, and has been making up for it ever since ... Still, the

rats of Scotland breed faster than ever, and God sent Grieve to exterminate them.

> *Lewis Grassic Gibbon, on Hugh Mac-Diarmid (C. M. Grieve, 1892–1978), quoted in Hugh MacDiarmid,* Lucky Poet *(1943)*

121 Yet Knox himself was of truly heroic mould; had his followers, far less his allies, been of like mettle, the history of Scotland might have been strangely and splendidly different.

> *Lewis Grassic Gibbon,* Scottish Scene

122 The 'heroic young queen' in question had the face, mind, manners and morals of a well-intentioned but hysterical poodle.

> *Lewis Grassic Gibbon,* Scottish Scene, *on Mary I*

123 'Sir, I reckon that man's the quaintest work of Almighty God.'

> *Visiting American on the Rev. Charles Barr MP, reciting Charles Murray's* The Whistle, *quoted in Gibbon and MacDiarmid,* Scottish Scene, *(1934)*

124 I am certanely persuaded that his gratious, humane and courteous fredome of behaviour, being certanly acceptable before God as well as men, was it that wann him so much renoune and inabled him cheifly, in the love of his followers, to goe through so great interprysses.

> *Patrick Gordon (c.1600–c.1660),* Britanes Distemper, *on the Marquis of Montrose*

125 A dinner partner asked him: 'Is it true that there is royal blood in your family?'
'Madam,' replied Cunninghame Graham, 'if I had my rights I should be king of England – and what a two weeks that would be!'

> *R. B. Cunninghame Graham, quoted in C. Fadiman,* The Little, Brown Book of Anecdotes *(1985)*

126 On the 'plainstones'– the only pavement then in Glasgow – in the middle of the street fronting the Trongate piazza, those Virginia traders – known as tobacco lords – strutted in business hours, clad in scarlet cloaks, cocked hats, and powdered wigs, bearing with portly grace gold-headed canes in their hands.

> *H. Grey Graham,* The Social Life of Scotland in the Eighteenth Century *(1899)*

127 ... the cheerful clatter of Sir James Barrie's cans as he went round with the milk of human kindness.

> *Philip Guedalla (1889–1944),* Some Critics, *on J. M. Barrie (1860–1937)*

128 She stuck hard to her thankless task, yet with such success that good Scottish historians to this day bless her name ... And as far as these Highland parts are concerned, her reforms slowly but surely spread until theirrom feudalistic groundwork blossomed in the flame-bright flower of the Clearances.

> *Neil Gunn (1891–1973),* Off in a Boat, *on Queen Margaret, consort of Malcolm Canmore*

129 I am of that unfortunate class who never knew what it was to be a child in spirit. Even the memories of boyhood and young manhood are gloomy.

> *James Keir Hardie (1856–1915), quoted in K. O. Morgan,* Keir Hardie

130 Born into the ranks of the working class, the new King's most likely fate would have been that of a street-corner loafer.

> *James Keir Hardie on King George V, 1910*

131 Nine quarteris large he was in lenth indeed,
Thrid part lenth in shouldris braid was he,
Richt seemly, strang and lusty for to see.

> *'Blind Harry' (fl. 1490s)* Wallace

132 Of riches he keepit no proper thing,
Gave as he wan, like Alexander the king.
In times of peace, meek as a monk was he,
Whar weir approachit, the richt Ector was he.

> *'Blind Harry',* Wallace

133 Wallace, that has redeemit Scotland,
The best is callit this day beltit with brand.

> *'Blind Harry',* Wallace

134 When Adam Ferguson, minister and sometime infantryman, found that gaining the Edinburgh chair of philosophy meant that he had to teach physics and not, as he had

thought, ethics, he set to and kept himself a fortnight ahead of his class.

> *Christopher Harvie (1944–)*, Scotland and Nationalism

135 ... the most indolent of mortals and of poets. But he was also one of the best both of mortals and of poets.

> *William Hazlitt (1778–1830)*, Lectures on the English Poets, *on Thomas Campbell (1771–1844)*

136 Out of his nose the meldrop fast can rin;
With lippis blae, and cheekis lean and
thin.

> *Robert Henryson (c.1425–c.1500)*, The Testament of Cresseid

137 Bot in her face seemit great variance,
Whiles perfyt truth, and whiles
inconstance.

> *Robert Henryson*, The Testament of Cresseid

138 Now hait, now cold, now blyth, now full
of woe,
Now green as leaf, now witherit and ago.

> *Robert Henryson*, The Testament of Cresseid

139 'What a wonderful boy he is!' said my mother.
'I'm feared he turn out to be a conceited gowk,' said old Barnet, the minister's man.

> *James Hogg (1770–1835)*, The Private Memoirs and Confessions of a Justified Sinner

140 Tall was the plume that waved over the brow
Of that dark reckless Borderer, Wat o' the Cleuch.

> *James Hogg*, Wat o' the Cleuch

141 The very worst play she wrote is better than the best o' any ither body's that hasna kickt the bucket.

> *James Hogg (1770–1835)*, in Christopher North *(John Wilson, 1785–1854)*, Noctes Ambrosianae, *on Joanna Baillie (1762–1851)*

142 McADAM, hail!
Hail Roadian! hail Colossus, who dost stand
Striding ten thousand turnpikes in the

land!
O universal Leveller, all hail!

> *Thomas Hood (1799–1845), on John Loudon McAdam (1756–1836)*

143 A sober, discreet, virtuous, regular, quiet, good-natured man of a bad character.

> *David Hume (1711–1776), letter to Dr Clephane, on himself*

144 O Knox he was a bad man
he split the Scottish mind.
The one half he made cruel
and the other half unkind.

> *Alan Jackson (1938–)*, Knox

145 ... he was mainly impressed by what seemed to him the utter futility of the world he surveyed.

> *E. O. James, in* Dictionary of National Biography, *on Sir James G. Frazer (1854–1941), author of* The Golden Bough

146 When these two godlike men met, they embraced and kissed each other, and having first satiated themselves with the spiritual banquet of divine words, they refreshed themselves with bodily food ... they exchanged pastoral staves in pledge and testimony of their mutual love in Christ.

> *Jocelyn of Furness*, Life of St Kentigern, *on the meeting between St Kentigern (Mungo) and St Columba*

147 ... for you know he lives among savages in Scotland, and among rakes in London.

> *Samuel Johnson (1709–1784), to John Wilkes, on James Boswell, in Boswell's* Life of Johnson

148 I do not believe that Burnet intentionally lied; but he was so much prejudiced that he took no pains to determine the truth.

> *Samuel Johnson, quoted in Boswell's* Life of Johnson, *on Bishop Gilbert Burnet (1643–1715)*

149 Hardie was a collier, a journalist, an agitator who held fast to his faiths in all the storms and tempests of an agitator's life; an incorruptible if ever there was one.

> *Thomas Johnston (1881–1965)*, Memories, *on James Keir Hardie (1856–1915)*

150 The classic instance of the man who lingered overlong in public affairs is Ramsay Macdonald.

> *Thomas Johnston*, Memories

151 She never fails to hang out a bonny white washing.

> *Jessie Kesson (Jessie Grant McDonald, 1915–1994)*

152 That poltron and vile knave Davie was justlie punished.

> *John Knox (c.1513–1572)*, History of the Reformation in Scotland, *on the murder of David Riccio*

153 We call her nott a hoore . . . but sche was brought up in the company of hooremongaris . . . what sche was and is, her self best knowis, and God (we doubt nott) will farther declair.

> *John Knox*, History of the Reformation in Scotland, *on Mary I*

154 None I haif corrupted, none I haif defrauded, merchandise haif I not maid.

> *John Knox, quoted in L. Maclean Watt*, Scottish Life and Poetry *(1912)*

155 That evershifting politician, Robert Bruce.

> *Andrew Lang (1844–1912)*, A History of Scotland

156 If I am a great man, then all great men are frauds.

> *Andrew Bonar Law (1858–1923), quoted in Lord Beaverbrook*, Politicians and the War *(1930)*

157 He doesnae juist drap a name
or set it up and say grace wi't,
he lays it oot on his haun
and hits ye richt in the face wi't.

> *T. S. Law (1916–)*, Importance

158 Lord Kelvin – being Scotch, he didn't mind damnation, and he gave the sun and the whole solar system only ninety million more years to live.

> *Stephen Leacock (1869–1944)*, My Discovery of England

159 . . . that richt redoutit Roy,
That potent prince gentle King James the Ferde.

> *Sir David Lindsay (1490–1555)*, The Testament of the Papyngo, *on James IV*

160 He was the glory of princely governing.

> *Sir David Lindsay*, The Testament of the Papyngo

161 James the Feird unhappilie slaine in this manner, with manie of his nobles . . . by the kingis awin wilful misgovernance, who wold use no counsall of his nobles in defence of his honour, and preserving of his armie: bot used his awin sensuall plesoure, quhilkis war the cause of his utter ruine.

> *Robert Lindsay of Pitscottie (c.1532–1580)*, Historie and Cronicles of Scotland, *on James IV and Flodden (1513)*

162 Hugh Skene was a poet whose work had excited more controversy than any Scottish writer had been flattered by for many years. Those who admired his writing declared him to be a genius of the highest order, and those who disliked it, or did not understand it, said he was a pretentious versifier who concealed his lack of talent by a ponderous ornamentation of words so archaic that nobody knew their meaning . . . The title poem of his new volume, *The Flauchter-Spaad*, was strikingly polyglot, and after three hours' study Magnus was unable to decide whether it was a plea for Communism, a tribute to William Wallace, or a poetical rendering of certain prehistoric fertility rites.

> *Eric Linklater (1899–1974)*, Magnus Merriman *(satirising Hugh MacDiarmid)*

163 She looks like a million dollars, but she only knows a hundred and twenty words and she's got only two ideas in her head.

> *Eric Linklater*, Juan in America

164 To sum all up, he was a learned, gallant, honest, and every other way well-accomplished gentleman; and if ever a man proposes to serve and merit well of his country, let him place his courage, zeal and constancy as a pattern before him, and think himself sufficiently applauded and rewarded by obtaining the character of being like Andrew Fletcher of Saltoun.

> *George Lockhart of Carnwath (1673–1731)*, The Lockhart Papers

165 The Judas of his country and the bane of Scotland in general.

> *George Lockhart of Carnwath*, Memoirs

Concerning the Affairs of Scotland in
1707, *on the Earl of Stair*

166 When Hogg entered the drawing-room,
Mrs Scott, being at the time in a delicate
state of health, was reclining on a sofa.
The Shepherd, after being presented, and
making his best bow, forthwith took possession of another sofa placed opposite to
hers, and stretched himself thereupon at
all his length; for, as he said afterwards, 'I
thought I could never do wrong to copy
the lady of the house.'

> *John Gibson Lockhart (1794–1854),* Life
> of Scott, *on James Hogg (1775–1835),
> patronised as 'The Ettrick Shepherd'*

167 The government decreed that
on the anniversary of his birth
the people should observe
two minutes pandemonium.

> *Norman MacCaig (1910–1996),* After
> His Death, *on Hugh MacDiarmid*

168 She was brown eggs, black skirts
and a keeper of threepenny bits
in a teapot.

> *Norman MacCaig,* Aunt Julia

169 There's a lesson here, I thought, climbing
into the pulpit I keep in my mind.

> *Norman MacCaig,* Country Dance

170 Mary was depressed,
She wanted real life, and here she was
acting in a play, with real blood in it.
And she thought of the years to come,
and of the frightful plays that would be
   written
about the play she was in.

> *Norman MacCaig,* Queen of Scots

171 My job, as I see it, has never been to lay a
tit's egg; but to erupt like a volcano, emit-
ting not only flame, but a load of rubbish.

> *Hugh MacDiarmid (C. M. Grieve,
> 1892–1978), letter to George Bruce,
> June 1964*

172 But Stumpie believ't nor in Gode nor
   man –
Thocht life but a fecht without ony plan,
An' the best nae mair nor a flash i' the
   pan.

> *James Pittendrigh MacGillivray
> (1886–1938),* Mercy o' Gode

173 In the College of Edinburgh about the
middle or later part of the seventeeenth

century there was a strange, vain, pedantic
librarian, whose name, I think, was Henderson . . . The North wall of the College
then, as it continued to do even in my lifetime, like the Tower of Pisa leaned very
much outwards off the perpendicular; and
there was a traditionary prediction that it
was to fall on the wisest man in the College. Henderson would never pass this wall
for fear of its falling on him.

> *Henry Mackenzie (1745–1831), quoted in
> H. W. Thomson,* The Anecdotes and
> Egotisms of Henry Mackenzie

174 He was a student at the University of Edinburgh, and his circumstances obliged him
to have a sharer of his humble apartment
whom Thomson's late sitting up, reading
or writing, much incommoded; but his
chum contrived to force Thomson into
bed by blowing out the candle and working on his terror for ghosts.

> *Henry Mackenzie,* The Anecdotes and
> Egotisms of Henry Mackenzie, *on
> James Thomson (1700–1748)*

175 Mediocrity weighed dully on his mind,
like a migraine. He felt seedy with
mundanities.

> *William McIlvanney (1936–),* A Gift
> from Nessus

176 Henry VIII approached as nearly to the
ideal standard of perfect wickedness as the
infirmities of human nature will allow.

> *Sir James Mackintosh (1765–1832),* His-
> tory of England

177 A dungeon of wit.

> *Isabella Maclean, Lady Lochbuie, noted in
> James Boswell's* Journal, *October 1773,
> on Samuel Johnson*

178 My heart is a lonely hunter, that hunts on a
lonely hill.

> *Fiona MacLeod (William Sharp,
> 1856–1905),* From the Hills of Dream

179 It seems that he had a marked reluctance
to take off his skin-boots more than once a
year, for the ritual annual feet-washing on
Maundy Thursday . . . It sounds almost too
revolting to contemplate; but Bede justi-
fies this conspicuous disregard for hygiene
on the ground that 'he had so far withdrawn his mind from the care of his body
and fixed it on the care of his soul alone
that, having once been shod with the boots

of skin that he was accustomed to use, he would wear them for whole months together'.

> *Magnus Magnusson,* Lindisfarne, *on St Cuthbert (c.635–687)*

180 Of Liddisdale the common thievis
Sa pertlie stealis now and reivis,
That nane may keep
Horse, nolt, not sheep
Nor yet dar sleep for their mischiefis.

> *Sir Richard Maitland (1496–1586),*
> Aganis the Thievis of Liddisdale

181 On returning to Buchanan's bedside, he meekly enquired of us, 'Have I told the truth?' My uncle replied, 'Yes, Sir, I think so.' All that the patient could utter was, 'Pray to God for me, Melvyll, and let him direct all.'

> *James Melville (1556–1614),* Diaries,
> *on the death of George Buchanan
> (1517–1583)*

182 . . . ere he had done with his sermone, he was sa active and vigorous that he was like to ding the pulpit in blads, and flie out of it.

> *James Melville,* Life of John Knox, *on
> the preaching of the frail and elderly Knox*

183 Scot had answered unto Scot: an eccentric had elaborated a prodigy.

> *H. Miles, Introduction to* Life and Death
> of the Admirable Crichton, *by Sir
> Thomas Urquhart (1611–1660)*

184 He was not insensible to pleasures; but he deemed very few of them worth the price which, at least in the present state of society, must be paid for them.

> *John Stuart Mill (1806–1873),* Auto-
> biography, *on his father, James Mill
> (1773–1836)*

185 Must we not regard him as a kind of intellectual monster – a sort of moral centaur! His character is wonderful, not in any of its single parts, but in its incongruity as a whole.

> *Hugh Miller (1802–1856),* Notes and
> Legends of the North of Scotland, *on
> Sir Thomas Urquhart (1611–1660)*

186 Lovat's head i' the pat,
Horns and a' thegither,

We'll mak brose o' that
An' gie the swine their supper.

> *Hugh Miller,* Notes and Legends of the
> North of Scotland, *on Lord Lovat*

187 There was another Highlander who resided near Kessock, who had vowed, immediately after the battle of Preston, that he would neither cut nor comb the hair of his head until Charles Stuart was placed on the throne of his ancestors. And he religiously observed this vow. My grandfather saw him twenty years after the battle. He was then a strange, grotesque-looking thing, not very unlike a huge cabbage out a-walking.

> *Hugh Miller,* Notes and Legends of the
> North of Scotland

188 And washed his hands, and watched his
    hands, and washed
his hands, and watched his hands, and
    washed his hands.

> *Edwin Morgan (1920–),* Pilate at
> Fortingall

189 James Hutton, that true son of fire.

> *Edwin Morgan,* Theory of the Earth

190 Bell's mind was fir'd
With ardent light, mankind to bless.

> *Edward Morris, panegyric on Henry
> Bell (1767–1830), inventor and engineer,
> quoted in B. D. Osborne and R. Arm-
> strong,* Scotch Obsessions *(1996)*

191 What Knox really did was to rob Scotland of all the benefits of the Renaissance.

> *Edwin Muir (1887–1959),* John Knox

192 The death-mask . . . shows the face of a man who, after struggling courageously and drawing on his powers to the end, has found that that is not enough; so that all the features are fixed in painful surprise. The mouth is pulled down like that of a hurt child; but the rest of the face expresses steady offence.

> *Edwin Muir,* Scottish Journey, *on Sir
> Walter Scott*

193 If a celestial journalist, notebook in hand, had asked her what kind of woman she was, she would have replied, with some surprise, that she was a minister's sister.

> *Willa Muir (1890–1970),* Imagined
> Corners

194 I knew he was one of the Macfarlanes. There were ten Macfarlanes, all men, except one, and he was a valet, but the family did their best to conceal the fact, and said he was away on the yachts.

> *Neil Munro (1864–1930)*, The Vital Spark

195 'Hurricane Jeck was seldom very rife wi' money, but he came from Kinlochaline, and that iss ass good ass a Board of Tred certuficate.'

> *Neil Munro*, In Highland Harbours with Para Handy

196 'He iss not a brat of a boy, I admit,' said the Captain, 'but he's in the prime o' life and cheneral agility.'

> *Neil Munro*, In Highland Harbours with Para Handy

197 'I'm nae phenomena; I'm jist Nature; jist the Rale Oreeginal.'

> *Neil Munro*, Erchie

198 'Fat does he dee? Ye micht as weel speir fat I dee mysel,'
The things he hisna time to dee is easier to tell.'

> *Charles Murray (1864–1941)*, Docken Afore His Peers

199 A penniless lass wi' a lang pedigree.

> *Lady Nairne (1766–1845)*, The Laird o' Cockpen

200 She's been embalmed inside and out –
And sautéd to the last degree –
There's pickle in her very snout,
Sae caper-like and cruetie,
Lot's wife was fresh compared to her.

> *George Outram (1805–1856)*, The Annuity

201 With one hand he put a penny in the urn of Poverty, and with the other he took a shilling out.

> *Robert Pollok (1798–1827)*, The Course of Time, *on a landlord*

202 And do not believe that the blessed state of the heroes and demigods of the Elysian Fields was anything to do with asphodel, or ambrosia, or nectar, or whatever our old-time writers say. It lay, in my opinion, with the fact that they wiped their arses with a gosling. Such, moreover, is also the belief of Master John of Scotland.

> *François Rabelais (c.1494–c.1553)*, Gargantua, *translated by David Ross*

203 Imprimis, then, for tallness, I
am five feet and four inches high;
A black-a-vic'd, snod, dapper fallow,
Nor lean, nor overlaid with tallow.

> *Allan Ramsay (1686–1758)*, on himself, quoted in L. Maclean Watt, Scottish Life and Poetry *(1912)*

204 He scorned carriages on the ground of its being unmannerly to 'sit in a box drawn by brutes'.

> *Dean E. B. Ramsay (1793–1872)*, Reminiscences of Scottish Life and Character, *on Lord Monboddo*

205 In the Clerk Maxwell household the young scientist always had some 'experimental philosophy' going forward. His results were known collectively as 'Jamsie's durts'.

> *J. T. R. Ritchie*, The Singing Street *(1964)*, on James Clerk Maxwell

206 You know that his mind was elegance itself – He sometimes hinted his uneasiness at the thought of becoming, silly, or slovenly, or squalid . . . his wish was completely gratified – for life must have ceased without a pang.

> *John Robison (1739–1805)*, letter to James Watt, December 1799, on the death of Joseph Black

207 His baptismal register spoke of him pessimistically as John Henry, but he left that behind with the other maladies of infancy.

> *Saki (H. H. Munro, 1870–1916)*, Adrian

208 And this is aa the life he kens there is.

> *Tom Scott (1918–1995)*, Auld Sanct-Aundrians

209 And dar'st thou then,
To beard the lion in his den,
The Douglas in his hall?

> *Sir Walter Scott (1771–1832)*, Marmion

210 In these far climes it was my lot
To meet the wondrous Michael Scott;
A Wizard, of such dreaded fame,
That when in Salamanca's cave,

Him listed his magic wand to wave,
The bells would ring in Notre Dame!

> *Sir Walter Scott*, The Lay of the Last
> Minstrel

211 His step is first in peaceful ha',
His sword in battle keen.

> *Sir Walter Scott*, Jock o' Hazeldean
> *(additional verses)*

212 Donald Caird can lilt and sing,
Blithely dance the Highland fling,
Drink till the gudeman be blind,
Fleech till the gudewife be kind;
Hoop a leglin, clout a pan,
Or crack a pow wi' ony man.

> *Sir Walter Scott*, Donald Caird's Come
> Again

213 My foot is on my native heath, and my
name is MacGregor.

> *Sir Walter Scott*, Rob Roy

214 O young Lochinvar is come out of the
West,
Through all the wide Border his steed was
the best.

> *Sir Walter Scott*, Lochinvar

215 And there was Claverhouse, as beautiful as
when he lived, with his long, dark, curled
locks streaming down over his laced buff-
coat, and his left hand always on his right
spule-blade, to hide the wound that the
silver bullet had made.

> *Sir Walter Scott*, Redgauntlet

216 High though his titles, proud his name,
Boundless his wealth as wish can claim, –
Despite those titles, power, and pelf
The wretch, concentred all in self,
Living, shall forfeit fair renown,
And doubly dying shall go down
To the vile dust from whence he sprung,
Unwept, unhonoured and unsung.

> *Sir Walter Scott*, The Lay of the Last
> Minstrel

217 The honest grunter.

> *Sir Walter Scott*, Journal *(December
> 1825), on James Hogg*

218 A rattle-skulled half-lawyer, half-sports-
man, through whose head a regiment of
horse has been exercising since he was five
years old.

> *Sir Walter Scott, on himself, quoted in
> L. Maclean Watt*, Scottish Life and
> Poetry *(1912)*

219 Up to her University days she carried the
conviction that there was something about
Scotland in the Bible.

> *Nan Shepherd (1893–1981)*, Quarry
> Wood

220 I'm lame, feeble and foolish; the wrinkles
are wonderful – no concertina is so wonderfully folded and convoluted. I'm a wee,
wee wifie, very little buikit but I grip on
well none the less.

> *Mary Slessor (1848–1915), letter to
> Friends, September 1912, quoted in James
> Buchan*, The Expendable Mary Slessor
> *(1980)*

221 Lord Charlemont described the expression
of his mouth as imbecilic, that of his eyes
as vacant, and the corpulence of his frame
as befitting rather a 'turtle-eating alder-
man' than a philosopher.

> *Alastair Smart*, The Life and Art of
> Allan Ramsay *(1952), on David Hume
> (1711–1776)*

222 He has less nonsense in his head than any
man living.

> *Adam Smith (1723–1790), quoted in
> Lord Brougham*, Lives of Men of
> Letters and Science in the Reign
> of George III, *on Joseph Black
> (1728–1799)*

223 Upon the whole, I have always considered
him, both in his lifetime and since his
death, as approximating as nearly to the
idea of a perfectly wise and virtuous man,
as perhaps the nature of human frailty will
permit.

> *Adam Smith, letter to William Strachan,
> 1776, on David Hume (1711–1776)*

224 I would rather be remembered by a song
than by a victory.

> *Alexander Smith (1830–1867),*
> Dreamthorp

225 Well, never mind, never mind . . . Never
mind his damning the North Pole. *I* have
heard him speak disrespectfully of the
Equator.

> *Sydney Smith (1771–1845), quoted in
> J. Sutherland*, The Oxford Book of
> Literary Anecdotes, *on Francis Jeffrey
> (1773–1850), refusing to back Sir John
> Ross' Polar expedition*

226 There ye gang, ye daft
And doitit dotterel, ye saft
Crazed outland skalrag saul.
> *Sydney Goodsir Smith (1915–1975)*, The
> Grace of God and the Meths Drinker

227 A Renaissance man, if only we'd had a
renaissance.
> *W. Gordon Smith*, Mr Jock *(1987), on
> King James IV*

228 John Paul Jones demonstrates, better than
anybody, that endearing protean quality
of the Scot, to be all things to all men, providing the price is right.
> *W. Gordon Smith*, Mr Jock

229 Too coy to flatter, and too proud to serve,
Thine be the joyless dignity to starve.
> *Tobias Smollett (1721–1771)*, Advice

230 He was formed for the ruin of our sex.
> *Tobias Smollett*, Roderick Random

231 In bane he was sma'-boukit,
But had a muckle beard
And whan he gar'd it waggle
Baith men and beast were feared.
> *William Soutar (1898–1943)*,
> John Knox

232 My faither's deid, my mither's dottle,
My tittie's cowpit the creel;
My only brither is the bottle
And I've aye lo'ed him weel.
> *William Soutar*, Cadger Jimmy

233 From my experience of life I believe my
personal motto should be 'Beware of men
bearing flowers'.
> *Muriel Spark (1918–)* Curriculum
> Vitae

234 ... the nicest boy who ever committed the
sin of whisky.
> *Muriel Spark*, A Sad Tale's Best for
> Winter

235 To this day his name smacks of the
gallows.
> *Robert Louis Stevenson (1850–1894)*,
> Some Portraits by Raeburn, *on Lord
> Braxfield*

236 Poor Matt! He's gone to Heaven no doubt,
but he won't like God.
> *Robert Louis Stevenson, quoted in Jona-
> thon Green*, The Dictionary of Insult-
> ing Quotations *(1996) on Matthew
> Arnold (1822–1888)*

237 ... an austerity of which he was quite
unconscious, and a pride which seemed
arrogance, and perhaps was chiefly shyness,
discouraged and offended his companions.
> *Robert Louis Stevenson*, Weir of
> Hermiston

238 Heedious! I never gave twa thoughts to
heediousness, I have no call to be bonny.
I'm a man that gets through with my day's
business, and let that suffice.
> *Robert Louis Stevenson*, Weir of
> Hermiston

239 Sellar, daith has ye in his grip;
Ye needna think he'll let ye slip,
Justice ye've earned, and by the Book,
A warm assize ye winna jouk.
The fires ye lit to gut Strathnaver,
Ye'll feel them now, and roast for ever.
> *Recorded from Andrew Stewart of Mel-
> ness, 1958, and quoted in* The Arm-
> strong Nose, Letters of Hamish Hend-
> erson, *edited by Alec Findlay (1996),
> referring to Patrick Sellar's part in the
> Sutherland Clearances*

240 He was too large to stand in the ranks
and generally stood at the right of the regiment when in line and marched at the head
when in column, but was always accompanied by a mountain deer of uncommon
size. This animal was so much attached
to him that whether on duty with his regiment or on the streets, the hart was always
at his side.
> *David Stewart of Garth (1772–1829)*,
> Sketches of the Highlanders, *on
> Sergeant Samuel MacDonald of the
> Sutherlands*

241 The wisest fool in Christendom.
> *Ascribed to the Duc de Sully (1559–1641),
> also to Henri IV of France (1553–1610): a
> comment on King James VI (1565–1625)*

242 ... lanely I stray, in the calm simmer
gloamin',
To muse on sweet Jessie, the flower o'
Dunblane.
> *Robert Tannahill (1774–1810)*, Jessie,
> the Flower o' Dunblane

243 An haena ye heard man, o' Barochan Jean,
How death an starvation cam' ower
the haill nation:

She wrocht such mischief wi' her twa
pawky e'en.

   Robert Tannahill, Barochan Jean

244 Friend more than Servant,
Loyal, truthful, brave.
Self less than Duty,
Even to the Grave.

   *Lord Tennyson (1809–1892), lines writ-
   ten for Queen Victoria's monument to
   John Brown (1826–1883) at Balmoral*

245 I dinna like McFarlane, I'm safe enough
tae state.
His lug wad cast a shadow ower a
sax-fit gate.
He's saft as ony goblin and sliddery
as a skate,
McFarlane o' the Sprots o' Burnieboozie.

   G. Bruce Thomson, McFarlane o' the
   Sprots o' Burniboozie

246 He has been known to have lectured for
the hour before reaching the subject of the
lecture.

   J. J. Thomson, Recollections and Reflections, *on Lord Kelvin (1824–1907)*

247 The Queen united such strictness to her
sweetness and such sweetness to her strictness that all who were in her service, men
as well as women, while fearing her loved
her and while loving feared her.

   Turgot (c.1060–c.1115), The Life of
   St Margaret, Queen of Scotland

248 . . . he and his works very soon settled
down to the position of being names and
nothing more, except to the student whom
nothing can daunt.

   *Lauchlan Maclean Watt, on William
   Wilkie (1721–1772), author of* The
   Epigoniad, *in* Scottish Life and Poetry
   (1912)

249 'Five foot six, an unlucky thirteen stone . . .
a sixth rate mathematician, a second-rate
physicist, a second-rate engineer, a bit of
a meteorologist, something of a journalist, a plausible salesman of ideas, liking to
believe that there is some poetry in my
physics and some physics in my poetry'.

   *Sir Robert Watson-Watt (1892–1973), in
   a radio broadcast, about himself*

250 He had rather spend £10,000 on Embassies
to keep or procure peace with dishonour,

than £10,000 on an army that would have
forced peace with honour.

   *Sir Anthony Weldon (fl. early 17th cen-
   tury)*, The Court and Character of
   King James, *on King James VI*

251 He was so monstrously ill-favoured as to
possess some of the attractiveness of a gar-
goyle. He had neither dignity, nor what a
Roman would have called gravity. As Lord
Chancellor, he distinguished himself by
belching from the Woolsack.

   *Esmé Wingfield-Stratford, on Lord
   Brougham (1778–1868)*

Philosophy, Political Economy and Social Science

1 Metaphysics I detested. The science appeared to me an elaborate, diabolical
invention for mystifying what was clear,
and confounding what was intelligible.

   W. E. Aytoun (1813–1865)

2 Were na my heart light, I wad dee.

   Lady Grizel Baillie (1665–1746), Were
   Na My Heart Light, I Wad Dee

3 Kant, as we all know, compared moral
law to the starry heavens, and found them
both sublime. On the naturalistic hypothesis we should rather compare it to the
protective blotches on a beetle's back, and
find them both ingenious.

   A. J. Balfour (1848–1930), Foundations
   of Belief

4 Yes, yes, I grant the sons of earth
Are doom'd to trouble from their birth.
We all of sorrow have our share;
But say, is yours without compare?

   A. J. Beattie (1735–1803), The
   Question

5 Thou must be true thyself
If thou the truth would'st teach.

   Horatius Bonar (1808–1889), Be True

6 Personally I am a great believer in bed, in
constantly keeping horizontal.

   *Sir Henry Campbell-Bannerman
   (1836–1908), letter to Mrs Whiteley*

7 I don't pretend to understand the Universe.
It's a great deal bigger than I am.

   Thomas Carlyle (1795–1881)

8 Misery of any kind is not the *cause* of Immorality, but the effect thereof.

Thomas Carlyle, Count Cagliostro

9 Everywhere the human soul stands between a hemisphere of light and another of darkness; on the confines of two ever-lasting hostile empires, Necessity and Freewill.

Thomas Carlyle, Essays

10 . . . what we might call, by way of emi-nence, *the dismal science*.

Thomas Carlyle, The Nigger Question, *referring to Political Economy*

11 . . . the canting moralist
Who measures right and wrong.

John Davidson (1857–1909), A Ballad of a Poet Born

12 They felt that if any large portion of the subjects of her Majesty were to be impressed with a belief that they had a right to rely upon the interposition of the State in order to supply them with food, the strongest motives to foresight, indus-try and frugality would be withdrawn, and a principle would be laid down, inconsist-ent with the well-being of scociety.

Committee of Contributors for the Relief of Those Suffering from Destitution in the Highlands and Islands (1836–37), quoted in Charles Withers, Gaelic Scotland *(1988)*

13 He who will not reason, is a bigot; he who cannot is a fool; and he who dares not, is a slave.

William Drummond (1585–1649), Aca-demical Question

14 It should seem, therefore, to be the happi-ness of man to make his social dispositions the ruling spring of his occupations; to state himself as the member of a commu-nity, for whose general good his heart may glow with an ardent zeal . . . We need not enlarge our communities to to enjoy these advantages. We frequently obtain them in the most remarkable degree, where nations remain independent, and are of a small extent.

Adam Ferguson (1723–1816), An Essay on the History of Civil Society

15 Town-planning is not mere place-planning, nor even work-planning. If it is to be suc-cessful it must be folk-planning . . . its task is to find the right places for each sort of people; places where they will really flour-ish. To give people in fact the same care that we give when transplanting flowers, instead of harsh evictions and arbitrary instructions to 'move on'.

Sir Patrick Geddes (1854–1932), quoted in J. Tyrwhitt, Patrick Geddes in India *(1947)*

16 . . . if you'd all the same money one day what would it be the next? – Rich and Poor again!

Lewis Grassic Gibbon (James Leslie Mitchell, 1901–1935), Sunset Song

17 Now, my own suspicion is that the Uni-verse is not only queerer than we suppose, but queerer than we *can* suppose.

J. B. S. Haldane (1892–1964), Possible Worlds

18 Every day a big lorry loaded with Perrier Water bound for Scotland will pass a big lorry loaded with Highland Spring Water bound for England.

Christopher Harvie (1944–), Cultural Weapons

19 Avarice, the spur of industry.

David Hume (1711–1776), Of Civil Liberty

20 Reason is and ought to be the slave of the passions and can never pretend to any other office than to serve and obey them.

David Hume, Essays

21 A State is never greater than when all its superfluous hands are employed in the service of the public.

David Hume, Essays

22 We are placed in this world, as in a great theatre, where the true springs and causes of every event are concealed from us; nor have we sufficient wisdom to foresee, or power to prevent, those ills with which we are constantly threatened.

David Hume, The Natural History of Religion

23 An object may exist, and yet be nowhere.

David Hume, A Treatise of Human Nature

24 Generally speaking, the errors in religion are dangerous; those in philosophy only ridiculous.

> *David Hume*, A Treatise of Human Nature

25 'Tis not contrary to reason to prefer the destruction of the whole world to the scratching of my finger.

> *David Hume*, A Treatise of Human Nature

26 The great end of all human industry is the attainment of happiness.

> *David Hume*, The Stoic

27 I am apt in a cool hour to suspect, in general, that most of my reasonings will be more useful by furnishing hints and exciting people's curiosity, than as containing any principles that would augment the stock of knowledge.

> *David Hume, letter to Francis Hutcheson*

28 'The fall in the value of kelp,' observed Lord MacDonald's North Uist factor in 1839, 'renders . . . a change in the management of the North Uist estate necessary. The tenants have hitherto been accustomed to pay for the greater part of their rents by their labour as kelpers. Kelp is not now a productive manufacture. The population of the estate is greater than the land, the kelp being abandoned, can maintain. The allotments of land held by the small tenants are so small that they cannot maintain their families and pay the proprietor the rents which the lands are worth if let in larger tenements. It becomes necessary, therefore, that a number of small tenants be removed . . .'

> *James Hunter*, The Making of the Crofting Community *(1976), quoting from the MacDonald Papers*

29 That action is best, which procures the greatest happiness for the greatest numbers.

> *Francis Hutcheson (1694–1746)*, A System of Moral Philosophy

30 For the ultimate notion of right is that which tends to the universal good; and when one's acting in a certain manner has this tendency he has a right thus to act.

> *Francis Hutcheson*, A System of Moral Philosophy

31 If there is no moral sense, which makes rational Actions appear Beautiful, or Deform'd; if all Approbation be from the Interest of the Approver, 'What's Hecuba to us, or we to Hecuba?'

> *Francis Hutcheson*, An Inquiry into the Original of Our Ideas of Beauty and Virtue

32 Logic is to language and grammar what mathematics is to common sense. Logic is etherealised grammar . . . More ships are lost through bad logic than through bad seamanship.

> *Lord Kelvin (1824–1907), presidential address to the Birmingham and Midland Institute*

33 He comprehended at last how the whole world of will was doomed to eternal anguish in order that one Being might feel joy.

> *David Lindsay (1878–1945)*, A Voyage to Arcturus

34 Hauf his soul a man may use
Indulgin' in illusions:
And hauf in gettin' rid o' them,
And comin' to conclusions

> *Hugh MacDiarmid (1892–1978)*

35 Scotland – Scottish genius – has scarcely begun to recover yet from the fact that Scotland accepted Dugald Stewart and rejected David Hume, and has been dominated by the philosophy of 'common sense' ever since.

> *Hugh MacDiarmid*, Lucky Poet

36 We must do the thing we *must*
Before the thing we *may*;
We are unfit for any trust
Till we can and do obey.

> *George Macdonald (1824–1905)*, Willie's Question

37 Say not the will of man is free
Within the limits of his soul –
Who from his heritage can flee?
Who can his destiny control.

> *Donald A. Mackenzie (b.1879)*, Free Will

38 If it becomes necessary for me, as I fear it will, to carry through the measure of dispossessing a population overgrown and daily becoming more burdensome to pave the way for the grand improvement of the introduction of mutton in lieu of man, the

numbers almost appal me and will astonish you.

> *Stewart Mackenzie of Seaforth, letter asking for financial assistance with the transportation of Lewis tenants, 1819, quoted in James Hunter,* The Making of the Crofting Community *(1976 and 2000)*

39 Hume possessed powers of a very high order; but regard for truth formed no part of his character . . . the object of his reasonings was not to attain truth, but to show it was unattainable.

> *John Stuart Mill (1806–1873), in* Westminster Review, *(1824), on David Hume*

40 For when I dinna clearly see
I always own I dinna ken:
And that's the way wi' wisest men.

> *Allan Ramsay (1686–1758)*

41 The belief of a material world is older, and of more authority, than any principles of philosophy. It declines the tribunal of reason, and laughs at all the artillery of the logician.

> *Thomas Reid (1710–1796),* An Inquiry into the Human Mind

42 Men are often led into error by the love of simplicity, which disposes us to reduce things to few principles, and to conceive a greater simplicity in nature than there really is.

> *Thomas Reid,* An Inquiry into the Human Mind

43 The Epicurean view is the only possible one – that we are born because the great Order of Things has so decreed, and that we continue to exist because the sum of our pleasures exceeds the sum of our sorrows.

> *Sir Ronald Ross (1857–1932),* Memoirs

44 All decent people live beyond their incomes nowadays, and those who aren't respectable live beyond other people's. A few gifted individuals manage to do both.

> *Saki (H.H. Munro, 1870–1916),* The Chronicles of Clovis

45 I'm living so far beyond my income that we may be almost said to be living apart.

> *Saki,* The Chronicles of Clovis

46 There is such a thing as letting one's aesthetic sense override one's moral sense . . .

I believe you would have condoned the South Sea Bubble and the persecution of the Albigenses if they had been carried out in effective colour schemes.

> *Saki,* The Toys of Peace

47 *Scotch Optimism*
Through a gless,
Darkly
Scotch Pessimism
Nae
gless

> *Alexander Scott (1920–),* Scotched

48 I cannot tell how the truth may be;
I tell the tale as 'twas said to me.

> *Sir Walter Scott (1771–1832),* The Lay Of The Last Minstrel

49 We often find out what will do, by finding out what will not do; and probably he who never made a mistake never made a discovery.

> *Samuel Smiles (1812–1904),* Self-Help

50 He who spends all he gets is on his way to beggary.

> *Samuel Smiles,* On Thrift

51 Consumption is the sole end and purpose of production; and the interest of the producer ought to be attended to only so far as it may be necessary for promoting that of the consumer.

> *Adam Smith (1723–1790),* The Wealth of Nations

52 It is not from the benevolence of the butcher, the brewer, or the baker that we procure our dinner, but from their regard to their own interest. We address ourselves not to their humanity, but to their self-love, and never talk to them of our necessities but of their advantages.

> *Adam Smith,* The Wealth of Nations

53 No society can surely be flourishing and happy, of which the far greater part of the members are poor and miserable.

> *Adam Smith,* The Wealth of Nations

54 To found a great empire for the sole purpose of raising up a people of customers, may at first sight appear a project fit only for a nation of shopkeepers. It is, however, a project altogether unfit for a nation of shopkeepers; but extremely fit for a

nation whose government is influenced by shopkeepers.

Adam Smith, The Wealth of Nations

55 The natural effort of every individual to better his own condition, when suffered to exert itself with freedom and security, is so powerful a principle that it is alone and without any assistance, not only capable of carrying on the society to wealth and prosperity, but of surmounting a hundred impertinent obstructions with which the folly of human laws have too often encumbered its operations.

Adam Smith, The Wealth of Nations

56 There is no art which one government sooner learns of another than of draining money from the pockets of the people.

Adam Smith, The Wealth of Nations

57 It is the highest impertinence and presumption, therefore, in kings and ministers, to pretend to watch over the economy of private people, and to restrain their expense . . . They are themselves always, and without any exception, the greatest spendthrifts in society . . . If their own extravagance does not ruin the state, that of their subjects never will.

Adam Smith, The Wealth of Nations

58 I consider the world as made for me, not me for the world. It is my maxim therefore to enjoy it while I can, and let futurity shift for itself.

Tobias Smollett (1721–1771), Roderick Random

59 Little live, great pass,
Jesus Christ and Barabbas
Were found the same day.
This died, that went his way.

C. H. Sorley (1895–1915), All the Hills and Vales Along

60 You could read Kant by yourself, if you wanted, but you must share a joke with someone else.

Robert Louis Stevenson (1850–1894), Virginibus Puerisque

61 If thy morals make thee dreary, depend upon it they are wrong.

Robert Louis Stevenson, A Christmas Sermon

62 An elegant sufficiency, content,
Retirement, rural quiet, friendship, books

Ease and alternate labour, useful life,
Progressive virtue, and approving Heaven!

James Thomson (1700–1748), The Seasons

63 What, what is virtue, but repose of mind?
A pure ethereal calm that knows no storm,
Above the reach of wild ambition's wind,
Above those passions that this world deform.

James Thomson, The Castle of Indolence

64 I find no hint throughout the universe
Of good or ill, of blessing or of curse;
I find alone, necessity supreme.

James Thomson (1834–1882), The City of Dreadful Night

65 If there is anything that isn't clear I refer you to the chronicles of Zarathustra or to the Chieh-hein of the Llama Swingitup.
If you can't get hold of these, *see me*, please.

Alexander Trocchi (1925–1984), A Little Geography Lesson for my Sons and Daughters

66 Still, failure, success, what is it? Whae gies a fuck. We aw live, then we die, in quite a short space ay time n aw. That's it; end ay fuckin story.

Irvine Welsh (1957–), Trainspotting

Places: Real

(In alphabetical order of name)

1 Blyth Aberdeen, thou beriall of all tounis,
The lamp of bewtie, bountie and blythness.

William Dunbar (c.1460–c.1520), On Aberdeen

2 Glitter of mica at the windy corners
. . . the sleek sun flooding
The broad abundant dying sprawl of the Dee.

G. S. Fraser (1915–1980), Hometown Elegy, *on Aberdeen*

3 Aberdeen a thin-lipped peasant woman who has borne eleven and buried nine.

Lewis Grassic Gibbon (James Leslie Mitchell, 1901–1935), Scottish Scene

4 Aberdeen impresses the stranger as a city of granite palaces, inhabited by people as definite as their building material.

   H. V. Morton (1892–1979), In Search of Scotland

5 The sea-gray toun, the stane-gray sea . . .
   And kirks and crans clamjamfrie,
   Heav'n and haven inter-maxtered heave
   To the sweel o' the same saut tide.

   Alexander Scott (1920–), Aberdeen, Heart of Stone

6 It was only in Aberdeen that I saw . . . the kind of tartan tight-fistedness that made me think of the average Aberdonian as a person who would gladly pick a halfpenny out of a dunghill with his teeth . . . a cold, stony-faced city.

   Paul Theroux, A Kingdom by the Sea *(1983)*

7 Now summer blinks on flow'ry braes,
   And o'er the crystal streamlet plays;
   Come let us spend the lightsome days,
   In the birks of Aberfeldy.

   Robert Burns (1759–1796), The Birks of Aberfeldy

8 A'll awa' to Alloa,
   and A'll awa' the noo.
   A'll awa' to Alloa
   to buy a pund o' oo.

   Traditional, Awa' to Alloa

9 A fine, bright, self-confident little town.

   Thomas Carlyle (1795–1881), Reminiscences, *on Annan*

10 This grey, grim, sea-beaten hole.

   Robert Louis Stevenson (1850–1894), letter to his mother, 1868, on Anstruther

11 Arran of the many stags,
    The sea reaches to its shoulder.

   Anonymous, translated from Gaelic by Kenneth Jackson

12 It is an ageless sang this auld isle sings
    In the burn born alang the scree fute
    By riven craigs where the black raven brings
    The still-born lamb to its nest by the rowan-rute.

   Robert Maclellan (1907–1985), Arran

13 You feel, even if you cannot explain exactly why, that you are on a peculiar island.

   Moray McLaren, Arran, *in E. Molony*, Portraits of Islands *(1951)*

14 It was a true, sterling, gospel sermon – it was striking, sublime, and awful in the extreme. He finally made out the IT, mentioned in the text, to mean, properly and positively, the notable town of Auchtermuchty. He proved all the people in it, to their perfect satisfaction, to be in the gall of bitterness and the bond of iniquity.

   James Hogg (1770–1835), The Private Memoirs and Confessions of a Justified Sinner

15 Auld Ayr, wham ne'er a toon surpasses,
    For honest men and bonny lasses.

   Robert Burns (1759–1796), Tam o' Shanter

16 Happy the man who belongs to no party,
    But sits in his ain house, and looks at Benarty.

   Sir Michael Malcolm of Lochore, at the time of the French Revolution, 1789

17 In all the Hebrides, Benbecula is the sea's dearest child. That is why the returning tide races so quickly over the sand, hurrying with pouted lips to kiss its shore. And when the night's embraces are over, the sea leaves Benbecula again, like a mother bird going to forage for its young.

   Hector MacIver (1910–1966), The Outer Isles , *in G. Scott-Moncrieff*, Scottish Country *(1936)*

18 Your kindly slope, with bilberries and blaeberries, studded with cloudberries that are round-headed and red; wild garlic clusters in the corner of rock terraces, and abounding tufted crags; the dandelions and pennyroyal, and the soft white bog-cotton and sweet grass there on every part of it, from the lowest level to the topmost edge of the peaks.

   Duncan Bàn MacIntyre (1724–1812), Ben Doran, *from Gaelic*

19 O Brignall banks are wild and fair,
    And Greta woods are green,
    And you may gather garlands there,
    Would grace a summer's queen.

   Sir Walter Scott (1771–1832), Rokeby

20 'We're buryin' Annie,' says I.
   'Whatna Annie?' says Mr Sutherland.
   'Animosity,' says I – ony auld baur'll pass
   in Brora.

   Neil Munro (1864–1930), Jimmy Swan,
   The Joy Traveller

21 I am glad to have seen the Caledonian
   Canal, but don't want to see it again.
   Matthew Arnold (1822–1888), Letters

22 . . . a the sweets that ane can wish
   Frae Nature's han, are strewed on thee.
   Robert Tannahill (1774–1810), Bonnie
   Wood o' Craigielea

23 Crianlarich is the most signposted nowhere
   on the planet.
   Jim Crumley (1947–), Gulfs of Blue Air

24 Ye lover of the picturesque, if ye wish to
      drown your grief,
   Take my advice and visit the ancient town
      of Crieff.
   William McGonagall (1825–1902), Beau-
   tiful Crieff

25 If Dingwall was in its ordinary state, it
   must be an excellent place for sleeping a
   life away in.
   Henry Thomas Cockburn (1779–1854),
   Circuit Journeys

26 It was a kind of cowboy town, but I liked
   that aspect of it, buying stuff out of vans, a
   ragman coming in a wee green van.
   Billy Connolly (1942–), on Drumchapel,
   quoted on the Billy Connolly Website,
   1998

27 It is an east coast town with a west coast
   temperament.
   George Blake, The Heart of Scotland
   (1934), on Dundee

28 Dundee . . . had for generations dedicated
   itself to a kind of commercial single-mindedness that had come to fruition, in my
   day, in black and terrible industrial depression. Even then I felt . . . an absence of
   grace so total that it was almost a thing of
   wonder.
   James Cameron (1911–1985), Point of
   Departure

29 Dundee, the palace of Scottish blackguardism, unless perhaps Paisley be entitled to
   contest this honour with it.
   Henry Thomas Cockburn (1779–1854),
   Circuit Journeys

30 Dundee, a frowsy fisherwife addicted to
   gin and infanticide.
   *Lewis Grassic Gibbon (James Leslie
   Mitchell, 1901–1935)*, Scottish Scene

31 Dundee . . . As men have made it, it stands
   today perhaps the completest monument
   in the entire continent of human folly, avarice and selfishness.
   *Fionn McColla (Thomas Douglas Macdon-
   ald, 1906–1975)*, in G. Scott-Moncrieff,
   Scottish Country (1934)

32 The town is ill-built and is dirty beside,
   For with water it's scantily, badly supplied
   . . . And abounds so in smells that a
      stranger supposes
   The people are very different in noses.
   Thomas Stuart, Dundee (1815)

33 What Benares is to the Hindoo, Mecca to
   the Mohammedan, Jerusalem to the Christian, all that Dunfermline is to me.
   Andrew Carnegie (1835–1919), Our
   Coaching Trip

34 It was a roadsign, the name of a village
   – Dunino – where no village is.
   A scatter of farms, a school, and one
      red telephone box.
   Stephen Scobie, Dunino

35 Was there e'er sic a parish, a parish, a
      parish,
   Was there e'er sic a parish as that o'
      Dunkeld?
   They've stickit the minister, hanged
      the precentor,
   Dung doun the steeple, and drucken the
      bell.
   *Anonymous, but the original form prob-
   ably referred to Kinkell in Strathearn*

36 Duns dings a'.
   Traditional Duns saying

37 Who indeed, that has once seen Edinburgh, with its couchant lion crag, but
   must see it again in dreams, waking or
   sleeping?
   Charlotte Bronte (1816–1855), Letters

38 It was a patriarchial Fife laird, Durham of
Largo, who had the honour of giving to
Edinburgh the *sobriquet* of 'Auld Reekie'.
It appears that this old gentleman was
in the habit of regulating the time of
evening worship by the appearance of the
smoke of Edinburgh . . . saying – 'It's time
noo, bairns, to tak the buiks, and gang to
our beds, for yonder's Auld Reekie, I see,
putting on her nightcap.'

Robert Chambers (1802–1871), quoted in
George Blake, Scottish Treasure-Trove
(undated)

39 Your burgh of beggaris is ane nest,
To shout the swengouris will nocht rest,
All honest folk they do molest,
Sa piteously they cry and rame.

William Dunbar (c.1460–c.1530), Satire
on Edinburgh

40 To imagine Edinburgh as a disappointed
spinster, with a hare-lip and inhibitions, is
at least to approximate as closely to the
truth as to image the Prime Mover as a
Levantine Semite.

Lewis Grassic Gibbon (James Leslie
Mitchell, 1901–1935), Scottish Scene

41 If the world comes to an end, Edinburgh
will never notice.

Jo Grimond (1913–1993), interview in
The Scotsman (October 1979)

42 Isna Embro a glorious city!

James Hogg (1770–1835), in Christopher
North (John Wilson), Noctes
Ambrosianae

43 Edinburgh's soul is Bible-black, pickled in
boredom by centuries of sermons, swad-
dled in the shabby gentility of the Kirk.

Tom Nairn (1932–), Festival of the
Dead, in New Statesman, September
1967

44 Most of the denizens wheeze, snuffle and
exude a sort of snozzling whnoff whnoff,
apparently through a hydrophile sponge.

Ezra Pound (1885–1972), quoted in Hugh
MacDiarmid, Lucky Poet (1943)

45 The Castle looms – a fell, a fabulous ferlie.
Dragonish, darksome, dourly grapplan
the Rock
wi' claws o' stane.

Alexander Scott (1920–1989), Haar in
Princes Street

46 This braw, hie-heapit toun.

Lewis Spence (1874–1955), The Prows o'
Reekie

47 To none but those who have themselves
suffered the thing in the body, can the
gloom and depression of our Edinburgh
winters be brought home.

Robert Louis Stevenson (1850–1894), Pic-
turesque Notes on Edinburgh

48 One day, when I was taking tea with a
well-known Scottish divine in Glasgow,
the conversation turned on Edinburgh, its
charm, its menace, its appeal. Suddenly my
companion leant forward over the table,
a strange gleam in his eyes. 'They say
there are more amateur tarts in Edinburgh
than anywhere else,' he said, with a grave
intensity.

George Malcolm Thomson, The Re-Dis-
covery of Scotland

49 The impression Edinburgh has made on
me is very great; it is quite beautiful, totally
unlike anything else I have ever seen; and
what is even more, Albert, who has seen
so much, says it is unlike anything he ever
saw.

Queen Victoria (1819–1901), Letters

50 Three crests against the saffron sky
Beyond the purple plain.

Andrew Lang (1844–1912), Twilight on
Tweed, on the Eildon Hills

51 Outby, across a water not so wide but that
in May-time you shall hear the cuckoo
from the one shore to the other, a mountain lies sunk to the shoulders. This water
is the Kyles, and that yonder, Father Allan's
Island.

Amy Murray, Father Allan's Island, on
Eriskay (1936)

52 Fish guts and stinkin' herrin
Are bread and milk for an Eyemouth
bairn.

Old rhyme

53 We seemed to stand an endless while,
Though still no word was said,
Three men alive on Flannan Isle,
Who thought on three men dead.

Wilfred Gibson (1878–1962), Flannan
Isle

54 Outposts in the Atlantic, they had about
them that air of the remote and wild, shut

off by incalculable seas, sustaining the shock of thunderous water, pierced by the myriad screaming birds, and haunted by an unknown unhuman loneliness that has to be felt to be dimly understood.

> *Neil Gunn (1891–1973)*, Highland Pack, *on the Flannan Isles*

55 'For the sake o' business I've had to order suits in places no' the size o' Fochabers, where they put rabbit-pouches in your jacket whether ye poach or no'.

> *Neil Munro (1864–1930)*, Jimmy Swan, The Joy Traveller

56 Fort Augustus
Did disgust us,
And Fort William
Did the same.
At Letterfinlay
We fared thinly;
At Ballachulish
We looked foolish,
Wondering why we thither came.

> *William Wordsworth (1770–1850)*, *quoted in Robert Southey*, Journal of a Tour in Scotland, *written in 1819*

57 'What', I inquired of my companion, 'are these kind people pitying me so very much for?'

'For your want of Gaelic, to be sure. How can a man get on in the world that wants Gaelic?'

'But do not they themselves,' I asked, 'want English?'

'Oh, yes,' he said. 'But what does that signify? What is the use of English in Gairloch?'

> *Hugh Miller (1802–1856)*, My Schools and Schoolmasters

58 Girvan – a cauld, cauld place. Naebuddy o' ony consequence was ever born here.

> *'Robin Ross' in* The Chiel, *January 1885, quoted in William Donaldson*, The Language of the People *(1989)*

59 This is the tree that never grew
This is the bird that never flew
This is the fish that never swam
This is the bell that never rang.

> *Traditional rhyme associated with Glasgow's coat of arms*

60 Glasgow is not for me.
I do not see the need for such a crowd.

> *Gaelic poet, quoted in Alasdair Maclean*, Night Falls on Ardnamurchan *(1989)*

61 'Heaven seems vera little improvement on Glesga,' a Glasgow man is said to have murmured, after death, to a friend who had predeceased him. 'Man, this is no Heaven,' the other replied.

> *Anonymous*

62 Glasgow, that damned sprawling evil town.

> *G. S. Fraser (1915–1980)*, Meditation of a Patriot

63 I belong to Glasgow,
Dear old Glasgow toon . . .
But when I get a couple o' drinks on a Saturday,
Glasgow belongs to me!

> *Will Fyffe (1885–1947)*, I Belong to Glasgow

64 Glasgow is one of the few places in Scotland which defy personification . . . The monster of Loch Ness is probably the lost soul of Glasgow, in scales and horns, disporting itself in the Highlands after evacuating finally and completely its mother-corpse.

> *Lewis Grassic Gibbon (James Leslie Mitchell, 1901–1935)*, Scottish Scene

65 Glasgow . . . the vomit of a cataleptic commercialism.

> *Lewis Grassic Gibbon*, The Thirteenth Disciple

66 Glas Chu! Glasgow! The dear green place! Now a vehicular sclerosis, a congestion of activity.

> *Archie Hind (1928–)*, The Dear Green Place

67 Then there is a grand picture gallery,
Which keepers thereof are paid a very large salary;
Therefore, citizens of Glasgow, do not fret or worry,
For there is nothing like it in Edinburry.

> *William MacGonagall (c.1825–1905)*, The Beautiful City of Glasgow

68 It's Scotland's Friendliest Market-Place.
Watch Your Handbags, Ladies, Please.

> *Gerald Mangan (1951–)*, Heraclitus at Glasgow Cross

69 A town with guts – you see some on the pavement.

> *Forbes Masson (1964–) and Alan Cumming (1965–), Glasgow Song, in S. Maguire and D. Jackson Young, Hoots (1997)*

70 '... all the wise men in Glasgow come from the East – that's to say, they come from Edinburgh.'
'Yes, and the wiser they are the quicker they come.'

> *Neil Munro (1864–1930), Erchie*

71 We have not been able to build up any proof of the hitch-hiker stopping a car on the road outside Lisbon and asking the driver where he was going and on being told 'Edinburgh', turned away saying, 'That's nae use. I'm going to Glasgow.'

> *John Rafferty, Celtic in Europe, from I. Archer and T. Royle, We'll Support You Evermore (1976)*

72 A sacredness of love and death
Dwells in thy noise and smoky breath.

> *Alexander Smith (1830–1867), Glasgow*

73 City! I am true son of thine ...
From terrace proud to alley base
I know thee as my mother's face.

> *Alexander Thomson (1830–1867), Glasgow*

74 This grey town
That pipes the morning up before the lark
With shrieking steam ...
This old grey town, this firth, the further strand
Spangled with hamlets, and the wooded steeps,
Whose rocky tops behind each other press,
Fantastically carved like antique helms ...
Is world enough for me.

> *John Davidson (1857–1909), A Ballad in Blank Verse: Greenock*

75 Alas my native place! That Goddess of dullness has strewed on it all her poppies.

> *Jane Welsh Carlyle (1801–1866), letter to Eliza Stoddart (1824), on Haddington*

76 Hamilton is notoriously a dull place; if a joke finds its way into our neighbourhood, it is looked upon with as much surprise as a comet would be.

> *The Hamilton Hedgehog, October 1856 (see also Motherwell, below)*

77 What about the glamorous Hebrides, you ask? You think you will find a wonderful sensitiveness to nature – and to the supernatural – there? Not a bit of it. That is the bunkum of the Celtic Twilight. There is nothing morek detestable, perhaps, than this Tibetization of the Hebrides.

> *Hugh MacDiarmid (C. M. Grieve, 1892–1978), Lucky Poet*

78 There's nothing here but Hielan' pride,
An' Hielan' scab and hunger:
If Providence has sent me here,
'Twas surely in an anger.

> *Robert Burns (1759–1796), Epigram on the Inn at Inveraray*

79 Inverkip is so rough they put a date stamp on your head when they mug you so they don't do you twice in the one day.

> *Chic Murray (1919–1985), quoted in A. Yule, The Chic Murray Bumper Fun Book (1991)*

80 I will arise now, and go to Inverness,
And a small villa rent there, of lath and plaster built;
Nine bedrooms will I have there, and I'll don my native dress,
And walk around in a damned loud kilt.

> *Harry Graham (1874–1936), The Cockney of the North*

81 If justice were done to the inhabitants of Inverness, in twenty years' time there would be no-one left there but the Provost and the hang-man.

> *John Telford (d.1807), quoted in L. T. C. Rolt, Thomas Telford (1958)*

82 Iona of my heart, Iona of my love, instead of monks' voices shall be lowing of cattle, but ere the world comes to an end, Iona shall be as it was.

> *Saint Columba (521–597)*

83 That man is little to be envied, whose patriotism would not gain force upon the plain of Marathon, or whose piety would not grow warmer among the ruins of Iona.

> *Samuel Johnson (1709–1784), A Journey to the Western Islands*

84　I call you shrine of a nation yet to be,
　　A Scotland of a grander growth and fair.
　　　Archie Lamont, Iona

85　There is another Iona than the Iona of
　　sacred memories and prophecies; Iona the
　　metropolis of dreams. No one can under-
　　stand it who does not see it through its
　　pagan light, its Christian light, its singular
　　blending of paganism, romance and spirit-
　　ual beauty.
　　　*Fiona MacLeod (William Sharp,
　　1856–1905)*, Iona

86　To tell the story of Iona is to go back to
　　God, and end in God.
　　　Fiona MacLeod, Iona

87　A Kilmaurs whittle can cut an inch afore
　　the point.
　　　Traditional Kilmaurs saying

88　Slip a foot on frost-spiked stone
　　Above this rock-lipped Phlegethon,
　　And you shall have
　　The Black Rock of Kiltearn
　　For tombstone, grave
　　And trumpet of your resurrection.
　　　Andrew Young (1885–1971), The Black
　　Rock of Kiltearn

89　At kirk yetholm
　　there is a sign
　　that points three ways
　　at the same time
　　& each arm claims
　　the same destination.
　　It is an interesting
　　place to begin in.
　　　Dave Calder, At Kirk Yetholm, *quoted in*
　　H. Brown, Poems of the Scottish Hills
　　(1982)

90　I ken mysel' by the queer-like smell
　　That the next stop's Kirkcaddy!
　　　M. C. Smith (c.1869–1949), The Boy in
　　the Train

91　As I walked to the Taversoe of the evening,
　　I could see the lights of Kirkwall twin-
　　kling across the water, miles to the south
　　east. 'Ah,' I would think to myself, disap-
　　provingly, 'there's that Babylon of a place,
　　full of distraction and debauchery.'
　　　Will Self, The Rousay Effect *(1995)*

92　But the far-flung line o' the Lang Whang
　　　Road,
　　Wi' the mune on the sky's eebree,

An' naething but me an' the wind abroad,
Is the wuss that's hauntin' me.
　　　*Hugh Haliburton (J. Logie Robertson,
　　1846–1922)*, The Lang Whang Road

93　I have nowhere seen loveliness so intense
　　and so diverse crowded into so small a
　　place. Langholm presents the manifold
　　and multiform grandeur and delight of
　　Scotland in miniature.
　　　Hugh MacDiarmid (1892–1978), The
　　Thistle Rises

94　Lerwick, the capital of the Shetlands –
　　a place I avoid like the plague . . . it
　　would be difficult to find any place where
　　the citizens are more class conscious –
　　though not in the Marxian sense – more
　　purse-proud, more snooty towards their
　　supposed inferiors.
　　　Hugh MacDiarmid, Lucky Poet

95　I can na mair my silence hald
　　But mon put furth my mind
　　To speak of thee, O Lethington,
　　Whilk standis fair on Tyne,
　　Whais worthy praises and renown
　　Transcendis my ingyne.
　　　*Sir Richard Maitland of Lethington
　　(1496–1586)*, In Praise of Lethington

96　For Lochaber no more, Lochaber no
　　　more,
　　We'll maybe return to Lochaber no more.
　　　Allan Ramsay (1686–1758), Lochaber
　　No More

97　It is a far cry to Lochow.
　　　*Traditional Campbell slogan, quoted by Sir
　　Walter Scott (1771–1832) in* Rob Roy

98　Up amid the swells of London,
　　Mid the pomp of purple sinners,
　　Where many a kilted thane was undone
　　With dice, debauchery and dinners.
　　　John Stuart Blackie (1809–1895)

99　London, thou art the flour of Cities all.
　　　*William Dunbar (c.1460–c.1520),
　　ascribed*, To the City of London

100　I hate London, and I do not think that flat-
　　tery or profit can ever make me love it.
　　　*James Hogg (1770–1835), letter to his
　　wife, January 1832*

101　'Far be't fae me to lichtlie Macduff,' says
　　Peter, 'an noo fan ye speak o' Glasca, uncle,
　　if ye'll jist luik alang the quay to the east,

takin' in the buik shoppie there an' the baker's i' the corner, it reminds me in a vera mild wye o' the Broomielaw.'

William Alexander, Aberdeen Weekly Free Press *(1872), quoted in William Donaldson,* The Language of the People *(1989)*

102 If thou wouldst view fair Melrose aright,
Go visit it by the pale moonlight.

Sir Walter Scott (1771–1832), The Lay of the Last Minstrel

103 O Alva hills is bonny,
Tillicoultry hills is fair,
But to think on the Braes o' Menstrie
It maks my heart fu' sair.

Anonymous

104 The great round of sky, the wide links with their stretches of thyme and eyebright, the wild North Sea beating on sand dunes held together by tough pink liquorice and marram grass . . . was it not a setting where the wind of the spirit had freedom to blow?

Willa Muir (1890–1970), Belonging, *on Montrose*

105 What's Motherwell famous for? Coal and steel.
What's Hamilton famous for? Stealin' coal.

One-time Motherwell saying

106 Musselburgh was a burgh
When Edinburgh was nane;
And Musselburgh will be a burgh,
When Edinburgh's gane.

Traditional Musselburgh slogan

107 At Oban of discomfort one is sure,
Little the difference whether rich or poor.

A. H. Clough (1819–1861), Mari Magno, The Lawyer's Second Tale

108 Words cannot express how horrible Oban is . . . tacky beyond belief, full of disgusting shops selling Highland dancer dolls.

Tom Morton, Spirit of Adventure *(1985)*

109 Out of doors, Oban is not a bad representation of Vanity Fair. Every variety of pleasure-seeker is to be found there and every variety of costume.

Alexander Smith (1830–1867), A Summer in Skye

110 . . . seeing roaring seas from rocks rebound
By ebbs and streams of contrar routing tydes.

William Fowler (c.1560–1605), In Orknay

111 The bloody roads are bloody bad,
The bloody folks are bloody mad,
They'd make the brightest bloody sad,
In bloody Orkney . . .
No bloody sport, no bloody games,
No bloody fun: the bloody dames
Won't even give their bloody names
In bloody Orkney.

Hamish Blair, Bloody Orkney, *written in the Second World War, quoted in Arnold Silcock,* Verse and Worse *(1952)*

112 St Johnstoun is a merry toun
Whaur the water rins sae schire;
And whaur the leafy hill looks doun
On steeple and on spire.

William Soutar (1898–1943), St Johnstoun *(Perth)*

113 Sae ye Nine –
Gie inspiration that I may
Sing o' the bonnie sands o' Reay.

Henry Henderson (1883–1937), The Sands o' Reay

114 O! Rhynie is a Hieland place:
It doesna suit a Lowland loon!
Rhynie is a cauld clay hole,
It is na like my father's toun.

Traditional, Linten Lowren, *from Sir Harold Boulton and Miss A. C. Macleod,* Songs of the North

115 We a' lay doon tae tak our ease,
When somebody happened for tae sneeze –
An' he wakened hauf a million fleas
In a ludgin-hoose in Rothesay, O.

Anonymous, The Day We Went To Rothesay, O

116 Some towns have quietly died. Some have been murdered. The most striking case of murder is Roxburgh. On the map of Scotland one finds Roxburghshire, but the town is gone, sacked by the armies of Edward I of England.

Stephen Bone, Albion: an Artist's Britain *(1939)*

117 The pure and immaculate royal burgh of
    Rutherglen.
        Job Galt (1779–1839), The Ayrshire
        Legatees

118 St Andrews by the northern sea,
    A haunted town it is to me!
    A little city, worn and grey,
    The grey North Ocean girds it round.
    And o'er the rocks, and up the bay,
    The long sea-rollers surge and sound.
        Andrew Lang (1844–1912), Almae
        Matres

119 Old tales, old customs, and old men's
        dreams
    Obscure this town . . .
    The past sleeps in the stones.
        Edwin Muir (1887–1959), St Andrews,
        June 1946

120 The sea-gray town, the stane-gray sea.
        Alexander Scott (1920–), Heart of Stone,
        on St Andrews

121 And the sea below is still as deep
    As the sky above.
        Alexander Stewart (1829–1901), The
        St Kilda Maid's Song

122 . . . the people of Saltcoats – a sordid race.
        John Galt (1779–1839), The Ayrshire
        Legatees

123 A day oot o' Selkirk is a day wastet.
        *Selkirk saying, quoted in Donald Omand
        (ed.)* The Borders Book *(1995)*

124 What struck me in these islands was their
    bleakness, the number of ridiculous little
    churches, the fact that bogs do not require
    a level surface for their existence but can
    also run uphill, and that ponies sometimes
    have a black stripe like the wild ass.
        Norman Douglas (1869–1952), Looking
        Back *(on Shetland and Orkney)*

125 Speed, bonnie boat, like a bird on the
        wing
    Over the sea to Skye;
    Carry the lad who was born to be king
    Over the sea to Skye.
        Sir Harold Boulton (1859–1935), The
        Skye Boat Song

126 O great island, island of my love,
    Many a night of them I fancied
    the great ocean itself restless
    agitated with love of you

as you lay on the sea,
great beautiful bird of Skye.
    Sorley Maclean (1911–1996), The Island

127 If you are a delicate man,
    And of wetting your skin are shy,
    I'd have you know, before you go,
    You had better not think of Skye.
        Alexander Nicolson (1827–1893), Skye

128 And there was Stonehaven itself, the home
    of the poverty toffs, folk said, where you
    might live in sin as much as you pleased
    but were damned to hell if you hadn't a
    white sark.
        *Lewis Grassic Gibbon (James Leslie
        Mitchell, 1901–1935),* Sunset Song

129 There's nae greater luck that the heart
        could desire
    Than to herd the fine cattle in bonnie
        Strathyre.
        Sir Harold Boulton (1859–1935), Bonnie
        Strathyre

130 Stromness strikes the visitor as a cosmo-
    politan, sophisticated little port town with
    no provincialism about it.
        Libby Purves, Finn Folk and a Whisky-
        Coloured Cat *(1995)*

131 . . . on the road to Thurso there is a low
    suavity of line, a smoothness of texture, a
    far light-filled perspective that holds the
    mind to wonder and a pleasant silence.
        Neil Gunn (1891–1973), Highland Pack

132 Never have I seen desolation less abomina-
    ble: but desolation it is, Ulva.
        George Scott-Moncrieff (1910–), The
        Scottish Islands *(1952)*

133 This towne it stands within the sea,
    Five miles or thereabout,
    Upon no ile or ground, the sea
    Runnes all the streets throughout.
        King James VI (1566–1625), Lepanto,
        on Venice

134 Wick is . . . the meanest of men's towns,
    set on what is surely the baldest of God's
    bays.
        *Robert Louis Stevenson (1850–1894),
        letter to his mother, 1868*

Places: Imaginary

1 This is my Baikie.
A slate-grey township half as old as
  Peckham,
Grew in Italian villas, built in the fifties,
Auld Scots baronial mansions
Handy by train for the City,
For shipbuilders, stockbrokers, wholesale
  grocers to die in,
Lulled by the wash of the waves of the
  Clyde.

  *James Bridie (Osborne Henry Mavor,
  1888–1951)*, The Baikie Charivari

2 The freshness of the air, the smoke rising
thin and far above the red chimneys, the
sunshine glistering on the roofs and gables,
the rosy clearness of everything, above all
the quietness and peace, made Barbie, usually so poor to see, a very pleasant place to
look down at on a summer morning.

  *George Douglas (George Douglas Brown,
  1869–1902)*, The House With the
  Green Shutters

3 . . . he was to say it was the Scots countryside itself, fathered between a kailyard and
a bonnie brier bush in the lee of a house
with green shutters. And what he meant by
that you could guess at yourself if you'd a
mind for puzzles and dirt, there wasn't a
house with green shutters in the whole of
Kinraddie.

  *Lewis Grassic Gibbon (James Leslie
  Mitchell, 1901–1935)*, Sunset Song

4 Oh, Segget it's a dirty hole,
A kirk without a steeple,
A midden-heap at ilka door,
And damned uncivil people.

  Lewis Grassic Gibbon, Cloud Howe (borrowed from popular tradition)

5 Ye gang oot there for sixteen miles and ye
come to a signpost. On ae side it says 'You
are just entering Inversnecky,' and on the
ither, 'You are just leaving Inversnecky.'

  *Harry Gordon (Alexander Ross,
  1893–1957), quoted in Iain Watson,
  Harry Gordon, the Laird of Inversnecky (1993)*

6 'I am from Glaik. Have you heard of
Glaik?'
  'No. Tell me about it. Is it a small place?'
  'No, it's big. We manufacture fish-glue
and sweaters and process a lot of cheese.'

  Alasdair Gray (1934–), The Fall of
  Kelvin Walker

7 D'ye ken the big village of
  Balmaquhapple,
The great muckle village of
  Balmaquhapple?
'Tis steep'd in inquity up to the thrapple,
An' what's to become of poor
  Balmaquhapple?

  James Hogg (1770–1835), The Village
  of Balmaquhapple

8 High Street . . . was special . . . It was
a penal colony for those who had committed poverty, a vice which was usually
hereditary.

  William McIlvanney (1936–), Docherty

9 Graithnock is a town friendly and rough,
like a brickie's handshake.

  William McIlvanney, The Kiln

10 Battles have been fought, kings have
died, history has transacted itself; but all
unheeding and untouched, Dreamthorp
has watched apple-trees redden, and wheat
ripen, and smoked its pipe, and quaffed
its mug of beer, and rejoiced over its new-
born children, and with proper solemnity
carried its dead to the churchyard.

  Alexander Smith (1830–1867),
  Dreamthorp

Pleasures and Pastimes

1 We had some fun, haud awa' wi' the smell
At the muckin' o' Geordie's byre.

  Anonymous, The Muckin' o' Geordie's
  Byre

2 And if it shall happen any man to win any
sums of money at carding or dicing, attour
the sum of an hundred merks within the
space of twenty-four hours, or to gain in
wagers on horse races any sum attour the
said sum of an hundred merks, the superplus shall be consigned within twenty-four
hours thereafter in the hands of the treasurer for the Kirk . . . to be employed always

on the poor of the parish where such winning shall happen to fall out.

Act of Parliament of 1621, quoted in Agnes Mure Mackenzie, Scottish Pageant 1513–1625 (1948)

3 ... three farmers were dancing a barbaric dance, an extempore invention, in the middle of the room. So that they could dance the freer, they had stripped themselves entirely naked and were leaping fantastically between the shadows in the full glory of their manhood ... There is no doubt about it, the Scots have considerable heat in their blood.

John R. Allan, Summer in Scotland (1938)

4 But pleasures are like poppies spread,
You seize the flow'r, its bloom is shed;
Or like the snowfall on the river,
A moment white – then melts forever.

Robert Burns (1759–1796), Tam o' Shanter

5 There's some are fou' o' love divine;
There's some are fou' o' brandy;
And many jobs that day begin,
May end in 'houghmagandie'
Some ither day.

Robert Burns, The Holy Fair

6 The under-teacher keep the door and exact not more than twelve pennies Scots from each scholar for the benefit of bringing a cock to fight in the schoolroom; and that none to be suffered to enter that day except gentlemen and persons of note, from whom nothing is to be demanded; and what money is given is by the scholars, the under-teacher is to receive and apply to his own use for his pains and troubles; and that no scholar except who pleases shall furnish a cock; but that all scholars whether they have a cock or not can enter the school. Those that have none paying 2s Scots as forfeit.

From the regulations of Dumfries town council, 1725

7 When the noisy ten hours drum
Gars a' your trades gae dandering hame,
Gie a' to merriment and glee,
Wi' sang and glass they fley the power
O' care that wad harass the hour.

Robert Fergusson (1750–1774), Auld Reekie

8 I mend the fire, and beikit me about,
Then took ane drink my spreitis to comfort,
And armit me weill fra the cauld thereout;
To cut the winter nicht and mak it short,
I took ane quair, and left all other sport

Robert Henryson (c.1425–c.1500), The Testament of Cresseid

9 An example of concentrated joy was at Acharacle, when in front of a croft a young fellow was dancing the Highland Fling, with such whole-souled consuming zeal that I stood transfixed with wonder and awe. He was alone, and I came suddenly upon him at a sharp bend of the road. He threw his legs about him with such regardless glee that for a moment I was afraid that one of them might come spinning through the air to hit me. I watched him, fascinated, for fully ten minutes. When at length he saw me, the glory flowed suddenly off his legs; he subsided into a country bumpkin, and beat a hasty reatreat indoors.

D. T. Holmes, Literary Tours in the Highlands and Islands (1909)

10 There's a joy without canker or cark,
There's a pleasure eternally new,
'Tis to gloat on the glaze and the mark
Of china that's ancient and blue.

Andrew Lang (1844–1912), Ballade of Blue China

11 Roamin' in the gloamin', by the bonnie banks o' Clyde,
Roamin' in the gloamin' wi' my lassie by my side,
When the sun has gone to rest,
That's the time that I love best
O, it's lovely roamin' in the gloamin'.

Sir Harry Lauder (1870–1950), Roamin' in the Gloamin'

12 One feat which I never saw since was twisting the four legs from a cow, for which a fat sheep was offered as a prize. The cow was brought up and felled before the multitude, and the barbarous competition began, several men making the attempt. At last one man succeeded. After struggling for about an hour, he managed to twist off the four legs, and as a reward received his sheep, with a eulogistic speech from the chief in Gaelic.

Joseph Mitchell (1803–1883), Reminiscences of My Life in the Highlands

13 Driving their ba's frae whins or tee
    There's no ae gowfer to be seen,
    Nor doucer folk wying a-jee
    The byass bouls on Tamson's green.

    Then fling on coals, and ripe the ribs,
    And beik the house baith but and ben:
    That mutchkin stoup it hauds but drips,
    Then let's get in the tappit-hen.

    Allan Ramsay (1686–1758), To the Phiz:
    An Ode

14 Silence is, perhaps, the greatest hallelujah;
    the silent hosannas of the sun, the stars,
    the trees and the flowers. But silence is not
    enough – the innumerable songs of earth
    mingle with the acclamations of the serene
    witnesses. The wind, the water, the cries
    of bird and beast and the thoughful utter-
    ance of humanity: each day is life's messiah
    and at its feet are leaves and about its head
    are the canticles of joy.

    William Soutar (1898–1943), Diary

15 No one knows the stars who has not slept,
    as the French happily put it, *à la belle
    étoile*. He may know all their names and
    distances and magnitudes, and yet be igno-
    rant of what alone concerns mankind –
    their serene and gladsome influence on the
    mind.

    Robert Louis Stevenson (1850–1894),
    Travels With a Donkey

Poets and Poetry

1 Now I am not a poet
   Nor yet a learned man,
   But I will sing a verse or two,
   And spread them as I can.

   *Anonymous, from a bothy ballad, quoted in
   D. K. Cameron*, The Cornkister Days
   (1984)

2 Yuh wrote? A po-it? Micht ye no juist as
   weel hae peed inti thuh wund?

   *Anonymous Glaswegian to Maurice Lind-
   say, 'In a Glasgow Loo', noted in Robin
   Bell*, The Best of Scottish Poetry
   (1989)

3 Woody Morven, and echoing Sora, and
   Selma with its silent halls! we all owe them
   a debt of gratitude, and when we are unjust
   enough to forget it, may the Muse forget
   us!

   Matthew Arnold (1822–1888), Celtic

Literature, *on the impact of MacPherson's Ossian poems*

4 Who would not be
   The Laureate bold,
   With his butt of sherry
   To keep him merry
   And nothing to do but pocket his gold?

   W. E. Aytoun (1830–1865), The
   Laureate

5 Gie me ae spark o' Nature's fire,
   That's a' the learning I desire;
   Then, tho' I drudge thro' dub and mire
   At pleugh or cart,
   My Muse, tho' hamely in attire,
   May touch the heart.

   Robert Burns (1759–1796), Epistle to
   J. Lapraik

6 I pored over them, driving my cart or walking to labour, song by song, verse by verse,
   carefully noting the true, tender and sublime from affectation and fustian.

   *Robert Burns, letter to Dr John Moore,
   1787*

7 O thou whom poesy abhors,
   Whom prose has turned out of doors!
   Heardst thou that groan?
   Proceed no farther:
   'Twas laurelled Martial roaring murther.

   Robert Burns, On James Elphinston's
   Translation of Martial's 'Epigrams'

8 £5 10s per acct I owe to Mr Robert Burn,
   Architect, for erecting the stone over poor
   Fergusson . . . He had the *hardiesse* to
   ask me interest on the sum; but considering the money was due by one Poet, for
   putting a tombstone over another, he may,
   with grateful surprise, thank Heaven that
   he ever saw a farthing of it.

   Robert Burns, letter to Peter Hill, 1791

9 The said Hogg is a strange being, but of
   great, though uncouth, powers.

   *Lord Byron (1788–1824), letter to
   Thomas Moore, on James Hogg
   (1770–1835)*

10 Voltaire asked why no woman had 'written even a tolerable tragedy' (and) replied,
   'The composition of a tragedy requires testicles.' If this be true Lord knows what
   Joanna Baillie does – I suppose she bor-
   rows them.

   Lord Byron (1788–1824), on Joanna Bail-

*lie (1762–1851), quoted in Rupert Chris-
tiansen*, Romantic Affinities *(1985)*

11 And think'st thou, Scott! by vain conceit
     perchance,
   On public taste to foist thy stale
     romance . . .
   No! when the sons of song descend to
     trade,
   Their bays are sear, their former laurels
     fade.
   Let such forgo the poet's sacred name,
   Who rack their brains for lucre, not for
     fame.

   Lord Byron, English Bards and Scotch
   Reviewers

12 The Sabbath bard . . .
   Undisturbed by conscientious qualms
   Perverts the Prophets and purloins the
     Psalms.

   Lord Byron, English Bards and Scotch
   Reviewers, *on James Grahame's* The
   Sabbath *(1804)*

13 A vein of poetry exists in the hearts of all
   men.

   Thomas Carlyle (1795–1881), On
   Heroes, Hero-Worship, and the
   Heroic in History

14 The kind of man that Keats was gets
   ever more horrible to me. Force of hunger
   for pleasure of every kind, and want of
   all other force – such a soul, it would
   once have been very evident, was a chosen
   'vessel of hell'.

   Thomas Carlyle, on R. Monckton Milne's
   Life of Keats

15 Shelley is a poor creature, who has said or
   done nothing worth a serious man being at
   the trouble of remembering.

   Thomas Carlyle

16 Joanna Baillie is now almost totally forgotten, even among feminist academics
   dredging the catalogues for third-rate
   women novelists . . . Her life story is a
   quaint one, interesting for being so dull.

   Rupert Christiansen, Romantic Affinities *(1988)*

17 Mr Thomson makes one of his characters
   address Sophonisba in a line which some
   critics reckoned the false pathetic:
     O! Sophonisba! Sophonisba, oh!
   Upon which a smart from the pit cried
   out: *Oh! Jamey Thomson! Jamey Thomson,
   oh!*

   Colley Cibber (1671–1757), Lives, *on
   James Thomson's* Sophonisba

18 My feet ne'er filed that brooky hill
   Where ancient poets drank their fill . . .
   For I am verie apt to think
   There's als much vertue, sonce and pith
   In Annan, or the water of Nith.

   *William Cleland (c.1661–1689), quoted
   in L. Maclean Watt*, Scottish Life and
   Poetry *(1912)*

19 Beis weill advisit my werk or ye reprief;
   Consider it warely, read ofter than anis,
   Weill, at ane blenk, slee poetry nocht
     ta'en is.

   Gavin Douglas (1475–1522), Prologue
   to the Aeneid

20 So me behovit whilom, or than be dumb,
   Some bastard Latin, French or Inglis use,
   Where scant were Scottis; I had na other
     choiss.

   Gavin Douglas, Prologue to the Aeneid

21 Therefore, guid friendis, for ane gymp
     or a bourd,
   I pray you, note me not at every word.

   Gavin Douglas, Prologue to the Aeneid

22 He shouldn't have written in such small
   print.

   O. Douglas (Anna Buchan, 1877–1948)
   The Setons, *on Sir Walter Scott*

23 Allace for ane, quhilk lamp wes of this
     land,
   Of eloquens the flowand balmie strand
   And in our Inglis rethorik the rois:
   As of rubeis the carbunkel bein chois,
   And as Phebus dois Cynthia precell,
   So Gawane Dowglas, Bischop of Dunkell
   Had, quhen he wes into this land on lyve
   Abuve vulgare poetis prerogative.

   William Dunbar (c.1460–c.1520), Testament of the Papyngo

24 My poems should be Clyde-built, crude
     and sure,
   With images of those dole-deployed
   To honour the indomitable Reds,
   Clydesiders of slant steel and angled

cranes;
A poetry of nuts and bolts, born, bred,
Embattled by the Clyde, tight and impure.

> *Douglas Dunn (1942–),* Clydesiders
> *from* Love of Nothing

25 Now is the yaird kail boiled and hashed
While Muses feed in slums;
The Ball of Kirriemuir has smashed
The window-pane of Thrums.

> *A. H. Emslie-Smith,* Scottish Renais-
> sance, *quoted in Douglas Young,* Scottish
> Verse 1851–1951 *(1952)*

26 On Waterloo's ensanguined plain
Lie tens of thousands of the slain,
But none by sabre or by shot
Fell half so flat as Walter Scott.

> *Thomas, Lord Erskine (1750–1823), on
> Scott's* The Field of Waterloo

27 Ossian has superseded Homer in my head.
To what a world does the illustrious bard
transport me! To wander over pathless
wilds, surrounded by impetuous whirl-
winds, where by the feeble light of the
moon, we see the spirits of our ancestors:
to hear from the mountain-tops, mid the
roar of torrents, their plaintive sounds issu-
ing from deep caverns . . . I meet this bard
with silver hair: he wanders in the valley,
he seeks the footsteps of his fathers, and
alas! he finds only their tombs.

> *Johann Wolfgang von Goethe
> (1749–1832),* The Sorrows of Young
> Werther *(from German)*

28 The Scottish poets all felt competent
to teach the art of government to their
rulers.

> *M. M. Gray,* Scottish Poetry from Bar-
> bour to James VI *(1935)*

29 He offers the Muse no violence. If he
lights upon a good thought, he immediately drops it in fear of spoiling a good
thing.

> *William Hazlitt (1778–1830),* Lectures
> on the English Poets, *on Thomas Camp-
> bell (1777–1844)*

30 His hood was reid, heklit atour his crown,
Like to ane poet of the old fassoun.

> *Robert Henryson (c.1425–c.1500),* The
> Testament of Cresseid

31 . . . a similitude,
In dissimilitude, man's sole delight

And all the sexual intercourse of things,
Do most supremely hang.

> *James Hogg (1770–1835), parody of Wil-
> liam Wordsworth, quoted in Karl Miller
> (1931–),* Dark Horses *(1998)*

32 It is indeed strange that any man of sense
could have imagined it possible, that above
twenty thousand verses, along with num-
berless historical facts, could have been
preserved by an oral tradition during fifty
generations, by the rudest, perhaps, of all
the European nations, the most necessi-
tous, the most turbulent, and the most
unsettled.

> *David Hume (1711–1776), letter to
> Edward Gibbon, March 1776, with refer-
> ence to James MacPherson's* Ossian *poems*

33 Och, I wish you hadn't come right now,
You've put me off my balance:
I was just translating my last wee poem
Into the dear old Lallans.

> *Alan Jackson (1938–)* A Scotch Poet
> Speaks

34 This will never do!

> *Francis Jeffrey (1773–1850),* The Edin-
> burgh Review *(November 1814), on Wil-
> liam Wordsworth's* The Excursion

35 This we think has the merit of being
the worst poem ever seen imprinted in a
quarto volume.

> *Francis Jeffrey,* The Edinburgh Review
> *(October 1815), on William Wordsworth's*
> The White Doe of Rylstone

36 The whole soul of the peasant class breathes
in their burdens as the great sea resounds
in the shells cast up on the shores. Ballads
are a voice from secret places, from silent
peoples, and old times long dead.

> *Andrew Lang (1844–1912), quoted in
> L. Maclean Watt,* Scottish Life and
> Poetry *(1912)*

37 Search Scotland over, from the Pentland
to the Solway, and there is not a cottage-
hut so poor and wretched as to be without
its Bible; and hardly one that, on the same
shelf, and next to it, does not treasure a
Burns.

> *John Gibson Lockhart (1794–1854),* Life
> of Burns

38 Here lies the peerless peer Lord Peter
Who broke the laws of God and man and
metre.

> *John Gibson Lockhart*, Epitaph for Lord
> Robertson

39 Are my poems spoken in the factories
and fields,
In the streets o' the toon?
If they're no', then I'm failin' to doe
What I ocht to ha' dune.

> *Hugh MacDiarmid (C. M. Grieve,
> 1892–1978)*, Second Hymn to Lenin

40 . . . men wha through the ages sit,
And never move frae aff the bit,
Wha hear a Burns or Shakespeare sing,
Yet still their ain bit jingles string,
As they were worth the fashioning.

> *Hugh MacDiarmid*, A Drunk Man
> Looks at the Thistle

41 'A Scottish poet maun assume
The burden o' his people's doom,
And dee to brak' their livin' tomb.'

> *Hugh MacDiarmid*, A Drunk Man
> Looks at the Thistle

42 There were not many genteel Scottish writers before Scott; there have not been many
ungenteel ones since.

> *Hugh MacDiarmid, in* The Voice of
> Scotland, *quoted in* Lucky Poet *(1943)*

43 The essential beginning of all national
uprisings is that poets should believe.

> *A. G. Macdonell (1895–1941)*, My
> Scotland

44 He also . . . has a certain disregard for the
muse. 'I never met a white goddess in my
life and, when I find myself in the company of singing robes, hieratic gestures
and fluttering voices, I phone for a taxi.'

> *Norman MacCaig (1910–1996), inter-
> viewed by Michael Aitken*, The Scots-
> man *(June 1976)*

45 Poetry's my second wife.

> *Alastair Mackie (1925–1995)*, Bigamist

46 Oor Scots Pegasus
is a timmer naig
wi a humphy back and cockle een.
He ettles tae flee
but his intimmers are fu o the deid
chack . . .
The hert o the nut is this –

Naebody, damm't, kens the horseman's
wird.

> *Alastair Mackie*, Oor Scots Pegasus

47 A poet can disregard the internal combustion engine, but I doubt if he can disregard
Freud and the atom bomb.

> *Sorley Maclean (1911–1996)* Old Songs
> and New Poetry, *in K. Miller*, Memoirs
> of a Modern Scotland *(1969)*

48 I'll never hae a poet's name,
Nor in the gaudy house of fame,
Enjoy a wee bit garret;
The clinking I may hit, hooh, hoo,
As also could the cockatoo,
Or green Brazilian parrot.

> *John Mactaggart*, The Scottish Gallo-
> vidian Encyclopedia *(1824)*

49 Poetry never goes back on you. Learn as
many pieces as you can. Go over them
again and again till the words come of
themselves, and then you have a joy forever that cannot be stolen or broken or
lost.

> *Sir Patrick Manson (1844–1922), quoted
> in John Carey*, The Faber Book of Sci-
> ence *(1995)*

50 So late as the year 1750, a copy of Milton's *Paradise Lost*, which had been brought
to town by a sailor, was the occasion of
much curious criticism among them; some
of them alleging that it was heterodox,
and ought to be burnt, others deeming
it prophetic. One man affirmed it to be
a romance, another said it was merely a
poem; but a Mr Thomas Hood, a shop-
keeper of the place, set the matter at rest
by remarking that it seemed to him to be a
great book, full of mystery like the Revelation of St John, but certainly no book for
the reading of simple unlearned men like
him or them.

> *Hugh Miller (1802–1856)*, Notes and
> Legends of the North of Scotland

51 Every critic in the town
Runs the minor poet down;
Every critic – don't you know it?
Is himself a minor poet.

> *R. F. Murray (1863–1894)*, On Critics

52 Next to tartan and soldiers, poetry is the
greatest curse of contemporary Scotland.
It is the intellectuals' special form of dope,
which they can indulge in with a good con-

science while the crowds go mad up on the Castle esplanade.

> Tom Nairn *(1932–)*, Festival of the Dead, *in* New Statesman, *September 1967*

53 Bad poems try to offer solutions, while good poems leave a little more chaos, mystery, fear or wonder in the world than there was before.

> *Don Paterson (1963–) in* Dream State, *edited by D. O' Rourke (1994)*

54 These six or seven years past I have not wrote a line of poetry; I e'en gave o'er in good time, before the coolness of fancy that attends advanced years should risk the reputation I had acquired.

> *Allan Ramsay (1686–1758), letter to John Smibert, May 1736*

55 They say I'm only a poet,
Whose fate is as dead as my verse
(His father's a packman, you know it;
His father, in turn, couldn't boast).
They'd take a good field and plough it.
I can cut better poems than most.

> *William Ross (1762–1790)*, Oran Eile (Another Song), *translated by Iain Crichton Smith*

56 Ne'er
Was flattery lost on poet's ear;
A simple race! they waste their toil
For the vain tribute of a smile.

> *Sir Walter Scott (1771–1832)*, The Lay of the Last Minstrel

57 Who, noteless as the race from which he sprung,
Saved others' names, but left his own unsung.

> *Sir Walter Scott*, Waverley

58 Many a clever boy is flogged into a dunce; and many an original composition corrected into mediocrity . . . Somehow he wants audacity – fears the public, and, what is worse, fears the shadow of his own reputation.

> *Sir Walter Scott*, Journal, *referring to Thomas Campbell (1777–1844)*

59 The poet, whose vanity was at least equal to his genius . . . spoke of himself as one of 'the warld's wonders'.

> *Alastair Smart*, The Life and Art of

Allan Ramsay *(1952), on Allan Ramsay Senior (1686–1758)*

60 Reading Milton is like dining off gold plate in a company of kings; very splendid, very ceremonious, not a little appalling.

> *Alexander Smith (1830–1867)*, Dreamthorp

61 Poetry drives its lines into her forehead like an angled plough across a bare field.

> *Iain Crichton Smith (1928–1998)*, A Young Highland Girl Studying Poetry

62 Lea him at least outgang wi mockerie,
The Makar macironical!
A sang on his perjurit lips
And naething i the pouch
– Or i the hert, for that!

> *Sydney Goodsir Smith (1915–1975)*, 23rd Elegy: Farewell to Calypso

63 Now I can be a poet.

> *William Soutar (1898–1943)*, Journal, *October 1923, on learning he had osteoarthritis of the spine*

64 There are mair sangs that bide unsung nor aa that hae been wrocht.

> *William Soutar (1898–1943)*, The Makar

65 Poetry is a river that deepens into silence.

> *William Soutar, quoted in Alexander Scott*, Still Life: William Soutar *(1958)*

66 Of all my verse, like not a single line;
But like my title, for it is not mine.
That title from a better man I stole;
Ah, how much better, had I stol'n the whole!

> *Robert Louis Stevenson (1850–1894)*, Underwoods

67 Just how much Scotland's current hyper-vitality owes to the fertilising efforts of its twentieth-century versifiers is a question worth looking into.

> *John Sutherland*, The Times Literary Supplement, *August 1998*

68 Oh! If by any unfortunate chance I should happen to die,
In a French field of turnips or radishes I'll lie.
But thinking of it as really Scottish all the time,

Because my patriotic body will impart
goodness to the slime.

> *J. Y. Watson*, Pastiche of Rupert Brooke
> in the style of William McGonagall

69 It was unfortunate for the Scottish ballads
that so many who collected such things
were able to write creditable verse, while
the master of romance himself was the
head of the enterprise.

> *Lauchlan Maclean Watt*, Scottish Life
> and Poetry *(1912)*

70 As a poet Scott *cannot* live, for he has never
in verse addressed anything to the immortal part of man . . . What he writes in the
way of natural description is merely rhym-
ing nonsense.

> *William Wordsworth (1770–1850), con-*
> *versation reported by Mrs Davy, 1844*

71 All hail, Macpherson! hail to thee, Sire of
Ossian! The Phantom was begotten by the
snug embrace of an impudent Highlander
upon a cloud of tradition – it travelled
southward, where it was greeted with accla-
mation, and the thin consistence took its
course through Europe, upon the breath
of popular applause.

> *William Wordsworth, upon James*
> *Macpherson (1736–1796) and the success*
> *of his* Ossian *poems*

Politics and Protest

1 *Brodie:* No innocent blood in all his reign
was shed,
  Lillias: Save all Glencoe in one night
murdered.
  Brodie: He saved our country, and
advanced our trade.
  Lillias: Witness such product we from
Darien had.

> *Anonymous, supposed dialogue between the*
> *Laird of Brodie and Lillias Brodie on the*
> *death of William of Orange (1702), from*
> *Maidment's* Scottish Pasquils

2 Then up wi' Geordie, kirn-milk Geordie,
Up with Geordie high in a tow.
At the last kick o' a foreign foot
We'se a' be ranting roaring fou.

> *Anonymous*, Kirn-Milk Geordie, *Jaco-*
> *bite song from 1715*

3 'Didna ye hear? We're goin' to overturn
the Government.'
  'Oh, ye idiots,' I said. 'Ye may as weel try
to overturn God Almighty. If ye go to the
Cathkin Braes the sodgers'll blaw ye up
like the peelins o' onions.'

> *Eyewitness of the 'Radical war' of 1820,*
> *quoted in* Glasgow Weekly Mail, *Decem-*
> *ber 1887*

4 The fish that was yesterday miles away
from the land was claimed by the landlord
the moment it reached the shore. And so
also were the birds of the air the moment
they flew over his land. The law made it
so, because landlords themselves were the
lawmakers, and it was a wonder that the
poor man was allowed to breathe the air
of heaven and drink from the mountain
streams without having the factors and the
whole of the county police pursuing him
as a thief.

> *A member of the Highland Land Law*
> *Reform Association, Skye, 1884, quoted*
> *in James Hunter,* The Making of the
> Crofting Community *(1976 and 2000)*

5 Four and twenty blacklegs, working
    night and day,
Fed on eggs and bacon, getting double
    pay;
Helmets on their thick heads, bayonets
    gleaming bright,
If someone burst a sugar bag, the lot
    would die of fright.

> *Anonymous, student magazine of 1928,*
> *quoted in Roy M. Pinkerton*, Of Cham-
> bers and Communities, *in G. Donald-*
> *son*, Four Centuries: Edinburgh Uni-
> versity Life *(1983)*

6 The People of Scotland, as members of
one of the oldest nations in Europe, are
the inheritors, bearers and transmitters
of an historic tradition of liberty. They
have in common with the peoples of all
other nations an inherent right to determine their own destiny in accordance with
the principles of justice accepted by the
social conscience of mankind.

> Statement of Aim and Policy of
> the Scottish National Party, *December*
> *1946*

7 As I know my own heart to be entirely English, I can sincerely assure you there is not
anything you can expect or desire from

me which I shall not be ready to do for the happiness and prosperity of England.

> *Queen Anne (1665–1714), coronation address, 1702*

8 All political parties die at last of swallowing their own lies.

> *John Arbuthnot (1667–1735), quoted in R. Garnett*, Life of Emerson *(1988)*

9 Toleration is the cause of many evils, and renders diseases or distempers in the state more strong and powerful than any remedies.

> *Archibald, Marquis of Argyll (1598–1661)*, Maxims of State

10 My Lord, when I have justice dun me here and am told what to expect for going to Scotland, I shall be reddy to obey My Lord Treasurer's commands.

> *Iain, Duke of Argyll (1680–1743), letter to the Earl of Mar, July 1706*

11 . . . has not got the brains of a Glasgow bailie.

> *H. H. Asquith (1852–1928), to David Lloyd George, quoted in Frances Stevenson*, Diary *(November 1916), on Andrew Bonar Law (1858–1923)*

12 It really is a matter where the effulgence of two Dukedoms and the best salmon river in Scotland will go a long way.

> *A. J. Balfour (1848–1930), persuading the Duke of Richmond and Gordon to take on the new post of Secretary of State for Scotland in 1885, quoted in Christopher Harvie (1944–)*, Scotland and Nationalism

13 I am horribly ashamed at feeling a kind of illegitimate exhilaration at the catastrophe which has occurred.

> *A. J. Balfour, letter to Lady Salisbury, on his losing his seat (as Prime Minister) in the 1906 General Election*

14 I thought he was a young man of promise; but it appears he was a young man of promises.

> *A. J. Balfour, quoted in Randolph Churchill*, Winston Churchill, *Vol. 2, on Winston Churchill (1874–1965)*

15 But above all, My Lord, I think I see our Ancient Mother Caledonia, like Caesar sitting in the midst of our Senate, Rufully looking round about her, Covering her self

with the Royal Garment, attending the Fatal Blow, and breathing out her last with a *Et tu quoque mi fili.*

> *Lord Belhaven (1656–1708), speech to Parliament in the Union Debate, November 1706 ('And you too, my son')*

16 'A millionaire communist?'
'Why not? You've got penniless capitalists.'
'What'll happen to him when the Revolution comes?'
'He'll be commissar for Scotland, and you'll be sent to the salt mines of Ross and Cromarty.'

> *Chaim Bermant (1929–1998)*, Jericho Sleep Alone

17 Insolence in the few begets
Hate in the many; hatred breeds revolt,
Revolt where all are free to rise and rule
Breeds anarchy, whose wild chaotic reign
Calls in the despot . . . thus we reel
From vassalage to vassalage, through fits
Of drunken freedom – glorious for an hour.

> *J. S. Blackie (1809–1895)*, The Wise Men of Greece

18 The Clydesiders failed because they were not outstandingly intelligent and they had nothing whatever to say. Jimmy Maxton, his hair growing longer, lanker and greasier each year, ended as the most popular member of the Commons . . . rather a queer ending for the apostle of 'socialism in our time'.

> *Colm Brogan*, The Glasgow Story *(1952)*

19 No Chancellor until this one has come to the House and said that because he has money available to him the rich will get the benefits and the poor will make the sacrifices.

> *Gordon Brown (1951–), quoted in* The Observer *(May 1988), on Norman Lamont's budget*

20 Class-conscious we are, and class-conscious will be
Till our fit's on the neck o' the boorjoysie.

> *Socialist hymn quoted or parodied by John Buchan (1875–1940) in* Huntingtower

21 I remember a lady summing up the attitude thus: Tories may think they are better

born, but Liberals think they are born better.

>   *John Buchan*, Memory-Hold-the-Door

22 Now Sark rins over Solway sands,
    And Tweed rins to the ocean,
    To mark where England's province
        stands –
    Such a parcel of rogues in a nation!

>   *Robert Burns (1759–1796)*, Such a
>   Parcel of Rogues in a Nation

23 Who will not sing 'God Save the King'
    Shall hang as high's the steeple;
    But while we sing 'God Save the King',
    We'll ne'er forget THE PEOPLE.

>   *Robert Burns*, Does Haughty Gaul Inva-
>   sion Threat?

24 In Politics if thou wouldst mix,
    And mean thy fortunes be;
    Bear this in mind, be deaf and blind,
    Let great folk hear and see.

>   *Robert Burns*, In Politics if Thou
>   Wouldst Mix

25 What millions died, that Caesar might be great!

>   *Thomas Campbell (1777–1844)*, The
>   Pleasures of Hope

26 Aristocracy of Feudal Parchment has passed away with a mighty rushing; and now, by a natural course, we arrive at Aristocracy of the Moneybag.

>   *Thomas Carlyle (1795–1881)*, The
>   French Revolution

27 Within this Pandemonium sat the town-council, omnipotent, corrupt, impenetrable. Nothing was beyond its grasp; no variety of opinion disturbed its unanimity, for the pleasure of Dundas was the sole rule of every one of them . . . Silent, powerful, submissive, mysterious and irresponsible, they might have been sitting in Venice.

>   *Henry Thomas Cockburn (1779–1854)*,
>   Memorials of His Time

28 . . . that man is a maniac who, after a study of history, will stand up and deny that the Act of Union was an advantage.

>   *Sir Henry Craik, speech to the House of
>   Commons, 1924*

29 Wha the deil hae we got for a King,
    But a wee, wee German lairdie!

>   *Allan Cunningham (1784–1842)*, The
>   Wee, Wee German Lairdie

30 We have existed a conquered province these two centuries. We trace our bondage from the Union of the Crown and find it little alleviated by the Union of the Kingdoms.

>   *Lord Daer (1763–1794), letter to Charles
>   Grey, January 1795*

31 . . . that universal Aunt Sally of Scotland, the Department of Agriculture.

>   *Sir Frank Fraser Darling (1903–1979)*,
>   Natural History in the Highlands and
>   Islands

32 Distrust of authority should be the first civic duty.

>   *Norman Douglas (1868–1952)*, An
>   Almanac

33 'Peking, Alec, Peking,' his devoted wife Dorothy would repeat to him while walking behind him down the steps of the aeroplane while he was Foreign Secretary . . . in order to prevent him saying to his hosts, as he stood before the microphone, 'I'm very happy to be back in Montreal (or Rome or Washington or Moscow).'

>   *William Douglas-Home (1912– 1992)*,
>   Mr Home Pronounced Hume *(1979)*,
>   *on Lord Home*

34 *Socialism? These days?* There's the tree that never grew. *Och, a shower of shites.* There's the bird that never flew.

>   *Carol Ann Duffy (1955–)*, Politico

35 Sir, Yow are herby ordered to fall upon the rebells, the McDonalds of Glenco, and to putt all to the sword under 70. You are to have a special care that the old fox and his sons doe not escape your hands.

>   *Major Robert Duncanson, letter to Captain Robert Campbell of Glenlyon, ordering the Glencoe Massacre, 12 February 1692, quoted in W. C. Dickinson and G. Donaldson*, The Source Book of Scottish History, *Volume 3 (1954)*

36 By this time there should have turned up in post-war Scotland and, one would have hoped, from Edinburgh, some voice

expressing the search for Scottish renewal. Not a word!

> *Sir Alastair Dunnett (1908–1998)*, The Glasgow Herald, *August 1983*

37 No Language, no Nation.

> *Ruaraidh Stuart Erskine of Mar (1869–1960), Scottish nationalist slogan*

38 The late Oliver Brown . . . put it well. He said that when I won Hamilton, you could feel a chill along the Labour back benches, looking for a spine to run up.

> *Winnie Ewing (1933–), quoted in Kenneth Roy,* Conversations in a Small Country *(1989)*

39 The great danger in giving voting power to women is that those best qualified would hold aloof from those whose distorted views of their social duties and surroundings would lead them to seek a public life, and women's views would be represented by the noisiest and least womanly of their sex.

> *Countess of Galloway,* Women and Politics, *June 1866, quoted in M. Goodwin,* Nineteenth-Century Opinion *(1951)*

40 Everything I have done has been biocentric; for and in terms of life, both individual and collective; whereas all the machinery of state, public instruction, finance and industry ignores life when indeed it does not destroy it. The only thing that amazes me, therefore, is that I was not caught and hung many years ago.

> *Sir Patrick Geddes (1854–1932), quoted in Hugh MacDiarmid (1872–1978),* Lucky Poet

41 I would welcome the end of Braid Scots and Gaelic, our culture, our history, our nationhood under the heels of a Chinese army of occupation, if it could cleanse the Glasgow slums.

> *Lewis Grassic Gibbon (James Leslie Mitchell, 1901–1935),* Scottish Scene

42 *Mr Kirkwood:* What about Calton Jail – that is empty?

> *Duchess of Atholl:* If the Honourable Member would like to be returned as a representative of his constituents to the Calton Jail, he is quite welcome to do so.
> *Mr Kirkwood:* I have been there before.
> Hansard, *1924, quoted in Andrew Marr,* The Battle for Scotland *(1992)*

43 No better means for retaining all that is best in the life of a nation has yet been devised than that of a National Parliament, through which National sentiment finds expression and embodiment in the laws of the land.

> *James Keir Hardie (1856–1915), in* The Scots Independent *(1927–8), quoted in H. J. Hanham,* Scottish Nationalism *(1969)*

44 *Sir Robert Smith:* Politicians and the media look to what is happening in Sweden, Germany or other countries without recognising that they may learn from examining how things operate on the other side of the Border.

> *Mr John McAllion:* Like the poll tax.
> Hansard, *Proceedings of the Scottish Grand Committee, June 1998*

45 On Hardie's first day at the House of Commons, the policeman at the gate took one look at the former miner, dressed in his ordinary working clothes and cloth cap, and asked suspiciously, 'Are you working here?'

> 'Yes', replied Hardie.
> 'On the roof?'
> 'No,' said the new MP, 'on the floor.'
> *James Keir Hardie (1865–1915), attributed, in C. Fadiman,* The Little, Brown Book of Anecdotes *(1985)*

46 The Scottish Tories are an extreme case of necrophilia.

> *Christopher Harvie (1944–),* Cultural Weapons

47 . . . a new Scotland, neither urban nor rural, which straggles westwards from the fringes of the Firth of Forth to the lower Clyde. It is this unknown Scotland, not in the guidebooks, away from the motorway, seen fleetingly from the express, that holds the key to the modern politics of the country.

> *Christopher Harvie,* Scotland and Nationalism

48 Toryism is an innate principle o' human nature – Whiggism but an evil habit.

> *James Hogg (1770–1835, quoted in Christopher North (John Wilson, 1785–1854),* Noctes Ambrosianae

49 Our erles and lords, for their nobilitie,
How ignorant and inexpert they be.
*Alexander Hume (1560–1609), quoted in
L. Maclean Watt*, Scottish Life and
Poetry *(1912)*

50 A regard for liberty, though a laudable passion, ought commonly to be subordinate
to a reverence for established government.
David Hume (1711–1776), Essays
Moral and Political

51 It is therefore a just *political* maxim, *that
every man must be supposed a knave.*
David Hume, Essays Moral and
Political

52 No bishop, no King.
*King James VI (1566–1625), quoted in
W. Barlow*, Summary and Substance
of the Conference *(1604)*

53 What is betwixt the pride of a glorious Nebuchadnezzar and the preposterous humility
of our puritan ministers, claiming to their
parity, and crying, 'We are all but vile
worms'; and yet will judge and give law
to their king, but will be judged nor controlled by none. Surely there is more pride
under such a one's black bonnet than under
great Alexander's diadem.
King James VI, Basilikon Doron

54 I will govern according to the common
weal, but not according to the common
will.
*King James VI, reply to the House of
Commons, 1621*

55 Were it no for the workin man what wad
the rich man be?
What care some gentry if they're weel
though a' the puir wad dee?
Ellen Johnston (c.1835–c.1874), The
Last Sark

56 Generation after generation, these few
families of tax-gatherers have sucked the
life-blood of our nation; in their prides
and lusts they have sent us to war, family
against family, class against class, race
against race; that they might live in idleness and luxury, the labouring mass has
sweated and starved.
Thomas Johnston (1881–1965), Our
Scots Noble Families

57 Of course us artists aren't supposed to talk
about political issues, we are too idealistic,
we don't have a firm-enough grasp on reality . . . It's quite remarkable really the
different ways whereby the state requires
its artists to suck dummytits.
*James Kelman (1946–), lecture at the
Glasgow School of Art, 1996*

58 While all the Middle Classes should
With every vile Capitalist
Be clean reformed away for good
And vanish like a morning mist!
Andrew Lang (1844–1912), The New
Millennium

59 Ah! splendid Vision, golden time,
An end of hunger, cold and crime.
An end of Rent, and end of Rank,
An end of balance at the Bank,
An end of everything that's meant
To bring Investors five per cent.
Andrew Lang, The New Millennium

60 'I must follow them. I am their leader.'
*Andrew Bonar Law (1858–1923), quoted
in E. Raymond, Mr Balfour (1920), but
the story is first told of the 19th-century
French politician Ledru-Rollin*

61 After a long debate, Mr Harley said he
admired the debate should last so long.
'For have we not bought the Scots and a
right to tax them? And pray, for what did
we give the Equivalent?'
I took him up, and said I was glad to hear
the truth, which I never doubted, now publicly brought to light and owned: for the
Honourable gentleman acknowledged that
Scotland was bought and sold . . . I would
be extremely glad to know what this price
amounted to, and who received it.
George Lockhart (1673–1731), Memoirs,
*on the Parliamentary debate to tax linen
exports, 1710–11*

62 All government is a monopoly of violence.
*Hugh MacDiarmid (C. M. Grieve,
1892–1978)*, The Glass of Pure Water

63 The daughter of a base and brainless
breed
Is given what countless better women
sorely need . . .
Rope in the shameless hussy, let her be
Directed to factory work or domestic
service
Along with all the other spivs and drones.
Hugh MacDiarmid, Royal Wedding
Gifts *(1947)*

64 ... if I had my way
I would melt your gold payment,
pour it into your skull,
till it reached to your boots.

> *Ian Lom Macdonald (c.1620–c.1707),*
> Oran an Aghaidh an Aonaidh (Song
> Against the Union), *citing the bribe-
> takers*

65 Tomorrow every Duchess in London will
be wanting to kiss me!

> *J. Ramsay Macdonald (1866–1937), on
> forming the National Government, 1931,
> quoted in* Viscount Snowden, An
> Autobiography

66 All you folks are off your head
I'm getting rich from your sea bed

I'll go home when I see fit
All I'll leave is a heap of shit.

> *John McGrath (1935–),* The Cheviot,
> the Stag and the Black, Black Oil

67 We will not get true independence in a
oner. People want to see how a parliament
or assembly works before going for what
we want for Scotland.

> *Robert McIntyre, letter to Gordon Wilson
> (1989), quoted in Andrew Marr,* The
> Battle for Scotland *(1996)*

68 In the old days of the Tories we would
be standing about, talking, waiting for the
county council meeting to begin, and the
Earl of Elgin would say, 'Well, gentlemen,
maybe we should make a start.' But now
we have a Labour convener, and an official
comes smartly into the room and says, 'Be
upstanding for the County Convener.'

> *Fife miner, quoted in R. F. Mackenzie
> (1910–1987),* A Search for Scotland

69 The Commons, faithful to their system,
remained in a wise and masterly inactivity.

> *Sir James Mackintosh (1765–1832),* Vin-
> diciae Gallicae

70 A titled Nobility is the most undisputed
progeny of feudal barbarism.

> *Sir James Mackintosh*

71 *Sir Pertinax MacSycophant:* Why, you see,
sir, I have acquired a noble fortune, a
princely fortune, and how do you think I
raised it?
  Charles MacSycophant (his son): Doubtless,
sir, by your abilities.
  Sir Pertinax: Doubtless, sir, you are a
blockhead. Nae, sir, I'll tell you how I
raised it. Sir, I raised it by booing – booing,
sir ... Sir, I booed, and watched, and
hearkened, and ran about, backwards and
forwards, and dangled upon the then great
mon, till I got into the very bowels of
his confidence, and then, sir, I wriggled,
and wrought, and wriggled, till I wriggled
myself among the very thick of them. Ha!
I got my snack of the clothing, the forag-
ing, the contracts ... guin I could but have
spoken in the Hoose, I should have done
the deed in half the time; but the instant I
opened my mouth, they aw fell a-laughing
at me.

> *Charles Macklin (c.1697–1797),* The
> Man of the World *(1781)*

72 Scottish separation is part of England's
imperial disintegration.

> *John Maclean (1879–1923), election
> address, 1922*

73 'God forgie them; but God never let us die
till we have them in the same condition
they had us, and we are sure we would not
treat them as they treated us. We would
show them the difference between a good
and a bad cause.'

> *Donald MacLeod (Prince Charles Edward
> Stewart's guide after Culloden) and Mal-
> colm MacLeod, Jacobite prisoners, quoted
> in Robert Forbes,* The Lyon in Mourn-
> ing *(compiled 1746–75), on their English
> jailers*

74 My desire to disturb no man for conscience
sake is pretty well known, and, I hope, will
be had in remembrance.

> *Lord Mansfield (1705–1793), quoted in
> Bonamy Dobrée,* Anne to Victoria

75 The real question for Scotsmen is not
whether an independent Scotland would be
viable, but whether it would be bearable.

> *Arthur Marwick, in K. Miller,* Memoirs
> of a Modern Scotland *(1969)*

76 The working class is now the ruling class,
and it is not fitting or proper that the
ruling class should go in rags.

> *James Maxton (1885–1946), speech in
> Glasgow, 1924*

77 If you cannot ride two horses you have no
    right in the circus.

> *James Maxton, in the* Daily Herald, *Jan-
> uary 1931, opposing the disaffiliation of
> the Scottish Independent Labour Party
> from the Labour Party*

78 I do not believe in professional politicians,
    that is men who set out to make a career for
    themselves in politics . . . I believe in men
    and women throwing themselves into the
    Socialist movement wholeheartedly. If that
    sh ould result in throwing them into Parlia-
    ment or prison, good enough, but neither
    of these should be a prime objective.

> *James Maxton, letter to Mr Ibbotson,
> June 1944*

79 *Mr J. C. Wallace* (National Liberal, Dun-
    fermline): 'You were once a Liberal
    yourself.'
      Maxton (in mock horror): 'I have never
    concealed that, in my youth, I was a Con-
    servative, but never, in the depth of my
    ignorance or degradation, was I a Liberal.'

> *James Maxton (1885–1946), quoted in
> G. McAllister,* James Maxton: Portrait
> of a Rebel *(1935)*

80 'All the fine ladies, if you will except one or
    two,' says Lord President Forbes, 'became
    passionately fond of the young Adventurer,
    and used all their arts and industry for
    him in the most intemperate manner.'

> *Dugald Mitchell,* History of the High-
> lands and Gaelic Scotland *(1900),
> quoting Duncan Forbes of Culloden
> (1685–1747), on Prince Charles Edward
> in Edinburgh, 1745*

81 One is apt to ask, was the country better,
    or the people happier, under these grand
    ecclesiastics, who lived in the country, and
    devoted their time to religion and benefi-
    cence, than at the present time, when the
    chief part of the territory is possessed by
    two great lords, who interest themselves
    chiefly in politics, take little interest in the
    people, and have no practical experience
    of rural affairs?

> *Joseph Mitchell (1803–1883),* Reminis-
> cences of My Life in the Highlands

82 Scotland does not, in fact, belong to the
    people of Scotland. They are permitted to
    reside in it, and practise their callings, but
    they appear to be merely tenants at will . . .
    Although our kingdom contains upwards

of three and a half millions of inhabitants,
who are supposed from their education to
be the most enlightened and intelligent
people in Europe, yet they possess no
interest in the territory of Scotland. One-
half their country is owned by seventy
proprietors, while nine-tenths belongs to
seventeen hundred persons.

> *Joseph Mitchell,* Reminiscences of My
> Life in the Highlands

83 When our ashes are scattered by the winds
    of heaven, the impartial verdict of future
    times will rejudge your verdict.

> *Thomas Muir (1765–1799), to his judges,
> in the political trials of 1793*

84 This evil mélange of decrepit Presbyterian-
    ism and imperialist thuggery, whose spirit
    may be savoured by a few mornings with
    the Edinburgh *Scotsman* and a few eve-
    nings watching Scottish television, appears
    to be solidly represented in the SNP.

> *Tom Nairn (1932–),* Three Dreams
> of Scottish Nationalism, *in K. Miller,*
> Memoirs of a Modern Scotland *(1969)*

85 British 'Parliamentary cretinism' (to use
    Lenin's old phrase) has found its last abid-
    ing refuge within the Scottish National
    Party, where sectarian infantilism seems
    likely to keep the old thing warm until a
    true Doomsday comes.

> *Tom Nairn,* The Timeless Girn, *in
> O. D. Edwards,* A Claim of Right for
> Scotland *(1989)*

86 What is called 'Communism' in backward
    countries is hunger becoming articulate.

> *John Boyd Orr (1880–1971), quoted by
> Ritchie Calder in* Science Profiles

87 'A'm no' a man: a'm a Glasgow bailie.'

> *A. W. Petrie (c.1853–1937),* The
> Clincher, *March 1898, quoted in Wil-
> liam Donaldson,* The Language of the
> People *(1989)*

88 By the time the civil service has finished
    drafting a document to give effect to a
    principle, there may be little of the princi-
    ple left.

> *Lord Reith (1889–1971),* Into the Wind

89 Mak' your lick-fud bailie core
    Fa' down behint him – not afore,

His great posteriors to adore,
Sawney, now the king's come.

*Alexander Rodger (1784–1846), Sawney,
Now the King's Come, burlesque of Sir
Walter Scott's Carle, Now the King's
Come, on George IV's visit to Edinburgh,
1822*

90 Imperialism, sane Imperialism, as distinguished from what I may call mad-dog
Imperialism, is but this – a larger
patriotism.

*Lord Rosebery (1847–1929), speech to the
City of London Liberal Club, 1899*

91 A gentleman will blithely do in politics
what he would kick a man downstairs for
doing in ordinary life.

*Lord Rosebery, quoted in Jonathan Green,
Dictionary of Insulting Quotations
(1996)*

92 There is no word so prostituted as
patriotism.

Lord Rosebery, rectorial address to Edinburgh University, November 1882

93 Just say things are looking grim.

*William Ross, Secretary of State for
Scotland, 1964–70 and 1974–76, usual
instruction to his speech-writer, David
Kemp, recorded in Arnold Kemp, The
Hollow Drum (1993)*

94 We know that the organised workers of
the country are our friends. As for the rest,
they don't matter a tinker's cuss.

*Emmanuel Shinwell (1884–1986), speech
to the Electrical Trades Union Conference,
1947*

95 We weren't necessarily wrong. We were
just trying to push water uphill.

*Jim Sillars (1937–), founder of the Scottish Labour party, quoted in Arnold Kemp,
The Hollow Drum (1993)*

96 What signifies 't for for folks to chide
For what was done before them
Let Whig and Tory all agree . . .
To spend the night wi' mirth and glee,
And cheerful sing alang wi' me
The Reel o' Tullochgorum.

*John Skinner (1721–1807),
Tullochgorum*

97 (Ramsay) MacDonald nervously asked
Shinwell if there was an escape route to
the rear, and quickly shied away when a

burly six-footer wielding a heavy piece of
lead pipe jumped up next to him.
'Who's this?' MacDonald stammered.
'Oh, you've no need to worry about
him,' replied Shinwell. 'It's only McGovern. He's a pacifist.'
'He's the sort of pacifist I much prefer on
my side,' declared MacDonald.

Peter Slowe, Manny Shinwell (1993)

98 A'body kens oor nationalism
Is yet a thing o' sect and schism.

William Soutar (1898–1943), Vision

99 The general movement in favour of a
national rebirth has attracted some of the
finest and most generous spirits in Scotland – and many of the greatest cranks
in Christendom . . . if Scotland is to survive as a nation a strong curb must be put
upon the blatant egotism of so many of her
protagonists.

*Lewis Spence in The Scots Independent,
(1928–9), quoted in H. J. Hanham, Scottish Nationalism (1969)*

100 I think the clan Donell must be rooted
out, and Lochiel. Leave the McLeans to
Argyll . . . God knows whether the 12,000
£ sterling had been better employed to
settle the Highlands, or to ravage them;
but, since we will make them desperate, I
think we should root them out before they
can get the help they depend upon.

*The Master of Stair (Sir John Dalrymple,
1648–1707), letter to the Earl of
Breadalbane, December 1691, quoted in
W. C. Dickinson and G. Donaldson,
The Source-Book of Scottish History,
Volume 3 (1954)*

101 The McDonalds will fall in this net. That's
the only popish clan in the kingdom, and it
will be popular to take severe course with
them. Let me hear from you with the first
whether you think this is the proper season
to maul them in the cold long nights, and
what force will be necessary.

*The Master of Stair, letter to Lt. Col.
Hamilton at Fort William, December
1691, quoted in The Source Book of
Scottish History, Volume 3*

102 D. (Lloyd George) told us he had discovered the secret of Rosebery's limitations.
One night when there was an important
debate in the House of Lords, he overheard Rosebery's valet say to him, 'Your

grouse is done to a turn, my lord,' and Rosebery disappeared, leaving the debate to take care of itself.

> *Frances Stevenson*, Diary, *November 1934*

103 . . . if I had been acquainted with it in time, I had certainly done my best to prevent its being executed. If it was rash, I cannot but say it was a bold undertaking, and the courage and sentiments the Prince expresses on this occasion will always do him honour.

> *James Stewart, 'The Old Pretender' (1688–1766), letter to the Earl Marischal (1745) on Prince Charles Edward's landing in Scotland*

104 Blest Revolution, which creates Divided Hearts, united states.

> *Jonathan Swift (1667–1745), on the Union of Scotland and England*

105 There can be no doubt that we get nearly all the talents the northern kingdom produces, and the cause is not difficult to ascertain. It is not merely because parliament sits in London that England draws away the best brains from the other two kingdoms, but because Englishmen have thrown away those confined notions of nationality that still prevail in Scotland and Ireland . . . the more Scotland has striven to be a nation, the more she has sunk to be a province.

> The Times, *London, December 1856*

106 One may reasonably say that the arrangements under which Scotland was governed for a century and a quarter represented not so much a constitution as a bad joke elaborated with the careful logic of lunacy.

> *Colin Walkinshaw (James M. Reid)*, The Scots Tragedy *(1935)*

107 If the endurance and determination they displayed had been on the battlefield on behalf of our ruling class and the prevailing order of society, their struggle would be the central feature in the history books of our schools for centuries to come. As it is, they are blackguarded for their bravery.

> *John Wheatley (1873–1930), on the 1926 miners' strike*

108 We do not wish to take from what already is your own;
But let some law of equity to nations all be known;
Let one be to the other just as when the world began,
In universal fellowship and brotherhood of man.

> *Adam Wilson (b.1850)*, The Brotherhood of Man

Religion and the Church

1 A cold Church,
A thin wretched cleric;
The body in subjection shedding tears:
Great their reward in the eyes of the King of Heaven.

> *Anonymous, 12th century verse from Gaelic, quoted in Hugh Cheape and I. F. Grant*, Periods in Highland History *(1987), from Donald MacKinnon*, A Descriptive Catalogue of Gaelic Manuscripts *(1912)*

2 Lufe God abufe al, and yi nychtbour as yi self.

> *Inscription on 'John Knox's House', High Street, Edinburgh (16th century)*

3 Better keep the devil out, than have to put him out.

> *Anonymous*

4 There is more knavery among kirkmen than honesty among courtiers.

> *Anonymous*

5 St Andreus is an Atheist, and Glasgow is ane gouke:
A Vencher Brechin: Edinburgh of avarice a pocke.
To popery prone is Galloway: Dunkeld is rich in thesaure,
A courtier Rosse: but glutton lyke Argyle eats out of measure;
Dround Aberdeen in povertie: vagge Murrays subtile vitt,
Dunblane the criple, loves the Coupe: Jylles for all subject fitt.
Skill'd Orknay is in archerie, as Caithness is in droges,
O quhat a shame Christ's flocke to trust to such unfaithful doges.

> *Anonymous*, Pasquil against the Scottish Bishops, *c.1630; from James Maidment*, A Book of Scottish Pasquils *(1868)*

6 Not mellow voice, but fervent prayer;
Not music strings, but upright mind,
Not loud-toned voice, but love unfeigned,
Will reach the ears of the Divine.

Anonymous, from the Introduction to the
Metric Psalms *published by the Synod of*
Argyll (1694), from Gaelic

7 *Elspeth Buchan:* Come and toil in the garden
of the Lord!
Old man: Thank ye, but He wasna ower
kind to the first gairdner that he had.

Apocryphal anecdote of 'The Woman of
Revelation' (1738–1791)

8 I do believe in stone and lime,
a manse of large dimension,
Broad acres for a glebe and farm,
that is my church extension.
My folk may perish if they like –
Christ's name I rarely mention;
I take the stipend due by right
to men of good intention.

Anonymous, 18th century, quoted in
Gordon Donaldson, The Faith of the
Scots *(1990)*

9 The Free Kirk, the wee kirk,
The kirk without the steeple;
The Auld Kirk, the cauld kirk,
The kirk without the people.

Anonymous, rhyme on the Disruption of
1843

10 O Lord! Thou art like a mouse in a drystane dyke, aye keekin' out at us frae holes
and crannies, but we canna see Thee.

Anonymous Western minister, quoted in
Charles Mackay, Poetry and Humour
of the Scottish Language *(1882), from*
Rogers' Illustrations of Scottish Life

11 'We thank thee, O Lord, for all Thy mercies; such as they are.'

Anonymous Aberdeen minister, quoted in
William Power, Scotland and the Scots
(1934)

12 The Kingdom of God consists not in exuberance of eloquence, but in the abundant
blossoming forth of faith.

St Adamnan (679–704), The Life of
Saint Columba, *translated from Latin by*
Wentworth Huyshe

13 One is tempted almost to say that there
was more of Jesus in St Theresa's little
finger than in John Knox's whole body.

Matthew Arnold (1822–1888), Literature and Dogma

14 The Presbyterian faith is an incomparable
metaphor for the unity of creation, for the
inner conflict between our sense of freedom and our scientific understanding that,
in another way, we control nothing that
happens.

Neal Ascherson (1932–), Games With
Shadows

15 The grim Geneva ministers
With anxious scowl drew near.

William Edmonstone Aytoun
(1813–1865), The Execution of
Montrose

16 I thought God was actually floating somewhere overhead, a stern man with a
beard, something like Papa only of enormous dimension, infinitely powerful and
fearsome.
Fear indeed hung over me like a dark
cloud in my childhood.

John Logie Baird (1888–1946), Sermons,
Soap and Television

17 If there is no future life, this world is a bad
joke. But whose joke?

A. J. Balfour (1848–1930), attributed
death-bed remark

18 Nothing to pay,
No, nothing to pay . . .
Coatbridge to Glory,
And nothing to pay.

Baptist hymn, quoted by David Donaldson
(1916–), in Coatbridge to Glory, *from*
A. Kamm and A. Lean, A Scottish
Childhood *(1985)*

19 When this action came to the king's ears,
he asked the bishop as they were going
in to dine, 'My lord bishop, why did you
give away the royal horse which was necessary for your own use? Have we not many
less valuable horses or other things which
would have been good enough to give to
the poor, without giving away a horse that
I had specially selected for your personal
use?'
The bishop answered at once, 'What are
you saying, o king? Surely this son of a

mare is not dearer to you than that son of God?'

> *St Bede (c.673–735)*, Ecclesiastical History of the English People, *on St Aidan and King Oswiu of Northumbria*

20 Man's extremity is God's opportunity.

> *Lord Belhaven (1656–1708), speech to the Scottish Parliament, 1706*

21 'I know not truly what gold ye seek . . . but if it were permitted me to know, Christ permitting, never would these lips tell this to your ears. Savagely bring your swords, seize your hilts, and kill'.

> *St Blathmac (d.825), quoted in Walafrid Strabo*, Life of St Blathmac *(849), his last words to the Viking raiders on Iona (from Latin)*

22 Few are thy days and full of woe,
    O man of woman born;
    Thy doom is written, 'Dust thou art,
    And shalt to dust return.'

> *Michael Bruce (1746–1767), also claimed by John Logan (1748–1788)*

23 An atheist is a man with no invisible means of support.

> *John Buchan (1875–1940), quoted in H. E. Fosdick*, On Being a Real Person

24 'Is it true that under the Act there's a maternity benefit, and that a woman gets the benefit whether she's married or no?'
    'That is right.'
    'D'ye approve of that?'
    'With all my heart.'
    'Well, sir, how d'ye explain this? The Bible says the wages of sin is death and the Act says thirty shillin's.'

> *John Buchan*, Memory-Hold-the-Door

25 When the Scotch Kirk was at the height of its power, we may search history in vain for any institution that can compete with it, except the Spanish Inquisition.

> *Henry Thomas Buckle (1821–1862)*, History of Civilisation in England

26 That is not the best sermon which makes the hearers go away talking to one another, and praising the speaker, but which makes them go away thoughtful and serious, and hastening to be alone.

> *Gilbert Burnet (1643–1715)*, History of the Reformation

27 But Lord, remember me and mine
    Wi' mercies temporal and divine,
    That I for grace and gear may shine
    Excelled by none;
    And all the glory shall be thine,
    Amen! Amen!

> *Robert Burns (1759–1796)*, Holy Willie's Prayer

28 The sire turns o'er, with patriarchal grace,
    The big ha'-Bible, ance his father's pride:
    His bonnet reverently is laid aside,
    His lyart haffets wearing thin and bare:
    Those strains that once did sweet in
        Zion glide,
    He wales a portion with judicious care;
    And 'Let us worship God!' he says with
        solemn air.

> *Robert Burns*, The Cottar's Saturday Night

29 They never sought in vain that sought the Lord aright!

> *Robert Burns*, The Cottar's Saturday Night

30 O thou! Whatever title suit thee –
    Auld 'Hornie', 'Satan', 'Nick', or 'Clootie'

> *Robert Burns*, Address to the Deil

31 Some time ago two officers of the army had transgressed with two sisters at Stirling: one of these gentlemen seldom failed of going to kirk, the other never was there. The affair came to a hearing before a presbytery, and the result was, that the girl who had the child by the kirk-goer was an impudent baggage, and deserved to be whipped out of town for seducing an honest man; and that he who never went to kirk, was an abandoned wretch for seducing her sister.

> *Edmund Burt, (fl. early 18th century)*, Letters From a Gentleman in the North of Scotland *(1726–37)*

32 'Our neighbour nation will say of us, poor Scotland! beggarly Scotland! scabbed Scotland! Lousy Scotland! yea, but Covenanted Scotland! that makes amends for all.'

> *Robert Calder*, Scots Presbyterian Eloquence Displayed

33 I fear I have nothing original in me
    Excepting original sin.

> *Thomas Campbell (1777–1844)*

34 The Lord knows I go up this ladder with less fear and perturbation of spirit than ever I entered the pulpit to preach.

Donald Cargill (1619–1681), at his execution

35 Man's unhappiness, as I construe, comes of his Greatness, it is because there is an Infinite in him, which with all his cunning he cannot quite bury under the Finite.

Thomas Carlyle (1795–1881)

36 The three great elements of modern civilization, gunpowder, printing, and the Protestant religion.

Thomas Carlyle

37 His religion is at best an anxious wish – like that of Rabelais: a great Perhaps.

Thomas Carlyle, Essays (on Robert Burns)

38 For me as an individual the worst thing in this unhappy age in which I have grown old is that one was born into a faith which could not, without deceit or strain, be maintained.

Catherine Carswell (1879–1946), Lying Awake

39 Who cares about the Free Church, compared with the Christian good of Scotland? Who cares about any church but as an instrument of Christian good?

Thomas Chalmers (1780–1847)

40 We leave to others the passions and politics of this world, and nothing will ever be taught, I trust, in any of our halls which shall have the remotest tendency to disturb the existing order of things, or to confound the ranks and distinction which at present obtain in society. But there is one equality between man and man which will strenuously be taught – the essential equality of human souls; and that in the high count and reckoning of eternity, the soul of the very poorest of nature's children, the raggedest boy that runs along the pavement, is of like estimation in the eyes of heaven with that of the greatest and noblest of our land.

Thomas Chalmers, address on laying the foundation stone of New College, Edinburgh, June 1846

41 Then the folk were sair pitten aboot,
An' they cried, as the weather grew waur:
'Oh Lord! We ken we hae sinn'd,

But a joke can be carried owre far!'
Then they chapped at the ark's muckle door,
To speir gin douce Noah had room;
But Noah never heedit their cries;
He said, 'This'll learn ye to soom.'

W. D. Cocker (1882–1970), The Deluge

42 It is a mistaken belief that priestdom died when they spelled it Presbytery.

S. R. Crockett (1859–1914), Bog Myrtle and Peat

43 . . . the North, where Time stands still and Change holds holiday, where Old and New
welter upon the border of the world, and savage faith works woe.

John Davidson (1857–1909), Ballad of the Making of a Poet

44 The wark gangs bonnily on.

Attributed to David Dickson (c.1583–1663) in Henry Guthry, Memoirs of Scottish Affairs,Civil and Ecclesiastical (1702), on executions of opponents of the Covenanters, 1645

45 Hot Burning Coals of Juniper shall be
Thy Bed of Down, and then to Cover thee
A Quilt of Boyling Brimstone thou must take,
And Wrap thee in till thou full Payment make.

James Donaldson (late 17th century), The Voice of God

46 Whenever a young man was recommended to old Lord Stormont for one of his kirks, he used allways to ask, 'Is he good-natured in his drink?' and if that was the case he said he should be his man.

Quoted of Lord Stormont (d.1748), by Sir John Douglas in Charles Rodger, Boswelliana (1874)

47 The gods take wondrous shapes, sometimes.

Norman Douglas (1868–1952), Old Calabria

48 Eastern religions lose their finest strains when transplanted out of their native soil . . . Only the modern Scotsman, the Roman of the Republic, and a few other favoured races whose minds are constructed on the watertight-compartment system, can withstand the toxic effects

of certain speculations which in no wise
impair the sanity of those among whom
they originated.

> *Norman Douglas*, Siren Land

49 Who listen'd to his voice, obey'd his cry?
Only the echoes which he made relent,
Rung from their marble caves, 'Repent,
Repent!'

> *William Drummond (1585–1649)*, For
> the Baptist

50 *Ave Maria, gratia plena!*
Thy birth has with his blude
Fra fall mortall originall
Us raunsound on the rude.

> *William Dunbar (c.1450–c.1520)*, Ane
> Ballat of Our Ladye

51 'The truth is, my friends, you might as
weel expect to see my red coo climb the
muckle pear tree in the manse garden tail
first and whistle like a laverock!'

> *William Faichney (1805–1854), in a
> sermon about the rich entering the King-
> dom of Heaven, quoted in Hugh MacDiar-
> mid*, Lucky Poet *(1943)*

52 'It was the saying, sir, of one of the wisest
judges who ever sat on the Scottish bench,
that a *poor* clergy made a *pure* clergy; a
maxim which deserves to be engraven in
letters of gold on every manse in Scotland.'

> *Susan Ferrier (1782–1854)*, Destiny

53 An annibabtist is a thing I am not a member
of:– I am a Pisplikan just now and a Pris-
betern at Kercaldy my native town which
though dirty is clein in the country.

> *Marjory Fleming (1803–1811)*, Journals

54 Wha daur debait religion on a Sunday?

> *Robert Garioch (Robert Garioch
> Sutherland,1909–1981)*, And They
> were Richt

55 . . . a base impudent brazen-faced villain,
a spiteful ignorant pedant, a gross idolator,
a great liar, a mere slanderer, an evil man,
hardened against all shame . . . full of insolence and abuse, chicanery and nonsense,
ld detestable, misty, erroneous, wicked,
vile, pernicious, terrible and horrid doc-
trines, tending to corrupt the mind and
stupefy the conscience, with gross iniquity,

audacious hostility, pitiful evasion, base,
palpable and shocking deceit.

> *The Rev. Adam Gib (fl. 17th century),
> anti-Burgher leader, reviewing a work by
> the Rev. Archibald Hill, a Burgher min-
> ister, from a pamphlet printed in Perth
> (1782)*

56 'Religion – a Scot know religion? Half of
them think of God as a Scot with brosy
morals and a penchant for Burns. And the
other half are over damned mean to allow
the Almighty even existence.'

> *Lewis Grassic Gibbon (James Leslie
> Mitchell, 1901–1935)*, Cloud Howe

57 'Pisky, Pisky, Amen,
Doon on your knees and up again.'

> *Rude boys' chant to Episcopalian ministers,
> quoted in H. Grey Graham*, The Social
> Life of Scotland in the Eighteenth
> Century *(1899)*

58 I confess that, as an impartial outsider, I
hope that as long as there are an appre-
ciable number of Protestants, they will
be balanced by some Catholics; for, while
both bodies have been about equally hostile to truth, the Catholics have on the
whole been kinder to beauty.

> *J. B. S. Haldane (1892–1964)*, Science
> and Ethics

59 O for the days when sinners shook
Aneth the true Herd's righteous crook.

> *Henry Henderson (1883–1937)*, The
> Northern Muse

60 I think I had not then broken, that is, absolutely broken, above four out of the ten
commandments; but for all that, I had
more sense than to regard either my good
works, or my evil deeds, as in the smallest
degree influencing the eternal decrees of
God concerning me, either with regard to
my acceptance or reprobation.

> *James Hogg (1770–1835)*, The Private
> Memoirs and Confessions of a Justified
> Sinner

61 Nothing in the world delights a truly religious people so much as consigning them
to eternal damnation.

> *James Hogg*, The Private Memoirs and
> Confessions of a Justified Sinner

62 'Surely you are not such a fool,' said I, 'as to believe that the devil really was in the printing office?'

'Oo, gud bless you sir! saw him myself, gave him a nod, and good-day. Rather a gentlemanly personage – Green Circassian hunting coat and turban – Like a foreigner – Has the power of vanishing in one moment though – Rather a suspicious circumstance that. Otherwise, his appearance not much against him.'

> *James Hogg*, The Private Memoirs and Confessions of a Justified Sinner

63 Upon the whole, we may conclude, that the *Christian Religion* not only was at first attended by miracles, but even to this day cannot be believed by any reasonable person without one.

> *David Hume (1711–1776)*, An Enquiry Concerning Human Understanding

64 What strange objects of adoration are cats and monkeys? says the learned doctor. They are a least as good as the relics or rotten bones of martyrs.

> *David Hume*, The Natural History of Religion

65 In all ages of the world, priests have been enemies of liberty.

> *David Hume*, Of the Parties of Great Britain

66 Evangelicalism and the emergence of the modern crofting community are inseparable phenomena if only for the reason that it was through the medium of a profoundly evangelical faith that the crofters first developed a forward-looking critique of the situation created in the Highlands by the actions of the region's landowning and therefore ruling class.

> *James Hunter*, The Emergence of the Crofting Community: The Religious Contribution, *from* Scottish Studies *(1974)*

67 Do not be afraid of being free-thinkers. If you think strongly enough you will be forced by science to the belief in God, which is the foundation of all Religion. You will find science not antagonistic, but helpful to Religion.

> *Lord Kelvin (1824–1907), address to the Rev. Professor Henslow, London, 1903*

68 It was only later I came to the conclusion that Eve had been framed.

> *Helena Kennedy (1950–)*, Eve Was Framed: Women and British Justice

69 A man with God is always in the majority.

> *Attributed to John Knox (c.1513–1572); quoted also as 'God and one are always a majority' by Mary Slessor, in James Buchan*, The Expendable Mary Slessor *(1980)*

70 Seeing that impossible it is, but that either I shall offend God or else that I shall displease the world, I have determined to obey God, notwithstanding that the world shall rage thereat.

> *John Knox*

71 Some goes to church just for a walk,
Some go there to laugh and talk . . .
Some go there to doze and nod,
It's few goes there to worship God.

> *Sir James Cameron Lees*

72 Mr John, have you not once gotten your fill of blood?

> *David Leslie (1601–1682), Covenanting general, to the minister of Newmilns, who was demanding the slaughter of the women followers of Montrose's army after the Battle of Philiphaugh, 13 September 1645, quoted in C. Stewart Black*, Scottish Battles *(1936)*

73 There was a smug, trim, smooth little minister, making three hundred a year pimping for a God in whom his heart was too small to believe.

> *Eric Linklater (1899–1974)*, Magnus Merriman

74 . . . the reik of Maister Patrik Hammyltoun hes infected as many as it blew upoun.

> *John Lyndsay (fl. 16th century), letter to Archbishop Beaton on the burning of Patrick Hamilton, 1528, quoted in John Knox*, History of the Reformation in Scotland

75 Abide with me: fast falls the eventide;
The darkness deepens; Lord, with me abide.

> *Henry Francis Lyte (1793–1847)*, Abide With Me

76 Change and decay in all around I see.

> *Henry Francis Lyte*, Abide With Me

77   Ransomed, healed, restored, forgiven,
     Who like me His praise should sing?

     Henry Francis Lyte, Praise My Soul the
     King of Heaven

78   Religion? Huh!

     Hugh MacDiarmid (1892–1978), Two
     Memories

79   Let men find the faith that builds
        mountains
     Before they seek the faith that moves
        them.

     Hugh MacDiarmid, On a Raised Beach

80   I saw twa items on
     The TV programme yesterday.
     'General Assembly of the Church of
        Scotland'
     Said ane – the ither 'Nuts in May'.
     I lookit at the picters syne
     But which was which I couldna say.

     Hugh MacDiarmid, Nuts in May

81   The principal part of faith is patience.

     George Macdonald (1824–1905)

82   Love of our neighbour is the only door out
     of the dungeon of self.

     George Macdonald

83   The Lord is my Shepherd!
     I'm a puir man, I grant,
     But I am weel neiboured!

     George Macdonald, The Lord is my
     Shepherd

84   I find doing the will of God, leaves me no
     time for disputing about His plans.

     George Macdonald, The Marquis of
     Lossie

85   . . . the minister's voice
     spread a pollution of bad beliefs.

     Norman MacCaig (1910–1996), High-
     land Funeral

86   Among the Shieldaig party was a small boy
     of four or five summers who had been to
     church for the first time in his life. My
     grandfather, wishing to say something to
     the little chap, asked him what he saw in
     church, and his reply was much to the
     point: 'I saa a man baaling, baaling in a
     box, and no a man would let him out.'

     Osgood Mackenzie (1842–1922), A Hun-
     dred Years in the Highlands

87   The Scots had no reason to set any value
     on their Parliament. The Scots Parliament
     was a time-serving institution and echoed
     the voice of whoever was in power. It was
     to the General Assembly of the Church
     that the Scots looked for their liberty.

     Norman Maclean, The Years of Fulfil-
     ment *(1953), quoted in H. J. Hanham,*
     Scottish Nationalism *(1969)*

88   Courage, brother! do not stumble
     Though the path be dark as night
     There's a star to guide the humble,
     Trust in God, and do the right.

     Norman Macleod (1812–1872), Trust in
     God

89   O Love that will not let me go.

     George Matheson (1842–1906), O Love
     That Will Not Let Me Go

90   Make me a captive, Lord,
     And then I shall be free.

     George Matheson, Make Me a Captive,
     Lord

91   The brain of man most surely did invent
     That purging place, he answer'd me
        again;
     For greediness together they consent
     To say that souls in torment may remain
     Till gold and goods relieve them of their
        pain.

     Elizabeth Melville (fl. 1603), Ane
     Godlie Dreame Complit in Scottish
     Meter be M.M., Gentilwoman in Cul
     Ross, at the Request of Her Freindes
     (1606)

92   The Reformation was a kind of spiritual
     strychnine of which Scotland took an
     overdose.

     Willa Muir (1890–1970), Mrs Grundy
     in Scotland

93   'No man wi' any releegion aboot him
     would caal his canary a Wee Free.'

     Neil Munro (1864–1930), The Vital
     Spark

94   Then the minister made a comic speech wi'
     jokes in't, and tried to look as game as ony-
     thing; and the folk frae Clachnacudden
     leaned forrit on their sates and asked the
     wifes in front if they had mind when his
     mither used to work in the tawtie field . . .
     A' the time the puir minister was thinkin'

he was daein' fine, and wonderin' if the *Oban Times* was takin' doon a' his speech.

Neil Munro, Erchie

95 The gude auld Kirk o' Scotland,
She's nae in ruins yet!

George Murray (*1819–1868*), The Auld Kirk o' Scotland

96 By and large, it was the odious hell-religion of Scottish Calvinism which endured, and still endures as the cultural substratum of the country.

Tom Nairn (*1932–*), Festival of the Dead, *in* New Statesman, *September 1967*

97 I cannot praise the Doctor's eyes,
I never saw his glance divine;
He always shuts them when he prays,
And when he preaches, he shuts mine.

George Outram (*1805–1856*), Lines on the Doctor

98 Considering that the line and succession of our kings and rulers hath been against the power and purity of religion and godliness, and Christ's reigning over his church, and its freedom, and so against God, and hath degenerate from that virtue, moderation, sobriety and good government which was the tenor and right by which their ancestors held their crowns . . . into an idle and sinful magnificence where the all and only government is to keep up their own absoluteness and tyranny, and to keep on a yoke of thraldom upon the subjects, and to squeeze from them their substance to uphold their lustful and pompous superfluities.

The Queensferry Paper, *1680, Cameronian document quoted in Robert Wodrow,* Sufferings of the Church of Scotland (*1721*)

99 The Devil was sick – the Devil a monk would be;
The Devil was well – the Devil a monk was he.

François Rabelais, Gargantua and Pantagruel, *translated by Sir Thomas Urquhart (1611–1660)*

100 In the year 1784, when the great actress, Mrs Siddons, first appeared in Edinburgh, during the sitting of the General Assembly, that court was obliged to fix all its important business for the alternate days when she did not act.

Dean E. B. Ramsay (*1793–1872*), Reminiscences of Scottish Life and Character

101 The Rev. Mr Monro of Westray, preaching on the flight of Lot from Sodom, said: 'The honest man and his family were ordered out of the town, and charged not to look back; but the auld carlin, Lot's wife, looked owre her shouther, for which she was smote into a lump of sawt.' And he added with great unction, 'Oh, ye people of Westray, if ye had had her, mony a day since ye wad hae putten her in the parritch-pot!'

Dean E. B. Ramsay, Reminiscences of Scottish Life and Character

102 A young girl sat upon the cutty-stool at St Andrews . . . was asked who was the father of her child? How can I tell, she replied artlessly, amang a wheen o' Divinity students?

Dean E. B. Ramsay, Reminiscences of Scottish Life and Character

103 . . . the most considerable of the Druidical festivals is that of Beltane, or May-day, which was lately observed in some parts of the Highlands with extraordinary ceremonies . . . Like the other public worship of the Druids, the Beltane feast seems to have been performed on hills or eminences. They thought it degrading to him whose temple is the Universe, to suppose he would dwell in any house made with their hands.

John Ramsay of Ochteryre (*1736–1814*), quoted by Sir James Frazer (*1854–1941*), *in* The Golden Bough

104 Being in a minister's house, there was the minimum of religious consolation.

John Macnair Reid (*1895–1954*), Homeward Journey

105 Every conjecture we form with regard to the works of God has as little probability as the conjectures of a child with regard to the works of a man.

Thomas Reid (*1710–1796*), Inquiry into the Human Mind

106 Few forms of Christianity have offered an ideal of Christian perfection so pure as the Celtic Church of the sixth, seventh and

eighth centuries. Nowhere, perhaps, has God been better worshipped in spirit.

> *Ernest Renan (1823–1892)*, Etudes d'Histoire Réligieuse

107 Suffering is the professor's golden garment.

> *Samuel Rutherford (c.1600–1661), letter to Marion McNaught, 1637*

108 Scotland's judgement sleepeth not: awake and repent.

> *Samuel Rutherford, letter to his parishioners at Anwoth, 1637*

109 No man can be an unbeliever nowadays. The Christian apologists have left one nothing to disbelieve.

> *Saki (H. H. Munro, 1870–1916)*

110 I've read the secret name o' Knox's God. The gowd calf 'Getting On'.

> *Tom Scott (1918–1995), Fergus*

111 O ay! the Monks! the Monks, they did the mischief!
Theirs all the grossness, all the superstition,
Of a most gross and superstitious age.

> *Sir Walter Scott (1771–1832), The Monastery*

112 What has the Kirk given us? Ugly churches and services, identifying in the minds of the churchgoers ugliness with God, have stifled the Scottish arts almost out of existence . . . until the Kirk as it has been is dead Scotland will continue to be the Home of Lost Causes.

> *George Scott-Moncrieff (1910–), in D. C. Thomson, Scotland in Quest of her Youth: A Scrutiny (1932), quoted in H. J. Hanham, Scottish Nationalism (1969)*

113 It is lawful to prevent the murder of ourselves or our brethren, when no other way is left, by killing the murderers before they accomplish their wicked design, if they be habitually prosecuting it . . . It is lawful – to kill Tories or open murderers, as devouring beasts.

> *Alexander Shields, A Hind Let Loose (17th century), Cameronian tract quoted in Gordon Donaldson, The Faith of the Scots (1990)*

114 The soul of man is like the rolling world,
One half in day, the other dipt in night;

The one has music and the flying cloud,
The other, silence and the wakeful stars.

> *Alexander Smith (1830–1867), Horton*

115 Covenanters. Hopeless cases committed to hopeless causes. Ten thousand martyrs, but no saints. The sad thing is, there's practically no point now in trying to explain what they fought and died for.

> *W. Gordon Smith, Mr Jock (1987)*

116 The Pope was Giovanni, good Pope John. The Moderator was the great Dr Archie Craig. He'd gone to Rome to support the ecumenical movement. They had a cordial meeting, but both men realised the way ahead was rocky. As Dr Craig rose to go, the Pope shook him warmly by the hand. 'Arrivederci, Erchie.' Dr Caig turns at the door, 'Aye, an ca' canny, Giovanni.'

> *W. Gordon Smith, Mr Jock*

117 Must we not go on and admit that there is something very congenial to Calvinism in the Scottish psyche?

> *William Soutar (1898–1943), Diaries of a Dying Man*

118 We have been making a tub these forty years, and now the bottom thereof is fallen out.

> *Archbishop Spottiswoode on the Covenant, 1636*

119 Thou knowest that the silly snivelling body is not worthy even to keep a door in thy house. Cut him down as a cumberer of the ground; tear him up root and branch, and cast the wild rotten stump out of thy vineyard. Thresh him, O Lord, and dinna spare! O thresh him tightly with the flail of thy wrath, and mak a strae wisp o' him to stap the mouth o' Hell.

> *A Seceder minister preaching on the minister of Symington, in Statistical Account of Scotland (1791–99), quoted in Agnes Mure Mackenzie, Scottish Pageant 1707–1802 (1950)*

120 A generous prayer is never presented in vain.

> *Robert Louis Stevenson (1850–1894), The Merry Men*

121 The day returns and brings us the petty round of irritating concerns and duties. Help us to play the man, help us to perform them with laughter and kind faces; let cheerfulness abound with industry. Give

us to go blithely on our business all this day, bring us to our resting beds weary and content and undishonoured, and grant us in the end the gift of sleep. Amen.

Robert Louis Stevenson, Prayer

122 Nae schauchlin' testimony here –
We were a' damned, an' that was clear.
I owned, wi' gratitude an' wonder,
He was a pleisure to sit under.

Robert Louis Stevenson, The Scotsman's Return from Abroad

123 Work as though work alone thy end would gain,
But pray to God as though all work were in vain.

Sir D'Arcy Wentworth Thompson (1860–1948), Sales Attici

124 God was the private property of a chosen few
Whose lives ran carefully and correctly to the grave.

Ruthven Todd (1914–1978), In Edinburgh

125 . . . he was the minister after their heart who possessed such signs of grace as Mr Alexander Dunlop, who was renowned and envied as the possessor of a 'holy groan'.

Lauchlan Maclean Watt, Scottish Life and Poetry *(1912)*

126 The Lord God is my Pastor gude,
Abundantlie for me to feid:
Then how can I be destitute
Of ony gude thing in my neid?

The brothers James, John and Robert Wedderburn (fl. 16th century), Psalm 23 from The Gude and Godlie Ballatis

127 John, cum kis me now,
John, cum kis me now,
John, cum kis me by and by,
And mak no moir ado.
The Lord thy God I am,
That John dois the call;
John representis man
By grace celestiall . . .

The brothers James, John and Robert Wedderburn, remaking of an old song into a Gude and Godlie Ballat

128 The Bischop wald not wed ane wife,
The Abbot not persew ane,

Think and it was ane lustie life
Ilk day to haif a new ane.

The brothers Wedderburn, from The Paip, That Pagan Full of Pryde

129 The Eleventh Commandment: Thou shalt not be found out.

George Whyte-Melville (1821–1878)

130 There is a happy land,
Far, far away,
Where saints in glory stand,
Bright, bright as day.

Andrew Young (1807–1889)

131 There is a happy land
Down in Duke Street Jail,
Where all the prisoners stand
Tied to a nail.

Children's burlesque of the preceding item

Rivers

1 Annan, Tweed and Clyde
Rise aa oot o' ane hillside;
Tweed ran, Annan wan,
Clyde fell, and brak its neck owre Corra Linn.

Traditional

2 O river Clyde, baith deep and wide,
Thy streams are wonder strang.
Make me thy wrack as I come back,
But spare me as I gang.

Traditional

3 Tweed says to Till,
What gars ye rin sae still?
Till says to Tweed,
Though ye rin fast, and I rin slaw,
For ae man that ye droon,
I droon twa.

Traditional

4 She's socht him high, she's socht him low,
She's socht him near and far, O;
Syne in the clifting of a craig,
She's found him droon'd in Yarrow.

Anonymous, Fair Willie Droon'd in Yarrow

5 Naething but a perfect waste o' watter.

Anonymous Paisley native, on seeing Niagara Falls

6 Music o' bonny Dee as't cantly rummles doon,

Purlin' wi' lauchter whiles; an' syne a
  froon;
Flirtin' in eddies, kissin' mossy stanes,
Skirlin' again like happy skule-free weans.
  Anonymous, quoted in W. T. Palmer,
  Wanderings in Scotland *(1949)*

7 . . . the infant spilth
Assumes a voice, and, gathering as it goes,
A runnel makes: how beautiful the green
Translucent lymph, crisp curling, purling
  o'er
The floating duckweed, lapsingly away!
  Thomas Aird (1802–1876), St Mary's
  Well

8 Flow gently, sweet Afton, amang thy
  green braes,
Flow gently: I'll sing thee a song in thy
  praise.
  Robert Burns (1759–1796), Flow Gently,
  Sweet Afton

9 The twinkling Earn, like a blade in the
  snow.
  John Davidson (1857–1909), Winter in
  Strathearn

10 Stone-rolling Tay, Tyne tortoise-like
  that flows,
The pearly Don, the Dee, the fertile Spey,
Wild Naver which doth see our longest
  day,
Ness, smoking sulphur, Leave with
  mountains crowned,
Lomond for his floating isles renowned,
The Irish Ryan, Ken, the silver Ayr,
The snaky Dun, the Ore with rushy hair,
The crystal-streaming Nidd, the
  bellowing Clyde
  William Drummond (1585–1649), River
  of Forth Feasting, *composed for King
  James VI's return visit to Scotland, 1617*

11 . . . the Luggie with a plaintive song
Twists thro' a glen of greenest gloom,
  and gropes
For open sunshine; and the shadows past,
Glides quicker-footed thro' divided
  meads
With sliding purl.
  David Gray (1838–1861), The Luggie

12 . . . to the westward is Tweed's Well, where
in a meadow the first fountain of silvery
Tweed rises from 'its own unseen unfailing
spring', still bubbling up through sand and
pebbles, but altered in shape from what it

was when as a lad Dr John Brown peered
into its depths and saw 'on a gentle swelling like a hill of pure white sand, a delicate
column, rising and falling and shifting
in graceful measures as if governed by a
music of its own'.
  *Hugh MacDiarmid (C. M. Grieve,
  1892–1978),* Lucky Poet

13 The Rosa . . . must surely be one of the
most pellucid streams in Britain. For the
most part it flows over sand and pale rock.
The trout that inhabit it are almost impossible to catch, for it is impossible, even
when the river is in spate, to hide from
them. They have acquired a pale, protective colouring and if one is lucky enough
to catch one, one can scarcely believe it is a
trout; for its back is the colour of the faintest gold.
  Moray McLaren, Arran, *in E. Molony,*
  Portraits of Islands *(1951)*

14 The sparkling Clyde
splashing its local sewage at the wall.
  Ian Crichton Smith (1928–1998), You
  Lived in Glasgow

15 Oh, the Tweed! the bonnie Tweed!
O' rivers it's the best;
Angle here, or angle there,
Troots are soomin' ilka where,
Angle east or west.
  Thomas Tod Stoddart (1810–1880)

16 All day I heard the water talk
From dripping rock to rock
And water in bright snowflakes scatter
On boulders of the dark Whitewater.
  Andrew Young (1807–1889), Loch
  Brandy

Science and the Scientific Approach

1 Operations were started by the purchase
of a tea chest, an old hat box, some darning
needles, and a bullseye lens from a local
shop, also a plentiful supply of sealing wax
and Seccotine glue.
  John Logie Baird (1888–1946), Sermons,
  Soap and Television

2 Science is of no party.
  A. J. Balfour (1848–1930), Politics and
  Political Economy

3   The scientific man is the only person who has anything new to say and who does not know how to say it.

>   *Sir J. M. Barrie (1867–1930)*

4   Millions, millions – did I say millions? Billions and trillions are more like the fact.
Millions, billions, trillions, quadrillions, Make the long sum of creation exact,

>   *J. S. Blackie (1809–1895)*, Song of Geology, *quoted in C. P. Finlayson, The Symposium Academicum, in G. Donaldson, Four Centuries: Edinburgh University Life (1983)*

5   He devoured every kind of learning. Not content with chemistry and natural philosophy, he studied anatomy, and was one day found carrying home for dissection the head of a child that had died of some hidden disorder.

>   *Lord Brougham (1778–1868)*, Lives of Men of Literature and Science in the Age of George III, *on James Watt (1736–1819)*

6   A trend is a trend is a trend, But the question is, will it bend? Will it alter its course Through some unforeseen force And come to a premature end?

>   *Sir Alexander Cairncross (1911–1998)*, Stein Age Forecaster, *in* Economic Journal, *1969*

7   The citizen is told that ignorance of the law is no excuse; ignorance of science should not be either.

>   *Ritchie Calder (1906–1982)*, Science Profiles

8   He ever loved the Mathematics, because he said even God Almighty works by geometry.

>   *S. R. Crockett (1859–1914)*, The Raiders

9   He had to an unusual degree the almost intuitive faculty for original investigation coupled with a high degree of technical inventiveness and skill. He had in fact most of the qualities that make a great scientist: an innate curiosity and perceptiveness regarding natural phenomena, insight into the heart of a problem, technical ingenuity, persistence in seeing the job through, and that physical and mental toughness that is essential to the top-class investigator.

>   *R. Cruickshank*, Journal of Pathology and Bacteriology, *1956, on Sir Alexander Fleming (1881–1955)*

10   'How often have I said to you that when you have eliminated the impossible, whatever remains, *however improbable*, must be the truth?'

>   *Sir Arthur Conan Doyle (1859–1930)*, The Sign of Four

11   'It is a capital mistake to theorise before one has data. Insensibly one begins to twist facts to suit theories, instead of theories to suit facts.'

>   *Sir Arthur Conan Doyle*, A Scandal in Bohemia

12   'Is there any other part to which you would wish to draw my attention?'
'To the curious incident of the dog in the night-time.'
'The dog did nothing in the night-time.'
'That was the curious incident,' remarked Sherlock Holmes.

>   *Sir Arthur Conan Doyle*, Silver Blaze

13   Since Maxwell's time, Physical Reality has been thought of as represented by continuous fields, governed by partial differential equations, and not capable of any mechanical interpretation. This change in the concept of Reality is the most profound and the most fruitful that physics has experienced since the time of Newton.

>   *Albert Einstein (1879–1955)*, *in* James Clerk Maxwell: A Commemorative Volume

14   It is the lone worker who makes the first advance in a subject: the details may be worked out by a team, but the prime idea is due to the enterprise, thought and perception of an individual.

>   *Sir Alexander Fleming (1881–1955)*, rectorial address to Edinburgh University, *1951*

15   There was a time, still within the memory of living men, when a handful of ardent original observers here in Edinburgh carried geological speculation and research to such a height as to found a new, and, in the end, a dominant school of Geology.

>   *Sir Archibald Geikie (1835–1924)*, The Scottish School of Geology

16 When the great English physicist Joule, who was one of Kelvin's staunch friends, was visiting his lordship's workshops, he came across a large coil of piano wire, and asked for what purpose it was to be used. When Kelvin replied it was for sounding, Joule asked, 'What note?' 'The deep C,' said Kelvin slyly, as it was for taking soundings in the ocean.

Charles Gibson, Heroes of Science *(1913), on Lord Kelvin (1824–1907)*

17 The Creator, if he exists, has a specific preference for beetles.

J. B. S. Haldane (1892–1964), Lecture, April 1951

18 No testimony is sufficient to establish a miracle, unless the testimony be of such a kind that its falsehood would be more miraculous than the fact which it endeavours to establish.

David Hume (1711–1776), An Enquiry Concerning Human Understanding

19 A bag of gravel is a history to me, and . . . will tell wondrous tales . . . mind, a bag of gravel is worth a bag of gold.

James Hutton (1726–1797)

20 No powers are to be employed which are not natural to the globe. no action to be admitted of except those of which we know the principle . . . Nor are we to proceed in feigning causes when those appear insufficient which occur in our experience.

James Hutton, Theory of the Earth

21 Maxwell, by a train of argument which seems to bear no relation at all to molecules, or to the dynamics of their movements, or to logic, or even to ordinary common sense, reached a formula which according to all precedents and all the rules of scientific philosophy, ought to have been hopelessly wrong. In actual fact it was subsequently shown to be exactly right.

Sir James Jeans, quoted in J. W. N. Sullivan, J. C. Maxwell, *in Massingham*, The Great Victorians, Vol. 1 *(1932)*

22 . . . when you can measure what you are speaking about, and express it in numbers, you know something about it.

Lord Kelvin (1824–1907), lecture to the Institution of Civil Engineers (1883)

23 When I say a few million, I must say at the same time, that I consider a hundred millions as being a few.

Lord Kelvin, On Geological Time

24 I was very anxious he should admire a beautiful picture of Glen Sannox, with mist resting among the mountains; but he remarked that it was an unfortunate time to choose, and the artist ought to have waited till the mist had cleared away, and all the outlines of the mountains were distinctly seen.

Agnes G. King, Kelvin the Man *(1925)*

25 Like any other martyr of science, I must expect to be thought importunate, tedious, and a fellow of one idea, and that idea wrong. To resent this would show great want of humour, and a plentiful lack of knowledge of human nature.

Andrew Lang (1844–1912), Magic and Religion

26 He clings to statistics as a drunken man clings to a lamp-post; for support rather than illumination.

Attributed to Andrew Lang, perhaps in conversation

27 We may anticipate with confidence that many edifices and implements of human workman-ship, and the skeletons of men, and casts of the human form, will continue to exist when the great part of the present mountains, continents and seas have disappeared.

Sir Charles Lyell (1797–1875), Principles of Geology *(1830–33)*

28 A million stars decide the place
Of any single star in space,
And though they draw it divers ways,
The star in steady orbit stays.

Ronald Campbell Macfie (1867–1931), A Moral

29 In every thought, in every part,
Made is he of a million slain,
Blood of the dead is in his heart,
Dreams of the dead are in his brain.

Ronald Campbell Macfie, Man in Evolution

30 Spawn was he in the steamy mire,
Fins he was in a primal sea,

Wings he was in the feathered choir,
Or ever he came a man to be.
   Ronald Campbell Macfie, War

31   Diffused knowledge immortalises itself.
       Sir James Mackintosh (1765–1832), Vin-
       diciae Gallicae

32   Never refuse to see what you do not want
       to see or what might go against your own
       cherished hypothesis or against the view
       of authorities. Here are just the clues to
       follow up . . . The thing you cannot get a
       pigeon-hole for is the finger-post showing
       the way to discovery.
       *Sir Patrick Manson (1844–1922), quoted
       in Philip Manson-Bahr*, Patrick Manson
       (1962)

33   I have made a tetrahedron, a dodecahe-
       dron, and two more hedrons that I don't
       know the right names for.
       *James Clerk Maxwell (1831–1879), letter
       to his father, June 1844*

34   Gin a body meet a body
       Flyin' through the air,
       Gin a body hit a body,
       Will it fly? and where?
       Ilka impact has its measure,
       Ne'er an ane hae I,
       Yet a' the lads they measure me,
       Or, at least, they try.
       James Clerk Maxwell, In Memory of
       Edward Wilson: Rigid Body (Sings)

35   I come from fields of fractured ice
       Whose wounds are cured by squeezing;
       Melting they cool, but in a trice
       Get warm again by freezing
       . . . I come from empyrean fires –
       From microscopic spaces,
       Where molecules with fierce desires
       Shiver in hot embraces.
       James Clerk Maxwell, To the Chief
       Musician Upon Nabla: A Tyndallic
       Ode

36   In fact, whenever energy is transmitted
       from one body to another in time, there
       must be a medium or substance in which
       the energy exists after it leaves one body
       and before it reaches the other.
       James Clerk Maxwell, Treatise of Elec-
       tricity and Magnetism

37   Each molecule therefore throughout the
       universe bears impressed upon it the stamp
       of a metric system as distinctly as does

the metre of the Archives at Paris, or
the double royal cubit of the temple of
Karnac.
   No theory of evolution can be formed
to account for the similarity of molecules,
for evolution necessarily implies continuous change, and the molecule is incapable
of growth or decay.
       James Clerk Maxwell, Discourse on
       Molecules

38   Dr Black dreaded nothing so much as error
       and Dr Hutton dreaded nothing so much
       as ignorance; the one was always afraid of
       going beyond the truth and the other of
       not reaching it.
       John Playfair (1748–1819), Life of
       Dr Hutton, *in* Transactions of the
       Royal Society of Edinburgh, *on Joseph
       Black and James Hutton*

39   I shall find out things, yes, yes!
       *Sir Ronald Ross (1857–1932), last words,
       quoted in John Carey*, The Faber Book
       of Science *(1995)*

40   I had the chloroform for several days in
       the house before trying it . . . The first
       night we took it Dr Duncan, Dr Keith and
       I all tried it simultaneously, and were all
       'under the table' in a minute or two.
       *Sir James Young Simpson (1811–1870),
       letter to Mr Waldie, November 1847*

41   Science is the great antidote to the poison
       of enthusiasms and superstition.
       Adam Smith (1723–1790), The Wealth
       of Nations

42   For the harmony of the world is made man-
       ifest in Form and Number, and the heart
       and soul and all the poetry of Natural Phi-
       losophy are embodied in the concept of
       mathematical beauty.
       *Sir D'Arcy Wentworth Thompson
       (1860–1948)*, Growth and Form *(edi-
       tion of 1942)*

43   I was thinking upon the engine at the
       time, and had gone as far as the Herd's
       house when the idea came into my mind,
       that as steam was an elastic body, it would
       rush into a vacuum, and if a communica-
       tion was made between the cylinder and an
       exhausted vessel, it would rush into it, and
       might there be condensed without cooling
       the cylinder.
       James Watt (1736–1819), quoted in H. W.

Dickinson, James Watt, Craftsman and Engineer *(1935), evolving the thought of the steam condenser*

44 The point is to establish that I was the inventor that the invention was perfect as to the *saving steam and fuel* at the time of the patent 1769 . . . I did not invent this method piecemeal but all at once in a few hours in as 1765 I believe.

> *James Watt, letter to John Robison, October 1796*

The Sea and Seafaring

1 The waves have some mercy, but the rocks have no mercy at all.

> *Gaelic Proverb*

2 Than ane of the marinalis began to haul and to cry, and al the marinalis answeirit of that samyn sound.
Hou hou, hou hou,
Pull weill a', pull weill a',
Bollein a', bollein a'.
Dart a', dart a',
Hard out steif, hard out steif,
Afoir the wind, afoir the wind,
God send, send
Fair wethir, fair wethir,
Monie prisis, monie prisis,
Guid foirland, guid foirland,
Stow, stow, stow, stow,
Make fast and belay

> *Anonymous, from* The Complaynt of Scotland *(1549), a hauling shanty*

3 Along the quay at Peterhead the lasses stand around,
With their shawls all pulled about them and the salt tears running down;
Don't you weep, my bonny lasses, though you be left behind,
For the rose will grow in Greenland's ice before we change our mind.
So it's cheer up, my lads,
Let your hearts never fail,
As the bonnie ship the *Diamond*
Goes a-fishing for the whale.

> *Traditional,* The Bonnie Ship, the Diamond *(19th century)*

4 Into the pit-mirk nicht we northwart sail
Facin the bleffarts and the gurly seas.

> *J. K. Annand (1908–1993),* Arctic Convoy

5 In the bay the waves pursued their indifferent dances.

> *George Mackay Brown (1921–1996),* A Winter Bride

6 The boats drove furrows homeward, like ploughmen
In blizzards of gulls.

> *George Mackay Brown,* Hamnavoe

7 A wet sheet and a flowing sea,
A wind that follows fast,
And fills the white and rustling sail,
And bends the gallant mast.

> *Allan Cunningham (1791–1839),* A Wet Sheet and a Flowing Sea

8 . . . the sea's horizon soars into the firmament.

> *Norman Douglas (1868–1952),* Siren Land

9 O weel may the boatie row,
That fills a heavy creel,
And cleads us a' frae head to feet,
And buys our parritch meal.

> *John Ewen (1741–1821),* O Weel May the Boatie Row

10 I cast my line in Largo Bay,
And fishes I caught nine,
'Twas three to boil and three to fry,
And three to bait the line.

> *John Ewen,* O Weel May the Boatie Row

11 A hunder year sin syne
Shetland men sailed der smacks
Nort to da Faroe bank.
Dere dey shot der lang-lines
Deep i da green dyoob,
Doon amang da steedin cod.
Da mirl an da yark on da line
Liftet der herts as dey haeled –
'Licht i da lum,'
'White upo white,'
Owre da heildin gunnel
Dey cam sprikklin.

> *John Graham,* Jakobsen *(1936)*

12 Over the gunwale over into our deep lap
The herring come in, staring from their scales.

> *W. S. Graham (1917–1986),* The Nightfishing

13 They forgot all about the ship; they forgot everything, except the herrings, the lithe silver fish, the swift flashing ones, hun-

dreds and thousands of them, the silver darlings.

> *Neil Gunn (1891–1973)*, The Silver Darlings

14 In and out of the bay hesitates the Atlantic.

> *Norman MacCaig (1910–1996)*, Neglected Graveyard, Luskentyre

15 The sea-shell wants to whisper to you.

> *George Macdonald (1824–1905)*, Summer Song

16 The tide was dark and heavy with the burthen that it bore.
   I heard it talkin', whisperin', upon the weedy shore.

> *Fiona MacLeod (William Sharp,1855–1905)*, The Burthen of the Tide

17 The wild sea-weed went moaning, sooing, moaning o'er and o'er.
   The deep sea-heart was brooding deep upon its ancient lore,
   I heard a sob, the sooing sob, the dying sob at its core.

> *Fiona Macleod*, The Burthen of the Tide

18 At mouth of day,
   The hour of buds,
   Stood Columba
   On the great white strand:
   'O King of Storms,
   Home sail the boat
   From far away:
   Thou King on High,
   Home sail the boat!'

> *Kenneth Macleod (1871–1955)*, A Blessing on the Boat

19 Sore sea-longing in my heart,
   Blue deep Barra waves are calling;
   Sore sea-longing in my heart.

> *Kenneth Macleod*, Sea-Longing

20 Perhaps other seas have voices for other folk, but the western sea alone can speak in the Gaelic tongue and reach the Gaelic heart.

> *Kenneth Macleod, Introduction to Marjory Kennedy-Fraser*, Songs of the Hebrides

21 What care we though white the Minch is?
   What care we for wind or weather?

Let her go, boys! Every inch is
Wearing home, home to Mingulay.

> *Sir Hugh S. Roberton (1874–1952)*, The Mingulay Boat Song

22 No pipes or drum to cheer them on
   When siccar work to do:
   'Tis the music of the tempest's song
   Leads on the lifeboat crew.

> *R. Robertson*, The Aith Hope Lifeboat Crew *(1899)*

23 Alang the shore
   The greinan white sea-owsen ramp and roar.

> *Tom Scott (1918–1995)*, Auld Sanct-Aundrians

24 It's no fish ye're buying: it's men's lives.

> *Sir Walter Scott (1771–1832)*

25 Farewell, merry maidens, to song, and to laugh,
   For the brave lads of Westra are bound to the Haaf;
   And we must have labour, and hunger, and pain,
   Ere we dance with the maids of Dunrossness again.

> *Sir Walter Scott*, Song of the Zetland Fishermen

26 Vague wishless seaweed floating on a tide.

> *Iain Crichton Smith (1928–)*, Old Woman

27 . . . my kinsmen and my countrymen,
   Who early and late in the windy ocean toiled
   To plant a star for seamen.

> *Robert Louis Stevenson (1850–1894)*, Skerryvore, *on the lighthouse-builders*

Seasons, Wind and Weather

1 'I will go tomorrow,' said the king.
   'You will wait for me,' said the wind.
   Gaelic Proverb

2 Perhaps the Moon is shining for you
   In the far country –
   But the skies there are not island skies;
   You will not remember the salt smell of the sea,
   And the little rain.

> *Anonymous*, Island Moon, *from Gaelic*

3 You journey on your course, you steer the
flood-tides, you light up your face, new
moon of the seasons.

　　Queen of guidance, queen of good luck,
queen of my love, new moon of the
seasons!

　　*Gaelic folk prayer, translated by Kenneth
　　Jackson*

4 Be it wind, be it weet, be it hail, be it sleet,
Our ship maun sail the faem.

　　Anonymous, Sir Patrick Spens

5 They hadna sailed a league, a league,
A league but barely three,
When the lift grew dark, and the wind
　　blew loud,
And gurly grew the sea.

　　Anonymous, Sir Patrick Spens

6 West wind to the bairn
When ga'an for its name;
And rain to to the corpse
Carried to its lang hame.
A bonny blue sky
To welcome the bride
As she gangs to the kirk
Wi' the sun on her side.

　　Traditional

7 Though raging storms movis us to shake,
And wind makis waters overflow;
We yield thereto bot dois not break
And in the calm bent up we grow.

　　Anonymous, The Reeds in the Loch
　　Sayis, *from the Maitland Manuscript,
　　quoted in M. M. Gray*, Scottish Poetry
　　from Barbour to James VI *(1935)*

8 There were twa doos sat in a dookit,
The rain cam' doun and they were
　　drookit.

　　*Traditional nursery song, quoted in
　　Charles Mackay (1814–1889)*, Poetry
　　and Humour of the Scottish Language

9 It's dowie in the hint o' hairst,
At the wa-gang o' the swallow,
When the win' grows cauld, and the
　　burns grow bauld,
And the wuds are hingin' yellow.

　　Hew Ainslie (1792–1877), The Hint o'
　　Hairst

10 And saftly, saftly, ower the hill,
Comes the sma', sma' rain.

　　Marion Angus (1886–1946), The Lilt

11 'And besides, the winters here aren't winters,' said Moss. 'Not compared to Russia.
In fact, if you dress warmly enough, you
can manage without lighting a fire from
one end of the year to the other. The
important thing is the underwear.'

　　Chaim Bermant (1929–1998), The
　　Patriarch

12 James Payn, who settled there in 1858 as
editor of *Chambers's Journal*, made as much
ado about its east wind as he did about
the Edinburgh Sunday. In vain Robert
Chambers assured him that the same isothermal band passed through Edinburgh
and London.

　　'I know nothing about isothermal bands,'
was Payn's reply, 'but I know I never saw
a four-wheeled cab blown upside-down in
London.'

　　James Bone, The Perambulator in Edin-
　　burgh *(1926)*

13 'Thu'll be shoors, lang-tailed shoors, an'
rain a' 'tween, an' it'll ettle tae plump; but
thu'll no be a wacht o' weet.'

　　*Border farmer's weather forecast, quoted
　　by J. Brown in W. Knight*, Some Nine-
　　teenth-Century Scotsmen *(1903)*

14 . . . nowadays, we say 'it rains'. The old
Orkneymen had a range of words for every
kind and intensity of rain – a driv, a rug, a
murr, a hagger, a dagg, a rav, a hellyiefer.

　　George Mackay Brown (1921–1996), An
　　Orkney Tapestry

15 In the north, on a showery day, you can
see the rain, its lovely behaviour over an
island – while you stand a mile off in a
patch of sun.

　　George Mackay Brown, An Orkney
　　Tapestry

16 Of a' the airts the wind can blaw,
I dearly like the west,
For there the bonnie lassie lives,
The lassie I lo'e best.

　　Robert Burns (1759–1796), Of A' the
　　Airts the Wind Can Blaw

17 O wert thou in the cauld blast,
On yonder lea, on yonder lea,
My plaidie to the angry airt,
I'd shelter thee, I'd shelter thee.

　　Robert Burns, O Wert Thou in the
　　Cauld Blast

18 . . . yellow Autumn, wreath'd with nodding corn.

> *Robert Burns,* The Brigs of Ayr

19 And bleak December's winds ensuin',
Baith snell an' keen!

> *Robert Burns,* To a Mouse

20 And weary winter comin' fast.

> *Robert Burns,* To a Mouse

21 The win' blaws oot o' Orkney
A winter month or twa,
An' rievin' ower the Moray Firth
It lifts the gangrel snaw,
An' sets it doon on Badenoch
A hunder mile awa.

> *William Moir Calder (b.1881),* Moray Sang

22 Would ye partake of harvest's joys,
The corn must be sown in Spring.

> *Thomas Carlyle (1795–1881),* The Sower's Song

23 Arthur o' Bower has broken his bands,
And he's come roaring owre the lands;
The king o' Scots, and a' his power
Canna turn Arthur o' Bower.

> *Chambers'* Popular Rhymes *(1841), on the wind*

24 Is there any light quite like the June sun of the North and West? It takes trouble out of the world.

> *Sir Frank Fraser Darling (1903–1979),* Island Days

25 On window-sill and door-post,
On rail and tramway rust,
Embroidery of hoar-frost
Was sown like diamond dust.

> *John Davidson (1857–1909),* A Frosty Morning

26 The licht begouth to quinkle out and fail,
The day to darken, decline and devaill . . .
Up goes the bat, with her pelit leathern flycht,
The lark descendis from the skyis hycht
Singand her complin song efter her guise.

> *Gavin Douglas (1475–1522),* Prologue to the Aeneid, *on a June Evening*

27 The rage and storm our welter and wally seas,

Riveris ran reid on spate with water broun,
And burnis hurlis all their bankis doun

> *Gavin Douglas,* Prologue to the Aeneid, *on Winter*

28 In this congealit season sharp and chill,
The caller air penetrative and pure,
Dazing the blood in every creature.

> *Gavin Douglas,* Prologue to the Aeneid, *on Winter*

29 In to thir dark and drublie dayis
Whone sabill all the Hevin arrayis,
With mystie vapouris, cluddis and skyis,
Nature all curage me denyis.

> *William Dunbar (c.1460–c.1520),* Meditation in Winter

30 For mirth of May, wyth skippis and wyth hoppis
The birdis sang upon the tender croppis,
With curiouse note, as Venus chapell-clerkis.

> *William Dunbar,* The Golden Targe

31 Lusty May, that moder is of flouris.

> *William Dunbar,* The Thistle and the Rose

32 Snow is its own country.

> *Douglas Dunn (1942–),* Snow Days

33 Now mirk December's dowie face
Glow'rs owre the rigs wi' sour grimace.

> *Robert Fergusson (1750–1774),* The Daft Days

34 The rain falling Scotchly, Scotchly.

> *Ian Hamilton Finlay (1925–),* Black Tomintoul

35 St Kilda is a home of clouds: it is a cloud-maker, in a part of the Atlantic where there is plenty of material to make clouds from. Soay and Hirta and Boreray comb and rake the sky with their rugged fangs, and the weather spills out of it. On a fine day they have crowns of cloud, blowing away with the wind, and making as they blow . . . When Boreray makes dark clouds it looks like a smoking anvil.

> *James Fisher,* St Kilda, *in E. Molony,* Portraits of Islands *(1951)*

36 She was a dour bitch o' a back-end, yon.

> *Flora Garry,* Ae Mair Hairst, *quoted in D. K. Cameron,* Cornkister Days *(1984)*

37 My words go through the smoking air
Changing their tune on silence.
W. S. Graham (1918–1986), Malcolm
Mooney's Land

38 Tangled woods and hawthorn dale
In many a songful snatch prevail;
But never yet, as well I mind,
In all their verses can I find
A simple tune, with quiet flow,
To match the falling of the snow.
David Gray (1838–1861), The Luggie

39 This, I suppose, was a genuine scotch mist;
and as such it is well enough to have experienced it, though I would willingly never
see it again.
Nathaniel Hawthorne (1804–1864)

40 Cold is the wind over Islay
that blows on them in Kintyre.
George Campbell Hay (1915–1984),
Meftah baktum es-sabar

41 The northern wind had purifyit the air,
And shed the misty cloudis fra the sky
Robert Henryson (c.1425–c.1500), The
Testament of Cresseid

42 I' the back end o' the year,
When the clouds hang laigh wi' the
weicht o' their greetin'.
Violet Jacob (1863–1946), Craigo
Woods

43 . . . the shilpit sun is thin
Like an auld man deein' slow.
Violet Jacob, The Rowan

44 . . . creeping over Rannoch, while the
God of moorland
walks abroad with his entourage of
freezing fog,
his bodyguard of snow.
Kathleen Jamie (1962–), The Way We
Live

45 The world's a bear shrugged in his den.
It's snug and close in the snoring night.
And outside like chrysanthemums
The fog unfolds its bitter scent.
Norman McCaig (1910–1996), Novem-
ber Night, Edinburgh

46 I hear the little children of the wind
Crying solitary in lonely places.
*Fiona MacLeod (William Sharp,
1856–1905)*, Little Children of the
Wind

47 In a Gaelic story or poem-saga clouds are
called 'The Homeless Clan'. But they are
not homeless whom the great winds of the
upper world eternally shepherd, who have
their mortal hour in beauty and strength
and force, and, instead of the graves and
secret places of the earth, know a divine
perpetual renewal.
Fiona MacLeod, quoted in W. T. Palmer,
Wanderings in Scotland (1949)

48 Now skaills the skyis
The night is neir gone.
Alexander Montgomerie (c.1545 -c.1610),

49 Mournfully, oh, mournfully,
The midnight wind doth sigh.
William Motherwell (1797–1835), The
Midnight Wind

50 Oh, the blessed enchantment of these Saturday runaways in the prime of the spring!
How our young wondering eyes reveled in
the sunny, breezy glories of the hills and
the sky, every particle of us thrilling and
tingling with the bees and the glad birds
and glad streams.
John Muir (1838–1913), The Story of
My Boyhood and Youth

51 Father called us out into the yard in
front of the house where we had a wide
view, crying, 'Come! Come, mother; come,
bairns! And see the glory of God! All the
sky is clad in a robe of red light. Look
straight up to the crown where the folds
are gathered. Hush and wonder and adore,
for surely this is the clothing of the Lord
himself.'
*John Muir, The Story of My Boyhood
and Youth, on the spectacle of the Aurora
Borealis, in Wisconsin*

52 Storms are never counted among the
resources of a country, yet how far they go
towards making brave people.
John Muir, from L. M. Wolfe, John
of the Mountains: The Unpublished
Journals of John Muir (1938)

53 We lost no time in getting out, to see,
amidst the flying shower and broken moonlight, the wraith of a rainbow hanging
frost-white, melting as we gazed . . .
Peering into the shower, we saw nothing
more . . . Then, as it drew away all at once

the great white bow sprang out against it,
so near it arched the croft.

> *Amy Murray*, Father Allan's Island
> (1936)

54 Noo that cauldrife Winter's here
There's a pig in ilka bed . . .
Doddy mittens we maun wear,
Butter skites an' winna spread.

> *Charles Murray (1864–1941)*, Winter

55 The thunder crack'd, and flauchts did rift
Frae the black vizard o' the lift.

> *Allan Ramsay (1686–1758)*, The Vision

56 Butter, new cheese, and beer in May,
Comamis, cokkilis, curds and whey,
Lapstaris, limpettis, mussellis in shells.

> *Alexander Scott (c.1520–c.1590)*, Of May

57 And wind, that grand old harper, smote
His thunder-harp of pines.

> *Alexander Smith (1830–1867)*, A Life
> Drama

58 In their wrack the brackens lie
Black whaur they fell:
Thereis nae mair to tell:
Summer is by.

> *William Soutar (1898–1943)*, Summer
> is By *(from the Irish)*

59 Silence is in the air:
The stars move to their places.
Silent and serene the stars move to their
places.

> *William Soutar*, The Children

60 It was a glorious October day; the light had
that angelic radiance of a Scottish autumn
and its tingling freshness, so welcome to
people who enjoy feeling cold, as the Scots
often do.

> *William Soutar*, Symposium

61 Autumnal frosts enchant the pool
And make the cart-ruts beautiful.

> *Robert Louis Stevenson (1850–1894)*,
> The House Beautiful

62 Wee Davie Daylicht keeks owre the sea,
Early in the mornin', wi' a clear e'e;
Waukens all the birdies that are sleepin'
soun':
Wee Davie Daylicht is nae lazy loon.

> *Robert Tennant (1830–1879)*, Wee
> Davie Daylicht

63 A fresher gale
Begins to wave the wood and stir
the stream,
Sweeping with shadowy gust the fields
of corn,
While the quail clamours for his running
mate.

> *James Thomson (1700–1748)*, The
> Seasons

64 Through the hushed air the whitening
shower descends,
At first thin-wavering; till at last the
flakes
Fall broad and wide and fast, dimming
the day
With a continual flow.

> *James Thomson*, The Seasons

65 . . . As to my childhood's sight
A midway station given
For happy spirits to alight,
Betwixt the earth and heaven.

> *James Thomson*, To the Rainbow

66 O mither, John Frost cam' yestreen,
And owre a' the garden he's been,
He's on the kail-stocks,
And my twa printed frocks,
That Mary left out on the green.

> *David Wingate (fl. 19th century)*, John
> Frost

67 And long wan bubbles groped
Under the ice's cover,
A bridge that groaned as I crossed over.

> *Andrew Young (1885–1971)*, The
> Mountain

The Spirit of Scotland

1 My son, I tell thee truthfully,
No good is like to liberty
Then never live in slavery.

> *Traditional, dictum ascribed to William
> Wallace (c.1270–1305)*

2 But after all, if the prince shall leave these
principles he hath so nobly pursued, and
consent that we or our kingdon be subjected to the king or people of England, we
will immediately endeavour to expel him
as our enemy, and as the subverter both
of his own and our rights, and will make
another king who will defend our liberties.
For as long as there shall but one hundred

of us remain alive, we will never consent
to subject ourselves to the dominion of the
English. For it is not glory, it is not riches,
neither is it honour, but it is liberty alone
that we fight and contend for, which no
honest man will lose but with his life.

*The Declaration of Arbroath, 1320, from
Latin*

3 From the lone sheiling on the misty island
Mountains divide us, and a waste of seas –
Yet still the blood is true, the heart is
   Highland,
And we in dreams behold the Hebrides.

Anonymous, Canadian Boat Song

4 For we have three great advantages;
The first is, we have the richt,
And for the richt ilk man suld ficht,
The tother is, they are comin here . . .
To seek us in our awn land . . .
The thrid is that we for our livis
And for our childer and our wifis
And for the fredome of our land
Are strenyeit in battle for to stand.

John Barbour (c.1320–1395), The Brus

5 A! fredome is a noble thing!
Fredome maiss man to haif liking:
Fredome all solace to man giffis,
He levis at ease that freely levis!
A noble heart may haif nane ease,
Nae ellis nocht that may him please,
Gif fredome failye

John Barbour, The Brus

6 'Gude king, forouten mair delay,
To-morn, as soon as ye see day,
Ordain you haill for the battaile,
For doubt of deid we sall not fail,
Na nane pain sall refusit be
Till we have made our country free.'

John Barbour, The Brus, *describing the
eve of the Battle of Bannockburn, June
1314*

7 A people that might match the world for
energy, and who have heretofore stood in
the first rank of nations, sinking under
a combination of increasing evils – the
efforts of ministers paralysed – our universities locked up, dwarfed, and comparatively
inefficient – crime increasing – drunkenness and Sabbath-breaking making
progress . . . the Parliament of England

despising us, our natural guardians join-
ing in the oppression.

James Begg, National Education for
Scotland Practically Considered *(1850)*

8 My Lords, patricide is a greater crime than
parricide, all the world over.

*Lord Belhaven (1656–1708), speech in
Parliament, 1706*

9 None can destroy Scotland, save Scotland's
self.

*Lord Belhaven, speech in Parliament, the
Union Debate,1706*

10 She's a puir auld wife wi' little to give,
And rather stint o' caressin';
But she's shown us how honest lives we
   may live,
And sent us out wi' her blessin'.

William Black (1841–1898), Shouther
to Shouther

11 I am by birth a *North Briton*, as a *Scotchman*
must now be called.

James Boswell, Letter to the Public
Advertiser, *April 1779*

12 And for my dear lov'd Land o' Cakes,
I pray with holy fire:
Lord, send a rough-shod troop o' Hell
O'er a' wad Scotland buy or sell,
To grind them in the mire!

Robert Burns (1759–1796), Election
Ballad

13 Auld Scotland has a raucle tongue;
She's just a devil wi' a rung;
An' if she promise auld or young
To tak their part,
Tho' by the neck she would be strung,
She'll no desert.

Robert Burns, The Author's Earnest
Cry and Prayer to the Right Honourable and the Honourable, the
Scotch Representatives in the House
of Commons

14 . . . the story of Wallace poured a Scottish
prejudice in my veins which will boil along
there till the floodgates of life shut in eternal rest.

*Robert Burns, letter to Dr John Moore,
August 1787*

15 And though, as you remember, in a fit
Of wrath and rhyme, when juvenile and
   curly,
I rail'd at Scots to show my wrath and wit,

Which must be own'd was sensitive and
surly,
Yet 'tis in vain such sallies to permit,
They cannot quench young feelings fresh
and early:
I 'scotch'd not kill'd' the Scotchman in my
blood,
And love the land of 'mountain and of
flood'.

> *Lord Byron (1788–1824), Don Juan*

16 This is where the children of honest
poverty have the most precious of all advantages over those of wealth. The mother,
nurse, cook, governess, teacher, saint, all
in one; the father, exemplar, guide, counsellor and friend! Thus were my brother
and I brought up. What has the child of
millionaire or nobleman that counts compared to such a heritage?

> *Andrew Carnegie (1835–1918),*
> *Autobiography*

17 Land of polluted river,
Bloodshot eyes and sodden liver
Land of my heart forever
Scotland the Brave.

> *Billy Connolly (1942–), quoted in*
> *Jonathan Margolis, The Big Yin (1994)*

18 At the first performance of *Douglas*, when
young Norval was busy giving out one
of his rodomontading speeches, a canny
Scot, who had been observed to grow more
and more excited as the piece progressed,
unable to contain his feelings, called out
with evident pride, 'Whaur's yer Wully
Shakespeare noo!'

> *James C. Dibdin, Annals of the Edin-*
> *burgh Stage (1888), referring to Home's*
> *play, performed in Edinburgh in Decem-*
> *ber 1756*

19 In the garb of old Gaul, wi' the fire of
old Rome,
From the heath-covered mountains of
Scotia we come.

> *Henry Erskine (1720–1765), In the*
> *Garb of Old Gaul*

20 The Scots deserve no pity, if they voluntarily surrender their united and separate
interests to the Mercy of an united Parliament, where the English have so vast a
Majority.

> *Andrew Fletcher of Saltoun (1656–1716),*
> *State of the Controversy Betwixt*
> *United and Separate Parliaments*
> *(1706)*

21 It is only fit for the slaves who sold it.

> *Andrew Fletcher of Saltoun, quoted in*
> *G. W. T. Ormond, Fletcher of Saltoun*
> *(1897), on Scotland after the Union*

22 Lord have mercy on my poor country, that
is so barbarously oppressed.

> *Andrew Fletcher of Saltoun, dying words*
> *as quoted by his nephew, Andrew Fletcher,*
> *in a letter to Henry Fletcher, September*
> *1716*

23 The world is neither Scottish, English, nor
Irish, neither French, Dutch nor Chinese,
but *human*, and each nation is only the
partial development of a universal humanity . . . England will not be better by
becoming French, or German, or Scottish,
but by becoming more truly and more
nobly English; and Scotland will never be
improved by being transformed into an
inferior imitation of England, but by being
made a better and truer Scotland.

> *James Grant (1822–1887), Report of*
> *the Society for Vindication of Scottish*
> *Rights (1852)*

24 It grows near the seashore, on banks, in
clefts, but above all on the little green
braes bordered with hazel-woods. It rarely
reaches more than two feet in height, is
neither white nor cream so much as old
ivory; unassuming, modest, and known as
the white rose of Scotland.

> *Neil Gunn (1891–1973), Highland Pack*

25 Forty-eight Scottish kings buried in this
tumbled graveyard – *before* the Norman
conquest of England in 1066. And today
should a man be bold enough to refer to
the Scottish nation, he is looked upon as a
bit of a crank.

> *Neil Gunn, Off in a Boat*

26 The small nation has always been humanity's last bulwark for the individual against
that machine, for personal expression
against impersonal tyranny, for the quick
freedom of the spirit against the flattening
steamroller of the mass.

> *Neil Gunn, Nationalism and Interna-*
> *tionalism, from A. McCleery, Land-*
> *scape and Light (1987)*

27 So many Scots, forgetting that one of the
great features of our history is the mobil-

ity between classes, have lapsed into the English habit of thought best expressed in the words, 'I wouldn't presume. I hope I know my place.' I always presume. I have never known my place.

> *Ian Hamilton (1925–), quoted in Ludovic Kennedy,* In Bed With an Elephant *(1995), on his part in the removal of the Stone of Destiny from Westminster Abbey in 1950*

28 Towering in gallant fame,
Scotland, my mountain hame –
High may your proud banners gloriously wave!

> *Cliff Hanley (1922–1999),* Scotland the Brave

29 In a Scotch village, and still more in these lonely clachans which defy the tempests of the Atlantic, there is no sense whatsoever of obedience to authority as such.

> *W. R. Lawson,* The Poetry and Prose of the Crofter Question, *from* National Review *(1885)*

30 ... swordless Scotland, sadder than its psalms,
Fosters its sober youth on national alms
To breed a dull provincial discipline,
Commerce its god, and golf its anodyne.

> *Eric Linklater (1899–1974), quoted in Hugh MacDiarmid (1892–1978),* Lucky Poet

31 It is now the duty of the Scottish genius
Which has provided the economic freedom for it
To lead in the abandonment of creeds and moral compromises
Of every sort.

> *Hugh MacDiarmid (1892–1978),* Stony Limits and Other Poems

32 He canna Scotland see wha yet
Canna see the Infinite,
And Scotland in true scale to it.

> *Hugh MacDiarmid,* A Drunk Man Looks at the Thistle

33 ... the rouch dirl o' an auld Scots strain,
– A dour dark burn that has its ain wild say
Thro' a' the thrang bricht babble o' Earth's flood.

> *Hugh MacDiarmid,* Gairmscoile

34 Above all, it must be remembered that the Scottish spirit is in general brilliantly improvisatory.

> *Hugh MacDiarmid,* Scottish Eccentrics

35 It has suffered in the past, and is suffering now, from too much England.

> *A. G. Macdonell (1895–1941),* My Scotland

36 So if ever ye come on a Stane wi' a ring
Just sit yersel' doon and proclaim yersel' King.
For there's nane wid be able tae challenge yer claim
That ye'd crowned yersel' King on the Destiny Stane.

> *Johnny McEvoy,* The Wee Magic Stane *(1951)*

37 ... the little band striving
When giving in would be good sense.

> *Sorley Maclean (1911–1996),* A Poem Made When the Gaelic Society of Inverness Was 100 Years Old

38 No other country has fallen so hard for its own image in the funfair mirror. Tartan rock, and a Scottie dog for every pot.

> *Candia MacWilliam (1957–),* A Case of Knives

39 Fecht for Britain? Hoot, awa!
For Bonnie Scotland? Imph, man, na!
For Lochnagar? Wi' clook and claw!

> *J. C. Milne, quoted in H. Brown,* Poems of the Scottish Hills *(1982)*

40 It seems to me you are bound to assume that a self-governing Scotland is going to be immediately morally better, and I don't see it *unless there has also been a revolution.* I can't see how the people who are likely to govern Scotland under any democratic system are going to be any different from the undoubted Scots who are in positions of local power.

> *Naomi Mitchison (1897–1998), letter to Roland Muirhead, 1953*

41 Must we be thirled to the past,
To the mist and the unused shieling?
Over love and home and the Forty-Five,
Sham tunes and a sham feeling?

> *Naomi Mitchison,* The Cleansing of the Knife

42 The Thistle, Scotland's badge,
Up from Freedom's soil it grew,

Her foes aye found it hedged round
With rosemarie and rue.

> *David Macbeth Moir (1798–1851)*, The
> Blue Bell of Scotland

43 When a man was convinced that his language was a barbarism, his lore was filthy
rags, and that the only good thing about
him – his land – was, because of his general worthlessness, to go to a man of
another race and anotheer tongue, what
remained . . . that he should fight for?

> *John Murdoch, in evidence to the Napier
> Commission, 1884, from James Hunter,*
> For the People's Cause: From the Writ-
> ings of John Murdoch *(1986)*

44 Though thirty thousand pounds they gie,
There is nane that wad betray.

> *Lady Nairne (1766–1845)*, Will Ye No
> Come Back Again

45 We can't for a certainty tell
What mirth may molest us on Monday,
But at least to begin the week well,
We can all be unhappy on Sunday.

> *Lord Neaves (1800–1876)*, Songs and
> Verses

46 Of Scotland's king I haud my hoose,
He pays me meat and fee;
And I will keep my gude auld hoose,
While my hoose will keep me.

> *Attributed to 'Black' Agnes Randolph,
> Countess of March (fl. 14th century), to
> the besiegers of Dunbar Castle*

47 The solitudes of land and sea assuage
My quenchless thirst for freedom
     unconfined;
With independent heart and mind
Hold I my heritage.

> *Robert Rendall (1898–1964)*, Orkney
> Crofter

48 There is a storm coming that shall try your
foundations. Scotland must be rid of Scotland before the delivery come.

> *James Renwick (1662–1688), Camero-
> nian leader, at his execution*

49 If we don't have some self-respect we
Might as well be in the ground
If we've got nothin' else at least
We've got our pride.

> *Tony Roper*, Pride, *from* The Steamie
> *(1987)*

50 Hou sall aa the folk I've been ere meet
And bide in yae wee house?
Knox wi' Burns and Mary, Wishart and
     Beaton
Aa be snod and crouse?
Campbell and MacDonald be guid feirs,
The Bruis sup wi Comyn?
By God, I dout afore sic love appears,
Nae man sall kiss a woman!

> *Tom Scott (1918–1995)*, Fergus

51 Front, flank and rear, the squadrons
     sweep
To break the Scottish circle deep,
That fought around their king . . .
The stubborn spearmen still made good
Their dark impenetrable wood,
Each stepping where his comrade stood,
The instant that he fell.

> *Sir Walter Scott (1771–1832)*, Marmion

52 Breathes there the man with soul so dead
Who never to himself hath said,
This is my own, my native land!

> *Sir Walter Scott* , The Lay of the Last
> Minstrel

53 O Caledonia! stern and wild,
Meet nurse for a poetic child!
Land of brown heath and shaggy wood;
Land of the mountain and the flood!

> *Sir Walter Scott*, The Lay of the Last
> Minstrel

54 Mons Meg is a monument of our pride
and poverty. The size is immense, but six
smaller guns would have been made at the
same expense, and done six times as much
execution as she could have done.

> *Sir Walter Scott*, Journal, *March 1829*

55 Resentment of my country's fate
Within my filial breast shall beat;
And, spite of the insulting foe,
My sympathising verse shall flow,
'Mourn, hapless Caledonia, mourn
Thy banish'd peace, thy laurels torn.'

> *Tobias Smollett (1721–1771)*, The Tears
> of Scotland

56 Return to your friends, and tell them that
we came with no peaceful intent, but ready
for battle, and determined to avenge our
own wrongs and set our country free. Let
your masters come and attack us; we are
ready to meet them beard to beard.

> *Sir William Wallace (c.1270–1305),
> attributed saying to mediators before the*

Battle of Stirling Brig (11 September 1297), quoted in C. Stewart Black, Scottish Battles *(1936)*

57 I resolved to spare no strain to drive out of this kingdom every single Englishman; and had I not been met at every turn by the opposition of our nobles, 'tis beyond a doubt that I would have done it.

Sir William Wallace, attributed saying to Robert Bruce in John Major (1469–1550), Historia Majoris Britanniae, *translated from Latin*

58 . . . my young nephew Patrick, the taciturn Scot of all the Scots; he who, at the age of three, held up before a mirror by his grandmother and asked by her, 'Wha's that?' had lived up to the highest tradition of the Scots by his riposte, 'Wha wad it be?'

Sir Robert Watson-Watt (1892–1973), Three Steps to Victory

59 O Flower of Scotland
When will we see your like again?
That fought and died for
Your wee bit hill and glen . . .
These days are past now
And in the past they must run,
But we can still rise now,
And be a nation again.

Ronald Williamson, The Flower of Scotland *(1969)*

60 The Scottish spirit abhors standardisation.

Douglas Young (1913–1973), Introduction to *Scottish Verse 1851–1951*

Sports and Pastimes

1 Brissit brawnis and broken banis,
Stride, discord, and waistie wanis;
Crukit in eild, syne halt withal –
Thir are the bewties of the fute-ball.

Anonymous, The Bewties of the Fute-Ball

2 The Scots invented golf, it's said,
And also good malt whisky;
If wearied when the first is played,
The other keeps them frisky.

Anonymous

3 Follow! Follow! We will follow Rangers,
Anywhere, everywhere, we will follow on:

Ibrox, Parkhead, Hampden or Tynecastle,
Anywhere they lead us till the Cup is won.

Anonymous, Rangers supporters' song

4 Sing high, sing low
Wherever we go
We'll follow the Jam Tarts
Wherever they go.

Heart of Midlothian supporters' song

5 'At a big fitba' match . . . when the crowd wave their hankies for the ambulance men to come, and then the man's taken along the touchline to the pavilion – on a stretcher, ken – well, if he's carried heid foremost he's a' right, but if he's feet foremost, he's deid!'

Anonymous football lore, quoted in James Ritchie, The Singing Street *(1964)*

6 Everywhere we go-o!
People want to know-ow
Who the hell we a-are
And where we come from.
We're the Tartan Army,
We're mental and we're barmy

Anonymous, Everywhere We Go, *quoted in Ian Black*, Tales of the Tartan Army *(1997)*

7 Sure it's a grand old team to play for,
Sure it's a grand old team to see.

Celtic supporters' Song

8 The grouse shooters were often rather pathetic people, going through a ritual imposed on them because they could afford it . . . They were stung, by everything and everybody.

John R. Allan, Farmer's Boy

9 Th' athletic fool to whom what Heav'n denied
Of soul is well compensated in limbs . . .
The men of better clay and finer mould
Know nature, feel the human dignity,
And scorn to vie with oxen or with apes.

John Armstrong (c.1709–1779), The Art of Preserving Health

10 Tully produced a complimentary admission ticket from the waistband of his playing shorts during a game in which he was getting the better of his immediate opponent, the fearsome full-back Don Emery. He handed it to Emery, with

the observation, 'Here, would you not be better watching from the stand?'

Peter Burns and Pat Woods, Oh, Hampden in the Sun *(1997), on Charlie Tully, Celtic star of the late 1940s*

11 In Glasgow half the fans hate you and the other half think they own you.

Tommy Burns (1956–), quoted in Kenny MacDonald, Scottish Football Quotations *(1994)*

12 No party politics around our Tee,
For Whig and Tory on the ice agree;
Glory we play for, may it be our lot,
To gain the Bonspiel by a single shot.

John Cairney (18th century)

13 I support Partick Thistle. They'll be in Europe next year. If there's a war on.

Billy Connolly (1941–), quoted in D. Campbell, Billy Connolly: The Authorised Version *(1976)*

14 My son was born to play for Scotland. He has all the qualities, a massive ego, a criminal record, an appalling drink problem, and he's not very good at football.

'Mrs Alice Cosgrove', quoted on the back cover of Stuart Cosgrove, Hampden Babylon *(1991)*

15 If FIFA ever got round to creating an identikit picture of national footballing types, the Scottish player would be short, stocky, aggressive and ginger-haired. He would have a fiery temper, a bad disciplinary record and a passionate spirit. He would come from a rough housing scheme in Stirling and his name would be Billy Bremner.

Stuart Cosgrove, Hampden Babylon *(1991)*

16 There is hardly any pleasure like good oarmanship. In rowing, the human machine works more cleanly and completely than in any other work.

S. R. Crockett (1859–1914), The Glistering Beaches

17 The channel-stane,
The bracing engine of a Scottish arm.

David Davidson, from a poem on Curling (1789)

18 Football management these days is like a nuclear war. No winners, only survivors.

Tommy Docherty (1928–), quoted in Peter

Ball and Phil Shaw, The Umbro Book of Football Quotations *(1993)*

19 I've had more clubs than Jack Nicklaus.

Tommy Docherty, quoted in Call the Doc *(1981)*

20 I've been in more courts than Bjorn Borg.

Tommy Docherty, quoted in S. Cosgrove, Hampden Babylon *(1991)*

21 To the Scot, football's a lovely incurable disease.

Tommy Docherty, It's Only a Game, *BBC TV, 1985*

22 He says, 'Who are you?' I says, 'Albion Rovers.' He says, 'Never heard of them.' I said, 'You ignorant bugger.' But it was a natural thing, I mean, it wisnae him alone – there were other people who'd never heard of Albion Rovers.

Tom Fagan of Albion Rovers, on a FIFA meeting, 1985, quoted in K. Macdonald, Scottish Football Quotations *(1994)*

23 If Johnson had deliberately intended an attack on the referee, his right foot would not have missed the target.

F. A. Disciplinary Report on Willie 'Wee Bud' Johnson (1976), quoted in S. Cosgrove, Hampden Babylon *(1991)*

24 The doctor said, 'This child's very ill. Have to get him to hospital.' 'I canny take him,' the man says. 'Celtic are playing Leeds United tonight.'

Hugh Ferrie, Celtic supporter, quoted in S. Walsh, Voices of the Old Firm *(1995)*

25 "Twas the short fourteenth,' the Duke was saying. 'Need I tell thee what 'tis like? A hint of slice and you're dead. I laid my pitch pin-high, and damme if Paterson didn't miss the putt.'
'Codso!' exclaimed King Charles.

George Macdonald Fraser, The Pyrates *(1994)*

26 Play Up, Play Up, And Get Tore In.

George Macdonald Fraser, title of short story

27 They christened their game golf because they were Scottish and revelled in meaningless Celtic noises in the back of the throat.

Stephen Fry (1957–), Paperweight

28 Would you also be good enough to
    bring your ball with you in case of any
    breake down, and thus prevent interrup-
    tion. Hoping the weather will favour the
    Thistle and Queen.

> *Robert Gardner, letter to the Secretary of*
> *Thistle FC, Glasgow, June 1867, arrang-*
> *ing the first known inter-club football*
> *game in Scotland*

29 Bi' ma knees is skint and bluddan,
    an ma breeks they want the seat,
    jings! ye get mair nir ye're eftir,
    pleyan fi'baw in the street.

> *Robert Garioch (Robert Garioch Suther-*
> *land, 1909–1981), Fi'baw in the Street*

30 Strange to say, the clergy who were ready
    to denounce all carnal pleasure, even in
    the decorous form of a minuet, uttered no
    complaint against the coarse and demor-
    alising sport of cock-fighting. Why this
    ecclesiastical reticence? Obviously because
    everyone had been accustomed to that
    sport at every parish school. Every minis-
    ter in his boyish days had himself indulged
    in it, when on Fastern Eve or Shrove
    Tuesday he had proudly brought his own
    favourite cock under his arm to pit against
    those of his schoolmates, while the master
    looked on and annexed the corpses of the
    slaughtered fowls to replenish his scanty
    table.

> *H. Grey Graham, The Social Life of*
> *Scotland in the Eighteenth Century*
> *(1899)*

31 . . . near and more near the sounding
        stones,
    Some winding in, some bearing straight
        along,
    Crowd jostling all around the mark, while
        one,
    Just slightly touching, victory depends
    Upon the final aim: long swings the stone,
    Then with full force, careering furious on,
    Rattling, it strikes aside both friend and
        foe,
    Maintains its course, and takes the
        victor's place.

> *James Graham, Thoughts on the Sea-*
> *sons: January (1809), on curling*

32 In this district old people have told me
    of their fathers' stories of the New Year
    shinty match. The ball was hit off on the
    high road at the old boundary between the
    parishes of Moy and Dalarossie. The game

was over walls and fields until darkness
fell or, as occasionally happened, the game
ended in a free fight in which almost the
entire male population joined.

> *I. F. Grant, Highland Folk Ways (1961)*

33 . . . the Partick Thistle supporters' anthem
    goes like this:
    'We hate Roman Catholics,
    We hate Protestants too,
    We hate Jews and Muslims:
    Partick Thistle we love you . . .'

> *Alasdair Gray (1934–), The Trende-*
> *lenburg Position, in S. Maguire and*
> *D. Jackson Young, Hoots (1967)*

34 . . . an intensely Presbyterian activity. In
    golf, you do not play against an opponent.
    You may play alongside him, but he can't
    touch your ball or interefere with your
    swing. You are on your own, one man
    matching his effort and his conscience
    against the enigma of life. You may lie
    about the number of strokes you took to
    kill a snake in the heather; but you know,
    and so does the Big Handicapper in the
    Sky from Whom nothing is hidden.

> *Cliff Hanley (1922–1999), The Scots*

35 Referees are following rules made by men
    who don't pay to watch football. These
    rules are ruining the game for those who
    do.

> *David Hay, of St Mirren, August 1991,*
> *quoted in K. Macdonald, Scottish Foot-*
> *ball Quotations (1994)*

36 There was a woman there with the blue
    eye-shadow and the red lipstick and I was
    walking off and she called me a big dirty
    Fenian bastard. I turned and said, 'Oh,
    come on,' and she said, 'Nothing personal,
    I know your Auntie Annie.'

> *Tony Higgins, Hibernian striker, in Only*
> *a Game, BBC TV, 1985*

37 'Compare fists – Mine's the biggest, but ma
    faith, sir, yours is as bonny a bunch o' fives
    as ever was pitched into a bread-basket.'

> *James Hogg (1770–1835), in Christopher*
> *North (John Wilson, 1785–1854),*
> Noctes Ambrosianae

38 Even in the Foreign Office I could set my
    watch by the evening flight of the ducks
    from St James's Park – over the Horse
    Guards Parade to the Thames estuary –

and select a right and a left with my imaginary gun.

> *Lord Home (1903–1995)*, Border Reflections

39 In spite of all I've said, I'm not the man to see my own side lose for want of a little help (for I'm an 'Uppie'). Some other day the ba' may be pushed into the Harbour and hoisted topmast by the 'Doonies', but not this day if I can be of any use.

> *David Horne*, The Brutality of the Ba', *on the Kirkwall Ba' Game*

40 . . . English football players have been quoted as saying that the Hampden Roar is the equivalent of two goals for Scotland. Unfortunately this has not always proved true.

> *Jack House (1906–1991)*, The Third Statistical Account of Scotland: Glasgow (1958)

41 He never had a day's illness, he didn't smoke, he didn't drink and he used to do all the training himself. I remember when we got in at the end of training and he walked in and said: 'You know something, boys – when I die I want to be the fittest man ever to die.'

> *Emlyn Hughes, quoted in Roddy Forsyth*, The Only Game (1990), *on Bill Shankly*

42 The secret of my success over the four hundred metres is that I run the first two hundred metres as hard as I can. Then, for the second two hundred metres, with God's help, I run faster.

> *Eric H. Liddell (1902–1945), on winning the Olympic gold medal (1924)*

43 The wee bit pat, nae mair nor that,
The canny touch, scarcely sae much.
The stroke that sends the ballie in,
O that's the stroke to gar you win!

> *Wallace Martin Lindsay (1858–1937)*, A Song of Putting

44 All I've got against it is that it takes you so far from the clubhouse.

> *Eric Linklater (1899–1974)*

45 . . . at its best, Rugby is a game that all the gods of Greece might crowd the northern skies to see.

> *Eric Linklater*, Magnus Merriman

46 A shinty-stick is a fine weapon. There was a man called Alastair Mhor, and he stopped

at one time and said 'What's this on my stick?' And then he saw it was a man's eyebrow he had knocked off.

> *Eric Linklater*, Magnus Merriman

47 Five grand a week? That's my kind of pressure.

> *Lou Macari, quoted in K. Macdonald*, Scottish Football Quotations, *1994*

48 . . . the soccer fan attending his first Rugby International at Murrayfield who, puzzled and indignant at the constant kicking to touch, at last bellowed to one of the fullbacks who had just found touch with a magnificent long kick – 'Hi, keep the ba' in the park, youse!'

> *Hugh MacDiarmid (C. M. Grieve, 1892–1978)*, Lucky Poet

49 That isn't just a stadium – it's a weapon.

> *Alex Macdonald, of Heart of Midlothian, on Ibrox Stadium, from K. Macdonald*, Scottish Football Quotations *(1994)*

50 The thunderbolt struck him in the midriff like a red-hot cannonball upon a Spanish galleon, and with the sound of a drumstick on an insufficiently stretched drum. With a fearful oath, Boone clapped his hands to his outraged stomach, and found the ball was in the way. He looked at it for a moment in astonishment and then threw it down angrily and started to massage the injured spot while the field rang with applause at the brilliance of the catch.

> *A. G. Macdonell (1895–1941)*, England, Their England

51 Oh, he's football crazy, he's football mad
And the football it has robbed him of
    the wee bit sense he had.
And it would take a dozen skivvies, his
    clothes to wash and scrub,
Since our Jock became a member of that
    terrible football club.

> *Jimmy MacGregor (1932–)*, Football Crazy

52 . . . the game is hopelessly ill-equipped to carry the burden of emotional expression the Scots seek to load upon it. What is hurting so many now is the realisation that something they believed to be a metaphor for their pride has all along been a metaphor for their desperation.

> *Hugh McIlvanney (1933–)*, McIlvanney on Football

53 *Eck:* . . . This is where I come to do what
the Scots are best at.
Willie: Shinty?
Eck: Moping.
   John McKay, Dead Dad Dog *(1988)*

54 If I ask the players for less than perfection
they'll definitely give me less.
   *Jim Mclean, football manager, quoted in
   K. Macdonald,* Scottish Football Quotations *(1994)*

55 I am convinced that there was something
odd about the way the ball 'flew' in
Argentina.
   Ally MacLeod, The Ally MacLeod Story
   (1979)

56 I am a very good manager who just happened to have a few disastrous days, once
upon a time, in Argentina.
   Ally MacLeod, The Ally MacLeod Story

57 Get up, get up, ilk Highland wight,
The clouds are off, the morn is bright;
So seize your camach, grasp it tight,
And haste awa' to shinty.
   Ossian Macpherson (c.1818–c.1874)

58 Up at Tannadice
Framed in woodwork cool as ice
Keeping out the wolves in his particular
   way
A smile and a wave, a miraculous save
   they say
Out runs Hamish and the ball's in
   Invergowrie Bay.
   Michael Marra, Hamish

59 One would throw two pennies up in the
air, and all the other members of the
group would bet they would come down
as tails . . . It reminds me of the visitor
who came to a mining village and said
the miners had a queer kind of religion;
a group of miners stood in a ring every
Sunday morning and they all looked up at
the sky and looked down on the ground
and together they would say, 'Jesus, tails
again.'
   Abe Moffat, My Life With the Miners,
   quoted in T. C. Smout, A Century of the
   Scottish People, 1830–1950 *(1986)*

60 Oh Lord, heap blessings on the soup,
Heap blessings on the stovies,
Heap blessings on the popes and jews,
The moslems and jehovies,
Heap blessings on all gathered here,

On absent friends and strangers,
And if you've any blessings left,
For Christ's sake *bless the Rangers*.
   *Chic Murray (1919–1985), quoted in
   A. Yule,* The Chic Murray Bumper
   Fun Book *(1991)*

61 Would you like to see a city given over
Soul and body to a tyrannising game?
If you would there's little need to be a
   rover,
For St Andrews is the abject city's name.
   R. F. Murray (1863–1893), The Scarlet
   Gown

62 Among the Scots, licking of wounds is
second only to football as a national sport,
ecstasy occurring when the two activities
merge (as they often do) into one.
   Tom Nairn (1936–), The Guardian,
   May 1986

63 The team is currently struggling in Europe.
The lack of competition from other clubs
in the Scottish League appears to be affecting the ability of world-class players to
reach their best in European matches.
   Rangers FC Official Website, 1998

64 Golf is not a relaxation, golf is everything,
golf is a philosophy, it's a religion, absolutely, I mean really absolutely.
   Sir Bob Reid, quoted in the Sunday
   Times *(November 1989)*

65 Then strip, lads, and to it, though sharp
   be the weather,
And if, by mischance, you should happen
   to fall,
There are worse things in life than a
   tumble on heather,
And life is itself but a game of foot-ball.
   Sir Walter Scott (1771–1832), Lines on
   the Lifting of the Banner of the House
   of Buccleuch, At a Great Foot-ball
   Match on Carterhaugh

66 Three things are thrown away on a bowling green, namely, time, money and oaths.
   Sir Walter Scott, The Fortunes of Nigel

67 Some people think football is a matter of
life and death . . . I can assure them it is
much more serious than that.
   Bill Shankly (1914–1981), quoted in The
   Guardian *(1973)*

68 I don't drop players. I make changes.

Bill Shankly, quoted in The Guardian *(1973)*

69 If you're in the penalty area and don't know what to do with the ball, put it in the net and we'll discuss the options later.

Bill Shankly, quoted by Alastair Mackay in The Scotsman *(July 1998)*

70 The trouble with referees is that they know the rules but do not know the game.

Bill Shankly, quoted by Alastair Mackay in The Scotsman *(July 1998)*

71 If it's gold, I'm a 28.

Bill Shankly, on hearing that Adidas wanted to present him with a Golden Boot

72 The ultimate Scottish international team would be: Knox, Wallace, Bruce, Burns, Montrose, Dunbar, Adam, Napier, Smith, Telford and Stewart. Absolute certainty of salvation in goal; tigerish tackling and devilish cunning at full back; a centre back of legendary courage . . . the left winger can be Charles Edward, Lachie, or Jackie, they could all shift a bit when the going was good or bad.

W. Gordon Smith, This is My Country *(1976)*

73 Shankly, who once played for a very minor Scottish team called Glenbuck Cherrypickers, is also alleged to have put his head round the door of the visitors' dressing-room after a goalless game and announced: 'The better team drew.'

W. Gordon Smith, This Is My Country

74 In the fields called the Links, the citizens of Edinburgh divert themselves at a game called Golf, in which they use a curious kind of bats tipped with horn and small elastic balls of leather, stuffed with feathers, less than tennis balls but of much harder consistency; this they strike with such force and dexterity from one hole to another that they will fly to an incredible distance.

Tobias Smollett (1721–1771), The Expedition of Humphrey Clinker

75 We all end up yesterday's men in this business.

Jock Stein (1922–1985), quoted in Archie Macpherson, The Great Derbies: Blue and Green *(1989)*

76 Glaswegian definition of an atheist – a man who goes to a Celtic–Rangers match to watch the football.

Sandy Strang, quoted in S. Walsh, Voices of the Old Firm *(1995)*

77 We've no chance, I thought, you never do at Hampden against one of the Old Firm, with the crowd and the referees firmly behind the establishment clubs.

Irvine Welsh (1957–), Trainspotting

78 Who's the best team, you'd ask us, crushing, digging or twisting harder. No respite for me until ah sais: Hearts. Even after we'd fucked you seven-nil on New Year's Day at Tynecastle, you still made me say Hearts.

Irvine Welsh, Trainspotting

79 Any defeat is hard to take for about an hour. Then you forget it . . . If you're a Hibby you know you're better than anyone else so defeats in football matches are actually useful to remind you that you're only human.

Irvine Welsh, interview on ErinWeb, *1997*

80 Yet the finest golfers are also the least loquacious. It is said of the illustrious Sandy McHoots that when, on the occasion of his winning the British Open Championship, he was interviewed by the leading daily papers as to his views on Tariff Reform, Bimetallism, The Trial by Jury System, and the Modern Craze for Dancing, all they could extract from him was the single word 'Mphm'.

P. G. Wodehouse (1881–1975)

Television, Radio and Cinema

1 It is a strange fact that, when one broadcasts, there is no sensation of loneliness and no sensation of talking into nothing.

William Barclay (1907–1978), Testament of Faith

2 *Braveheart* is pure Australian shite.

Billy Connolly (1942–)

3 I went to Scotland but I could find nothing that looked like Scotland.

Arthur Freed, producer of Brigadoon, *quoted in Forsyth Hardy,* Scotland in Film *(1990)*

4 I'm terrified, terrified, of the celebration of mediocrity in Scotland . . . You just have to watch the Scottish BAFTAs to want to kill yourself.

Muriel Gray (1959–), interview in Scotland on Sunday, *14 January 1996*

5 Comedy when it begins to be really good is, like tragedy, too large an affair altogether for the commercial conditions which determine the film business.

John Grierson (1898–1972), Everyman *(1931)*

6 . . . so basic is its appeal to our Scottish minds that we get to thinking that all the stories in the tradition belong to us personally . . . when I produced *Laxdale Hall* there was the same curious illusion. I had, of course, to show it to Linklater but I found myself wondering what the devil he was doing there.

John Grierson, Arts Review, BBC TV, *1959*

7 Film-making belongs like all show business to that magical world in which two and two can make five, but also three and even less. It is, by that token, not a business to which the presbyterian mind is natively and nationally attuned.

John Grierson , quoted in Forsyth Hardy, John Grierson's Scotland *(1979)*

8 I suppose I coined the word [documentary] in the sense that I wasn't aware of its being used by anybody else.

John Grierson, interviewed by Elizabeth Sussex in Rise and Fall of the British Documentary *(1975)*

9 Within the dominant narrative, Scotland is heavily feminised, languorously awaiting the phallic embrace of the outsider.

Colin McArthur, Scotland and the Braveheart Effect, *from* Journal for the Study of British Cultures *(1998)*

10 *Willie:* Naebody Scottish works for the BBC.
Eck: Plenty do. Plenty.
Willie: Like who?
Eck: Em, Mary Marquis.
Willie: She's no Scottish. She's just English pretendin.'

John McKay, Dead Dad Dog *(1988)*

11 It is said of a cinema in Leith that, in the absence of WCs, young patrons were expected to relieve themselves on the seats in front, being sprayed with disinfectant by ushers in the aisles. In Tain, patrons were expected to use the walls outside.

Charles McKean, The Scottish Thirties

12 Broadcasting is in no sense to be regarded as a substitute for the reading of good books or the study of good music.

Lord Reith (1889–1971), Broadcast over Britain

13 At least he shall never read the Epilogue.

Lord Reith, quoted in Ned Sherrin, Theatrical Anecdotes *(1991), on a BBC announcer who was divorced*

14 . . . some tragic attempts at the filming of Scottish history. There was one that dealt with Mary Queen of Scots, where that lady paraded in a Glengarry and very abbreviated kilt.

The Scots Magazine, quoted in L. G. Gibbon and H. MacDiarmid, Scottish Scene *(1934)*

15 The film western isn't something that needs immaculate research or anything like that . . . And I always put Scotsmen into them. You know, the first westerns with Greenockian-type people in them. A new art form.

Alan Sharp, quoted in W. Gordon Smith, This Is My Country *(1970)*

Thoughts, Wishes and Reflections

1 I heard the cuckoo, with no food in
    my stomach,
I heard the stock dove on the top of
    the tree . . .
I saw the wheatear on a dike of holes,
I saw the snipe while sitting bent.
And I foresaw that the year
Would not go well with me.

Omens, from Gaelic

2 What is hotter than fire? The face of an hospitable man, when strangers come, and there is nought to offer.

Anonymous, from Fionn's Questions, *quoted by Amy Murray in* Father Allan's Island *(1936)*

3 I would I were where Helen lies,
   Night and day on me she cries.
   I would I were where Helen lies,
   On fair Kirkconnel lea.

   Anonymous

4 'Sa lang as I may get gear to steal, I never
   will wirk.'

   Anonymous, How the First Hielandman
   was Made

5 O that the peats would cut themselves,
   The fish jump on the shore,
   And that I in my bed could lie
   And sleep for ever more.

   Anonymous, The Crofter's Prayer

6 There's many a horse has snappit and fa'n,
   And risen an' gane fu' rarely;
   There's many a lass has lost her lad,
   An' gotten anither richt early.

   Traditional, Mormond Braes

7 Even to be happy is a dangerous thing.

   Sir William Alexander (c.1567–1640),
   Darius

8 My father told me, that if you saw a man
   in a Rolls Royce, you could be sure he
   was not a gentleman, unless he was the
   chauffeur.

   Lord Arran (1938–)

9 Life is much easier, being an Earl. It has
   changed me a lot. I'm much nastier now.

   Lord Arran, quoted in The Sunday
   Times, *January 1967*

10 Its all one thing, both tends unto one
   Scope
   To live upon Tabacco and on hope,
   The one's but smoake, the other is but
   wind.

   Sir Robert Aytoun (1569–1638), Upone
   Tabacco

11 It is unfortunate, considering that enthusiasm moves the world, that so few
   enthusiasts can be trusted to speak the
   truth.

   *A. J. Balfour (1848–1930), letter to Mrs
   Drew, 1918*

12 God if ye knew the stait that I am in!

   *Hugh Barclay (c.1560–1597), To Alexan-
   der Montgomerie*

13 Endurance is not just the ability to bear a
   hard thing, but to turn it into glory.

   William Barclay (1907–1978), in The
   British Weekly

14 As soon as you can say what you think, and
   not what some other person has thought
   for you, you are on the way to being a
   remarkable man.

   Sir J. M. Barrie (1860–1937), Tommy
   and Grizel

15 All things to all men only fools will tell,
   Truth profits none but those who use it
   well.

   John Stuart Blackie (1809–1895), The
   Wise Men of Greece

16 All things are wonderful; who wonders
   not
   Hath eyes and sees not; wonder is the key
   Of knowledge and of worship to the wise.

   John Stuart Blackie, The Wise Men of
   Greece

17 I said it was not true that the world is grown
   old and no good men now to be found as
   in former times, for new men of worth are
   always appearing. He answered . . . 'Yes,
   yes, the pot is continually boiling, and
   there's always fresh broth.' I love such metaphorical sallies.

   James Boswell (1740–1795), Journal

18 Hawick. Mr Christian showed me there
   an inscription upon a house which he had
   observed in coming to Scotland:
   All was others.
   All will be others.
   1775
   We could not explain the meaning of
   this. We applied to the proprietor . . .
   and with some wonder at our slowness of
   understanding he told us the meaning was
   the great truth that property changes from
   one to another. 'One generation cometh
   and another goeth,' he said, 'but the earth
   abideth'.

   James Boswell, Journal

19 The Big House of the bairn, so enormous,
   majestic, what is it?
   Just decently earning its keep as a farm.
   Oh, never revisit!

   Ivor Brown (1891–1974), Never Go
   Back

20 Little acquainted with other minds . . . she
   concluded that all mankind were like her-

self engaged in a constant endeavour after
excellence.

> *Mary Brunton (1778–1818)*, Self-
> Control

21 I'll be merry and free,
I'll be sad for naebody;
Naebody cares for me,
I care for naebody.

> *Robert Burns (1759–1796)*, I Hae a
> Wife

22 O wad some Power the giftie gie us
To see oursels as ithers see us!
It wad frae monie a blunder free us,
And foolish notion.

> *Robert Burns*, To a Louse

23 Contented wi' little, and cantie wi' mair,
Whene'er I forgather wi' Sorrow and
Care,
I gie them a skelp as they're creepin alang,
Wi' a cog o' gude swats and an auld
Scottish sang.

> *Robert Burns*, Contented Wi' Little and
> Cantie Wi' Mair

24 'Tis distance lends enchantment to the
view.

> *Thomas Campbell (1777–1844)*, The
> Pleasures of Hope

25 Like pensive beauty, smiling in her tears.

> *Thomas Campbell*, The Pleasures of
> Hope

26 Like angel visits, few and far between.

> *Thomas Campbell*, The Pleasures of
> Hope

27 Silence is the element in which great things
fashion themselves together.

> *Thomas Carlyle (1795–1881)*, Sartor
> Resartus

28 The man who dies rich dies disgraced.

> *Andrew Carnegie (1835–1918)*, The
> Gospel of Wealth

29 I'll mount Phoebus' chair
Having ne'er a hat on,
All my hair a-burning
In my journeying;
Hurrying through the air.
Fain would I hear his fiery horses
neighing
And see how they on foamy bits
are playing,
All the stars and planets I will be

surveying!
Hallo my fancy, whither wilt thou go?

> *William Cleland (c.1661–1689)*, Hallo
> My Fancy

30 I've seen the smiling of Fortune
beguiling,
I've tasted her favours and felt her decay.

> *Alison Cockburn (1712–1794)*, The Flow-
> ers of the Forest

31 Me, made after the image o' God?
Jings, but it's laughable, tae.

> *Joe Corrie (1894–1968)*, Miners' Wives

32 Three things by distance still grow
dearer –
Our loves, our native land, our mother
tongue.

> *Sir William Craigie (1867–1957)*,
> Autumn in Denmark

33 Oh, Thou who dost forbear
To grant me motherhood,
Grant that my brow may wear
Beneath its maiden's snood
Love to distressed Mankind,
And helpful sympathy
For all whom Fate doth bind
In Sorrow's company.

> *Helen B. Cruickshank (1886–1975)*, A
> Prayer

34 Secure your birthright; set the world
at naught;
Confront your fate; regard the naked
deed;
Enlarge your Hell; preserve it in repair;
Only a splendid Hell keeps Heaven fair.

> *John Davidson (1857–1909)*, The Testa-
> ment of an Empire-Builder

35 Feel Like a Boy Again.

> *Norman Douglas (1868–1952)*, *telegram
> to a friend*

36 Man alone is a perennial drudge. Yet many
of us would do well to *mediterraneanise* ourselves for a season, to quicken those ethic
roots from which has sprung so much of
what is best in our natures.

> *Norman Douglas*, Siren Land

37 He was a wight of high degree
And knew how many beans make five,
But now he's not a patch on me,
For he is dead and I'm alive.

> *T. L. Douglas*, A Living Dog

38 And three measures of slenderness . . .
    in which the eye, the ear and the
        mind meet: the slimness of a boy's
        ankle while he is alive to dance,
    the whisper that draws a hill across
        a strath,
    and that which separates self-respect from
        self-regard.

    Adam Drinan (Joseph Macleod, 1903–),
    Measures

39 I know that all beneath the moon decays,
    And what by mortals in this worlds is
        brought
    In Time's great periods shall return to
        nought.

    William Drummond (1585–1649),
    Passed Joy

40 Thrice happy he, who by some shady
        grove,
    Far from the clamorous world, doth live
        his own.

    William Drummond, Urania

41 What sweet delight a quiet life affords
    And what it is from bondage to be free,
    Far from the madding worldlings' hoarse
        discords.

    William Drummond, The Cypresse
    Grove

42 Excess of thocht does me mischeif.

    William Dunbar (c.1460–c.1520), To
    the King

43 I will nae priests for me shall sing,
    Dies illa dies irae,
    Nor zit nae bells for me to ring,
    Sicut semper solet fieri,
    But a bag-pyp to play a spring
    Et unum ale-wisp *ante me.*

    William Dunbar, The Testament of
    Mr Andro Kennedy

44 The sea, I think, is lazy,
    It just obeys the moon.

    Ian Hamilton Finlay (1925–), Mansie
    Considers the Sea, in the Manner of
    Hugh MacDiarmid

45 Conflict is one of the givens of the uni-
    verse. The only way it can ever be tamed
    or managed or civilised is within culture.
    You cannot pretend that it does not exist.

    Ian Hamilton Finlay, quoted in Alec
    Finlay, Wood Notes Wild: Essays on
    the Poetry and Art of Ian Hamilton
    Finlay *(1995)*

46 To every man the hardest form of slavery
    is to serve as a slave in one's own native
    country, there where one was wont to be
    free lord.

    John Fordun (d.1385), Scotichronicon,
    translated from Latin

47 . . . good triumphs and the villain bites the
    dust. If anyone believes that, the story of
    the Border Reivers should convince him
    otherwise. Its moral is clear: there is little
    justice to be had. The good man survives,
    if he is lucky, but the villain becomes the
    first Lord Roxburgh.

    George Macdonald Fraser, The Steel
    Bonnets *(1971)*

48 The posters show my country blonde
        and green,
    Like some sweet siren, but the travellers
        know
    How dull the shale sky is, the airs how
        keen

    G. S. Fraser (1916–1980), Meditation
    of a Patriot

49 I wish I were an exile and I rave:
    With Byron and with Lermontov
    Romantic Scotland's in the grave.

    G. S. Fraser, Meditation of a Patriot

50 It was the old Scotland that perished then,
    and we may believe that never again will
    the old speech and the old songs, the old
    curses and the old benedictions, rise but
    with alien efforts to our lips.

    Lewis Grassic Gibbon (James Leslie
    Mitchell, 1901–1935), Sunset Song

51 I take it Africa was brought about in sheer
    ill-humour. No-one can think it possible
    that an all-wise God (had he been in his
    sober senses) would create a land and fill
    it full of people destined to be replaced by
    other people from across the seas.

    Robert B. Cunninghame Graham
    (1852–1936), Bloody Niggers, *from*
    Selected Writings, *edited by Cedric Watt*
    (1981)

52 When I was a buoy it seemed
    Craft of rare tonnage
    Moored to me. Now
    Occasionally a skiff

Is tied to me and tugs
At the end of its tether.

> W. S. Graham (1918–1986), Implements in Their Places

53 Now up in the mornin's no for me,
Up in the mornin' early;
When snaw blaws into the chimley cheek,
Wha'd rise in the mornin' early?

> John Hamilton (1761–1814), Up in the Morning Early

54 Tiresome 'tis to be a dreamer.
When will it be time to dine?

> James Hedderwick (b.1814), The Villa by the Sea

55 And all in care translatit is my joy.

> Robert Henryson (c.1425–c.1500), The Testament of Cresseid

56 'How had you the audacity, John,' said a Scottish laird to his servant, ' to go and tell some people that I was a mean fellow, and no gentleman?'
'Na, na, sir,' was the candid answer, 'you'll no catch me at the the likes o' that. I aye *keep my thoughts to mysel''.*

> Alexander Hislop, The Book of Scottish Anecdote (1883)

57 I carena muckle for folk that bairns and dogs dinna like.

> James Hogg (1770–1835), *quoted in Margaret Garden*, Memorials of James Hogg

58 From my heart I can say I like no such titles & if you value your own comfort & my peace of mind you will at once, if offered to you, refuse it.

> Margaret Hogg (1790–1870), *letter to her husband James in London, who had been speculating on whether he would be offered a knighthood (March 1832)*

59 What pleasure were to walk and see
Endlang a river clear,
The perfite form of every tree
Within the deep appear.

> Alexander Hume (c.1550–1609), Of the Day Estivall

60 O, then it were a seemly thing,
While all is still and calm,

The praise of God to play and sing,
With cornet and with shalm!
All labourers draw home at even,
And can till other say,
Thanks to the gracious God of heaven,
Whilk sent this summer day.

> Alexander Hume, Of the Day Estivall

61 An' what'll I get when my mither kens.

> Violet Jacob (1863–1946), The End o't.

62 O besy goste! ay flickering to and fro,
That never art in quiet nor in rest,
Til thou cum to that place thou cam fro.

> King James I (1394–1437), Animula, Vagula, Blandula

63 The museums of Scotland are wrang.
– They urnae arraheids
but a show o grannies' tongues,
the hard tongues o grannies
aa deid an gaun.

> Kathleen Jamie (1962–), Arraheids

64 Pass the sick-bag, Alice.

> John Junor (1919–1997), The Sunday Express

65 John Knox, with his one foot in the grave.

> Signature of a letter from John Knox (c.1513–1572), to Sir William Cecil, 1570

66 Farewell, be glad, forget:
There is no need to say 'forget' I know,
For youth is youth, and time will have it so.

> Andrew Lang (1844–1912), Good-bye

67 Then men till other did record,
Said Lyndsay wald be made ane lord.
Thou hes made lordis, schir, be Sanct Geill,
Of some that has nocht servit so weill.

> Sir David Lindsay (1490–1555), The Complaynt of Schir David Lyndsay

68 The party's almost over. Though at times a trifle odd,
I've thoroughly enjoyed it. Thank you for having me, God.

> Maurice Lindsay (1918–), To Catch the Last Post

69 What more lovely than to be alone
With a Teasmade, a radio and a telephone?

> Liz Lochhead (1947–), Heartbreak Hotel

70 Mars is braw in crammasy,
    Venus in a green silk goun,
    The auld mune shak's her gowden
        feathers,
    Their starry talk's a wheen o' blethers,
    Nane for thee a thochtie sparin',
    Earth thou bonnie broukit bairn!
    – But greet, an' in your tears ye'll droun
    The haill clamjamfrie!
        Hugh MacDiarmid (C. M. Grieve,
        1892–1978) ,The Bonnie Broukit Bairn

71 Nae man or movement's worth a damn
        unless
    The movement 'ud gang on withoot him
        if
    He de'ed the morn.
        Hugh MacDiarmid, Depth and the
        Chthonian Image

72 I'll ha'e nae hauf-way hoose, but aye be
        whaur
    Extremes meet – it's only way I ken
    To dodge the curst conceit o' bein' richt
    That damns the vast majority o' men.
        Hugh MacDiarmid, A Drunk Man
        Looks at the Thistle

73 Reflecting on these islands – on, say, Barra
    or Iona – on the attainments of past ages . . .
    It must seem that the world has lost some-
    thing it once possessed, that Europe at
    any rate has been living for the past fif-
    teen hundred years or a little more under a
    grave misapprehension as to the nature of
    things, perhaps deliberately brought about
    by those who ought to have known better.
        Hugh MacDiarmid, The Islands of
        Scotland

74 Naebody kens what the auld fowk are
    thinkin'.
        George Macdonald (1824–1905), What
        the Auld Fowk are Thinkin'

75 I think that nothing made is lost;
    That not a moon has ever shone,
    That not a cloud my eyes hath crossed
    But to my soul is gone.
        George Macdonald, A Prayer for the
        Past

76 Of noise alone is born the inward sense
    Of silence; and from action springs alone
    The inward knowledge to true love and
    faith.
        George Macdonald, Within and
        Without

77 They sang that never was sadness
    But it melted and passed away;
    They sang that never was darkness
    But in came the conquering day.
        George Macdonald, The Old Garden

78 To be trusted is a greater compliment than
    to be loved.
        George Macdonald, The Marquis of
        Lossie

79 Golden-heided, ripe an' strang,
    Shorn will be the hairst ere lang,
    Syne begins a better sang!
        George Macdonald, Ane by Ane

80 It's only when at home that I forgo
    The luxury of knowing who I am.
        Alasdair Maclean (1926–), Home
        Thoughts from Home

81 Joy that is clothed with shadow
    Is the joy that is not dead
    For the joy that is clothed with the
        rainbow
    Shall with the bow be sped.
        Fiona MacLeod (William Sharp,
        1855–1905), The Sorrow of Delight

82 O what is this wild song I sing,
    With meanings strange and dim?
    No soul am I, a wave am I,
    And sing the Moon-Child's hymn.
        Fiona MacLeod, The Moon-Child

83 It is loveliness I seek, not lovely things.
        Fiona MacLeod

84 People talk of early morning in the country
    with bleating sheep, singing larks and purl-
    ing brooks. I prefer the roar which greets
    my ears when a thousand hammers, thun-
    dering on boilers of steam vessels which
    are to bridge the Atlantic or Pacific, usher
    in a new day – the type of a new era.
        Norman McLeod (1812–1872), quoted
        in R. Ferguson, George MacLeod,
        Founder of the Iona Community
        (1990)

85 Therefore put quite away
    All heaviness of thocht
    Thoch we murne nicht and day
    It will avail us nocht.
        Sir Richard Maitland (1496–1586),
        Advice to Leesome Merriness

86 O grant me, Heaven, a middle state,
    Neither too humble nor too great;

More than enough for nature's ends,
With something left to treat my friends.
> *David Mallett (c.1705–1765)*, Imitation
> of Horace

87 ... no-one need expect to be original
simply by being absurd. There is a cycle in
nonsense ... which ever and anon brings
back the delusions and error of an earlier
time.
> *Hugh Miller (1802–1856)*, The Testi-
> mony of the Rocks

88 Too late I knaw, wha hewis too hie,
The spail sall fall into his e'e;
Too late I went to schoolis.
Too late I heard the swallow preach,
Too late Experience does teach –
The school-maister of foolis.
> *Alexander Montgomerie (c.1545–c.1611)*,
> The Cherry and the Slae

89 We let the day grow old among the grass.
> *Edwin Morgan (1920–)*, From a City
> Balcony

90 The thochts o' bygane years
Still fling their shadows ower my path,
And blind my een wi' tears.
> *William Motherwell (1797–1835)*, Jeanie
> Morrison

91 And all the kings before
This land was kingless,
And all the singers before
This land was songless,
This land that with its dead and living
Awaits the Judgement Day.
> *Edwin Muir (1887–1959)*, Scotland's
> Winter

92 We bear the lot of nations,
Of times and races,
Because we watched the wrong
Last too long
With non-committal faces.
> *Edwin Muir*, The Refugees

93 And without fear the lawless roads
Run wrong through all the land.
> *Edwin Muir*, Hòlderlin's Journey

94 On one occasion he declared that he was
richer than magnate E. H. Harriman: 'I
have all the money I want and he hasn't.'
> *John Muir (1838–1914)*, quoted in
> C. Fadiman, The Little, Brown Book
> of Anecdotes *(1985)*

95 Gin I was God, sittin' up there abeen,
Weariet nae doot noo a' my darg was deen,
Deaved wi' the harps an' hymns oonendin'
ringin ...
I'd ... Start a' thing ower again, gin I
was God.
> *Charles Murray (1864–1941)*, Gin I was
> God

96 There's meikle good done in the dark.
> *Allan Ramsay (1686–1758)*, The
> Marrow Ballad

97 We find that nonsense of every kind is
received with applause, when it happens to
drop from what is called *a great Name*; and
that it is sometimes, on the same account,
transmitted from age to age, like the toe-
nail parings of st nicholas, with religious
veneration and astonishment.
> *Allan Ramsay Jr (1713–1784)*, On the
> Naturalisation of Foreigners

98 'Ach, it's sair cheenged times at Castle
Grant, when gentlemans can gang to bed
on their ain feet.'
> *Dean E. B. Ramsay (1793–1872)*,
> Reminiscences of Scottish Life and
> Character

99 Whit trasherie will I turn up the day?
> *Christopher Rush (1944–)*, Monday
> Morning

100 Sorrow remembers us when day is done.
> *Iain Crichton Smith (1928–1998)*, When
> Day is Done

101 There's a gude time coming.
> *Sir Walter Scott (1771–1832)*, Rob Roy

102 Vengeance to God alone belongs;
But, when I think on all my wrongs,
My blood is liquid flame!
> *Sir Walter Scott*, Marmion

103 It isna what we hae done for oursels, but
what we hae done for ithers, that we think
on maist pleasantly.
> *Sir Walter Scott*, The Heart of
> Midlothian

104 We do that in our zeal our calmer moments
would be afraid to answer.
> *Sir Walter Scott*, Woodstock

105 Vacant heart, and hand, and eye,
Easy live and quiet die.

    Sir Walter Scott, The Bride of
Lammermoor

106 But THOU hast said, The blood of goat,
The flash of rams I will not prize;
A contrite heart, a humble thought,
Are mine accepted sacrifice.

    Sir Walter Scott, Rebecca's Hymn, *from*
Ivanhoe

107 Lift not the festal mask!– enough to know
No scene of mortal life but teems with
    mortal woe.

    Sir Walter Scott, The Lord of the Isles

108 Still if the question was eternal company
without the power of retiring within yourself or solitary confinement for life I should
say, 'Turnkey, lock the cell.'

    Sir Walter Scott, Journal, *December 1825*

109 Self-respect is the noblest garment with
which a man may clothe himself, the most
elevating feeling with which the mind can
be inspired.

    Samuel Smiles (1816–1904), Self Help

110 We ever new, we ever young,
We happy creatures of a day!

    C. H. Sorley (1895–1915), Untitled
Poem

111 Darkness is your only door;
Gang doun wi' a sang, gang doun.

    William Soutar (1898–1943), Song

112 Ah! forgive me, fellow-creatures,
If I mock when you are gone;
And if sometimes at life's concert
I would rather sit alone.

    William Soutar, Impromptu in an Ere-
mitic Mood

113 Was Jesus no a jiner (and a poet)?
And wudna Jesus, noo, be on the dole?

    William Soutar, Saint Andra's Day

114 A lane man in a lanely land.

    William Soutar, The Solitary Place

115 Nae day sae dark; nae wud sae bare;
Nae grund sae stour wi' stane;
But licht comes through; a sang is there;
A glint o' grass is seen.

    William Soutar, Nae Day Sae Dark

116 ... there's aye the bluid o' puir folk
On the sarks o' gentilities.

    William Soutar, My Grannie

117 How easily a small inconvenience can cover
the sun and make us forget the misery
of a universe; and the tragic element in
self-pity is this, that at last the power
of maintaining proportion between the
world and the self is lost, and is not known
to have been lost.

    William Soutar, Diary of a Dying Man

118 But oh! what a cruel thing is a farce to
those engaged in it!

    Robert Louis Stevenson (1850–1894),
Travels With a Donkey

119 Selfishness is calm, a force of nature: you
might say the trees were selfish.

    Robert Louis Stevenson, Ethical Studies

120 Truth in spirit, not truth to letter, is the
true veracity.

    Robert Louis Stevenson, Truth of
Intercourse

121 The world is so full of a number of things
I'm sure we should all be as happy as
    kings.

    Robert Louis Stevenson, Happy Thought

122 Little Indian, Sioux or Crow,
Little frosty Eskimo,
Little Turk or Japanee,
O! don't you wish that you were me?

    Robert Louis Stevenson, Foreign
Children

123 Sing me a song of a lad that is gone,
Say, could that lad be I?
Merry of soul, he sailed on a day
Over the sea to Skye.

    Robert Louis Stevenson, Songs of Travel

124 It's deadly commonplace, but, after all, the
commonplaces are the great poetic truths.

    Robert Louis Stevenson, Weir of
Hermiston

125 At the First Supper
The guests were but one:
A maiden was the hostess,
The guest her son.

    Jan Struther (J. Anstruther, 1901–1953),
The First Supper

126 The feeling of temporal urgency cannot
be artificially produced, any more than the
feeling of financial distress.
> *Jan Struther*, Mrs Miniver

127 It took me forty years on earth
To reach this sure conclusion:
There is no Heaven but clarity;
No Hell except confusion.
> *Jan Struther*, All Clear, *from* The Glass-
> Blowers and Other Poems

128 This warl's a tap-room owre and owre,
Whaur ilk ane tak's his caper,
Some taste the sweet, some drink the sour,
As waiter Fate sees proper.
> *Robert Tannahill (1774–1810)*, The Tap-
> Room

129 What the future may have in store, no-one
can tell; we are bound to say *ignoramus*,
but not *ignorabimus*.
> *Sir J. Arthur Thomson*, The Wonder of
> Life, *in F. Mason*, The Great Design
> *(1934) (we do not know; we shall not
> know)*

130 What, what is Virtue, but Repose of
Mind? . . .
The Best of Men have ever loved Repose;
They hate to mingle in the filthy Fray.
> *James Thomson (1700–1748)*, The
> Castle of Indolence

131 . . . a cold rage seizes one at whiles
To show the bitter old and wrinkled truth
Stripped naked of all vesture that beguiles
False dreams, false hopes, false masks and
modes of youth.
> *James Thomson (1834–1882)*, The City
> of Dreadful Night

132 The world rolls round for ever like a mill;
It grinds out death and life and good and
ill;
It has no purpose, heart or mind or will.
> *James Thomson*, The City of Dreadful
> Night

133 Forty years old today. Cold; third day of
fog. Congenial natal weather. No marvel
one is obscure, dismal, bewildered, and
melancholy.
> *James Thomson, note made on 23 Novem-
> ber 1874*

134 My son's whorled ear was once my father's,
then mine;
I am the map of a campaign, each ancestor
has his flag
Marking an advance or a retreat. I am
their seed.
> *Ruthven Todd (1914–1978)*, Personal
> History: For My Son

135 Aye, it's on the highways
The feck o' life maun gang:
But aye it's frae the byways
Comes hame the happy sang.
> *Walter Wingate (1865–1918)*, Highways
> and Byways

Time

1 Our life's a flying shadow, God's the pole,
The Index pointing at Him is our soul;
Death the horizon, when our sun is set,
Which will through Christ a resurrection
get.
> *Inscription on a sundial, Glasgow
> Cathedral*

2 Ae day gie me o' youthful life
At the back o' Benachie.
> *Anonymous*, Where Gadie Rins

3 Oh no, sad and slow,
And lengthened on the ground
The shadow of our trysting bush,
It wears so slowly round . . .
Oh no, sad and slow,
The time will ne'er be gane:
The shadow of the trysting bush
Is fixed like ony stane.
> *Joanna Baillie (1762–1851)*, The Tryst-
> ing Bush

4 How long ago it may seem since
yesterday!
> *J. M. Barrie (1860–1937)*, Sentimental
> Tommy

5 The present moment is our ain,
The neist we never saw.
> *James Beattie (1735–1803), stanza added
> to Mickle's* The Sailor's Wife

6 Nae man can tether Time nor Tide,
The hour approaches Tam maun ride.
> *Robert Burns (1759–1796)*, Tam o'
> Shanter

7 The wan Moon is setting behind the
white wave,
And Time is setting with me, oh
Robert Burns, Open the Door to
Me, Oh

8 Time but th'impression stronger makes,
As streams their channels deeper wear.
Robert Burns, To Mary in Heaven

9 The social hours, swift wing'd, unnotic'd
fleet.
Robert Burns, The Cottar's Saturday
Night

10 When o'er the hill the eastern star
Tells bughtin' time is near, my jo.
Robert Burns, My Ain Kind Dearie

11 I watch the wheels of Nature's mazy plan,
And learn the future by the past of man.
Thomas Campbell (1777–1844), The
Pleasures of Hope

12 That great mystery of TIME, were there
no other; the illimitable, silent, never-rest-
ing thing called Time, rolling, rushing on,
swift, silent, like an all-embracing ocean-
tide, on which we and all the Universe
swim like exhalations, like apparitions
which *are*, and then *are not*; this is forever
very literally a miracle; a thing to strike
us dumb,– for we have no word to speak
about it.
Thomas Carlyle (1795–1881), On
Heroes, Hero-Worship, and the
Heroic in History

13 Here hath been dawning
Another blue Day;
Think, wilt thou let it
Slip useless away?
Carlyle, To-Day

14 Yesterday
Was once the date of every lasting change.
John Davidson (1857–1909), Bruce

15 The sun is bright on heaven's brow,
The world's fresh blood runs fleet;
Time is as young as ever now,
Nature as fresh and sweet.
John Davidson, A Ballad of Euthanasia

16 ... on I go,
My head erect beneath the tragic years.
John Davidson, I Felt the World A-spin-
ning on its Nave

17 I know that all beneath the moon decays,
And what by mortals in this world is
brought
In Time's great periods shall return to
naught.
William Drummond (1585–1649), I
Know That All Beneath the Moon
Decays

18 Time Tryeth Trothe.
Kenneth Grahame (1859–1932), The
Golden Age, *sundial inscription*

19 For evermore I wait, and longer too.
Robert Henryson (c.1425–c.1500), The
Town Mouse and the Country Mouse

20 The sun-dial was so aged
It had gathered a thoughtful grace;
'Twas the round-about of the shadow
That had so furrowed its face.
George Macdonald (1824–1905), The
Old Garden

21 Mourn not, my friends, that we are
growing old:
A fresher birth brings every new year in.
George Macdonald, Death

22 The slow weary drip of the slow weary
years.
*Fiona MacLeod (William Sharp,
1855–1905)*, The Bugles of Dreamland

23 Take time in time, ere time be tint,
For time will not remain.
Alexander Montgomerie (c.1545–c.1610),
The Cherry and the Slae

24 Time is not progress, but amount;
One vast accumulating store,
Laid up, not lost!
Alexander Montgomery (1771–1854),
Time

25 Time's a fire-wheel whose spokes the
seasons turn,
And fastened there we, Time's slow
martyrs, burn.
Edwin Muir (1887–1959), The Fire-
Wheel

26 A hundred pipers canna blaw
Our trauchled times awa.
Alexander Scott (1920–1989), Calvinist
Sang

27 Before my breath, like blazing flax,
Man and his marvels pass away;

And changing empires wane and wax,
Are founded, flourish, and decay.

> *Sir Walter Scott (1771–1832)*, The Antiquary

28 Time that has dinged doun castels
and hie toures,
And cast great crouns like tinsel in
the fire,
That halds his hand for palace nor
for byre,
Stands sweir at this, the oe of Venus'
boures.

> *Lewis Spence (1874–1955)*, The Queen's Bath-House, Holyrood

29 The obscurest epoch is today.

> *Robert Louis Stevenson (1850–1894)*, Ethical Studies

30 Over me pass the days and months and
years
Like squadrons and battalions of the foe.

> *James Thomson (1834–1882)*, To Our Ladies of Death

Toasts and Greetings

1 May the best ye've ever seen
Be the worst ye ever see.

> *Traditional*

2 May the mouse never leave our meal pock
wi' the tear in its eye.

> *Traditional*

3 Would it not be the beautiful thing now
If you were coming instead of going?

> *Traditional island farewell, from Gaelic*

4 Here's to the king, sir,
Ye ken wha I mean, sir.

> *Jacobite toast*

5 The King ower the Water.

> *Jacobite toast*

6 The little gentleman in black velvet.

> *Jacobite toast, to the mole on whose hill King William II's horse stumbled, causing his death*

7 Here's to the horse wi' the four white
feet,
The chestnut tail and mane –

A star on his face and a spot on his breast,
An' his master's name was Cain.

> *Traditional horsemen's toast*

8 Grace be here, and grace be there,
And grace be on the table;
Ilka one tak' up their speen,
An' sup a' that they're able.

> *Anonymous bothy grace, from D. K. Cameron*, The Cornkister Days *(1984)*

9 For auld lang syne, my dear,
For auld lang syne,
We'll tak' a cup o' kindness yet,
For auld lang syne.

> *Robert Burns (1759–1796)*, Auld Lang Syne

10 John Barleycorn was a hero bold,
Of noble enterprise;
For if you do but taste his blood,
'Twill make your courage rise.

Then let us toast John Barleycorn,
Each man with glass in hand;
And may his great posterity
Ne'er fail in old Scotland!

> *Robert Burns*, John Barleycorn

11 Fair fa' your honest sonsie face,
Great chieftain o' the pudding-race!

> *Robert Burns*, Address to a Haggis

12 Napoleon is a tyrant, a monster, the sworn
foe of our nation. But gentlemen – he once
shot a publisher.

> *Thomas Campbell (1777–1844), proposing a toast to Bonaparte at a writers' dinner*

13 Every glass during dinner had to be dedicated to someone. It was thought sottish and rude to take wine without this, as if forsooth there was nobody present worth drinking with.

> *Henry Thomas Cockburn (1779–1854)*, Memorials

14 In ancient times the tenants of Lord Breadalbane having applied to him for a reduction of rent, had occasion to dine together, before their landlord and chief had sent his reply. When they proposed his health, therefore, they gave it in these cautious words, – 'Breadalbane – , till we see.'

> *Alexander Hislop*, The Book of Scottish Anecdote *(1883)*

15 Good night, and joy be wi' you a';
    We'll maybe meet again the morn.

> *James Hogg (1770–1835)*, Good Night,
> and Joy Be Wi' You

16 May the hills lie low,
    May the sloughs fill up
    In thy way.

> *Kenneth Macleod (1871–1955)*, Blessing
> of the Road, *in* The Road to the Isles

17 Highland honours are one foot on the
    chair and the other on the table, with the
    exclamation of 'Neish, neish, shouterish,
    shouterish, hurrah!' which is translated
    'Now, now, again, again, hurrah!' the
    company brandishing and emptying their
    glasses, and then throwing each glass into
    the fire. The latter part of the ceremony
    was omitted in this case, but I have seen
    it done. Being inconvenient and expensive,
    it is not generally adopted, particularly if
    there is a lady in the house.

> *Joseph Mitchell (1803–1883)*, Reminis-
> cences of My Life in the Highlands

18 The traditional Orkney invitation to a visi-
    tor was, 'Put in thee hand.'

> *Edwin Muir (1887–1959)*,
> Autobiography

19 I'll drink a cup to Scotland yet,
    Wi' a' the honours three!

> *Henry Scott Riddell (1798–1870)*, The
> Three Honours of Scotland

20 Plenty herring, plenty meal,
    Plenty peat to fill her creel –
    Plenty bonny bairns as weel,
    That's the toast for Mairi.

> *Sir Hugh S. Roberton (1874–1952)*, The
> Lewis Bridal Song

Transport and Travel

1 The king sits in Dunfermline town,
   Drinking the bluid-red wine;
   'O where will I get a skeely skipper,
   To sail this new ship o' mine?'

> *Anonymous*, Sir Patrick Spens

2 Had you seen these roads before they
       were made,
   You would lift up your hands and bless
       General Wade.

> *Anonymous, lines on the military roads*

*constructed under General George Wade
during 1726–37*

3 The earth belongs unto the Lord,
   And all that it contains;
   Except the Western Isles alone,
   And they are all MacBrayne's.

> *Anonymous rhyme on the MacBrayne
> Steamship Company, 20th century*

4 The bonnie wee *Sultana*,
   The bully of the Clyde –
   She's gone and took the *Jeanie Deans*,
   And laid her on her side.

> *Boys' rhyme on rival Clyde steamers,
> quoted in George Blake (1893–1961)*,
> Down to the Sea: The Romance of the
> Clyde

5 Anyone can go. It's just a question of looking at the horizon and deciding whether
   you really want to go.

> *Sir Chay Blyth (1940–), on single-handed
> sailing round the world, interview with
> Herb McCormick in* Cruising World,
> *March 1997*

6 No problems there. Except I couldn't sail
   or navigate. But I figured it wouldn't be
   that difficult.

> *Sir Chay Blyth, interview in* Cruising
> World

7 I am travelling with a general desire to
   improve myself.

> *James Boswell (1740–1795), letter to
> Jean-Jacques Rousseau, December 1764*

8 I'm now arriv'd – thanks to the gods!
   Thro' pathways rough and muddy:
   A certain sign that makin' roads
   Is no this people's study.
   Altho' I'm not wi' Scripture cram'd,
   I'm sure the Bible says
   That heedless sinners shall be damn'd,
   Unless they mend their *ways*.

> *Robert Burns (1754–1796)*, Epigram on
> Rough Roads

9 The little crib of a place which I had
   glanced at two hours before and found
   six beds in had now developed itself by
   hinge-shelves (which in the day were parts
   of sofas) and iron brackets into the practical sleeping-place of at least sixteen of the
   gent species. There they all lay, my crib
   the only empty one; a pile of clothes up
   to the very ceiling, and all round it gent
   packed on gent, few inches between the

nose of one gent and the nape of the other gent's neck; not a particle of air, all orifices closed. And five or six of said gents already raging and snoring. And a smell! *Ach Gott!* I suppose it must resemble the slave-ships in the middle passsage. It was positively immoral to think of sleeping in such a receptacle of abominations.

> *Thomas Carlyle (1795–1881)*, Letters

10 If any man wants to be happy, I advise him to get a public allowance for travelling.

> *Henry Thomas Cockburn (1779–1854)*,
> Circuit Journeys

11 This train was off for Scotland. It had started from the home of one accent to the home of another accent. It was going from manner to manner, from habit to habit, and in the minds of these London spectators there surely floated dim images of the traditional kilts, the burring speech, the grouse, the canniness, the oat-meal, all the elements of a romantic Scotland.

> *Stephen Crane (1871–1900)*, Men,
> Women and Boats

12 Jokes were made about the Highland Railway . . . You heard, until you were sick of it, about the Highland mail train from Inverness which reached Helmsdale twelve hours late and, when it finally arrived at Wick, was mistain ken for the next day's train running to time.

> *C. Hamilton Ellis*, The Trains We
> Loved *(1947)*

13 You could recognise *Cardean* miles away down the valley of the Annan. At both Carlisle and Glasgow Central, she had her regular fans who gathered to see her off again and again; Driver Gibson was a popular hero – almost a demigod to boys, who used to speculate on whether the two brilliant coins mounted, amid elaborate brazen filigree, on her regulator, were bright ha'pennies or in very truth sovereigns, and to fanatics the former suggestion was not in entirely good taste.

> *C. Hamilton Ellis*, The Trains We
> Loved

14 On the platform of the Waverley Station at Edinburgh may be witnessed every evening in summer a scene of confusion so chaotic that a sober description of it is incredible to those who have not themselves survived it. Trains of caravan length come in portentously late from Perth, so that each is mistaken for its successor; these have to be broken up and remade on inadequate sidings, while bewildered crowds of tourists sway up and down amongst equally bewildered porters . . . the higher officials stand lost in subtle thought . . . while the hands of the clock with a humorous air survey the abandoned sight, till at length, without any obvious reason and with sudden stealth, the shame-stricken driver hurries his packed passengers off into the dark.

> *Professor Foxwell*, Express Trains English and Foreign *(1899)*

15 On one occasion the *Lochmor* was in the vicinity of Canna Pier, enveloped in thick fog, and Captain Robertson was on the bridge while his First Officer was stationed in the bow, peering into the murk . . .

Captain to First Officer: 'Can you see anything, Mr Mate?'

'No Captain, but I can hear ducks.'

'Can you see if they are walking or swimming? Because if they're walking, we're in trouble.'

> *Christopher Fraser*, Christie Boy *(1994)*

16 The minister of Dolphinton, being eager to have a railway through his parish, set himself to ascertain the number of cattle that passed along the road daily in front of his manse. He was said to have counted the same cow many times in the same day.

> *Sir Archibald Geikie (1835–1924)*, Scottish Reminiscences

17 A worthy countryman who had come from the north-east side of the kingdom by train to Cowlairs, was told that the next stoppage would be Glasgow. He at once began to get all his little packages ready, and remarked to a fellow-passenger,'I'm sailin' for China this week, but I'm thinkin' I'm by the warst o' the journey noo.'

> *Sir Archibald Geikie*, Scottish Reminiscences

18 I remember a crofter on the island of Eigg, who, when asked when the steamer would arrive, replied at once, 'Weel, she'll be comin' sometimes sooner, and whiles earlier, and sometimes before that again.'

> *Sir Archibald Geikie*, Scottish Reminiscences

19 But I need the rides most, hurling warm through all weathers and seasons, with a paperback thriller on my lap, and always Scotland outside the window in more changes of scenery in ten miles than England in fifteen or Europe in twenty, or India, America or Russia in a hundred.

Alasdair Gray (1934–), 1982, Janine

20 ... Out there was at least one class of criminals from which Scotland was exempt, and that was of highwaymen. That fraternity, so large and prosperous beyond the border, was here unknown; they would have grown weary of waiting for passengers to waylay, and died of poverty from finding so little to plunder from their persons.

H. Grey Graham, The Social Life of Scotland in the Eighteenth Century *(1899)*

21 'Beyond the Wild Wood comes the wide world,' said the Rat. 'And that's something that doesn't matter either to you or me. I've never been there, and I'm never going, nor you either, if you've got any sense at all. Don't ever refer to it again, please.'

Kenneth Grahame (1859–1932), The Wind in the Willows

22 To the rail, to the rail, now the pent-up desires
Of the pale toiling million find gracious reply.
On the pinions of steam they shall fly, they shall fly.

Janet Hamilton (1795–1873), The Sunday Rail, *on the first running of Sunday trains on the North British Railway*

23 In the Outer Islands, Watt's machine is unknown, and many of the roads which imaginative cartographers have inserted in their maps will perhaps be finished when the last trump is about to sound.

D. T. Holmes, Literary Tours in the Highlands and Islands *(1909)*

24 I always think of it when I read the Ninth Ode in Horace's first book! Outside were snow-sheeted mountains and the moon gazing through a screen of haze. From end to end of the train resounded the rhythmic beat of cold-footed passengers striving to bring some warmth to the toes.

D. T. Holmes, Literary Tours in the Highlands and Islands, *on a train stalled in Drumochter Pass*

25 There was a naughty boy,
And a naughty boy was he –
He ran away to Scotland,
The people for to see.
But he found,
That the ground was as hard,
That a yard was as long,
That a song
Was as merry,
That a cherry
Was as red ...
And a door was as wooden, as in England

John Keats (1795–1821), There Was a Naughty Boy

26 And all chatter on the subject of motor cars a mere bagatelle, a trumpery, a flumpery, a frumpery, fump.

James Kelman (1946–), A Disaffection

27 But the whole notion of standing at bus stops! Awful. The whole notion of a bus even! Because he required the exact sum of money for the fare. If he didni have this exact sum the driver would refuse to give him change, he would just take the entire £1 or £5 or whatever it was and keep it on behalf of the transport company that employed him.

A situation fraught with awkwardidity.

James Kelman, A Disaffection

28 A general perfume of nausea and unhappy half-sleeping humanity – the crossing had been rough – filled the saloon; a fitful, piercing odour of pickles blew through it when a door opened. Women and children, too ill to undress, lay in the stuffy cabins, and commercial travellers slept stertorously on sofas.

Eric Linklater (1899–1974), White-Maa's Saga

29 Hammered like a bolt
diagonally through Scotland (my
small dark country) this
train's a
swaying caveful of half-
seas over oil-men (fuck
this fuck that fuck
everything) bound for Aberdeen and
North Sea Crude

Liz Lochhead (1947–), Inter-City

30 No doubt he'd come home by instinct, the poor man's taxi.
    Brian McCabe (1951–), The Other McCoy

31 I don't like this, being carried sideways through the night. I feel wrong and helpless – like a timber broadside in a fast stream.
    Norman MacCaig (1910–1996), Sleeping Compartment

32 I'll tak ye on the road again,
    When yellow's on the broom.
    Adam McNaughton, When Yellow's On the Broom

33 They started a coach between Edinburgh and Aberdeen. Their coaches were luxurious and handsome, the horses beautifully matched and of the first character, harness in good taste and of the best quality . . . the mail and other coaches were obliged to follow suit, and travel with equal speed and punctuality. But true to red tapeism, the cramped form and colour of the mail coach never changed, and until the last it retained the iron skid instead of the screw brake.
    Joseph Mitchell (1803–1883), Reminiscences of My Life in the Highlands

34 . . we were graciously received by Lady Seafield, to whom we explained the purport of our visit. She very decidedly told us she 'hated railways',–a they brought together such an objectionable variety of people. Posting, in her opinion, with four horses, was the perfection of travelling.
    Joseph Mitchell, Reminiscences of My Life in the Highlands

35 The *Vital Spark*, I confessed, was well known to me as the most uncertain puffer that ever kept the Old New Year in Upper Lochfyne.
    Neil Munro (1864–1930), The Vital Spark

36 May God bless the bark of Clan-Ranald
    The first day she floats on the brine:
    Himself and his strong men to man her –
    The heroes whom none can outshine.
    Alexander Nicolson (1827–1893), The Galley of Clanranald, *from the Gaelic of Alastair Macdonald*

37 While exploring a particularly wild and uncultivated region of Africa, Mungo Park unexpectedly came across a gibbet. 'The sight of it', he later remarked, 'gave me infinite pleasure, as it proved that I was in a civilised society.'
    Mungo Park (1771–1806), quoted in C. Fadiman, The Little, Brown Book of Anecdotes *(1985)*

38 The tale is told of a hiker who saw his rucksack and all his kit engulfed by the clear waters of a Highland loch. The skipper turned to the ferryman responsible for the accident, and chided him gently for his mistake.
    'Ach, James,' he said, 'you will really have to be more careful in future.'
    Tom Patey (1932–1970), One Man's Mountains

39 'You attend to the driving, Cheorge', she said at the approach to every bend, and on the most distant sight of approaching traffic, 'and I'll see to the horn.' . . . What she said to all passengers before setting out on an excursion was, 'Now remember, if we are going up a hill and the motor suddenly stops, you jump out, clever, and put that stone under the back wheel.'
    Alastair Phillips, My Uncle George *(1954)*

40 The end of the world is near when the Mac-Brayne's ship will be on time.
    Iain Crichton Smith (1928–1998), Thoughts of Murdo

41 The silent ferryman standing in the stern-clutching his coat about him like old iron.
    Iain Crichton Smith, By Ferry to the Island

42 Faster than fairies, faster than witches,
    Bridges and houses, hedges and ditches;
    And charging along like troops in a battle,
    All through the meadows the horses
       and cattle,
    All the sights of the hill and the plain
    Fly as thick as driving rain.
    Robert Louis Stevenson (1850–1894), From a Railway Carriage

43 I travel not to go anywhere, but to go. I travel for travel's sake. The great affair is to move.
    Robert Louis Stevenson, Travels with a Donkey

44 To travel hopefully is a better thing than
to arrive.
Robert Louis Stevenson, Virginibus
Puerisque

45 All I ask, the heavens above,
And the road below me.
Robert Louis Stevenson, The Vagabond

46 No 224. This was the engine that had
gone down with the Tay Bridge on 27th
December 1879, had been recovered, and
had spent part of 1880 at Cowlairs being
refurbished. Someone christened her 'The
Diver', and she was known by that name
until the end of her long career.
John Thomas, The Springburn Story
(1964)

47 Will someone ever rise to write the saga
of the 'Flying Scotsman'? There would be
sardonic stories in that book, like that of
the two enterprising ladies who, during
the war years, drove a thriving trade cater-
ing for the amorous needs of men going on
and returning from leave, and who must
have been the most consistent passengers
the London and North-Eastern Railway
ever had.
George Malcolm Thomson, The Rediscovery of Scotland

48 As we rush, as we rush in the train,
The trees and the houses go wheeling
back,
But the starry heavens above the plain
Come flying in on our track.
James Thomson (1834–1882), The Train

49 The bus station concourse is like a Social
Security office turned inside out and
doused with oil.
Irvine Welsh (1957–), Trainspotting

50 Highways for eident feet,
That hae their mile to gae.
Walter Wingate (1865–1918), Highways
and Byways

Universities

1 The Principal, it is especially requisite,
must be an upright and godly man . . . well
versed in the Scriptures . . . He must also
be skilled and learned in languages, and
especially in Hebrew and Syriac . . .
He shall also . . . set forth all the rest
of Physiology from the Greek text of
Aristotle, to which he shall add a short
explanation of Anatomy. He shall also
expound Geography, History and the outlines of Astronomy. Moreover, he shall
also add Hebrew Grammar, together with
some practice in the rules.
*From the foundation charter of Marischal
College, Aberdeen (1593)*

2 I went to the Royal Technical College in
Glasgow, filled with zeal and enthusiasm,
and feeling quite sure I would distinguish
myself. I found it not so easy. There were
plenty of other youths there, filled with
zeal and enthusiasm. How those youths
worked!
John Logie Baird (1888–1946), Sermons,
Soap and Television

3 What's a' your jargon o' your schools –
Your Latin names for horns and stool?
If honest Nature made you fools,
What sairs your grammars?
Ye'd better ta'en up spades and shools,
Or knappin-hammers.

A set o' dull, conceited hashes
Confuse their brains in college classes!
They gang in stirks, and come out asses,
Plain truth to speak;
And syne they think to climb Parnassus
By dint o' Greek!
Robert Burns (1754–1796) Epistle to
J. Lapraik

4 The true university these days is a collection of books.
Thomas Carlyle (1795–1881), On
Heroes, Hero-Worship and the Heroic
in History

5 Discipline at the University was of the most
relaxed sort; the tutorial system unknown.
It was characteristic of the Scots to leave
the young men to themselves, to teach
them self-management and self-discipline.
*Benjamin Constant (1767–1830), on his
student years in Edinburgh*

6 In a generation which has seen students
become so much more vocal and aggressive in their criticism of University policy
and their demands for a share in deci-
sion-making, and so militant in some
activities to press their claims, they have

become incomparably more docile in the classroom.

> Gordon Donaldson, Some Changes in the Classroom in the Twentieth Century, *in* Four Centuries: Edinburgh University Life *(1983)*

7   It was a grim experience for youth, and would damp the ardour of not a few; they had no fire in winter and would sit over their books wrapped in their plaid. The food was both coarse and monotonous. The dining hall served *pot-au-feu* and stale bread. But in its own way this college was a university in the original sense of the term. It was not training men simply to earn a living. It was not a vocational training, but a liberal education that fits a free man for a full life whatever his calling.

> Arnold Fleming, The Medieval Scots Scholar in France *(1952), on the Scots College in Paris*

8   A kep and goun – what dae they maitter?
A kep and bells wad suit him better.

> Robert Garioch (Robert Garioch Sutherland, 1909–1981), Garioch's response Til George Buchanan

9   We want 'safe' men here, you know, and we generally get them.

> Sir Patrick Geikie, letter to Victor Branford, September 1910, on Edinburgh University

10 From my window I see the rectangular blocks of man's
Insolent mechanical ignorance rise, with hideous exactitude,
against the sun
against the sky.
It is the University

> Alan Jackson (1938–), From My Window

11 . . . a university which does not have a philosophy section has lost the right to be known as a university.

> James Kelman (1946–), letter in Scotland on Sunday *(January 1989), on Strathclyde University*

12 The discipline of colleges and universities is in general contrived, not for the benefit of the students, but for the interest, or more properly speaking, the ease of the masters.

> Adam Smith (1723–1790), The Wealth of Nations

13 Sanctuaries for obsolete systems and exploded prejudices.

> Adam Smith, on Oxford and Cambridge Universities, quoted in Kenneth White, On Scottish Ground (1998)

14 You could go tae University.
  – Whit fir?
  Geoff had to think for a while. He had recently graduated with a degree in English Literature and was on the dole. So were most of his fellow graduates. – It's a good social life, he said.

> Irvine Welsh (1957–), Trainspotting

15 . . . a sort of high-grade liberal arts college on its bold bluff beside the chill North Sea.

> Douglas Young (1913–1973), Scotland, on St Andrews University

War and Men of War

1   'Thou shalt not yield to lord nor loun,
Nor yet shalt thou to me;
But yield thee to the bracken bush
Grows on yon lily-lee.'

> Anonymous, The Battle of Otterburn

2   This fray was fought at Otterbourne,
Between the night and the day;
Earl Douglas was buried at the bracken bush,
And the Percy led captive away.

> Anonymous, The Battle of Otterburn

3   In doubtsome victory they dealt;
The bludy battle lasted long;
Ilk man his neighbour's force there felt
The weakest oft-times got the wrong.

> Anonymous, The Battle of Harlaw

4   'Fight on, my men,' says Sir Andrew Barton,
'I am hurt, but I am not slain;
I'le lay me down and bleed awhile,
And then I'le rise and fight again.'

> Anonymous, Sir Andrew Barton

5   *Teribus ye teri odin,*
Sons of heroes slain at Flodden,

Imitating Border bowmen,
Aye defend your rights and common.

*Traditional Hawick rhyme, quoted in
Charles Mackay,* Poetry and Humour of
the Scottish Language *(1882)*

6 O are ye come to drink the wine,
As ye hae doon before, O?
Or are ye come to wield the brand,
On the dowie houms o' Yarrow?

Anonymous, The Dowie Houms o'
Yarrow

7 Of this sort the said galliasse in schort
tyme cam on windwart of the tothir schip.
Than eftir that thay had hailit utheris, thay
maid them reddie for batail. Than quhair
I sat I herd the cannonis and gunnis maik
monie hideous crak, duf duf duf duf duf
duf. The bersis and falconis cryit tirdif,
tirdif, tirdif, tirdif, tirdif, tirdif. Then the
small artailzie cryit tik tak, tik tak, tik tak,
tik tak, tik tak. The reik, smuik, and the
stink of the gun pulder fylt all the air.

Anonymous, The Complaynt of Scotland *(1549), account of a sea battle*

8 It fell on a day, and a bonnie simmer day,
When green grew aits and barley,
That there fell out a great dispute
Between Argyll and Airlie.

Anonymous, The Bonny House o' Airlie

9 Some had halbards, some had durks,
Some had crooked swords like Turks,
Some had slings, and some had flails
Knit with eel and oxen tails,
Some had spears, some had pikes,
Some had spades which delvit dykes,
Some had guns with rustie ratches,
Some had fiery peats for matches,
Some had bows, but wanted arrows,
Some had pistols without marrows,
Some the coulter of a plough,
Some had scyths, men and horse to hough,
And some with a Lochaber axe
Resolved to gie Dalziel his paiks.

*Anonymous, lines on the Covenanters'
Army at Rullion Green, 24 November
1666, from James Maidment,* A Book of
Scottish Pasquils *(1868)*

10 I faught at land, I faught at sea,
At hame I faught my aunty, O;
But I met the devil and Dundee,
On the braes o' Killiecrankie, O

Anonymous, quoted in Dugald Mitchell,
History of the Highlands and Gaelic

Scotland *(1900), on the battle of Killiecrankie (26 July 1689)*

11 Everybody else took the road he liked
best.

*Contemporary comment on the end of the
1715 Rising, following the secret departure
of the 'Old Pretender' and the Earl of
Mar, quoted in C. Stewart Black,* Scottish Battles *(1936)*

12 A Gordon for me, a Gordon for me:
If you're no' a Gordon you're nae use to
me.
The Black Watch are braw, the Seaforths
and a',
But the cocky wee Gordon's the pride o'
them a'.

Anonymous, A Gordon for Me

13 The wind may blaw, the cock may craw,
The rain may rain, and the snaw may
snaw;
But ye winna frichten Jock McGraw,
The stoutest man in the Forty-Twa.

Anonymous, The Stoutest Man in the
Forty-Twa

14 'They're a' out o' step but oor Jock!'

*Apocryphal mother looking through the
railings of a Glasgow barracks*

15 So 'list, bonnie laddie,
And come awa' wi' me.

Anonymous, Twa Recruiting Sergeants

16 Weep no more, my soldier laddie,
There is peace, where there was once
was war;
Weep no more, my soldier laddie –
There is peace now the battle's o'er.

Anonymous, Now The Battle's O'er

17 Had I been there with sword in hand,
And fifty Camerons by,
That day through high Dunedin's streets
Had pealed the slogan-cry.

W. E. Aytoun (1813–1865), The Execution of Montrose

18 For the king had said him rudely
That ane rose of his chaplet
Was fallen.

John Barbour (c.1320–1395), The Brus,
*Bruce's rebuke to the Earl of Moray on the
field of Bannockburn, 1314*

19 'Beis not abasit for their schor,
Bot settis speris you before

And back to back set all your rout
And all the speris pointis out'.

John Barbour, The Brus

20 'I wot not what mair sall say I?
Ye wot weill all what honour is:
Conteyn you therefore on sic wise
That your honour aye savit be.'

John Barbour, The Brus

21 Like a hedehog with its quills, so would
you see a Pict bristling all round with the
arrows that had pierced him, yet still brandishing his sword, and in blind madness
rushing foreward, now smiting a foe, now
beating the air with vain blows.

C. Stewart Black, Scottish Battles
*(1936), quoting 'an eye-witness account' of
the Galwegians at the Battle of the Standard, 22 August 1138*

22 Henry V . . . ordered the plunder of the
shrine of Saint Fiacre, the holy son of an
ancient Scottish king. For this sacrilege
he was smitten by the saint with a kind
of leprosy, and shortly died of it, cursing
the Scots, and lamenting that 'I can go
nowhere without the finding the Scots at
my beard, dead or alive.'

C. Stewart Black, Scottish Battles

23 'Fight on!' he cried to them. 'Fight on!
Stand ye fast by the Cross of Saint
Andrew!'

C. Stewart Black, Scottish Battles, *quoting the last words of Sir Andrew Barton
(d.1511)*

24 There is no such things as an inevitable
war. If war comes it will be from failure of
human wisdom.

Andrew Bonar Law (1858–1923), speech

25 Scots, wha hae wi' Wallace bled,
Scots, wham Bruce has aften led,
Welcome to your gory bed,
Or to victory.

Robert Burns (1759–1796), Bruce's
Address to His Army Before
Bannockburn

26 Now's the day and now's the hour,
See the front o' battle lour . . .
Wha for Scotland's king and law
Freedom's sword would strongly draw,

Freeman stand, and freeman fa' –
Let him on wi' me!

Robert Burns, Bruce's Address to His
Army Before Bannockburn

27 I am a son of Mars who have been in many
wars,
And show my cuts and scars wherever I
come;
This here was for a wench, and that other
in a trench,
When welcoming the French at the sound
of the drum.

Robert Burns, The Jolly Beggars

28 I once was a maid, tho' I cannot tell when,
And still my delight is in proper young
men;
Some one of a troop of dragoons was
my daddie,
No wonder I'm fond of a sodger laddie.

Robert Burns, The Jolly Beggars

29 Cock up your beaver, and cock it fu'
sprush,
We'll over the Border and gie them a
brush.

Robert Burns, Cock Up Your Beaver

30 O Kenmure's lads are men, Willie,
O Kenmure's lads are men;
Their hearts and swords are metal true,
And that their foes shall ken.

Robert Burns, Kenmure's On and Awa',
Willie

31 Ye hypocrites! are these your pranks?
To murder men, and gie God thanks!
For shame! Gie o'er – proceed no farther –
God won't accept your thanks for
murther.

Robert Burns, Verses Written on a Pane
of Glass on the the Occasion of a
National Thanksgiving for a Naval
Victory

32 And wild and high the 'Cameron's
gathering' rose!
The war-note of Lochiel, which Albyn's
hills
Have heard, and heard, too, have her
Saxon foes:–
How in the noon of night that pibroch
thrills,
Savage and shrill! But with the breath
that fills
Their mountain-pipe, so fill the
mountaineers

With the fierce native daring which instils
The stirring memory of a thousand years,
And Evan's, Donald's fame rings in each
   clansman's ears!

> *Lord Byron (1788–1824),* Childe
> Harold's Pilgrimage, *on the Battle of
> Waterloo*

33 'Ninety-third! Ninety-third! Damn all that
eagerness.'

> *Sir Colin Campbell to the 'Thin Red
> Line' at Balaclava, quoted in C. Wood-
> ham-Smith,* The Reason Why *(1953)*

34 When was a war not a war? When it was
carried on by means of barbarism.

> *Sir Henry Campbell-Bannerman
> (1836–1908), Speech to the National
> Reform Union Dinner, June 1901, on the
> Boer War*

35 For a moment the Spaniards seemed taken
by surprise as though unwilling to believe
that so small a crew would have the audacity to board them; but soon recovering
themselves they made a rush to the waist
of the frigate where the fight was for some
minutes gallantly carried on. Observing
the enemy's colours still flying, I directed
one of our men immediately to haul them
down, when the Spanish crew, without
pausing to think by whose orders the
colours had been struck, and naturally
believing it the act of one of their own officers, gave in, and we were in possession.

> *Thomas Cochrane, Earl of Dundonald
> (1775–1860),* The Autobiography of a
> Seaman, *on naval warfare in 1800–01*

36 It was during this time that Billy joined
the Parachute Regiment of the Territorial
Army, seeking adventure, and trying to
make himself windswept and interesting.
Billy claims that at the medical exam, the
doctor said, 'You're not very big downstairs, are you?' to which Billy quipped, 'I
thought we were only going to fight them.'

> *Billy Connolly (1942–), quoted by James
> McGowan,* The Billy Connolly Website,
> *1998*

37 I cannot reproach myself; the manner in
which the enemy came on was quicker
than could be described, and . . . possibly
was the cause of our men taking a most
destructive panic.

> *Sir John Cope (c.1690–1760), reporting*

*to Lord Tweeddale after the battle of
Prestonpans (20 September 1745)*

38 On fut should be all Scottis weir,
By hill and moss thaimself to steir,
Lat woodis for wallis be bow and speir,
That enemyis do thaim na deir.
In strait placis keip all store,
And burn the planeland thaim befoir . . .
This is the counsail and intent
Of Guid King Robert's Testament

> *John Fordun (d.1385),* Scotichronicon,
> *translation from Latin written in the
> margin of a copy belonging to Hector Boece
> (c.1465–1536)*

39 . . . when the Scots saw the Englishmen
recoil and yield themselves, then the Scots
were courteous and set them their ransoms
and every man said to his prisoner, Sir, go
and unarm you and take your ease: I am
your master, and so made their prisoners
as good cheer as if they had been brothers,
without doing them any damage.

> *Jean Froissart (c.1333–c.1404),* Chro-
> niques, *on the Battle of Otterburn, 1388,
> translated from French*

40 Victory belongs to those who hold out the
longest.

> *Field Marshal Earl Haig (1861–1928),
> order to the British Expeditionary
> Force, April 1918*

41 Never volunteer for nothing.

> *Hamish Henderson (1919–), Fort
> Capuzzo*

42 In the battle of Inverkeithing, between
the Royalists and Oliver Cromwell, five
hundred of the followers of the Laird of
Maclean were left dead on the field. In
the heat of the conflict, seven brothers of
the clan sacrificed their lives in defence
of their leader, Sir Hector Maclean. Being
hard pressed by the enemy, he was supported and covered from their attacks by
these intrepid men; and as one brother fell,
another came up in succession to cover
him, crying, 'Another for Hector!'

> *Alexander Hislop,* The Book of Scottish
> Anecdote *(1883), quoting David Stewart
> of Garth (1772–1829)*

43 'There's equal quackery in a' things alike.
Look at a sodger – that is, an offisher –
a' wavin' wi' white plumes, glitterin' wi'
gowd, and ringin wi' iron . . . and a' the

stopped street stares . . . at school that symbol o' extermination was ca'd Fozie Tam.'

James Hogg (1770–1835), quoted in Christopher North (John Wilson, 1785–1854), Noctes Ambrosianae

44   Lock the door, Lariston, lion of
       Liddisdale,
     Lock the door, Lariston, Lowther comes on.

James Hogg, Lock the Door, Lariston

45   'Oh Scotia my dear, my native land.' That line, penned by Sir Walter Scott . . . can be read on a stone at Coldstream bridge midway across the Tweed . . . At the beginning of the war . . . Coldstream council had the slab removed because they feared the verse inscribed thereon might be of help to any German parachutist who happened to land on the bridge.

William Douglas Home (1912–), Old Men Remember

46   Like Douglas conquer, or like Douglas die.

John Home (1724–1808) Douglas

47   I do not now precisely remember how many days the dead bodies lay in the field to glut the eye of the merciless conqueror. But it is certain that there they lay until the stench oblig'd him to cause bury them.

Rev. George Innes (fl. 1750s), letter to Robert Forbes, Bishop of Ross and Caithness, (February 1750), quoted in Forbes' The Lyon in Mourning, on Culloden

48   I canna see the sergeant,
     I canna see the sergeant,
     I – canna – see the – sergeant:
     He's owre far awa'.

Joseph Lee (1878–1949), Ballads of Battle

49   Every bullet has its billet;
     Many bullets more than one.
     God! Perhaps I killed a mother,
     When I killed a mother's son.

Joseph Lee, The Bullet

50   Then the King broke out publicly, in these words, saying, 'O you who were wont to say that my Scotsmen were useless to the King and the kingdom, worth naught save as eaters of mutton and guzzlers of wine,

see now who have earned the honour, victory, and glory, of this battle.'

Liber Pluscardensis, quoting King Charles VII of France, on the Scots who fought at the Battle of Beaugé (1421), translated from Latin

51   The Captain whispered, 'Come on!' Merriman, lurching forward on his belly, thrust his bayonet stiffly in front of him and heard a muffled cry of pain.
     'What's the matter?' he asked.
     Another muted whimper answered him, and a moment later one of the patrol, in the broad, untroubled accents of Buchan, said hoarsely, 'Michty God, ye've fair ruined the Captain. You've stuck your bayonet clean up his airse!'

Eric Linklater (1899–1974), Magnus Merriman

52   They are a song in the blood of all true men.

Hugh MacDiarmid (C. M. Grieve, 1898–1972), The International Brigades

53   You remember the place called the Tawny Field?
     It got a fine dose of manure;
     Not the dung of sheep and goats,
     But Campbell blood, well congealed.

Iain Lom Macdonald (c.1620–c.1707), Las Inbhir Lochaidh (The Battle of Inverlochy)

54   'I will follow you to death, were there no other to draw a sword in your cause.'

Ranald MacDonald (fl. mid-18th century), quoted in Dugald Mitchell, History of the Highlands and Gaelic Scotland (1900), to Prince Charles Edward Stewart, on the Doutelle, July 1745

55   'We had an English subaltern once in our battery who used to run and extinguish fires in ammunition dumps . . . He said that shells cost five pounds each and it was everyone's duty to save government money.'
     'Where is he buried?' asked Cameron.

A. G. Macdonell (1895–1941), England, Their England

56   Duncan gave orders that if it came to fighting, every one of the ships must fight until she sank, and added that he had carefully noted the soundings, and the flags

could still fly though the ships were at the bottom . . . in fact he stopped the Dutch without losing a man.

Agnes Mure Mackenzie, Scottish Pageant, *1707–1802, on Admiral Lord Duncan in 1797*

57 Fat civilians wishing they
'Could go and fight the Hun.'
Can't you see them thanking God
That they're over forty-one?

E. A. Mackintosh (1893–1916),
Recruiting

58 Lads, you're wanted. Come and die.

E. A. Mackintosh, Recruiting

59 Lest we see a worse thing than it is to die,
Live ourselves and see our friends cold
    beneath the sky,
God grant that we too be lying there in
    wind and mud and rain
Before the broken regiments come stum
    bling back again.

E. A. Mackintosh, Before the Summer

60 The only war that is worth waging is the Class War.

John Maclean (1879–1923), The
Vanguard

61 There's some say that we wan,
Some say that they wan,
Some say that nane wan at a', man;
But o' ae thing I'm sure,
That at Sheriffmuir,
A battle there was that I saw, man.
And we ran, and they ran,
And they ran, and we ran,
And they ran and we ran awa', man.

Murdoch MacLennan (fl. early 18th cen-
tury), Sheriffmuir *(1715)*

62 O children of Conn, remember
Hardihood in time of battle:
Be watchful, daring,
Be dextrous, winning renown,
Be vigorous, pre-eminent,
Be strong, nursing your wrath,
Be stout, brave,
Be valiant, triumphant . . .

MacMhuirich, Incitement to Clan Donald
before the Battle of Harlaw (1411), from
Gaelic, quoted in Hugh Cheape and I. F.
Grant, Periods in Highland History
(1987)

63 Tonight's the night – if the lads are the lads!

Macnab's rallying cry to his twelve sons,
quoted in Augustus Muir, Heather Track
and High Road *(1944)*

64 Our business is like men to fight,
And hero-like to die!

William Motherwell (1797–1835), The
Cavalier's Song

65 There's nothing noo in the heids o' the gyurls but sodgers. But ye canna blame the craturs! There's something smert aboot the kilt and the cockit bonnet.

Neil Munro (1864–1930), Hurricane
Jack of the Vital Spark

66 Gin danger's there, we'll thole our share,
Gi'es but the weapons, we've the will
Ayont the main to prove again,
Auld Scotland counts for something still.

Charles Murray (1864–1941), A Sough
of War

67 . . . some said the hair shirt rather than arms was their protection.

Guillaume de Nangis, Chronicon
(c.1315), quoted in Agnes Mure Macken-
zie, Scottish Pageant *55 BC–AD 1513*
(1946), on the Scots at Bannockburn,
from Latin

68 PECCAVI

Sir Charles James Napier (1782–1853),
attributed telegraphic message announcing
his capture of Sind (Latin for 'I have
sinned')

69 There are more than birds on the hill
    tonight,
And more than winds on the plain!
The threat of the Scotts has filled the
    moss,
'There will be moonlight again.'

Will H. Ogilvie (1869–1963), The
Blades of Harden

70 It was perhaps one of the most innocent and orderly hosts ever seen, considering they had no discipline and not much pay.

John Ramsay of Ochtertyre (1736–1814),
letter to Elizabeth Dundas, February
1810, on Prince Charles Edward Stewart's
army

71 In winter 1779, after Scotland had been exhausted by raising new levies, Sir William Augustus Cunningham boasted in

the House of Commons that 20,000 men might yet be raised in that country and never be missed . . . The Hon Henry Erskine said he believed it was true. But they must be raised from the churchyards.

Charles Rodger, Boswelliana (*1874*)

72 Who could be blind to the horrors, who could be dumb to the cries? The first man I saw was the bombing sergeant, with his head laid open, being carried back on a stretcher, moaning and pleading for water which could not assuage his thirst or moisten his parched throat. The bodies of two Black Watch pipers, their red kilts splashed with blood, lay near. Every little nook was filled by wounded men who had crawled there to die.

Robert B. Ross, The 51st in France, (*1918*)

73 Hail to the Chief who in triumph advances!

Sir Walter Scott (1771–1832), The Lady of the Lake

74 On right, on left, above, below,
Sprung up at once the lurking foe.

Sir Walter Scott, The Lady of the Lake

75 Come one, come all! This rock shall fly
From its firm base as soon as I.

Sir Walter Scott, The Lady of the Lake

76 . . . the stern joy which warriors feel
In foemen worthy of their steel.

Sir Walter Scott, The Lady of the Lake

77 . . . Flodden's fatal field,
Where shiver'd was fair Scotland's spear
And broken was her shield.

Sir Walter Scott, Marmion

78 I hae swaggered wi' a' thae arms, and muskets, and pistols, buff-coats and bandoliers, lang eneugh, and I like the pleugh-paidle a hantle better.

Sir Walter Scott, Old Mortality

79 England shall many a day
Tell of the bloody fray,
When the Blue Bonnets came over the
Border.

Sir Walter Scott, Border Ballad

80 'Aye, if ye had fower legs ye wouldnae stand there lang.'

Wat Scott of Harden (fl. late 16th century), quoted in G. M. Fraser, The Steel

Bonnets (*1971*), *remark made on passing an English haystack on the way home from a raid*

81 If that you will France win
Then with Scotland first begin.

William Shakespeare (c.1530–1601), Henry V

82 Now Johnnie, troth, ye are na blate
To come wi' the news o' your ain defeat,
And leave your men in sic a state,
Sae early in the morning.

Adam Skirving (1719–1803), Johnnie Cope

83 The security of every society must always depend, more or less, upon the martial spirit of the great body of the people.

Adam Smith (1723–1790), The Wealth of Nations

84 Doutless he deed for Scotland's life;
Doutless the statesmen dinna lee;
But och tis sair begrutten pride,
And wersh the wine o' victorie!

Sydney Goodsir Smith (1915–1975), The Mither's Lament

85 The captain's all right, really. A touch of the toasted tea-breid. You know the type.

W. Gordon Smith, Mr Jock (*1987*)

86 As a nation we've fallen in and marched behind some damned funny folk.

W. Gordon Smith, Mr Jock

87 Earth that blossom'd and was glad
'Neath the cross that Christ had,
Shall rejoice and blossom too
When the bullet reaches you.

C. H. Sorley (1895–1915), Untitled Poem

88 Machines of death from east to west
Drone through the darkened sky;
Machines of death from west to east
Through the same darkness fly . . .
They leave a ruin; and they meet
A ruin on return

William Soutar (1898–1943), Revelation

89 You can understand, from the look of him, that sense, not so much of humour, as of what is grimmest and driest in pleasantry, which inspired his address before the fight at Camperdown. He had just overtaken the Dutch fleet under Admiral de

Winter. 'Gentlemen,' says he, 'you see a severe Winter approaching; I have only to advise you to keep up a good fire.'

> *Robert Louis Stevenson (1850–1894),*
> Some Portraits by Raeburn, *on Admiral Lord Duncan (1731–1804)*

90   '. . . it may come to a fecht for it yet, Davie; and then, I'll confess I would be blythe to have you at my oxter, and I think you would be none the worse of having me at yours.'

> *Robert Louis Stevenson,* Catriona

91   I fear how lucidly I shall remember
That I dared contemplate a moment
       of time
Without compassion, when men rushed
       to dismember
Mutually their white harmonious limbs –

> *W. F. M. Stewart (1918–),* Poem

92   Wha would shun the field of danger?
Wha to fame would be a stranger?
Now, when Freedom bids avenge her,
Wha would shun her ca', lassie?

> *Robert Tannahill (1774–1810),* Loudon's
> Bonnie Woods and Braes

93   'A warrior,' said he, 'should not care for wine or luxury, for fine turbans or embroidered shulwars; his talwar should be bright, and never mind whether his papooshes are shining.'

> *W. M. Thackeray (1811–1863), of Sir*
> *Charles James Napier (1782–1853)*

94   'Men, remember there is no retreat from here. You must die where you stand.'
       To the Russian cavalry as they came on, the hillock appeared unoccupied, when suddenly, as if out of the earth, there sprang up a line two deep of Highlanders in red coats – the line immortalised in British history as 'the thin red line'.

> *Cecil Woodham-Smith,* The Reason
> Why *(1953), on Sir Colin Campbell*
> *(1792–1863), and the Argylls at Balaclava (October 1854)*

Words, Language and Speech

1   Words of affection, howsoe'er express'd,
The latest spoken still are deemed the
       best.

> *Joanna Baillie (1762–1851),* Address to
> Miss Agnes Baillie on Her Birthday

2   Let us treat children and fairies in a more summary manner . . . Nowadays if in reading a book I come across a word beginning with 'c' or 'f' I toss it aside.

> *J. M. Barrie (1860–1937), speech to the*
> Royal Literary Fund, *1930*

3   . . . we who live in Scotland are obliged to study English from books like a dead language which we can understand but cannot speak. Our style smells of the lamp and we are slaves of the language, and are continually afraid of committing gross blunders.

> *James Beattie (1735–1803), quoted in*
> Burton, Life of Hume *(1840)*

4   And while the bishop, who was not yet fluent in the English language, preached the Gospel, it was most delightful to see the king himself interpreting the word of God to his thanes and leaders; for he himself had obtained perfect command of the Scottish tongue during his long exile.

> *St Bede (c.673–735),* Ecclesiastical History of the English People, *on St Aidan*
> *and King Oswald of Northumbria (the*
> *'Scottish tongue' is Gaelic)*

5   A word, he says, is short and quick, but
       works
A long result.

> *John Stuart Blackie (1809–1895),*
> The Wise Men of Greece

6   Our school was in Scotland, in almost every respect a Scottish public school, and yet a strong Scottish accent was a real stigma . . . When people spoke with a strong Scottish accent we would make harsh retching sounds in the base of our throats or emit loose-jawed idiot burblings.

> *William Boyd,* Old School Ties, *on Gordonstoun School in the 1960s*

7   The tinkers have curious voices – angular outcast flashing accents like the cries of seagulls.

> *George Mackay Brown (1921–1996),*
> Five Green Waves

8   It is a word, blossoming as legend, poem, story, secret, that holds a community together and gives a meaning to its life . . .

Decay of language is always the symptom of a more serious sickness.

> *George Mackay Brown*, An Orkney Tapestry

9 Most words descend in value.

> *Ivor Brown (1891–1974)*, A Word in Your Ear

10 Glamour . . . this beautiful word has been bludgeoned to death by modern showmanship . . . an English importation from Scotland where it had long signified magic with magical effect.

> *Ivor Brown*, A Word in Your Ear

11 I can perceive without regret the gradual extinction of the ancient Scottish language, and cheerfully allow its harsh sounds to die away, and give place to the softer and more harmonious tones of the Latin.

> *George Buchanan (c.1506–1582), quoted in A. L. Williamson*, Scottish National Consciousness in the Age of James VI (1979)

12 The mair they talk I'm kend the better; E'en let them clash!

> *Robert Burns (1759–1796)*, The Poet's Welcome to His Bastart Wean

13 Strange encomiums I have heard from the natives upon the language of their country, although it be but a corruption of the Irish tongue; and, if you could believe some of them, it is so expressive, that it only wants to be better known to become universal.

> *Edmund Burt (fl. early 18th century)*, Letters From a Gentleman in the North of Scotland (1726–37)

14 I realised that Gaelic was a missing part of my world, since with the modern Gael I share a history but not a language . . . his history remains mine; written into my conscience in invisible ink, in a language I have forgotten how to understand.

> *James Campbell*, Invisible Country (1984)

15 The coldest word was once a glowing new metaphor.

> *Thomas Carlyle (1795–1881)*, Past and Present

16 Silence is deep as Eternity, speech is as shallow as Time.

> *Thomas Carlyle*, Sir Walter Scott

17 Speak not at all, in any wise, till you have somewhat to speak; care not for the reward of your speaking, but simply and with undivided mind for the truth of your speaking.

> *Thomas Carlyle*, Essays

18 Sarcasm I now see to be, in general, the language of the devil.

> *Thomas Carlyle*, Sartor Resartus

19 Great the blindness and the sinful darkness and ignorance and evil will of those who teach, write and foster the Gaelic speech; for to win for themselves the empty rewards of the world, they both choose and use more and more to make vain and misleading tales, lying and worldly, of the Tuath de Danann, of fighting men and champions, of Fionn MacCumhal and his heroes, and many more whom now I will not number.

> *John Carswell, Kirk Superintendent of Argyll (fl. mid-16th century), translated from Gaelic, in the Introduction to a Gaelic translation of the Liturgy of the English Congregation at Geneva, quoted in Agnes Mure Mackenzie*, Scottish Pageant 1513–1625 (1948)

20 . . . the Society's design was . . . not to continue the Irish language, but to wear it out, and learn the people the English tongue.

> *Committee of the Society for the Propagation of Christian Knowledge (1720), quoted in Agnes Mure Mackenzie*, Scottish Pageant 1707–1802 (1950)

21 Edinburgh, one of the few European capitals with no anti-semitism in its history, accepted them with characteristic cool interest. In its semi-slums they learned such English as they knew, which meant in fact that they grafted the debased Scots of the Edinburgh streets onto their native Yiddish to produce one of the most remarkable dialects ever spoken by man.

> *David Daiches (1912–1999)*, Two Worlds

22 Traist weill, to follow ane fixt sentence or matter
Is mair practic, difficil, and mair straiter,
Though thine ingyne be elevate and hie,
Than for to write all ways at libertie.

> *Gavin Douglas (1475–1522)*, Prologue to the Aeneid, *on translation*

23 Beside Latin our language is imperfite,
Whilk in some part is the cause and wyte
Why that of Virgillis verse the ornate
   beauty
Intill our tongue may not observit be.

   Gavin Douglas, Prologue to the Aeneid

24 The beauty of his ornate eloquence
May nocht all time be keepit with the
   sentence . . .
Wha haldis, quod he, of wordis the
   properteis
Full oft the verity of the sentence fleeis.

   Gavin Douglas, Prologue to the Aeneid

25 . . . the most interesting nicknames, and
the ones in which the Borderers obviously
took great pleasure, were those descriptive and often highly offensive appellations
referring to personal appearance, habits
and behaviour. Thus we find Curst Eckie,
Ill Will Armstrong, Nebless Clem Croser,
the two Elliot brothers, Archie and George,
who were familiarly known as 'Dog Pyntle'
and 'Buggerback'.

   George Macdonald Fraser, The Steel
   Bonnets *(1971)*

26 Telling the secret, telling, clucking and
   tutting,
Sighing, or saying it served her right,
the bitch! – the words and weather
   both are cutting
In Causewayend, on this November night.

   G. S. Fraser (1916–1980), Lean Street

27 . . . the fortunate circumstance of the
Scotch possessing the whole range of the
English language as well as their own, by
which they enjoy an uncommonly rich
vocabulary.

   John Galt (1779–1839), The
   Seamstress

28 For tho' 'tis true that Mither-tongue
Has had the melancholy fate
To be neglekit by the great,
She still has fun' an open door
Amang the uncorruptit poor . . .
A fouth o' flours may yet be fund
Wi' pains, on Caledonian grund.
Dig for their roots, or they be dead,
Fra Gretna Green to Peterhead;
And plant them quick, as soon as got,
In ae lexicographic pot;

I trou they'll soon baith live and thrive
And gie you flours eneuch belyve.

   Alexander Geddes (1737–1802), Epistle
   to the Society of Antiquaries *(1792)*

29 Chris would say they needn't fash, if
she said it in Scots the woman would
think, *Isn't that a common-like bitch at the
Manse?* If she said it in English the speak
would spread round the minister's wife
was putting on airs.

   *Lewis Grassic Gibbon (James Leslie
   Mitchell, 1901–1935)*, Cloud Howe

30 Three Lords of Justiciary were ordered to
appear at the Bar of the House of Lords
about the Porteous mob. 'Brethren,' said
Lord Dun pompously, as he supped with
his fellow-judges, 'I am sorry to say neither
of you will be understood by the House
tomorrow. I am, you well know, in a different situation, having made the English
language my particular study.' Tomorrow
came, when Lord Royston was hardly intelligible; as for my Lord Dun, Lord Kames
used gleefully to tell, 'Deil ae word from
beginning to end did the English understand of his speech.'

   H. Grey Graham, The Social Life of
   Scotland in the Eighteenth Century
   (1899)

31 What is the language
Using us for?
For the prevailing weather or words
Each object hides in a metaphor.

   W. S. Graham (1918–1986), What Is
   the Language Using Us For?

32 The fishermen have always had taboos on
certain words while at sea . . . The forbidden words in the north were priest or
minister, salmon, pig, hare, rats and rabbits (exactly like the east coast). Rabbits
were alluded to as 'little feeties'.

   I. F. Grant, Highland Folk Ways *(1961)*

33 A 'Gadgie' when he is a 'Chor',
A 'Jugal' always fears,
For 'Jugals' as a rule are kept
By 'Gadgies' with big 'keirs';
This means a man who goes to steal
A watchdog may expect;
'Tis mystifying all the same,
This Berwick dialect.

   Thomas Grey, Tweedmouth, *in* The
   Berwick Advertiser *(1910), quoted in*

J. Grant, Introduction to The Scottish National Dictionary *(1934)*

34 ... the old languageack ... was full of such names, not only for things but for men; particularly indeed for men, so that the name evokes each kind of man with an astonishing, almost laughable, magic. Naturally with thi-s go diminutives that are the finger-tips of fun, phrases that snare the heart with a hair. For love-making, it is a subtle tongue.

Neil Gunn (1891–1973), Butcher's Broom, *on Gaelic*

35 Words are well adapted for description and arousing of emotions, but for many kinds of precise thought, other symbols are much better.

J. B. S. Haldane (1892–1964)

36 'Whipping the cat', or, more enigmatically, 'flogging poussy' – it is of tailors we must be understood to speak – was simply a practice of going from farm-toun to farm-toun, even from cottar-house to cottar-house, and there working for, and meantime messing and lodging with, the inhabitants.

Hugh Haliburton (John Logie Robertson, 1846–1922), In Scottish Fields

37 The gude auld honest mither tongue!
They kent nae ither, auld or young;
The cottar spak' it in his yaird,
An' on his rigs the gawcie laird.

Hugh Haliburton, On the Decadence of the Scots Language, Manners and Customs

38 Would you repeat that again, sir, for it sounds sae sonorous that the words droon the ideas?

James Hogg (1770–1835), quoted in Christopher North (John Wilson,1785–1854), Noctes Ambrosianae

39 The regrettable thing about Gaelic is its hopelessly bewildering spelling. The sounds are pleasing and melodious in a high degree but they hide themselves behind most peculiar disguisements of print.

D. T. Holmes, Literary Tours in the Highlands and Islands *(1909)*

40 Since word is thrall, and thought is free,
Keep well thy tongue, I counsel thee.

King James VI (1566–1625), Ballad of Good Counsel

41 heh jimmy
yawright ih
stull wayiz urryi
ih

Tom Leonard (1944–), The Good Thief

42 what's your favourite word dearie
is it wee
I hope it's wee
wee's such a nice wee word

Tom Leonard, The Voyeur

43 awright fur
funny stuff
ur
Stanley Bax-
ter ur but
luv n science
n thaht naw

Tom Leonard, Unrelated Incidents

44 'Learn English!' he exclaimed, 'no, never; it was my trying to learn that language that spoilt my Scots; and as to being silent, I will promise to hold my tongue if you will make fools hold theirs.'

Dr John Leyden (1775–1811), quoted in John Reith, The Life of Dr John Leyden *(1909), when asked, on his arival in Bombay, not to discuss literature and to speak 'English'*

45 Douglas Young, anxious to demonstrate the living quality of Scots, held up his empty beer glass and called to the barman, 'Some mair.' To everyone's astonishment, the barman presently came across carrying a long pole and pulled open an upper window.

Maurice Lindsay (1918–), Thank You for Having Me

46 Its glory shall not fade in spite of guile
and strangers' bitter hate.
Scotland spoke it,
and Lowland carles did too,
our nobles, princes,
dukes of high degree.
In King's Council
when the court gave its decision

knotty problems
were solved with Gaelic precision.

*Alexander Macdonald (Alasdair Mac-
Maighstir Alasdair, c.1690–c.1770)*, In
Praise of Gaelic, *from Derick Thomson,*
An Introduction to Gaelic Poetry
(1974)

47 It's soon', no' sense, that faddoms the
    herts o' men,
    And by my sangs the rouch auld Scots
    I ken
    E'en herts that hae nae Scots'll dirl richt
    thro'
    As nocht else could – for here's a language
    rings
    Wi' datchie sesames, and names for name
    less things.

    Hugh MacDiarmid (1892–1978),
    Gairmscoile

48 I covet the mystery of our Gaelic speech
    In which *rugadh* was at once a blush,
    A promontory, a headland, a cape,
    Leadan, musical notes, litany, hair of the
    head,
    And *fonn*, land, earth, delight, and a tune
    in music.

    Hugh MacDiarmid, Direadh

49 'Tis the speech used in the Garden –
    Adam left it to mankind.

    Duncan Bàn MacIntyre (1724–1812),
    Rann Do 'N Ghaidhlig 'S Do 'N
    Phiob-Mhoir (Ode to Gaelic and the
    Great Pipe)

50 The Scotch is as spangled with vowels as a
    meadow with daisies in the month of May.

    Charles Mackay (1814–1889), The
    Poetry and Humour of the Scottish
    Language

51 To me it appears undeniable that the Sco-
    tish Idiom of the British Tongue is more
    fit for Pleading than either the English
    Idiom or the French Tongue; for certainly
    a Pleader must use a brisk, smart and quick
    way of speaking . . . Our Pronunciation is
    like ourselves, fiery, abrupt, sprightly and
    bold.

    Sir George Mackenzie (1636–1691),
    What Eloquence is Fit for the Bar

52 Lord Kelly, a determined punster, and his
    brother Andrew were drinking tea with
    James Boswell. Boswell put his cup to his
    head, 'Here's *t'ye*, my Lord.' – At that

moment, Lord Kelly coughed. – 'You have
a *coughie*', said his brother. – 'Yes', said
Lord Kelly, 'I have been like to *choak o'*
late.'

*Henry Mackenzie (1745–1831), recorded
in H. W. Thomson,* The Anecdotes and
Egotisms of Henry Mackenzie

53 It is natural for a poet to love his own lan-
    guage if it is the language of his ancestors
    and dying, even if it were a poor defective
    thing. Gaelic is not a poor language, in art
    at any rate.

    Sorley Maclean (1911–1996)

54 You could drive a train across the Firth of
    Forth on her vowels.

    Bruce Marshall (1899–1987), Teacup
    Terrace

55 The accent of the lowest state of Glaswe-
    gians is the ugliest one can encounter . . .
    it is associated with the unwashed and the
    violent.

    *Anonymous university lecturer (1975),
    quoted in Janet Menzies,* Investigation
    of Attitudes to Scots and Glaswegian
    Dialect Among Secondary School
    Pupils

56 Then I noticed that Scottish grammar was
    not English, and I made a Scotch Gram-
    mar showing that all the things that people
    called 'bad grammar' because they would
    be so in English, were 'good grammar' in
    Scotch.

    *Sir James Murray (1837–1915), letter to
    Dr Bryce, December 1903*

57 *Greitand doun in Gallowa*
    mar bu dual don *gallow breid*
    a' dranndail is ag cainntearachd
    le *my trechour tung*, gun teagamh
    that hes tane ane hyland strynd.

    (The habit of yon gallows breed
    muttering and deedling, piper-like
    with my traitor tongue, doubtless
    that has taken a Highland twist)

    William Neill (1922–), De A Thug Ort
    Sgriobhadh Ghaidhlig? (What Made
    You Write in Gaelic?)

58 I speak just the fine English now,
    My own ways left behind;
    The good schoolmasters taught me how;
    they purified my mind
    from the errors of any kind.

    William Neill, Dh' fhalbh sin is tha

'inig seo (That's Gone and This Has Come)

59 Anywhere in the world where there's a dying language, the neighbours say the people are lazy and prone to drink.

Sir Iain Noble (1935–), quoted in Kenneth Roy, Conversations in a Small Country (1989)

60 I was once down alone at the pier in Balintore, watching the boats come in, and fell in with some young fishermen . . . who tried some Gaelic on me. I had a quick ear. They made me repeat the phrase over and over again, and then said, 'Now away you and say that to the Minister.' That was the only time I suffered the ebony cane without knowing exactly – that is, word for word – what I was getting it for, but it made me wary of casual Gaelic.

Alastair Phillips, My Uncle George (1954)

61 . . . none can more sincerely wish a total extinction of the Scotish *colloquial* dialect than I do, for there are few *modern* Scoticisms which are not barbarisms.

John Pinkerton (1758–1826), Preface to Ancient Scotish Poems (1786)

62 A conscientious Chinaman who contemplated a thesis on the literary history of Scotland would have no doubt as to his procedure: 'I will learn a little Gaelic, and read all I can find about Gaelic literature . . .' He would be rather mystified when he found that historians of Scotland and its literature had known and cared as much about Gaelic as about Chinese.

William Power, Literature and Oatmeal

63 . . . sae saft a voice and slid a tongue.

Allan Ramsay (1686–1758), Eclogue

64 . . . the story was told of . . . Henry Dundas, applying to Mr Pitt for the loan of a horse 'the length of Highgate'– a very common expression in Scotland, at that time, to signify the distance to which the ride was to extend. Mr Pitt good-humouredly wrote back to say that he was afraid he had not a horse in his possession quite so long as Mr Dundas had mentioned, but he had sent the longest he had.

Dean E. B. Ramsay (1793–1872), Reminiscences of Scottish Life and Character

65 There is no greater impediment to the advancement of knowledge than the ambiguity of words.

Thomas Reid (1710–1796), Essays on the Intellectual Powers of Man

66 We've words afouth, that we can ca' our ain,
Tho' frae them now my childer sair refrain.

Alexander Ross (1699–1784), Helenore

67 His ready speech flowed fair and free,
In phrase of gentlest courtesy;
Yet seemed that tone and gesture bland
Less used to sue than to command.

Sir Walter Scott (1771–1832), The Lady of the Lake

68 Ae day laest ouk, whin I was gaen t' da sola,
I met wir skülmaister. I gees him da time o da day, an' spaeks back an' fore, dan he says to me, 'Fat's yer wee bit loonie deein', that he's nae been at skool syne Monday week?' Noo sir, haed I been askin' dis question I wid hae said, 'What's your peerie boy düin' 'at he's no been at skül frae last Moninday?' . . . we pay dem fur laernin' bairns English, no fur unlearnin' wir Shetlan' speech.'

Shetland Times, Recollections of the Past, (*November 1880*)

69 He who loses his language loses his world.

Iain Crichton Smith (1928–1998), Shall Gaelic Die?

70 'Transposing Greek to Gaelic is no toil.
They had their clans, their sea terms.
   And the style
Of the great O*dyssey* is what Gaelic knows.'

Iain Crichton Smith, Oban, 1955–82

71 . . . wi' sic clash
Gang up the slogans an' gab-gash
O' what-for-noes, fornents, forbyes,
Tae-hell-wi'-yous an' here-am-Is
That only glegest lugs are able
Frae oot the blethers oo' oor Babel
Tae wale a modicum o' wit.

William Soutar (1898–1943), Vision

72 Man is a creature who lives not by bread alone, but principally by catchwords.

Robert Louis Stevenson (1850–1894)

73 'Lallans' – a synthesised Burnsian esperanto; 'Plastic Scots' its enemies called it.

John Sutherland, The Times Literary Supplement (*August 1998*)

74 Many people think that Scots possesses a rich vocabulary, but this is a view not wholly borne out by a close examination . . . It is as if the Doric had been invented by a cabal of scandal-mongering beldams, aided by a council of observant gamekeepers.

George Malcolm Thomson, The Rediscovery of Scotland

75 Noo slings aboot an' stars a' oot, an'
auld moon chowin' sin,
Here ye wonner really at the din,
As fit aboot of ebbs salute, and fetters
all the score,
Hyfon pland often really soar.

Thomas Thomson (1837–1924), Hyfons, Hyfons

76 I am fascinated and frightened by the power and danger of words, which are so often grave obstacles to full honesty of thought.

Sir Robert Watson-Watt (1892–1973), Three Steps to Victory

Youth and Age

1 Welcome eild, for youth is gone.

Anonymous, Welcome Eild

2 I'm not young enough to know everything.

J. M. Barrie (1867–1930), The Admirable Crichton

3 I've seen sae monie changefu' years,
On earth I am a stranger grown;
I wander in the ways of men,
Alike unknowing and unknown.

Robert Burns (1759–1796), Lament for James, Earl of Glencairn

4 An' O for ane an' twenty, Tam!
And hey, sweet ane an' twenty, Tam!
I'll learn my kin a rattlin sang,
An' I saw ane an' twenty, Tam.

Robert Burns, O For Ane An' Twenty, Tam

5 The canty auld folk crackin' crouse,
The young ones rantin' through the house.

Robert Burns, The Twa Dogs

6 Heaven gives our years of fading strength
Indemnifying fleetness;
And those of Youth, a seeming length,
Proportioned to their sweetness.

Thomas Campbell (1777–1844), A Thought Suggested by the New Year

7 'Tis the sunset of life gives me mystical lore,
And coming events cast their shadows before.

Thomas Campbell, Lochiel's Warning

8 This day I am thirty years old. Let me now bid a cheerful adieu to my youth. My young days are now surely over, and why should I regret them? Were I never to grow old I might be always here, and might never bid farewell to sin and sorrow.

Janet Colquhoun (1781–1846), Diary, 17 April 1811, quoted in A Memory of Lady Colquhoun, by *James Hamilton (1851)*

9 The auld wife sat ayont her man,
But nae auld carle saw she;
And, gin he keekit owre at her,
An auld wife saw na he.
Wi' tousy head a cottar lad
Sat in the auld man's place,
And glowered, tongue-tackit, at the stars
That lauched in Jeanie's face.

A. M. Davidson, Auld Fowk

10 I wes in yowth on nureis knee
Dandely, Bischop, dandely;
And quhen that ege now dois me greif,
Ane simple vicar I can nocht be.

William Dunbar (c.1460–c.1520), To the King

11 To die is nothing very grand.
This world is delicate and misinformed.
It's growing old I've failed to understand.

Douglas Dunn (1942–), Stranger's Grief: i.m. Robert Lowell

12 Worldly prudence is very suitable at seventy, but at seventeen it is absolutely disgusting.

Susan Ferrier (1782–1854), letter to Walter Ferrier, in J. A. Doyle, Memoir and Correspondence of Susan Ferrier (*1898*)

13 . . . people who are forever consecrating the memory of the departed, and hold the virtues, nay the faults of their ancestors in such blind veneration, see much to love and revere in their own parents, that others never think of. They accumulate on these patriarchs all the virtues of their progenitors, and think the united splendour reflects a lustre on themselves.

Ann Grant (1755–1838), Letters from the Mountains

14 Eild comes owre me like a yoke on my craig.

George Campbell Hay (1915–1984), The Auld Hunter, *translated from Gaelic by Hugh MacDiarmid*

15 The moir of ege the nerrer hevynis bliss.

Robert Henryson (c.1425–c.1500), The Praise of Age

16 Our hearts are young 'neath wrinkled rind:
Life's more amusing than we thought.

Andrew Lang (1844–1912), Ballade of Middle Age

17 Youth having passed, there is nothing to lose but memory.

George Macdonald (1824–1905), Fifty Years of Freethought

18 Age is not all decay; it is the ripening, the swelling, of the fresh life within, that withers and bursts the husk.

George Macdonald, The Marquis of Lossie

19 Out of the Past, and on her old decay
The beauty of her childhood you can trace.

George Macdonald, On a December Day

20 After a certain age all of us, good and bad, are guilt-stricken because of powers within us which have never been realised; because, in other words, we are not what we should be.

Edwin Muir (1887–1959), Autobiography

21 My heart's still light, albeit my locks be grey.

Allan Ramsay (1686–1758), The Gentle Shepherd

22 Be sure ye dinna quit the grip
Of ilka joy, when ye are young,
Before auld age your vitals nip,
And lay ye twa-fold o'er a rung.

Allan Ramsay, Miscellany

23 . . . a bird
In song outside made evening suddenly splendid.
. . . I listened
Without a wound, accepting the song
I was given,
Content to accept it as song, the years gone over
When sight of a seagull's swoop upon grey water
Or petals fluttering butterfly-bright from flowers
Could solve at a stroke the puzzle of all existence.

Alexander Scott (1926–1989), Evensong

24 On his bold visage middle age
Had slightly press'd its signet sage,
Yet had not quench'd the open truth
And fiery vehemence of youth.

Sir Walter Scott (1771–1832), The Lady of the Lake

25 All sorts of allowances are made for the illusions of youth; and none, or almost none, for the disenchantments of age.

Robert Louis Stevenson (1850–1894), Virginibus Puerisque

26 Old and young, we are all on our last cruise.

Robert Louis Stevenson, Virginibus Puerisque

27 After a certain distance, every step we take in life we find the ice growing thinner below our feet, and all around us and behind us we see our contemporaries going through.

Robert Louis Stevenson, Virginibus Puerisque

28 For God's sake give me the young man who has brains enough to make a fool of himself.

Robert Louis Stevenson, Virginibus Puerisque

INDEX OF AUTHORS

INDEX OF KEYWORDS

This index is to help readers find quotations on particular topics within each section. Brief extracts are given to indicate the context in which the keyword appears; the keyword itself is repeated with the initial letter only, except when that spelling is a variant form.

A

Abbey: In Saxon strength that a. frowned **BUI 26**
our glorious Churches of Abbacies . . . knocking all down **BUI 17**

Abbot: The A. not persew ane **REL 128**
This Abbott tuik in hand to fly with wingis **MOM 25**

Abbotsford: a very strange house **BUI 23**

abeigh: Stand a., ye foolish forward folk **MUS 54**

Aberdeen: A. a thin-lipped peasant woman **PLA 3**
A. impresses the stranger as a city of granite palaces **PLA 4**
Blyth A., thou beriall of all tounis **PLA 1**
bound for A. and North Sea Crude **TRA 29**
cauld kail in A. **FOO 3**
cried in her thin A. **BAD 4**
High tea in A. is like no other meal on earth **FOO 59**
No jokes of any kind are understood here **HUMO 12**
Only in A. that I saw . . . tartan tight-fistedness **PLA 6**
started a coach between Edinburgh and A. **TRA 33**
Union Street has as much warmth **INS 43**
When A. and Ayr are baith ae toun **M-W 4**

Aberdeen University: late Principal of A. U. had contributed . . . to the expulsion of fairies **FANT 30**

Aberdonian: average A. as a person who would gladly pick a halfpenny out of a dunghill with his teeth **PLA 6**

Aberfeldy: let us spend the lightsome days In the birks of A. **PLA 7**

Aberlady: you might as well stick us a' in A. **M-W 97**

ablachs: A., and scrats, and dorbels o' a' kinds **INS 58**

abode: your happy a. **ADV 82**

abroad: when they went a., became the dynamic forces of the New World **PPL 83**

absences: A. are a good influence in love **LOVE 84**

abstinence: addressed the assembled rustics on the virtues of total a. **MOM 7**

Abyssinia: what musical instruments were used in A. **INS 83**

Academy: An A. of Painting was also established there **ART 7**
I bless the A. I found in Glasgow streets **ART 5**

accent: a. and gesture peculiar to that country **PPL 96**
a. of the lowest state of Glaswegians is the ugliest **WORD 55**
he will still have a strong Scotch a. of the mind **HIGH 45**
accidie: '*A?*' he queried **MIN 43**

accordion: they brought in a kind of a. **MUS 24**

Acharacle: example of concentrated joy was at A. **PLEAS 9**

Achnacarry: My stalker . . . at A. has seen it twice **MONS 16**

acquaintance: Of lordly a. you boast **INS 17**
Should auld a. be forgot **FRI 25**

act: get my a. across to a non-English-speaking audience **HUMO 1**
my first a. . . . was to kill my mother **PER 54**
obliged to fix its . . . business for the alternate days when she did not a. **REL 100**
under the A. there's a maternity benefit **REL 24**

Act of Union: man is a maniac who . . . will stand up and deny that the A. of U. was an advantage **POL 28**
There was no A. of U. **HIS 38**

action: from a. springs alone The inward knowledge to true love and faith **THO 76**
That a. is best, which procures the greatest happiness for the greatest numbers **PHIL 29**
When this a. came to the king's ears **REL 19**

actions: A. appear Beautiful, or Deform'd **PHIL 31**

actors: A. . . . tell tales of, for example, Macduff **ACT 3**
explain phallic comedy **ACT 11**
if we *didn't* perform **ACT 9**

Adam: As father A. first was fool'd **M-W 46**
I no great A. **M-W 113**
'Tis the speech used in the Garden – A. left it to mankind **WORD 49**

Adamnan, Saint: most remarkable thing I discovered in A.'s admirable record **FANT 32**

Adams: Scotsmen by the name of A. **PER 12**

adenoid: animated a. **BOO 24**

Adieu: A. for ay! This is a lang gude nicht! **LAM 44**

advance: lone worker who makes the first a. **SCI 14**

advice: answered 'Take a.' **MIN 37**

Advocaat: A., the alcoholic's omelette **FOO 40**

advocate: a. complaining . . . that his claims to a judgeship had been overlooked **LAW 28**

aeroplane: could probably have achieved more by sending an a. to drop £10 notes **COM 16**

aesthetic: letting one's a. sense override one's moral sense **PHIL 46**

affection: was embraced in his cold, wet arms with such a. **DEA 21**

Africa: I take it A. was brought about in sheer ill-humour **THO 51**
something which . . . will turn out for the true and permanent welfare of A. **HOP 10**
those rivers of A., which lose themselves in the burning sands **HIS 28**
While exploring a particularly wild and uncultivated region of A. **TRA 37**

Afton: Flow gently, sweet A. **RIV 8**

age: After a certain a., all of us . . . are guilt-stricken **YOU 20**
A. is not all decay **YOU 18**
allowances are made for the illusions of youth, and none . . . for the disenchantments of a. **YOU 25**

animal: a. . . . was between four and five feet long MONS 15

disease missed the a. and hit Alexander Douglas of Dalkeith MIN 25

distinguishing thing between an a. and a vegetable MIN 31

no other uncarapaced a. M-W 33

something so forlorn and miserable about the aspect of the a. FOO 128

somewhat appalling to persons of low a. spirits PER 13

use of the paunch of the a. . . . gives the touch of romantic barbarism FOO 92

Annan: A., Tweed and Clyde RIV 1

als much vertue, sonce and pith In Annan POET 18

fine, bright, self-confident little town PLA 9

where the Tweed, Clyde and A. rise MOM 6

You could recognise *Cardean* miles away down the valley of the A. TRA 13

Anne, Queen: treaty between A., Queen of Scots, and A., Queen of England HIS 38

Annie:' O A., A.,' loud he cried LOVE 8

Annie Laurie: for bonnie A.L., I'd lay me doun and dee LOVE 42

Anstruther: grey, grim sea-beaten hole PLA 10

answer: but a. came there none MOM 37

anxiety: smiling a. FAMI 25

you cannot conceive what a. I am in about you LOVE 40

apes: scorn to vie with oxen or with a. SPOR 9

aphorism: danger of ADV 53

apology: only a. which this work perhaps requires is with regard to the title BOO 30

apostle: queer ending for the a. of 'socialism in our time' POL 18

apothecary: better and wiser thing to be a starved a. INS 56

apparatus: Never did I see such a. got ready for thinking PER 76

apparitions: imposed upon by spectres and a. MIN 42

appearance: his first a. was somewhat appalling PER 13

a. is only sin deep ADV 106

otherwise, his a. not much against him REL 62

appetite: Scotland, the best place in the world to take an a. FOO 95

applause: like a banquet ACT 6

appraisal: they feel the glances of a. following them HIGH 17

architecture: direct expression of the needs and beliefs of man at the time of its creation BUI 19

how are you to judge a. BUI 21

It is not the bulk . . . but the proportion BUI 12

this useful and elegant art BUI 2

we should be less cosmopolitan and more national BUI 20

Argentina: few disastrous days, once upon a time, in A. SPOR 56

something odd about the way the ball 'flew' in A. SPOR 55

Argentocoxus: Caledonian M-W 27

argument: a. more attractive than whisky BAD 3

Argyll: there fell out a great dispute Between A. and Airlie WAR 8

aristocracy: A. of feudal parchment has passed away POL 26

about one half of the Scottish nation consciously regarded themselves as members of the a. PPL 50

arithmetic: he confessed himself deficient in A. BOO 68

peasantry . . . are . . . more or less skilful in writing and a. PPL 90

arithmeticians: many of my friends are poor a. BOO 58

ark: chapped at the a.'s muckle door REL 41

arm: *Strong* as his a. when he fights with his foes FOO 87

Armstrong, John: *see* John o' the Syde

Arnold, Matthew: Matt . . . won't like God PER 236

Arran: ageless sang this auld isle sings PLA 12

A. of the many stags PLA 11

Look, the peaks of A. MOU 20

You feel . . . you are on a peculiar island PLA 13

arse: devil . . . caused all the company kiss his a. FANT 50

lawland ers wald mak a bettir noyis INS 36

scratch-marks of itch at your a. INS 65

stuck your bayonet clean up his airse WAR 51

arselickers: we are a nation of a. PPL 45

arses: individuals bare their a. to each other FAMI 20

they wiped their a. with a gosling PER 202

art: a. and part LAW 2

a. may make a suit of clothes COS 38

A.'s a' the go in Gleska ART 23

but one a. – to omit BOO 66

called his harmless a. a crime MUS 71

dare not show your faces . . . in the practice of any one a. PPL 73

Gaelic is not a poor language, in a. at any rate WORD 53

I might not know what a. is ART 19

no a. that is not intellectual can be worthy of Scotland ART 34

poets all felt competent to teach the a. of government to their rulers POET 28

this useful and elegant a. BUI 2

to refine our taste with respect to the beauties of a. ART 18

With meikle a. could on the bagpipes play MUS 25

art editor: extremely little to do with a. JOU 11

Arthur o' Bower: A. o' B. has broken his bands SWW 23

artist: a. without sentiment ART 2

excited amateur who has to die . . . before the a. can be born ART 31 no native a. could be found **ART 15**

the Scots a. should . . . remain as it were beneath the salt **ART 26**

to be an a. and not know it **ART 1**

we need to give everyone the outlook of the a. **ART 14**

artists: As a. give me a little information of what is going on among the a. **ART 27**

Of course us a. aren't supposed to talk about political issues **POL 57**

two kinds of a. left **MUS 44**

arts: illusion that the Scots are really a cultured people, with an interest in the a. **FES 9**

May the devil fly away with the fine a. **ART 9**

stifled the Scottish a. almost out of existence **REL 112**

Who doubly plagues, and boasts two a. to kill **INS 90**

ashes: Scatter my A., throw them in the Air **HOP 13**

When our a. are scattered by the winds of heaven **POL 83**

aspiration: no upper limit to Scottish a. **FAMI 14**

asses: They gang in stirks, and come out a. **UNI 3**

atheist: a. is a man with **REL 23**

Glaswegian definition of an a. **SPOR 76**

he is a Jew and may be an a. **INS 10**

Athenians: A., indeed! **PPL 72**

Atholl: Cam' ye by A., lad wi' the philabeg? **MUS 38**

Atholl, Duchess of: If the Honourable Member would like to be returned . . . to the Calton Jail **POL 42**

Atlantic: entire Hebrides and Highland coast formed one A. principality **HIGH 35**

hammers, thundering on boilers of steam vessels which are to bridge the A. or Pacific **THO 84**

In and out of the bay hesitates the A. **SEA 14**

lonely clachans which defy the tempests of the A. **SPIR 29**

Outposts in the A., they had about them that air of the remote and wild **PLA 54**

part of the A. where there is plenty of material to make clouds from **SWW 35**

atom bomb: I doubt if he can disregard Freud and the a.b. **POET 47**

atmosphere: a. warm with that lovely heat **FAMI 25**

atoms: since Thou know'st where all these A. are **HOP 13**

attorneys: Here enter not A., Barristers **LAW 34**

Auchtermuchty: notable town of A. **PLA 14**

audacity: 'How had you the a., John . . . to go and tell some people I was a mean fellow **THO 56**

unwilling to believe that so small a crew would have the a. to board them **WAR 35**

Somehow he wants a. **POET 58**

auk: 'It is the great A, itself – we have found it!' **ANI 30**

the last of all the British great a.s . . . they thought it was a witch **ANI 36**

Whae's like us? **ANI 55**

auld acquaintance: Should a.a. be forgot **FRI 25**

Auld Lang Syne: To the peril of the passers and the tune of 'A.L.S.' **FES 10**

We'll tak' a richt gude willie-waught For A.L.S. **FOO 24**

Auld Nick: There sat A.N., in shape o' beast **MUS 16**

Auld Reekie: had the honour of giving to Edinburgh the *sobriquet* of 'A.R.' **PLA 38**

'Auld Robin Gray': her own ballad 'A.R.G.' sung to the accompaniment of the harp **MUS 34**

auld ways: a.w. are siccar **ADV 141**

Aunt Sally: universal A. S. of Scotland **POL 31**

Aurora borealis: bounded on the North by the arory-bory-Alice **LAND 50**

It was the a.b. **MOU 30**

austere: I strode on a. **HOP 22**

austerity: a. of which he was quite unconscious **PER 238**

Australian: young A., after meeting Cameron of Lochiel **PER 104**

Author: I replied brazenly, 'An A.' **BOO 7**

if an a. acknowledges his own blunders **BOO 56**

lack of memory of **ACT 2**

Let no woman who values peace of soul ever dream of marrying an a. **BOO 17**

only people free from routine **BOO 45**

perhaps the most dreadful fate that can be encountered **BOO 57**

authors: blizzard of a. sweeping through Glasgow **BOO 73**

authorities: unpermitted diversion, frowned on by the a. **HUMO 9**

authority: belief of a material world is . . . of more a. **PHIL 41**

distrust of a. should be the first civic duty **POL 32**

he's an a., he knows as much as any man alive about the life of the herring **LOVE 67**

no sense whasotever of obedience to a. **SPIR 29**

Such was the wisdom and authoritie of that old, little, crooked souldier **PER 31**

Autobiography: an attempted jail-break **BIO 6**

autumn: sadness of the land and sky in dark a. evenings **MUS 31**

yellow A., wreathed with nodding corn **SWW 18**

autumnal: A. frosts enchant the pool **SWW 61**

avarice: A. the spur of industry **PHIL 19**

his insatiable A. **INS 11**

awe: a. and dread with which the untutored savage contemplates his mother-in-law **FAMI 16**

awmrie: steek the a. **ADV 115**

Ayr: Auld A., wham ne'er a toon surpasses **PLA 15**

When Aberdeen and A. are baith ae toun
M-W 4
Ayr, River: the silver A. RIV 10

B

ba': Keep the ba' in the park, youse! SPOR 48
Some other day the ba' may be pushed into
the Harbour SPOR 39
ba's: Driving their b. frae whins or tee
PLEAS 13
babe: bonny babe's miss'd and awa' M-W 11
My b. is unborn LAM 10
babes: Smile na sae sweet, my bonny b. CHI 2
Babington, Rev. Dr: there is falsehood in his
looks INS 16
baby: he isn't mamma's b. any more CHI 4
hush thee, my babie, thy sire was a knight
CHI 39
What is man? A foolish b. M-W 58
When the first b. laughed for the first time
FANT 18
Where did you come from, B. dear? CHI 27
back: At the b. o' Benachie TIM 2
b. to b. set all your rout And all the speris
pointis out WAR 19
He can lie on his b., a posture long sustained
by no other uncaraped animal M-W 33
I lean'd my b. unto an aik LOVE 6
I took his body on my b. LAM 12
its b. is the colour of the faintest gold RIV 13
its b. was hollow, which is not the shape of any
fish MONS 16
No man could be charged with theft for as
much meat as he could carry on his b.
LAW 14
backwards: I b. cast my e'e HOP 3
bacon: not worth his weight in cold b. INS 24
bad: nothing To the badness of her badness when
she's b. PER 37
she was so good, and he was so b. M-W 124
two b. shepherds MOU 27
Badenoch: lifts the gangrel snaw, An' sets it
doon on B. SWW 21
badge: Thistle, Scotland's b. SPIR 42
Badinloskin: the old witch, she has lived too
long LAND 42
bag: b. of gravel is a history to me SCI 19
He filled the b. at a breath, and swung a
lover's arm round about it. MUS 62
Bagdad: similah gatherings in B. BUR 15
bagpipe: Experts have been puzzled by a new
kind of b. music MUS 65
impossible the b. could frighten any body
MUS 28
nae bells for me to ring, But ae Bag-pipe to
play a spring THO 43
bagpipes: Scottish spirit, trying to reproduce
the b. MOM 26
With meikle art could on the b. play MUS 25
Baikie: This my B. PLA2: 1

bailie: 'A'm no' a man, a'm a Glasgow b.' POL 87
do you realise I'm a b.? INS 13
not got the brains of a Glasgow b. POL 11
your lick-fud b. core POL 89
Baillie, Joanna: J.B. is now almost totally
forgotten POET 16
John Anybody would have stood higher with
the critics BOO 3
'The composition of a tragedy requires
testicles.' If this is true Lord knows what J.B.
does POET 10
bairn: and teachit by a b. LAM 18
Big House of the b., so enormous THO 19
Bolder b. was never born PER 2
bonnie, bonnie b. sits poking in the ase CHI 8
Come and tak' the b. CHI 6
Earth thou bonnie broukit b.! THO 70
Little ken I my b.'s father CHI 3
mitherless b. creeps up to his lane bed CHI 53
Ne'er, ne'er was sic a b. CHI 1
to make the cradle, That's to rock the b.
FANT 5
West wind to the b. SWW 6
bairnie: can ye sing ba-la-loo When the b.
greets? DAI 1
creep awa my b. ADV 17
let the b. sit CHI 14
wha the b.'s daddy is They dinna muckle mind
HUM 9
bairnies: Are a' the b. in their beds? CHI 31
O, b., cuddle doon CHI 7
We're only b. come to play FES 3
bairns: b. daurdna set up their gabs FAMI 13
birns of b. and gey muckle gear PPL 66
come, b.! And see the glory of God! SWW 51
I carena muckle for folk that b. and dogs
dinna like THO 57
Lord has pity on the b. Wha belang to
Caledonie PPL 89
Plenty bonny b. as weel, That's the toast for
Mairi TOA 20
to skelp the b. on Monday EDU 1
said *Cockadoodledo!* to some school b. MIN 26
time noo, b., to tak the buiks PLA 38
twa b. at scule EDU 27
twa Sweet b. were round me here DEA 63
underneath thy hearthstane, The tod shall
bring her bairnis hame CUR 23
we pay dem fur laernin' b. English WORD 68
We're a' John Tamson's b. PPL 81
what will ye leave to your b. and your wife?
FAMI 3
Ye Mauchline b., as on ye press EPI 16
Balintore: at the pier in B., watching the boats
come in WORD 60
ball (*see also* **ba'**): B. of Kirriemuir has smashed
The window-pane of Thrums POET 25
b. was hit off on the high road SPOR 32
clapped his hands to his outraged stomach
and found the b. was in the way SPOR 50
he can't touch your b. SPOR 34
If you're in the penalty area and don't know
what to do with the b. SPOR 69

Out runs Hamish and the b.'s in Invergowrie Bay **SPOR** 58

something odd about the way the b. 'flew' in Argentina **SPOR** 55

Would you also be good enough to bring your b. with you **SPOR** 28

Ballachulish: At B. we felt foolish **PLA** 56

ballads: B. are a voice from secret places **POET** 36

if a man were permitted to make all the b., he need not care who should make the laws **LAW** 11

unfortunate for the Scottish b. that so many who collected . . . were able to write creditable verse **POET** 69

Ballyhoo: tireless Scottish B. **PPL** 73

Balmaquhapple: D'ye ken the big village of B.? **PLA2**: 7

band: little b. striving When giving in would be good sense **SPIR** 37

bane: In b. he was sma'-boukit **PER** 232

Up wi' her on the bare b. dyke **PER** 1

we spak nae word Nor sinder'd b. frae b. **LOVE** 82

banes: Below thir stanes lie Jamie's b. **EPI** 19

Brissit brawns and broken banis **SPOR** 1

My sister gathered my b. **FANT** 14

Ower his white b. when they are bare **DEA** 2

Bangor: high, high notes o' *B's* tune **MUS** 6

bank: From b. to b. the water pouring **MONS** 1

Nort to da Faroe b. **SEA** 11

banks: Brignall b. are wild and fair **PLA** 19

burnis hurlis all their bankis doun **SWW** 27

by the bonnie b. o' Clyde **PLEAS** 11

By the bonny, bonny b. of Loch Lomond **MUS** 5

Far abune the bonnie b. o' Loch Lomond **MUS** 4

For we've established Shaving B. **DAI** 44

It grows near the seashore, on b., in clefts **SPIR** 24

obtained a signal victory on the b. of the Carun **PPL** 38

Ye b. and braes o' bonnie Doon **NAT** 3

banners: High may your proud b. gloriously wave **SPIR** 28

Bannockburn: your lemmans ye haue lost at Bannockysborne **BOA** 1

banshee: wail, such as a b. might be imagined to utter **MOM** 26

Barabbas: Jesus Christ and B. Were found the same day **PHIL** 59

barbarians: b. as well as Brethren, were greatly terror-struck **MONS** 6

B. who inhabit the banks of the Thames **INS** 49

basely stole what less b. won **INS** 22

barbarism: titled Nobility is the most undisputed progeny of feudal b. **POL** 70

When a man is convinced that his language is a b. **SPIR** 43

When was a war not a war? **WAR** 34

barbarisms: few *modern* Scoticisms which are not b. **WORD** 61

barbarity: their neighbours were fully satisfied of their *b*. **HIGH** 21

with unparalleled b. **INS** 8

barber: b. had drawn blood from his face for the third time **FOO** 56

Barbie: B., usually so poor to see **PLA2**: 2

bard: Iersche brybour b. **INS** 36

Sabbath b. . . . . Perverts the Prophets and purloins the Psalms **POET** 12

to the great b. erect a bust **BUR** 21

To what a world does the illustrious b. transport me! **POET** 27

barley: fermenters of b. have come **FOO** 83

Scotch broth, with b. and peas in it **FOO** 15

barmaid: calling the b. Dearie **BUR** 12

barn: My b. is to bigg **LAM** 10

Barochan: haena ye heard, man, o' B. Jean? **PER** 244

Barr, Rev Charles: quaintest work of Almighty God **PER** 123

Barra: Blue deep B. waves **SEA** 19

Reflecting on . . . say, B. or Iona **THO** 73

Barrie, Sir James .M.: cheerful clatter of Sir J. B.'s cans **PER** 128

'Sir J.B., I presume?' **INS** 12

With *Courage!* echoing in the ears of youth **EPI** 28

Barton, Sir Andrew: 'Fight on, my men,' says A.B. **WAR** 4

bastard: Believe him b. of a brighter race **CUR** 14

called me a big dirty Fenian b. **SPOR** 36

that b. land **LAND** 12

that b. verdict, *Not proven* **LAW** 29

ya parish-eyed, perishin' bastart **INS** 71

bastards: I think the Scots are a lazy set of b.s **DAI** 25

bat: Up goes the b., with her pelit leathern flycht **SWW** 26

bath: takin' them every mornin' just as if they were a cauld b. **FOO** 100

battle: at Sheriffmuir, A b. there was that I saw, man **WAR** 61

bludy b. lasted long **WAR** 3

charging along like troops in a b. **TRA** 42

children of Conn, remember Hardihood in time of b. **WAR** 62

for the fredome of our land Are strenyeit in b. **SPIR** 4

he never walked to b., More proudly than to die **PER** 28

his sword in b. keen **PER** 212

In the b. of Inverkeithing, between the Royalists and Oliver Cromwell **WAR** 42

Now's the day and now's the hour, See the front o' b. lour **WAR** 26

Ordain you haill for the battaile **SPIR** 6

see how have earned the honour . . . of this b. **WAR** 50

thay maid them ready for batail. Than quhair I sat I heard the cannonis **WAR** 7

There is peace now the b.'s o'er **WAR 16**
we came with no peaceful intent, but ready for
b. **SPIR 56**

battlefield: If the endurance . . . they displayed
had been on the b. **POL 107**

battlement: rocky summits . . . formed turret,
dome or b. **MOU 38**

baudrons: *see* **cat**

bauld: It makes a man baith gash and b.
FOO 105
When . . . the burns grow b. **SWW 9**

bawbee: Greetin' for anither b. **CHI 5**
jocose saying as well received as a b. **PER 112**

bawdry: great leaven that breaks through all
Scots b. **M-W 24**

Baxter, Stanley: awright fur funny stuff ur S.B.
WORD 43

bay: In and out of the b. hesitates the Atlantic
SEA 14
In the b., the waves pursued their indifferent
dances **SEA 5**
o'er the rocks, and up the b., The long sea-
rollers surge **PLA 118**

bays: their b. are sear, their former laurels fade
POET 11
what is surely the baldest of God's b. **PLA 134**

BBC: Naebody Scottish works for the BBC
TEL 10

bean: small portion about the size of a b. . . .
prevents them from feeling hunger **PPL 14**

beans: He . . . knew how many b. make five
THO 37
we spill the b. and we swill our gin **M-W 90**

bear: world's a b. shrugged in his den **SWW 45**

beard: his b. was flesh **ANI 5**

beast: As I came through the slochk . . . I
foregathered wi' the b. **PER 92**
Baith men and b. were feared **PER 231**
b. cam doun the hill **FANT 61**
b. which . . is called Leviathan **MONS 4**
There sat Auld Nick, in shape o' b. **MUS 16**

beasts: lawful to kill Tories . . . as devouring b.
REL 113
so many of these good birds and b. are . . .
extinct **NAT 20**

beaten: everybody represses you, if you but
propose to step out of the b. track **PPL 64**

Beaton, Cardinal: yon man that lyis so glorious
on yon wall head **FANT 42**

Beaton, Mary: *The Queen's Marie* **LAM 8**

Beaton medical family: **MIN 17**

beautiful: Actions appear B., or Deform'd
PHIL 31
And make the cart-ruts b. **SWW 61**
anxious he should admire a b. picture of Glen
Sannox **SCI 24**
B. railway bridge of the Silv'ry Tay **DEA 44**
Claverhouse, as b. as when he lived **PER 215**
Dr Joseph Black was a striking and b. person
PER 86
great b. bird of Skye **PLA 126**
How b. the green Translucent lymph **RIV 7**
I have never seen anything quite so b. **COS 58**

piece on crisps. Aye b. **FOO 76**
Would it not be the b. thing now If you were
coming instead of going **TOA 3**

beauty: b. and sadness **ADV 87**
b. of his ornate eloquence **WORD 24**
called *Picti* either from their b. . . . . or . . .
because they were so shabby **PPL 37**
Catholics on the whole have been kinder to
b. **REL 58**
derive none of their b. from paint **M-W 125**
embodied in the concept of mathematical b.
SCI 42
flowers have . . . a new b. **MOU 17**
lady in bour full of bewtie **DEA 30**
lamp of bewtie **PLA 1**
he who weeps for b. gone **ADV 130**
Like pensive b., smiling in her tears **THO 25**
of Virgillis verse the ornate b. Intill our
tongue may not observit be **WORD 23**
on her old decay, The b. of her childhood you
can trace **YOU 19**
secret b. born of the mists **MOU 16**
seen it . . . assume a new and delicate b. not of
this world **NAT 9**
she that b. lang had kend **PER 103**
singular blending of paganism . . . and
spiritual b. **PLA 85**
so much b. with so much horror **MOU 21**
To accept Life is to give it b. **DEA 64**
Woman's b. gies man true content **M-W 78**

bed: ' b., a b.,' Clerk Saunders said, 'A b. for you
and me' **M-W 7**
contrived to force Thomson into b. by
blowing out the candle **PER 174**
For my b. is prepared in the mossy graveyard
MUS 4
He rushes to his burning b. **MOM 40**
Hot Burning Coals . . . Sall be thy B. **REL 45**
I love in Isa's b. to lie **PER 108**
It's narrow, narrow, mak your b., And learn to
lie your lane **M-W 10**
lay in b. in their heather-thatched cabin
M-W 75
lie on a perpetual b. of roses **MIN 9**
lying in Prince Charles's b. **MOM 4**
mak my b. soon, For I'm weary wi' huntin'
DEA 4
Make the weans get out of b. **M-W 109**
mitherless bairn creeps up to his lane b.
CHI 53
My mother said always look under the b.
M-W 126
nicer to stay in b. **DAI 36**
Personally I am a great believer in b. **PHIL 6**
she was afraid we wanted to go to b. with her
M-W 30
that I in my b. could lie, And sleep for ever
more **THO 5**
There's a pig in ilka b. **SWW 54**
Welcome to your gory b., Or to victory
WAR 25
When a' the lave gang tae their b. **M-W 18**

bigot: he who will not reason is a b. ADV 61
bigots: b. of the iron time MUS 71
    land of brigands and b. PPL 31
billions: Millions, b., trillions, quadrillions
    SCI 4
Billy: That's the way for B. and me CHI 21
biocentric: Everything I have done has been b.
    POL 40
biography: B. should be written by an acute
    enemy BIO 1
birch (*see also* **birk**): One b. in particular I have
    in mind NAT 9
birches: extraordinary feeling of joy in being
    among the b. NAT 7
bird: b. in song outside made evening suddenly
    splendid YOU 23
    b. of the wilderness ANI 50
    b. of Christ ANI 74
    great beautiful b. of Skye PLA 126
    ilka b. sang o' his love LOVE 34
    inward gates of a b. are always open ANI 64
    b. . . . is only a song-machine ANI 65
    seed, the root, the b. – all are one MOU 40
    Seven years a b. in the wood DEA 3
    Speed, bonnie boat, like a b. on the wing
        PLA 125
    This is the b. that never flew PLA 59
birdies: Waukens all the b. SWW 62
birds: all the silent b. that sit In this snow-
    travelled wood MOM 54
    birdis sang upon the tender croppis SWW 30
    b. are older by far than your ancestors are
        ANI 53
    for the b. of the air had nests HUM 15
    more than b. on the hill tonight WAR 69
    pierced by the myriad screaming b. PLA 54
    so also were the b. of the air the moment they
        flew over his land POL 4
    so many of these good b. and beasts are . . .
        extinct NAT 20
    These b. are parasitic INS 60
    Thrilling . . . with the bees and the glad b.
        SWW 50
    When molested these b. have a characteristic
        and unpleasant trait MOU 34
birk: b.-stems were white, the b. leaves brown
    and gold NAT 27
    their hats were o' the b. FANT 3
birkie: Te see yon b. called a lord FAMI 7
birks: Lightsome days In the b. of Aberfeldy
    PLA 7
birth: from the moment of b. CHI 24
birth-place: the flummery of a b.p. BUR 13
bishop: Bischop wald not wed ane wyfe REL 128
    My lord b., why did you give away the royal
        horse REL 19
    No b., no King POL 52
    soul of a most holy b. FANT 2
    while the b. . . . preached the Gospel
        WORD 4
Bishops: such unfaithfull doges REL 5
bitch: 'Did he – the b.! BOO 41

Isn't that a common-like b. at the manse?
    WORD 29
    saying it served her right – the b.! WORD 26
    she was a dour b. o' a back-end, yon SWW 36
    such a bleth'rin' b. EPI 19
    'History' . . . Which is always a B. HIS 2
    I called John an impudent b. INS 40
    Ye stupid auld b. M-W 31
bitches: Fare ye a' weel, ye b. FRI 18
    that price that the b. of the world have earned
        PPL 63
Black, Joseph: died seated DEA 22
    Dr B. dreaded nothing so much as error
        SCI 38
    Dr J.B. was a striking and beautiful person
        PER 86
    less nonsense in his head than any man living
        PER 222
    trying snail soup FOO 66
black: b. as ony draff PPL 1
    brackens lie B. whaur they fell SWW 58
    fire that's blawn on Beltane een May weel be
        b. gin Yule LOVE 64
    fury of his enemies was b. and universally
        detested PER 58
    little gentleman in b. velvet TOA 6
    mists half-hiding the b. precipices MOU 14
    more pride under such a one's b. bonnet
        POL 53
    Pity I was not with the B.-haired Lad LOVE 2
    pointed out a b. thing in the water MONS 7
    She was brown eggs, b. skirts PER 168
    streaman cobbles b. wi rain MOM 46
black bun: inimical to life FOO 131
black dog: I was sadly worried by the b. d.
    MIN 43
black spot: shadow of ourselves ADV 39
Black Watch: B.W. are braw, the Seaforths and
    a' WAR 12
    bodies of two B.W. pipers . . . lay near
        WAR 72
blackbird: Nae a b. or a mavis, that hae pipin' for
    their trade MUS 63
Blackfriars Wynd: With her to room in B.W.,
    and twice HUM 3
Blackie, John Stuart: 'I hope you . . don't think
    we hate you?' J.S.B. asked PPL 48
blacklegs: Four and twenty b., working night
    and day POL 5
blackmail: get your succour where ye paid b.
    ADV 6
blackthorn: white bloom of the b., she LOVE 3
blade: I'm a rash and a roving b. PER 17
blasphemy: his b., libertinism and sentimentality
    are all Protestant BUR 18
    patchwork of b., absurdity and gross obscenity
        MUS 58
blast: b. has lopped my branches away LAM 39
    b. upon b. they blew MUS 10
blate: ye are na b., To come wi' the news o' your
    ain defeat WAR 82
Blawearie: there wasn't a cold soul in B. barn
    MUS 30

as steam was an elastic b., it would rush into a vacuum **SCI 43**

b. in subjection **REL 1**

b.-killing tyrants cannot kill The public soul **PPL 26**

chield's a decent-like b. **PER 14**

For harmis of bodie, handis and heid, The pottingar will purge the painis **LOVE 15**

called *Picti* . . . from . . . the graceful stature of their b. **PPL 37**

Gin a b. meet a b. **M-W 47; SCI 34**

'had so far withdrawn his mind from the care of his b.' **PER 179**

Head, arms and b. down to the middle like a human being **MONS 15**

here his b. lies fu' low **PER 65**

I took his b. on my back **LAM 12**

martial spirit of the great b. of the people **WAR 83**

misery n pain in your mind n b. **MIN 55**

My b. is full of bliss **LOVE 4**

she seemed in a mortal b. . . . a true goddess **PER 55**

silly snivelling b. is not worthy even to keep a door in thy house **REL 119**

very worst play she wrote is better than the best o' any ither b.'s **PER 141**

Will you pour a bottle of the Talisker over my dead b.? **FOO 84**

Boece, Hector: If you should bid me count the lies of H.'s history **HIS 20**

bog: need only arrange to be buried in a b. **NAT 29**

bog cotton: soft white b. c. **PLA 18**

Boghead: Here lies B. among the dead **EPI 18**

Bogie: For a' the wives in B. **FOO 3**

bogs: b. do not require a level surface for their existence **PLA 124**

bold: b. man who first swallowed an oyster **FOO 74**

Inspiring b. John Barleycorn **FOO 30**

bones (*see also* **banes**): Mountaineering lays one alongside the b. of mother earth. **MOU 9**

rotten b. of martyrs **REL 64**

their b. and yours are up for sale **LAND 15**

bonnet: b. blue, and laigh-heeled shoes **COS 28**

bridegroom stood dangling his b. **MOM 36**

clad in tartan new, B. and blackcock feather **MUS 10**

his b. reverently is laid aside **REL 28**

more pride under such a one's black b. than under great Alexander's diadem **POL 53**

something smert aboot the kilt and the cockit b. **WAR 65**

bonnets: Saw ye the lads wi' their b. and white cockades **MUS 38**

When the Blue B. came over the Border **WAR 79**

Bonny Dundee: Under the cake lies B.D. **PPL 52**

Up wi' the bonnets o' B.D. **BOA 16**

Bonny Mary of Argyle: I have watched thy heart, dear M. **LOVE 57**

Bonspiel: To gain the B. by a single shot **SPOR 12**

Bonxie: that noble Scua **ANI 61**

book: And a coloured fairy b. **PER 90**

Can anything be called a b. **BOO 25**

for several days after my first b. was published, I carried it about **BOO 8**

he wanted a b. out of the Advocates' Library **MOM 32**

I thought your b. an imposture **INS 50**

if a b. come from the heart **BOO 20**

If I had time to write a b. **MIN 53**

if in reading a b. I come across a word beginning with 'c' or 'f' **WORD 2**

it seemed to him to be a great b., full of mystery **POET 50**

man who has been able to furnish a b. which has been approved by the world **BOO 10**

No good b. shows its best face at first **BOO 22**

no quite good b. without a good morality **BOO 64**

one b. she'd thought fair daft, *Alice in Wonderland* it was **BOO 32**

so valuable . . . the b. was sent round by land **MIN 17**

books: all very well to be able to write b. **BOO 6**

b., Ease and alternate labour **PHIL 62**

Broadcasting is in no sense . . . a substitute for the reading of good b. **TEL 12**

by far the most momentous, wonderful and worthy **BOO 19**

feature in the history b. of our schools for centuries to come **POL 107**

few b. today are forgivable **BOO 42**

finer world within the world **BOO 59**

Here stand my b., line upon line **BOO 44**

instructive quarry . . . is worth many b. **EDU 19**

love of b., the Golden Key **BOO 43**

b. . . . . are a mighty bloodless substitute for life **BOO 63**

obliged to study English from b. **WORD 3**

some b. are lies frae end to end **BOO 16**

spare the golden bindings **BOO 15**

stupid, worn-out b. **BOO 72**

time noo, bairns, to tak the buiks **PLA 38**

true university these days is a collection of b. **UNI 4**

villanous profane and obscene b. **BOO 75**

boots: having once been shod with the b. of skin . . . he would wear them for whole months together **PER 179**

hill b., the sole rising sharply at the toe **COS 24**

I would melt your gold payment, pour it into your skull, till it reached to your b. **POL 64**

Rhynie loons wore tackety b. **COS 36**

boozing: element of degradation in all b. **FOO 82**

Border: Imitating B. bowmen, Aye defend your rights and common **WAR 5**

Old and New Welter upon the b. of the world **REL 43**

or answer by the B. law **BOA 2**

Scotland rises as the b. of the world **LAND 5**

she's o'er the B. and awa' **ADV 114**

That fraternity, so large and prosperous beyond the b. **TRA 20**

they may learn from examining how things operate on the other side of the B. **POL 44**

Through all the wide B. his steed was the best **PER 214**

wan water from the b. hills **MOM 24**

We'll over the B. and gie them a brush **WAR 29**

When the Blue Bonnets came over the B. **WAR 79**

Border Reivers: high midnight of the B.R. . . . was as cruel and horrible in its way as Biafra or Vietnam **HIS 16**

    story of the B.R. . . . its moral is clear: there is little justice to be had **THO 47**

Borderer: that dark reckless B., Wat o' the Cleuch **PER 140**

Borderers: grunt-punctuated silences which B. seem to inhabit **PPL 77**

    nicknames . . . in which the B. obviously took great pleasure **WORD 25**

    said to be a tradition among the B. **HIGH 19**

bore: always a b. being ahead of one's time **ADV 94**

Boreray: When B. makes dark clouds **SWW 35**

boring: kind, but so b. the Lord preserve them **PPL 11**

    She thought her relatives were so b. **FAMI 35**

borrow: With neichbours gladly lend and b. **DAI 22**

Bosjesmans: primitive performers **ACT 4**

bosom: health in the wild wind's b. **NAT 12**

    I would hold thee in my b. **LOVE 26**

    No feeling, save one, to my b. was dear **LOVE 38**

    to dismiss the choice of its children from its own b. **PPL 23**

Bosphorus: What a pity it is that I shall be beyond the B. **INS 21**

Boswell, James: B. put his cup to his head. 'Here's *t'ye*, my Lord' **WORD 52**

    B. was praising the English highly **INS 73**

    For thee, J. B., may the hand of Fate **INS 82**

    I thought he was a gentleman who had the misfortune to be mad **INS 76**

    Jemmy . . . thought not of his own Scotch snivel **INS 81**

    Servile and impertinent **INS 57**

boss: It's just the power of some to be a b. **DAI 18**

Boston: in a building at No 5, Exeter Place, B., that the first complete sentence was ever spoken by Bell **MOM 15**

Bothwell: said of her B. that she could follow him round the world in her nighty **LOVE 22**

bottle: b. that is both white and nappie **PER 10**

    provided . . . he has himself finished the b. in two sittings **FRI 17**

    My only brither is the b. **PER 232**

When the last big b.'s empty **FES 10**

will you pour a b. of the Talisker over my dead body? **FOO 84**

Yo-ho-ho, and a b. of rum **FOO 130**

bottles: Black b. of strong port were set down **LAW 9**

    fewer glasses and more b. **FOO 60**

    sauce-b. are filled with old blood **FOO 124**

    went to the stoups (for there was no b.) **FOO 102**

    you learned quickly to empty the b. **CHI 17**

bouls: wying a-jee the byass bouls **PLEAS 13**

bowels: I doubt If thou hast any b. **INS 53**

    I got into the very b. of his confidence **POL 71**

    keep your boo'els open **MIN 20**

    no complete misery . . . that does not emanate from the b. **MIN 14**

    upwards of thirty yards of b. squeezed under that girdle **MIN 3**

bower: I will twine thee a bow'r By the clear siller fountain **LOVE 85**

bowling green: Three things are thrown away on a b.g. **SPOR 65**

box: a man baaling, baaling in a b. **REL 86**

boxes: why do you propose these b. for our people? **BUI 35**

boy: b. Big B. took me into a lonely corner of the Field **M-W 79**

    b. flew at the oranges **FOO 111**

    brooding b. and sighing maid **M-W 116**

    FEEL LIKE A B. AGAIN **THO 35**

    'He iss not a brat of a b., I admit' **PER 196**

    he was a funny wee cunt when he was a b. **CHI 22**

    I ate so much crab and lobster as a b. **FOO 96**

    I never could stand a boily b. **CHI 37**

    Just at the age 'twixt b. and youth **CHI 38**

    Knox the b. that buys the beef **MIN 2**

    Luis was an ugly b. **CHI 9**

    Many a clever b. is flogged into a dunce **POET 58**

    nicest b. who ever committed the sin of whisky **PER 234**

    raggedest b. that runs along the pavement **REL 40**

    slimness of a b.'s ankle **THO 38**

    small b. . . . who had been to church for the first time **REL 86**

    There was a naughty b., And a naughty b. was he **TRA 25**

    wee b., and still he stude **INS 1**

    wee b.'s Drambuie **FOO 71**

    'What a wonderful b. he is!' said my mother **PER 139**

    what every b. ought to learn from his mother **FAMI 12**

    What's your peerie b. düin' 'at he's no' been at skül? **WORD 68**

    you can't expect a b. to be vicious until he's been to a really good school **EDU 35**

boyhood: Even the memories of b. and young manhood are gloomy **PER 129**

boys: I want these b. and girls to acquire the habit of looking honestly at life **EDU 29**
  Let her go, b.! **SEA 21**
bracken: b. buries the lea **FANT 62**
  brecken's waving feather **NAT 10**
  curled young b. unsheath their green claws **NAT 22**
  Earl Douglas was buried at the b. bush **WAR 2**
  Fast-rooted b. where the corn once ripened **LAND 17**
  lamb from the b. and doe from the glen **FOO 70**
  yield thee to the b. bush Grows on yon lily-lee **WAR 1**
brackens: In their wrack the b. lie **SWW 58**
brae: Jess sat in her chair and looked down the b. **MOM 2**
  that bonnie road, That winds about the ferny b. **FANT 9**
braes: b. abune it are dowf and whinny **FANT 62**
  I met the devil and Dundee, On the b. o' Killiecrankie **WAR 10**
  It grows . . . above all on the little green b. **SPIR 24**
  Ye banks and b. o' bonnie Doon **NAT 3**
braid: B. Claith lends fock an unco heese **COS 23**
  I would welcome the end of Braid Scots and Gaelic **POL 41**
  in the b. Scottish tongue **MUS 1**
  Thrid part lenth in shouldris b. was he **PER 131**
  warm Scotch heart, and a b. Scotch tongue **PER 34**
brain: b. of man most surely did invent **REL 91**
  man should keep his little b. attic stocked **BOO 27**
  We need thee still, thy moulding b. and hand **PER 22**
brains: b. enough to make a fool of himself **YOU 28**
  Confuse their b. in college classes **UNI 3**
  has not got the b. of a Glasgow bailie **POL 11**
  Let such forgo the poet's sacred name, Who rack their b. for lucre **POET 11**
brand: Or are ye come to wield the b. **WAR 6**
brassic: Ah'm fuckin b. until this rent cheque hits the mat the morn **DAI 61**
brave: how far they go towards making b. people **SWW 52**
  If it is for fame that men do b. actions **FAM 12**
  meed of the b. **ADV 102**
  Scotland the B. **SPIR 29**
Braveheart: B. is pure Australian shite **TEL 2**
bravery: blackguarded for their b. **POL 107**
  spread her b. **PER 84**
bravest: who was the b. man in the Grand Army . . . no man braver than Brigadier Gerard **BOA 6**
braw: assisting at a b. Scots nicht! **FES 10**
  Black Watch are b. **WAR 12**
  b. bride to bring hame **M-W 10**
  if ye can say, 'It's a b. bricht moonlicht nicht' **FOO 94**

Mars is b. in crammasy **THO 70**
This b., hie-heapit toun **PLA 46**
Tho' this was fair, and that was b. **LOVE 30**
brawly: b. could she frisk it **MUS 74**
Braxfield, Lord: his name smacks of the gallows **PER 235**
bread: begged his b. from door to door **MUS 71**
  Man is a creature who lives not by b. alone, but principally by catchwords **WORD 72**
  You are offered a piece of b. and butter that feels like a damp handkerchief **FOO 89**
Breadalbane, Earl of: 'B. – till we see' **TOA 14**
breakfast: no finer b. than flounders **FOO 42**
breast: From your b. to your gullet transfer the blue string **INS 9**
  gowd in the b. of the primrose pale **NAT 12**
  If happiness hae not her seat An' centre in the b. **HUM 4**
  In the human b., Two master-passions cannot co-exist **HUM 7**
  mist like hair hangs over One barren b. **MOM 53**
  Now is my breist with stormy stoundis stad **LAM 32**
  Sin a toom howe is in the breist O' their sair forjaskit mother **PPL 89**
  star on his face and a spot on his b. **TOA 7**
  Within my filial b. **SPIR 56**
breasts: And you sall hae my breists like stars **M-W 92**
  snowy daises, with their rounded b. of gold **NAT 24**
  Wear amber beads between her b. **FANT 59**
breath: Before my b., like blazing flax, Man and his marvels pass away **TIM 26**
  boldest held his b. **MOM 12**
  b. that fills their mountain-pipe **WAR 32**
  but the b. of kings **PPL 22**
  Here I can blow a garden with my b. **NAT 28**
  His b.'s like a burst lavy **INS 85**
  Judges, destroyers, with an unjust b. **LAW 34**
  sacredness of love and death Dwells in thy noise and smoky b. **PLA 72**
breathing: trick is to keep b. **ADV 67**
breeches: the pale grey b. cast a gloom on us **COS 42**
breed: daughter of a base and brainless b. **POL 63**
  dour provincial thocht That merks the Scottish b. **PPL 60**
  rats of Scotland b. faster than ever **PER 120**
breeks: lang-leggit callants gaun wanting the b. **HIGH 40**
  ma b. they want the seat **SPOR 29**
  With thy Canigait breikis **INS 78**
  ye'd better hae stuck to b. **COS 49**
  ye'se get my b. to keep in trim **LOVE 72**
breeze: riches galore in the b. of the vale **NAT 12**
  When next the summer b. comes by **CHI 40**
Bremner, Billy: his name would be B.B. **SPOR 15**

brethren: 'B. . . . I am sorry to say neither of you will be understood by the House' **WORD 30**
> lawful to prevent the murder of ourselves or our b. **REL 113**
> taunt which northern pipers hurl to this day at their inferior b. **MUS 50**

brewer: I wish I were a b.'s horse **MUS 7**

brier-bush: fathered between a kailyard and a bonnie b.-b. in the lee of a house with green shutters **PLA2: 3**
> There grows a bonnie b.-b. in our kail-yard **MUS 64**

bride: bonny blue sky To welcome the b. **SWW 6**
> Busk ye, busk ye, my bonnie b. **LOVE 49**
> I'll wed ye to my youngest son, And ye shall be his b. **LOVE 9**
> I'm gaun far owre the sea, Fair Annie, A braw b. to bring hame **M-W 10**
> Out ran his bonnie b., Reaving her hair **LAM 10**
> 'Tis a pleasant thing to be a b. **CHI 36**
> This night sall ye lig within my arms, Tomorrow my b. sall be **M-W 9**

bridegroom: b. stood dangling his bonnet and plume **MOM 36**
> 'You are very late, Mr Baird,' said the b. **PER 32**

brides: I'll woo her as the lion woos his b. **LOVE 55**

Bridie, J.M.: praise, damn you **ACT 12**

bridge: any German parachutist who happened to land on the b. **WAR 45**
> b. that groaned as I crossed over **SWW 67**
> steam vessels which are to b. the Atlantic or Pacific **THO 84**

brig: I'll be a b. when ye're a shapeless cairn **BUI 6**

Brignall: B. banks are wild and fair **PLA 19**

British: B. 'Parliamentary cretinism' **POL 85**
> immortalised in B. history as 'the thin red line' **WAR 94**
> most shining period of the B. history **PPL 38**

broadcloth: the fine frogged b. **COS 15**

brochen: And there will be fadges and b. **FOO 120**

broken-hearted: Never met – or never parted, We had ne'er been b.-h. **LOVE 36**

broo: scads itsel' wi' b. **CHI 36**

brooches: I will make you b. and toys for your delight **LOVE 83**

broom: Gallowa' hills are covered wi' b. **MOU 3**
> he's in the b., That's waiting for me **LOVE 41**
> I'll tak ye on the road again, When yellow's on the b. **TRA 32**
> maid shanna go to the bonny b. And a maiden return **M-W 8**

Broomielaw: it reminds me in a verra mild wye o' the B. **PLA 101**

Brora: ony old baur'll pass in B. **PLA 20**

brose: dine on a dishfu' o' b. **FOO 133**
> I've seen the day ye buttered my b. **M-W 51**
> Lovat's head i' the pat . . . We'll mak b. o' that **PER 186**

our forefathers' dose, to swill down their b. **FOO 122**

broth: Dr Johnson ate several platefulls of Scotch b. **FOO 15**
> I think b. is always better the second day **FOO 86**
> there's always fresh b. **THO 17**
> they'd b., it was good **FOO 58**

brother: come to announce to his mother that his father and b. had been slain **MOM 52**
> Courage, b., do not stumble **REL 88**
> gently scan your b. man **ADV 28**
> he has the honour to be my b. **LAND 4**
> his facetious professional b. **LAW 12**
> Judas, your own b. **INS 66**
> My only brither is the bottle **PER 232**
> Thus were my b. and I brought up **SPIR 16**

brotherhood: can still rise into some glow of b. over food and wine **FOO 37**
> universal fellowship and b. of man **POL 108**

brothers: gamekeeper resembled him so closely they might almost be b. **M-W 77**
> made their prisoners as good cheer as if they had been b. **WAR 39**
> man to man, the world o'er, Shall b. be **HOP 5**
> seven b. of the clan sacrificed their lives in defence of their leader **WAR 42**
> some of the attractiveness of a gargoyle **PER 251**

brow: Grant that my b. may wear . . . Love to distressed Mankind **THO 33**
> Her b. grew bleak **PPL 76**
> Her b. is like the snawdrift **LOVE 42**

Brown, Dr John: as a lad Dr J.B. peered into its depths **RIV 12**

Brown, John: Friend more than Servant **PER 244**

brows: Gathering her b. like gathering storm **M-W 40**

browst: the b. which the gudewife of Lochrin produced **FOO 93**

Bruce, James, of Kinnaird: B. was talking away **INS 83**

Bruce, Robert: This is the counsail . . . Of Guid King Robert's Testament **WAR 38**
> Scots, wham B. has aften led **WAR 25**
> That evershifting politician, R.B. **PER 155**

Buccleuch: Or answer to the bauld B. **BOA 2**

bubbly-jock: thraw the neck of the b.j. **FES 5**

buckies: there will be partans and b. **FOO 120**

Buachaille: mystic twilight . . . of B. **MOU 32**
> two bad shepherds . . . B.Etive Mor and B. Etive Beag **MOU 27**

Buchanan, George: On returning to B.'s bedside, he meekly enquired **PER 181**
> This caused B. to exclaim: 'Look at him!' **PER 105**

Buddha: synthetic goddess, vast and bland as B. **HIS 6**

Buddhism: nothing in Christianity or B. that quite **FOO 113**

buffers: B. like yon would stop the Flying Scotsman **M-W 96**

bul-bul: male of the coo-coo ANI 48
bull: lyke ane boisteous b. INS 54
bullet: Earth . . . shall rejoice and blossom too
When the b. reaches you WAR 87
  Every b. has its billet WAR 49
  to hide the wound the silver b. made PER 215
bulls: great b. mellow to the touch ANI 63
bung: Ye'll need tae gie us a b. DAI 61
bungalows: lowness of ceilings BUI 18
buoy: When I was a b. THO 52
Burke: B.'s the butcher MIN 2
burn: dour, dark b. that has its ain wild say
SPIR 33
  In the b. born alang the scree-fute PLA 12
  in the sheiling by the b. PPL 65
Burnet, Gilbert: I do not believe that B.
intentionally lied PER 148
burnie: muirlan' b., purple-fringed NAT 10
Burns, Robert (*see also* dedicated R.B. Section):
and next to it, does not treasure a B. POET 37
  beneath this lowly thatch love's sweetest bard
  was born BUI 15
  God . . . with a penchant for B. REL 56
  Wha hear a B. or Shakespeare sing, Yet still
  their ain bit jingles string POET 40
burns: burnis hurlis all their bankis doun
SWW 27
  Whan big as b. the gutters rin FOO 50
  When . . . the b. grow bauld SWW 9
bus: b. station concourse is like a Social Security
office turned inside out TRA 49
  But the whole notion of standing at b. stops!
  Awful. TRA 27
bush: Earl Douglas was buried at the bracken b.
WAR 2
  shadow of our trysting b., It wears so slowly
  round TIM 3
  what saw ye there At the b. aboon Traquair?
  NAT 26
  yield thee to the bracken b. Grows on yon
  lily-lee WAR 1
business: B. – the sale of lies DAI 19
  Comedy . . . too large an affair altogether
  for . . . the film b. TEL 5
  deil had b. on his hand MOM 9
  For the sake o' b. I've had to order suits
  PLA 55
  Give us to go blithely on our b. REL 121
  'Hokey!' said the youth. 'When Ah'm in the b.,
  Ah'll have the times!' DAI 21
  I'm a man that gets through with my day's b.
  PER 239
  not a b. to which the presbyterian mind is
  natively . . . attuned TEL 7
  not by any means certain that a man's b. is the
  most important thing DAI 57
  our b. in the world is not to succeed DAI 54
  our b. is like men to fight WAR 64
  our Scots way to do little b. but squeeze up
  high prices COM 9
  Scotland . . . increasingly unprofitable sphere
  in which to conduct various b. DAI 37

Those who think composing a Scotch song is
a trifling b. MUS 18
Virginia traders – known as tobacco lords –
strutted in b. hours PER 126
was obliged to fix all its important b. for the
alternate days REL 100
We all end up yesterday's men in this b.
SPOR 75
bustard: goose, or b. rather . . . Cocks up its
shitepoke INS 64
busy: I'm b. too, an' skelpin' at it DAI 8
but and ben: beik the house baith b. and b.
PLEAS 13
  I can hardly stotter b.a.b. FOO 32
  There's a wee wifie waitin, In a wee b.a.b.
  FOO 94
butcher: ae fat b. fried the ither INS 7
  Burke's the b. MIN 2
  not from the benevolence of the b. . . . that we
  procure our dinner PHIL 52
Bute, Earl of: O B., if instead of contempt INS 9
butler: beam, cool as a b. MOM 43
  but my father was your mother's b. M-W 79
butter: B., new cheese and beer in May SWW 56
  b. skites an' winna spread SWW 54
  seasoned the whole . . . with a reasonable
  proportion of b., pepper and salt! FOO 109
  You are offered a piece of bread and b.
  FOO 89
buttock: lusty like a good broad female b.
M-W 24
butts: while you to b. were striding LAND 17
byre: Time . . . halds his hand for palace nor for
b. TIM 28
  We had some fun, haud awa' wi' the smell, At
  the muckin' o' Geordie's b. PLEAS 1
  whistlin' ower the travise to the baillie in the
  b. MUS 63
Byron: A Burns is infinitely better educated than
a B. BUR 4

C

cabbage: for Beef and C. . . . no body excels me
FOO 73
  not very unlike a huge c. out a-walking
  PER 187
  Who knows what agonies the c. suffers
  FOO 9
caddy-spoon: c.-s. was a special shape FOO 127
Cady: I remember when they were so numerous
BIO 9
Caesar, Julius: Great J., that tribute gat of a'
HIS 19
  like C. sitting in the midst of the Senate
  POL 15
  What millions died, that C. might be great
  POL 25
cailleach: 'famine of the farm' . . . in the shape of
an imaginary old woman FANT 24
Cain: An' his master's name was C. TOA 7

carline: auld carlin, Lot's wife **REL 101**
   c. wife's three sons cam' hame **FANT 3**
   ilka c. swat and reekit **MUS 17**
Carlyle, Thomas: entirely devoid of interest in
   the arts **ART 13**
     misreading of *Poems of a Painter* **BOO 31**
     very good of God to Let C. and Mrs C. marry
     one another **PER 68**
     When C.'s thunder had been followed by his
     wife's sparkle **INS 84**
Carmichael, Marie: *The Queen's Marie* **LAM 8**
carriages: He scorned c. **PER 204**
cars: all chatter on the subject of motor c. a mere
   bagatelle **TRA 26**
cart: Drivin' intae Glesca on the soor milk c.
   LOVE 58
   I pored over them, driving my c. or walking
     to labour **POET 6**
   his gurling c. **LAND 28**
   though I drudge thro' dub and mire At pleugh
     or cart **POET 5**
case: c. that's still too common **M-W 46**
   In just about every c. . . . I've wanted to
     implicate as many people as I could **LAW 22**
cash: smartest bidder buys for ready c. **LAND 15**
castle: biggin' c. in the air **CHI 8**
   C. looms – a fell, a fabulous ferlie **PLA 45**
   equally honoured in c., farm and croft
     FOO 92
   I find I have only been in an enchanted c.
     MIN 42
   lighted upon the c. . . . and brak in sunder
     FANT 41
   no symptom of decay about its huge shell
     BUI 14
   sacrilegiously cutting down the old timber
     about the c. **MOM 34**
   yon castel braw . . . is the Scottis Glamourie
     FANT 62
Castle Grant: sair cheenged times at C.G.
   THO 98
castles: c. of the chiefs were inconvenient and
   rude **BUI 22**
   Time that has dinged doun castels and hie
     toures **TIM 28**
cat: c. may look at a king **ANI 87**
   c. on the clootie rug **MOM 16**
   efforts to shift the disease . . . to a c. or dog
     MIN 25
   He's noticed once or twice **ANI 46**
   I'll bell the c. **ADV 51**
   I'm a little black c. and I'm not very well
     ANI 96
   only mystery about the c. **ANI 71**
   puir pussy baudrons **ANI 10**
   the ideal literary companion **ANI 32**
   the muckle c. sat doon and grat **ANI 1**
   There was a Presbyterian c. **ANI 3**
   They bought a c. and taught it to bark
     FAMI 31
   those poor souls who claim to own a c.
     ANI 84
   Touch not the c. bot a glove **MOTT 16**

untrammeled liberty of primal savagery
   ANI 85
When we wold go in the liknes of ne c.
   FANT 29
'Whipping the c.', or, more enigmatically,
   'flogging poussy' **WORD 36**
catastrophe: a kind of illegitimate exhilaration
   at the c. which has occurred **POL 13**
cathedral: mankind was never so happily
   inspired as when it made a c. **BUI 32**
Cathkin Braes: If ye go to the C.B. the
   sodgers'll blaw ye up **POL 3**
Catholics: I hope they will be balanced by some
   C. **REL 58**
   cats: his body would be devoured by these
     very c. **ANI 93**
   What strange objects of adoration are c. and
     monkies **REL 64**
cattle: All through the meadows the horses and
   c. **TRA 42**
   instead of monks' voices shall be lowing of c.
     PLA 82
   Men . . . are kittle c. **M-W 66**
   And shamble-wards nae c.-beast e'er passes
     ANI 62
   had a soft wild beauty that held the eye
     ANI 47
   to herd the fine c. in bonnie Strathyre
     PLA 129
   Vast presences come mincing in **ANI 56**
cauld: armit me weill fra the c. thereout
   PLEAS 8
   Auld Kirk, the c. kirk **REL 9**
   Girvan – a c., c. place **PLA 58**
   Good claret best keeps out the c. **FOO 105**
   O wert thou in the c. blast **SWW 17**
   Rhynie is a c. clay hole **PLA 114**
   When the win' grows c., and the burns grow
     bauld **SWW 9**
   when 'tis auld, it waxeth c. **LOVE 6**
cause: c. is not difficult to ascertain . . . she has
   sunk to be a province **POL 105**
   I despise both the c. and the judges **LAW 4**
   I will follow you to death, were there no other
     to draw a sword in your c. **WAR 54**
   nae c. to sing **LAM 42**
   No c. so vile **ADV 58**
   value your c. **ADV 71**
   we would show them the difference between a
     good and a bad c. **POL 73**
causes: Hopeless cases committed to hopeless c.
   REL 115
   Nor are we to proceed in feigning c. **SCI 20**
Causewayend: words and weather both are
   cutting In C. **WORD 26**
caution: it sometimes sends native c. by the
   board **COM 12**
   Myths about a nation's history should be
     treated with considerable c. **HIS 13**
cave: O Merlin, in your crystal c. **CUR 20**
caves: echoes . . from their marble c. **REL 49**
Celt: C. . . . has felt, Like a religion, ties and dues
   of blood. **PPL 86**

to pass adolescence under the care of a deaf, offhand old centaur in a cave **EDU 5**

house where a c. is about to be born **FAMI 25**

What has the c. of millionaire or nobleman **SPIR 16**

with the birth of each c. you lose two novels **BOO 50**

childe: c. with the graip hurls it steady **LAND 28**

childer: c., wi' a fastin' mou' **CHI 15**

for our c. and our wifis . . . Are strenyeit in battle **SPIR 4**

We've words afouth . . Tho' frae them now my c. sair refrain **WORD 66**

childhood: As to my c.'s sight A midway station given **SWW 65**

fear . . . like a dark cloud in my c. **REL 16**

on her old decay, The beauty of her c. you can trace **YOU 19**

tear down c.'s cheek that flows **CHI 40**

'Twas but a piece of c. thrown away **LAM 27**

zones of c. through which we pass **CHI 34**

children: all the c. came shouting to the market **MOM 20**

c. as a rule have not been encouraged to speak their minds **HIGH 17**

c. of Conn, remember Hardihood in time of battle **WAR 62**

born teacher loves c. **EDU 31**

census of head-lice among the c. of handloom weavers **HIS 39**

even c. lisp the Rights of Man **M-W 45**

give our c. what they desire easily and endlessly **HIS 6**

I hear the little c. of the wind **SWW 46**

isle . . . Belonged as a dwelling to the C. of the Gael **LAND 39**

man who applauds and encourages all the vices of his c. **CHI 30**

these c. are happy **CHI 19**

c. whether big or small, Should always have a smiling face **CHI 41**

c. with their melancholy looks **LAM 38**

community should have to dismiss the choice of its c. **PPL 23**

Cruel c., crying babies **CHI 49**

his dearest wish and prayer to have his c. under his own eye **EDU 10**

Let c. walk with nature **DEA 52**

Let us treat c. and fairies in a more summary manner **WORD 2**

Listen to the little c., Praying God their souls to keep **MOM 1**

My c. from the youngest to the eldest loves me and fears me **CHI 52**

Not at all like proper c. **CHI 48**

our c. are conscripts **EDU 14**

Parents learn from their c. about coping with life **CHI 47**

see our c. die in Hunger **LAM 55**

she's had five c. and she's as barren as Rannoch Moor **FAMI 24**

soul of the very poorest of nature's c. **REL 40**

That race is gone, but still their c. breathe **PPL 25**

thousand schemes of petulance and pride Despatch her scheming c. **PPL 24**

where the c. of honest poverty have the most precious of all advantages **SPIR 16**

Women and c., too ill to undress **TRA 28**

chimpanzees: individuals bare their arses to each other **FAMI 20**

China: 'I'm sailin' for China this week' **TRA 17**

china: c. that's ancient and blue **PLEAS 10**

chips: I don't like my c. back-het **FOO 86**

chloroform: I had the c. for several days in the house before trying it **SCI 40**

I set him above even the inventor of C. **CUR 15**

chocolate: I have been like to *choke o' late* **WORD 52**

chocolates: those who prefer hard-centre c. **FOO 82**

choice: if it ever came to the c. between living and dying **CHI 23**

Chopin: C. hated the English **PPL 11**

chords: c. that vibrate sweetest pleasure **MUS 12**

Her fingers witched the c. **MUS 21**

Chris Colquhoun: C. would say they needn't fash **WORD 29**

Christ: *And Christe receive thy saule* **DEA 1**

C. born into Virginitie Succour Scotland **LAM 2**

C. Jesus the King, and his kingdom the kirk **MOM 33**

C. permitting, never would these lips tell **REL 21**

C.'s name I rarely mention **REL 8**

Earth that blossomed . . . 'Neath the cross the C. had **WAR 87**

For C.'s sake *bless the Rangers* **SPOR 60**

in pledge and testimony of their mutual love in C. **PER 146**

Our souls triumph with C. our glorious Heid **EPI 9**

sacred among the Gael before C. was born **FANT 47**

Which will through C. a resurrection get **TIM 1**

Christendom: many of the greatest cranks in C. **POL 99**

Christian: C. apologists have left nothing to disbelieve **REL 109**

C. Religion not only was at first attended by miracles **REL 63**

church but as an instrument of C. good **REL 39**

early C. gets the fattest lion **ADV 107**

Christianity: Few forms of C. have offered an ideal . . . so pure **REL 106**

nothing in C. . . . matches the sympathetic unselfishness of an oyster **FOO 113**

Christians: no enemies except . . . all the Christians **FRI 16**

Christmas: I'd spent a merry C. **FES 8**

clock: Between the clicking of the c. A star dies
  MOM 48
close: Up the c. and doun the stair MIN 2
clothes: Art may make a suit of c. COS 38
  cows munching c. on the line MOM 45
  Do I like women's c. more than their bodies?
    COS 34
  fine c. . . . are tossed into a corner INS 80
  is it not to C. that most men do reverence?
    COS 15
  it would take a dozen skivvies, his c. to wash
    and scrub SPOR 51
  my mother's c. came from a dress agency
    COS 44
  Trust not the heart of that man for whom Old
    C. are not venerable COS 16
  wanderer . . . that his c. might not be wet, held
    them up a great deal too high PER 50
cloud: dark c. came suddenly over the sun
  LAW 26
  fear indeed hung over me like a dark c.
    REL 16
  lonely paths, through mist, and c., and foam
    MOM 44
  little wee c. in the world its lane FANT 35
  not a c. my eyes hath crossed, But to my soul
    is gone THO 75
  one has music and the flying c. REL 114
  snug embrace of an impudent Highlander
    upon a c. of tradition POET 71
clouds: 'Homeless Clan' SWW 47
  mystie vapours, cluddis and skyis SWW 29
  St Kilda is a home of c. SWW 35
  shed the misty cloudis fra the sky SWW 41
  when c. rise from the waste of the waves
    LAM 39
  When the c. hang laigh SWW 42
  Winds and c. for ever going EPI 21
clout: Without a c. to interrupt them HIGH 15
club: Since our Jock became a member of that
  terrible football c. SPOR 51
clubs: crowd and the referees firmly behind the
  establishment c. SPOR 77
  I've had more c. than Jack Nicklaus SPOR 19
  lack of competition from other c. in the
    Scottish League SPOR 63
Clyde, River: Annan, Tweed and C., Rise oot o'
  ane hillside RIV 1
  bellowing C. RIV 10
  bonnie wee *Sultana*, The bully of the C.
    TRA 4
  Lulled by the wash of the waves of the C.
    PLA2: 1
  My native C., thy once romantic shore
    COM 4
  new Scotland . . . straggles westwards . . . to
    the lower C. POL 47
  O river C., baith deep and wide RIV 2
  poetry . . . Embattled by the C. POET 24
  Roamin' in the gloamin', by the bonnie banks
    o' C. PLEAS 11
  sparkling C., splashing its local sewage
    RIV 14

  where the Tweed, C. and Annan rise MOM 6
Clydesiders: C. failed because POL 18
  C. of slant steel POET 24
coach: They started a c. between Edinburgh and
  Aberdeen TRA 33
coals: Hot Burning C. of Juniper shall be Thy
  Bed of Down REL 45
  Then fling on c., and ripe the ribs PLEAS 13
coat: c., breeches and stockings all knitted by his
  wife COS 45
  clutching his c. about him like old iron
    TRA 41
  crisp in his mulberry-coloured kerseymere c.
    COS 19
  his waistcoat was white and his c. it was blue
    COS 50
  I should rather wear a worse gown than you
    should appear in a shabby c. COS 37
  nane o' them can dae wi'oot a c. or a sark
    DAI 49
Coatbridge: C. to glory REL 18
coats:her c. were kiltit, and did sweetly shaw Her
  straight bare legs COS 52
  peel off their c., and dip them in the butter
    FOO 12
cobbler: more the c. plies his trade, The broader
  grow his thumbs ADV 7
cobbles: streaman c. black wi rain MOM 46
cock: c. doth craw, the day doth daw FANT 4
  C. up your beaver, and c. it fu' sprush
    WAR 29
  proudly brought his own favourite c.
    SPOR 30
  twelve pennies Scots from each scholar for
    the benefit of bringing a c. to fight PLEAS 6
  up and crew the milk-white c. FANT 7
  wind may blaw, the c. may craw WAR 13
cock-fighting: clergy . . . uttered no complaint
  against . . . c. SPOR 30
cockernony: her c. snooded up fou' sleek COS 52
cod: Doon amang da steedin' c. SEA 11
coffee: and a cup of good strong c. FOO 76
  c. and whist HUM 3
coffins: c. stood round, like open presses
  FANT 22
cogie: bring a c. mair FOO 31
  But I maun hae my c. FOO 3
  coggie o' yill and a pickle aitmeal FOO 122
Coigach: Wagnerian Devil wrote the C. score
  MOU 24
Coire na Caime: From the deeps of C.n.C.
  MOU 26
cold, common: MIN 15
Coldstream: That line . . . can be read on a stone
  at C. bridge WAR 45
Coleridge, Samuel Taylor: Mr C. was in bad
  health INS 37
Coll: where the hills grip the beaches in strong
  pink talons LAND 48
colleagues: he . . . must deride himself and his
  c. MIN 10
college: I went to the Royal Technical C. in
  Glasgow, filled with zeal UNI 2

matching his effort and his c. against the enigma of life SPOR 34

My desire to disturb no man for c. sake is pretty well known POL 74

Conservative: in my youth, I was a C. POL 79

Constantine, King: His was the fair long reign PER 43

constituency: And it's in the c. too NAT 14

constitution: not so much a c. as a bad joke POL 106

consumer: interest of the producer ought to be attended to only so far as it may be necessary for promoting that of the c. PHIL 51

content: c., Retirement, rural quiet PHIL 62

He hes aneuch, that is c. ADV 64

Not c. with chemistry and natural philosophy SCI 5

Wumman's beauty gies man true c. M-W 78

contented: C. wi' little, and cantie wi' mair THO 23

contentment: it ne'er was wealth That coft c. LOVE 37

continent: When we have discovered a c. HOP 21

contradictions: heart of man was made to reconcile c. HUM 10

conversation: marrriage is one long c. M-W 118

cook: c. was a good c., and as good cooks go, she went FOO 112

c. was too filthy an object to be described FOO 33

need of a canny c. FOO 106

Cookery: Science to which I intend to addict the remaining years of my life FOO 73

cooper: There was a wee c. who lived in Fife DAI 3

Cope, Sir John: Now Johnnie, troth, ye are na blate WAR 82

copulation: C. is a sweet and necessary act BOO 12

corduroys: the well-worn rear of my c. COS 47

corn: c. must be sown in Spring SWW 22

c. was driven on to the teeth by the swinging reaper flails LAND 26

Fast-rooted bracken where the c. once ripened LAND 17

My c. is unshorn LAM 10

Sweeping with shadowy gust the fields of c. SWW 63

wreath'd with nodding c. SWW 18

corp: in the chalmer whaur the c. was hangin' FANT 64

girn on her face like an unsteakit c. FANT 63

corpse: rain to the c. SWW 6

corpses: master . . . annexed the c. of the slaughtered fowls SPOR 30

Corra Linn: Clyde . . . brak its neck owre C.L. RIV 1

corrie: disappeared over the ridge into the c. MOU 19

Corsican dress: so fine a fellow COS 8

cost: brooding on the Lord Krishna and the c. of living MOM 11

cotillion: Nae c., brent new frae France MUS 15

cottar: c. spak' it in his yaird WORD 37

Wi' tousy head a c. lad Sat in the auld man's place YOU 8

couch: c. where infant beauty sleeps CHI 13

Coulter's candy: To buy some C.c. CHI 5

counsel: Sage c. in cumber LAM 54

This is the counsail . . . Of Guid King Robert's Testament WAR 38

those of his own country whose right it was to c. him PER 101

counsellors: my c., my comforters, and guides FRI 23

counsels: how mony c. sweet, . . . the husband frae the wife despises! M-W 41

Sic counsels ye gave to me CUR 8

counterpane: the pleasant land of c. CHI 51

countries: all the c. that contributed towards the civilisation we now know LAND 59

'Communism' in backward c. POL 86

For these c., one should be amphibian LAND 35

indebted to other C. for those Accomplishments PPL 4

country: boasted that 20,000 men might yet be raised in that c. WAR 71

c. above all others . . . in which a man . . . may carve out his own pleasures LAND 61

c.'s looking very green HUMO 14

death and c. and love . . . comes out in these songs MUS 39

determined to avenge our own wrongs, and set our c. free SPIR 56

dressed . . . in the barbaric fashion of the savages of her c. PER 55

drunken mannners of this c. are very bad FOO 16

fine c. to grow old in PPL 44

great is the scandal to your c. that such a brute did grow in it INS 66

Hame to my ain countrie! LAND 18

he never had much affection for those of his own c. whose right it was to counsel him PER 101

He saved our c., and advanced our trade POL 1

he subsided into a c. bumpkin PLEAS 9

I am not apt to confide in the professions of gentlemen of that c. PPL 51

I am not sure whether Scotland . . . is not the finest c. in the world LAND 33

I am . . . very glad to be able to live in and enjoy my own c. HIGH 42

I believe Scotland would be the c. I should choose to end my days in LAND 23

if any one c. is endowed with a superior partition of sense PPL 99

if ever a man proposes to serve and merit well of his c. PER 164

It was then we had a King and Court and C. of our ain LAM 43

Lord have mercy on my poor c. SPIR 22

Moon is shining for you In the far c. SWW 2

crags: Oh for the c. that are wild and majestic!
HIGH 14
  Your kindly slope, with . . . abounding tufted
  c. PLA 18
Craig, Archie: Moderator was the great Dr A.C.
REL 116
craig: I . . . dirkit him, and syne whittled his c.
PER 92
  Eild comes owre me like a yoke on my c.
  YOU 13
  in the cleaving of a c., She found him droon'd
  in Yarrow DEA 6
Craigielea: a the sweets that ane can wish Frae
Nature's han PLA 22
craigs: riven c. where the black raven brings The
still-born lamb PLA 12
  time to sharp the maiden for shearing o' c.
  HUM 12
crammasy: Mars is braw in c. THO 70
crap: aye maist sawn o' the best c. M-W 106
cratur: 'Sit doon, ye useless c.' MUS 32
craw: c. killed the pussie, O ANI 1
  Happy the c. That biggs in the Trotten shaw
  LAM 15
  Three c. sat upon a wa' ANI 2
cream: tea kettle . . . and marmalade and c.
FOO 91
creation: incomparable metaphor for the unity
of c. REL 14
  long sum of c. SCI 4
  whole affair of her c. was an afterthought
  M-W 65
creator: C. if he exists, has a specific preference
for beetles SCI 17
creature: any c. who seems to be doing the work
of the Almighty MIN 10
  c. was basking on the surface MONS 16
  extraordinary humped back of some huge
  living c. MONS 10
  funny thing about the c. was she believed
  none spoke ill of her PER 116
  glass of wine is a glorious c. FOO 116
  Let me have my own way . . and a sunnier . . .
  c. does not exist PER 78
  Man is a c. who lives . . . principally by
  catchwords WORD 72
  overdose of the c. FOO 118
  poor c., who has said or done nothing
  worth . . . remembering POET 15
creatures: Ah! forgive me, fellow-c. THO 112
  One of the most perfect c. that ever was seen
  PER 40
  they are very precarious c. PER 92
  these monstrous c. of God MOU 21
  We happy c. of a day! THO 110
creeds: guid auld c., That met a simple people's
needs LAM 28
  To lead in the abandonment of c. SPIR 31
creel: Plenty peat to fill her c. TOA 20
  weel may the boatie row, That fills a heavy c.
  SEA 9
crème de la crème: all my pupils are the *c.*
CHI 46

Crianlarich: C., the most signposted nowhere
PLA 23
Crichton, the Admirable: an eccentric had
elaborated a prodigy PER 183
Crieff: flesher Rob that lived in C. M-W 108
  Take my advice and visit the ancient town of
  C. PLA 24
crime: c. increasing – drunkenness . . . making
progress SPIR 7
  end of hunger, cold and c. POL 59
  If suicide be supposed a c. DEA 40
  patricide is a greater c. than parricide SPIR 8
  sheep-stealing, which was at this time a
  capital c. DEA 48
criminals: one class of c. from which Scotland
was exempt TRA 20
crinoline: at last . . . she had the whole c.
adjusted to her satisfaction COS 51
crisps: a packet of potato c. which he can stuff
FOO 76
Critic: cut-throat bandits on the path of fame
BOO 14
  Every c. in the town Runs the minor poet
  down POET 51
  hedgehogs courting BOO 48
  scandalous what I was doing with the hose-
  nozzle ACT 11
critics: John Anybody would have stood higher
with the c. BOO 3
Criticism: it isn't c. you want ACT 12
croft: equally honoured in castle, farm and c.
FOO 92
  great white bow . . . arched the c. SWW 53
  in front of a c. a young fellow was dancing the
  Highland Fling PLEAS 9
  In his wee thatched c. he wore awa' DEA 55
crofter: Could we analyse the soul of a Highland
c. HIGH 22
  c. girls' underclothing BOO 29
  c. . . . when asked when the steamer would
  arrive TRA 18
  These c. carles may cross the sea LAND 8
  They burned the rest of them; and this c.'s
  was the last LAND 13
  typical Lewis c.'s house BUI 10
crofters: c. call it 'gress' NAT 23
  c. first developed a forward-looking critique
  REL 66
  hardship and poverty of the thousands of c.
  LAND 41
crony: His ancient, trusty, drouthy c. FRI 9
cross: after making the salutary sign of the C.
MONS 6
  as c. as two sticks ADV 117
  Earth that blossom'd . . . 'Neath the c. that
  Christ had WAR 87
  'Stand ye fast by the C. of Saint Andrew!'
  WAR 23
crouse: canty auld folk crackin' c. YOU 5
  Knox wi' Burns and Mary . . . Aa be snod and
  c.? SPIR 50
  we canna bide sae c. HUM 16
crowdie: drammock and c. FOO 120

whack o' crumpy-c. **FOO** 125

crown: I had the honour to set the c. on the king's head **DEA** 9

Look straight up to the c. where the folds are gathered **SWW** 51

We trace our bondage from the Union of the C. **POL** 30

crowns: cast great crouns like tinsel in the fire **TIM** 28

right by which their ancestors held their c. **REL** 98

cruel: he split the Scottish mind. The one half he made c. **PER** 144

cruise: we are all on our last c. **YOU** 26

Cruithneach: after slaughtering C. **LAM** 17

cuck-stool: when a well-known offender sat on a c. **LAW** 15

cuckoo (*see also* **gowk**): He would return, even as the c. comes **EPI** 28

I heard the c., with no food in my stomach **THO** 1

you shall hear the c. from the one shore to the other **PLA** 51

cucumber: The pale c. **BATH** 5

sometimes, when c. is added to it **FOO** 89

Cuillin: individuality of the C. is . . . not the mystery of clearness **MOU** 16

Cuillins: the far C. that are puttin' love on me **LAND** 43

Cul Beag: frieze of mountains **MOU** 23

Cul Mor: frieze of mountains **MOU** 23

God was Mozart when he wrote C.M. **MOU** 24

Culloden, Battle of: **FANT** 21

culture: generation being educated to know nothing of our history and c. **EDU** 11

Cumberland, Duke of: bluidy Duke cam trysting thither **INS** 7

Here continueth to stink **INS** 8

May there be no joy on his hearth **CUR** 25

merciless conqueror **WAR** 47

Cumbraes: bless the Greater and Lesser C. **BOA** 17

cummers: If he expected the c. of Aberlady to sympathise . . . he got a drop **M-W** 97

C.'s Feast . . . where each gentleman brought a pint of wine **FOO** 102

cunt: he was a funny wee c. **CHI** 22

kis the c. of ane kow **INS** 79

cup: Anywhere they lead us till the C. is won **SPOR** 3

Boswell put his c. to his head **WORD** 52

I'll drink a c. to Scotland yet **TOA** 19

We'll tak' a c. o' kindness yet, For auld lang syne **TOA** 9

curd: c. from the pen **FOO** 70

cure: Best c. in the world for whooping cough **MIN** 33

c. for which there is no disease **FOO** 49

Hope's . . . sad c. **HOP** 9

Work is a grand c. **DAI** 14

curiosity: innate c. and perceptiveness **SCI** 9

curl: Though it crawl on the c. of a Queen! **INS** 17

curlew: his troubled note dwells mournfully **ANI** 33

curse: c. his new hoose, his business, his cigar **CUR** 19

c. of Hell frae me sall ye bear **CUR** 8

First on the head of him who did this deed, My c. shall light **CUR** 14

I c. their head and all the hairs of their head **CUR** 16

My c. upon your venom'd stang **MIN** 13

no hint throughout the universe . . . of blessing or of c. **PHIL** 64

printing-press is either the greatest blessing or the greatest c. **JOU** 1

curses: the old c. and the old benedictions **THO** 50

cursit: thair evil deeds generalie c. . . . with the GREIT CURSING **CUR** 17

cushat: I heard the c. croon Thro' the gowden afternoon **NAT** 26

cushions: O can ye sew c.? **DAI** 1

custocks: c. in Strathbogie **FOO** 3

custom: C., then, is the great guide of human life **DAI** 33

customers: To found a great empire for the sole purpose of raising up a people of c. **PHIL** 54

Cuthbert, Saint: **FANT** 2

C. had a marked reluctance to take off his skin-boots more than once a year **PER** 179

cutty sark: her c.s., o' Paisley harn **COS** 10

cutty-stool: young girl sat upon the c.-s. **REL** 102

cycled: as if I had suddenly c. into an alternative town **FANT** 65

cynicism: I hate c. a great deal worse than I do the Devil **BAD** 16

cypress: The Minister said it wald dee, The cypress buss I plantit **BOA** 25

D

dad: stacher through To meet their d. **CHI** 12

daddy: wha the bairnie's d. is They dinna muckle mind **HUM** 9

My d. is a cankered carle **LOVE** 41

My mimmie me slew, My d. me chew **FANT** 14

rantin' dog the d. o't **M-W** 39

Some one of a troop of dragoons was my daddie **WAR** 28

Daddy Darkness: Auld D.D. is no wantit yet **CHI** 14

daft: no' much use in bein' d. if ye're no' tae be weel peyed **HUMO** 10

ye d. And doitit dotterel **PER** 226

daftie: off to the asylum they hurled the d. **MIN** 26

Daily Record: joined the *D.R.* as Art Editor **JOU** 11

daisies: crimson dockens, snowy d. **NAT 24**
Scotch is as spangled with vowels as a meadow
with d. **WORD 50**
daisy: d. did onbreid her crownell small **NAT 8**
dagger: Then strake the d. untill his heart
M-W 6
Dalarossie: old boundary between the parishes
of Moy and D. **SPOR 32**
Dalhousie: Alas, Lord and Lady D. are dead
BATH 18
Thou, D., thou great God of War **BATH 2**
Dalziel: gie D. his paiks **WAR 9**
dame: our sulky, sullen d. **M-W 40**
Dame Nature: D.N.'s petticoat is not so easily
lifted **NAT 13**
dames: Let dorty d. say Na! **M-W 105**
damnation: being Scotch, he didn't mind d.
PER 158
Nothing in the world delights a truly
religious people so much **REL 61**
damned: d. they wadna fry beside him **INS 7**
worms even d. him **INS 18**
dance: ae best d. e'er came to the land **MUS 14**
Blithely d. the Highland fling **PER 212**
d. gaed thro' the lichted ha' **MUS 11**
d. to your shadow when it's good to be living
MUS 53
Ere we d. with the maids of Dunrossness
again **SEA 25**
slimness of a boy's ankle while he is alive to
d. **THO 38**
three farmers were dancing a barbaric d.
PLEAS 3
dancers: rapturous yelp, which . . . escapes the
male d. **MUS 45**
dances: the enthusiasm and earnestness they put
into their national d. **PPL 91**
waves pursued their indifferent d. **SEA 5**
dancing: d. on each chimney top I saw a
thousand darling imps **FANT 58**
found they were d. in the proper patterns
MUS 46
young fellow was d. the Highland Fling, with
such . . . consuming zeal **PLEAS 9**
Dandy Doctors: 'D.D.s' clad in long black
cloaks **CHI 33**
danger: friends, By social d. bound **FRI 29**
Gin d.'s there, we'll thole our share **WAR 66**
I am fascinated and frightened by the . . . d. of
words **WORD 76**
Wha would shun the field of D.? **WAR 92**
dangers: What d. thou canst make us scorn
FOO 30
Darien: such product we from D. had **POL 1**
dark: And history leans by a d. entry **HIS 23**
boulders of the d. Whitewater **RIV 16**
d. blue is her e'e **LOVE 42**
d. cloud came suddenly over the sun **LAW 26**
dour, d. burn that has its ain wild say **SPIR 33**
eddies sleep, Calm and silent, d. and deep
MONS 17
fear indeed hung over me like a d. cloud
REL 16

his eyes d., clear and large **PER 85**
how dolorous, bitter and d. that unlooked-for
day **LAM 3**
if ever a soul had seen her at rest when the d.
was done **PER 118**
in an instant, all was d. **MOM 10**
In to thir d. and drublie days **SWW 29**
meikle good done in the d. **THO 96**
Nae day sae d., nae wud sae bare **THO 115**
on the left flank, a huge d. blotch **MONS 10**
sadness of the land . . . in d. autumn evenings
MUS 31
Scotland (my small d. country) **TRA 29**
shame-stricken driver hurries his packed
passengers off into the d. **TRA 14**
sitting d. there and terrible **MOM 17**
steep frowning glories of d. Loch na Garr
HIGH 14
Suilven, throwing its d. shadow **MOU 48**
that d. reckless Borderer, Wat o' the Cleuch
PER 140
Though the path be d. as night **REL 88**
tide was d. and heavy **SEA 16**
turning Round in the quay-lit d. **FAMI 18**
When I roved a young Highlander o'er the d.
heath **LOVE 38**
ye dungeons d. and strong **LAM 21**
dark glasses: d.g. hide dark thoughts **ADV 131**
'Dark Lochnagar': I used ance to could nearly
play't **MUS 61**
darkness: and a d down on the land he loved
better than his soul **LAND 25**
d. deepens **REL 75**
D. is your only door **THO 111**
game was over walls and fields until d. fell
SPOR 32
Great the blindness and sinful d. . . . . of
those who teach, write and foster the Gaelic
speech **WORD 19**
human soul stands between a hemisphere of
light and another of d. **PHIL 9**
In the silence and the d. **MOM 1**
Machines of death from west to east Through
the same d. fly **WAR 88**
never was d., But in came the conquering day
THO 77
darling: he's jist a perfect darlin' **CHI 42**
darlings: silver d. **SEA 13**
daughter: d. of a base and brainless breed
POL 63
dochter as black as Old Nick **FAMI 5**
messenger said it was ane fair dochter **HIS 22**
thirty yards of bowels squeezed under that
girdle of your d.'s **MIN 3**
daughters: Fame is rot: d. are the thing **FAM 2**
David Balfour: It may come to a fecht for it yet,
Davie **WAR 90**
dawn: d. creeps grey and cold **FES 10**
dark there and terrible, beneath the radiant
arch of d. **MOM 17**
You get up at the crack of d. **M-W 109**
day: Ae d. gie me o' youthful life At the back o'
Benachie **TIM 2**

days: Few are thy d. and full of woe **REL 22**
Football management these d. is like a nuclear war **SPOR 18**
I do not now precisely remember how many d. the dead bodies lay **WAR 47**
I dout my d. are on the trot **MIN 49**
I think that your d. are now shorter **LAM 20**
In case that his d. are dune **FAMI 2**
In to thir dark and drublie d. **SWW 29**
King might well have escaped, but he made to let it stop well three d. afore **HIS 26**
lightsome d. In the birks of Aberfeldy **PLA 7**
Nae after d. are like the d. When we were at the scule **EDU 24**
O for the d. when sinners shook **REL 59**
obliged to fix all its important business for the alternate d. **REL 100**
O'er me pass the d. and months and years **TIM 30**
Scotland would be the country I should choose to end my d. in **LAND 23**
They have got no meat these two d. **LAM 55**
true university these d. is a collection of books **UNI 4**
very good manager who just happened to have a few disastrous d. **SPOR 56**
When d. of refinement came, old topers mourned **FOO 60**
When it is twenty d. bottled drink it **MIN 27**
within few d. he sall ly as shamfull as he lyis glorious now **FANT 42**
dead: and hold high converse with the mighty d. **DEA 68**
as though our universe were . . . not a d. thing **MOU 31**
d. sleep cam over me **FANT 17**
Ballads are a voice from . . . old times long d. **POET 36**
Breathes there the man with soul so d. **SPIR 52**
deny to the spirits of their d. the welcome which they gave to the cows? **DEA 32**
Dig for their roots, or they be d. **WORD 28**
Fifteen men on a d. man's chest **FOO 130**
For he is d., and I'm alive **THO 37**
I'm only a poet, Whose fate is as d. as my verse **POET 55**
Here lies Boghead among the d. **EPI 18**
heroes of the Clan of Conn are d. **LAM 41**
hint of slice, and you're d. **SPOR 25**
History's easy. D. easy. **HIS 36**
I can go nowhere without finding the Scots at my beard, d. or alive **WAR 22**
I do not now precisely remember how many days the d. bodies lay **WAR 47**
I'm not d. yet **HOP 1**
I am not d., but gone before **EPI 4**
I saw a d. man win a fight **FANT 13**
Joy that is clothed with shadow Is the joy that is not d. **THO 81**
like a d. language which we can understand but cannot speak **WORD 3**
living or the d. No mercy find **PER 69**

Living were wearied in the burying of the D. **LAM 55**
rest is for the d. **DAI 17**
shaw'd the d. in their last dresses **FANT 28**
Sluagh, host of the d. **FANT 54**
strake the dagger untill his heart, And fell d. by her side **M-W 6**
these people (all d., born d. in fact) **INS 60**
This land that with its d. and living Awaits the Judgement Day **THO 91**
Three men alive on Flannan Isle, Who thought on three men d. **PLA 53**
Until the Kirk as it has been is d. **REL 112**
What a pity it is, mother, that you're now d. **DEA 34**
When Alysandyr our King was dede **LAM 2**
wife's niece dresses d. corpses **DEA 7**
with proper solemnity carried its d. to the churchyard **PLA 2: 10**
dead-born: it fell *dead-born* from the press **BOO 38**
Dearg the Fierce: Brimful was Alban east and west, During the reign of D. the F. **PER 44**
dearie: My ain kind d. **LOVE 32**
dears: the lovely d. Her noblest work she classes **M-W 38**
Death: adds a new terror to d. **BIO 4**
after d. you have no choice at all **DEA 25**
at the very idea of the general grief which must have attended his d. **DEA 59**
beautiful blending and communion of d. and life **DEA 52**
Cruel as d. **DEA 67**
d. and country and love . . . comes out in these songs **MUS 39**
d. and starvation came ower the haill nation **PER 243**
D. has murdered Johnny **PER 65**
d.'s a market where everyone meets **EPI 3**
D. is a grim creditor **DEA 33**
D. is the port where all may refuge find **DEA 8**
D. the horizon, when our sun is set **TIM 1**
d.-dirge of the ready-handed men **LAM 1**
Did he die a natural d.? **MIN 1**
found his mother . . . at the point of d. **MOM 52**
God says, 'To d. with them' **INS 44**
guarantees us a place in the front of the queue for d. certificates **PPL 87**
holds the power of life and d. over helpless persons **MIN 10**
lands I was to travel in; The d. I was to dee **LAM 8**
I will follow you to d., were there no other **WAR 54**
Machines of d. from east to west **WAR 88**
Mr Cockburn, on whom were the sweats of d., beg'd me to lie down with him **DEA 21**
Morag, harbinger of d. **MONS 5**
news of the d. of the Queen of Great Britain and Ireland **JOU 13**

Devil: All in all he's a problem must puzzle the d. **HUM 5**
as to believe that the d. really was in the printing-office? **REL 62**
Better keep the d. out **REL 3**
deil had business on his hand **MOM 9**
d., clad in a black gown, with a black hat **FANT 50**
D. ruled the woman **M-W 46**
d. sae devit was with thair yell **INS 33**
D. was sick **REL 99**
deeil a minute div ye get **DAI 12**
deevil a shilling I awe, man **DAI 10**
fly away with the fine arts **ART 9**
found myself wondering what the d. he was doing there **TEL 6**
I met the d. and Dundee, On the braes o' Killiecrankie **WAR 10**
I shall goe in the Divellis nam **FANT 29**
onlye woman, who by the dieuls perswasion **FANT 15**
Sarcasm I now see to be . . . the language of the d. **WORD 18**
She's just a d. wi' a rung **SPIR 13**
Tho' the d. piss in the fire **ADV 32**
To raise the wind in the divellis name **FANT 26**
Wagnerian D. wrote the Coigach score **MOU 24**
Wha the deil hae we got for a King **POL 29**
Whatever title suit thee **REL 30**
Wi' usquabae, we'll face the d.! **FOO 30**
devils: change o' deils is lichtsome **DEA 41**
Open your doors, ye d. **INS 33**
dew: fades away like morning d. **LOVE 6**
like the d. on the mountain **DEA 60**
Mountain D., *clear* as a Scot's understanding **FOO 87**
white fetlocks all wet with the d. **MOM 35**
dews: thro' your pores the d. distil **FOO 28**
dialect: none can more sincerely wish a total extinction of the Scotish *colloquial* d. than I do **WORD 61**
one of the most remarkable d. ever spoken by man **WORD 21**
'Tis mystifying all the same, This Berwick d. **WORD 33**
Diamond: bonny ship the *D.* **SEA 3**
die: And hero-like to d. **WAR 64**
easy live and quiet d. **THO 105**
every little nook was filled by . . . men who had crawled there to d. **WAR 72**
glad did I live and gladly d. **DEA 66**
great and good do not d. even in this world
he apparently couldn't d., even at the age of 84 **PER 110**
he never walked to battle, More proudly than to d. **PER 28**
I think no man fit to live that is not fit to d. **DEA 11**
I want to be the fittest man ever to d. **SPOR 41**
If after that they choose to d., What's that to me! **MIN 24**

If someone burst a sugar bag, the lot would d. of fright **POL 5**
It must couple or must d. **HUM 17**
Lads, you're wanted. Come and d. **WAR 58**
Lest we see a worse thing than it is to d. **WAR 59**
Let them alone, and they will all d. of themselves **FRI 20**
no retreat from here. You must d. where you stand **WAR 94**
nor fret for few who d. before I do **DEA 35**
old have been left to d. **LAM 37**
or like Douglas d. **WAR 46**
political parties d. at last of swallowing their own lies **POL 8**
see our children d. in Hunger **LAM 55**
there can be no entry for the day on which I d. **DEA 64**
to d. is nothing very grand **YOU 11**
to d. will be an awfully big adventure **DEA 12**
to d. young . . . the giving over of a Game **DEA 27**
died: dwined and d. of it, while the original patient was made whole **MIN 25**
fought and d. for Your wee bit hill and glen **SPIR 59**
he d., seated with a bowl of milk on his knee **DEA 22**
he d. at hame, like an auld dug **HIGH 11**
This d., that went his way **PHIL 59**
unless the movement 'ud gang on withoot him if He de'ed the morn **THO 71**
What millions d., that Caesar might be great! **POL 25**
Yea, I have d. for love **LOVE 21**
dies: d. on the banks of the Earn **LAM 17**
d. to win a lasting name **ADV 60**
man is born, a man d. **LAM 31**
man who d. thus rich d. disgraced **THO 28**
diet: Our d. was a curious one **FOO 96**
digestioun: helpis to the . . . guid d. **FOO 64**
dignity: He had neither d. nor . . . gravity **PER 251**
men of better clay and finer mould . . . feel the human d. **SPOR 9**
Thine be the joyless d. to starve **PER 229**
dilemmas: nivir any real d. wi junk **BAD 18**
dine: MacNeil of Barra has dined – the rest of the world may d. **BOA 12**
When will it be time to d.? **THO 54**
Dingwall: D. . . . an excellent place for sleeping a life away in **PLA 25**
dinner: At d., Dr Johnson ate several platefulls of Scotch broth **FOO 15**
David Hume ate a swinging great d. **PER 38**
d. at Fortune's **HUM 3**
d. partner asked him, 'Is it true that there is royal blood in your family?' **PER 125**
Every glass during d. had to be dedicated to someone **TOA 13**
In d. talk it is perhaps allowable **FOO 10**
not from the benevolence of the butcher . . . that we procure our d. **PHIL 52**

Dio: pleasant story from M-W 27
Diormit: D., his attendant . . . waited the arrival of the troublesome guest PER 21
dirt: the more d. the less hurt ADV 70
dirty: above anything d. or mean M-W 37
disappointment: few live exempt from d. ADV 129
    in spite of acid D. LOVE 24
discipline: considering they had no d. and not much pay WAR 70
    D. at the University was of the most relaxed sort UNI 5
    d. . . . for the interest . . . of the masters UNI 12
discomfort: d. arises from the feeling that you are outside of everything MOU 43
discoveries: being present while the first philosopher of the age was the historian of his own d. PER 56
    d. which lengthen life . . . are of infinitely more importance MIN 40
discovery: grand d., that in order to enjoy leisure, it is absolutely necessary it should be preceded by occupation DAI 47
    he who never made a mistake never made a d. PHIL 49
disease: asked how I was. Ill; a serious d. MIN 43
    cure for which there is no d. FOO 49
    efforts to shift the d. . . . to a cat or dog MIN 25
    Hope's sweet d. HOP 9
disgrace: a d. to be seen drunk FOO 102
dish: D. or no d., rejoined the Caledonian FOO 18
    fowl in a lordly d.is carried in FOO 128
    in a river and in a d. I hate that ubiquitous blasted fish FOO 85
    no d. was attempted that was not national FOO 61
    'Tis an inexpensive d. FOO 48
    thoroughly democratic d. FOO 92
dishes: some highly disparaging remarks on Scottish d. FOO 109
disjaskit: never such a d. rascal as yourself LAW 33
disputes: marriage is one long conversation, chequered by d. M-W 118
Disraeli, Benjamin, Lord Beaconsfield: cursed old Jew INS 24
distance: Three things by d. still grow dearer THO 32
    'Tis d. lends enchantment to the view THO 24
distillers: singed d. with their tubes FOO 83
distracted: d. man, a d. subject, in a d. time PER 25
distress: indure In dolour and d. LOVE 75
    their d. Comis for the peoples wickedness HUM 11
ditch: It neither grew in syke nor d. FANT 3
    Like ony d. FOO 29
diversion: an unpermitted d., frowned on by the authorities HUMO 9
divine: I never saw his glance d. REL 97

    love unfeigned Will reach the ears of the D. REL 6
    mercies temporal and d. REL 27
divinity students: 'How can I tell amang a wheen o' D. s.?' REL 102
dockens: crimson d., snowy daisies NAT 24
doctor: Any really good d. ought to be able to tell MIN 8
    I cannot praise the D.'s eyes REL 97
    or was the d. sent for? MIN 1
    They didn't like the idea of a woman d. MIN 12
    when the d. crossed an arm of the sea MIN 17
doctors: d. and kirkyards would go out o' fashion FOO 67
documentary: I suppose I coined the word (d.) TEL 8
dog: as dotit d. that damys INS 35
    curious incident of the d. in the night-time SCI 12
    efforts to shift the disease . . . to a cat or d. MIN 25
    gude sign o' a dowg ANI 49
    He is nae D.; he is a Lam PER 98
    he was a gash and faithfu' tyke ANI 21
    I wanted a d. FAMI 31
    Is thy servant a d., that he should do this thing? ART 20
    kicked an Edinbro dug-luver's dug ANI 40
    Madame, ye hev a dangerouss D.! PER 97
    'My long d. there turned him' PER 92
    one of the executioners . . . espied her little d. ANI 11
    rantin' d. the daddy o't M-W 39
    Scottie d. for every pot SPIR 38
doggies: Do d. gang to heaven? CHI 11
dogs: destroyers . . . of honest men, Like d. LAW 34
    d. are barking MOM 45
    I carena muckle for folk that bairns and d. dinna like THO 57
    What are these d. *doing?* CHI 16
    doings: d. here below That mortal ne'er should ken FANT 38
dollar: a puckle d. bills will aye preive Hiram Teufelsdrockh A septary of Clan McKay COS 27
    ye canny spend a d. when ye're deid ADV 89
dollars: She looks like a million d., but she only knows a hundred and twenty words PER 163
dolour: in d. thy dayis to endure CUR 18
Dolphinton: minister of D., being eager to have a railway TRA 16
dominions: His majesty's d., on which the sun never sets ADV 98
Donald Caird: D.C. can lilt and sing PER 212
donkey: a diminutive she-ass, not much bigger than a dog ANI 95
doo: I grew and grew, To a milk-white D. FANT 14
doos: twa d. sat in a dookit SWW 8
dool: for a' my d. and care, It's wantonness for evermair M-W 52

dools: covenanting fools, Wha erst ha'e fash'd us
  wi' unnumbered d. PER 102
doom: Had *Cain* been Scot, God would have
  changed his d. PPL 27
    must it thus be my d. To spend my prime in
    maidhood's joyless state? M-W 122
    Scottish poet maun assume The burden of his
    people's d. POET 41
    Thy d. is written REL 22
Doon: Ye banks and braes o' bonnie D. NAT 3
'Doonies': ba' may be . . . hoisted topmast by the
  'D.' SPOR 39
door: begged his bread from d. to d. MUS 71
    But he found . . . a d. was as wooden, as in
    England TRA 25
    chapped at the ark's muckle d. REL 41
    Darkness is your only d. THO 111
    d. of the Fionn is always open FANT 1
    not worthy even to keep a d. REL 119
    only d. out of the dungeon of self REL 82
    She still has fun' an open d. WORD 28
    she ope'd the d., she loot him in M-W 121
    stick a piece of steel . . . in the d. FANT 29
    under-teacher keep the d. PLEAS 6
    Vain are all things when death comes to your
    d. DEA 45
doors: O thou . . . whom prose has turned out
  of d. POET 7
Doric: It is as if the D. had been invented by a
  cabal of scandal-mongering beldams WORD 74
Dornoch Cathedral: mausoleum for the
  remains of her late husband BUI 25
doublet: thair meit doublet does thaim rejois
  COS 3
douce: even the d. grey concrete lamp-posts
  FANT 65
Douglas: dar'st thou then, To beard . . . the D. in
  his hall? PER 209
    doughty D. on a steed Rode all his men before
    PER 2
    Like D. conquer, or like D. die WAR 46
Douglas: At the first performance of *D.* SPIR 18
Douglas, Alfred, Lord: fatal lover of Oscar
  Wilde INS 92
Douglas, Gavin: as Phebus dois Cynthia precell,
  So Gawane Dowglas, Bischop of Dunkell
  POET 23
    opposed by a shower of shot BUI 1
Douglas, Norman: He was a . . . sort of Field
  Marshal Sir Douglas Haig turned inside out
  PER 110
Doune: lang may his lady Look owre the Castle
  D. DEA 5
dour: d. bitch o' a back-end SWW 36
    d., dark burn that has its ain wild say SPIR 33
    I am the half that is d. and practical and canny
    PER 36
    surface of d. practical integrity PPL 45
    to giff a doublett he is als doure, As it war off
    ane futt syd frog PER 97
dowie: mirk December's d. face SWW 33
    Near some lamp-post, wi' dowy face PER 103
    On the d. houms o' Yarrow WAR 6

    d. in the hint o' hairst SWW 9
Downa-do: D.-d.'s come o'er me now M-W 51
dowry: as d. with his wife . . . he got two
  thousand Herbridean Scots PPL 29
draff: Hielandman, black as ony d. PPL 1
dragons: every honest person believes in d.
  ANI 43
dragon-flies: like arrows go ANI 66
dram: after a d. of good wholesome Scots spirits
  FOO 91
    Fat say ye till a d.? FOO 103
    We'll have a d. to keep out the wet FOO 81
drammock: d. and crowdie FOO 120
drams: source o' joy below . . . Was drinkin' d.
  FOO 104
Drambuie: seaweed suppers . . . and draught D.
  LAND 39
    wee boy's D. FOO 71
drappie: dainty wee d. o' whisky FOO 122
    just a d. in our e'e FOO 22
drawers: I hope you have got warm d. COS 39
    tore off these beastly d. COS 26
dream: d. had no sound FAMI 18
    From the dim blue Hill of D. FANT 44
    I hae dreamed a dreary d. FANT 13
    Last night I dreamed a ghastly d. FANT 53
    old Bob in the d. that was Chris's snorted and
    shied FANT 28
dreamer: Tiresome 'tis to be a d. When will it be
  time to dine? THO 54
    young d.'s biggin' castles in the air CHI 8
Dreamthorp: D. has watched apple-trees redden,
  and wheat ripen PLA2: 10
Dreams: All schemes of Industry to be executed
  in that Country are idle D. COM 11
    D. come true HOP 16
    False d., false hopes, false masks THO 131
    Iona the metropolis of d. PLA 85
    put legs to your d. ADV 23
    we in d. behold the Hebrides SPIR 3
drink: And d. up all the beer MUS 7
    appalling d. problem, and he's not very good
    at football SPOR 14
    D. till the gudeman be blind PER 212
    gin my wife wad d. hooly and fairly M-W 25
    I can d. and nae be drunk BOA 3
    I should be let in; For my food and my d.
    FES 4
    I'll d. a cup to Scotland yet TOA 19
    If it was a fine day, why then, 'We'll d. its
    health.' FOO 81
    Is he good-natured in his d.? REL 46
    'It's an awful thing the d.!' FOO 56
    neighbours say the people are lazy and prone
    to d. WORD 59
    O are ye come to d. the wine WAR 6
    Scotch do not d. FOO 77
    Some taste the sweet, some d. the sour
    THO 128
    That I may d. before I go, A service to my
    bonie lassie FOO 21
    took ane d. my spreitis to comfort PLEAS 8
    We'll d. it in strong and in sma'! FES 7

When it is 20 days bottled d. it **MIN 27**

drinking: after that it's apt to degenerate into d. **FOO 4**

as if forsooth there was nobody present worth d. with **TOA 13**

At a prolonged d. bout **DEA 54**

Debauchery and d. **FOO 20**

D. the blood-red wine **TRA 1**

Oh the dreadfu' curse o' d.! **FOO 63**

Sweitin, sweirin, fechtin, drinkin **DAI 30**

What harm in d. can there be **FOO 14**

drinks: Than culit thai thair mouthis with confortable drinkis **FOO 46**

when I get a couple o' d. on a Saturday, Glasgow belongs to me! **PLA 63**

drooned: I ne'er lo'ed a lad but ane, And he's d. in the sea **LAM 7**

She found him d. in Yarrow **DEA 6**

droukit: Gin ye hae catcht a d. skin **FOO 50**

rain came down and they were drookit **SWW 8**

drublie: In to thir dark and d. days **SWW 29**

drudge: Man alone is a perennial d. **THO 36**

drum: No pipes or d. to cheer them on **SEA 22**

noisy ten hours d. **PLEAS 7**

sound of a drumstick on an insufficiently stretched d. **SPOR 50**

When welcoming the French at the sound of the d. **WAR 27**

Drumchapel: D., where dreams come true **HOP 16**

kind of cowboy town **PLA 26**

Drumossie: Oh! D., thy bleak moor shall . . . be stained with the best blood **FANT 21**

drunk: disgrace to be seen d. **FOO 102**

exac proportion . . . that ought to be d. every day **FOO 67**

I can drink and nae be d. **BOA 3**

I did not get d.; I was, however, intoxicated **FOO 16**

Mustn't-get-d., mustn't-get-d. **FOO 39**

Wonderful man! I long to get d. with him **PER 57**

drunkards: amassed a fortune by plundering d. **FOO 83**

drunken: blustering, d. blellum **INS 19**

d. manners of this country are very bad **FOO 16**

Scotland . . . most d. nation on the face of the earth **FOO 114**

through fits Of d. freedom **POL 17**

drunkenness: d. and Sabbath-breaking making progress **SPIR 7**

Duchess: every D. in London will be wanting to kiss me! **POL 65**

ducks: 'Can you see anything, Mr Mate?' 'No, Captain, but I can hear d.' **TRA 15**

D. are a-dabbling **ANI 44**

eider-d. have arrived **ANI 76**

I could set my watch by the evening flight of the d. from St James's Park **SPOR 38**

duddies: coost her d. on the wark **MUS 17**

Duke: Before a D. came **LAND 40**

''Twas the short fourteenth,' the D. was saying **SPOR 25**

Duke Street Jail: Down in D.S.J. **REL 131**

dukedoms: the effulgence of two D.s . . . will go a long way **POL 12**

Dukes: D. that you dined with yestreen **INS 17**

dule: forecasting such a time of unrest and d. **LAM 3**

dumb: d. monsters sadden and perplex **MOU 43**

me behovit whilom, or than be d., Some bastard Latin, French or Inglis use **POET 20**

Many of his opponents will now rail . . . who were d. before him **PER 87**

Dumfries: people of D. . . . with their pompous mausoleum **BUR 27**

westland warlock when he was at D. **MIN 25**

Dumfries, Lady: L.D. . . . asked him with a smile of contempt **INS 95**

Dun, River: snaky D. **RIV 10**

Dunblane: the flower o' D. **PER 242**

Duncan, Admiral Lord: D. gave orders that . . . every one of the ships must fight until she sank **WAR 56**

that sense . . . of what is grimmest and driest in pleasantry **WAR 89**

Dundas, Henry: H.D., applying to Mr Pitt for the loan of a horse **WORD 64**

pleasure of D. was the sole rule of every one of them **POL 27**

Dundee: D., a frowsy fishwife addicted to gin and infanticide **PLA 30**

D. . . . for generations dedicated itself to a kind of commercial single-mindedness **PLA 28**

D., the palace of Scottish blackguardism **PLA 29**

D. . . . completest monument in the entire continent of human folly **PLA 31**

east coast town with a west coast temperament **PLA 27**

Then some D. cake **FOO 59**

town is ill-built **PLA 32**

Until that night I never for a moment imagined that there were so many veritable fiends **BIO 8**

Dundee, Viscount (*see also* **Claverhouse**): I met the devil and D. On the braes o' Killiecrankie **WAR 10**

Dunedin: That day through high D.'s streets Had pealed the slogan-cry **WAR 17**

Dunfermline: king sits in D. toun, Drinking the blood-red wine **TRA 1**

What Benares is the Hindoo . . . D. is to me **PLA 33**

dung-heap: year they hauled the old woman out on to the d.h. **HUM 15**

dungeon: d. of self **REL 82**

d. of wit **PER 177**

dungeons: Farewell, ye d. dark and strong **LAM 21**

Dunino: D. – where no village is **PLA 34**

Dunkeld: minster was the scene of violence
  BUI 1
  Was there e'er sic a parish as that o' D.?
  PLA 35
Dunlappie: Oh! John Carnagie in D. **PER 10**
Dunlop, Alexander: possessor of a 'holy groan'
  REL 125
Dunmore, Countess of: attempts destruction of
  a *sheela-na-gig* **BUI 24**
Dunrossness: Ere we dance with the maids of D.
  again **SEA 25**
Duns: D. dings a' **PLA 36**
Duns Scotus: **EPI 15**
dust: D. thou art **REL 22**
  good triumphs and the villain bites the d. If
    anyone believes that **THO 47**
  hoar-frost Was sown like diamond d.
    SWW 25
  vile d. from whence he sprung **PER 216**
dustman: his life as a whole would have
  discredited a d. **BUR 7**
Dutch: He had just overtaken the D. fleet
  WAR 89
  in fact he stopped the D. without losing a man
    WAR 56
duty: Distrust of authority should be the first
  civic d. **POL 32**
  no d. we so much under-rate as the d. of being
    happy **DAI 55**
  now the d. of the Scottish genius **SPIR 31**
  Scotch method **ADV 96**
  Self less than Duty **PER 244**
  The hangman . . . only does his d. **DEA 15**
  You would not think any d. small, If you
    yourself were great **DAI 38**
dyke: like a mouse in a drystane d. **REL 10**

E

eagerness: Damn all that e.! **WAR 33**
eagle: E. and alpine veronica are part of the
  mountain's wholeness **MOU 40**
  even the eagle Forbears **ANI 61**
earl: Life is much easier, being an E. **THO 9**
Earl of Moray: They hae slain the E. o' M., And
  hae laid him on the green **DEA 5**
earls: Our erles and lords . . . How ignorant and
  inexpert they be **POL 49**
Earn: he dies on the banks of the E. **LAM 17**
  twinkling E., like a blade in the snow **RIV 9**
earth: a' the thrang bricht babble o' E.'s flood
  SPIR 33
  As the chill snow is friendly to the e. **MIN 36**
  e. belongs unto the Lord **TRA 3**
  E., e. on Oran's eyes **FANT 49**
  e. eats everything there is **LAND 53**
  e. goeth on e. **ADV 5**
  E. that blossomed and was glad 'Neath the
    cross that Christ had **WAR 87**
  E. thou bonnie broukit bairn! **THO 70**
  e., tideless and inert **LAM 16**

everything created In the bounds of e. and sky
  HUM 17
fonn, land, e., delight **WORD 48**
For happy spirits to alight, Betwixt the e. and
  heaven **SWW 65**
High tea in Aberdeen is like no other meal on
  e. **FOO 59**
I am a jingo patriot of planet e. **PER 119**
I grant the sons of e. Are doom'd to trouble
  PHIL 4
In all the e. like unto me is none **LAM 19**
innumerable songs of e. mingle with the
  acclamations of the serene witnesses
  PLEAS 14
is full of graves **DEA 26**
lays one alongside the bones of mother e.
  MOU 9
little foull earthe taid **INS 78**
lowest form ay vermin on goad's e. **PPL 100**
most drunken country on the face of the e.
  FOO 114
night hush of e. is expectant **MOU 31**
not possible to hope for more from any
  princess of the e. **PER 40**
On e. I am a stranger grown **YOU 3**
playing: 'Farewell to Scotland, and the rest of
  the e.' **MUS 47**
receptive to the influences of e. and sky
  MOM 21
that garret of the e. **LAND 55**
the various e. of which you are made **ADV 95**
thistle well betrays the niggard e. **LAND 12**
the most sentimental and emotional people on
  e. **PPL 20**
when the dust returns to the e. once more
  DEA 50
ease: every man said to his prisoner, Sir, go and
  unarm you and take your e. **WAR 39**
  high grasslands . . . are e. to the feet **MOU 17**
  in our hours of e., Uncertain, coy and hard to
    please **M-W 111**
  We a' lay doon to tak' our e. **PLA 115**
east: as much ado about its e. wind as he did
  about the Edinburgh Sunday **SWW 12**
  Beloved land of the E. **LAND 1**
  bounded . . . on the E. by the rising sun
    LAND 51
  Machines of death from e. to west Drone
    through the darkened sky **WAR 88**
  She sought him e., she sought him west
    DEA 6
  Some e., some west, some everywhere but
    north **PPL 24**
easy: e. live and quiet die **THO 105**
eat: Men . . . can sympathetically e. together
  FOO 37
eccentric: an e. had elaborated a prodigy
  PER 183
eccentrics: those intelligent e. of whom Scotland
  has the manufacturing secret **PER 49**
echoes: Only the e. which he made relent
  REL 49
economics: love o' e. **ADV 85**

elves: when e. at midnight hour are seen
FANT 43
embalmed: She's been e. inside and out **PER 200**
emblem: *Primula Scotica* might be an even better
e. NAT 30
Emery, Don: the fearsome full-back, D.E.
SPOR 10
emigration: thanks to . . . e., Londonism, and
the eruption of crude industrialism **PPL 74**
emotional life: reading of novels the most
effective training for BOO 1
employment: to rob was thought at least as
honourable an e. as to cultivate the soil
HIGH 23
enchantment: blessed e. of these Saturday
runaways SWW 50
    day kept up its e. as I walked up the bridle-
    path NAT 27
    'Tis distance lends e. to the view THO 24
end: all . . . from the beginning to the e., gave
over themselves to be guided by him **PER 31**
    And come to a premature e. SCI 6
    e. of hunger, cold and crime POL 59
    e. of the world is near when the MacBrayne's
    ship will be on time TRA 40
    ere the world comes to an e., Iona shall be as
    it was PLA 82
    grant us in the e. the gift of sleep REL 121
    great e. of all human industry is the
    attainment of happiness PHIL 26
    I would welcome the e. of Braid Scots and
    Gaelic POL 41
    I' the back e. of the year SWW 42
    In my e. is my beginning MOTT 21
    Keep right on to the e. of the road ADV 82
    Someone christened her The Diver, and she
    was known by that name until the e. of her
    long career TRA 46
    We all e. up yesterday's men in this business
    SPOR 75
    Whoredom her trade, and vice her e. PER 103
    without lighting a fire from one e. of the year
    to the other SWW 11
    Work as though work alone thy e. would gain
    REL 123
endurance: E. is not just the ability to bear a
hard thing THO 13
enemies: fury of his e. was black and universally
detested PER 58
    I am dying as fast as my e., if I have any, could
    wish DEA 39
    I have no e., except indeed, all the Whigs, all
    the Tories, and all the Christians FRI 16
    king of Scots was skilled . . . in inflicting
    damage on the e. he fought PER 101
    Lallans . . . 'Plastic Scots' its e. called it
    WORD 73
    Lat woodis for wallis be bow and speir, That
    enemyis do thaim na deir WAR 38
    priests have been e. of liberty REL 65
    to strike 'unallowed' blows upon his family's
    e. HIGH 19

when asked why he carried a sword, that it was
to kill his e. **FRI 20**
When I came into Scotland, I knew well
enough what I was to expect from my e.
FRI 28
worst e. are our own kin in the east HIGH 5
enemy: Being hard-pressed by the e., he was
supported . . . by these intrepid men WAR 42
    Biography should be written by an acute e.
    BIO 1
    He was . . . the violentest e. I ever had PER 59
    manner in which the e. came on was quicker
    than could be described WAR 37
    No e. is half so fatal FRI 11
    Observing the e.'s colours still flying WAR 35
    we will . . . endeavour to expel him as our e.
    SPIR 2
engine: I was thinking upon the e. at the time
SCI 43
    This was the e. that had gone down with the
    Tay Bridge TRA 46
engines: clanking e. gleam COM 4
England: bounded on the South by E. LAND 51
    country to reckon with as long as she was not
    incorporated with E. LAND 21
    E. shall mony a day Tell of the bloody fray
    WAR 79
    E. will not be better by becoming . . . Scottish
    SPIR 23
    he found . . . a door was as wooden, as in E.
    TRA 25
    'If I had my rights I should be king of E.'
    PER 125
    is suffering now, from too much E. SPIR 35
    King of E. and his accomplices PER 53
    more changes of scenery in ten miles than E.
    in fifteen TRA 19
    not anything you can expect . . . which I shall
    not be ready to do for . . . E. POL 7
    Parliament of E. despising us SPIR 7
    Poor E.! when such a despicable abortion is
    named genius PER 77
    To mark where E.'s province stands POL 22
    treated direct with the kings of Scotland, E.
    and Europe HIGH 35
English: Ah don't hate the E. They're just
wankers INS 97
    apt to upbraid the E. with being a
    composition of all nations HIGH 10
    bishop, who was not yet fluent in the E.
    language WORD 4
    As I know my own heart to be entirely E.
    POL 7
    E., as a people, are very little inferior to the
    Scots PPL 71
    E. football players have been quoted SPOR 40
    Glamour . . . an E. importation from Scotland
    WORD 10
    He had recently graduated with a degree in E.
    literature and was on the dole UNI 14
    his ear continues to remark the E. speech
    HIGH 45

e. we do – alas! that the world should love it
  so **LAM 4**
Glasgow, that damned sprawling e. town
  PLA 62
Whiggism but an e. habit **POL 48**
With his depths and his shallows, his good
  and his e. **HUM 5**
evils: Toleration is the cause of many e. **POL 9**
evolution: No theory of e. can be formed **SCI 37**
ewe: We'll sune hae neither cow nor e. **PPL 3**
ewes: Milk the e., Lassie! **LOVE 70**
ewie: My e. wi' the crookit horn! **ANI 90**
  pot still has passed into tradition as the 'e. wi'
  the crookit horn' **FOO 38**
examinations: to learn our lessons and pass the
  e. **EDU 26**
excellence: constant endeavour after e. **THO 20**
exile: had obtained perfect command of the
  Scottish tongue during his long e. **WORD 4**
  I wish I were an e. **THO 49**
experience: E. the best of schoolmasters
  EDU 12
  E. . . . schoolmaister of foolis **THO 88**
  From my e. of life **PER 233**
  grim e. for youth **UNI 7**
  Hope's . . . sad cure, dear-bought E. **HOP 9**
  no worldly pleasure . . . Which by e. doth not
  folly prove **LOVE 20**
  teaches that it doesn't **ADV 84**
  Practical wisdom is only to be learned in the
  school of e. **DAI 51**
experiment: mouthful or two satisfied both that
  the e. was a failure **FOO 66**
  trying all my life to like Scotchmen . . .
  obliged to desist from the e. in despair
  PPL 53
eye: dead bodies lay in the field to glut the e. of
  the merciless conqueror **WAR 47**
  dark blue is her e'e **LOVE 42**
  Early in the mornin', wi' a clear e'e **SWW 62**
  Light in the e., and it's goodbye to care
  MUS 69
  May the mouse never leave our meal pock wi'
  the tear in his e'e **TOA 2**
  shy, rare glance of her e. **LOVE 3**
  steal me a blink o' your bonnie black e'e
  LOVE 35
  There was lustre in his e. **PER 28**
  three measures of slenderness . . . in which the
  e., the ear and the mind meet **THO 38**
  To find a friend one must close one e. **FRI 12**
  Though his richt e'e doth skellie **LOVE 16**
  Vacant heart, and hand, and e. **THO 105**
  With a smile on her lips, and a tear in her eye
  LOVE 77
  with that e., no-one could answer for his
  temper **PER 30**
eyes: always to have the fear of the Laird before
  our ees **MIN 20**
  And the young fair maidens Quiet e.
  HIGH 43
  appearance of the face of a human being, with
  very hollow e. **MONS 15**

described the expression of his . . . e. as vacant
  PER 221
eject a foul-smelling odour into the face and
  e. **MOU 34**
his e. dark, clear and large **PER 85**
I cannot praise the Doctor's e. **REL 97**
I looked straight into his smiling face and e.
  MOM 13
leant forward over the table, a strange gleam
  in his e. **PLA 48**
mud wherein we stand Up to the e. **PPL 30**
not a cloud my e. hath crossed **THO 75**
of like estimation in the e. of heaven **REL 40**
our young wondering e. reveled **SWW 50**
reward in the e. of the King of Heaven **REL 1**

F

face: As soon as they saw her weel-faur'd f.
  FANT 11
  Bot in her f. seemit great variance **PER 137**
  death-mask . . . shows the the f. of a man . . .
  fixed in painful surprise **PER 192**
  determination to f. the facts **DAI 37**
  eject a foul-smelling odour into the f. and
  eyes **MOU 34**
  f. of an hospitable man, when strangers come,
  and there is nought to offer **THO 2**
  Fair fa' your honest, sonsie f. **TOA 11**
  flow'rs did smile, like those upon her f.
  LOVE 43
  for the first time he saw its f. **MONS 15**
  girn on her f. like an unsteakit corp **FANT 63**
  glowered, tongue-tackit, at the stars That
  lauched in Jeanie's f. **YOU 9**
  Hail in each crag a friend's familiar f.
  HIGH 13
  he lays it oot on his haun, and hits ye richt in
  the f. wi't **PER 157**
  He lookit on her ugly leper f. **MOM 22**
  Her f. it is the fairest That e'er the sun shone
  on **LOVE 42**
  'heroic young queen' . . . had the f. of a . . .
  hysterical poodle **PER 122**
  his f. was terrible **FANT 50**
  his wee round f. **CHI 8**
  I have asked grace at a graceless f. **LAM 9**
  I looked straight into his smiling f. **MOM 13**
  I will pluck the yarrow fair, That kindlier
  shall be my f. **CUR 5**
  lumpis haw appearand in thy f. **CUR 18**
  mirk December's dowie f. **SWW 33**
  nae smile was seen on Kilmeny's f. **FANT 36**
  on her f. That look which seems to say,
  'Industry is the noblest plan' **DAI 23**
  sceptical look which still lingered on the
  Minister's f. **LOVE 67**
  star on his f. and a spot on his breast **TOA 7**
  'Twas the round-about of the shadow That
  had so furrowed its f. **TIM 20**
  Wha called ye partan-f.? **INS 14**

families: these few f. have sucked the lifeblood of
our nation **POL 56**
family: bloated with f. pride **INS 57**
f. did their best to conceal the fact **PER 194**
honest men, and very careful of their f.
HIGH 11
'Is it true that there is royal blood in your f.?'
PER 125
small f. in the congregation of Europe **PPL 62**
to strike 'unhallowed' blows upon his f.'s
enemies **HIGH 19**
wasn't the place to display arses. This was f.
FAMI 20
We were a f., a tribe, a people **HIS 30**
when she could not get bread for her f., she
was forced to hire them out **LAND 4**
famine: 'f. of the farm' *(gort a bhaile)* **FANT 24**
'In his flesh there's a f.' **INS 18**
fan: soccer f. attending his first Rugby
International **SPOR 48**
fancy: day and night my f.'s flight Is ever with my
Jean **LOVE 31**
I e'en gave o'er in good time, before the
coolness of f. **POET 54**
my existence is chiefly conditioned by the
powers of f. and sensation **PER 52**
not a maid . . whose fancy any man . . . could
not conquer **M-W 65**
She fairly won my f. **LOVE 58**
fans: At both Carlisle and Glasgow Central, she
had her regular f. **TRA 12**
In Glasgow, half the f. hate you **SPOR 11**
farce: what a cruel thing is a f. to those engaged
in it **THO 118**
farewell: Fare ye a' weel, ye bitches! **FRI 18**
F., ye dungeons **LAM 21**
Fair weill, my lady bricht **LAM 50**
farm: Big House . . . decently earning its keep
as a f. **THO 19**
equally honoured in castle, f. and croft
FOO 92
having the 'famine of the f.' **FANT 24**
farmers: three f. were dancing a barbaric dance
PLEAS 3
farmer's wife: 'come awa' in to your parritch'
FOO 8
Faroe: Nort to da F. bank **SEA 11**
fart: I will not gif . . . an sowis fart **INS 55**
fash: Chris would say they needn't f. **WORD 29**
f. your thumb **ADV 29**
fashion: doctors and kirkyards would go out o'
f. **FOO 67**
dressed . . . in the barbaric f. of the savages of
her country **PER 55**
He comes out . . . with the latest f. from
France **INS 80**
however desirous to be in f., every Scots lady
had . . . the plaid **COS 33**
intellectual refinement, entirely independent
of the f. of their lower garments **HIGH 21**
Like to ane poet of the old fassoun **POET 30**
Silence is the element in which great things f.
themselves together **THO 27**

to talk, after the Scottish f., of the funeral
DEA 24
fashionable: if they wish to be f., they must
resemble two blown bladders **COS 21**
fate: Confront your f.: regard the naked deed
THO 34
He either fears his f. too much **BOA 13**
helpful sympathy For all whom F. doth bind
THO 33
I'm only a poet, Whose f. is as dead as my
verse **POET 55**
Resentment of my country's f. Within my
filial breast shall beat **SPIR 55**
Some taste the sweet, some drink the sour, As
waiter F. sees proper **THO 128**
father: ance his f.'s pride **REL 28**
An' lea'e the carle, your f. **LOVE 72**
come to announce to his mother that his f.
and brother had been slain **MOM 52**
F. called us out into the yard **SWW 51**
f., exemplar, guide, counsellor and friend
SPIR 16
f. I can never get mair **FAMI 1**
f. thundered at her, that way he had **M-W 70**
her f. did fume **MOM 36**
his f.'s a packman, you know it **POET 55**
It was my f. standing As real as life **FAMI 18**
My f. had a strong dislike for marriages of
necessity **PER 32**
My f. told me, that if you saw a man in a Rolls-
Royce **THO 8**
my f. was your mother's butler **M-W 77**
My f.'s deid, my mither's dottle **PER 232**
My son's whorled ear was once my f.'s
THO 134
'Nonsense,' her f. had countered **MIN 33**
O tread ye lightly on his grass – Perhaps he
was your f.! **EPI 16**
sangs my f. loved to hear **MUS 1**
was asked who was the f. of her child.
REL 102
'Ye maun gang to your f., Janet' **FAMI 2**
fathers: awful things that f. and mothers did
M-W 79
f.s' stories of the New Year shinty match
SPOR 32
he seeks the footsteps of his f. **POET 27**
Our f. all were poor **PPL 69**
fatness: F. is the only quality you can ascribe to
him **BUR 17**
faults: greatest of f. . . . . to be conscious of none
HUM 8
fause: But my f. lover staw my rose **LOVE 34**
She's fair and f. **M-W 34**
favour: something about me that interests most
people at first sight in my f. **PER 51**
favours: I've felt all its f. and found its decay
LAM 24
fear: always to have the f. of the Laird before our
ees **MIN 20**
bonny grey mare she swat for f. **MONS 1**
F. indeed hung over me like a dark cloud
REL 16

forward, though I canna see, I guess, and f.
HOP 3

I f. I have nothing original in me REL 33

I go up this ladder with less f. REL 34

I have als littil to f. HOP 8

No hope could have no f. HOP 22

to behold thereon I quoke for f. FANT 39

Untutor'd by science, a stranger to f.
LOVE 38

without f. the lawless roads THO 93

feared: 'I'm f. he turn out to be a conceited gowk'
PER 139

We're a' sae f. to speak our mind PPL 82

feast: Liberty's a glorious f. LAW 8

you need not ask who is the master of the f.
FOO 72

fecht: an we f., I'll get the waur M-W 12

F. for Britain? Hoot, awa'! SPIR 39

it may come to a f. for it yet, Davie WAR 90

Stumpie . . . Thocht life a f. without ony plan
PER 172

feed: 'f. 'em at both ends,' replied my
grandmother M-W 115

if you f. your good man well FOO 6

feeding: deal o' fine confused feedin' FOO 18

feeling: extraordinary f. of joy in being among
the birches NAT 7

f., pensive hearts NAT 2

most elevating f. with which the mind can be
inspired THO 109

Sham tunes and a sham f. SPIR 41

they were the growth of . . . true f. MUS 26

feet: at its f. are leaves and about its head are the
canticles of joy PLEAS 14

behold, there was a pair of cloven f. MONS 13

cleads us a' frae head to f. SEA 9

every turf beneath their f. Shall be a soldier's
sepulchre LAM 23

Here's to the horse wi' the four white f.
TOA 7

Highways for eident f. TRA 50

if he's f. foremost, he's deid! SPOR 5

many . . . losing the Use of Hands and F.
LAM 55

My f. ne'er filed that brooky hill POET 18

Oft I embrace her f. of lillys But she has goton
all the pillies PER 108

there lies gude Sir Patrick Spens Wi' the
Scots lords at his f. LAM 5

They are ease to the f. MOU 17

warning to all young People to take care of
Wet f. FOO 54

we find the ice growing thinner below our f.
YOU 27

when gentlemans can gang to bed on their ain
f. THO 98

fellow: black-a-vic'd snod, dapper fallow
PER 203

glimmers of a smile to the f. musicians
MUS 40

'He was a great f. my friend Will' PER 93

if the f. was to be thrown against the wall, he
would stick to it FOO 33

old f. younder sternly said FES 4

one-eyed f. in blinkers PER 115

to go and tell some people that I was a mean
f. THO 56

ugly, cross-made . . . little dumpling of a f.
PER 48

very weak f., I'm afraid INS 45

We have no damned f.-feeling at all PPL 59

young f. was dancing the Highland Fling
PLEAS 9

fellowship: universal f. and brotherhood of man
POL 108

female: He was very awkward in f. dress PER 50

to satiate the lecherous f. kind INS 5

feminist: f. academics dredging the catalogues
for third-rate women novelists POET 16

Fenian: called me a big dirty F. bastard SPOR 36

Fergus: F., the first King of Scots, had no other
law HIS 25

Ferguson, Adam: trying snail soup FOO 66

When A.F. . . . found he had to teach physics
PER 134

Fergusson, Robert: erecting the stone over poor
F. POET 8

Ferlas Mor: Scotland's Abominable Snowman
MONS 8

ferlie: a fell, a fabulous f. PLA 45

ferret: with the enthusiasm of a f. finding the
rabbit family at home FOO 111

ferry: I wish I had him to f. over Loch Lomond
CUR 13

ferryman: silent f. standing in the stern TRA 41

skipper turned to the f. . . . and chided him
gently TRA 38

festive: We gather round the f. board FES 2

fetters: Furth Fortune and fill the f. MOTT 22

feud: all the membris are at feid LOVE 15

Food today, and f. tomorrow FOO 1

in time of f. he would be better equipped to
strike 'unhallowed' blows HIGH 19

Fhairshon: F. had a son, Who married Noah's
daughter PER 29

fickle: oh! the f., faithless quean M-W 74

fiction: F. is to the grown man what play is to the
child BOO 65

fiddle: And some to buy my f. MUS 3

Long Rob's f. bow was darting and
glimmering MUS 30

fiddler: I am a f. to my trade MUS 13

fiddles: made the people break and burn their
pipes and f. MUS 29

fidelity: He pursues us with malignant f. FRI 5

fidgety: Breakin' my heart, ye f. bairn CHI 1

field: dead bodies lay in the f. to glut the eye of
the merciless conqueror WAR 47

his mither used to work in the tawtie f.
REL 94

In f. of gold he stude full myghtely HER 2

Wha would shun the f. of danger? WAR 92

You remember the place called the Tawny F.?
WAR 53

fields: game was over walls and f. until darkness
fell SPOR 32

In the f. called the Links, the citizens of Edinburgh divert themselves at a game called golf **SPOR 74**

Physical reality has been thought of as represented by continuous f. **SCI 13**

Sweeping with shadowy gust the f. of corn **SWW 63**

fiend: foulest f. there doughtna bide him **INS 7**

Fife: They say in Fife **M-W 13**

fig: f. for those by law protected **LAW 8**

fight: every one of the ships must f. until she sank **WAR 56**

'F. on!' he cried to them. 'F. on!' **WAR 4**

for the richt ilk man suld ficht **SPIR 4**

game ended in a free f. **SPOR 32**

'I'le lay me down and bleed awhile, And then I'le rise and f. again' **WAR 4**

Our business is like men to f. **WAR 64**

waist of the frigate where the f. was for some minutes gallantly carried on **WAR 35**

what remained . . . that he should f. for? **SPIR 43**

fighter: 'am I no a bonny f.?' **BOA 19**

film: commercial conditions which determine the f. business **TEL 5**

F.-making belongs . . . to that magical world in which two and two can make five, but also three and even less **TEL 7**

f. western isn't something that needs immaculate research **TEL 15**

Fingal: F. is said to have commanded the Caledonians **PPL 38**

finger: more of Jesus in St Theresa's little f. **REL 13**

to prefer the destruction of the whole world to the scratching of my f. **PHIL 25**

fingers: Her f. witched the chords **MUS 21**

'I'd do so if my f. had not been after the skate' **MUS 50**

to take potatoes from the pot with his f. **FOO 12**

Fionn MacCumhal: vain and misleading tales of . . . F.M. **WORD 19**

fire: and yet I burn as f. **BATH 4**

'Better is the small f. that warms on the little day of peace' **MUS 29**

brandishing and emptying their glasses, and then throwing each glass into the f. **TOA 17**

cast great crouns like tinsel in the f. **TIM 28**

cat on the clootie rug Afore the f. **MOM 16**

f. of their temper not always latent **PER 83**

f. that's blawn on Beltane een **LOVE 64**

fling any faggot rather than let the f. go out **FOO 10**

follows on a woman throw the f. **LAM 18**

Furnace of f., with stink intolerable **FANT 34**

Gie me ae spark o' Nature's f. **POET 5**

Glowerin' in the f. wi' his wee round face **CHI 8**

had no f. in winter and would sit . . . wrapped in their plaid **UNI 7**

his look full of dignity and composed f. **PER 86**

I have only to advise you to keep up a good f. **WAR 89**

I mend the f., and beikit me about **PLEAS 8**

I pray with holy f. **SPIR 12**

James Hutton, that true son of f. **PER 189**

light of the peat-f. flame **HIGH 27**

Nothing now my heart can f. **HOP 11**

porridge that were hott'rin' on the f. **MUS 63**

running round the playground striking f. and thunder off the surface **COS 36**

Stir the f. till it lowes **CHI 14**

in the nor-east ane gritt fir upoun the sea **FANT 41**

there is now the tea-kettle put to the f. **FOO 91**

What is hotter than f.? **THO 2**

wi' the f. of old Rome **SPIR 19**

Without one spark of intellectual f. **CUR 14**

you can manage without lighting a f. from one end of the year to the other **SWW 11**

fires: f. ye lit to gut Strathnaver **PER 239**

used to run and extinguish f. in ammunition dumps. **WAR 55**

fireside: nane half so sure as ane's ain f. **HOM 3**

Firth of Forth: new Scotland . . . straggles westwards from the F. of F. to the lower Clyde **POL 47**

You could drive a train across the F.o.F. on her vowels **WORD 54**

fish: bonny f. and halesome fairin' **DAI 42**

f. jump on the shore **THO 5**

f. of divers sort **ANI 18**

f. that was yesterday miles away from the land **POL 4**

goodly f. **ANG 12**

halesomest and nicest gear Of f. or flesh **FOO 51**

I hate that ubiquitous blasted f. **FOO 85**

I saw, in a radiant raincoat, the woman from the f.-shop **PPL 76**

In quakin' quaw or f.-currie **NAT 16**

it can be served up as f., fowl or flesh **FOO 97**

'It's a fush that's chust sublime' **FOO 99**

It's no f. ye're buying: it's men's lives **SEA 24**

its back was hollow, which is not the shape of any f. **MONS 16**

Let us praise the humble f. **FOO 48**

Scotland rich in f. **LAND 6**

Seven years a f. in the flood **DEA 3**

silver scalit f. **ANG 3**

slowest f. swims faster **M-W 35**

sticky state of his fingers after having eaten some of that f. **MUS 50**

tang of . . . smoked f., of pine-woods **MOM 5**

thair wes ane monstrous fische in Loch Fyne **MONS 11**

This is the f. that never swam **PLA 59**

'We manufacture f.-glue and sweaters' **PLA2: 6**

fisherman: Strange things happen to a lone f. **ANG 4**

fishermen: f. have always had taboos on certain words **WORD 32**

I . . . fell in with some young f. . . . who tried some Gaelic on me **WORD 60**

fishes: f. I caught nine **SEA 10**

fists: 'Compare f. – Mine's the biggest' **SPOR 37**

fit: in a f. Of wrath and rhyme **SPIR 15**
  only f. for the slaves who sold it **SPIR 21**

fitba: 'At a big f. match' **SPOR 5**
  ye get mair nir ye're eftir, pleyan fi'baw in the street **SPOR 29**

Fitz-James: F.-J. alone wore cap and plume **MOM 39**

flags: f. could still fly though the ships were at the bottom **WAR 56**

flame: light of the peat-fire f. **HIGH 27**

Flannan Isle: Outposts in the Atlantic **PLA 54**
  Three men alive on F.I., Who thought on three men dead **PLA 53**

flattery: Ne'er Was f. lost on poet's ear **POET 56**

flax: stalks of the old nettle are as good as f. **NAT 4**

fleas: he wakened hauf a million f. **PLA 115**

flees: f.'ll be droonin' themselves in your milk bowl **FOO 8**
  lines And f. that were my pride **ANG 15**

flesh: blood of goat, The f. of rams I will not prize **THO 106**
  in spite of their entire dependence on cheese, f., and milk **HIGH 16**
  it can be served up as fish, fowl or f. **FOO 97**
  league between us written . . . in the f. and skin of men **HIS 12**
  nicest gear Of fish or f. **FOO 51**

flesher: f. Rob that lived in Crieff **M-W 108**

Fletcher of Saltoun, Andrew: think himself sufficiently applauded and rewarded by obtaining the character of being like A.F. of S. **PER 164**

Flodden: by some slight accident he was missing from the battle of F. **PER 120**
  F.'s fatal field, Where shiver'd was fair Scotland's spear **WAR 77**
  Sons of heroes slain at F. **WAR 5**
  thanks to . . . F. and the English raids **PPL 74**

Flood: nearly spoil'd ta F., By trinking up ta water **PER 29**

flounder: he trampled on a beautiful little fair f. **ANI 29**

flower: And every flour unlappit in the dale **NAT 8**
  bonnie Earl o' Moray Was the f. amang them a' **DEA 5**
  flame-bright f. of the Clearances **PER 128**
  Flooer o' the gean **LOVE 50**
  f. of stone **ADV 130**
  O F. of Scotland When will we see your like again? **SPIR 59**
  Out of this ugliness may come . . . so beautiful a f. **FANT 52**
  sweet Jessie, the f. o' Dunblane **PER 242**
  You seize the flow'r, its bloom is shed **PLEAS 4**

flowers : 'Beware of men bearing f.' **PER 233**
  f. did smile, like those upon her face **LOVE 43**

f. have great variety and a new beauty **MOU 17**

f. of the Forest are a' wede away **LAM 25**

fouth o' flours may yet be fund **WORD 28**

give people in fact the same care that we give when transplanting f. **PHIL 15**

good machair . . . grows not grass but f. **NAT 23**

I was suddenly aware of some f. **MOM 29**

I'll cover it o'er Wi' the f. o' the mountain **LOVE 85**

May, that moder is of flouris **SWW 31**

petals fluttering butterfly-bright from f. **YOU 3**

silent hosannas of the f. **PLEAS 14**

smells (known as the 'f. of Edinburgh') filled the air **DAI 28**

fly: Machines of death . . . through the same darkness f. **WAR 88**
  On the pinions of steam they shall f. **TRA 22**
  This rock shall f. From its firm base as soon as I **WAR 75**

Flying Scotsman: 'Buffers like yon would stop the F.S. going full tilt' **M-W 94**
  Will someone ever rise to write the saga of the 'F.S.'? **TRA 47**

flyte: Wha'll f. us for a lack o' lair **INS 91**

Fochabers: For the sake o' business I've had to 'order suits in places no the size o' F.' **PLA 55**

foe: above, below, Sprung up at once the lurking f. **WAR 74**
  better it is To bide a friend's anger than a f.'s kiss **FRI 6**
  days and months and years Like squadrons and battalions of the f. **TIM 30**
  direst f. of courage **ADV 88**
  Napoleon is . . . the sworn f. of our nation **TOA 12**
  now smiting a f., now beating the air with vain blows **WAR 21**

foemen: f. worthy of their steel **WAR 76**

foes: f. in the forum in the field were friends **FRI 29**
  He was . . . a heckle to his f. **PER 11**
  Her f. aye found it hedged around, With rosemarie and rue **SPIR 42**
  many f. but none like thee **FAMI 8**
  Their hearts and swords are metal true, And that their f. shall ken **WAR 30**

fog: f. unfolds its bitter scent **SWW 45**
  his entourage of freezing f. **SWW 44**
  in the vicinity of Canna Pier, enveloped in thick f. **TRA 15**
  obscurity which hangs over the beginnings of all history – a kind of . . . f. **HIS 29**

Foinne Bheinn: on the snows of F. B. a ptarmigan rose **MOU 19**

folk (*see also* **fowk**): All honest f. they do molest **PLA 39**
  aye the bluid o' puir f. On the sarks o' gentilities **THO 116**
  be deaf and blind, Let great f. hear and see **POL 24**

behave yoursel' before f. **ADV 103**

canty auld f. crackin' crouse **YOU 5**

country f. are kind **HUM 9**

f. frae Clachnacudden leant forrit **REL 94**

f. were sair pitten aboot **REL 41**

F. wha say their say and speir their speir **PPL 66**

f. who wrought and fought and were learnéd **LAND 27**

Hou sall aa the folk I've been ere meet And bide in yae wee hoose? **SPIR 50**

I carena muckle for folk that bairns and dogs dinna like **THO 57**

My f. may perish if they like **REL 8**

not . . . the most immediately lovable f. **HIGH 18**

'Stand abeigh, ye foolish forward f.' **MUS 54**

still my thoughts return To my ain f. ower yonder **PPL 65**

that is why some f. make pilgrimage to the Western Isles **HIGH 30**

Town-planning . . . must be f.-planning **PHIL 15**

we weemen f. will only be helpit when we help oorsels **M-W 93**

We're either in or oot wi' f. **PPL 6**

we've fallen in and marched behind some damned funny f. **WAR 86**

Where are the f. like the f. of the West? **PPL 79**

'Woe to the f. of Scotland' **LAM 3**

folks: All your f. are off your head **POL 66**

Some folks are wise **ADV 127**

What signifies 't for f. to chide **POL 96**

What will the auld f. . . . say **M-W 108**

folly: completest monument in the entire continent of human f. **PLA 31**

f. of human laws **PHIL 55**

sweetest f. in the world is love **LOVE 20**

food: can still rise into some glow of brotherhood over f. and wine **FOO 37**

f. was both coarse and monotonous **UNI 7**

give our children what they desire easily and endlessly – f., sex, excitement **HIS 6**

having first satiated themselves with . . . divine words, they refreshed themselves with bodily f. **PER 146**

I heard the cuckoo, with no f. in my stomach **THO 1**

I should be let in; For my f. and my drink **FES 4**

F. fills the wame **FOO 25**

F. today, and feud tomorrow **FOO 1**

O English F.! How I adore you **FOO 80**

right to rely on the interposition of the state in order to supply them with f. **PHIL 12**

Fool: athletic f., to whom what Heav'n denied **SPOR 8**

brains enough to make a f. of himself **YOU 28**

fond fule, fariar **PPL 2**

f. and his money **ADV 27**

f. who cried 'Nothing but heather!' **LAND 37**

'not such a f. as to believe . . . the devil really was in the printing-office' **REL 62**

you were shamed and a f. to say that in Scotland **LOVE 46**

Whatten ane glaikit fule am I **LOVE 74**

wisest f. in Christendom **PER 241**

foolish: I'm lame, feeble and f. **PER 220**

fools: All things to all men only f. will tell **THO 15**

covenanting f., Wha erst ha'e fash'd us wi' unnumbered dools **PER 102**

human bodies are sic f. **HUM 6**

I will promise to hold my tongue if you will make f. hold theirs **WORD 44**

If honest Nature made you f., What sairs your grammars? **UNI 3**

Thirty million, mostly f. **INS 26**

foot: And sleep thegither at the f. **M-W 49**

At the last kick o' a foreign f. We'se a' be ranting roaring fou **POL 2**

Fleet f. on the correi **LAM 54**

his right f. would not have missed the target **SPOR 23**

His very f. has music in't **LOVE 62**

John Knox, with his one f. in the grave **THO 65**

Let us f. it out together **MUS 68**

My f. is on my native heath **PER 213**

On fut sould be all Scottis weir **WAR 38**

Till our fit's on the neck o' the boor-joysie **POL 20**

football: and he's not very good at f. **SPOR 14**

atheist – a man who goes to a Celtic–Rangers match to watch the f. **SPOR 76**

defeats in f. matches are actually useful to remind you that you're only human **SPOR 79**

F. management these days is like a nuclear war **SPOR 18**

f.'s a lovely incurable disease **SPOR 21**

game is hopelessly ill-equipped to carry the burden of emotional expression **SPOR 52**

I don't drop players **SPOR 68**

If you're in the penalty area and don't know what to do with the ball **SPOR 69**

In the excitement of playing f. **BAD 14**

licking of wounds is second only to f. as a national sport **SPOR 62**

life is itself but a game of foot-ball **SPOR 65**

Oh he's f. crazy, he's f. mad **SPOR 51**

rules made by men who don't pay to watch f. **SPOR 35**

Some people think f. is a matter of life and death **SPOR 67**

strange, defiant cry heard from some of Scotland's f. terraces **PPL 57**

We all end up yesterday's men **SPOR 75**

Forbes of Culloden: greatest part of his guests . . . cannot go at all **FOO 34**

force: 'Every f. evolves a form' **PPL 61**

forefathers: our f.'s dose to swill down their brose **FOO 122**

forest: flowers of the F. are a' wede away
LAM 25
He is lost to the f. LAM 54
in my hand a f. lies asleep NAT 28

forests: of great f., of honey-scented heather hills
NAT 17
Stripping f. from hill and mountain
LAND 24

forever: from today till tomorrow, and from that
f. LAW 20

foremost: he thought rather to be with the f.
than with the hindermost PER 109

forget: I never forgive but I always f. PER 33

forgive: I never f. but I always forget PER 33
F. me, Sire, for cheating your intent PER 71

forkytails: a hundred f. seethed from under it
ANI 19

formula: Maxwell . . . reached a f. which . . .
ought to have been hopelessly wrong SCI 21

fornication: kilt is an unrivalled garment for f.
HIGH 29

Fort Augustus: F.A. did disgust us PLA 56

Fort William: And F.W. did the same PLA 56

Forth: caller herrin', New-drawn frae the F.
DAI 42

Forth Bridge: A monument o strength and grace
BUI 29

Fortingall: And washed his hands PER 188

fortune: amassed a f. by plundering drunkards
FOO 83
F.! if thou'll but gie me still Hale breeks
FAM 4
F. is not so blind as men are FAM 11
Furth F. and fill the fetters MOTT 22
gif evir God send me a f. HOP 8
hopes to ken their f. FANT 43
I have acquired a noble f., a princely f. POL 71
I've seen the smiling of F. beguiling LAM 24
saddest sight that f.'s inequality exhibits
DAI 15
She's but a bitch FAM 3
there shall not be born forever, One who had
more f. or greatness PER 45

forty: f. days and f. nights He wade thro' red
blude to the knee FANT 10

Forty-Five: love and home and the F.-F. SPIR 41

Forty-Twa: stoutest man in the F.-T. WAR 13

forward: And f., though I canna see, I guess, and
fear HOP 3

fou: At the last kick o' a foreign foot We'se a' be
ranting roaring f. POL 2
every Piper was f. MUS 10
he was f. at the time FOO 79
some are fou' o' love divine; There's some are
fou' o' brandy PLEAS 5
We are na f., we're nae that f. FOO 22

foundation: What though their f. is built on the
sand? COM 1

foundations: precious articles of our national
belief not to be given up without danger of
sapping the f. of society HIS 27
storm coming that shall try your f. SPIR 48

fountain: first f. of silvery Tweed rises RIV 12

I will twine thee a bow'r By the clear siller f.
LOVE 85

fouth: f. o' flours may yet be fund WORD 28

fowk: Naebody kens what the auld f. are thinkin'
THO 74
some f. like parritch, and some f. like
paddocks FOO 109

fowl: f. in a lordly dish is carried in FOO 128
it can be served up as fish, f. or flesh FOO 97

fox: have a special care the old f. and his sons doe
not escape POL 35
pure case of the f. that lost its tail HIGH 5

foxes: My blessing with the f. dwell HIGH 26

France: If that you will F. win WAR 81
Nae cotillion, brent new frae F. MUS 15
that nobill and most puissant kingdom of F.
HER 1

frankness: If you wish to preserve your secret,
wrap it in f. ADV 125

Frazer, J.G.: mainly impressed by what seemed
to him the utter futility of the world he
surveyed PER 145
Thinking of Helensburgh, J.G.F. Revises
flayings PER 91

fredome: for the fredome of our land Are
strenyeit in battle SPIR 4
f. is a noble thing! SPIR 5

free: determined to avenge our own wrongs, and
set our country f. SPIR 56
F. Kirk, the wee k. REL 9
'f. men of the hills' stuff MOU 46
game ended in a f. fight SPOR 32
His ready speech flowed fair and f. WORD 67
I'll be merry and f. THO 21
I'm a lassie f. LOVE 68
liberal education that fits a f. man for a full
life UNI 7
nane pain sall refusit be Till we have made
'our country f.' SPIR 6
Say not the will of man is f. PHIL 37
they would have all men bound . . . and they
for to be f. M-W 110
to serve as a slave . . where one was wont to
be f. lord THO 46
what it is from bondage to be f. THO 41
word is thrall, and thought is f. WORD 40

Free Church: F. Kirk, the wee kirk REL 9
Who cares about the F.C.? REL 39

freedom: conflict between our sense of f. and our
scientific understanding REL 14
fredome is a noble thing SPIR 5
quick f. of the spirit SPIR 26
F. and whisky gang thegither FOO 26
My quenchless thirst for f. unconfined
SPIR 47
Now, when F. bids avenge her WAR 92
Up from F.'s soil it grew SPIR 42
Wha for Scotland's king and law, F.'s sword
would strongly draw WAR 26
women's f. in having intercourse M-W 27

free-thinkers: Do not be afraid of being f.
REL 67

Freewill: two everlasting hostile empires, Necessity and F. **PHIL 9**

French: as the F. happily put it, *à la belle étoile* **PLEAS 15**

various abominations served up . . . under F. names **FOO 61**

welcoming the F. at the sound of the drum **WAR 27**

French, Alfred: trial for murder of **INS 10**

French Revolution: Mill had borrowed that first volume of my poor *F.R.* **MOM 14**

Frenchman: F. offended the old Scottish peeress **FOO 109**

Freud: I doubt if he can disregard F. and the atom bomb **POET 47**

friend: better it is, To bide a f.'s anger **FRI 6**

father, exemplar, guide, counsellor, and f. **SPIR 16**

F. more than servant **PER 244**

Gin ye ca' me seelie wicht, I'll be your f. both day and nicht **FANT 16**

Hail in each crag a f.'s familiar face **HIGH 13**

He was the coldest f. and the violentest enemy I ever had **PER 59**

I leave my f. . . . twelve dozen of my old claret **FRI 17**

may I ever have a f., In whom I safely may depend **FRI 3**

'My ae fauld f. when I was hardest stad!' **LAM 29**

No enemy Is half so fatal as a f. estranged **FRI 11**

no man is useless while he has a f. **FRI 26**

offer of marriage . . . made on behalf of a shy f. **LOVE 45**

to be with the mountain as one visits a f. **MOU 41**

To find a f. one must close one eye **FRI 12**

no treasure which may be compared Unto a faithful f. **FRI 4**

When I came to my f.'s house of a morning **FOO 91**

friendless: All, all forsook the f. guilty mind **HOP 6**

friends: dearest f. are the auldest f. **FRI 27**

discovers he has merely opened a tavern for his f. **FAMI 11**

foes in the forum in the field were f. **FRI 29**

F. are lost by calling often **FRI 2**

F. given by God in mercy and in love **FRI 23**

glimmers of a smile to the . . . f. and acquaintances in the audience **MUS 40**

guid friendis, for ane gymp or a bourd, I pray you, note me not at every word **POET 21**

He was a hedge unto his f. **PER 11**

Heap blessings on all gathered here, On absent f. and strangers **SPOR 60**

'I am dying . . . as easily . . . as my best f. could desire' **DEA 39**

I like to taste my f. **FRI 14**

I little foresaw what I meet with from my f. **FRI 28**

Here's to the f. we can trust **FRI 15**

Live ourselves and see our f. cold beneath the sky **WAR 59**

men see their f. Drop off **DEA 13**

Mourn not, my f., that we are growing old **TIM 21**

My northern f. have accused me . . . of personality **INS 21**

organised workers of the country are our f. **POL 94**

Return to your f., and tell them we came with no peaceful intent **SPIR 56**

Warm as his heart to the f. he has chosen **FOO 87**

With something left to treat my f. **THO 86**

friendship: chain of f., however bright **FRI 24**

faithful nation, a people most worthy of f. **HIS 12**

Matrimony . . . a sort of f. recognised by the police **FAMI 34**

two things which are peculiarly fatal to f. **FRI 19**

friendships: 'This world's f. . . .' 'Are as cheap as crockery' **FRI 22**

frieze: f. of mountains, filed on the blue air **MOU 23**

fright: I have never forgotten the unearthly f. **MOU 22**

If someone burst a sugar bag, the lot would die of f. **POL 5**

frocks: my twa printed f. **SWW 66**

frogs (*see also* **puddock**): their ballet dancer's legs **ANI 59**

Joseph-coated, they ambled and jumped **ANI 60**

frost: black heart-killing f. **MIN 36**

f.. was sufficient to freeze the water-vapour **MOU 19**

shattered by the lightning and f. of ages **MOU 37**

frosts: Autumnal f. enchant the pool **SWW 61**

fruits: dried f. and sweetmeats at the sides **FOO 102**

uther strange fructis delicious **FOO 78**

Fuath: Spirit of Terror **FANT 54**

fucker: Ya knee-crept, Jesus-crept, swatchin' little f. **INS 71**

fucking: Aye fukkand lyk ane furious fornicatour **INS 54**

fugitive: to meet in with a f. Coming from Ben Cruachan **LAM 13**

fun: We had some f., haud awa wi' the smell **PLEAS 1**

funeral: bereaved relatives enquiring about f. arrangements were referred to the 'Refuse' section **DEA 62**

it was arranged the customary f. dinner should be held **DEA 49**

to talk, after the Scottish fashion, of the f., before the anticipated corpse **DEA 24**

funnels: A hunner f. bleezin, reekin **DAI 30**

funny: f. thing about the creature was she believed none spoke ill of her **PER 116**

F.-peculiar or f. ha-ha? **HUMO 8**

I dinna think I was ever what could be called a f. man **PER 112**

nothing very f. about Scotland **HUMO 16**

she was really made from his f.-bone **M-W 27**

Furnace: 'You don't need tickets for a F. baal' **MUS 59**

fushionless: a f. woman **M-W 103**

fute-ball: Thir are the bewties of the f. **SPOR 1**

futility: mainly impressed by what seemed to him to be the utter f. of the world **PER 145**

future: And learn the f. by the past of man **TIM 11**

confidence i wir ain f. **HOP 7**

life is not a rehearsal **ADV 46**

What the f. may have in store, no-one can tell **THO 129**

'you will really have to be more careful in f.' **TRA 38**

futurity: let f. shift for itself **PHIL 58**

Fyvie: F., thou's ne'er thrive ye **CUR 22**

G

gaberlunzie: blithe be the auld g.-man **PER 34**

gable-ends: g.-e. o' time **BUI 31**

gadgie: A 'G.', when he is a 'Chor' **WORD 33**

Gael: isle . . . Belonged as a dwelling to the Children of the G. **LAND 40**

many a G. bred up in the Land of Mists **HIGH 28**

Stone of Destiny, sacred among the G. **FANT 47**

thanks to . . . the schism between G. and Lowlander **PPL 74**

with the modern G. I share a history but not a language **WORD 14**

Gaelic: a subtle tongue **WORD 34**

'be dacent and speak aboot it in the Gaalic' **LOVE 65**

east-coaster who has lost . . . his G. **HIGH 5**

G. is not a poor language **WORD 53**

G. periphrase for 'I love' **LOVE 61**

Great the blindness . . . of those who teach, write and foster the G. speech **WORD 19**

How can a man get on in the world that wants G.? **PLA 57**

I covet the mystery of our G. speech **WORD 48**

I realised that G. was a missing part of my world **WORD 14**

'I will learn a little G.' **WORD 62**

I would welcome the end of Braid Scots and G. **POL 41**

Lilium Medicinae was very soon afterwards translated into G. **MIN 17**

Mrs Kennedy-Fraser's travesties of G. songs **INS 70**

Poverty hath the G. and Greek **PPL 98**

problems were solved with G. precision **WORD 46**

regrettable thing about G. is its hopelessly bewildering spelling **WORD 39**

Scottish G. song is the chief artistic glory of the Scots **MUS 51**

'so long as you ken the man at the door and talk the Gaalic at him' **MUS 59**

some young fishermen . . . tried some G. on me **WORD 60**

staunch Lowlander carries on his back a G. . . . heritage **HIGH 47**

There lives no man who understands his G. **INS 67**

Transposing Greek to G. is no toil **WORD 70**

'used to greet in the twa languages, Gaalic and Gleska' **CHI 35**

western sea alone can speak in the G. tongue **SEA 20**

with a eulogistic speech from the chief in G. **PLEAS 12**

Gairloch: 'What is the use of English in G.?' **PLA 57**

gait: And gang their ain g. wi' a lach or a spit or a sweir **PPL 66**

Gallowa': *Greitand doun in Gallowa* **WORD 57**

Oh, the G. hills are covered wi' broom **MOU 3**

Galloway: there is nane in G., There's nane at a' for me **LAM 7**

Galloway, Earl of: Bright ran thy line, o G. **INS 15**

Gallowgate: Up the G., down the Green **LOVE 17**

gallows: habit of yon g. breed **WORD 57**

McPherson's time will not be long On yonder g. tree **LAM 21**

To this day his name smacks of the g. **PER 235**

galore: riches g. in the breeze of the vale **NAT 12**

game: citizens of Edinburgh divert themselves at a g. called Golf **SPOR 74**

city given over Soul and body to a tyrannising g. **SPOR 61**

g. in which he was getting the better of his immediate opponent **SPOR 10**

g. is hopelessly ill-equipped to carry the burden of emotional expression **SPOR 52**

g. that all the gods of Greece might crowd the northern skies to see **SPOR 45**

g. was over walls and fields until darkness fell **SPOR 32**

life is itself but a g. of foot-ball **SPOR 65**

put his head round the door of the visitors' dressing-room after a goalless g. **SPOR 73**

referees . . . know the rules but do not know the g. **SPOR 70**

to die young . . . is but the giving over of a G. **DEA 27**

These rules are ruining the g. **SPOR 35**

They christened their g. golf **SPOR 27**

'What sort of g.are ye after, Mackintosh?' **PER 92**

gamekeeper: g. resembled him so closely **M-W 77**

gangrel: rievin' ower the Moray Firth, it lifts the
g. snaw **SWW 21**
   To play the gangrel p. **ADV 10**
gannet: I have never tasted a g. **FOO 97**
garden: Come and toil in the g. of the Lord
REL 7
   Here I can blow a g. with my breath **NAT 28**
   owre a' the g. he's been **SWW 66**
   though the G. of thy Life be wholly waste
DEA 70
   'Tis the speech used in the G. **WORD 49**
Gardy loo: passengers beneath would
agonisingly call out **DAI 28**
garland: I'll mak' a g. o' thy hair **LAM 11**
garret: That g. of the earth **LAND 55**
Garry, River: Down by the Tummel or banks o'
the Gary? **MUS 38**
gas: learnin', fame, g., . . . a' mere shams
FOO 104
gash: he was a g. and tousy tyke **ANI 21**
   It makes a man baith g. and bauld **FOO 105**
gaslicht: the g. flichtered on the stair **MOM 46**
Gaul: In the garb of old G. **SPIR 19**
gay: 'Poor little g. men' **INS 44**
gear: He'll no twine with his g. **LOVE 41**
   our stamacks fou O gusty g. **FES 7**
   'Sa lang as I may get g. to steal, I never will
wirk' **THO 4**
   That I for grace and g. may shine **REL 27**
Geddes, Jenny: J.G. and her stool are precious
articles of our national belief **HIS 27**
geese: Cruel children . . . all grow up as g. or
gabies **CHI 49**
   far abune the Angus straths I saw the wild g.
flee **ANI 51**
   wi' weird unyeirdly cry **ANI 89**
   wild spirits, knowing what they know **ANI 99**
General Assembly: G.A. of the Church of
Scotland . . . 'Nuts in May' **REL 80**
   great actress . . . appeared in Edinburgh
during the sitting of the G.A. **REL 100**
   It was to the G.A. . . . that the Scots looked for
their liberty **REL 87**
General Election: Sourock's wife had never
forgiven . . . the way she voted at the G.E.
COS 30
generation: floated down on the stream of oral
tradition, from g. to g. **MUS 37**
   G. after g., these few families . . . have sucked
the life-blood of our nation **POL 56**
   In a g. which has seen students become so
much more vocal and aggressive **UNI 6**
   One g. cometh and another goeth **THO 18**
   'What is the rising g. coming to?' **PER 105**
generosity: Good humour and g. carry the day
HUM 13
   He had . . . the most abundant generosity
PER 100
Geneva: grim G. ministers **REL 15**
genius: hot-bed of g. **ADV 128**
   It is now the duty of the Scottish g. **SPIR 31**
   Land . . . where G. is lost **INS 89**
   O' stature short, but g. bright **PER 63**

Poor England! when such a despicable
abortion is named g. **PER 77**
Scottish g. – has scarcely begun to recover
from the fact that Scotland . . . rejected
David Hume **PHIL 35**
talent instantly recognises g. **ADV 59**
Those who admired his writing declared him
to be a g. **PER 162**
whose vanity was at least equal to his g.
POET 59
womankind not of g., but of *character*
M-W 101
gent: sleeping-place of at least sixteen of the g.
species **TRA 9**
   you couldn't but laugh at the joke of the g.
PPL 40
genteel: not many g. Scottish writers before
Scott **POET 42**
gentil: ane mechanyc plebien, beand verteous, he
is ane gentil man **FAMI 4**
   Our gentyl men are all degenerate **PPL 55**
gentle: Ah, g. dames! it gars me greet **M-W 41**
   That potent prince g. King James the Ferde
PER 159
   thence comes a' our g. blood **FAMI 32**
   Wi g. glances aye she socht me **LOVE 50**
gentleman: blustering about the dignity of a
born g. **INS 57**
   each g. brought a pint of wine **FOO 102**
   'G. who had the misfortune to be mad' **INS 76**
   g. willl blithely do in politics what he would
kick a man downstairs for **POL 91**
   great deal rests on this g.'s credibility **INS 10**
   little g. in black velvet **TOA 6**
   only God Almighty can make a g. **FAMI 19**
   Right Honourable G. is indebted to his
memory for his jests **INS 87**
   this attenuated philosophical g. **DEA 22**
   'to go and tell some people that I was a mean
fellow, and no g.' **THO 56**
   When Montaigne was made G. of the
Bedchamber to Henry II of France **PER 105**
gentlemen: But g. – he once shot a publisher
TOA 12
   G., Gigmen, and Men **M-W 59**
   'G.,' says he, 'you see a severe winter
approaching' **WAR 89**
   I am not apt to confide in the professions of g.
of that country **PPL 51**
   no finer G. in the world, than that Nation can
justly boast of **PPL 4**
   none to be suffered to enter . . . except g. and
persons of note **PLEAS 6**
   one of these g. seldom failed of going to kirk
REL 31
   'sair cheenged times . . . when gentlemans can
gang to bed on their ain feet' **THO 98**
   two g. were passing the scene of these
improvements **MOM 34**
   usual for two g. . . . to sleep together **M-W 71**
   Women . . . find it extremely difficult to
behave like g. **FAMI 27**

town with guts – you see some on the
pavement **PLA** 69

vomit of a cataleptic commercialism **PLA** 65

Watch Your Handbags, Ladies, Please **PLA** 68

Glasgow Cathedral: nane o' yer whigmaleeries
BUI 27

Glasgow Central: At both Carlisle and G.C.,
she had her regular fans **TRA** 13

Glasgow Empire: except at the G.E. **HUMO** 1

Glasgow Orpheus Choir: dank euphonies of the
G.O.C. **MUS** 75

Glasgow Royal Infirmary: **MIN** 39

glass: anxious to demonstrate the living quality
of Scots, held up his empty beer g. **WORD** 45

  Every g. during dinner had to be dedicated to
someone **TOA** 13

  g. of wine is a glorious creature **FOO** 116

  let us toast John Barleycorn, Each man with g.
in hand **TOA** 10

  Nae gless **PHIL** 47

  single Scotch nothing more than a dirty g.
FOO 47

  square foot of g. where Jess sat in her chair
MOM 2

  then throwing each g. into the fire **TOA** 17

  Through a gless, Darkly **PHIL** 47

  Wi' sang and g. they fley the power O' care
PLEAS 7

glasses: Black bottles of strong port . . . with g.
LAW 9

  'fewer g. and more bottles' **FOO** 60

Glaswegians: accent of the lowest state of G. is
the ugliest one can encounter **WORD** 55

glee: Gie a' to merriment and g. **PLEAS** 7

  male dancers in the height of their g. **MUS** 45

  See Social-life and G. sit down **FOO** 20

  threw his legs about him with such regardless
g. **PLEAS** 9

  To spend the night wi' mirth and g. **POL** 96

  wheels o' life gang down-hill . . . Wi' rattlin'
g. **FOO** 25

glen: lamb from the bracken, and doe from the
g. **FOO** 70

  laverock's note . . . Lilting wildly up the g.
LAM 48

  Twists thro' a g. of greenest gloom **RIV** 11

  We are the men Who own your g. **LAND** 38

  Your wee bit hill and g. **SPIR** 59

Glen Coe: all Glencoe in one night murdered
POL 1

  wide shimmering curtain across Glencoe
MOU 30

Glen Orchy: their heather-thatched cabin in G.
O. **M-W** 75

Glen Sannox: beautiful picture of G.S. **SCI** 24

Glen Tilt: stretch of G.T. that comes to the
mind **NAT** 27

Glendale & Co: themselves part and parcel a
product of G. **DAI** 27

Glengarry: lady paraded in a G. and very
abbreviated kilt **TEL** 14

  produced out of my pocket my grey G.
MOM 13

When G. came to Inverness, the people
looked upon him with awe **COS** 46

Glenlivet: Gie me the real Glenleevit **FOO** 67

  Had ta mixture peen Only half G. **PER** 29

glens: green g., the fine g., we knew **LAM** 47

  O little Morag . . . Descending g. **CUR** 7

  what are the bens and g. but manifold
qualities **HIGH** 38

Glesca: Drivin' intae G. on the soor milk cart
LOVE 58

  for a' they misca'd Gleska, . . . ye couldna get
yin o' them to gang back **HIGH** 34

  'Heaven seems verra little improvement on
Glesga' **PLA** 61

  'kind of a plain piper going aboot the streets of
Gleska' **MUS** 60

  'noo fan ye speak o' Glasca, uncle' **PLA** 101

gloaming: An' fond lovers meet in the gloamin'
MUS 4

  Late, late in a gloamin' **FANT** 35

  Roamin' in the g., by the bonnie banks o'
Clyde **PLEAS** 11

gloom: g. and depression of our Edinburgh
winters **PLA** 47

  a glen of greenest g. **RIV** 11

gloomy: have not looked too exclusively on the
g. side **HUMO** 5

glories: steep frowning g. of dark Loch na Garr
HIGH 14

  sunny, breezy g. of the hills and the sky
SWW 50

glorious: drunken freedom, g. – for an hour
POL 17

  glass of wine is a g. creature **FOO** 116

  Isna Embro a g. city! **PLA** 42

  Liberty's a g. feast **LAW** 8

  pride of a g. Nebuchadnezzar **POL** 53

  Tam was g. **MOM** 8

  'yon man that lyis so g. on yon wall head'
FANT 42

glory: all the g. shall be thine **REL** 27

  Coatbridge to G. **REL** 18

  come, bairns! And see the g. of God! **SWW** 51

  fall of the Asturians in their g. **PPL** 63

  Gaelic song is the chief artistic g. of the Scots
MUS 51

  g. crowns them with redoubled wreath **PPL** 25

  g. flowed suddenly off his legs **PLEAS** 9

  g. of the sun will be dimmed **LAM** 16

  He was the g. of princely governing **PER** 160

  it is not g. . . . that we fight and contend for
SPIR 2

  'my inlet to g.' **DEA** 10

  not just the ability to bear a hard thing, but to
turn it into g. **THO** 13

  There was g. on his forehead **PER** 28

  Where saints in g. stand **REL** 130

glove: Touch not the cat bot a g. **MOTT** 16

gloves: decorated with long g. a bright vermilion
colour **COS** 54

  Thair gluvis perfumit in thair hand **COS** 3

  Their gluvis were of the raffell richt **COS** 1

glow-worm: g.-w. lights her little spark **ANI** 77

only G. Almighty can make a gentleman
   FAMI 19
our kings and rulers hath been . . . against G.
   REL 98
Our life's a flying shadow, G.'s the pole **TIM 1**
Pharisee who thanked G. he was not as this
   Publican **INS 93**
pimping for a G. in whom his heart was too
   small to believe **REL 73**
place commanded us by G. **LAND 45**
praised be G., it was in such a sort That I
   revived **LOVE 21**
pray to G. as though all work were in vain
   REL 123
'Pray to G. for me, Melvyll' **PER 181**
rats of Scotland . . . G. sent Grieve to
   exterminate them **PER 120**
repugnant to Nature; contumelie to G.
   M-W 84
Saint Peter said to G., in ane sport word **PPL 1**
Scottish writers on terms of informal
   intimacy with **BOO 74**
second two hundred metres, with G's help, I
   run faster **SPOR 42**
secret name o' Knox's G. **REL 110**
spirit to G. who gave it **DEA 50**
Stumpie believed nor in Gode nor man
   PER 172
surely the baldest of G.'s bays **PLA 134**
Thank you for having me, G. **THO 68**
thanks be to G., I despise death **DEA 47**
Thanks to the gracious G. of heaven **THO 60**
thou ne'er had a true heart, To G. or King
   INS 6
to imagine he is a g. **MIN 10**
To murder men, and gie G. thanks! **WAR 31**
To tell the story of Iona is to go back to G.
   PLA 86
Trust in G., and do the right **REL 88**
Vengeance to G. alone belongs **THO 102**
what sche was . . . her self best knowis, and
   G. . . . will farther declair **PER 153**
We don't get G. saying 'Poor little gay men'
   INS 44
We'll have what G. in His mercy may send to us
   M-W 70
Who will not sing 'G. Save the King' **POL 23**
'Ye might as weel try to overturn G. Almighty'
   POL 3
goddess: 'I never met a white g. in my life'
POET 44
   Progress is a g. **HIS 6**
   she seemed in a mortal body . . . a true g.
      PER 55
   That G. of dullness has strewed on it all her
      poppies **PLA 75**
gods: game that all the g. of Greece might crowd
   the northern skies to see **SPOR 45**
   g. take wondrous shapes **REL 47**
   now arriv'd – thanks to the g. **TRA 8**
   where g. and goddesses walked side by side
      with mankind **FANT 57**
gold: bag of gravel is worth a bag of g. **SCI 19**

birk leaves brown and g. **NAT 27**
huddled all the harvest g. away **HIS 31**
'I know not truly what g. ye seek' **REL 21**
I would melt your g. payment, pour it into
   your skull **POL 64**
In field of g. he stude full myghtely **HER 2**
its back is the colour of the faintest g. **RIV 13**
like dining off g. plate in a company of kings
   POET 60
'maxim which deserves to be engraved in
   letters of g.' **REL 52**
nothing to do but pocket his g.? **POET 4**
Our g. was changyd into lead **LAM 2**
This town . . . was charged with g. **FANT 65**
To a shower of g. **ADV 43**
golden: letting the g.hours slip by **ADV 18**
   splendid Vision, golden time **POL 59**
golden eagle: overtaken by a g. e. **ANI 42**
Golden Wonder: G.W. has entered their souls
   NAT 1
golf: citizens of Edinburgh divert themselves at a
   game called g. **SPOR 74**
   G. is not a relaxation, g. is everything
      SPOR 64
   g. its anodyne **SPIR 30**
   In g., you do not play against an opponent
      SPOR 34
   it takes you so far from the clubhouse
      SPOR 44
   nor so relaxing as g. **BUR 11**
   Scots invented g., it's said **SPOR 2**
   They christened their game g. **SPOR 27**
   tyrannising game **SPOR 61**
golfers: finest g. are also the least loquacious
   SPOR 80
goloch: A g. is an awesome beast **ANI 7**
good (*see also* **guid**) : After a certain age, all of us,
   g. and bad, are guilt-stricken **YOU 20**
   all the Middle Classes should . . . Be clean
      reformed away for g. **POL 58**
   Broadcasting . . . in no sense a substitute for
      the reading of g. books or the study of g.
      music **TEL 12**
   church but as an instrument of Christian g.
      REL 39
   dan he played da god gabber reel **MUS 2**
   g. man survives if he is lucky, but the villain
      becomes the first Lord Roxburgh **THO 47**
   hardly any bad luck in the mountains, only g.
      MOU 28
   I e'en gave o'er in g. time, before the coolness
      of fancy **POET 54**
   I find no hint throughout the universe Of g.
      or ill **PHIL 64**
   'I have only to advise you to keep up a g. fire'
      WAR 89
   I speak just the fine English now . . . the g.
      schoolmaster taught me how **WORD 58**
   If he lights upon a g. thought, he immediately
      drops it **POET 29**
   made their prisoners as g. cheer as if they had
      been brothers **WAR 39**
   meikle g. done in the dark **THO 96**

We let the day grow old among the g. THO 89
grate: or else Get up and clean the g. M-W 73
grave: An open g. is a furrow syne DEA 37
Dig the g., and let me lie DEA 66
Don't let the awkward squad fire over my g.
DEA 18
g. has no victory, for it never fights DEA 52
g.'s lang, lanely hame EPI 24
g.'s most holy peace is ever sure DEA 69
I digg'd a g., and laid him in LAM 12
I hae dug a g. and dug it deep DEA 37
hungry as the g. DEA 67
John Knox, with his one foot in the g.
THO 65
judge has sentenced himself to a suicide's g.
LAW 21
man could go on being a man till he dropped
into his g. M-W 83
On the third day, Columba caused the g. to be
opened FANT 49
One small g. is all he gets M-W 58
restful rapture of the inviolate g. DEA 71
Romantic Scotland's in the g. THO 49
Self less than Duty, Even to the G. PER 244
She asked him but to stand beside her g.
BATH 25
to the g. descend I must EPI 14
When shall it dawn on the night of the g.?
BATH 7
Whose lives ran carefully and correctly to the
g. REL 124
worms ev'n damned him when laid in his g.
INS 18
gravel: bag of g. is worth a bag of gold SCI 19
graves: about the g. of the martyrs the whaups
are crying LAND 58
her ancestors raged in their g. PPL 77
we dig each day our g. with our teeth
FOO 123
gravity: began with the utmost g. to play on it
the most atrocious tunes MUS 24
Gray, Dr: Dr G. attended as Ambassador of
Scotland. PER 106
great: g. and good die not BIO 12
greit men reignis at their awin libertie HIS 21
great auk: *see* auk
Great Grey Man of Ben Macdhui: MONS 8
greatness: We have not the love of g., but the
love of the love of g. FAM 5
greed: clansmen and chiefs whose empassioned g.
and blindness HIGH 48
Greegory's Mixtur': A big cup o' G.M. MIN 7
Greek: cried in the G. *The ships of Pytheas!*
FANT 28
syne they think to climb Parnassus By dint o'
G.! UNI 3
Transposing G. to Gaelic is no toil WORD 70
green: A'comely clad in glisterin' g. M-W 2
bracken unsheath their g. claws NAT 22
byass bouls on Tamson's g. PLEAS 13
Deep i da g. dyoob SEA 11
'Dinna ye think they're a little g.?' FOO 66
Glasgow! The dear g, place! PLA 66

Greta woods are g. PLA 19
hazels o' g. Inverarnan MUS 4
little g. braes bordered with hazel-woods
SPIR 24
Meg up and walloped ower the g. MUS 74
nane sae green tho' grander MOU 5
Now g. as leaf, now witherit and ago PER 138
posters show my country blonde and g.
THO 48
Venus in a g. silk goun THO 70
Greenland: rose will grow in G.'s ice SEA 3
Greenock: This old grey town, this firth, the
further strand PLA 74
Greenockian: first westerns with G.-type people
TEL 15
greet: Ah, gentle dames! It gars me g. M-W 41
Grumble and g., and mak an unco mane
CHI 15
can ye sing ba-la-loo When the bairnie
greets? DAI 1
sair did we g., and mickle did we say LOVE 60
greeting: clouds hang laigh wi' the weicht o'
their greetin' SWW 42
Greitand doun in Gallowa WORD 57
Though the waefu' may cease frae their
greetin' LAM 14
Gregor: One who will give me news of Clan G.
LAM 13
Greta: G. woods are green PLA 19
Gretna Green: Dig for their roots . . . fra G.G.
to Peterhead WORD 28
grew: I never see them but they gar me g.
MOU 38
greybeard: I'll not take a g. while you come to
my mind LOVE 2
grief: bitter to our heart is the g. for them
LAM 41
Grieve, C. M.: acquainted with G. BOO 52
rats of Scotland . . . God sent G. to
exterminate them PER 120
grouse: g. shooters were often rather pathetic
people SPOR 8
I got 99 and a half brace of g. NAT 20
Your g. is done to a turn, my lord POL 102
grue: *see* grew
guid: dandlin' wi' the business sae faur as the real
guid o' the masses are concerned M-W 93
Dinna speak to me of the g. auld days BIO 3
how can I be destitute Of ony gude thing
REL 126
I will keep my gude auld hoose SPIR 46
There's a gude time coming THO 101
Wi' a cog o' gude swats THO 23
gudeman: Drink till the g. be blind PER 212
kind g., and twa Sweet bairns were round me
here DEA 63
little pleasure in the hoose, When our g.'s awa'
M-W 96
sho gat ane meikle rung And the g. made to
the door M-W 12
to maintain an easy life, I aft maun yield,
though I'm g. M-W 14
Yellow-haired Laddie shall be my g. LOVE 70

guest: awaited the arrival of the troublesome g.
  PER 21
  At the First Supper . . . A maiden was the
    hostess, The g. her son THO 125
guests: greatest part of his g. . . . cannot go at
  all FOO 34
guides: My counsellors, my comforters, and g.
  FRI 23
guidmen: G. I've kistit twa DEA 41
guidwife: browst which the gudewife of Lochrin
  produced FOO 93
  Fleech till the gudewife be kind PER 212
  Gudewife, count the lawin FOO 31
  muckle thocht our gudewife to hersell HUM 1
  Rise up, g. and shake yir featers FES 3
guilty: All, all forsook the friendless g. mind
  HOP 6
  found g. by his master . . . and put into the
    pit LAW 16
  one of the most notable pieces of
    impertinence of which the press has lately
    been g. INS 37
  One who is not proven g. is innocent LAW 29
guinea: g,'s stamp ADV 31
  I must go and earn this damned g. DAI 34
gulls: blizzards of g. SEA 6
gumption: hasn't got the g. of a louse INS 47
gun: select a right and a left with my imaginary
  g. SPOR 38
Gunn, Neil: a brilliant novelist from Scotshire
  BOO 34
guns: I herd the cannonis and gunnis mak monie
  hideous crak WAR 7
gunwale: Over the g. into our deep lap SEA 12
gurly: and g. grew the sea SWW 5
  and the g. seas SEA 4
guts: Oor g. maun glorify your name INS 91
  town with g. PLA 69

H

haberdashery: Never underestimate the
  importance of h. COS 20
habit: h. of looking honestly at life EDU 29
  h. of yon gallows breed WORD 57
  lapsed into the English h. of thought SPIR 27
  we called Johnny 'Mother Superior' because
    ay . . . his h. BAD 17
  Whiggism but an evil h. POL 48
habits: contracted ideas and h., quite
  incompatible with the customs of regular
  society PPL 56
  indifferent about the modes and h. of the
    modern world PER 83
  their h. are . . . averse to pleasure INS 46
Haddington: That Goddess of dullness has
  strewed on it all her poppies PLA 75
haddock: O'er oysters and a dram o' gin, Or h.
  lug FOO 50
haemorrhoids: h. you call your poems INS 64
haffets: His lyart h. REL 28

haggis: and a h., And scadlips to sup till ye spue
  FOO 120
  cauld kail . . . preaching against hot h. INS 93
  equally honoured in castle, farm and croft
    FOO 92
  I was like the first puff of a h. INS 23
  photo of Mrs MacTavish winning the h.
    JOU 7
  what's hetter than a h.? FOO 68
Haig, Earl: committed suicide twenty-five years
  after his death PER 41
hail: be it h., be it sleet SWW 4
hair: All my h. a-burning THO 29
  had lost his h. and wore a wig about which he
    was sensitive PER 113
  his h. carefully powdered, though there was
    little of it PER 85
  I'll mak' a garland o' thy h. LAM 11
  in my h. forget, The seed o' a' the men
    M-W 92
  islands are as the wayward tendrils of a
    sweetheart's h. HIGH 24
  Jimmy Maxton, his h. growing longer, lanker
    and greasier POL 18
  Leadan, musical notes, litany, h. of the head
    WORD 48
  mist like h. hangs over One barren breast
    MOM 53
  more h. on their thievish faces than clothes
    PPL 41
  She cocks a purple tammie on a stook o yalla
    h. COS 5
  She'd reddish h., and high, skeugh nose
    PER 118
  some said the h. shirt rather than arms was
    their protection WAR 67
  would neither cut nor comb the h. of his head
    PER 187
hairdresser: I was not above six hours in the
  hands of the h. COS 57
hairst: auld rusty lass linking at a bluidy h.
  HUM 12
  dowie in the hint o' h. SWW 9
  Shorn will be the h. ere lang THO 79
half: h. owre, h. owre to Aberdour 'Tis fifty
  fathoms deep LAM 5
hall: dance gaed thro' the lichted ha' MUS 11
  His step is first in peaceful ha' PER 211
  never be equality in the servants' h. PPL 13
  To beard . . . the Douglas in his h. PER 209
hallelujah: Silence is, perhaps, the greatest h.
  PLEAS 14
Hallowe'en: H., when fairy sprites Perform their
  mystic gambols FANT 43
  H. . . . when souls of the departed were
    supposed to revisit their old homes DEA 32
ham: just be daein' wi' h. and eggs FOO 100
Hame: And far we were from h. LAM 51
  aye it's frae the byways Comes h. the happy
    sang THO 135
  corpse Carried to its lang h. SWW 6
  Far frae my h. I wander, but still my thoughts
    return PPL 65

for it's hame, my dear, no more **LAM 47**
gin ye'll just come h. wi' me **LOVE 72**
H., h., h., h., fain wad I be! **LAND 18**
H.'s h., be it ever sae hamely **ADV 11**
He dy'd at h., lik an auld dug **HIGH 11**
I'm gaun far owre the sea, Fair Annie, A braw
  bride to bring h. **M-W 10**
mosses, waters, slaps and styles, That lie
  between us and our h. **LAND 11**
our h., Where sits our sulky, sullen dame
  M-W 40
Scotland, my mountain h. **SPIR 28**
ten hours drum Gars a' your trades gae
  dandering h. **PLEAS 7**
we're a' noddin' at our house at h. **HOM 4**
When the kye come h. **LOVE 52**
hamely: Hame's hame, be it ever sae h. **HOM 1**
My Muse, tho' h. in attire **POET 5**
Hamilton: H. is notoriously a dull place **PLA 76**
What's H. famous for? **PLA 105**
when I won H., you could feel a chill along
  the Labour back benches **POL 38**
Hamilton, Patrick: reik of Maister Patrik
  Hammyltoun **REL 74**
Hampden: H. Roar is the equivalent of two goals
  for Scotland **SPOR 40**
We've no chance . . . you never do at H.
  against one of the Old Firm **SPOR 77**
hand: a' the sweets . . . Frae Nature's han **PLA 22**
deil had business on his h. **MOM 9**
declared he would kill the first man that put a
  h. on him **LAW 16**
designing God Hath put into my h. a
  wondrous thing **MIN 44**
Each in his cauld h. held a light **FANT 22**
For he lifted his h, not only against the King
  of England **PER 53**
Had I been there with sword in h., And fifty
  Camerons by **WAR 17**
h. in h. we'll go **M-W 49**
h. prescribing, or the flattering quill **INS 90**
h. that skelped her way through life **PER 118**
He doesnae juist drap a name . . . he lays it oon
  on his haun **PER 157**
He's . . . got the h. of Kate Dalrymple
  LOVE 16
his h. would have burnt you **BUR 9**
his left h. always on his right spule-blade
  PER 215
his right h. should be excluded from the
  ceremony **HIGH 19**
hyacinth I wish'd me in her h. **LOVE 43**
let us toast John Barleycorn, Each man with
  glass in h. **TOA 10**
Life lifts his h. to turn his hour-glass round
  MOM 47
neck and h. in the pillory **LAW 15**
One lovely h. she stretched for aid **LOVE 39**
Pope shook him warmly by the h. **REL 116**
Red h. in the foray **LAM 54**
Seer's h. is put on the Inquirer's head
  FANT 40

Time . . . halds his h. for palace nor for byre
  TIM 28
Traditional Orkney invitation to a visitor was,
  'Put in thee h.' **TOA 18**
took it out of my h., and said, 'Pshaw'
  HUMO 7
Vacant heart, and h., and eye **THO 105**
Vine of Death, within easy reach of thy h.
  DEA 70
We need thee still, thy moulding brain and h.
  PER 22
when the hour o' reckoning's at h. **DEA 33**
Who climb, a desperate lover, with h. and
  knee **MOM 53**
handicap: As the offspring of a nun, he suffered
  a formidable h. **PER 106**
handkerchief: bread and butter that feels like a
  damp h. **FOO 89**
hands: and washed his h., and watched his h.
  PER 188
as he came he wrung his h. **FANT 28**
bearing with portly grace gold-headed canes
  in their h. **PER 126**
clapped his h. to his outraged stomach
  SPOR 50
For harmis of bodie, handis and heid, The
  pottingar will purge the painis **LOVE 15**
h. of the clock with a humorous air survey the
  abandoned sight **TRA 14**
have a special care that the old fox and his
  sons doe not escape your hands **POL 35**
Lookit on her ugly leper face . . . Wringand
  his h. **MOM 22**
manner . . . is like a man washing his h.
  INS 88
many . . . losing the Use of H. and Feet
  LAM 55
State is never greater than when all its
  superfluous h. are employed **PHIL 21**
superplus shall be consigned . . . in the h. of
  the treasurer for the Kirk **PLEAS 2**
to suppose he would dwell in any house made
  with their h. **REL 103**
handwriting: dawn of legibility in his h. **EDU 21**
hanged: Come up quietly and be h. **LAW 16**
hanging: *nevertheless* he is deserving of hanging
  LAW 10
ye'll be nane the waur o' a h. **LAW 7**
hangman: h. . . . took off his hat and made a low
  bow towards the prisoner **DEA 15**
h. was a distinguished and awful functionary
  DEA 48
hantle: h. o' miscellawneous eating about a pig
  FOO 107
happiness: great end of all human industry is the
  attainment of h. **PHIL 26**
h. of man to make his social dispositions the
  ruling spring of his occupations **PHIL 14**
I consider the capacity to labour as part of the
  h. **DAI 46**
If h. hae not her seat An' centre in the breast
  HUM 4
Of a' roads to h. ever were tried **HOM 3**

action is best, which procures the greatest h. for the greatest numbers **PHIL 29**

happy: aye it's frae the byways Comes hame the h. sang **THO 135**

duty of being h. **DAI 55**

Even to be h. is a dangerous thing **THO 7**

For h. spirits to alight **SWW 65**

h. may ye be **FES 1**

H. the man who belongs to no party **PLA 16**

how do you keep men h.? **M-W 115**

I am sure we should all be as h. as kings **THO 121**

If any man wants to be h., I advise him to get a public allowance for travelling **TRA 10**

most h. state, that never takes revenge **HOP 9**

Never shall I forget the h. days I passed there **LAND 54**

No society can surely be . . . h., of which the far greater part of the members are poor and miserable **PHIL 53**

There is a h. land **REL 130**

Thrice h. he, who by some shady grove **THO 40**

We h. creatures of a day! **THO 110**

harangue: If you awakened him . . . he immediately began a h. **PER 76**

harbinger: Morag, h. of death **MONS 5**

Hardie, James Keir: 'Are you working here?' **POL 45**

H. was . . . an incorruptible if ever there was one **PER 149**

never knew what it was to be a child in spirit **PER 129**

hardship: the true h. is to be a dull fool **DAI 59**

Hare, William: H.'s the thief **MIN 2**

hare: Even the h. tramples on the fallen lion **MOTT 20**

harm: if we gang to sea, master, I fear we'll come to h. **FANT 12**

harmonies: God-imprisoned h., That out in gracious motions go **MUS 49**

harmony: h.. of the world is made manifest in Form and Number **SCI 42**

h. is now no more **MUS 27**

harp: 'Auld Robin Gray' sung to the accompaniment of the h. **MUS 34**

H. and carp, Thomas, h. and carp **FANT 8**

He touched his h., and nations heard, entranced **MUS 67**

Which of ye all Touched his h. with that dying fall **MUS 72**

harper: wandering h., scorned and poor **MUS 71**

wind, that grand old h. **SWW 57**

harps: Deaved wi' the h. and hymns oonendin' ringin **THO 95**

harridan: I am wild-eyed, unkempt, hellbent, a h. **M-W 87**

Harris: I have often seen a little hill in H. **MOU 25**

harvest: huddled all the h. gold away **HIS 31**

in h. there was a struggle to escape being the last done **FANT 24**

Would ye partake of h.'s joys **SWW 22**

harvests: Our h. are not in the ordinary months **LAM 55**

hat: devil, clad in a black gown, with a black h. upon his head **FANT 50**

I'll mount Phoebus' chair Having ne'er a h. on **THO 29**

May he never prosper . . That'll wear twa faces under his h. **M-W 129**

Operations were started by the purchase of . . . an old h. box **SCI 1**

sat wi' his h. on his heid afore the best in the land **FAMI 13**

wisp-headed scowler, without h. or wig **INS 65**

hate: Ah don't h. the English . . . Ah h. the Scots **INS 97**

give us the grace to h. Our unemancipated state **M-W 127**

I do not h. him nearly as much as I fear I ought to **FRI 10**

Insolence in the few begets H. in the many **POL 17**

how hot Are Love and H. **BUR 25**

little amusement . . . but a Scotchman to h. **INS 52**

We h. Roman Catholics . . . Protestants . . . Jews and Muslims **SPOR 33**

hats: their h. were o' the birk **FANT 3**

they wat their h. aboon **COS 2**

hauf: Hauf his soul a man may use Indulgin' in illusions **PHIL 34**

Says I to him, 'Will ye hae a h.?' **FOO 5**

haunted: I find I'm h. with a busie mind **MIN 6**

Hawick: H. Mr Christian showed me there an inscription upon a house **THO 18**

hawk: captured by guile **ADV 4**

Hawkie: Lest witches should obtain the power Of H.'s milk **CUR 3**

Hay, Matthew: sentenced to death by Lord Kames **LAW 18**

hazards: game: g. that after never so many H. must be lost **DEA 27**

hazels: 'Mang the h. o' green Inverarnan **MUS 4**

hazelwoods: little green braes bordered with h. **SPIR 24**

head (*see also* **heid**): about its h. are the canticles of joy **PLEAS 14**

all you folks are off your h. I'm getting rich from your sea-bed **POL 66**

bombing sergeant, with his h. laid open **WAR 72**

Boswell put his cup to his h. **WORD 52**

carrying home for dissection the head of a child **SCI 5**

h., arms and body down to the middle like a human being **MONS 15**

I'd turn my h. where tail should be **MUS 7**

Its h. resembled that of a horse **MONS 16**

Leadan, musical notes, litany, hair of the h. **WORD 48**

less nonsense in his h. than any man living **PER 222**

Lovat's h. i' the pat, Horns and a' **PER 186**

marched at the h. when in column **PER 240**

master of romance himself was the h. of the enterprise **POET 69**

My h. erect beneath the tragic years **TIM 16**

Ossian has superseded Homer in my h. **POET 27**

place my pur-boil'd H. upon a Stake **HOP 13**

Seer's hand is put on the Inquirer's h. **FANT 40**

she had no place in which to lay her h. **HUM 15**

she's only got two ideas in her h. **PER 163**

There's the wolf's h. **PER 92**

they put a date stamp on your h. when they mug you **PLA 79**

through whose h. a regiment of horse has been exercising **PER 218**

True humour springs not more from the h. than from the heart **HUMO 4**

would neither cut nor comb the hair of his h. **PER 187**

Yon that ye thocht was the h. yestreen **MOU 45**

heads: cleads us a' frae h. to feet **SEA 9**

Helmets on their thick h. **POL 5**

live immersed in swamps with only their h. above water **PPL 14**

tearing the clothes off their H., crying **LAM 55**

Their h., their necks, their legs and thighs Are influenced by the skies **HIGH 15**

health: h. in the wild wind's bosom **NAT 12**

Here's a h. and here's a heartbreak **LAM 47**

I keep my h. better in these wild mountains **MIN 51**

if it was a fine day, why then, 'We'll drink its h.' **FOO 81**

man's h. depends on trifles **MIN 23**

never met a healthy person who worried much about his h. **MIN 29**

hearse: we have forgotten the h. **DEA 49**

we've got a braw new h. outby **DEA 24**

Heart: And opened new fountains in the human h. **MUS 67**

As I know my own h. to be entirely English **POL 7**

blacker faa awaits the h. Where first fond love grows cool **LOVE 64**

blood is true, the h. is Highland **SPIR 3**

broken h. kens nae second Spring **LAM 14**

Bountiful Primroses, With outspread h. **NAT 19**

cheery h. **ADV 10**

community, for whose general good his h. may glow **PHIL 14**

contrite h., a humble thought, Are mine accepted sacrifice **THO 106**

dan he played da god gabber reel Da meicht ha made a sick hert hale **MUS 2**

'D'ye approve of that?' 'With all my h.' **REL 24**

Every . . . member . . . must have a frank, honest, open h. **M-W 37**

every Scottish heart should beat high and proud today **BATH 13**

Firm as a stone, but of a h. contrite **EPI 13**

frightens folk out of the husk of their h. **FANT 54**

From my h. I can say I like no such titles **THO 58**

garland o' thy hair, Shall bind my h. for evermair **LAM 11**

God in whom his h. was too small to believe **REL 73**

Good humour and generosity carry the day with the popular h. **HUM 13**

gude ale hauds my h. aboon **FOO 2**

h. handsomely pieced again **BIO 11**

he . . . That feedis in his hairt a mad desire **LAM 18**

he was always with me, for I had him by h. **BUR 20**

he was the minister after their h. **REL 125**

h. and soul and all the poetry of Natural Philosophy **SCI 42**

H. inform'd The moral page **BOO 70**

h. of man is made to reconcile contradictions **HUM 10**

hert o' the nut is this **POET 46**

He's won the h . . . of Kate Dalrymple **LOVE 16**

his h. is rank poison **INS 18**

How bitter to our h. is the grief for them **LAM 41**

I heard her hert Gang soundin' wi' my ain **LOVE 82**

I have watched thy h., dear Mary **LOVE 57**

I shall die with a true h. **DEA 11**

If only the h. beat true to the lilt of the song **HIGH 39**

Iona of my h. **PLA 82**

it was more than his fond h. could brook **BATH 14**

Its grandeur draws back the h. **MOU 26**

let your h. be strong **ADV 82**

Lourd on my hert like winter lies The state that Scotland's in **LAM 34**

May they live in our songs and be nearest our h. **FRI 15**

Mony a hert will brak in twa, Should he ne'er come back again **LAM 48**

mouth that did my h. beguile **FANT 58**

My beloved sall ha'e this he'rt tae break **LOVE 18**

My h. is a lonely hunter, That hunts on a lonely hill **PER 178**

My h. is heich abufe **LOVE 4**

My h. remembers how! **LAND 58**

My h.'s a boat in tow **MUS 8**

My h.'s in the Highlands **HIGH 9**

My h.'s still light, albeit my locks be grey **YOU 21**

My hert, my will, my nature and my mynd Was changit **LOVE 56**

My Muse, tho' hamely in attire, May touch the h. **POET 5**

nae greater luck that the h. could desire
PLA 128

naething i the pouch – Or i the hert POET 62

noble h. may haif nane ease . . . Gif fredome
failye SPIR 5

Nothing now my h. can fire HOP 11

Nowhere beats the h. so kindly As beneath
the tartan plaid PPL 10

Oppressit hairt, indure In dolour and distress
LOVE 75

pictures . . . gain the h. by slow degrees
ART 21

reticulations of its h. are shredded FOO 9

She fairly won my fancy, and stole away my
h. LOVE 58

Sore sea-longing in my h. SEA 19

strake the dagger untill his h. M-W 6

That smells sharp and sweet – and breaks the
h. NAT 18

The world . . . has no purpose, h. or mind or
will THO 132

thou ne'er had a true h. To God or King
INS 6

to think on the Braes o' Menstrie, It maks my
h. fu' sair PLA 103

True humour springs not more from the head
than from the h. HUMO 4

Vacant h., and hand, and eye THO 105

Warm as his h. to the friends he has chosen
FOO 87

warm Scotch h., and a braid Scotch tongue
PER 34

Was ever h. more human? BUR 10

wee soup drink dis unco weel To had the h.
aboon FOO 52

Were na my h. light, I wad dee PHIL 2

western sea alone can . . . reach the Gaelic h.
SEA 20

Wi' lightsome h. I pu'd a rose LOVE 34

with a pain at my h., and pride and fondness
MOM 2

with . . . inflexible hardness of h. INS 8

yark on da line Liftet der herts SEA 11

Heart of Midlothian F.C.: Even after we'd
fucked you seven-nil . . . you still made me say
Hearts SPOR 78

hearts: barbarian sounds, bad suppers, excellent
h. LAND 54

Blest Revolution, which creates Divided H.
POL 104

feeling, pensive h. NAT 2

Our h. are all yours from the very first swing!
INS 9

Our h. are young 'neath wrinkled rind
YOU 15

Our h. were sair, our purse was bare LAM 51

Their h. and swords are metal true WAR 30

To live in h. we leave behind, Is not to die
DEA 19

It's soon', no' sense, that faddoms the herts o'
men WORD 47

vein of poetry exists in the h. of all men
POET 13

heath: gloomy spaces . . . most disagreeable when
the h. is in bloom MOU 11

From the h.-covered mountains of Scotia
SPIR 19

Land of brown h. and shaggy wood SPIR 53

My foot is on my native h. PER 213

heather: By h. tracks wi' heaven in their wiles
LAND 43

h. bells, in bonnie bloom MOU 3

h. sticking out of their ears INS 75

hinny-scented h. NAT 10

honey-scented h. hills NAT 17

number of strokes you took to kill a snake in
the h. SPOR 34

Out with you and put some h. on M-W 75

She's as sweet as the h. LOVE 59

Tangled tufts of purple h. NAT 24

where the h., waving, Gives fragrance to the
day. HIGH 33

With the hills of home before us, And the
purple of the h. MUS 68

heathery: mossy howes, the h. knowes LAND 3

heave: H. awa', boys! I'm not dead yet HOP 1

Heaven: But I'll be in H. afore him MUS 4

By heather tracks wi' h. in their wiles
LAND 43

For happy spirits to alight, Betwixt the earth
and h. SWW 65

gone to H. no doubt, but he won't like God
PER 236

he may . . . thank H. that he ever saw a
farthing of it POET 8

H. can boil the pot ADV 32

H. gives our years of fading strength
Indemnifying fleetness YOU 6

H. reflected in thy wave no more COM 4

H. seems verra little improvement on Glesga
PLA 61

if such as he in heav'n may be EPI 18

in the cleft of h. I scan The giant form of a
naked man FANT 37

love is h., and h. is love LOVE 78

moir of ege the nerrer hevynis bliss YOU 15

no H. but clarity THO 127

O grant me, H., a middle state THO 86

Only a splendid Hell keeps H. fair THO 34

Progressive virtue, and approving H.!
PHIL 62

sun is bright on h.'s brow TIM 15

Though all the wood under the h. that growis
M-W 1

through the opened h. . . . . he had seen angels
FANT 2

When our ashes are scattered by the winds of
h. POL 83

Whone sabill all the Hevin arrays SWW 29

wonder that the poor man was allowed to
breathe the air of h. POL 4

Work . . . in which his progressive advance
towards H. is to lie DAI 53

heavenly: heard a h. melody and sound MUS 35

heavens: All I ask, the h. above, And the road
below me TRA 45

starry h. above the plain Come flying in on
our track **TRA 48**
Hebrides: entire H. . . . formed one Atlantic
principality **HIGH 35**
we in dreams behold the H. **SPIR 3**
What about the glamorous H., you ask
PLA 77
Hebrides: this was the manner in which the
overture, *The H.*, took its rise **MUS 43**
Hector: 'Another for H.!' **WAR 42**
hedgehog: Like a h. with its quills, so would you
see a Pict bristling **WAR 21**
heels: bowing and knocking their h. in the air
MUS 46
strathspeys and reels Put life and mettle in
their h. **MUS 15**
heid: Fra harmis of bodie, handis and h., The
pottingar will purge the painis **LOVE 15**
if he's carried h. foremost, he's a'richt **SPOR 5**
like a stallion, Wha's h. hauds up a horn
FANT 61
monstrous fische . . . havand greit ein in the h.
thereof **MONS 11**
nocht a king, nor a lord, nor a h. **MOM 33**
What way hae ye sic a muckle, muckle h.?
MONS 2
heids: nothing noo in the h. o' the gyurls but
sodgers **WAR 65**
height: carried geological speculation and
research to such a h. **SCI 15**
h. for h. it is considerably more spectacular
MOU 33
Kirk was at the h. of its power **REL 25**
lark descendis from the skyis hycht **SWW 26**
male dancers in the h. of their glee **MUS 45**
heights: More h. before him than he left
behind **MOU 18**
Helen: O H. fair, beyond compare **LAM 11**
Helensburgh: Thinking of H., J.G. Frazer
PER 90
Hell: and H., nae doot **BUR 15**
And stappit him in the dub o' H. **INS 7**
Can . . . fiend from H., More hateful, more
malignant be **M-W 22**
chosen 'vessel of h.' **POET 14**
curse of H. frae me sall ye bear **CUR 8**
every seven years, They pay the teind to H.
FANT 17
in the depest pot of h. He smorit thame
INS 33
lest we gang to H. **COM 3**
make a strae wisp o' him to stap the mouth
o' H. **REL 119**
No H. except confusion **THO 127**
nor is h. what it has been described **FANT 49**
Of all the miscreants ever went to h. **INS 2**
Only a splendid H. keeps Heaven fair
THO 34
People want to know-ow Who the h. we a-are
SPOR 6
send a rough-shod troop o' H. **SPIR 12**
seven lang years in the flames o' H. **DEA 3**
ugly pit as deep as ony h. **FANT 39**

helm: if the pilot slumber at the h. **ADV 116**
Helmsdale: mail train from Inverness which
reached H. twelve hours late **TRA 12**
Help: H. us to play the man **REL 121**
I do indeed come from Scotland, but I cannot
h. it **MOM 3**
not the man to see my own side lose for want
of a little h. **SPOR 39**
for the second two hundred metres, with
God's h., I run faster **SPOR 42**
thy h. is fastlie brought to ground **LAM 30**
feared the verse . . . might be of h. to any
German parachutist **WAR 45**
we should root them out before they can get
the h. they depend upon **POL 100**
Henry VIII: H. approached as nearly to the ideal
standard of perfect wickedness **PER 176**
hens: get the h. to put their heids together and
invent a new kind o' fancy egg **FOO 98**
hereafter: Curse . . . if he has yin, his h. **CUR 19**
herd: Aneth the true H.'s righteous crook
REL 59
nae greater luck that the heart could desire,
Than to h. the fine cattle in bonnie
Strathyre **PLA 129**
Who o'er the h. would wish to reign **PPL 84**
whistle that the wee h. made **MUS 63**
heritage: With independent heart and mind
Hold I my h. **SPIR 47**
hero: Driver Gibson was a popular h. **TRA 13**
h. of 1,000 blunders **PER 80**
In all times and places the H. has been
worshipped **FAM 6**
John Barleycorn was a h. bold **TOA 10**
like men to fight, And h.-like to die **WAR 64**
man who can overcome his own terror is a h.
and more **ADV 88**
heroes: h. whom none can outshine **TRA 36**
Past is the race of h. **BATH 10**
Sons of h. slain at Flodden **WAR 5**
vain and misleading tales . . . of Fionn
MacCumhal and his h. **WORD 19**
heroic: 'H. young queen' . . . well-intentioned
but hysterical poodle **PER 122**
heroin: at least with h. they got an early death
BAD 8
heron: a h. was hungry and needin' tae sup
ANI 27
Herrin': herrin's heid, a loaf o' breid **ANI 4**
like the h. . . . you don't get them fresh in
Gleska **MUS 60**
not mich that iss wholesomer than a good h.
FOO 99
herring: he knows as much as any man alive
about the life of the h. **LOVE 67**
h. come in, staring from their scales **SEA 12**
no h. on the menu **FOO 41**
Plenty h., plenty meal, Plenty peat to fill her
creel **TOA 20**
herrings: cried for them all packed there like h.
in a barrel **MUS 23**
forgot everything except the h. **SEA 13**

By h. and moss thaimself to steer **WAR 38**

Blythe hae I been on yon h. **MOU 10**

I have often seen a little h. in Harris collapse
to half its size **MOU 25**

if we are going up a h. and the motor suddenly
stops **TRA 39**

like a h. of pure white sand **RIV 12**

more than birds on the h. tonight **WAR 69**

My heart is a lonely hunter, That hunts on a
lonely h. **PER 178**

rivers row, And mony a h. between **LOVE 31**

saftly, saftly, ower the hill **SWW 10**

that brooky h., Where ancient poets drank
their fill **POET 18**

Tweed, Clyde and Annan rise in one h.
MOM 6

When o'er the h. the eastern star Tells
bughtin' time is near **TIM 10**

whisper that draws a h. across a strath
THO 38

Your wee bit h. and glen **SPIR 59**

hills: Beltane feast . . . performed on h. **REL 103**

conveyed into the mind by the h. **MOU 31**

expert mountaineers accustomed to h. at
night **MONS 8**

'free men of the h.' stuff has its tragic
moments **MOU 46**

grey-faced nation, That swept our h. with
desolation **HIGH 26**

Hielan' h. – I never see them but they gar me
grew **MOU 39**

honey-scented heather h. **NAT 17**

lordly ones, Who dwell in the h. **FANT 46**

May the h. lie low . . . In thy way **TOA 16**

O Alva h. is bonny **PLA 103**

sunny, breezy glories of the h. and the sky
SWW 50

What h. are like the Ochil H.? **MOU 5**

When he some heaps of h. hath overwent
MOU 18

Who has the h. as lover **MOU 4**

With the h. of home before us **MUS 68**

hinny: her artless smile's mair sweet, Than
hinny **LOVE 53**

h.-scented heather **NAT 10**

My hinnie and my succour, O shall we dae the
thing ye ken **M-W 16**

hips: kis my hippis **INS 79**

we swing ungirded h. **FANT 60**

Hirta: boat arriving first should have the right to
claim H. **BOA 7**

make clouds from. Soay and H. **SWW 35**

historians: good Scottish h. to this day bless her
name **PER 128**

h. of Scotland and its literature had known . . .
as much about Gaelic as about Chinese
WORD 62

h. repeat each other **HIS 5**

history: And h. leans by a dark entry **HIS 23**

'H.', a Big Subject **HIS 2**

Ben Laoghal play . . . on the legendary stuff
of h. **MOU 22**

generation being educated to know nothing of
our h. and culture **EDU 11**

ghastly turned-inwards energy, which is after
all the h. of Scotland, pre-unification
PPL 95

glance at their h. . . . . reveals what lies under
PPL 52

high midnight of the Border Reiver as a
stirring, gallant episode in British h. It was
not like that **HIS 16**

H., as it lies at the root of all science **HIS 11**

H. does not repeat itself **HIS 5**

h. of Scotland is the most romantic, the most
incredible **HIS 18**

h. of Scotland might have been strangely and
splendidly different **PER 121**

h. of the world is but the biographies of great
men **HIS 10**

H.'s easy. Dead easy **HIS 36**

I am occupiit in writing of our historie **HIS 8**

If you should bid me count the lies of Hector's
H. **HIS 20**

immortalised in British h. as 'the thin red line'
WAR 94

It gave me the beginnings of a sense of h.
HIS 24

most shining period of the British h. **PPL 38**

Myths about a nation's h. should be treated
with considerable caution **HIS 13**

obscurity which hangs over the beginnings of
all h. **HIS 29**

one of the few European capitals with no anti-
semitism in its h. **WORD 21**

one of the great features of our h. is the
mobility between classes **SPIR 27**

our h. may be summed up in this one sentence
HIS 17

Scots are beset by Scottish h. **HIS 14**

Scottish historiography has been for too long
bogged down in a preoccupation with the
myriad aspects of the Labour movement
HIS 39

Scottish versions of h. seem to oscillate **HIS 4**

sentimentality that encumbers Scottish h.
HIS 35

Their h. is a varying record of heroism,
treachery, persistent bloodshed **PPL 70**

we should look upon this . . not as essentially
belonging to music, but to h. **MUS 70**

What is the h. of Scotland? **HIS 7**

with the modern Gael I share a h. but not a
language **WORD 14**

hoar-frost: Embroidery of h.-f. **SWW 25**

hoast: Sic a h. hae I got **MIN 49**

hobby: Man, that's ma hobby **FOO 5**

Hogg, James: honest grunter **PER 217**

The said H. is a strange being **POET 9**

When H. entered the drawing-room, Mrs
Scott . . . was reclining on a sofa **PER 166**

hoggie: my joy, my pride, my h. **ANI 24**

Hogmanay: So up and gie's our H. **FES 3**

winning the haggis at a H. dance **JOU 7**

auld black h. sat on his rump **ANI 6**

Can ye nocht mak a Hielandman of this h. turd? **PPL 1**

deid sleep cam over me, And frae my h. I fell **FANT 17**

Hame cam' his gude h., But never cam' he **LAM 10**

Here's to the h. wi' the four white feet **TOA 7**

h. *'the length* of Highgate' **WORD 64**

I wish I were a brewer's h. **MUS 7**

If he were a h., nobody would buy him **PER 30**

Its head resembled that of a h. **MONS 16**

Many a h. has snappit and fa'n **THO 6**

she had the fiercie and the fleuk **ANI 17**

surely ye widnae steal my h. **INS 13**

Through whose head a regiment of h. has been exercising **PER 218**

two creatures I would envy **ANI 26**

why did you give away the royal h. **REL 19**

horseman: naebody, damm't, kens the h.'s wird **POET 46**

horses: All through the meadows the h. and cattle **TRA 42**

and swung the h. down the bout **LAND 26**

Fain would I hear his fiery h. neighing **THO 29**

God forbid that I should go to any heaven where there are no h. **DEA 23**

great beasts, shining with health and care **ANI 14**

h. beautifully matched and of the first character **TRA 33**

h. of memory, thundering through **MOM 35**

If you cannot ride two h., you have no right in the circus **POL 77**

late in the evening the strange h. came **ANI 79**

On the Sabbath-day wash the h.s' legs **DAI 4**

Posting . . . with four h., was the perfection of travelling **TRA 34**

hose: gude ale gars me sell my h. **FOO 2**

hospital: almost unavoidable error in the h. physician **MIN 10**

hospitality: h. was exuberant **M-W 71**

hostess: maiden was the h., The guest her son **THO 125**

my h. (who was regarded locally as a great musician) **MUS 24**

hotel: I thought this was a temperance h.? **FOO 17**

houghmagandie: many jobs that day begin, May end in 'h.' **PLEAS 5**

hour: care, that wad harass the h. **PLEAS 7**

dreaded h. when the domestic abominations were flung out **DAI 28**

drunken freedom, glorious for an h. **POL 17**

h. after the appointed time, in stalked Pollochok **PER 92**

h. approaches Tam maun ride **TIM 6**

I am apt, in a cool h., to suspect **PHIL 27**

It is the wish'd, the trysted h. **LOVE 29**

lectured for the hour without reaching the subject **PER 246**

men will wonder at that h. **FANT 52**

One crowded h. of glorious life **FAM 10**

One little h.! **MOM 44**

This is the day of change And this the hour **MOM 47**

when the h. o' reckoning's at hand **DEA 33**

hours: I did not invent this method piecemeal but all at once in a few h. **SCI 44**

in our h. of ease, Uncertain, coy, and hard to please **M-W 111**

social h., swift wing'd, unnoticed fleet **TIM 9**

'Ten miles.' 'Say it in h.' 'Six h.' **MOU 46**

house: beik the h. baith but and ben **PLEAS 13**

Being in a minister's h., there was the minimum of religious consolation **REL 104**

Big H. of the bairn, so enormous **THO 19**

gaudy h. o' fame **POET 48**

gazed with blanched faces at the H. with the Green Shutters **MOM 17**

hoose is but a puppet-box **BUI 31**

Hou sall aa the folk I've been . . . bide in yae wee hoose? **SPIR 50**

h. where a child is about to be born **FAMI 25**

his ain sate in his ain hoose **FAMI 13**

I had the chloroform for several days in the h. **SCI 40**

I thought I could never do wrong to copy the lady of the h. **PER 166**

I'll hae nae hauf-way hoose **THO 72**

inscription upon a h. which he had observed **THO 18**

kept a warm h. and drove a plentiful trade **LAND 4**

Me and John will get a new H. in Drumchapel **HOP 16**

nae luck aboot the hoose **M-W 96**

not worthy even to keep a door in thy h. **REL 119**

Of Scotland's king I haud my h. **SPIR 46**

pleaded . . . to be left in the h. till his wife was well **LAND 13**

pulling down and burning of the h. . . . in which was lying his wife's mother **LAND 42**

there was a great din heard in the h. **MIN 25**

thing about a h. without a woman **FAMI 122**

to suppose he would dwell in any h. made with their hands **REL 103**

we're a' noddin at our h. at hame **HOM 4**

Why do you propose these boxes for our people? **BUI 35**

Young ones rantin' through the h. **YOU 5**

House of Commons: On Hardie's first day at the H. of C. **POL 45**

Sir William Augustus Cunningham boasted in the H. of C. that 20,000 men might yet be raised in that country **WAR 71**

House of Lords: an important debate in the H. of L. **POL 102**

Three Lords of Justiciary were ordered to appear at the Bar of the H.o.L. **WORD 30**

houses: h. were incommodious and hospitality was exuberant **M-W 71**

over ten thousand h., each as proud and as
    nobly descended PPL 50
trees and the h. go wheeling back TRA 48
hovel: 'Tis but a cot roofed in with straw; a hovel
built of clay BUI 15
human: And opened new fountains in the h.
heart MUS 67
    approximating as nearly to the idea of a
        perfectly wise and virtuous man, as perhaps
        the nature of h. frailty will permit PER 223
    completest monument in the entire continent
        of h. folly PLA 31
    defeats in football . . . are actually useful to
        remind you that you're only h. SPOR 79
    folly of h. laws PHIL 55
    great end of all h. industry is the attainment
        of happiness PHIL 26
    he has the power of making any Scotsman . . .
        more h. BUR 19
    head, arms and body down to the middle like
        a h. being MONS 15
    Henry VIII approached as nearly to the
        ideal standard of perfect wickedness as the
        infirmities of h. nature will allow PER 176
    how rich and strange the h. lot BUR 25
    h. bodies are sic fools HUM 6
    h. soul stands between a hemisphere of light
        and another of darkness PHIL 9
    'h. stories' which by definition concerned
        animals JOU 2
    I hold to be the first of h. joys LOVE 24
    I would make the h. mind as plain as the road
        from Charing Cross MIN 53
    if the h. species fails ADV 49
    If war comes it will be from failure of h.
        wisdom WAR 24
    In rowing, the h. machine works more cleanly
        SPOR 16
    In the h. breast, Two master-passions cannot
        co-exist HUM 7
    its use was perverted . . . to internal h.
        consumption FOO 43
    men of better clay . . . feel the h. dignity
        SPOR 9
    O painted piece of h. clay EPI 14
    Persisted . . . in the practice of Every H. Vice
        INS 11
    Sir James Barrie's cans . . . as he went round
        with the milk of h. kindness PER 127
    something that has no care for h. life MOU 9
    to step aside is h. ADV 28
    thing nae man can bide, An' he be h.
        M-W 103
    Toryism is an innate principle o' h. nature
        POL 48
    usual infirmity of h. nature MOM 6
    we hardly conceive of our parents as h.
        FAMI 29
    world is neither Scottish, English . . . but *h.*
        SPIR 23
humanity: In spite of all motives to lenity, That
policy or h. could suggest INS 8
    reconciles poor h. to itself FOO 116

small nation has always been h.'s last bulwark
    SPIR 26
thoughtful utterance of h. PLEAS 14
unhappy half-sleeping h. TRA 28
We address ourselves not to their h., but to
    their self-love PHIL 52
humble: contrite heart, a h. thought THO 106
    I have never before seen a h. king PER 42
    middle state, Neither too h. nor too great
        THO 86
    There's a star to guide the h. REL 88
humbug: It's all h. MONS 18
Hume, David: D.H. ate a swinging great dinner
    PER 38
    H. possessed powers of a very high order
        PHIL 39
    perfectly wise and virtuous man PER 223
    rather a 'turtle-eating alderman' PER 221
    Scotland rejected D.H. PHIL 35
humility: preposterous h. of our puritan
    ministers POL 53
humorist: Scot . . . is . . . a secret h. HUMO 9
humour: Caledonian woman showed a biting h.
    in her reply M-W 27
    flash of eternity HUMO 13
    Good h. and generosity carry the day
        HUM 13
    peculiar element in Scotch h. HUMO 11
    Scots have been distinguished for h.
        HUMO 5
    sense, not so much of h. . . . as of what is
        grimmest and driest in pleasantry WAR 89
    True h. springs not more from the head
        HUMO 4
    Without h., you cannot run a sweetie-shop
        HUMO 3
hunger: end of h., cold and crime POL 59
    Hielan' scab and hunger PLA 78
    How shall we go home and see our children
        die in H.? LAM 55
    h. becoming articulate POL 86
    h. for pleasure of every kind, and want of all
        other force POET 14
    small portion, about the size of a bean . . .
        prevents them from feeling h. PPL 14
    You stand convicted of sickness, h.,
        wretchedness, and want LAW 31
hungry: h. as the grave DEA 67
hunter: A h.'s fate is all I would be craving
    HIGH 33
Hurricane Jack: 'H. Jeck was seldom very rife wi'
    money' PER 195
husband: how mony lengthened, sage advices,
    The h. frae the wife despises! M-W 41
    indignant h. explained the reason for his
        wrath M-W 97
husbands: absolute mistresses of . . . their h.
    M-W 21
    how many h. had she had? HIGH 11
hush: awe-inspiring mid-day h. MOM 18
    H. and wonder and adore SWW 51
    In the h. of night-time I hear them go by
        MOM 35

magic moment when . . . the h. descends
MOM 11

night h. of earth is expectant MOU 31

huts: their h. are floorless except for earth
HIGH 4

Hutton, James: Dr H. dreaded nothing so much
as ignorance SCI 38

J.H., that true son of fire PER 189

hyacinth: h. I wish'd me in her hand LOVE 43

Hypocrisy: affording only Pedantry . . . and H.
PPL 4

Every Human Vice, Excepting . . . H. INS 11

oil to the wheels ADV 22

hypocrite: I was in no sense a h. ADV 36

hypocrites: Ye h.! are these your pranks?
WAR 31

hypothesis: what might go against your own
cherished h. SCI 32

I

I: I'm all right ADV 21

I am far better read . . . than they are BOA 10

I no great Adam M-W 113

'I too am here' M-W 54

Iain Dall: Macrimmon asked the other lad why
he did not play like I. D. MUS 50

ice: desperate struggles . . . with i. MOU 14

frozen moisture fell as delicate spicules of i.
MOU 19

long wan bubbles groped Under the i.'s cover
SWW 67

people's will moves slowly, as the i. PPL 67

rose will grow in Greenland's i. SEA 3

we find the i. growing thinner below our feet
YOU 27

Iceland: its tail would have touched I. MONS 4

Icolmkill: Sweeter still doth I. Fall on a
Scotsman's ear HIGH 36

idea: i. came into my mind, that as steam was an
elastic body SCI 43

man's really fine i. becomes an empty balloon
COM 12

prime i. is due to the enterprise . . . of an
individual SCI 14

their only i. of wit HUMO 15

ideas: i. and habits, quite incompatible with the
customs of regular society PPL 56

only two i. in her head PER 163

sae sonorous that the words droon the i.
WORD 38

identity: dis'll only happen if we hae an
awaarness o wir ain i. HOP 7

idleness: a faculty for i. implies a catholic
appetite DAI 56

idlers: why should a people be branded with the
name of idlers DAI 11

ignorance: Dr Hutton dreaded nothing so much
as i. SCI 37

harmless as long as i. and crassness are
considered failings INS 70

i. of the law is no excuse; i. of science should
not be either SCI 7

rectangular blocks of man's Insolent
mechanical i. UNI 10

ignorant: Our erles and lords . . . How i. and
inexpert they be POL 49

spiteful i. pedant REL 55

ill: I find no hint throughout the universe Of
good or i. PHIL 64

she believed none spoke i. of her PER 116

The world . . . grinds out death and life and
good and i. THO 132

ill-luck: men lamenting their i.-l. are only
reaping the consequence of their own neglect
DAI 52

illness: a seasonable fit of i. MIN 47

He never had a day's i. SPOR 41

ills: O'er a' the i. o' life victorious MOM 8

those i. with which we are constantly
threatened PHIL 22

imagination: indebted to his memory for his
jests, and to his i. for his facts INS 87

man of i. may carve out his own pleasures
LAND 61

must be employed . . . like the i. HUM 14

immorality: Misery of any kind is not the *cause*
of I. PHIL 8

immortality: littleness and hugeness of our
briefness and i. FANT 65

imp: Gin ye ca' me i. or elf FANT 16

imperialism: sane I., . . . a larger patriotism
POL 90

impertinence: highest i. and presumption . . . in
kings and ministers PHIL 57

one of the most notable pieces of i. INS 37

impertinent: hundred impertinent obstructions
PHIL 55

Servile and i. INS 57

important: i. thing is the underwear SWW 11

impossible: When you have eliminated the i.,
whatever remains . . . must be the truth SCI 10

imps: I saw a thousand imps FANT 58

Improvement: And call they this I.? COM 4

Heaven seems verra little i. on Glesga PLA 61

improvements: two gentlemen were passing the
scene of these i. MOM 34

impudence: His matchless I. INS 11

impudent: base i. brazen-faced villain REL 55

begotten by the snug embrace of an i.
Highlander upon a cloud of tradition
POET 71

I called John an I. Bitch INS 40

i. baggage, and deserved to be whipped
REL 31

your foolish and i. letter INS 50

income: living so far beyond my i. PHIL 45

incomes: all decent people live beyond their i.
PHIL 44

independence: We will not get true i. in a oner
POL 67

independent: not whether an i. Scotland would
be viable, but whether it would be bearable
POL 75

What struck me in these i. was their bleakness
PLA 123
Islay: Cold is the wind over I. SWW 40
Jura And I. lie near LAM 40
isle: ageless sang this auld i. sings PLA 12
low-lying i. . . . Belonged as a dwelling to the
Children of the Gael LAND 40
Isles: people . . . that dwelleth in the I., and are
utterly barbarous HIGH 20
that is why some folk make pilgrimage to the
Western I. HIGH 30
isothermal: same i. band passed through
Edinburgh and London SWW 12
ivory: neither white nor cream so much as old i.
SPIR 24

J

jackal: Next prowls the wolf, the filthy j. last
INS 22
jacket: My blue j. seemed . . . to have picked a
quarrel with the wrists COS 47
Jacob: J. made for his wee Josie, A tartan coat to
keep him cosie COS 18
like blessed J. the patriarch FANT 2
Jacobites: anxious to have portraits of Mary
Queen of Scots ART 16
jade: A souple j. she was M-W 43
jail: and j. the lot of us LAW 17
Jam Tarts: We'll follow the J.T. Wherever they
go SPOR 4
James IV: J. the Feird unhappilie slaine . . . by
the kingis awin wilful misgovernance PER 161
glory of princely governing PER 160
not a good captain PER 27
had a wonderful intellectual power PER 100
that richt redoutit Roy PER 159
James VI: He had rather . . . procure peace with
dishonour PER 250
wisest fool in Christendom PER 241
jazz: way a seated j. musician gets him or
herself . . . prepared MUS 40
jealousy: comes without seeking ADV 2
Jeanie Deans: She's gone and took the *J.D.*, And
laid her on her side TRA 4
Jeannie McColl: bonnie wee J.M. LOVE 47
Jeffrey, Francis, Lord: great literary
anthropophagus INS 21
J., pertest of the train INS 20
Jenny: J. wi' the airn teeth CHI 6
There's a J. for ilk Jock FOO 63
Jericho: first urban . . . community, had been
flourishing at J. for more than a thousand years
HIS 33
jersey: j. haps her shouthers COS 5
Jerusalem: Scotland would be way ahead . . .
except maybe J. LAND 59
Jess: where J. sat in her chair and looked down
the brae MOM 2
Jessie: sweet J., the flower o' Dunblane PER 242
jester: Charlemagne . . . that j. INS 39

jests: indebted to his memory for his jests INS 87
Jesus Christ: 'J., tails again' SPOR 59
J.C. and Barabbas Were found the same day
PHIL 59
more of J. in Saint Theresa's little finger
REL 13
muckle he made o' that LAW 6
neither J.C. nor Douglas Fairbanks PER 18
Was J. no a jiner? THO 113
wasn't a woman who betrayed J. M-W 61
Jew: cursed old J. INS 24
He is a J. and may be an atheist INS 10
jewel: Lest my j. I should tine LOVE 26
jig: That's the way to dance a j. MUS 77
jigs: hornpipes, j., strathspeys and reels MUS 15
job: persistence in seeing the j. through SCI 9
woman's j. to make the best of them. M-W 66
jobs: many j. that day begin, May end in
'houghmagandie' PLEAS 5
Jock: a' oot o' step but oor J. WAR 14
Jock Elliott: ma name it's wee J.E., And wha
daur meddle wi' me? PER 5
Jock McGraw: ye winna frichten J.M. WAR 13
Jock o' Hazeldean: aye she loot the tear doon fa'
for J. o' H. LOVE 9
Jockie: Will ye wed a muirlan' J.? LOVE 44
John Anderson: J.A., my jo M-W 51
John Barleycorn: Inspiring bold J.B. FOO 30
J.B. was a hero bold TOA 10
John Bull: LAND 4
John Ells: Next to the skin they wore J.E.s
COS 24
John Frost: J.F. cam' yestreen SWW 66
John Guthrie: then J.G. cried *Get up!* LAND 26
John Henry: baptismal register spoke of him
pessimistically as J.H. PER 207
John o' Groats Head: Its snout rested at
J.o'G.H. MONS 4
John o' the Syde: He is weil kend, J.o' the S.
PER 6
John Tamson: We're a' J.T.'s bairns PPL 81
Johnson, Samuel: As Dr J. never said PPL 12
Dr J. and I afterwards were merry on it
M-W 43
he needed J. as an ivy needs an oak PER 88
J. no sooner saw Smith than he attacked him
INS 86
'Mr J.,' said I, 'I do indeed come from
Scotland' MOM 3
To see Mr S.J. salute Miss Flora Macdonald
MOM 4
Johnson, Willie 'Wee Bud': If J. had deliberately
intended an attack SPOR 23
joke: bad j. elaborated with the careful logic of
lunacy POL 106
if a j. finds its way into our neighbourhood, it
is looked upon with as much surprise as a
comet PLA 76
j. can be carried owre far! REL 41
requires a surgical operation to get a j. well
into a Scotch understanding HUMO 15
To crack a j., or tell a tale FRI 3
world is a bad j. REL 17

kebbucks: Fell k., three year auld FES 12
keeper: I've crackit wi' the k., pockets packed wi' pheasants' eggs ANG 8
Kelly, Lord: L.K., a determined punster WORD 52
kelp: fall in the value of k. . . . renders a change . . . necessary PHIL 28
kelpie: Ghost, k., wraith MONS 9
    Kelpy has risen from the fathomless pool MONS 17
Kelvin, Lord: L.K., being Scotch, he didn't mind damnation PER 158
    'The deep C,' said K. slyly SCI 16
Kelvin, River: I tore off these beastly drawers and hurled them into the R. K. COS 26
Kenmore: Frae K. to Ben More The land is a' the Marquis's LAND 3
Kenmure, Viscount: K.'s lads are men, Willie WAR 30
Kennedy, Walter: Cuntbittin crawdoun K. INS 36
Kennedy-Fraser, Marjorie: Mrs K.-F.'s travesties of Gaelic songs INS 70
Keppoch: The Laird of K. . . . gave orders for rolling a snowball to lay under his head BOA 4
Kerr, Deborah: forget you ever wanted to go on the stage ACT 7
kettle: when the k. came to the boil, you kept it simmering FOO 127
key: k. keeps the castle ADV 80
    Love of Books, the golden K. BOO 43
    wonder is the k. Of knowledge THO 16
kidneys: you won't mind if I pass it through the k. first FOO 84
Kildonan: going down towards bleak K., I unthinkingly glanced over my shoulder MOU 22
kill: he would k. the first man that put a hand on him LAW 16
    My first act . . . was to k. my mother PER 54
    number of strokes you took to k. a snake in the heather SPOR 34
    seize your hilts, and k. REL 21
    watch the Scottish BAFTAs to want to k. yourself TEL 4
Killiecrankie: I met the devil and Dundee, On the braes o' K. WAR 10
Kilmaurs: K. whittle can cut an inch afore the point PLA 87
Kilmeny: nae smile was seen on K.'s face FANT 36
kilt: Hielan' man he wears the k. COS 32
    k. is . . . an aphrodisiac BOA 18
    I'll don my native dress, And walk around in a damned loud k. PLA 80
    if the king wore the k., she did not know what the ladies would do COS 35
    k. . . . . failed him only once COS 6
    k. is an unrivalled garment for fornication and diarrhoea HIGH 29
    lady paraded in a Glengarry and very abbreviated k. TEL 14

    Let others boast . . . Of k. and tartan plaid COS 55
    my k. and tartan stockings I was wearing COS 43
    paraphernalia of my national costume COS 9
    Sir William Curtis in a k. COS 13
    something smert aboot the k. WAR 65
    this dress is called the *quelt* COS 11
Kiltearn: Black Rock of K. For tombstone, grave And trumpet of your resurrection PLA 88
kilted: Who is so trim as a k. laddie? COS 41
kilts: their red k. splashed with blood WAR 72
    they wore nothing under their k. COS 39
kin: curious abyss that divides the closest k. FAMI 9
    I'll learn my k. a rattlin sang YOU 4
    Of kith and of k. we're one HIGH 39
    our worst enemies are our own k. in the east HIGH 5
    She wadna card and she wadna spin, For shamin' o' her gentle k. DAI 3
    Though a' her k. suld hae bin deid LOVE 13
kind: changit clene rycht in ane other k. LOVE 56
    wasna ower k. to the first gairdner REL 7
kindliness: characteristic touch of Scots k. LAW 14
kindly: Had we never loved sae k. LOVE 36
kindness: na k. at court ADV 93
    Sir James Barrie's cans . . . as he went round with the milk of human k. PER 127
king: And Snowdoun's Knight is Scotland's K. MOM 39
    and yet will judge and give law to their k. POL 53
    calling the K. bot Goddis sillie vassal MOM 33
    Carry the lad who was born to be k. PLA 125
    courageous, even more than a k. should be PER 27
    Cursed be the k. who stretched our stockings COS 40
    entended and put in hand the K.'s Maiesties death FANT 15
    For the k. had said him rudely That ane rose of his chaplet Was fallen WAR 18
    Gave as he wan, like Alexander the k. PER 132
    Gude k., forouten mair delay SPIR 6
    Guid K. Robert's testament WAR 38
    had we all been loyal to the k. who appealed to us COS 42
    He was K. of France and Germany, But he ne'er ruled Polmadie HIS 1
    Here's to the k., sir. Ye ken wha I mean, sir TOA 4
    I had the honour to set the crown on the k.'s head DEA 9
    I wadna caa the k. my cuisin LOVE 19
    I was K.'s Advocat and had sold the K. INS 51
    'I will go tomorrow,' said the k. SWW 1
    If I had my rights I should be k. of England PER 125

every egg being cautiously examined by the
l. **DAI 29**

Fare weill, my l. bricht **LAM 50**

hard to believe a l. had to jump into her
crinoline **COS 51**

he has ta'en that gay l., An' there he did her
burn **M-W 3**

He taikis . . . The l. in bour full of bewtie
DEA 30

How daur ye set your fit upon her – Sae fine
a l.? **ANI 22**

'I thought I could never do wrong to copy the
l. of the house' **PER 167**

If doughty deeds my l. please **LOVE 48**

lad may luve ane l. of estate **LOVE 5**

lang may his l. Look owre the Castle Doune
DEA 5

liked nothing better than to attack a l. from
the rear **ANI 41**

Nobody could sit down like the L. of
Inverleith **PER 84**

this resourceful l. appears to be the sheet-
anchor of many a foreigner's knowledge of
Scottish Church History **PER 94**

out there came a l. sheen **M-W 2**

Thy mother a l. both lovely and bright **CHI 39**

Were you to hear a Scots l. repeat . . . any of
the true original songs **MUS 79**

Why weep ye by the tide, ladye? **LOVE 9**

Wi' modest face, sae fu' o' grace, replies the
bonnie l. **M-W 16**

wren is . . . 'The L. of Heaven's hen' **ANI 39**

young l. with the . . . appetite of a ploughman
ADV 65

laigh: Speak well of the Hielands, but live in the
l. **HIGH 1**

laird: begging a charity of a Lowland l.'s lady
HIGH 11

Come up quietly and be hanged, and do not
anger the l. **LAW 16**

cottar spak' it . . . An' on his rigs the gawcie
laird **WORD 37**

five hundred of the followers of the L. of
Maclean were left dead **WAR 42**

'How had you the audacity, John,' said a
Scottish l. to his servant, 'to go and tell
some people I was a mean fellow' **THO 56**

I wass frightened they might be the l.'s salmon
ANG 9

l. of ancient title who had it pointed out
to him that his gamekeeper resembled him
so closely they might almost be brothers
M-W 77

l. is nae what you would call very intelligent
INS 69

L. of Keppoch . . . gave orders for rolling a
snowball **BOA 4**

l. wore coat, breeches and stockings all
knitted by his wife **COS 45**

Wha could refuse the L. wi' a' that? **COS 50**

What gars the L. of Garskadden luik sae gash?
DEA 54

lairdie: Wha the deil hae we got for a king, But a
wee, wee German l. **POL 29**

lairds: I've woo'd wi' lords, and woo'd wi' l.
LOVE 17

laith: O l., l. were our gude Scots lords **COS 2**

Lallans: I was just translating my last wee poem
Into the dear old L. **POET 33**

'L.' – a synthesised Burnsian esperanto
WORD 73

lamb: He is nae Dog; he is a Lam **PER 98**

I am come with a l. to sell **FES 4**

paladin in mental fight with the presence of a
Larry the L. **INS 61**

where the black raven brings The still-born l.
to its nest **PLA 12**

lament: L. him, Mauchline husbands a' **EPI 16**

Whom to l. first, he knew not **MOM 52**

land: Allace for ane, quhilk lamp wes of this l.
POET 23

Beloved l. of the East, Alba of marvels
LAND 1

day is aye fair, In the l. o' the leal **DEA 53**

every bit of fat or value they have grabbed
with L. Law from us **LAND 45**

Freed the hail l. frae covenanting fools
PER 102

game which represented a raid on the
debatable l. **CHI 43**

genial partiality for the wine of his native l.
PER 114

God send the l. deliverance Frae every reiving,
riding Scot **PPL 3**

his l. was to go to a man of another race
SPIR 43

humble of every l. were deceived by ruling
class, State and Civil Law **PPL 63**

I am heartily tired of this L. of Indifference
and Phlegm **INS 89**

I faught at l., I faught at sea **WAR 10**

I hae nae l., and you would give your . . .
barony for a square yard of rock **MOM 42**

I . . . love the l. of 'mountain and of flood'
SPIR 15

It is a stone l. **LAND 46**

l. of Calvin, oatcakes and sulphur **LAND 55**

L. of the mountain and the flood! **SPIR 53**

l. he loved better than his soul or God
LAND 25

l. is a' the Marquis's **LAND 3**

Land o' Cakes **HIGH, SPIR 12**

L. of polluted river **SPIR 17**

l. was forever, it moved and changed below
you **LAND 27**

lane man in a lanely l. **THO 114**

like lords o' the l. **COM 1**

many a Gael Bred up in the L. of Mists
HIGH 28

mountain-l. which spurned the Roman chain
PPL 25

My ancestors waiting, unborn, in the waves,
In the l. beyond **FANT 48**

no l. in which a man may live more pleasantly
and delicately **LAND 16**

ploughman lad's a jolly lad . . . and when he meets a bonny l., he taks her on his knee M-W 19

lasses: Along the quay at Peterhead the l. stand around SEA 3

Her prentice han' she tried on man, And then she made the l. M-W 38

tell the country l., if they wish to be fashionable COS 21

Auld Ayr, wham ne'er a toon surpasses, For honest men and bonny l. PLA 15

When lads and l. tartan wore MUS 27

lassie: Her cutty sark . . . That while a l. she had worn COS 10

highest joy That the heart of man can frame: My bonnie, bonnie l. LOVE 52

I love a l., a bonnie, bonnie l. LOVE 59

Ilka l. has her laddie LOVE 28

'Is't a laddie or a l.?' said the gardener M-W 106

L. wi' the yellow coatie, Will ye wed a muirlan' Jockie? LOVE 44

My love she's but a l. yet LOVE 33

needless to speer for the l. That's woo'd and married an a' ADV 104

Roamin' in the gloamin' wi' a l. by my side PLEAS 11

That I may drink before I go, A service to my bonie l.0 FOO 21

there the bonie l. lives, the l. I lo'e best SWW 16

What can a young l. do wi' an auld man? M-W 35

wind blew the bonnie l.'s plaidie awa' M-W 108

Ye're a bonny lad, and I'm a l. free LOVE 68

Yellow-haired Laddie . . . Cried 'Milk the ewes, L.!' LOVE 70

lassies: Bad luck to the lad that'll coort twa l. M-W 129

l. loup as they were daft When I blaw up my chanter MUS 73

trying hard to reach them gars The l.. burst their stays MUS 6

Latin: a' your jargon . . . Your L. names for horns and stools UNI 3

Beside L. our language is imperfite WORD 23

Scottish language . . . give place to the softer . . . tones of the L. WORD 11

So me behovit . . . Some bastard L. . . . use Where scant were Scottis POET 20

laud: Nocht is your famous l. ADV 75

Lauder, Sir Harry: Gang hame and practise, H. ACT 8

laugh: tartan tred wad gar ye lauch COS 27

use of Scots taken . . . as a signal to l. ACT 5

laughing: I saw by his teeth he was lauchin' at me ANG 10

L. at the fuffin' lowe CHI 8

laughter: Curse . . . abune a', his hearty l. CUR 19

help us to perform them with l. and kind faces REL 121

it issues not in l., but in still smiles HUMO 4

She burst into a l. so extreme COS 13

something so forlorn and miserable about the animal that we both roar with l. FOO 128

Their l. puts the leap upon the lame LAND 43

This idea sent him into a fit of l. quite merry to behold FRI 8

Laureate: Who would not be The L. bold POET 4

laurels: Mourn, hapless Caledonia . . . Thy l. torn SPIR 55

Ochon, the day! That clarty barm should stain my l. PER 64

when the sons of song descend to trade . . . their former l. fade POET 11

laverock: my red coo climb the muckle pear tree . . . and whistle like a l.! REL 51

Sweet's the l.'s note and lang, Lilting wildly up the glen LAM 48

laverocks: cry of *Caller Laverocks* was always heard in severe winters FOO 90

law: all the membris are at feid Quhair that the l. of luve remainis LOVE 15

bring me prisoners, and I'll find them l. LAW 5

every bit of fat or value they gave grabbed with Land L. from us LAND 44

Fergus, the first King of Scots, had no other l. HIS 25

fig for those by l. protected LAW 8

humble of every land were deceived by ruling class, State and Civil L. PPL 63

If the Lord Chancellor knew only a little l. PER 15

L. is a Bottomless Pit LAW 3

l. knows it can either say 'It's against the l. to go on strike' LAW 17

l. made it so, because the landlords themselves were the lawmakers POL 4

let some l. of equity to nations all be known POL 108

luve has no uthir l. LOVE 5

My look is l. CHI 52

One who is not proven guilty is innocent in the eye of l. LAW 29

she had totally succumbed to the l. of gravity INS 92

they both 'died for the l.' HIGH 11

Wha for Scotland's king and l. Freedom's sword would strongly draw WAR 26

Ye daurna swear aboot the toon, It is against the l. BAD 1

lawin': Gudewife, count the l. FOO 31

lawless: In quest of l. gain they issue forth PPL 24

without fear the l. roads Run wrong through all the land THO 93

Lawnmarket: Up the L., And doun the West Bow LAW 1

laws: folly of human l. PHIL 55

Liberal: never, in the depth of my ignorance . . .
was I a L. **POL 79**

liberality: education . . . a battlefield between l.
and illiberality **EDU 4**

Liberals: Tories think they are better born; but
L. think they are born better **POL 21**

liberty: In all ages . . . priests have been enemies
of l. **REL 65**

it is l. alone that we fight and contend for
SPIR 2

It was to the General Assembly . . . that the
Scots looked for their l. **REL 87**

L.'s a glorious feast **LAW 8**

No good is like to l. **SPIR 1**

regard for l., . . . ought commonly to be
subordinate to a reverence for established
government **POL 50**

library: rest he can put away in the lumber-room
of his l. **BOO 27**

vice and obscenity fearfully propagated
BOO 75

Liddesdale: I saw a man from L . . . hanged for
horse-stealing **DEA 20**

Of Liddisdale the common thievis **PER 180**

lie: And dinna tell a lee **CHI 44**

Doutless the statesmen dinna lee **WAR 84**

he said, *you lie!* **INS 86**

'It's a damned l.,' said Goodall, starting out of
his sleep **MOM 32**

L. over to me from the wall or else Get up and
clean the grate **M-W 73**

l. so obvious it was another way of telling the
truth **BAD 9**

takes a wise man to handle a l. **BAD 2**

They tell their master is a knave, And sure
they do not l. **INS 16**

When . . . the last damned l. is told **FES 10**

You may l. about the number of strokes you
took **SPOR 34**

lies: all l. and trash anyway **JOU 8**

All political parties die at last of swallowing
their own l. **POL 8**

Business . . . is the sale of l. **DAI 19**

cruellest l. are often told in silence **BAD 15**

Here l. Durham **EPI 11**

If you should bid me count the l. of Hector's
History **HIS 20**

so folk said, but they tell such l. **BAD 5**

some books are l. frae end to end **BOO 16**

life: act his part all his l. **ACT 13**

Ae day gie me o' youthful l. At the back o'
Benachie **TIM 2**

And l. is never the same again **LAM 35**

And this is aa the l. he kens there is **PER 208**

As if a word our l. wad bind **PPL 82**

beautiful blending and communion of death
and l. **DEA 52**

Books are . . . a mighty bloodless substitute
for l. **BOO 63**

castles of the chiefs . . . contained very few of
the comforts . . . of modern l. **BUI 22**

Curse . . . A' thing included in his l. **CUR 19**

discoveries which lengthen l. . . . of infinitely
more importance **MIN 40**

Doutless he deed for Scotland's l. **WAR 84**

each day is l.'s messiah **PLEA 14**

earth is full of graves, and mine was there
Before my l. began **DEA 26**

Ease and alternate labour, useful l. **PHIL 62**

excellent place for sleeping a l. away in
PLA 25

For I have enjoyed a long l. through **MOU 6**

For in my l. I couth never sing a note **MUS 36**

forgive me . . . if sometimes at l.'s concert I
would rather sit alone **THO 113**

Give me a girl at an impressionable age, and
she is mine for l. **EDU 37**

great l. if you don't weaken **ADV 25**

hand that skelped her way through l. **PER 118**

he knows as much as anybody alive about the l.
of the herring **LOVE 67**

his l. as a whole would have discredited a
dustman **BUR 7**

His one desire is to be Master of the Art of
L. **PER 105**

hoose is but a puppet-box To keep l.'s images
frae knocks **BUI 31**

hornpipes, jigs, strathspeys and reels Put l.
and mettle in their heels **MUS 15**

how warm the tints of L. **BUR 25**

hung on to the mundane for grim l. **FAMI 35**

I thank God for preserving my l. where so
many have fallen **HOP 10**

I tremble from the edge of l. **DEA 36**

If I kiss thy comely mouth, Thy days of l. will
not be long **FANT 6**

if l. were a thing money could buy **EPI 3**

If there is no future l. **REL 17**

if you feed your good man well He'll love you
all your l. **FOO 6**

In l. it is your privilege to choose **DEA 25**

In the choosing of a line of l. **DAI 40**

It grinds out death and l. and good and ill
THO 133

keeping a journal. I once in my l. thought of
doing so **BIO 10**

Let them beg through l. **FAMI 3**

liberty . . . which no honest man will lose but
with his l. **SPIR 2**

L. is much easier, being an Earl **THO 9**

L. is not a rehearsal **ADV 46**

L. lifts a hand to turn his hour-glass round
MOM 47

l. must have ceased without a pang **PER 206**

l. of every man is a diary **BIO 2**

l. of the people was moulded . . . by hidden
forces **FANT 57**

l.'s great lottery **DAI 44**

matches one's skill . . . against something that
has no care for human l. **MOU 9**

mode of l. is not different from that of African
negroes **HIGH 4**

most effective training for emotional l.
BOO 1

my father standing As real as l. **FAMI 18**

on the road to Thurso there is a low suavity
of l. **PLA 131**
Three to boil, and three to fry, And three to
bait the l. **SEA 10**
twenty Highland cattle . . . drawn out in a l.
ANI 47
When . . . the l. flies out with a squeal **ANG 1**
lines: That I aince mair may view the l. and flees
ANG 15
Whose l. are mottoes of the heart **BUR 3**
Linklater, Eric: I had of course to show it to L.
TEL 6
Mr E. L. is a lost Norseman with a tendency
to go berserk **BOO 35**
Linlithgow: post cam out of L., schowing the
king good tidings **HIS 22**
linnet: little l. fondly prest **ANI 23**
lion: And dar'st thou then, to beard the l. in his
den? **PER 209**
early Christian gets the fattest l. **ADV 107**
Edinburgh, with its couchant l. crag **PLA 37**
Even the hare tramples on the fallen l.
MOTT 20
I'll woo her as the l. woos his brides **LOVE 55**
So, when the l. quits his fell repast **INS 22**
See also lyon
literature: deadening blow was inflicted on our
rural l. **MUS 37**
he is the greatest loss . . . that Scottish l. has
suffered in this century **BOO 34**
I will . . . read all I can find about Gaelic l.
WORD 62
pleasures of l. . . . which most require to be
preached **BOO 4**
Style . . . is the immortal thing in l. **BOO 60**
We cultivate l. on a little oatmeal **JOU 15**
literary: cat is the ideal l. companion **ANI 32**
Chinaman who contemplated a thesis on the l.
history of Scotland **WORD 62**
In the true L. Man there is thus ever . . . a
sacredness **BOO 21**
L. criticism is constantly attempting a very
absurd thing **BOO 23**
majority of l. critics . . . recall to me
that extraordinary chirruping conversation
BOO 48
Never l. attempt was more unfortunate
BOO 38
Scots are incapable of considering their l.
geniuses purely as writers **BOO 69**
their great l. anthropophagus **INS 21**
little: l. ones were always compelled to be
English **CHI 43**
l. wee cloud in the world its lane **FANT 35**
Our Mother feedeth thus our l. life **DEA 72**
sometimes gets so l. that there's none of him
at all **CHI 48**
This l. life is all we must endure **DEA 69**
live: all l. together . . . like pigs **HIGH 4**
Easy l. and quiet die **THO 105**
Glad did I l. and gladly die **DEA 66**
Here's to the friends we can trust . . . May
they l. in our songs **FRI 15**

I think no man fit to l. that is not fit to die
DEA 11
'Industry is the noblest plan, By which to l.
you may' **DAI 23**
it is good to l. with the gods for a bit
HIGH 30
l. in the laigh **HIGH 1**
We l. only by the death of others **FOO 9**
liver: land of the sodden l. **SPIR 17**
Work and wait, a sturdy l. **BATH 9**
lives: guid auld l. O' leal and thrifty men and
wives **LAM 28**
It's no fish ye're buying: it's men's l. **SEA 24**
living: if it ever came to the choice between l.
and dying **CHI 23**
Work, eh. What a stupid way to earn a l.
DAI 43
load: As step I wi' the sunlight for my l.
LAND 42
mony a l. on shore may be skailed at sea
ADV 79
loaf: Herrin's heid, a l. o' breid **ANI 4**
loaning: Now they are moaning on ilka green l.
LAM 25
lobster: I ate so much crab and l. as a boy that I
have not been able to enjoy them since **FOO 96**
lobsters: presented no bad resemblance to a pair
of gigantic l. **COS 54**
loch: all his kit engulfed by the clear waters of a
Highland l. **TRA 38**
Loch Arkaig: creature was basking on the
surface **MONS 16**
Loch Awe: *see* **Lochow**
Loch Coruisk: You cannot feel comfortable at L.
C. **MOU 43**
Loch Fyne (*see also* **Lochfyne**): thair wes ane
monstrous fische in L. F. **MONS 11**
Loch Katrine: that filthy hole L.K. **CUR 13**
Loch Lomond: By the bonny, bonny, banks o' L.
L. **MUS 5**
Far abune the bonnie banks o' L.L. **MUS 4**
I wish I had him to ferry over L.L. **CUR 13**
in L. Lommond there are fishes without fins
LAND 49
Loch Maree: Birds-nesting expeditions were
also made to the islands of L.M. **ANI 73**
Loch Morar: Giant swimmer in deep-green M.,
The loch that has no bottom **MONS 5**
L.M. Monster as *A'Mhorag* **MONS 12**
Loch na Garr: The steep frowning glories of
dark L. na G. **HIGH 14**
Loch Ness: L.N. Monster was spoken of as *An
Niseag* **MONS 12**
Loughness never freezes **LAND 49**
monster of L.N. is probably the lost soul of
Glasgow **PLA 64**
visitor viewing L.N. Met the Monster
MONS 3
Loch Rannoch: by Tummel and L.R. and
Lochaber I will go **LAND 42**
Loch Shiel: L.S. Monster as *An Seileag*
MONS 12

My L., patricide is a greater crime than parricide SPIR 8

Our erles and l., for their nobilitie, How ignorant and inexpert they be POL 49

Princes and l. are but the breath of kings PPL 22

There lies good Sir Patrick Spens, Wi' the Scots l. at his feet LAM 5

They dash and they dare like l. o' the land COM 1

Three L.'s of Justiciary were ordered to appear WORD 30

lordship: respect his l.'s taste, And spare the golden bindings! BOO 15

lore: deep sea-heart was brooding deep upon its ancient l. SEA 17

his l. was filthy rags SPIR 43

'Tis the sunset of life gives me mystical l. YOU 7

lorry: Every day a big l. loaded with Perrier Water bound for Scotland PHIL 18

Lothian Road: ever-glorious L.-R. M-W 117

lottery: you, who are but useless blanks In life's great l. DAI 44

lourd: L. on my hert as winter LAM 34

louse: gutless wonder, that hasn't got the gumption of a l. INS 47

lovable: not . . . the most immediately l. folk in the United Kingdom HIGH 18

Lovat, Lord: L.'s head i' the pat, Horns and a' thegither PER 186

love: Absences are a good influence in l. LOVE 84

afore sic l. appears, Nae man sall kiss a woman! SPIR 50

all the membris are at feid Quhair that the law of luve remainis LOVE 15

all you l. and are dreaming of ADV 82

And ilka bird sang o' his l. LOVE 34

At lufis lair gin thou will lear LOVE 51

bands and bliss o' mutual l. LOVE 37

best to be off wi' the old l. Before ye be on wi' the new LOVE 79

Better to l. in the lowliest cot ADV 139

birds . . . made l. and made war ere the making of Man ANI 53

blacker faa awaits the heart Where first fond l. grows cool LOVE 64

But I hae parted frae my l., Never to meet again LOVE 66

Convuls'd in L.'s tumultuous throes LOVE 23

evil we do – alas! that the world should l. it so LAM 4

exchanged pastoral staves in pledge . . . of their mutual l. in Christ PER 146

far Cuillins that are puttin' l. on me LAND 43

first it bow'd, and syne it brak, Sae my true l. did lightly me LOVE 6

Follow l., and it will flee LOVE 1

Friends given by God in mercy and in l. FRI 23

from action springs alone The inward knowledge to true l. and faith THO 76

Grant that my brow may wear . . . L. to distressed Mankind THO 33

here, beneath this lowly thatch l.'s sweetest bard was born BUI 15

how hot Are L. and Hate BUR 25

I am set in lufe As weill as I wald wiss LOVE 4

I bow before thine altar, L. LOVE 81

I gat it frae the lad I lo'e COS 4

I l. a lassie, a bonnie, bonnie lassie LOVE 59

I l. my little son, and yet CHI 26

If I ever really l. it will be like Mary Queen of Scots LOVE 22

if you feed your good man well He'll l. you all your life FOO 6

If you're goin' to speak aboot l., be dacent and speak aboot it in the Gaalic LOVE 65

lad may luve ane lady of estate LOVE 5

leeze me on . . . Gaelic periphrase for 'I l.' LOVE 61

L. is like a dizziness LOVE 54

L., joy and patriotism are their inspiration MUS 26

L. makes the world go round? Not at all FOO 88

l. o' economics is the mainspring ADV 85

L. of Books, the Golden Key BOO 43

L. of our neighbour is the only door REL 82

l. of the fair is the meed of the brave ADV 102

l. of the l. of greatness FAM 5

L. rules the court, the camp, the grove LOVE 78

L. swells like the Solway, but ebbs like its tide LOVE 76

l., they say, gives one an air LOVE 80

Lufe God abufe al REL 2

me and my true l. will never meet again By the bonny, bonny banks of Loch Lomond MUS 5

My l. she's but a lassie yet LOVE 33

My luve is like a red, red rose LOVE 27

No force can hinder a woman from vengeance, when she is impelled there by l. M-W 85

No! nor fettered L. from dying In the knot there's no untying M-W 55

Not loud-toned voice, but l. unfeigned REL 6

O L. that will not let me go REL 89

On L.'s eager pinions borne, Harriet Beecher Stowe's come! BATH 6

ploughman poet, who . . . has a most enthusiastic heart of L. BUR 6

sacredness of l. and death Dwells in thy noise and smoky breath PLA 72

sheer l. of every inch and particle of the soil HIGH 24

So ferre I falling into lufis dance LOVE 56

sweetest folly in the world is l. LOVE 20

tell me how to woo thee, L. LOVE 48

there the bonie lassie lives, The lassie I lo'e best SWW 16

Thus with me began L. and Poesy LOVE 24

To see her is to l. her PER 61

True humour . . . its essence is l. **HUMO 4**
vast and bland as Buddha, but without l. or
   tenderness **HIS 6**
We always believe our first l. is our last, and
   our last l. our first **LOVE 86**
what he gives out is l. **EDU 32**
When Paradise is quit of heavenly hue, She
   whom I luve sall steadfast be and true
   M-W 4
who long to recognise . . . a look like l. **ANI 84**
Yes, I have died for l., as others do **LOVE 21**
loved: Had we never lov'd sae kindly **LOVE 36**
   she liked him, l. him as they said in the soppy
   English books **LOVE 46**
   To be trusted is a greater compliment than to
   be l. **THO 78**
lovely: atmosphere warm with that l. heat
   FAMI 25
   Kilmeny looked up wi' a l. grace **FANT 36**
   lady both l. and bright **CHI 39**
   l. dears, Her noblest work she classes **M-W 38**
   L. wee thing, wert thou mine **LOVE 26**
   O, it's l. roamin' in the gloamin' **PLEAS 11**
   One l. hand she stretched for aid **LOVE 39**
   rain, its l. behaviour over an island **SWW 15**
   What a l., l. moon **NAT 14**
   What more l. than to be alone With a
   Teasmade, a radio and a telephone? **THO 69**
   whose empassioned greed and blindness Made
   desolate these lonely l. places **HIGH 48**
lover: must be a professed l. of one or more of the
   female sex **M-W 37**
   Her l. vanished in the air **FANT 7**
   me, Who climb, a desperate l., With hand and
   knee **MOM 53**
   my fause l. staw my rose **LOVE 34**
   O Wallace, peerless l. of thy land **PER 22**
   One lovely hand she stretched for aid, And
   one was round her l. **LOVE 39**
   Who has the hills as l., Will find them
   wondrous kind **MOU 4**
lovers: And fond l. meet in the gloamin' **MUS 4**
   luifaris takis no rest **LOVE 63**
   tender curiosity appropriate to l. **FAMI 19**
   True l. I can get many an ane **FAMI 1**
   wow! but they were l. dear **LOVE 7**
loves: Three things by distance still grow dearer,
   Our l. **THO 32**
loving: But what is the best way of l.? **CHI 30**
   warmth of tenderness and l. souls **FAMI 25**
lowe: Laughin' at the fuffin' l. **CHI 8**
Lowland: begging a charity of a L. laird's lady
   HIGH 11
   In L. families, children . . . have not been
   encouraged to speak **HIGH 17**
   lawland ers wald mak a bettir noyis **INS 36**
   L. Scot has no unconscious mind **HIGH 8**
   whether the blood be Highland or L. or no'
   HIGH 39
Lowlander: from his compatriot in the south the
   L. stands consciously apart **HIGH 45**
   Highlander, L., and Border-men, are a' ae
   man's bairns **HIGH 41**

I suppose I am now much more a L. **HIGH 42**
L. finds himself the sentimental countryman
   of the Highlander **HIGH 44**
staunch L. carries . . . a Gaelic biological and
   linguistic heritage **HIGH 47**
Lowlanders: L. call their part of the country the
   land of cakes **HIGH 12**
Lowlands: Ye Hielands and ye Lawlands, O,
   whaur hae ye been? **DEA 5**
lowlands: across the glistening l. Slant the
   moonbeams' silver bars **MOM 1**
Lowther: Lock the door, Lariston, L. comes on
   WAR 44
loyal: had we all been l. to the king who appealed
   to us **COS 42**
loyalty: such devoted l. to the family of my
   ancestors **BOA 23**
luck: there is hardly any bad l. in the mountains
   MOU 28
Luckie Middlemist: To L.M.'s loup in, And sit
   fu' snug **FOO 50**
lucky: good man survives, if he is l. **THO 47**
   It . . . vexed me that a man I disliked so much
   should be so l. **FRI 7**
Lucky Macleary: under the sooty rafters of
   L.M.'s only apartment **FOO 119**
lug: until he summoned resolution to 'tear away
   the l. wi' the gristle' **LAW 15**
   your venom'd stang . . . thro' my l. gies mony
   a twang **MIN 13**
lugs: only glegest l. are able . . . Tae wale a
   modicum o' wit **WORD 71**
Luggie, River: L. with a plaintive song **RIV 11**
luif: Land on my l., an' bring Siller tae me **ANI 8**
Luss: everybody goes to see . . . Loch Katrine,
   then comes round by L. **CUR 13**
luxuries: Our diet was . . . a great number of l.
   which we did not know to be l. **FOO 96**
luxury: l. which only a highly developed
   civilisation can command **ANI 85**
   only when I'm at home that I forgo The l. of
   knowing who I am **THO 80**
   that they might live in idleness and l., the
   labouring mass has starved **POL 56**
   warrior . . . should not care for wine or l.
   WAR 93
   Wherever l. ceases to be innocent **ADV 77**
lyon: ane reid Lyoun rampand in ane field of gold
   HER 1
lyric: sacrifice a million people any day for one
   immortal l. **BOA 9**

M

McAdam: M., hail! Hail Roadian! **PER 142**
Mac an t-Saoir, Donnchadh Bàn: D.B.M.,
   commonly known as Duncan Bàn MacIntyre,
   wrote a song **M-W 75**
MacBrayne's: end of the world is near when the
   M. ship will be on time **TRA 40**

Except the Western Isles alone, And they are all M. TRA 3

McConnachie: M. . . . name I give to the unruly half of myself PER 36

MacCrimmon: M. asked the other lad why he did not play like Iain Dall MUS 50
    M. would write down a tune on the wet sand MUS 33
    Patrick Mor M. and Duncan Ban M. in the centre MUS 47

MacDonald: I think the clan Donell must be rooted out POL 100

Macdonald, Flora: To see Mr Samuel Johnson salute Miss F.M. was a wonderful romantic scene MOM 4

Macdonald, J. Ramsay: classic instance of the man who lingered overlong in public affairs PER 150
    every Duchess in London will be wanting to kiss me! POL 65
    largest amount of words into the smallest amount of thought PER 81
    M. nervously asked Shinwell if there was an escape route to the rear POL 97

MacDonalds: approached Hirta with the M. leading by a few yards BOA 7
    M. will fall in this net POL 101
    Yow are herby ordered to fall upon the rebells, the M. of Glenco POL 35

Macduff: Actors . . . tell tales of, for example, M. ACT 3
    'Far be't fae me to lichtlie M' PLA 101

McFarlane: I dinna like M., I'm safe enough tae state PER 245

Macfarlanes: I knew he was one of the M. PER 194

MacGregor: My foot is on my native heath, and my name is M. PER 213

MacInnes, Hamish: 'How do you know this rope is safe, H.?' MOU 35

McKay: Hiram Teufelsdrockh A septary of Clan McKay COS 27
    I . . . give to Mackay a right to Kilmahunaig LAW 20

Mackenzie: Yonder's the tomb o' wise M. fam'd PER 102

Mackintosh, Charles Rennie: M. was never merely original ART 25

Mackintosh: 'What sort of game are ye after, M.?' PER 92

Mackintosh of Raigmore: he begged to intimate to him that he *was* M. of R. MOM 34

Maclean, Sir Hector: Another for H.! WAR 42

McLeans: Leave the M. to Argyll POL 100

Macleods: M. of Harris and the MacDonalds of Uist, both desirous of owning St Kilda BOA 7

Macneill: M. of Barra has dined – the rest of the world may dine now BOA 12

MacPherson, James: M.'s time will not be long On yonder gallows tree LAM 21

MacPherson, James: All hail, M.! Hail to thee, Sire of Ossian! POET 71

Mr J.M., I received your foolish and impudent letter INS 50

machair: good m. . . . grows not grass but flowers NAT 23

machines: M. of death from west to east WAR 88

mad: half the people standing one day at the Cross of Edinburgh were m. MIN 38
    one half of the nation is mad MIN 46
    Some deemed him wondrous wise, and some believed him m. PER 39

madman: he is a m. who has the misfortune not to be a Gentleman INS 76

madness: as great m. as to starve ourselves FAM 8
    If he is to avoid m., he must . . . deride himself and his colleagues MIN 10
    liquid m. FOO 36
    m. is but one of God's pale winters MIN 36
    M. need not be all breakdown MIN 35

Mag: 'What, what?' quo' M., 'must it thus be my doom' M-W 122

Maggie: Blaw your warst, ye wind and rain, Since M., now, I'm in aside ye M-W 121

maggots: Ye m., make your windings BOO 15

magic: it had long signified m. with magical effect WORD 10
    lightsome play of every m. fraud PER 23
    m. moment when the sun balances on the rim of the world MOM 11
    Wee M. Stane SPIR 36
    when in Salamanca's cave, Him listed his m. wand to wave PER 210

magnetic: if there is not a distinct m. sense, I say it is a very great wonder MIN 32

Magnus Merriman: M., lurching forward on his belly, thrust his bayonet WAR 51

Magnus, St: jewel of great price, St M. Cathedral BUI 5

maid: 'A laddie,' said the m. M-W 106
    brooding boy and sighing m., Wholly fain and half afraid M-W 116
    Don't grow up a nervous old m. ADV 120
    I once was a m., tho' I cannot tell when WAR 28
    not a m., wife or widow whose fancy any man, if he set himself to it, could not conquer M-W 65
    sweetest still to wife or m., Was Whistle o'er the lave o't MUS 13
    when eer ye meet a pretty m., And two miles from a town M-W 89

maiden: asked by two m. ladies . . . what I was to be BOO 7
    Grant that my brow may wear Beneath its m.'s snood Love to distressed Mankind THO 33
    m. was the hostess, The guest her son THO 125
    time to sharp the m. for shearing o' craigs and thrapples HUM 12
    sweetest m. I ever kissed DEA 10
    whom it would be possible to mistake for the m. sister of the curate PER 89

maidens: And the young fair m. Quiet eyes
HIGH 43
   Farewell, merry m. SEA 25
   Maydens of England, sore may ye morne
   BOA 1
   Of all thir m. mild as meid LOVE 13
maids: She cam' tripping adown the stair, And
all her m. before her FANT 11
   We must have labour, and hunger . . . Ere
   we dance with the m. of Dunrossness again
   SEA 25
Mairi: Plenty bonny bairns as weel, That's the
toast for M. TOA 20
Majesty: His M.'s dominions, on which the sun
never sets ADV 98
makar: Lea him at last outgang wi mockerie,
The M. macaronical! POET 62
maker: Garskadden's been with his M. these twa
hours DEA 54
   thumb-mark of his M. was wet in the clay of him
   PER 93
male: when a m. child was christened, his right
hand should be excluded HIGH 19
malison: My m. light ilka day On them that
drink and dinna pay CUR 21
malisons: All the malesouns and waresouns that
ever gat warldlie creature CUR 17
   M., m., mair than ten ANI 39
Malkies: Whit'll ye dae when the wee M. come
BOA 14
Mally: M.'s meek, M.'s sweet PER 62
malt: fine m. . . . not too strongly reminiscent of
the peat FOO 55
malts: single m. must be drunk with
circumspection FOO 62
mamma: he isn't m.'s baby any more CHI 4
mammal: most important m. of all ANI 47
mammy: his m.'ll gie him cockie-ridey-rosey
CHI 42
   Sittin' on your m.'s knee CHI 5
Mamore: Between us and the mountains of M.
lay the Leven valley MOU 30
man: always look under the bed . . . To see if
there's a m. about M-W 126
   architecture . . . expression of the needs and
   beliefs of m. BUI 19
   as nearly to the idea of a perfectly wise and
   virtuous m. PER 223
   'ass long ass ye ken the m. at the door and talk
   the Gaalic' MUS 59
   Before my breath . . . M. and his marvels pass
   away TIM 27
   bold m. who first swallowed an oyster FOO 74
   brain of m. most surely did invent REL 91
   Burns of all poets is the most a M. BUR 22
   Burns summed up what the common poor m.
   feels BUR 5
   country above all . . . in which a m.
   of imagination may carve out his own
   pleasures LAND 61
   Death! the poor m.'s dearest friend DEA 17
   declared he would kill the first m. that put a
   hand on him LAW 16

distracted man . . . in a distracted time
PER 25
even children lisp the Rights of M. M-W 45
Every m. has a sane spot somewhere MIN 50
Every m. proper for a member of this Society
must have a frank, honest, open heart
M-W 37
Every m. that is high up loves to think he has
done it himself M-W 26
Few are thy days and full of woe, O m.
REL 22
first of all problems for a m. to find out what
kind of work he is to do DAI 13
Give a m. a pipe he can smoke BOO 71
give me the young m. who has brains enough
to make a fool of himself YOU 28
God to m. doth speak in solitude HIGH 6
Good claret . . . makes a m. baith gash and
bauld FOO 105
Good lord, what is m.? HUM 5
He has never in verse addressed anything to
the immortal part of m. POET 70
he was a good m. to her FAMI 17
He was a m. of no smeddum in discourse
PER 111
He was a strong m., grimly silent DEA 20
heart of m. was made to reconcile
contradictions HUM 10
Help us to play the m. REL 121
Her prentice han' she tried on m., And then
she made the lasses M-W 38
Here lies a m. a woman rul'd M-W 46
Himself and his strong men to m. her TRA 36
I am a very promising young m. PER 20
'I am patient, young m.,' Munro bagger said
MOU 6
I can lie wi' another m.'s lass BOA 3
I dinna think I was ever what could be called a
funny m. PER 112
I heard an auld m. blaw his horn ANI 5
I saw a dead m. win a fight FANT 13
I see the rectangular blocks of m.'s insolent
mechanical ignorance rise UNI 10
I think no m. fit to live that is not fit to die
DEA 11
If a m. were permitted to make all the ballads
LAW 11
If any m. wants to be happy . . . get a public
allowance for travelling TRA 10
if ever a m. proposes to serve and merit well of
his country PER 164
If I am a great m., then all great men are
frauds PER 156
I'm a m. that gets through with my day's
business PER 238
I'm not the m. to see my own side lose for
want of a little help SPOR 39
In marriage, a m. becomes slack and selfish
M-W 119
in the cleft of heaven I scan The giant form of
a naked m. FANT 37
In the true Literary M., there is thus ever . . .
a sacredness BOO 21

Instinct right, reflection wrong, When you get a m. to sing a song **MUS 48**

It is indeed strange, that any m. of sense could have imagined it possible **POET 32**

It takes a wise m. to handle a lie **BAD 2**

Jock McGraw, The stoutest m. in the Forty-Twa **WAR 13**

less nonsense in his head than any m. living **PER 222**

Let one be to the other just as when the world began, In universal fellowship and brotherhood of m. **POL 108**

liberty . . . which no honest m. will lose but with his life **SPIR 2**

life of every m. is a diary **BIO 2**

like a little old m. with enormous white eyebrows **ANI 30**

like a m. washing his hands **INS 88**

little society is necessary to show a m. his failings **PPL 94**

made love and made war ere the making of M. **ANI 53**

M. alone is a perennial drudge **THO 36**

M. alone seems to be the only creature . . . arrived to the natural size **PPL 43**

m. could go on being a m. till he dropped into his grave **M-W 83**

m. does well to rid himself of a turd **INS 38**

m. gazing at the stars **ADV 124**

m. has fought blindly for his own ultimate interest **LAND 24**

M.! I'm lookin weel **ANI 92**

M. is a creature who lives . . . principally by catchwords **WORD 72**

m. is born, a man dies **LAM 31**

m. had gone between it and its mother **ANI 47**

M. thinks more, woman feels more **M-W 69**

m. to m., the world o'er, Shall brothers be **HOP 5**

m. was made to mourn **LAM 22**

m. who can overcome his own terror is a hero **ADV 88**

m. who has been able to furnish a book **BOO 10**

m. who is shouting beyond the strait is not a m. of refined sentiment **PER 21**

M. will go down into the pit and all his thoughts will perish **LAM 16**

m. with God is always in the majority **REL 69**

M.'s extremity is God's opportunity **REL 20**

M.'s unhappiness . . . comes of his Greatness **REL 35**

most romantic, the only romantic, m. I have ever met **LOVE 67**

My sharp tongue will shrivel any m. **M-W 87**

Nature must produce a m. **COS 38**

No great m. lives in vain **HIS 10**

no m. could be charged with theft of as much meat as he could carry **LAW 14**

no m. is useless while he has a friend **FRI 26**

No m. is wiser than another **ADV 91**

no mood to which a m. may not administer the appropriate medicine **BOO 5**

not a maid, wife or widow whose fancy any m. . . . could not conquer **M-W 65**

not many works . . . worth the price of a pound of tobacco to a m. of limited means **BOO 63**

not perhaps before time that I asked myself what that m. had to do with my life **MOM 23**

not true that woman was made from m.'s rib **M-W 25**

O Knox he was a bad m. **PER 144**

Of the things which m. can do or make here below **BOO 19**

one equality between m. and m. which will strenuously be taught **REL 40**

one of the most remarkable dialects ever spoken by m. **WORD 21**

only happy m. **ADV 105**

or ever he came a m. to be **SCI 30**

poor m.'s richest legacy **EPI 24**

prisoner killit not the particular m. aforesaid **LAW 10**

rotting on the ground, of little use to M. or Beast **LAM 55**

Self-respect is the noblest garment with which a m. may clothe himself **THO 109**

similitude In dissimilitude, M.'s sole delight **POET 31**

skin of a m. of letters is peculiarly sensitive **BOO 61**

sober, discreet . . . good-natured m. of a bad character **PER 143**

soul of m. is like the rolling world **REL 114**

stand my ground as long as I have a m. remaining with me **BOA 20**

Stumpie believ't nor in Gode nor m. **PER 173**

sun is thin Like an auld m. deein slow **SWW 43**

That m. is little to be envied . . . whose piety would not grow warmer among the ruins of Iona **PLA 83**

that m.'s the quaintest work of Almighty God **PER 123**

That title from a better m. I stole **POET 66**

There lives no m. who understands his Gaelic **INS 67**

There was a m. lived in the moon **PER 19**

therefore a just *political* maxim, that *every m. must be supposed a knave* **POL 51**

thing nae m. can bide, An' he be human **M-W 103**

to rock the bairn, That's to grow a m., That's to lay me **FANT 5**

Tree of Life between M. and Woman **M-W 53**

Turn them out the best you can, Then dae the same thing for your m. **M-W 109**

uttered part of a m.'s life . . . bears to the unuttered a small . . . proportion **MIN 16**

Vanity . . . outlives the m. **ADV 32**

What is m.? A foolish baby **M-W 58**

Wonderful m.! I long to get drunk with him **PER 57**

she seemed in a mortal body . . . a true
goddess **PER 55**

Montaigne . . . met M. as favourite daughter-
in-law of the King **PER 105**

one that dealt with M.Q.o.S. when that lady
paraded in a Glengarry **TEL 14**

'Queen M. was a strumpet and a murtherer'
MOM 32

thanks be to God, I despise death **DEA 47**

we call her nott a hoore **PER 153**

well-intentioned but hysterical poodle
PER 122

mask: stupendous m. shaped like a beak **ANI 30**

Maskull: 'What's that?' called out M. **MOM 26**

master: An' his m.'s name was Cain **TOA 7**

beyond a certain point T'nowhead was m. in
his own house **FOO 12**

Blackamoor first to m. me **FANT 58**

gude sign o' a dowg . . . when his face grows
like his m.'s **ANI 49**

His one desire is to be M. of the Art of Life
PER 105

I ken when I hae a gude m. **DAI 48**

if we gang to sea, m., I fear we'll come to
harm **FANT 12**

ilka maister o' a faamily had his ain sate
FAMI 13

In good company you need not ask who is m.
of the feast **FOO 72**

maid maister but in mows **INS 36**

m. looked on and annexed the corpses of the
slaughtered fowls **SPOR 30**

m. race and it's almost run **ADV 78**

They tell their m. is a knave **INS 16**

Those crofter carles may cross the sea, but we
are m. here **LAND 8**

unfortunate for the Scottish ballads that . . .
the m. of romance himself was head of the
enterprise **POET 69**

masters: Let your m. come and attack us: we are
ready to meet them **SPIR 56**

masturbation: Spiritual m. of the worst
description **INS 63**

mate: Great Artificer made my m. **BATH 26**

In spouseless solitude without a m. **M-W 122**

mathematics: He ever loved the M. **SCI 8**

matrimony: M . . . no more than a sort of
friendship recognised by the police **FAMI 34**

Mauchline: Lament him, M. husbands a' **EPI 16**

mausoleum: object of the Duchess . . . was to
provide a m. **BUI 25**

people of Dumfries . . . with their pompous
m. **BUR 27**

Maxton, James: Jimmy M., his hair growing
longer, lanker and greasier each year **POL 18**

May: Butter, new cheese, and beer in M.
SWW 56

For mirth of M., wyth skippis and wyth
hoppis **SWW 30**

Lusty M., that moder is of flouris **SWW 31**

spangled with vowels as a meadow with
daisies in the month of M. **WORD 50**

meadow: in a m. the first fountain of silvery
Tweed rises **RIV 12**

My m. lies green, And my corn is unshorn
LAM 10

On the m. and the mountains Calmly shine
the winter stars **MOM 1**

Meadowbank, Lord: When L.M. was yet Mr
Maconochie **LAW 12**

meadows: All through the m. the horses and
cattle **TRA 42**

Teviot round his m. flowing **EPI 21**

meal: it is the m. of the day, the m. par excellence
FOO 59

Means Test Man: Don't try to dodge me if you
can . . . I'm the M.T.M. **PER 18**

Mearns: He . . . lit a fire in the M. that illumines
Scotland **EPI 20**

meat: No man could be charged with theft of as
much m. as he could carry **LAW 14**

Of Scotland's king I haud my hoose, He pays
me m. and fee **SPIR 46**

Some hae m. and canna eat **FOO 19**

They have got no m. these two days, and we
have nothing to give them **LAM 55**

mechanics: M., not microbes, are the menace to
civilisation **MIN 22**

medical: at the m. exam, the doctor said, 'You're
not very big downstairs' **WAR 36**

Beaton m. family in Skye **MIN 17**

His m. interest and sympathy were aroused
MIN 43

m. men all over the world having merely
entered into a tacit agreement **MIN 15**

medicine: in m . . . an almost unavoidable error
in the hospital physician **MIN 10**

no mood to which a man may not administer
the appropriate m. **BOO 5**

seasonable fit of illness is an excellent m.
MIN 47

mediocrity: I'm terrified . . . of the celebration of
m. in Scotland **TEL 4**

many an original composition corrected into
m. **POET 58**

M. knows nothing higher than itself **ADV 59**

M. weighed dully on his mind, like a migraine
PER 175

Such M. was ne'er on view, Bolster'd by
tireless Scottish Ballyhoo **PPL 73**

meed: love of the fair is the m. of the brave
ADV 102

meek: In times of peace, m. as a monk was he
PER 132

in wealth be meik **ADV 73**

Mally's m., Mally's sweet **PER 62**

Meg: M. up and walloped ower the green, For
brawly could she frisk it **MUS 74**

Weel mounted on his grey mare, M. **ANI 25**

melancholy: No marvel one is m. **THO 133**

One cannot but be conscious of an underlying
m. in Scotswomen **PPL 91**

Sour M. night and day provokes Her own
eternal wound **MIN 4**

Whatten ane glaikit fule am I To slay myself
with m. LOVE 74

Where I entombed in m. sink LAM 19

melody: He heard a heavenly m. and sound
MUS 35

My luve is like a m. That's sweetly play'd in
tune LOVE 27

melon: the moist m. BATH 5

Melrose: If thou would'st view fair M. aright
PLA 102

Melville, Andrew: Knox and M. clapped their
preaching palms HIS 31

'Pray to God for me, Melvyll' PER 181

member: annibaptist is not a thing I am a m. of
REL 53

happiness of man . . . to state himself as the m.
of a community PHIL 14

M. of Parliament, naked among the branches
of a tree MOM 27

members: about one half of the Scottish nation
regarded themselves as m. of the aristocracy
PPL 50

like a man washing his hands; the Scotch m.
don't know what he is doing INS 88

no society can surely be flourishing . . . of
which the far greater part of the m. are poor
and miserable PHIL 53

obvious itch in your privie m. INS 5

our nation is unjust to half its m. M-W 95

People of Scotland, as m. of one of the oldest
nations in Europe POL 6

taking great care not to confront . . . stares
from m. of the ordinary people MUS 40

memories: leave their m. to resurrect it when
they find their own thoughts inadequate
EDU 20

memory: deathless names by this dead snake
defiled Bid m. spit upon him BIO 13

fierce native daring which instils The stirring
m. of a thousand years WAR 32

Here continueth to stink The m. of the Duke
of Cumberland INS 8

I shall carry its m. as well as its marks to the
grave BIO 8

I've a grand m. for forgetting ADV 135

In the hush of the night-time I hear them go
by, The horses of m. MOM 35

indebted to his m. for his jests, and to his
imagination for his facts INS 87

m. of Burns – I am afraid heaven and earth
have taken too good care of it BUR 8

people who are forever consecrating the m. of
the departed YOU 13

there is nothing to lose but m. YOU 17

Things past belong to m. alone ADV 76

men: All things to all m. only fools will tell
THO 15

all things to all m., providing the price is right
PER 228

And still my delight is in proper young m.
WAR 28

Best of M. have ever loved Repose THO 130

best opposite sex that m. have got M-W 107

'Beware of m. bearing flowers' PER 233

Clever m. are good, but they are not the best
M-W 56

Converse with m. makes sharp the glittering
wit HIGH 6

even steam . . . will in m.'s eyes A trifle seem
FANT 51

Fortune is not so blind as m. are FAM 11

four classes: noblemen, gentlemen, gigmen,
and m. M-W 59

great m. says that their distress Comis for the
peoples wickedness HUM 11

greit m. reignis at thair awin libertie HIS 21

hardy and intrepid race of m. HIGH 37

Himself and his strong m. to man her TRA 36

history of the world is but the biographies of
great m. HIS 10

I am washing the shrouds of the fair m.
LAM 1

I have asked grace at a graceless face, But
there is nane for my m. and me LAM 9

I wander in the ways of m., Alike unknowing
and unknown YOU 3

If I am a great man, then all great m. are
frauds PER 156

If it is for fame that m. do brave actions
FAM 12

is it not to Clothes that most m. do reverence?
COS 15

league between us written in . . . flesh and
skin of m. HIS 12

leal and thrifty m. and wives LAM 28

Let m. find the faith that builds mountains
REL 79

Love rules . . . m. below and saints above
LOVE 78

medical m. . . . having merely entered into a
tacit agreement MIN 15

M. and m.'s government are only daidlin' and
dandlin' wi' the business M-W 93

m. are immortal till their work is done
ADV 83

m. are never so good or so bad as their
opinions ADV 90

m. . . . can sympathetically eat together
FOO 37

M., even the good ones, are kittle cattle
M-W 66

m. of better clay and finer mould Know
nature SPOR 9

m. of sorrow, and acquainted with Grieve
BOO 52

'M., remember there is no retreat from here'
WAR 94

m. were just a perfect nuisance M-W 83

m. who don't pay to watch football SPOR 35

Multitude of Wights, like furious hardie M.
FANT 40

my mother asked . . . how do you keep m.
happy M-W 115

O Kenmure's lads are m., Willie WAR 30

Our business is like m. to fight WAR 64

real leader of m. . . . afraid to go anywhere by himself **ADV 72**

saddle your horses, and call out your m. **BOA 16**

seed o' a' the m. that in My virgin womb ha'e met **M-W 92**

slaughtered m. Fight fiercer in their orphans o'er again **PPL 26**

souls of m. that pave their hell-ward path with women's souls lose immortality **M-W 64**

They are a song in the blood of all true m. **WAR 52**

They would have all m. bound and thrall **M-W 110**

To . . . leave your m. in sic a state **WAR 82**

20,000 m. might yet be raised in that country **WAR 71**

vein of poetry exists in the hearts of all m. **POET 13**

We are the m. Who own your glen **LAND 38**

We have intercourse openly with the best m. **M-W 27**

We want 'safe' m. here, you know **UNI 9**

wham ne'er a toon surpasses, For honest m. and bonny lasses **PLA 15**

whan he gar'd it waggle, Baith m. and beast were feared **PER 231**

wind inflate in other mennis ears **ADV 75**

You come to London to wrestle with so many celebrated m. **ART 8**

Mendelssohn-Bartholdy, Felix: M.'s sisters asked him to tell them something about the Hebrides **MUS 43**

Menstrie: to think on the Braes o' M. It maks my heart fu' sair **PLA 103**

Mephistopheles: tufted eyebrows that went up at the corners like those of M. **PER 113**

mercies: all thy m., such as they are **REL 11**

remember me and mine, Wi' m. temporal and divine **REL 27**

Salmon . . . one of the m. best taken with an uninquisitive appetite **ANG 11**

Mercury: these guides or messengers . . . exercised the functions of M. **BIO 9**

mercy: at the m. of the puddles in the road **ADV 124**

living or the dead No m. find **PER 69**

Lord have m. on my poor country **SPIR 22**

waves have some m., but the rocks have no m. at all **SEA 1**

We'll have what God in his m. may send us, woman **M-W 70**

merit: I sought for m. wherever it was to be found **HIGH 37**

if ever a man proposes to . . . m. well of his country **PER 164**

Rights of Woman m. some attention **M-W 45**

Merlin: O M. in your crystal cave **CUR 20**

mermaids: shore was cold with m. and angels **FANT 19**

merry: Be m., man **ADV 62**

fit of laughter quite m. to behold **FRI 8**

I felt not unpersuaded . . . That I'd spent a m. Christmas **FES 8**

I'll be m. and free. I'll be sad for naebody **THO 21**

king sat down and began to be m., but Aidan . . . began to shed tears **PER 42**

m. m. shriek of the reel **ANG 1**

truly ludicrous. Dr Johnson and I afterwards were m. on it **M-W 30**

With his butt of sherry To keep him m. **POET 4**

messages: M. run down this close **COM 2**

Mester Stoorworm: M.S., the largest . . . of all sea serpents **MONS 4**

metaphor: coldest word was once a glowing new m. **WORD 15**

Each object hides in a m. **WORD 31**

Presbyterian faith is an incomparable m. **REL 14**

something they believed to be a m. for their pride **SPOR 52**

metaphysics: M. I detested . . . an elaborate, diabolical invention **PHIL 1**

method: At last David said, 'I think I have a m. of waking him' **MOM 32**

I did not invent this m. piecemeal but all at once **SCI 44**

my own m. of controlling them was by slavish bribery **ANI 45**

Scotch m. of making every duty dismal **ADV 96**

usewall M. . . . is to put his left Foot under the Wizard's right Foot **FANT 40**

middle-class: m.-c. if you wore your dentures in mid-week **FAMI 36**

'm.c.' , that is, people with ideas above their station **FAMI 30**

midges: mitches are troublesome **ANI 83**

midnight: elves at m. hour are seen **FANT 43**

nightingale, That sits up till m. without any ale **ANI 54**

tendency to regard the high m. of the Border Reiver as a stirring, gallant episode **HIS 16**

milk: flees 'll be droonin' themselves in your m. bowl **FOO 8**

he died, seated, with a bowl of m. on his knee **DEA 22**

he went round with the m. of human kindness **PER 127**

I'll m. it for all its worth **ART 19**

in spite of their entire dependence on cheese, flesh and m. **HIGH 16**

Lest witches should obtain the power Of Hawkie's m. **CUR 3**

M. the ewes, Lassie! Let nane o' them gae! **LOVE 70**

say they inhabit a land of m. and honey **HIGH 12**

Mill, James: In 1817 J.M. was beginning to plan the *Analysis of the Human Mind* **MIN 53**

Mill, John Stuart: M. had borrowed that first volume of my poor *French Revolution* **MOM 14**

mill: Aboon the neuk frae Sprottie's m. **FAMI 5**

m. of Dolphinton, being eager to have a railway through his parish **TRA 16**

m. made a comic speech **REL 94**

M. said it wald dee, The cypress buss I plantit **BOA 25**

m.'s voice spread a pollution of bad beliefs **REL 85**

'Now away you and say that to the M.' **WORD 60**

'Oh,' said the m., '. . . there's a hantle o' miscellawneous eating aboot a pig' **FOO 107**

on the scaffold he said goodbye to the m. **BOO 9**

she was a m.'s sister **M-W 98**

smug, trim, smooth little m. **REL 73**

they will say, I wish we had the m. in the midst of it **FOO 35**

They've stickit the m., hanged the precentor **PLA 35**

two classes that mek ahl the mischief . . . are weemen and meenisters **PPL 15**

What a pity . . . you're now dead, for here's the m. come to see you **DEA 34**

when the last m. is strangled with the last copy of the *Sunday Post* **JOU 14**

ministers: good m. and elders . . . broke and burned their instruments **MUS 29**

highest impertinence . . . in kings and m., to pretend to watch over the economy of private people **PHIL 57**

preposterous humility of our puritan m. **POL 53**

minny: little did her auld m. ken **LOVE 14**

minstrels: Hearken, my m.! **MUS 72**

miracle: No testimony is sufficient to establish a m., unless **SCI 18**

Time . . . is forever very literally a m. **TIM 12**

miracles: *Christian Religion* not only was at first attended by m. **REL 63**

m. are the light in legendary form **FANT 32**

'Nonsense,' her father had countered, for he had no faith in m. **MIN 33**

misery: How easily a small inconvenience can . . . make us forget the m. of a universe **THO 117**

it being the mean to finish my sin and m. **DEA 10**

M. of any kind is not the *cause* of Immorality **PHIL 8**

no complete m. . . . . that does not emanate from the bowels **MIN 14**

omnipresent m. n pain in your mind n body **MIN 55**

missiles: some throwing of objectionable . . . m. **BIO 8**

mission: human sacrifice would be necessary for his m. **FANT 49**

mist: Alas, before we could reach the hilltop the m. swept in **MOU 19**

land of meanness, sophistry and m. **LAND 12**

m. like hair hangs over One barren breast **MOM 53**

Must we be thirled to the past, to the m. and the unused shieling? **SPIR 41**

on lonely paths, through m., and cloud, and foam **MOM 44**

On Tintock-tap there is a m. **MOU 1**

picture of Glen Sannox, with m. resting among the mountains **SCI 24**

Something of a doubtful m. hangs over these Highland traditions **PPL 38**

they lasted but as a breath, a m. of fog in the hills **LAND 27**

This, I suppose, was a genuine scotch m. **SWW 39**

mistake: capital m. to theorise before one has data **SCI 11**

he who never made a m. never made a discovery **PHIL 49**

mistresses: They are absolute m. of their houses **M-W 21**

misty: From the lone shieling on the m. island **SPIR 3**

in Skye, Over the m. sea, oh **ANI 52**

northern wind had . . . shed the m. cloudis fra the sky **SWW 41**

mither: curse of hell frae me sall ye bear, M., m. **CUR 8**

Down ran his old m., Greetin' fu' sair **LAM 10**

gude auld honest m. tongue! They kent nae ither, auld or young **WORD 37**

I gave her ma m.'s engagement ring **LOVE 47**

if they had mind when his m. used to work in the tawtie field **REL 94**

little did my m. ken, The day she cradled me **LAM 8**

my sweetheart's m. is a moolie besom **FAMI 26**

O my m., John Frost cam' yestreen **SWW 66**

Sic a toom howe is in the breist O' their sair forjaskit m. **PPL 89**

We're first fittin' ma m. **FES 13**

What'll I get when ma m. kens? **THO 61**

Mither-tongue: M.-t. Has had the melancholy fate **WORD 28**

moaning: What is that melodious m. we hear in the west? **ANI 72**

mob: former hangman . . . had died from severe treatment by a m. **DEA 48**

moderation: hypocrisy, in m., is oil to the wheels **ADV 22**

M. is my rule **FOO 4**

Moderator: M. was the great Dr Archie Craig **REL 116**

modern: absurd to think it is the duty of the m. architect to make believe he is living . . . one thousand years before **BUI 19**

all the novelists ancient and m. **BOO 12**

castles of the chiefs . . . contained very few of the comforts . . . of m. life **BUI 22**

few *m.* Scoticisms which are not barbarisms **WORD 61**

indifferent about the modes and habits of the m. world **PER 83**

Mackintosh invented . . . almost the whole vocabulary of the m. movement **ART 25**

not the remotest reason why the majority of
  m. Scottish writers should be considered
  Scots at all **BOO 33**
Only the m. Scotsman . . . and a few other
  favoured races **REL 48**
printing press is either the greatest blessing or
  the greatest curse of m. times **JOU 1**
That's very m., and I dare say very clever
  HUMO 14
their role in m. Scotland is non-existent
  FAMI 15
modest: As I took particular pleasure in the
  company of m. women **M-W 81**
  Mally's m. and discreet **PER 62**
  unassuming, m. . . . the white rose of Scotland
    SPIR 24
  Wi' m. face, sae fu' o' grace, replies the
    bonnie lady **M-W 16**
modesty: They feared the loss of something . . .
  m.? **MIN 12**
molecule: Each m. . . . bears impressed upon it
  the stamp of a metric system **SCI 37**
molecules: Maxwell, by a train of argument
  which seems to bear no relation at all to m.
  SCI 21
  m. with fierce desires **SCI 35**
  No theory of evolution can . . . account for the
    similarity of m. **SCI 37**
moment: I dared contemplate a m. of time
  Without compassion **WAR 91**
  I was, at that m., in possession of . . . the
    principal object of my ambition **MOM 6**
  magic m. when the sun balances on the rim of
    the world **MOM 11**
  Or like the snowfall on the river, A m. white
    PLEAS 4
  present m. is our ain, The neist we never saw
    TIM 5
moments: We do that in our zeal our calmer m.
  would be afraid to answer **THO 104**
  what the common poor man feels in widely-
    severed m. of exaltation, insight and
    desperation **BUR 5**
Monach Isles: good machair, like that of
  Berneray, or of the M.I. **NAT 23**
monarch: good-natured m. cried heartily
  himself **DEA 59**
  Gothic m. and the Pictish peer **INS 22**
  unfortunate m., whose head was executed as
    ruthlessly on canvas **ART 16**
Monday: he's no been at skül frae last Moninday
  WORD 68
money: Business . . . becomes the sale of m.
  DAI 19
  club would make more m. if we *didn't* perform
    ACT 9
  considering the m. was due by one Poet, for
    putting a tombstone over another **POET 8**
  fool and his m. are soon parted **ADV 27**
  I have all the m. I want and he hasn't **THO 94**
  if life were a thing m. could buy **EPI 3**
  if you'd all the same m. one day, what would it
    be the next? **PHIL 16**

No Chancellor until this one has . . . said that
  because he has m. available . . . the rich will
  get the benefits **POL 19**
monk: Devil was sick – the Devil a m. would be
  REL 99
  In times of peace, meek as a m. was he
    PER 132
monks: instead of m.s' voices shall be lowing of
  cattle **PLA 82**
  O ay, the M., the m., they did the mischief!
    REL 111
Mons Meg: M. M. is a monument of our pride
  and poverty. **SPIR 54**
monster: m. of Loch Ness is probably the lost
  soul of Glasgow **PLA 64**
  m., which was lying in the river bed . . .
    suddenly comes up **MONS 6**
  Thou many-headed m.-thing, O who would
    wish to be thy king? **PPL 84**
Montrose: place existing parallel to M. and yet
  fundamentally different **FANT 65**
  setting where the wind of the spirit had
    freedom to blow? **PLA 104**
Montrose, Marquis of: fell out on me
  publikye . . . that I had killed erle of M. **INS 51**
  his behaviour . . . was as great and firm to the
    last **PER 58**
monument: Abbotsford . . . surely the strangest
  and saddest m. that Scott's genius created
  BUI 23
  Dundee . . . completest m. in the entire
    continent of human folly **PLA 31**
  Mons Meg is a m. of our pride and poverty
    SPIR 54
  m. o' strength and grace Til the dour age o'
    coal and steam **BUI 29**
mood: no m. to which a man may not administer
  the appropriate medicine **BOO 5**
moon: auld m. chowin' sin **WORD 75**
  auld mune shak's her gowden feathers
    THO 70
  by the feeble light of the m., we see the spirits
    of our ancestors **POET 27**
  Good claret . . . heaves his saul beyond the
    m. **FOO 105**
  Good even, good fair m., good even to thee
    CUR 24
  He fell as the m. in a storm **LAM 39**
  He saw neither sun nor mune **FANT 10**
  I know that all beneath the m. decays **TIM 17**
  I saw the new m. late yestreen, Wi' the auld m.
    in her arm **FANT 12**
  line o' the Lang Whang Road, Wi' the mune
    on the sky's eebree **PLA 92**
  like a full m. seen through a dark haze **COS 47**
  No soul am I, a wave am I, And sing the
    M.-Child's hymn **THO 83**
  Nor hear the clapper o' the mune **FANT 61**
  not a m. has ever shone . . . But to my soul is
    gone **THO 75**
  Perhaps the M. is shining for you **SWW 2**
  sea, I think, is lazy, It just obeys the m.
    THO 44

There was a man lived in the m. **PER 19**
wan m. is setting behind the white wave
  DEA 16
What a lovely, lovely m. **NAT 14**
wood was sere, the m. i' the wane **FANT 35**
you light up your face, new m. of the seasons
  SWW 3
moonlight: On her consummate forehead lay
  The m. of eternal peace **BATH 3**
  'There will be m. again' **WAR 69**
moons: like m. in a misty sky **ANI 13**
moor: thy bleak m. . . . shall be stained with the
  best blood **FANT 21**
moorland: heavy on the slumber of the m. The
  hardship and poverty **LAND 41**
  Sweet be thy matin o'er m. and lea! **ANI 50**
  while the God of m. walks abroad **SWW 44**
moorlands: m. infinitely rich in little-
  appreciated beauties **NAT 17**
moors: Blows the wind on the m. today and now
  LAND 58
moose: she caught a m. within the hoose **ANI 3**
Morag: M., harbinger of death **MONS 5**
  O little M. A-climbing bens **CUR 7**
morality: no quite good book without a good m.
  BOO 64
morals: If thy m. make thee dreary **PHIL 61**
Moray Firth: rievin' ower the M.F. It lifts the
  gangrel snaw **SWW 44**
morn: brassic till the rent cheque hits the mat
  the m. **DAI 61**
  kept the same with great groaning and
    torment till the m. **MIN 25**
  Let me have your answer, aff or on, the m.,
    and nae mair about it **M-W 32**
  This m. is merry June, I trow **LAM 53**
  We'll maybe meet again the m. **TOA 15**
morning: but on the next m. **DEA 61**
  But with the m. cool repentance came
    MOM 38
  dew sat chilly on her breast, Sae early in the
    m. **ANI 23**
  Early in the mornin', wi' a clear e'e **SWW 62**
  group of miners stood in a ring every Sunday
    m. **SPOR 59**
  I wakened in the m., On an alien lobby mat
    FES 8
  Let m. walks . . . have an end **ADV 65**
  love . . . fades away like m. dew **LOVE 6**
  magnificent to rise in the m. in such a place
    MOU 17
  New-laid eggs every m. by me **COM 2**
  Oh, it's nice to get up in the mornin' **DAI 36**
  On a cold and frosty m. **ANI 2**
  People talk of early m. in the country
    THO 84
  To come wi' the news o' your ain defeat . . .
    Sae early in the m. **WAR 82**
  tyrant on the throne is the m. and evening
    press **JOU 6**
  up in the mornin's no for me **THO 53**
Morningside: all around Newington and M., the
  dismallest structures keep springing up **BUI 33**

mortal: doings here below That m. ne'er should
  ken **FANT 38**
  No scene of m. life but teems with m. woe
    THO 107
  she seemed in a m. body . . . a true goddess
    PER 55
mortals: barrenest of all m. is the sentimentalist
  M-W 57
  most indolent of m. and of poets **PER 135**
  what by m. in this world is brought In Time's
    great periods shall return to naught **TIM 17**
Morven: And climbed thy steep summmit, oh M.
  of snow! **LOVE 38**
  like an ancient oak on M., I moulder alone in
    my place **LAM 39**
  Woody M., and echoing Sora . . . we owe them
    all a debt of gratitude **POET 3**
mosquitoes: 'I have seen something very
  promising indeed in my new m.' **MIN 44**
mother (*see also* **mither**): Come till his bonnie,
  bonnie m.'s **CHI 42**
  First bought his m. for a prostitute **INS 2**
  From terrace proud to alley base I know thee
    as my m.'s face **PLA 73**
  God! Perhaps I killed a m., When I killed a
    m.'s son **WAR 49**
  He had come to announce to his m. that his
    father and brother had been slain **MOM 52**
  He trauchles his m. **CHI 20**
  heard my m. say . . . nettle cloth more durable
    than any other species of linen **NAT 4**
  Her silent watch the mournful m. keeps
    CHI 13
  His m. sank without another care To that
    dread state **CHI 26**
  his wife's m., an old bed-ridden woman of
    nearly 100 years **LAND 42**
  house without a woman, her m. often said
    FAMI 22
  I hae been to the wild wood, m., mak my bed
    soon **DEA 4**
  I think I see our Ancient M. Caledonia, like
    Caesar sitting in the midst of our Senate
    POL 15
  man had gone between it and its m. **ANI 47**
  m. and a nurse for the youth . . . of Scotland
    COM 13
  m., nurse, cook, governess, teacher, saint
    SPIR 16
  Mountaineering lays one alongside the bones
    of m. earth **MOU 9**
  My first act . . . was to kill my m. **PER 54**
  my m. asked . . . 'how do you keep men
    happy?' **M-W 115**
  My m. said always look under the bed
    M-W 126
  My m.'s clothes came from a dress agency
    COS 44
  Our M. feedeth thus our little life **DEA 72**
  Poor m. . . . had five children and she's as
    barren as Rannoch Moor **FAMI 24**
  said she: 'My m. bore me' **CHI 10**
  sangs my m. sung **MUS 1**

mouths: should not be taking the bread out of
other people's m. **BOO 2**
their m., indeed, are open **INS 73**
movement: Nae man or m.'s worth a damn
unless The m. 'ud gang on withoot him if He
de'ed the morn **THO 71**
Moy: ball was hit off . . . at the old boundary
between the parishes of M. and Dalarossie
SPOR 32
Mozart: God was M. when he wrote Cul Mor
MOU 24
Muck: chattering magpie on the Isle of M.
INS 82
muck: 'M. makes luck' **ADV 70**
mug: skelpit aff to find some other m. **ANI 40**
muir: shining like a negro's teeth through the
black m. **BUI 11**
syne our a muir, with thornis thick and sharp
FANT 33
muirlan': muirlan' burnie, purple-fringed
NAT 10
Will ye wed a muirlan' Jockie **LOVE 44**
Mull of Kintyre: thought that Boat of Garten
and M. of K. must be clan chiefs too **PER 104**
multitude: considering the m. of mortals that
can handle the pen **BOO 18**
he will see a M. of Wights, like furious hardie
Men **FANT 40**
m. of rivers, each with its own distinct music
NAT 17
Mungo, Saint: When these two godlike men
met **PER 146**
Munro: 'I am patient, young man,' M. bagger
said **MOU 6**
Munros: By the time you have topped a hundred
M. **MOU 8**
murder: God won't accept your thanks for
murther **WAR 31**
It is lawful to prevent the m. of ourselves
REL 113
laurell'd Martial roaring murther **POET 7**
Murray, Sir James: J.M. combs the dialect from
his beard **PER 91**
Murrayfield: soccer fan attending his first Rugby
International at M. **SPOR 48**
muse: He also . . . has a certain disregard for the
m. **POET 44**
He offers the M. no violence **POET 29**
My m. 'gan weep **COS 13**
My M., tho' hamely in attire, May touch the
heart **POET 5**
names to the M. dear **HIGH 36**
when we are unjust enough to forget it, may
the M. forget us! **POET 3**
muses: Now is the yaird kail boiled and hashed,
While M. feed in slums **POET 25**
museums: m. of Scotland are wrang **THO 63**
music: as the m. went on, they found they were
dancing to the proper patterns **MUS 46**
Broadcasting is in no sense to be regarded as
a substitute for . . . the study of good m.
TEL 12

Experts have been puzzled by a new kind of
bagpipe m. **MUS 65**
Here the m. has remained a spectacle, as in
the earliest times **MUS 22**
His very foot has m. in't **LOVE 62**
multitude of rivers, each with its own distinct
m. **NAT 17**
m. of the tempest's song Leads on the lifeboat
crew **SEA 22**
Not m. strings, but upright mind **REL 6**
Of sic m. to write I do but dote **MUS 36**
one has m. and the flying cloud **REL 114**
person doesn't make a life singing Scottish
traditional m. on a basis of charm **MUS 39**
Put no faith in aught that bears the name of m.
while you are in Scotland **MUS 66**
Saft m. rang on ilka shore **MUS 27**
Scotland has not only reached the level of
Ireland, but in science and skill of m. has far
surpassed it **MUS 20**
shifting in graceful measures as if governed
by a m. of its own **RIV 12**
Thy distant m. lulls and stills, And moves to
quiet tears **MOM 24**
wild m. . . . not as essentially belonging to m.,
but to history **MUS 70**
Musselburgh: M. was a burgh, When
Edinburgh was nane **PLA 106**
mystery: an adventure . . . in . . . the m. of
Scotland's self-suppression **BIO 7**
I covet the m. of our Gaelic speech **WORD 48**
only m. about the cat **ANI 71**
great m. of Time **TIM 12**
myths: M. about a nation's history should be
treated with considerable caution **HIS 13**

N

naebody: N. cares for me, I care for n. **THO 21**
naething: little to spend, and n. to lend **DAI 10**
n. but a moolie besom **FAMI 26**
N. but a perfect waste o' watter **RIV 5**
n. but me and the wind abroad **PLA 92**
naked: bitter, old and wrinkled truth Stripped n.
of all vesture **THO 131**
Confront your fate; regard the n. deed
THO 34
I scan The giant form of a n. man **FANT 37**
Member of Parliament, n. among the
branches of a tree **MOM 27**
old joke about the Highlander liking two
things to be n. **FOO 62**
So that they could dance the freer, they had
stripped themselves entirely n. **PLEAS 3**
name: agreement to call all sorts of maladies . . .
by one n. **MIN 15**
An' his master's n. was Cain **TOA 7**
Curs'd be the tribe who . . slew one o' th' n.,
and slew not all **CUR 9**
He doesnae juist drap a n. **PER 157**

McConnachie . . . n. I give to the unruly half of myself **PER 36**

My foot is on my native heath, and my n. is MacGregor **PER 213**

My n. is Rob the Ranter **MUS 73**

nonsense . . . is received with applause, when it happens to drop from . . . *a great N.* **THO 97**

Oor guts maun glorify your n. **INS 91**

poor man's richest legacy . . . an honest n. **EPI 24**

Someone christened her The Diver and she was known by that n. until the end of her long career **TRA 46**

To this day his n. smacks of the gallows **PER 235**

who dies to win a lasting n. **ADV 60**

Who hath not glow'd above the page where fame Hath fixed high Caledon's unconquer'd n. **PPL 25**

worth an age without a n. **FAM 10**

names: here's a language rings Wi' . . . n. for nameless things **WORD 47**

Saved others' n., but left his own unsung **POET 57**

two more hedrons that I don't know the right n. for **SCI 33**

Napoleon: N. is a tyrant **TOA 12**

N. was an emperor **HIS 1**

nation: about one half of the Scottish n. . . . regarded themselves as members of the aristocracy **PPL 50**

As a n. we've fallen in and marched behind some damned funny folk **WAR 86**

death an' starvation cam' ower the haill n. **PER 243**

each n. is only the partial development of a universal humanity **SPIR 23**

eternal Scots problem, the integration of . . . historical experience into a civilised n. **HIS 34**

faithful n. **HIS 12**

history of a very poor n. **HIS 7**

I call you shrine of a n. yet to be **PLA 84**

It is beginning to be hinted that we are a n. of amateurs **PPL 80**

more Scotland has striven to be a n., the more she has sunk to be a province **POL 105**

most accomplished n. in Europe **PPL 99**

most drunken n. on the face of the earth **FOO 114**

Myths about a n.'s history should be treated with considerable caution **HIS 13**

n. of shopkeepers **ADV 123**

n. whose government is influenced by shopkeepers **PHIL 54**

No better means for retaining all that is best in the life of a n. has yet been devised than that of a National Parliament **POL 43**

no finer Gentlemen in the World, than that N. can justly boast of **PPL 4**

No Language, no N. **POL 37**

normal development of a n. is founded solidly on its past **HIS 32**

one half of the n. is mad – and the other not very sound **MIN 46**

our n. is unjust to half its members **M-W 95**

'Our neighbour n. will say of us, poor Scotland!' **REL 32**

sheep, a grey-faced n. **HIGH 26**

should a man be bold enough to refer to the Scottish n. **SPIR 25**

small n. has always been humanity's last bulwark **SPIR 26**

Such a parcel of rogues in a n.! **POL 22**

these few families of tax-gatherers have sucked the life-blood of our n. **POL 56**

To witness 'gainst the n.'s perjury **EPI 9**

truth is, we are a n. of arse-lickers **PPL 45**

we can still rise now, And be a n. again **SPIR 59**

national: essential beginning of all n. uprisings is that poets should believe **POET 43**

For such a n. work no native artist could be found **ART 15**

general movement in favour of a n. rebirth has attracted some of the finest . . . and many of the greatest cranks **POL 99**

licking of wounds is second only to football as a n. sport **SPOR 62**

N. Parliament, through which N. sentiment finds expression **POL 43**

paraphernalia of my n. costume **COS 9**

precious articles of our n. belief **HIS 27**

soil which is the natural base of our n. life **HIGH 24**

There is an incurable nosiness in the n. character **PPL 47**

we should be a little less cosmopolitan and rather more n. in our architecture **BUI 20**

that essential part of n. costume, the plaid **COS 33**

nationalism: oor n. Is yet a thing o' sect and schism **POL 98**

nations: He touched his harp and n. heard, entranced **MUS 67**

let some law of equity to n. all be known **POL 108**

Most n. are forgeries **HIS 3**

People of Scotland, as members of one of the oldest n. in Europe **POL 6**

people . . . who have heretofore stood in the first rank of n. **SPIR 7**

rudest, perhaps, of all the European n. **POET 32**

situation and manners of the contending n. might amuse a philosophic mind **PPL 39**

Sometimes we think of the n. lying asleep **LAM 46**

these advantages We frequently obtain . . . where n. remain independent, and are of a small extent **PHIL 14**

We bear the lot of n., Of times and races **THO 92**

native: Alas my n. place! **PLA 75**

'Are you n. born?' 'No sir, I am a Scotchman'
    PER 79
fierce n. daring which instils The stirring
    memory of a thousand years WAR 32
genial partiality for the wine of his n. land
    PER 113
hardest form of slavery is to serve . . . in one's
    own n. country THO 46
How could he compose a song lacking skill
    and n. wit? INS 67
Kercaldy my n. town REL 53
My foot is on my n. heath PER 213
my n. Clyde, thy once romantic shore COM 4
no n. artist could be found ART 15
'O Scotia my dear, my n. land' WAR 45
This is my own, my n. land! SPIR 52
when a Justice of Peace court was sitting in my
    n. town LAW 26
Nature: A' the sweets that ane can wish Frae N.'s
han PLA 22
And hear, 'mid reverent N.'s hush, The water-
    closet's frequent flush BUI 34
approached as nearly to . . . perfect
    wickedness as the infirmities of human n.
    will allow PER 176
approximating as nearly to the idea of a
    perfectly wise and virtuous man, as perhaps
    the n. of human frailty will permit PER 223
Auld N. swears, the lovely dears Her noblest
    work she classes M-W 38
better the works of n. are understood, the
    more they will be ever admired NAT 11
Dame N.'s petticoat is not so easily lifted
    NAT 13
error . . . to conceive a greater simplicity in n.
    than there really is PHIL 42
Europe has been living . . . under a grave
    misapprehension as to the n. of things
    THO 73
Ever since I have been enquiring into the
    works of n., I have always admired . . . the
    simplicity of her ways NAT 15
fornicatour by natour INS 79
Gie me ae spark o' N.'s fire POET 5
Grant me . . . More than enough for n.'s ends
    THO 86
He appeared to take it for granted that all
    n. . . . was in a conspiracy PER 47
History . . . first distinct product of man's
    spiritual n. HIS 11
I watch the wheels of N.'s mazy plan TIM 11
If honest N. made you fools, What sairs your
    grammars UNI 3
I'm nae phenomena; I'm jist N. PER 197
indifference, which, from the usual infirmity
    of human n., follows . . . complete enjoyment
    MOM 6
indiscriminating n. of his praise FAMI 17
Let children walk with n. DEA 52
let N. have fair play, and you will have no
    need of my advice MIN 3
Men of Angus do not understand a n.-lover's
    ecstasies NAT 1

Men of better clay and finer mould Know n.
    SPOR 9
My earliest impressions are of an almost
    tropical luxuriance of n. NAT 17
My hert, my will, my n. and my mind Was
    changit clene LOVE 56
N. admits no lie ADV 41
N. all curage me denyis SWW 29
n. made her what she is, And never made
    anither! PER 61
N. must produce a man COS 38
N., which is the time-vesture of God NAT 5
O N.! A' thy shows and forms NAT 2
people who succeeded in clawing an existence
    from n.'s harshness PPL 83
rude and violent manifestations of the active
    power of N. MOU 16
Selfishness is calm, a force of n. THO 119
Time is as young as ever now, N. as fresh and
    sweet TIM 15
Tir'd n. must at last repose LOVE 23
To promote a Woman to beare rule . . . is
    repugnant to N. M-W 84
To resent this would show . . . lack of
    knowledge of human n. SCI 25
Toryism is an innate principle o' human n.
    POL 48
When evening closes N.'s eye ANI 77
Where N.'s face is banished and estranged
    COM 4
Women, destined by n. to be obedient
    M-W 82
Work . . . element in which his n. was ordained
    to develop itself DAI 53
You think you will find a wonderful
    sensitiveness to n . . . there? PLA 77
naughty: 'N. but nice' ADV 55
There was a n. boy TRA 25
nausea: general perfume of n. and unhappy half-
    sleeping humanity TRA 28
Naver, River: Wild N. which doth see our
    longest day RIV 10
neb: his n. was horn ANI 5
necessity: I find alone, n. supreme PHIL 64
two everlasting hostile empires: N. and
    Freewill PHIL 9
neck: and class-conscious will be Till our fit's on
    the n. o' the boor-joysie POL 20
there was Janet . . . wi' her n. thrawn
    FANT 63
Tho' by the n. she would be strung, She'll no
    desert SPIR 13
need: He is gone on the mountain . . . When our
    n. was the sorest LAM 54
how can I be destitute Of ony gude thing in
    my neid? REL 126
'let Nature have fair play, and you will have no
    n. of my advice' MIN 3
of no more has he n. ADV 74
needle: stick a n., or a fish-hook, in the door
    FANT 27
They taik delyt in nedill wark COS 3

Then sinks at once – and all is n. MOM 40

They've only been assisting at a Braw Scots Nicht! FES 11

Things wept for beside the sheep-buchts, remembered at night MUS 31

This ae nighte DEA 1

This fray was fought at Otterbourne, Between the n. and the day WAR 2

Thoch we murne nicht and day It will avail us nocht THO 85

Tonight's the n. – if the lads are the lads! WAR 63

used to sit up at n. and greet in the two languages CHI 35

we gather round the festive board To spend a jolly n. FES 2

Wi' hopes to ken their fortune By freets that n. FANT 43

nightingale: I'll not be a fool like the n. ANI 54

nights: For two n. did that woman sleep in a sheep-cot LAND 13

your n. longer, since you have lost that princess who was your light LAM 20

Ninety-Third: 'N.-t.! N.-t.! Damn all that eagerness!' WAR 33

Nith, River: als much vertue, sonce and pith In Annan, or the water of N. POET 18

Noah: But N. never heedit their cries REL 41

nobility: titled N. is the most undisputed progeny of feudal barbarism POL 70

nobles: gang of corrupt n. ADV 126

had I not been met at every turn by the opposition of our n. SPIR 57

nocht: N. is your fairness ADV 75

noise: Of n. alone is born the inward sense Of silence THO 76

nightingale . . . making a n. with his nose ANI 54

sacredness of love and death Dwells in thy n. and smoky breath PLA 72

There is n. and abandon ANI 31

noises: discordant n. blend into harmony with the deep voice of the sea ANI 31

nonsense: n. of every kind is received with applause, when it happens to drop from . . . *a great Name* THO 98

There is a cycle in n. THO 87

Noran: Up the N. water, The country folk are kind HUM 9

Norseman: Mr Eric Linklater is a lost N. with a tendency to go berserk BOO 35

North: forbidden words in the n. were priest or minister WORD 32

Is there any light quite like the June sun of the N. and West? SWW 24

men o' the N. are a' gone gyte PPL 34

Nort to da Faroe bank SEA 11

N. Briton, as a *Scotchman* must now be called SPIR 11

N. face of Liathach lives in the mind MOU 26

N., where . . . savage faith works woe REL 43

Some east, some west, some everywhere but n., In quest of lawless gain they issue forth PPL 24

Their only idea of wit, which prevails occasionally in the n. HUMO 15

There cam a wind oot of the N. FANT 17

North Pole: Never mind his damning the N.P. PER 225

North Sea: bound for Aberdeen and N.S. Crude TRA 29

sort of high-grade liberal arts college . . . beside the chill N.S. UNI 15

wild N.S. beating on sand dunes PLA 104

North Uist: 'fall in the value of kelp . . . renders a change in the management of the N.U. estate necessary' PHIL 28

Norval: My name is N. LAND 30

Young N. was busy giving out SPIR 14

nose: clap a sticking-plaster, covering mouth and n. CHI 33

Falkland sampled it with n. and tongue FOO 55

making a noise with his n. ANI 54

'next time I meet you I shall pull your n.' ART 28

Out of his n. the meldrop fast can rin PER 136

rub your little n. with a little mutton-fat ANI 96

She'd reddish hair, and a high, skeugh n. PER 118

Not Proven: that Caledonian *medium quid* LAW 29

note: For in my life I couth never sing a n. MUS 36

His troubled n. dwells mournfully ANI 33

notes: First he played da notes o noy MUS 2

high, high n. o' *Bangor's* tune Are very hard to raise MUS 6

n. would appear only the accents of the language made . . . musical MUS 79

nothing: Coatbridge to Glory, And n. to pay REL 18

dread state of n. but life itself CHI 26

I think that n. made is lost THO 75

mediocrity knows n. higher than itself ADV 59

Never volunteer for n. WAR 41

no meat these two days, and we have n. to give them LAM 55

no sensation of talking into n. TEL 1

n., in my opinion, can be more unbecoming ADV 65

N. in the world delights a truly religious people so much REL 61

n. on earth like it . . . a cliff of sea-birds ANI 31

n. original in me, Excepting original sin REL 33

n. to lose but memory YOU 17

they were n. under their kilts COS 39

notion: But the whole n. of standing at bus stops! TRA 27

ultimate n. of right is that which tends to the
universal good PHIL 30

novelist: Mr Gunn is a brilliant n. from
Scotshire BOO 34

novelists: Copulation . . . much better described
in the physiological textbooks than in all the
works of all the n. BOO 12

dredging the catalogues for third-rate women
n. POET 16

novels: reading of n. is probably the most
effective training for emotional life BOO 1

Walter Scott has no business to write n.
BOO 2

With the birth of each child you lose two n.
BOO 50

novelty: n. and variety of the following designs
will . . . justify our conduct BUI 2

November: In Causewayend, on this N. night
WORD 26

nowhere: most signposted n. on the planet
PLA 23

N., perhaps, has God been better worshipped
in spirit REL 106

object may exist, and yet be n. PHIL 23

nuisance: men were just a perfect n. M-W 83

number: harmony of the world is made manifest
in Form and N. SCI 42

I have been the means, under God, of
haanging a great n. LAW 33

world is so full of a n. of things I'm sure we
should all be as happy as kings THO 121

numbers: when you can . . . express it in n., you
know something about it SCI 22

nun: As the offspring of a n., he suffered a
formidable handicap PER 106

nurse: earthly nourrice sits and sings CHI 3

I wes in yowth on nureis knee Dandely,
Bischop, dandely YOU 10

mother and a n. for the youth . . . of Scotland
COM 13

O Caledonia! . . . Meet n. for a poetic child
SPIR 53

O

oak: he needed Johnson as an ivy needs an o.
PER 88

like an ancient o. on Morven, I moulder alone
in my place LAM 39

oatcakes:land of Calvin, o., and sulphur
LAND 55

they'd broth, it was good, and the o. better
FOO 58

oatmeal: We cultivate literature on a little o.
JOU 15

Oban: At O. of discomfort one is sure PLA 107

not a bad representation of Vanity Fair
PLA 109

Words cannot express how horrible O. is
PLA 108

Oban Times: wonderin' if the *O.T.* was takin'
doon a' his speech REL 94

object: cook was too filthy an o. to be described
FOO 33

Each o. hides in a metaphor WORD 31

every o. you produce must have a strong mark
of individuality ART 22

o. may exist, and yet be nowhere PHIL 23

o. of his reasonings was not to attain truth
PHIL 39

objects: What strange o. of adoration are cats
and monkeys REL 64

obscenity: patchwork of blasphemy, absurdity
and gross o. MUS 58

vice and o. fearfully propagated BOO 75

obscurity: o. which hangs over the beginnings of
all history HIS 29

obsequies: I'll sing thine o. with trumpet sounds
LAM 45

occasions: perpetual series of o. for hope ANG 2

occupations: they have yet in their . . . o. a
characteristic acuteness ART 34

Odyssey: style Of the great *O.* is what Gaelic
knows WORD 70

oil: richly butyraceous o. BATH 8

old: geologists . . . call it the O. Boy LAND 48

It's growing o. I've failed to understand
YOU 11

Mourn not, my friends, that we are growing
o. TIM 21

O. and young, we are all on our last cruise
YOU 26

O. have been left to die LAM 37

Old Firm: no chance . . . you never do at
Hampden against one of the O.F. SPOR 77

Old Man of Hoy: considerably more spectacular
MOU 33

ollamh: heroes . . . are dead . . . It is time for the
o. to go after them LAM 41

open: Every man proper for a member of this
Society must have a frank, honest, o. heart
M-W 37

door of the Fionn is always o. FANT 1

he has laid o. the slopes to be parched
LAND 24

inward gates of a bird are always o. ANI 64

o. people! their mouths, indeed, are o. INS 73

operation: o. . . . . To remove the haemorrhoids
you call your poems INS 64

operations: O. were started by the purchase of a
tea-chest SCI 1

opinion: 'My o. . . . . is that this good woman
should be suffered to return home' LAW 25

no variety of o. disturbed its unanimity
POL 27

'nothing, in my o., can be more unbecoming'
ADV 65

Public o. in a Scotch playground was a
powerful influence EDU 28

You ask my o. about keeping a journal BIO 10

opinions: Men are never so good or bad as their
o. ADV 90

opponent: his immediate o., the fearsome full-
back Don Emery **SPOR 10**
    In golf, you do not play against an o. **SPOR 34**
    never ascribe to an o. motives meaner than
    your own **ADV 19**
    will spring with tiger-like ferocity on its o.
    ANI 35
optimism: *Scotch O.* Through a gless, Darkly
PHIL 47
oral: It is indeed strange that any man of
sense could have imagined it possible, that
above twenty thousand verses . . . could have
been preserved by an o. tradition during fifty
generations **POET 32**
    Listening to the o. tradition of the wind
    LAND 14
    These songs had floated down on the stream
    of o. tradition **MUS 37**
Oran, Saint: 'Earth, earth, on O.'s eyes'
FANT 49
oranges: boy flew at the o. with the enthusiasm
of a ferret **FOO 111**
Ore, River: O. with rushy hair **RIV 10**
organise: O., o., o. **ADV 45**
original: almost intuitive faculty for o.
investigation **SCI 9**
    no-one need expect to be o. simply by being
    absurd **THO 87**
    nothing original in me Excepting o. sin
    REL 33
originality: O. is not necessarily a mark of
genius **ART 25**
Orkney: bloody O. **PLA 111**
    great ark of the people of O. **BUI 5**
    roaring seas from rocks rebound **PLA 110**
    traditional O. invitation to a visitor was, 'Put
    in thee hand' **TOA 18**
    win' blaws oot o' O. **SWW 21**
ornaments: enriched with a few o. properly
disposed **BUI 12**
    Loveliness Needs not the foreign aid of o.
    COS 60
orphans: slaughtered men Fight fiercer in their o.
o'er again **PPL 26**
orra: aye a bit pickle in the pat, For onie o. body
FOO 125
Ossian: Hail to thee, Sire of O. **POET 71**
    if we could . . indulge the pleasing supposition,
    that . . . O. sung **PPL 39**
osprey: Birds-nesting expeditions were also
made . . . after o.s' eggs **ANI 73**
otter: Near the o.'s track on the snows of Foinne
Bheinn **MOU 19**
Otterburn: This fray was fought at Otterbourne
WAR 2
outlook: We need to give everyone the o. of the
artist **ART 14**
owl: I almost understand Thy o. **ANI 70**
owls: drunk as o. **FOO 129**
ownership: o. is really custodianship **LAND 19**
Oxford: 'I hope you in O. don't think we hate
you?' **PPL 48**

oxter: I would be blythe to have you at my o.
WAR 90
oyster: gathered the venom . . . in an Oister shell
FANT 15
    he was a bold man who first swallowed an o.
    FOO 74
    I would envy . . an o. **ANI 26**
oysters: his death . . . was entirely owing to
eating Raw o. **FOO 54**
    Neptune's caller cheer, New o. fresh **FOO 51**
    sit fu' snug O'er o. and a dram o' gin **FOO 50**

P

pacifist: 'He's the sort of p. I much prefer on my
side' **POL 97**
paddocks: some fowk like parritch, and some
fowk like p. **FOO 109**
See also puddock, frog
page: had the name of Marmontel or Richardson
been on the title p., I should have wept **BOO 49**
    Heart inform'd The moral p. **BOO 70**
paint: it is like trying to p. a sunset in lamp-black
BOO 23
    they derive none of their beauty from p.
    M-W 125
    'to p. well it is necessary to have warm feet'
    ART 7
    You can't p. from a vacuum **ART 3**
painter: artist without sentiment is a p. without
colours **ART 2**
    I called on Mr Donaldson, the p. **ART 6**
    'My dear —,' wrote the p. in reply, 'the next
    time I meet you I shall pull your nose'
    ART 28
    Raeburn was a born p. of portraits **ART 30**
painting: judge architecture . . . as you judge p.
or sculpture **BUI 21**
Paisley: Her cutty sark, o' P. harn **COS 10**
    palace of Scottish blackguardism, unless
    perhaps P. be entitled to contest this honour
    PLA 29
panic: O, what a p.'s in thy breastie **ANI 20**
    they never p. so much that they fail to make
    stylish triangles **ANI 59**
pantaloon: buffoon tartan p. **COS 14**
pantalooons: took off her p. and set to in grim
earnest **COS 51**
papers: something aboot it every ither nicht in
the p. **ART 23**
paradise: in the howe o' P. That birk grew fair
eneuch **FANT 3**
    that dreary and barren land . . . a flourishing
    p. **LAND 34**
Paradise Lost: copy of Milton's *P.L.* . . . was the
occasion of much curious criticism **POET 50**
parent: If one with wit the p. brood disgrace
CUR 14
    never a problem child . . . only a problem p.
    EDU 30
parents: 'Intern all p.,' he enjoined **EDU 5**

My p. were wonderful **FAMI 31**

P. consider Learning . . . as of little Moment to the Girls **EDU 3**

P. learn a lot from their children **CHI 47**

Paurents were paurents then **FAMI 13**

people who are forever consecrating the memory of the departed . . . see much to love and revere in their own p. **YOU 13**

their p. and their p. before them **CHI 24**

We hardly conceive of our p. as human **FAMI 29**

parish: cursedest p. that ever God put breath into **FOO 35**

eager to have a railway through his p. **TRA 16**

everyone had been accustomed to that sport at every p. school **SPOR 30**

superplus shall be . . . employed always on the poor of the p. **PLEAS 2**

Was there e'er sic a p. as that o' Dunkeld? **PLA 35**

Park, Mungo: While exploring a particularly wild . . . region of Africa **TRA 37**

parliament: People want to see how a P. . . . works **POL 67**

Scots had no reason to set any value on their P. **REL 87**

Parnassus: syne they think to climb P., By dint o' Greek! **UNI 3**

parritch: 'come awa' in to your p.' **FOO 8**

mony a day since ye wad hae putten her in the p. pot **REL 101**

some fowk like p., and some fowk like paddocks **FOO 109**

though we're a' fearfu' fond o' oor p. in Scotland **FOO 100**

Weel may the boatie row, That . . . buys our p. meal **SEA 9**

See also porridge

parrots: five hundred grey p. who were set up . . . to cry 'Drink Pattison's Whisky!' **COM 18**

part: themselves p. and parcel a product of Glendale & Co **DAI 27**

Scot has to act his p. all his life **ACT 13**

partan: Wha called ye p.-face? **INS 14**

partans: there will be partens and buckies **FOO 120**

Partick: gaun tae a party in P. **FES 12**

Partick Thistle: I support P.T. They'll be in Europe next year **SPOR 13**

P.T. supporters' anthem goes like this **SPOR 33**

party: game . . . in which each p. tried to rob the other **CHI 43**

Happy the man who belongs to no p. **PLA 16**

many of his own p. chatter, who were dumb before him **PER 87**

p.'s almost over **THO 68**

Science is of no p. **SCI 2**

we're gaun tae a p. in Partick **FES 12**

passages: I was a good deal affected with some very trifling p. **BOO 49**

passenger: Halt, curious p. **EPI 9**

passengers: most consistent p. the London and North Eastern Railway ever had **TRA 47**

p. underneath would agonisingly call out 'Haud your hand' **DAI 28**

shame-stricken driver hurries his packed p. off into the dark **TRA 14**

would have grown weary of waiting for p. to waylay **TRA 20**

passion: certain delicious P., which . . . I hold to be the first of human joys **LOVE 24**

hap your hurdies with the p. pleats **BOA 18**

my p. rose to a pitch I could not quite command **M-W 29**

regard for liberty, though a laudable p. **POL 50**

seasonable fit of illness is an excellent medicine for the turbulence of p. **MIN 47**

passions: Above those p. which this world deform **PHIL 63**

Reason is and ought to be the slave of the p. **PHIL 20**

We leave to others the p. and politics of this world **REL 40**

past: derricks rise tae the northern skies, And the p. is gane forever **PPL 34**

gave me . . . a feeling for the p. *in which I had ancestors* **HIS 24**

Haud fast to the p. **ADV 108**

I . . . learn the future by the p. of man **TIM 11**

It has suffered in the p. . . . from too much England **SPIR 35**

Must we be thirled to the p.? **SPIR 41**

normal development of a nation is founded solidly on its p. **HIS 32**

Out of the P. . . . The beauty of her childhood you can trace **YOU 19**

p. sleeps in the stones **PLA 119**

We can pay our debts to the p. **ADV 26**

patience: principal part of faith is p. **REL 81**

patient: All that the p. could utter was, 'Pray to God for me, Melvyll' **PER 181**

Any really good doctor ought to be able to tell before a p. has fairly sat down **MIN 8**

'I am p., young man,' Munro bagger said **MOU 6**

original p. . . . was made whole **MIN 25**

used to say, as we were entering the p.'s room together, 'Weel, Mr Cooper' **MIN 20**

patients: going to see his p. accompanied by a pet sheep and raven **MIN 19**

Whenever patients come to I **MIN 24**

patriot: I am a jingo p. of planet earth **PER 119**

patriotic: Because my p. body will impart goodness to the slime **POET 68**

patriotism: education . . . a battlefield . . . between cosmopolitanism and p. **EDU 4**

Imperialism, sane Imperialism, is but . . . a larger p. **POL 90**

Love, joy and p. are their inspiration **MUS 26**

no word so prostituted as p. **POL 92**

part of p. to stare at the hill till there's a cow on it **MOU 25**

pattle: Wi' murderin' p. **ANI 20**

pay: considering they had no discipline and not much p. WAR 70

Four and twenty blacklegs, working night and day, Fed on eggs and bacon, getting double p. POL 5

no lodging to p. ADV 140

shepherd's plaiding, and a beggar's p. HIGH 33

them that drink and dinna p. CUR 21

We'll p. for it, we'll p. for it, we'll p. for it PPL 76

peace: 'Better is the small fire that warms on the little day of p.' MUS 29

Celestial p. was pictured in her look PER 73

He had rather . . . keep or procure p. with dishonour PER 250

if you value your own comfort and my p. of mind THO 58

In p. and war he suffered overmuch EPI 29

In times of p., meek as a monk was he PER 132

it ne'er was wealth, That coft contentment, p. or pleasure LOVE 37

Justice may nocht have dominatioun, But where P. makis habitatioun LAW 19

Let no woman who values p. of soul ever dream of marrying an author BOO 17

'Mourn, hapless Caledonia . . . Thy banish'd p.' SPIR 55

ne'er will be p. till the warld again Has learned to sing . . . We're John Tamson's bairns PPL 81

There is p. now the battle's o'er WAR 16

peasant: Aberdeen, a thin-lipped p. woman PLA 3

p., a poet, a patriot and a king BUR 16

whole soul of the p. class breathes in their burdens POET 36

peasantry: p. in the southern districts . . . possess a laudable zeal for knowledge PPL 90

This advantage . . . the p. of no other European country enjoyed HIGH 21

peat: fine malt . . . not too strongly reminiscent of the p. FOO 55

light of the p.-fire flame HIGH 27

must have been born with the p.-reek in your nostrils BATH 12

tang of so many Scottish things . . . of pine-woods and of p. MOM 5

pedagogue: presumptuous, self-conceited p. INS 48

Peden, Alexander: A.P., who made the strangest . . . wedding address ever heard in Scotland FANT 20

Hoodicrow P. in the blighted corn HIS 31

pedigree: If any can boast of a p. higher EPI 6

penniless lass wi' a lang p. PER 199

peep: there wasn't a p. out of her after that ACT 11

peeps: took surreptitious p. at it BOO 8

peer: Pictish p. . . . basely stole what less barbarians won INS 22

Pegasus: Oor Scots P. is a timmer naig POET 46

Peggy: My P. is a young thing, And I'm nae very auld LOVE 69

pelf: thy warldis p. ADV 73

pen: cream from the bothy, and curd from the p. FOO 70

I have seen his p. gang as fast ower the paper as ever it did . . . when it was in the grey goose's wing BOO 55

John kept his p. to the paper without interruption BOO 46

multitude of mortals that can handle the p. BOO 18

pens: Though all the wood . . . were crafty pennis convenient to write M-W 1

Pentland Firth: Search Scotland over, from the P. to the Solway, and there is not a cottage-hut . . . without its Bible POET 37

people: All decent p. live beyond their incomes nowadays PHIL 44

All the p. in Scotland are not so void of taste COM 8

and so make only two p. miserable instead of four PER 68

Authors and uncaptured criminals . . . only p. free from routine BOO 45

Before a Duke came or any of his p. LAND 40

But while we sing 'God Save the King', We'll ne'er forget THE P. POL 23

cannot bear the thought of other p. becoming losers by my schemes DAI 60

chief artistic glory of . . . all p. of Celtic speech MUS 51

chief part of the territory is possessed by two great lords, who . . . take little interest in the p. POL 81

Considderand the p. and the ground, That riches suld nocht in this realm redound PPL 54

draining money from the pockets of the p. PHIL 56

Education makes a p. easy to lead, but difficult to drive EDU 8

English, as a p., are very little inferior to the Scots PPL 71

English . . . were a fine, open p. INS 73

free p. who first gave power to the king HIS 25

exceedingly proud to be thought an unmixed p. HIGH 10

granite palaces, inhabited by p. as definite as their building material PLA 4

great ark of the p. of Orkney BUI 5

great men say that their distress Comis for the p.'s wickedness HUM 11

grouse shooters were often rather pathetic p. SPOR 8

guid auld creeds, That met a simple p.'s needs LAM 28

half the p. standing one day at the Cross of Edinburgh were mad MIN 38

Happy the p. whose annals are blank HIS 9

He ran away to Scotland, The p. for to see TRA 25

person: as soon as you can say what you think, and not what some other p. has thought **THO 14**

average Aberdonian as a p. who would gladly pick a halfpenny out of a dunghill with his teeth **PLA 6**

Dr Joseph Black was a striking and beautiful p. **PER 85**

fine clothes worn on his p. . . . tossed into a corner **INS 80**

'I am Mr Skirving, the p. who laid out the improvements' **MOM 34**

I am out looking out for a wife, and I thought you just the p. that would suit **M-W 32**

level spoonful of tea for each p., and one for the pot **FOO 127**

never met a healthy p. who worried much about his health **MIN 29**

only p. . . . expelled from the Communist Party for being a Scottish Nationalist **PER 72**

p. doesn't make a life singing Scottish traditional music on a basis of charm **MUS 39**

scientific man is the only p. who has anything new to say **SCI 3**

walks about looking for a p. proper to be a model **ART 12**

persons: holds the power of life or death over helpless p. **MIN 10**

Perth (*see also* **St Johnstoun**): trains . . . come in portentously late from P. **TRA 14**

pessimism: *Scotch P* Nae gless **PHIL 47**

pessimist: p. with a mechanical smile **EDU 31**

pest: war and the p. will gar ye sleep **DEA 37**

pet: going to see his patients accompanied by a p. sheep **MIN 19**

My sister wanted a cat for a p., I wanted a dog **FAMI 31**

Tell me, p., were you angry at me **M-W 114**

Peter, Saint: S.P. said to God . . . 'Can ye nocht mak a Hielandman?' **PPL 1**

Peterhead: Along the quay at P. the lasses stand around **SEA 3**

Dig for their roots, or they be dead, Fra Gretna Green to P. **WORD 28**

petticoat: Dame Nature's p. is not so easily lifted **NAT 13**

Ladies in walking . . . exhibited the p. **COS 17**

so particular with her rumpt gown and p. **COS 57**

they wear the p. so very short **COS 11**

pheasants: pockets packed wi' p.s' eggs **ANG 8**

philabeg: Cam' ye by Atholl, lad wi' the p.? **MUS 38**

Let others boast of philibeg **COS 55**

P. aboon his knee **COS 28**

philosopher: He looked like a p. from Lapland **PER 86**

present when the first p. of his age was the historian of his own discoveries **PER 56**

philosophers: past phases of humanity, from fishes to p. **CHI 54**

philosophical: at once decorative – contemplative – p. **ANI 32**

never stopped till he told you all he knew . . with the utmost p. ingenuity **PER 75**

this attenuated p. gentleman **DEA 22**

philosophy: belief of a material world is . . . of more authority, than any principles of p. **PHIL 41**

errors in religion are dangerous; those in p. only ridiculous **PHIL 24**

formula which, according to . . . the rules of scientific p., ought to have been hopelessly wrong **SCI 21**

gaining the Edinburgh chair of p. meant that he had to teach physics **PER 134**

Scotland . . . has been dominated by the p. of 'common sense' **PHIL 35**

university which does not have a p. section **UNI 11**

photography: Blessed be the inventor of P.! **CUR 15**

physician: old Scotch p. . . . used to say **MIN 20**

physics: gaining the Edinburgh chair of philosophy meant that he had to teach p. **PER 135**

This change . . . most profound that p. has experienced since the time of Newton **SCI 13**

pibroch: Hark to the p.'s pleasing note! **MUS 19**

How in the noon of night that p. thrills **WAR 32**

I asked the piper, 'How long does it take to learn to play a p.?' **MUS 9**

pickle: aye a bit p. in the pat For onie orra body **FOO 125**

There's p. in her very snout **PER 200**

Pict: P. bristling all round with the arrows that had pierced him **WAR 21**

Picts: foul hordes of Scots and P. **PPL 42**

Some maintain that the . . . Picts were called *Picti* . . . from their beauty **PPL 37**

picture: How idyllic is the p. of a small society and its handicraft **DAI 32**

person proper to be a model . . . in his p. **ART 12**

p. it . . . right there at the top of the glen, beautiful vista **LAND 38**

Then there is a grand p. gallery **PLA 67**

pictures: hunders o' p. oot in yon place at Kelvingrove **ART 23**

my price having been raised since I painted that p. **ART 33**

P. there are that do not please With any sweet surprise **ART 21**

Statues and p. and verse may be grand **ART 32**

piece: p. on crisps. Aye beautiful **FOO 76**

You are offered a p. of bread and butter **FOO 89**

pietas: sort of *p*. I had towards the whole world of life **MOM 29**

piety: weaker sex, to p. more prone **M-W 20**

pig: He took a young p. as a pet **ANI 82**

players: affecting the ability of world-class p. to reach their best **SPOR 63**
I don't drop p. **SPOR 68**
If I ask the p. for less than perfection **SPOR 54**
playmate: I have no p. but the tide **FANT 45**
pleasant: Barbie, usually so poor to see, a very p. place . . . on a summer morning **PLA2: 2**
During the whole of two or three p. weeks . . . I never on any occasion saw whisky made use of as a beverage **FOO 77**
far light-filled perspective that holds the mind to wonder and a p. silence **PLA 131**
p. land of counterpane **CHI 51**
P. was the youth to me, Brimful was Alban **PER 44**
'Tis a p. thing to be a bride **CHI 36**
pleasure: can there greater p. be Than see sic wee tots **CHI 36**
Chords that vibrate sweetest p. **MUS 12**
clergy who were ready to denounce all carnal p. **SPOR 30**
Force of hunger for p. of every kind **POET 14**
gibbet. 'The sight of it . . . gave me infinite p.' **TRA 37**
hardly any p. like good oarsmanship **SPOR 16**
He was a pleisure to sit under **REL 122**
his awin sensuall plesoure . . . cause of his utter ruine **PER 161**
I took a particular p. in the company of modest women **M-W 83**
it ne'er was wealth, That coft contentment, peace or p. **LOVE 37**
It would give me the greatest p. if you would take the trouble to write **ART 27**
My p. shall consist . . in establishing to myself that name in the world for wisdom and knowledge **HOP 12**
no worldly p. here below, Which by experience doth not folly prove **LOVE 20**
'one vice, but it's given me more p. than all my virtues' **FOO 79**
p. of Dundas was the sole rule of every one of them **POL 27**
Their climate, their religion and their habits are equally averse to p. **INS 46**
There's a p. eternally new **PLEAS 10**
There's little p. in the hoose, When our gudeman's awa' **M-W 98**
We take . . . a malicious p., . . . in pricking bubbles **PPL 18**
pleasures: But p. are like poppies spread **PLEAS 4**
country above all . . . in which a man of imagination may carve out his own p. **LAND 61**
He was not insensible to p.; but he deemed very few of them worth the price **PER 185**
p., and not the profits . . . of literature which most require to be preached **BOO 4**
we continue to exist because the sum of our p. exceeds the sum of our sorrows **PHIL 43**
plight: most glorious p. in the world **ART 1**

plough: I like the pleugh-paidle a hantle better **WAR 78**
Poetry drives its lines into her forehead like an angled p. across a bare field **POET 61**
They'd take a good field and p. it **POET 55**
tho' I drudge thro' dub and mire At pleugh or cart **POET 5**
ploughman: But the plooman laddie's my delight **M-W 18**
Nor sauce, nor state that I could see Mair than an honest p. **PER 66**
p. lad's a jolly lad **M-W 19**
Success the p.'s wages crown **DAI 5**
town is at present agog with the p.-poet **BUR 6**
twenty pints o' p.'s drinkie **FOO 93**
young lady . . . with the appetite of a p. **ADV 65**
ploughmen: boats . . . Like p. in blizzards of gulls **SEA 6**
plum-tree: higher up the p.-t. grows **ADV 7**
pocket: after my first book was published, I carried it about in my p. **BOO 8**
And nothing to do but p. his gold **POET 4**
pockets: p. packed wi' pheasants' eggs **ANG 8**
waistcoat with large old-fashioned p. **COS 19**
What are ye feel-feelin for . . . ass if they had pockets **ANG 9**
poem: I was just translating my last wee p. Into the dear old Lallans **POET 33**
title-p. of his new volume, *The Flauchter-Spaad* **PER 162**
poems: Are my p. spoken in the factories and fields? **POET 39**
Bad p. try to offer solutions **POET 53**
haemorrhoids you call your p. **INS 64**
I can cut better p. than most **POET 55**
My p. should be Clyde-built **POET 24**
Poems of a Painter: P. of a P., which Carlyle . . . took to be *Poems of a Printer* **BOO 31**
poesy: O thou whom p. abhors **POET 7**
Thus with me began Love and P. **LOVE 24**
poet: As a p. Scott *cannot* live **POET 70**
considering the money was due by one P., for putting a tombstone over another **POET 8**
Every critic in the town Runs the minor p. down **POET 51**
He has fame and fortune enough as a p. **BOO 2**
His hood was reid . . . Like to ane p. of the old fassoun **POET 30**
I'll ne'er hae a p.'s name **POET 48**
It is natural for a p. to love his own language **WORD 53**
Let such forgo the p.'s sacred name, Who rack their brains for lucre **POET 11**
Ne'er was flattery lost on p.'s ear **POET 56**
Now I am not a p., Nor yet a learned man **POET 1**
Now I can be a p. **POET 63**
p. can disregard the internal combustion engine **POET 47**

When a p. man was found guilty . . . and put into the pit **LAW 16**

wonder that the p. man was allowed to breathe the air of heaven **POL 4**

poortith: constantly on p.'s brink **DAI 9**

Pope: better than to be the P.'s nephew **ADV 48**

The Paip, That Pagan Full of Pryde **REL 128**

P. was Giovanni, good P. John **REL 116**

population: dispossessing a p. overgrown and daily becoming more burdensome **PHIL 38**

p. . . . is greater than the land . . . can maintain **PHIL 28**

porridge (*see also* **parritch**): He was whistlin' to the p. that were hott'rin' on the fire **MUS 63**

neither so nourishing as p., or stimulating as whisky **BUR 11**

rock is like p. **MOU 36**

port: Black bottles of strong p. were set down beside them **LAW 9**

Death is the p. where all may refuge find **DEA 8**

until you bring your ship into p. **ADV 1**

very wind that wafts us towards the p. **ADV 116**

port-a-beul: in the *p.-a-b.* song comes the line: 'all the sheep have milk but the ewe with the crooked horn has a gallon' **FOO 38**

porter: asked if he considered p. a wholesome beverage **FOO 108**

portion: He wales a p. with judicious care **REL 28**

portraits: Jacobites . . . were anxious to have p. of Mary, Queen of Scots **ART 16**

Raeburn was a born painter of p. **ART 30**

posset: cosy and tosh, from a p.-masking **FOO 57**

There was an eating p. in the middle of the table **FOO 102**

pot: aye a bit pickle in the pat For onie orra body **FOO 125**

Heaven can boil the p. **ADV 32**

in the deepest p. of hell He smorit thame **INS 33**

level spoonful of tea for each person, and one for the p. **FOO 127**

Lovat's head i' the pat **PER 186**

old p. seething with dissatisfaction **PPL 68**

plant them . . . In ae lexicographic p. **WORD 28**

'p. is continually boiling and there's always fresh broth' **THO 17**

put about a pound of tea into a tolerably large-sized p. **FOO 110**

Scottie dog for every p. **SPIR 38**

potato: before Winter there will not be one sound Potatoe in all the Highlands **FOO 7**

But he does have a packet of p. crisps **FOO 76**

the grossly overrated p. **FOO 45**

potatoes: growing p. so long that the Golden Wonder has entered into their souls **NAT 1**

What he did was to take p. from the pot with his fingers **FOO 12**

Who knows now what it was like to be fed only on three meals of p. a day? **PPL 88**

pottingar: p. will purge the painis **LOVE 15**

poverty: Be glaid in wilfu' povertie **ADV 73**

characteristic touch of Scots kindliness and sympathy with p. **LAW 14**

died of p. from finding so little to plunder **TRA 20**

hardship and p. of the thousands of crofters and the lowly of the lands **LAND 41**

home of the p. toffs **PLA 128**

penal colony for those who had committed p. **PLA2: 8**

P. hath the Gaelic and Greek In my land **PPL 98**

P. parts good company **ADV 13**

their own affording only Pedantry, P., Brutality, and Hypocrisy **PPL 4**

where the children of honest p. have the most precious of all advantages **SPIR 16**

We know they can remedy their p. when they set about it **PPL 49**

With one hand he put a penny in the urn of P. **PER 201**

power: Despite those titles, p., and pelf **PER 216**

free people who first gave p. to the king **HIS 25**

great danger in giving voting p. to women **POL 39**

he dealt in an article of which kings were said to be fond – P. **PER 100**

He had a wonderful intellectual p. **PER 100**

he holds the p. of life or death over helpless persons **MIN 10**

I am fascinated . . . by the p. and danger of words **WORD 76**

king o' Scots, and a' his p. **SWW 23**

line . . . of our kings . . . hath been against the p. and purity of religion **REL 98**

nor have we sufficient . . . p. to prevent, those ills **PHIL 22**

O wad some P. the giftie gie us To see oursels as ithers see us! **THO 22**

p. of some to be a boss **DAI 18**

Scots Parliament . . . echoed the voice of whoever was in p. **REL 87**

that will never be richtly mended till weemen get the pooer **M-W 93**

Thy p. . . . . Is nocht but very vanitie **ADV 73**

When the Scotch Kirk was at the height of its p. **REL 25**

Wi' sang and glass they fley the p. O' care that wad harass the hour **PLEAS 7**

powers: guilt-stricken because of p. within us which have never been realised **YOU 20**

strange being, but of great though uncouth p. **POET 9**

practice: deprived of their position by sharp p. **COM 10**

one sort of treatment may serve for all, and their p. . . . . simplified **MIN 15**

taken action to end a recent insensitive p. **DEA 62**

praise: Flow gently, I'll sing thee a song in thy p. RIV 8

Let us p. the humble fish FOO 48

overstepped the bounds by the indiscriminating nature of his p. FAMI 17

p., damn you ACT 12

Who like me His p. should sing? REL 77

pranks: Ye hypocrites! are these your p.? WAR 31

prayer: generous p. is never presented in vain REL 120

Not mellow voice, but fervent p. REL 6

presbyterian: intensely P. activity. In golf . . . you are on your own SPOR 34

not a business to which the p. mind is natively . . . attuned TEL 7

P. faith is an incomparable metaphor REL 14

There was a P. cat ANI 3

mistaken belief that priestdom died when they spelled it P. REL 42

presences: Vast p. come mincing in ANI 56

press: natural, nay . . . the necessary effect of a free p. JOU 12

P. is the Fourth Estate of the realm JOU 4

tyrant on the throne Is the morning and evening p. JOU 6

pressure: Five grand a week? That's my kind of p. SPOR 47

pretty: he is a very p. weoman ANI 38

prey: Presbyterian cat Went seeking for her p. ANI 3

price: all things to all men, providing the p. is right PER 228

He was not insensible to pleasures; but he deemed very few of them worth the p. PER 184

jewel of great p.: St Magnus Cathedral BUI 5

my p. having been raised since I painted that picture ART 33

Scotland was bought and sold . . . I would be extremely glad to know what this p. amounted to, and who received it POL 61

that p. that the bitches of the world have earned PPL 63

prices: Scots way to do little business but squeeze up high p. COM 9

pride: better thing than starved p. ADV 14

big ha'-Bible, ance his father's p. REL 28

bigot and a sot, bloated with family p. INS 57

Caracalla fled from his arms along the fields of his p. PPL 38

cocky wee Gordon's the p. of them a' WAR 12

fient a p., nae p. had he PER 66

glanced with anxious p. at their knees COS 39

If we've got nothin' else at least We've got our p. SPIR 49

It's p. puts a' the country doun HUM 2

lines And flees that were my p. ANG 15

Mons Meg is a monument of our p. and poverty SPIR 54

My joy, my p., my hoggie! ANI 24

nothing here but Hielan' p. PLA 78

pain at my heart, and p. and fondness too MOM 2

p. which seemed arrogance, and perhaps was chiefly shyness PER 237

sentimentality . . . has done very little to give us any sensible p. HIS 35

she preserved . . . a certain decent p. LAND 4

something they believed to be a metaphor for their p. SPOR 52

taken in the pitch of p. BIO 11

thousand schemes of petulance and p. Despatch her scheming children far and wide PPL 24

'tis sair begrutten p. WAR 84

What is betwixt the p. of a . . . Nebuchadnezzar and the preposterous humility of our puritan ministers POL 53

priest: Churches built to please the p. LAW 8

forbidden words in the north were p. or minister WORD 32

he is . . . the world's P. BOO 21

I will nae p. for me shall sing THO 43

priests: In all ages . . . p. have been enemies of liberty REL 65

prime: he's in the p. o' life and cheneral agility PER 196

must it thus be my doom To spend my p. in maidhood's joyless state? M-W 122

One's p. is elusive CHI 45

p. idea is due to the enterprise . . . of an individual SCI 14

these Saturday runaways in the p. of the spring! SWW 50

Prime Minister: He has all the qualifications for a great Liberal P.M. INS 29

Prime Ministers: We all know P.M.s are wedded to the truth BAD 13

primrose: gowd in the breast o' the p. pale NAT 12

primroses: Bountiful p., With outspread heart NAT 19

wild woods Where the p. blaw NAT 6

Primula Scotica: P.S. might be an even better emblem for Scotland NAT 30

prince: But after all, if the p. shall leave these principles SPIR 2

courage and sentiments the P. expresses . . . will always do him honour POL 103

P. of warriors, Oscur my son! LAM 39

sone of ane p. beand distitut of vert is no gentil man FAMI 4

That potent p. gentil King James the Ferde PER 159

princely: He was the glory of p. governing PER 160

princes: p. and lords are but the breath of kings PPL 22

princess: Nature's petticoat is not so easily lifted as that of the P. Obrea NAT 13

not possible to hope for more from any p. of the earth PER 40

since you have lost that p. who was your light LAM 20

Principal: P. . . . must be an upright and godly man UNI 1

principle: By the time the civil service has finished drafting a document to give effect to a p., there may be little of the p. left POL 88

so powerful a p. that it is alone . . . capable of carrying on the society to wealth and prosperity PHIL 55

Toryism is an innate p. o' human nature POL 48

principles: But after all, if the prince shall leave these p. SPIR 2

belief of a material world is . . . of more authority, than any p. of philosophy PHIL 41

error . . . which disposes us to reduce things to few p. PHIL 42

I have some fixed p. PER 52

most of my reasonings will be more useful as furnishing hints . . . than as containing any p. PHIL 27

right to determine their own destiny in accordance with the p. of justice accepted by the social conscience of mankind POL 6

print: He shouldn't have written in such small p. POET 22

his vulgarity beats p. BOO 28

prisoner: every man said to his p., Sir, go and unarm you WAR 39

p. killit not the particular man aforesaid LAW 10

prisoners: bring me p. and I'll find them law LAW 5

privilege: In life it is your p. to choose DEA 25

privy: entered low down among the ordure of the p. HIS 26

prize: We do not run for p. . . . . we run because we must FANT 60

problem: All in all he's a p. must puzzle the devil HUM 5

born teacher is not a p. EDU 31

eternal Scots p. HIS 34

never a p. child EDU 30

problems: first of all p. for a man to find out what kind of work he is to do DAI 13

No p. there. Except I couldn't sail or navigate TRA 6

prodigy: eccentric had elaborated a p. PER 183

production: Consumption is the sole end and purpose of p. PHIL 51

profanities: if ye use p., Then ye'll be putten awa' BAD 1

profession: Journalism is not and never has been a p. JOU 3

Journalism suits the Scot as it is a p. into which you can crawl without enquiry as to your qualifications JOU 5

no qualifications for any p. . . . . so he resolved to try his fortune as a journalist JOU 10

worst paid And the most richly rewarded P. in the world EDU 22

professor: Suffering is the p.'s golden garment REL 107

professors: p. . . . admit that I am far better read BOA 10

profit: enlarge the business, have the p. COM 9

profits: not the p. . . . of literature, which most require to be preached BOO 4

programme: If your p. is to achieve artistic success ART 22

progress: P. is a goddess who . . . has looked after her children well HIS 6

Time is not p., but amount TIM 24

promise: I thought he was a young man of p. POL 14

pronunciation: Our P. is like ourselves, fiery, abrupt WORD 51

proper: And still my delight is in p. young men WAR 28

Every man proper for a member of this Society M-W 37

Not at all like p. children CHI 48

Of riches he keepit no p. thing PER 132

only p. go, was drinkin' drams FOO 104

person p. to be a model ART 12

they found they were dancing to the p. patterns MUS 46

property: mistresses of their houses and . . . the administration of their p. M-W 21

his songs . . . are the p. and solace of mankind BUR 8

misapplied is a'body's p. BUR 15

sacredness of p. COM 7

proportion: It is not the bulk of a fabric . . . that give the grace . . . but the p. of the parts BUI 12

Provand's Lordship: P.L., was built in 1471 and still standing BUI 8

property: Things future are the p. of hope ADV 76

prospects: I backwards cast my e'e On p. drear! HOP 3

prosperity: not anything you can expect . . . which I shall not be ready to do for the happiness and p. of England POL 7

principle . . . capable of carrying on the society to wealth and p. PHIL 55

These qualities have made that dreary . . . land a home of p. LAND 34

Protestant: gunpowder, printing, and the P. religion REL 36

proud: High may your p. banners gloriously wave SPIR 28

High though his titles, p. his name PER 216

p. as a Scot PPL 75

proverb: Don't quote your p. ADV 1

old p. says *Piscinata Scotia* LAND 6

proverbs: people one of whose p. is 'Every force evolves a form' PPL 61

Providence: If P. has sent me here, 'Twas surely in an anger PLA 78

'We must leave that to P.' ADV 99

province: more Scotland has striven to be a nation, the more she has sunk to be a p. POL 105

To mark where England's p. stands POL 22

quarter: She's twisted right, she's twisted left, To balance fair in ilka q. **PER 67**

quarters: Nine quarteris large he was in lenth **PER 131**

quean: But oh! the fickle, faithless q. **M-W 74**

queen: at the broken altar Mary was crowned Q. of Scotland **MUS 57**

> good tidings, that the q. was deliverit **HIS 22**
> 'heroic young q.' . . . had the face, mind, manners and morals of a well-intentioned but hysterical poodle **PER 122**
> international treaty between Anne, Q. of Scots, and Anne, Q. of England **HIS 38**
> news of the death of the Q. of Great Britain and Ireland **JOU 13**
> Q. of guidance, q. of good luck **SWW 3**
> Q. united such strictness to her sweetness **PER 247**
> Though it crawl on the curl of a Q.! **INS 17**
> though the Q. maks muckle o' me **FANT 17**
> warst o' them might ha' been his q. **M-W 2**
> Yestreen the Q. had four Maries **LAM 8**
> you may gather garlands there Would grace a summer's q. **PLA 19**

Queen Bess: Q.B. a maiden-life should reign **CUR 9**

Queen Mary: 'Q.M. was a strumpet and a murtherer' **MOM 32**

queens: Q. should be cold and wise, And she loved little things **PER 24**

quelt: This dress is called the *quelt* **COS 11**

question: Bruce hesitated, not being prepared for the q. **INS 83**

> dog is out of the q. **ANI 32**
> haed I been askin' dis q. I wid hae said **WORD 68**
> if the q. was eternal company . . . or Solitary confinement for life **THO 108**
> it's just a q. of looking at the horizon and deciding whether you really want to go **TRA 5**
> Just how much Scotland's current hyper-vitality owes to . . . its twentieth-century versifiers is a q. worth looking into **POET 67**
> publications, of which the value is so obvious as to admit of no q. **BOO 30**

questions: Above all, not to ask q. **EDU 26**

quill: hand prescribing, or the flattering q. **INS 90**

Quiraing: Q. is frozen terror **MOU 44**

R

Rabelais, François: His religion . . . like that of R.: a great Perhaps **REL 37**

rabbit: they put r.-pouches in your jacket whether ye poach or no' **PLA 55**

rabbits: For r. young and for r. old, For r. hot and for r. cold **FOO 53**

> R. were alluded to as 'little feeties' **WORD 32**

race: Believe him bastard of a brighter r. **CUR 14**

common to all men, and found in no other r. of animals **COM 15**

earth . . . will no longer tolerate the r. which has for a moment disturbed its solitude **LAM 16**

hardy and intrepid r. of men **HIGH 37**

her people, notwithstanding their awkwardness, the greatest r. **LAND 33**

his land was to go to a man of another r. **SPIR 43**

noteless as the r. from whence he sprung **POET 57**

r. of true Scotswomen . . . seems to be facing extinction **M-W 91**

r. that was hard as the Spartans **BOA 11**

simple r.! they waste their toil For the vain tribute of a smile **POET 56**

strong have fainted in the r. for life **LAM 37**

The r. is gone, but still their children breathe **PPL 25**

There was a singular r. of excellent Scotch old ladies **PER 83**

they have sent us to war . . . r. against r. **POL 56**

races: Only the modern Scotsman . . . and a few other favoured r. **REL 48**

> We bear the lot of nations, Of times and r. **THO 92**

racism: One of the great delusions of Scottish society . . . that r. is a problem confined to England's green and unpleasant land **FAMI 10**

radio: alone With a Teasmade, a r., and a telephone **THO 69**

Raeburn, Sir Henry: R. was a born painter of portraits **ART 30**

rage: cold rage seizes one at whiles **THO 131**

ragged: Wha ran barefitted in r. claes **BIO 3**

railway: Beautiful r. bridge of the Silv'ry Tay **DEA 44**

> eager to have a r. through his parish **TRA 16**
> fellow-passenger in the r., took it into his head to smile **MOM 13**
> Jokes were made about the Highland R. **TRA 12**

railways: She very decidedly told us she 'hated r.' **TRA 34**

rain: All the sights of the hill and the plain Fly as thick as driving r. **TRA 42**

> And then comes a mist and a weeping r. **LAM 35**
> Blaw your warst, ye wind and r., Since Maggie, now, I'm in aside ye **M-W 121**
> God grant that we too be lying there in wind and mud and r. **WAR 59**
> In the north . . . you can *see* the r. **SWW 15**
> lang-tailed shoors, an' r. a' 'tween **SWW 13**
> like a wet pebble, with the colours brought out by the r. **ART 4**
> Old Orkneymen had a range of words for every kind . . . of r. **SWW 14**
> r. cam' doun, and they were drookit **SWW 8**
> r. falling Scotchly, Scotchly **SWW 34**
> r. is on our lips **FANT 60**

gunpowder, printing, and the Protestant r.
REL 36

His r. is at best an anxious wish REL 37

line . . . of our kings . . . hath been against the
power and purity of r. REL 98

miners had a queer kind of r. SPOR 59

No man wi' any releegion . . . would caal his
canary a Wee Free REL 93

odious hell-r. of Scottish Calvinism REL 96

'R.? A Scot know r.?' REL 56

'R.? Huh!' REL 78

Their climate, their r. and their habits are
equally averse to pleasure INS 46

Wha daur debait r. on a Sunday? REL 54

remede: Succour Scotland and r. That stad is in
perplexytie LAM 2

Renaissance: R. man, if only we'd had a r.
PER 227

What Knox really did was to rob Scotland of
all the benefits of the R. PER 191

rent: fuckin brassic till this r. cheque hits the mat
DAI 61

tenants of Lord Breadalbane having
applied . . . for a reduction of r. TOA 14

repose: The Best of Men have ever loved R.
THO 130

reptile: Sic a r. was Wat INS 18

reptiles: most scandalously cringing of r. INS 99

Republic: I like the thought of a Scots R. COS 31

resolution: I have taken a firm r. to conquer or
to die BOA 20

respectable: has established himself as a r.
character in distant society BOO 10

rest: end of labour, entry into r. DEA 8

if ever a soul had seen her at r. . . . he'd died of
the shock PER 118

He is adapted primarily for r. M-W 33

R. is for the dead DAI 17

till the floodgates of life shut in eternal r.
SPIR 14

restful: r. rapture of the inviolate grave DEA 71

resurrection: They'll know at R. Day CUR 10

revenge: he . . . was therefore justified in taking
his r. beforehand PER 47

reverence: is it not to Clothes that most men do
r.? COS 15

revolution: Blest R,. which creates Divided
Hearts, united states POL 104

we have brought about . . . a kind of r. in . . .
this useful and elegant art BUI 2

reward: Great their r. in the eyes of the King of
Heaven REL 1

Rhynie: O! R. is a Hieland place, It doesna suit a
Lowland loon PLA 114

rib: not true that woman was made from man's
r. M-W 25

Riccio, David: That poltron and vile knave
Davie PER 152

No Chancellor until this one POL 19

rich: No Chancellor until this one POL 19

if you'd all the same money one day what
would it be the next? – R. and poor again!
PHIL 116

poor could not live, and the r. never die EPI 3

poor country, neighbour to a r. one LAND 21

R. and poor four or five times – Once on the
verge of ruin BIO 11

too old, too fat, too lazy, and too r. BOO 39

O what a glorious sight, Warm-reekin', r.
FOO 29

Were it no for the workin man what wad the
r. man be? POL 55

riches: I marvel greatlie . . . that r. suld nocht in
this realm redound PPL 54

Of r. he keepit no proper thing, Gave as he
wan, like Alexander PER 132

'Our r. will soon be equal,' said the beggar
MOM 42

There's r. galore in the breeze o' the vale
NAT 12

ridge: continually hoping the next r. . . . will be
the summit MOU 12

ptarmigan . . . disappeared over the r. into the
corrie MOU 19

yon that ye thought was the head . . . is the
third r. fae the tap only MOU 45

right: They have . . . an inherent r. to determine
their own destiny POL 6

three great avantages; The first is, we have
the richt SPIR 4

Trust in God, and do the r. REL 88

ultimate notion of r. is that which tends to the
universal good PHIL 30

rights: even children lisp the R. of Man M-W 45

R. of Woman merit some attention M-W 45

river: As some vast r. of unfailing source . . . his
numbers flowed MUS 67

in a r. and in a dish, I hate that ubiquitous
blasted fish FOO 85

Land of polluted r. SPIR 17

Like the foam on the r. . . . Thou art gone
DEA 60

Or like the snowfall on the r., A moment
white – then melts for ever PLEAS 4

monster, which was lying in the r. bed
MONS 6

Up the r. and over the lea CHI 21

What pleasure were to walk and see, Endlang
a r. clear THO 59

rivers: like those r. of Africa which lose
themselves in the burning sands HIS 28

marsh and fountains, upon comparison with
the rise of many of our r., became now a
trifling object MOM 6

multitude of r. each with its own distinct
music NAT 17

O' r. it's the best RIV 15

riveris ran reid on spate SWW 27

wild woods grow, and r. row LOVE 31

road: All I ask, the heavens above, And the r.
below me TRA 45

Everybody else took the r. he liked best
WAR 11

far-flung line o' the Lang Whang R. PLA 92

he'll gang the hie r. and I'll gang the low
MUS 4

r. as the rocks where my infancy grew
LOVE 38

Thy birth has . . . Us raunsound on the r.
REL 50

very rock of the pinnacle seemed to be
vibrating . . . at our r. onslaught MOU 37

rue: He ne'er has gi'en me cause to r. COS 4

Her foes aye found it hedged around With
rosemarie and r. SPIR 42

rugby: R. is a game that all the gods of Greece
might crowd . . . to see SPOR 45

soccer fan attending his first R. International
SPOR 48

ruin: formed for the ruin of our sex PER 230

his awin sensuall plesoure . . . cause of his
utter ruine PER 161

It is for our sin that widespread r. now enters
in LAM 4

Once on the verge of r. BIO 11

place is, of course, technically a r. BUI 14

They leave a r., and they meet A r. on return
WAR 88

Wantonness has been my r. M-W 52

Whether should a r. be in the Gothic or
Grecian form? BUI 16

ruins: gude auld Kirk o' Scotland, She's nae in
r. yet! REL 95

rule: I think the warld is a' gane wrang, When
ilka wife her man wad rule M-W 14

made it a r. when in company never to talk of
what he understood BOO 11

No woman bore . . . A king whose r. will be
greater over Alban PER 45

pleasure of Dundas was the sole r. of every
one of them POL 27

To promote a Woman to beare r. . . . is
repugnant to Nature M-W 84

You have adopted the r. and course that
Judas . . . followed INS 66

rulers: schools are . . . agencies of the r. EDU 26

rules: r. made by men who don't pay to watch
football SPOR 35

rushes: All along the backwater, Through the r.
tall ANI 44

Ruskin, John: not a man: he's an emetic INS 32

Rutherglen: pure and immaculate royal burgh of
R. PLA 117

S

Sabbath: ninety lives have been taken away On
the last S. day of 1879 DEA 44

On the S.-day wash the horses' legs DAI 4

S. bard . . . Perverts the Prophets and purloins
the Psalms POET 12

She caught a moose . . . Upon the S. Day
ANI 3

Who knows now what it was like . . . to
experience as a child the rigours of the
Scottish s. PPL 88

sacredness: s. of love and death Dwells in thy
noise and smoky breath PLA 72

Upon the s. of property civilisation itself
depends COM 7

sacrifice: contrite heart, a humble thought, Are
thine accepted s. THO 106

I . . . would s. a million people any day for one
immortal lyric BOA 9

it was revealed . . . that a human s. would be
necessary FANT 49

J. G. Frazer Revises flayings and human s.
PER 90

sad: Aidan on the contrary grew so s. that he
began to shed tears PER 42

And now his look was most demurely s.
PER 39

And the sadness of her sadness when she's s.
PER 37

I sit on a knoll, all sorrowful and s. LAM 40

I'll be s. for naebody THO 21

Oh and alas, right s. was our case LAM 51

Oh no, s. and slow . . . The time will ne'er be
gane TIM 3

We would all . . . tell our s. stories LAW 22

sadness: And the s. of her s. when she's sad
PER 37

Beauty and s. always go together ADV 87

Bowed with s. many a Gael HIGH 28

how strange was the s. of Scotland's singing
MUS 31

They sang that never was s. But it melted and
passed away THO 77

safe: Make me s. for ever CUR 1

sailor: Home is the s., home from sea EPI 30

saint: Detested, shunn'd by s. and sinner ANI 22

it was revealed to the s. that a human sacrifice
would be necessary FANT 49

on hearing this word of the S., the monster . . .
fled away MONS 6

S., sitting in his little hut PER 21

St Aidan: A. on the contrary grew so sad PER 42

St Andrew: A. 'Stand ye fast by the Cross of St A.!'
WAR 23

St Andrews: ane gritt fir . . . appeared to him
upoun the cittie of Sanct Andros FANT 41

cauld kail in Aberdeen (or should we say St A.)
INS 93

girl sat upon the cutty-stool at St A. REL 102

Old tales . . . Obscure this town PLA 119

St A. by the northern sea, A haunted town it
is to me! PLA 118

St A. is the abject city's name SPOR 61

sea-gray town, the stane-gray sea PLA 120

St Columba: At mouth of day . . . stood C. On
the great white strand SEA 18

St Fiacre: St F., the holy son of an ancient
Scottish king WAR 22

St Johnstoun: St J. is a merry toun Whaur the
water rins sae schire PLA 112

St Kilda: Macleods of Harris and the
MacDonalds of Uist, both desirous of owning
St K. BOA 7

St K. is a home of clouds: it is a cloud-maker
SWW 35
sea below still as deep as the sky above
PLA 121
St Kildans: last of all the British great auks
was . . . beaten to death by the St K. ANI 36
St Theresa: more of Jesus in St T.'s little finger
than in John Knox's whole body REL 13
saints: Ten thousand martyrs, but no s. REL 115
To murder S. was no sweet play CUR 10
Where s. in glory stand, Bright, bright as day
REL 130
sale: Business . . . is the s. of lies DAI 19
's.'s a sublime thing' DAI 41
salmon: An' a ten-pun' saumon hangin' doun in
baith my trouser-legs ANG 8
birr! a whirr! a s.'s on, A goodly fish! ANG 12
effulgence of two dukedoms and the best s.
river in Scotland POL 12
every s. Dougie would be . . . feeling it all
over ANG 9
Finn saw the flashing silver of the s. ANG 5
I saw his sides a-gleamin', The King o' the
Saumon ANG 10
S. . . . is one of the mercies best taken with an
uninquisitive appetite ANG 11
salt: I sometimes wonder if . . . the Scots artist of
real calibre should not choose . . . to remain . . .
beneath the s. ART 26
Saltcoats: people of S. – a sordid race PLA 122
Saltoun, Lady: L.S. who said that if the King
wore the kilt . . . she did not know what the
ladies would do COS 35
salvation: Here lies Boghead . . . In hopes to get
s. EPI 18
my s. is that I'm bad ADV 68
sand: What tho' their foundations are built on
the s. COM 1
sands: I will luve thee still, my dear, While the s.
o' life shall run LOVE 27
sandwich: applause is like a banquet . . . thanks
for the cheese s. ACT 6
sane: Every man has a s. spot somewhere
MIN 50
s. imperialism . . . a larger patriotism POL 90
sang: But aye to me he sings ae s. LAM 48
Gang doun wi' a s., gang doun THO 111
I'll learn my kin a rattlin s., An' I saw ane an'
twenty, Tam YOU 3
aye it's frae the byways Comes hame the
happy s. THO 135
Nae day sae dark . . . But licht comes through;
a s. is there THO 115
s. on his perjurit lips And naething i the
pouch POET 62
Shorn will be the hairst ere lang, Syne begins
a better s. THO 79
There's . . . the s. o' a siller bell intil't
FANT 62
Wi' a cog o' gude swats and an auld Scottish
s. THO 23
sangs: by my s. the rouch auld . . . Scots'll dirl
richt through WORD 47

He . . . kens a' the auld s. that ever were sung!
PER 34
mair s. that bide unsung nor aa that hae been
wrocht POET 64
O sing to me the auld Scotch s. MUS 1
sark: coost her duddies to the wark, And linkit at
in her sark! MUS 17
Her cutty s., o' Paisley harn COS 10
Mealie was his s. M-W 15
might live in sin . . . but were damned to hell if
you hadn't a white s. PLA 128
nane o' them can dae wi'oot a coat or a s.
DAI 49
Thay gloir into that ruffit s. COS 3
Sark, River: Now S. rins over Solway sands . . .
To mark where England's province stands
POL 22
sarks: aye the bluid o' puir folk On the s. o'
gentilities THO 116
Sassunach: Nae S. drings'll daunton me INS 58
Satan: Auld S. cleekit him by the spaul INS 7
O S., when ye tak him, Gie him the schulin' o'
your weans EPI 17
O thou! Whatever title suit thee – REL 30
satin: black s. breeches with blue steel buttons
COS 19
Saturday: Oh, the blessed enchantments of
these S. runaways in the prime of the Spring!
SWW 50
When I get a couple of drinks on a S. PLA 63
sauce: Delightful . . . especially with mint s.
ANI 88
nae pride had he, Nor s., nor state that I could
see PER 66
saucy: She'll nae be half sae s. yet LOVE 33
Saunders: 'A bed, a bed,' Clerk S. said M-W 7
Saxon: In S. strength that abbey frowned BUI 26
saying: 'Is that a s.?' ' . . . it is one now' ADV 131
sayings: they enshrined their tastes in their s.
ADV 70
scadlips: s. to sup till ye spue FOO 120
scandal: S. . . . allowance which the gay make to
the humdrum BAD 12
Scarba: Where S. and Jura And Islay lie near
LAM 40
scene: At last I view the storied s. BUI 34
scenery: more changes of s. in ten miles than . . .
Russia in a hundred TRA 19
scenes: From s. like these, auld Scotia's grandeur
springs PPL 22
schemes: I cannot bear the thought of other
people becoming losers by my s. DAI 60
All s. of Industry to be executed in that
Country are idle Dreams COM 11
scholar: clap a sticking-plaster on the face of a
s. CHI 33
scholars: all s. whether they have a cock or not
can enter the school PLEAS 6
school: Arbiters of high style would sit on the s.
steps COS 36
can't expect a boy to be vicious until he's been
to a really good s. EDU 35
Every s. needs a debating society EDU 34

lesser s. with a few high points **ART 10**

Nae after days are like the days When we were at the scule **EDU 24**

Our s. was in Scotland . . . yet a strong Scottish accent was a real stigma **WORD 6**

Practical wisdom is only to be learned in the s. of experience **DAI 51**

Sweet time, sad time! twa bairns at scule **EDU 27**

Wherever there is access to a S., the Boys are . . . put to it **EDU 3**

wished like Katy she lived at a s. **BOO 32**

worn with the s. tie and baggy serge bloomers **COS 25**

schoolmaster: Ae day laest ouk . . . I met wir skúlmaister **WORD 68**

every severall Kirk have one School-maister appointed **EDU 13**

Experience The schoolmaister of foolis **THO 88**

I speak just the fine English now . . . The good s. taught me how **WORD 58**

s. is abroad, and I trust to him **EDU 8**

schoolmasters: Experience is the best of s. **EDU 12**

schools: But human bodies are sic fools, For a’ their colleges and s. **HUM 6**

s. are not on our side **EDU 26**

s. skailed, and all the children came shouting **MOM 20**

To close all the s . . . could not have any ill . . . effect **EDU 25**

What’s a’ your jargon o’ your s. **UNI 3**

science: luv n s. n thaht naw **WORD 43**

History . . . lies at the root of all s. **HIS 11**

If you think strongly enough you will be forced by s. to the belief in God **REL 67**

Like any other martyr of s., I must expect to be thought . . . wrong **SCI 25**

S. is of no party **SCI 2**

S. is the great antidote to the poison of enthusiasms **SCI 41**

What we might call . . . *the dismal s.* **PHIL 10**

scientific: I am a s. socialist **BOA 9**

s. man is the only person who has anything new to say and who does not know how to say it **SCI 3**

scientist: He had . . . most of the qualities that make a great s. **SCI 9**

scorn: better had they ne’er been born, Who read to doubt, or read to s. **BOO 54**

looking on all that was done to him with a noble s. **PER 58**

Scot: Argument to the S. is a vice more attractive than whisky **BAD 3**

But I am half a S. by birth, and bred a whole one **PER 70**

Had *Cain* been *S.*, God would have changed his doom **PPL 27**

I wondered not, when I was told, The venal S. his country sold **LAND 2**

John Paul Jones demonstrates . . . that endearing protean quality of the S. **PER 228**

Journalism suits the S. **JOU 5**

Mountain Dew, *clear* as a S.’s understanding **FOO 87**

my young nephew . . . the taciturn S. of all the Scots **SPIR 58**

‘One S. . . . was worth two of the Irish’ **PPL 29**

perfervid S. **PPL 78**

Proud as a S. **PPL 75**

Religion? A S. know religion? **REL 56**

S. had answered unto S.: an eccentric had elaborated a prodigy **PER 183**

S. has to act his part all his life **ACT 13**

S. . . . is very much what I choose to call a secret humorist **HUMO 9**

Trust yow no Skott **PPL 16**

Whatever blessing wait a genuine S., In double portion swells thy glorious lot **INS 20**

‘*Scozzeze.* What kind of animal is that?’ **PPL 33**

Scotch: all the things that people called ‘bad grammar’ . . . were ‘good grammar’ in S. **WORD 56**

Among ourselves, the S. . . . are particularly disagreeable **INS 46**

being S., he didn’t mind damnation **PER 158**

double S. is about the size of a small S. before the War **FOO 47**

Except in a real old-fashioned S. house **FOO 61**

he will still have a strong S. accent of the mind **HIGH 45**

He’s a warm S. heart, and a braid S. tongue **PER 34**

If you imagine a S. commercial traveller in a S. commercial hotel **BUR 12**

I adore . . . S. trifle at the North British Hotel **FOO 80**

‘I can go nowhere without finding the S. at my beard’ **WAR 22**

In a S. village . . . there is no sense whatsoever of obedience to authority **SPIR 29**

In our play-hours we amused ourselves . . . at ‘S. and English’ **CHI 43**

Jemmy . . . thought not of his own S. snivel **INS 81**

Mix the S. thistle with the English bays **INS 90**

O sing to me the auld S. sangs **MUS 1**

Permit me to begin with paying a just tribute to S. sincerity **PPL 51**

peculiar element in S. humour . . . if it is obvious it is of less account **HUMO 11**

Public opinion in a S. playground was a powerful influence **EDU 28**

requires a surgical operation to get a joke well into a S. understanding **HUMO 15**

S. are great charmers **PPL 102**

S. do not drink **FOO 77**

S. is as spangled with vowels as a meadow with daisies **WORD 50**

S. method of making every duty dismal **ADV 96**

S. songs are not 'pretty' **MUS 26**

There was a singular race of excellent S. old ladies **PER 83**

This, I suppose, was a genuine s. mist **SWW 39**

Those that think composing a S. song is a trifling business **MUS 18**

washing his hands; The S. members don't know what he is doing **INS 88**

Scotchly: rain falling S., S. **SWW 34**

Scotchman: 'Are you native born?' 'No sir, I am a S,' **PER 79**

I am by birth a *North Briton*, as a S. must now be called **SPIR 11**

I *scotch'd* not kill'd the *S.* in my blood **SPIR 15**

'Much . . . may be made of a S., if he be ate*caught* young' **EDU 7**

nine times out of ten there is a S. in the case **COM 10**

S. certainly does make one feel that underneath his greasy . . . civilisation the hairy simian sits and gibbers **INS 28**

S. is one of the proudest things alive **PPL 43**

very little amusement in the room but a S. to hate **INS 52**

Scotchmen: I have been trying all my life to like S. **PPL 53**

Scotia: From scenes like these, auld S.'s grandeur springs **PPL 22**

From the heath-covered mountains of S. we come **SPIR 19**

'Oh S. my dear, my native land' **WAR 45**

old proverb says *piscinata S.* **LAND 6**

Old S. is peerless in her magnificence **BATH 19**

On S.'s plains, in days of yore **MUS 27**

Scoticisms: few *modern* S. which are not barbarisms **WORD 61**

Scotland: after S. had been exhausted by raising new levies **WAR 71**

Ah, Kingdom of S., I think that your days are now shorter **LAM 20**

Alas, S., to whom sall thou complain **LAM 30**

All the people in S. are not so void of taste **COM 8**

And it's O for the kail-brose o' S. **FOO 33**

And weel the men o' S. kent It was the unicorn **FANT 61**

And you playing 'Farewell to S. and the rest of the earth' **MUS 47**

arrangements under which S. was governed . . . represented not so much a constitution as a bad joke **POL 106**

At the Council of Constance . . . Dr Gray attended as Ambassador of S. **PER 106**

Atlantic principality . . . whose ambassadors treated direct with the kings of S. **HIGH 35**

Auld S. has a raucle tongue **SPIR 13**

Before his arrival, S.'s history had been purely vegetable **HIS 37**

before the first savages set foot upon the soil of S. **HIS 33**

belief that S. is a tolerant and welcoming country **FAMI 10**

By this time there should have turned up in post-war S. . . . some voice expressing the search for Scottish renewal **POL 36**

Come S., tune your stock and horn **BATH 6**

'Congo's no' to be compared wi' the West o' S.' **ANI 80**

conscientious Chinaman who contemplated a thesis on the literary history of S. **WORD 62**

development of S. . . . bought at the expense of shedding one bit of its past after another **HIS 32**

Doutless he deed for S.'s life **WAR 84**

Duke of Cumberland Who . . . Endeavoured to ruin S. **INS 8**

effulgence of two Dukedoms and the best salmon river in S. will go a long way **POL 12**

Englishmen have thrown away those confined notions of nationality that still prevail in S. **POL 105**

even in S. the use of Scots is taken . . . as a signal to laugh **ACT 5**

Fecht for Britain? Hoot, awa'! For Bonnie S.? Imph, man, na! **SPIR 39**

For a brief period . . . S. enjoyed the largest educational system **EDU 39**

Great Grey Man . . . S.'s Abominable Snowman **MONS 8**

Great Julius . . . His winning was in S. bot full sma' **HIS 19**

gude auld Kirk o' S., She's nae in ruins yet! **REL 95**

had his followers . . . been of like mettle, the history of S. might have been strangely and splendidly different **PER 121**

Hammered like a bolt diagonally through S. . . . this train **TRA 29**

He canna S. see wha yet Canna see the Infinite **SPIR 32**

he lifted his hand . . . also against all the Kingdom of S. itself **PER 53**

he lives among savages in S., and among rakes in London **PER 147**

He would not allow S. to derive any credit from Lord Mansfield **EDU 7**

Highlands of S. contain mountain form of the finest . . . kind **MOU 115**

history of S. is the most romantic . . . of any country in Europe **HIS 18**

Holyrood, with its . . . effigies of crowned heads of S. **ART 15**

Honourable gentleman acknowledged that S. was bought and sold **POL 61**

how strange was the sadness of S.'s singing **MUS 31**

I am not sure whether S. . . . is not the finest country in the world **LAND 33**

I believe S. would be the country I should choose to end my days in **LAND 23**

I call you shrine of a nation yet to be, A S. of a grander growth **PLA 84**

'I do indeed come from S., but I cannot help it' **MOM 3**

I went to S. but I could find nothing that looked like S. **TEL 3**

If that you will France win, Then with S. first begin **WAR 81**

I'll drink a cup to S. yet, Wi' a' the honours three! **TOA 19**

I'm terrified . . . of the celebration of mediocrity in S. **TEL 4**

In my opinion S. is the great White Hope of European art **BOA 8**

In S. everybody represses you **PPL 64**

in S. I felt as if in a second home **LAND 34**

In S. I have eaten nettles, I have slept in nettle sheets **NAT 4**

Jenny Geddes . . . not to be given up without danger of sapping the foundations of society in our beloved S. **HIS 27**

Just how much S.'s current hyper-vitality owes to . . . its twentieth-century versifiers is a question worth looking into **POET 67**

Langholm presents . . . S. in miniature **PLA 93**

lark was never much used for the table in S. **FOO 90**

Let . . . plenty in S. aye abound, By labour of the ploughmen **DAI 5**

little white rose of S. That smells sharp and sweet **NAT 18**

Lourd on my hert as winter lies The state that S.'s in the day **LAM 34**

made the strangest . . . wedding address ever heard in S. **FANT 20**

Many a single county in S. has produced more men of original genius **PPL 32**

marriages of necessity, common enough at one time in S. **PER 32**

maxim which deserves to be engraven . . . on every manse in S. **REL 52**

movement in favour of a national rebirth has attracted some of the finest and most generous spirits in S. **POL 99**

museums of S. are wrang **THO 63**

My life has been . . . in the exploration of the mystery of Scotland's self-suppression **BIO 7**

My son was born to play for S. **SPOR 14**

new S., neither urban nor rural **POL 47**

no art that is not intellectual can be worthy of S. **ART 34**

None can destroy S., save S,'s self **SPIR 9**

not common everywhere like the Thistle; it is confined to S. **NAT 30**

nothing very funny about S. **HUMO 16**

O Flower of S. When will we see your like again **SPIR 59**

Of S.'s king I haud my hoose **SPIR 46**

On a clear day in central S. you can see Arran from any high place West of Tinto **MOU 20**

On the map of S. one finds Roxburghshire, but the town is gone **PLA 116**

One of S.'s misfortunes is that she was not conquered by the Roman **HIS 15**

Our school was in S. . . . yet a strong Scottish accent was a real stigma **WORD 6**

People of S. . . . are the inheritors . . . of an historic tradition of liberty **POL 6**

People want to see how a parliament . . . works before going for what we want for S. **POL 67**

poor S! beggarly S.! . . . yea, but Covenanted S.! **REL 32**

pre-commercial S., a land of brigands and bigots **PPL 31**

Put no faith in aught that bears the name of music while you are in S. **MUS 66**

rats of S. breed faster than ever **PER 120**

real question . . . is not whether an independent S. would be viable, but whether it would be bearable **POL 75**

Romantic S.'s in the grave **THO 49**

S. bore me, England adopted me **EPI 15**

S. can never be Old S. again **LAM 43**

S. does not, in fact, belong to the people of S. **POL 82**

S. has been . . . an increasingly unprofitable sphere **DAI 37**

S. has . . . a peculiar faculty in the production of womankind **M-W 101**

S. . . . has scarcely begun to recover yet from the fact that S. . . . rejected David Hume **PHIL 35**

S. is bounded . . . on the West by Eternity **LAND 51**

S. is indefinable **PPL 93**

S. is the country above all others . . . in which a man of imagination may carve out his own pleasures **LAND 61**

S. is the only country where six and half a dozen are never the same thing **LAND 56**

S. . . . most drunken nation on the face of the earth **FOO 114**

S. must be rid of S. before the delivery come **SPIR 48**

S. rich in fish **LAND 6**

S. rises as the border of the world **LAND 5**

S. small? **LAND 37**

S., the best place in the world to take an appetite **FOO 95**

S. was a country to reckon with as long as she was not incorporated with England **LAND 21**

S. will be reborn when the last minister is strangled with the last copy of the *Sunday Post* **JOU 14**

S. would be way ahead of anywhere except maybe Jerusalem **LAND 59**

S.'s an attitude of mind **LAND 36**

Search S. over . . . there is not a cottage-hut . . . without its Bible **POET 37**

she . . . loved him . . . you were shamed and a fool to say that in S. **LOVE 46**

So in S. witches used to raise the wind **FANT 26**

So this is your S. It is rather nice, but dampish **LAND 35**

Stands S. where it did? **LAND 50**

strange, defiant cry heard from some of S.'s football terraces **PPL 57**

Surely that exquisite aroma is essential S. **MOM 5**

Swordless S., sadder than its psalms **SPIR 30**

thair is twa kingis and twa kingdomis in S. **MOM 33**

that the nobillis of S. suld be the mair mindfull of the foirsaid League **HER 1**

that universal Aunt Sally of S. **POL 31**

theatre in S. has never been a powerful institution **ACT 13**

There is no land in which a man may live more pleasantly and delicately than in S. **LAND 16**

There was a naughty boy . . . he ran away to S., The people for to see **TRA 25**

These are the worthless creatures . . . who rule in the Highlands of S. **FOO 83**

these intelligent eccentrics of whom S. has the manufacturing secret **PER 49**

This train was off for S. **TRA 11**

Thistle, S.'s badge, Up from Freedom's soil it grew **SPIR 42**

three hours' sunshine in S. is worth three months' . . . in Cairo **ART 4**

Towering in gallant fame, S., my mountain hame **SPIR 28**

unassuming, modest, and known as the white rose of S. **SPIR 24**

Up to her University days she carried the conviction that there was something about S. in the Bible **PER 219**

Wallace, that has redeemit S. **PER 133**

we find the glories of ancient S. jostled by taverns **BUI 9**

We talked of S. . . . 'hard to paint when your feet are cold' **ART 7**

we who live in S. are obliged to study English in books like a dead language **WORD 3**

Wha for S.'s king and law Freedom's sword would strongly draw **WAR 26**

What is the history of S.? **HIS 7**

What, weneth the kynge of Englande So soone to haue wonne Scotlande? **BOA 1**

'What'll happen to him when the Revolution comes?' 'He'll be commissar for S.' **POL 16**

When Alysandyr our King was dede That S. led in luf and le **LAM 2**

when I . . . am told what to expect for going to S., I shall be reddy to obey **POL 10**

When I came into S. I knew well enough what to expect from my enemies **FRI 28**

when I did my fireman sketch in S. **ACT 11**

When shall I see S. again? **LAND 54**

while the Scotsman has often led . . . S. has no less often lagged **HIS 17**

Who cares about the Free Church, compared with the Christian good of S.? **REL 39**

Within the . . . narrative, S. is heavily feminised, languorously awaiting the phallic embrace of the outsider **TEL 9**

'Woe to the folk of S., for here is the beginning of all sorrow' **LAM 3**

Ye'll tak' the high road, and I'll tak' the low road, And I'll be in S. afore ye **MUS 5**

you are bound to assume that a self-governing S. is going to be . . . morally better, and I don't see it *unless there has also been a revolution* **SPIR 40**

You have talked unsparingly of S., and had better have kept silent **INS 66**

Scots: a' ae man's bairns when you are over the S. dyke **HIGH 41**

after a dram of good wholesome S. spirits **FOO 91**

ah don't hate the English . . . Ah hate the S. **INS 97**

Among the S., licking of wounds is second only to football as a national sport **SPOR 62**

by my sangs the rouch auld . . . S.'ll dirl richt through **WORD 47**

commonly our S. way to do little business but squeeze up high prices **COM 9**

Douglas Young, anxious to demonstrate the living qualities of S. **WORD 45**

English, as a people, are very little inferior to the S. **PPL 71**

eternal S. problem, the integration of Scottish historical experience **HIS 34**

every S. lady had that essential part of national costume **COS 33**

Fergus, the first King of S., had no other law **HIS 25**

foul hordes of S. and Picts **PPL 42**

grafted the debased S. of the Edinburgh streets onto their native Yiddish **WORD 21**

'have we not bought the S. and a right to tax them?' **POL 61**

'He is a Jew . . . We are honest S.' **INS 10**

I am S. – proud of it **HIGH 42**

'I think the S. are a lazy set of bastards, to be quite frank' **DAI 25**

I wonder if . . . the S. artist . . . should not choose deliberately as it were to remain beneath the salt **ART 26**

if she said it in S. the woman would think *Isn't that a common-like bitch at the manse* **WORD 29**

If the S. knew enough to go indoors when it rained **PPL 36**

imitated S. of the stage is seldom a happy imitation **ACT 10**

In pidgin English or in wild-fowl S. **BUR 15**

It is the Scottis Glamourie **FANT 62**

It was characteristic of the S. to leave the young men to themselves **UNI 5**

'it was trying to learn that language that spoiled my S.' **WORD 44**

king o' S., and a' his power Canna turn Arthur o' Bower **SWW 23**

king of S. was skilled in warfare **PER 101**

laith, laith were our gude S. lords To wat their cork-heeled shoon **COS 2** lang S. miles, The mosses, waters, slaps and styles **LAND 11**

many people think that S. possesses a rich vocabulary **WORD 74**

no sense among the S. that a working class man who has taken a degree has got above himself **FAMI 14**

not the remotest reason why the majority of modern Scottish writers should be considered S. all **BOO 33**

of the S. he said that they were ugly but good-natured **PPL 11**

On fut sould be all Scottis weir **WAR 38**

One factor that has made the S. 'a peculiar people' **PPL 103**

Oor S. Pegasus Is a timmer naig **POET 46**

overwhelmed with the burden of from six to ten pair of S. blankets **M-W 71**

rouch dirl o' an auld S. strain **SPIR 33**

S. are beset by Scottish history **HIS 14**

S. are incapable of considering their literary geniuses . . . as writers **BOO 69**

S. are not industrious **PPL 9**

S. deserve no pity, if they voluntarily surrender **SPIR 21**

S. had no reason to set any value on their parliament **REL 87**

S. have a strong . . . sense of history, yet . . . prefer the romantic myth **HIS 13**

S. have always been an unhappy people **PPL 70**

S. have been distinguished for humour **HUMO 5**

S. have never had a real chance to develop themselves **PPL 74**

S. invented golf, it's said **SPOR 2**

S., wha hae wi' Wallace bled **WAR 25**

Scottish Gaelic song is the chief artistic glory of the S. **MUS 51**

So many S. . . . . have lapsed into the English habit of thought **SPIR 27**

So me behovit . . . Some bastard Latin, French or Inglis use, Where scant were Scottis **POET 20**

They've only been assisting at a braw S. Nicht! **FES 11**

30,000 S. families that live incorporate in her bowels **COM 13**

this I have observed more frequently among the S. **PPL 96**

'This is where I come to do what the S. are best at.' 'Shinty?' 'Moping.' **SPOR 53**

touch of S. kindliness . . . in the law of the time **LAW 14**

use of S. is taken by audiences as a signal to laugh **ACT 5**

we have tested the faith of the S. in adverse times **HIS 12**

We S. need the English because otherwise we would have slaughtered each other **PPL 95**

Were you to hear a S. lady repeat the verses of any of the true original songs **MUS 79**

When the S. saw the Englishmen recoil and yield themselves, then the S. were courteous **WAR 39**

Whenever a venture appeared to be a forlorn hope . . . there were the S. battling for it **HIS 18**

Scotshire: Mr Gunn is a brilliant novelist from S. **BOO 34**

Scotsman: He has the power of making any S. . . . . more wholeheartedly himself **BUR 19**

Is there any S. without charm? **PPL 12**

never difficult to distinguish between a S. with a grievance and a ray of sunshine **PPL 101**

Only the modern S. . . . . can withstand the toxic effects of certain speculations **REL 48**

Wherever a S. goes, there goes Burns **BUR 20**

while the S. has often led the age, Scotland has no less often lagged **HIS 17**

Scotsmen: clever S., who complete their education at the University of Oxford **INS 94**

'O you who were wont to say that my S. were useless' **WAR 50**

real question for S. is not whether an independent Scotland would be viable **POL 75**

S. are metaphysical and emotional **PPL 97**

S. take all they can get, and a little more **PPL 58**

Scotswomen: One cannot but be conscious of an underlying melancholy in S. **PPL 41**

race of true S. . . . . seems to be facing extinction **M-W 91**

Scott, Michael: That other . . . Is M.S., who verily knew well The lightsome play of every magic fraud **PER 23**

wondrous M.S.; A Wizard, of such dreaded fame **PER 210**

Scott, Sir Walter: As a poet S. *cannot* live **POET 70**

none by sabre or by shot Fell half so flat as W.S. **POET 26**

not many genteel Scottish writers before S. **POET 42**

strangest and saddest monument that S.'s genius created **BUI 23**

That d – d Sir W.S.! **CUR 13**

think'st thou, Scott! by vain conceit perchance, On public taste to foist thy stale romance **POET 11**

W.S. has no business to write novels **BOO 2**

when Mr S.'s work appeared . . . a deadening blow was inflicted on our rural literature **MUS 37**

Scottie: Tartan rock, and a S. dog for every pot **SPIR 38**

Scotties: Croose London S. wi' their braw shirt fronts **BUR 15**

Scottish: a' the dour provincial thocht That merks the S. breed **PPL 60**

about one half of the S. nation . . . regarded themselves as members of the aristocracy **PPL 50**

There were not many genteel S. writers before
Scott **POET 42**

tragic attempts at the filming of S. history
TEL 14

Ugly churches and services . . . have stifled the
S. arts almost out of existence **REL 112**

ultimate S. international team would be
SPOR 72

touch of S. kindliness . . . in the law of the
time **LAW 14**

when I was taking tea with a well-known S.
divine **PLA 48**

Who knows what it was like . . . to experience
as a child the rigours of the S. sabbath
PPL 88

'Working-class Tenements! . . . inhabited by
the majority of the S. people **HOM 2**

world is neither S., English, nor Irish . . . but
human' **SPIR 23**

Scottish National Party: British 'Parliamentary
cretinism' . . . has found its last abiding refuge
within the S.N.P. **POL 85**

evil mélange of decrepit Presbyterianism and
imperialist thuggery . . . appears to be
solidly represented in the SNP **POL 84**

only person ever to have been expelled
from . . . the S.N.P. for being a communist
PER 72

Scotts: threat of the S, has filled the moss
WAR 69

Scotus, Duns: Scotland bore me **EPI 15**

scullions: S., hogge-rubbers, kenell brakers
BOA 22

sea: 'And if we gang to sea, master, I fear we'll
come to harm' **FANT 12**

Benbecula is the s.'s dearest child **PLA 17**

But he heard the roarin' o' the s. **FANT 10**

deep s.-heart was brooding deep upon its
ancient lore **SEA 17**

fishermen have always had taboos on certain
words while at s. **WORD 32**

God's might so peopled hath the s. **ANI 18**

Here, at three thousand feet above the s.
MOU 19

Home is the sailor, home from s. **EPI 30**

I look on the grey s. In mistiness clad
LAM 40

I never lo'ed a lad but ane, And he's drooned
in the s. **LAM 7**

I'm getting rich from your s.-bed **POL 66**

lift grew dark, and the wind blew loud, And
gurly grew the s. **SWW 5**

Looking from the sheiling, O, far away to s.
M-W 17

mony a load on shore may be skailed at s.
ADV 79

Of a' the fish that live in the s. The herrin' it is
the fish for me **ANI 4**

Over the s. to Skye **PLA 125**

salt s. we'll harry **FOO 70**

S. and sky and the folk who wrought . . . lasted
but as a breath **LAND 27**

s. below still as deep as the sky above **PLA 121**

s., I think, is lazy **THO 44**

s. of upturned faces **ADV 112**

s. reaches to its shoulder **PLA 11**

s.-gray town, the stane-gray s. **PLA 120**

s.'s horizon soars into the firmament **SEA 8**

solitudes of land and s. assuage My quenchless
thirst for freedom **SPIR 47**

sore s.-longing in my heart **SEA 19**

spoke the great Word over me, In the land
beyond the s. **FANT 58**

thair appeared unto him . . . ane gritt fir
upoun the s. **FANT 41**

These crofter carles may cross the s., but we
are masters here **LAND 8**

We twain have met like the ships upon the s.
MOM 44

Wee Davie Daylicht keeks owre the s.
SWW 62

western s. alone can speak in the Gaelic
tongue **SEA 20**

wet sheet and a flowing s. **SEA 7**

what grand's the smell ye'll get Frae the neep-
fields by the s.! **LAND 31**

You will not remember the salt smell of the
s. **SWW 2**

sea-birds: s. express their emotions with great
intensity **ANI 31**

sea-serpents: Mester Stoorworm . . . first, and
greatest of all s.-s. **MONS 4**

sea-shell: s.-s. wants to whisper to you **SEA 15**

sea-shore: It grows near the seashore, on banks,
in clefts . . . the white rose of Scotland **SPIR 24**

single excursion . . . to a . . . s.-s., is worth
many books **EDU 19**

sea-trout: landed from it a s.-t. as shining as a
swan **M-W 75**

sea-water: I weel believe I could mak drinkable
toddy out o' s.-w. **FOO 67**

Seafield, Lady: we were graciously received by
L.S. **TRA 34**

Seaforths: Black Watch are braw, the S. and a'
WAR 12

seals: But hark! . . . It is the singing of the s.
ANI 72

He would play a tune to the s. **ANI 100**

seas: From the lone sheiling on the misty island,
Mountains divide us, and a waste of s. **SPIR 3**

I will luve thee still, my dear, Till a' the s.
gang dry **LOVE 27**

Into the pit-mirk nicht we northwart sail
Facin the bleffarts and the gurly s. **SEA 4**

rage and storm ourwelterand wally s.
SWW 27

that air of the remote and wild, shut off by
incalculable s. **PLA 54**

season: In this congealit s. sharp and chill
SWW 28

Let me hear . . . whether you think this is the
proper s. to maul them **POL 101**

many of us would to well to *mediterraneanise*
ourselves for a s. **THO 36**

'only two gentlemen to guide all this blessed
s.' **CUR 13**

Whatever the s . . . eggs and fowls must be sent to the 'big house' **DAI 29**

seasons: I need the rides most, hurling warm through all . . . s. **TRA 19**

Time's a fire-wheel whose spokes the s. turn **TIM 25**

You light up your face, new moon of the s. **SWW 3**

Second Sight: S.S. is an unwelcome gift **FANT 31**

secret: Ballads are a voice from s. places **POET 36**

He that has a s. should . . . hide that he has something to hide **ADV 40**

I've read the s. name o' Knox's God **REL 110**

If you wish to preserve your s. **ADV 125**

inward gates of a bird are always open . . . That is the s. of its song **ANI 64**

Landlady and Tam grew gracious, Wi' s. favours **M-W 42**

s. beauty born of the mists **MOU 16**

s. of my success over the four hundred metres . . . with God's help, I run faster **SPOR 42**

those intelligent eccentrics of whom Scotland has the manufacturing s. **PER 49**

you allow yourselves to be seduced in s. **M-W 27**

seed: Ye'll no keep my s. frae faain in **DEA 37**

seer: S.'s hand is put on the Inquirer's Head **FANT 40**

Segget: S. it's a dirty hole **PLA2: 4**

seldom: Friends are lost by calling often; and . . . seldom **FRI 2**

self-control: prudent, cautious s.-c. is Wisdom's root **ADV 35**

self-discipline: characteristic of the Scots to leave the young men to themselves, to teach them . . . s.-d. **UNI 5**

self-pity: tragic element in s.-p. is this **THO 117**

self-respect: S.-r. is the noblest garment with which a man may clothe himself **THO 109**

selfishness: S. is calm, a force of nature **THO 119**

Selkirk: day oot o' S. is a day wastet **PLA 123**

Sellar, Patrick: S., daith has ye **PER 239**

sense: come it may . . . That S. and Worth o'er a' the earth Shall bear the gree **HOP 5**

grand, whunstane s. **ADV 137**

Here lies, of s. bereft – But s. he never had **EPI 25**

I dinna see the s. ava! **ANI 15**

There is no seventh s. of the mystic kind **MIN 32**

thou hast got By instinct wise much s. about thy lot **ANI 28**

senses: scared out of his seven s. **ADV 111**

sensuous: I have never . . . touched anything so s. before or since **COS 58**

sentence: nearest to a just s. any judge ever gave **LAW 21**

on March 10, 1876 . . . the first complete s. was ever spoken by Bell **MOM 15**

our history may be summed up in this one s. **HIS 17**

to follow ane fixt sentence . . . Is mair practic, difficil . . . Than for to write all ways at libertie **WORD 22**

Today, after dinner, my s. has been announced **DEA 47**

Wha haldis . . . of wordis the properteis Full oft the verity of the s. fleeis **WORD 24**

sentiment: artist without s. is like a painter without colours **ART 2**

great deal of what is called Scottish s. *is* funny **HUMO 2**

National Parliament, through which National s. finds expression **POL 43**

sentiments: I have heard higher s. from . . . uneducated men and women . . . than I ever yet met with out of the Bible **PPL 85**

sentimental: only thing that remains now is a s. legend **HIS 32**

though we are very s. ourselves, we like to pour cold water on other people's sentiment **PPL 18**

we are at bottom the most s. and emotional people on earth **PPL 20**

sentimentalist: barrenest of all mortals is the s. **M-W 57**

sentimentality: His ribaldry . . . and s. are all Protestant **BUR 18**

s. that encumbers Scottish history **HIS 35**

September: S.'s merry month is near, That brings in Neptune's caller chere **FOO 51**

serge: worn with the school tie and baggy s. bloomers **COS 25**

sergeant: first man I saw was the bombing s., with his head laid open **WAR 72**

I canna see the s. . . . . He's owre far awa' **WAR 48**

sermon: ere he had done with his sermone, he was sa active . . . he was like to ding the pulpit in blads **PER 182**

It was a true, sterling gospel s. **PLA 14**

not the best s. which makes the hearers go away . . . praising the speaker **REL 26**

they will go into a change-house after s. **FOO 35**

servant: asked me to sit to him, whereto I replied, 'Is thy s. a dog' **ART 20**

Friend more than S., Loyal, Truthful, Brave **PER 244**

'How had you the audacity, John?' said a . . . laird to his s. **THO 56**

I may bribe his s. to tie a rope across his staircase **FRI 8**

'If your honour disna ken when ye hae a gude s.' **DAI 48**

s. girls told us that 'Dandy Doctors' . . . prowled all night **CHI 33**

servants: there will never be equality in the s.s' hall **PPL 13**

warning call of 'Gardy loo' from s. **DAI 28**

service: I was inordinately ambitious . . . to be of s. **HOP 15**

servile: guided by s. ghillies to your sport
LAND 17
   most wretched, s., miserable, pathetic trash
   INS 97
   s. and impertinent, shallow and pedantic
   INS 57

sewer: sitting in a s., and adding to it INS 25

sex: formed for the ruin of our s. PER 230
   I am very strong and robust and not of the
   delicate s. PER 107
   must be a professed lover of one or more of
   the female s. M-W 37
   playing the pipes was not a substitute for s.
   MUS 41
   S. was not referred to at all CHI 16
   wanderer, forgetting his assumed s. PER 50
   weaker s., to piety more prone M-W 20
   Wisdom hath no s. M-W 28
   Women are the best opposite s. M-W 107
   women's views would be represented by
   the noisiest and least womanly of their s.
   POL 39

sexual: And all the s. intercourse of things
POET 31

shade: I said to him I was only a wandering s.
FANT 48

shadow: Dance to your s. when it's good to be
living, lad MUS 53
   Downward we drift through s. and light
   MONS 17
   He . . . fears the s. of his own reputation
   POET 58
   His lug wad cast a s. ower a sax-fit gate
   PER 245
   Joy that is clothed with s. Is the joy that is not
   dead THO 82
   Our life's a flying s., God's the pole TIM 1
   S. of our trysting bush, It wears so slowly
   round TIM 3
   'Twas the round-about of the s. That had so
   furrowed its face TIM 20

shadows: coming events cast their s. before
YOU 7
   hidden forces . . . which remain today as pale
   s. FANT 57
   thochts o' bygane years Still fling their s. ower
   my path THO 90

Shakespeare, William: Wha hear a Burns or
S. sing, Yet still their ain bit jingles string
POET 40
   Whaur's your Wully S. noo? SPIR 18

shameful: within few days he sall ly as shamfull
as he lyis glorious now FANT 42

Shankly, Bill: S. . . . announced: 'The better
team drew' SPOR 73

shanks: Wi' s. like that ye'd better hae stuck to
breeks COS 49

sharn: with the smell of the s. rising feuch! in her
face BOO 32

Sharp, William: whenever he was preparing to
write as Fiona MacLeod he dressed himself
entirely in women's clothes BOO 41

shearers: s. sweated phenomenally as they
worked COS 24

shearing: struggle to escape being the last done
with the s. FANT 24

sheep: bleatings of a s. INS 41
   going to see his patients accompanied by a pet
   s. MIN 19
   grey-faced nation HIGH 26
   two bad shepherds, hunched above their s.
   MOU 27
   virtuous to do a s. a good turn ADV 47

sheela-na-gig: a rarity, a *s.na.g.* BUI 24

Shelley, Percy Bysshe: S. is a poor creature
POET 15

shepherd: Lord is my s.! . . . I am weel
neiboured! REL 83
   s.'s plaiding, and a beggar's pay HIGH 33

shepherds: immediately awakening the s., he
described the wonderful vision FANT 2
   two bad s., hunched above their sheep
   MOU 27

Sheriffmuir: at S., a battle there was that I saw,
man WAR 61

Sherlock Holmes: It is most certainly to you
that I owe S.H. PER 96

sherry: the Laureate bold, With his butt of s. To
keep him merry POET 4

Shetland: hunder year sin syne S. men sailed der
smacks Nort to da Faroe bank SEA 11
   we pay dem fur laernin' bairns English, no fur
   unlearnin' wir Shetlan' speech WORD 68

Shetlands: Lerwick, capital of the S. . . . a place I
avoid like the plague PLA 94

sheugh: gash and faithfu' tyke, As ever lap a s.
or dyke ANI 21
   It neither grew in syke nor ditch, Nor yet in
   any s. FANT 3

Shieldaig: Among the S. party was a small boy
REL 86

shieling: From the lone s. on the misty island,
Mountains divide us SPIR 3
   still my thoughts return To my ain folk ower
   yonder, in the sheiling by the burn PPL 65
   Waiting at the sheiling, O M-W 17

shielings: low-lying isle, with its many s.
Belonged . . . to the Children of the Gael
LAND 40

shilling: deevil a s. I awe, man DAI 10

shilpit: s. sun is thin Like an auld man deein'
slow SWW 43

shinty: An' haste awa' to s. SPOR 57
   New Year shinty match . . . ended in a free
   fight SPOR 32
   'This is where I come to do what the Scots are
   best at.' 'S.?' 'Moping.' SPOR 53

ship: Be it wind, be it weet, be it hail, be it sleet,
Our s. maun sail the faem SWW 4
   Don't quote your proverb until you bring your
   s. into port ADV 1
   end of the world is near when the
   MacBrayne's s. will be on time TRA 40
   galliasse . . . cam on windwart of the tothir
   schip WAR 7

She would sail like a s. from Tarshish **PER 84**
They forgot all about the s., they forgot
   everything, except the herrings **SEA 13**
Where will I get a skeely skipper, To sail this
   new s. o' mine? **TRA 1**
ships: cried in the Greek *The s. of Pytheas!*
   FANT 28
   every one of the s. must fight until she sank
      WAR 56
   More s. are lost through bad logic than
      through bad seamanship **PHIL 32**
   no-one left to build s. **LAW 17**
   We twain have met like the s. upon the sea
      MOM 44
shirt: Then there was a thick woollen shirt and
   tweed trousers **COS 24**
shit: I'll go home when I see fit All I'll leave is a
   heap of s. **POL 66**
shite: Braveheart is pure Australian s. **TEL 2**
shoe: Ae wean fa's sick . . . anither tines his s.
   CHI 36
shoes: bright morocco shoes with silver or blue
   steel buckles **COS 19**
   I've got great s. . . . Try tartan s. **COS 20**
   Oh! to see his tartan trews, Bonnet blue, and
      laigh-heeled s. **COS 28**
   so, please your noble Grace, we make our
      shoois **COS 22**
   throwing back their hairy hooves till their
      bright s. caught the sunlight **ANI 14**
shoon: Gude ale gars me . . . pawn my s. **FOO 2**
   laith. laith, were our gude Scots lords To wat
      their cork-heeled s. **COS 2**
   Their s. were of the straitis **COS 1**
shopkeepers: nation of s. **ADV 123**
   nation whose government is influenced by s.
      PHIL 54
shopocracy: I cannot sit still . . . and hear you
   abuse the s. **COM 14**
shore: Alang the s. The greinan white sea-owsen
   ramp and roar **SEA 23**
   I heard it talkin', whisperin', upon the weedy
      s. **SEA 16**
   in May-time you shall hear the cuckoo from
      the one s. to the other **PLA 51**
   Lord Ullin reached the fatal s. **LOVE 39**
   My native Clyde, thy once romantic s. **COM 4**
   O that the peats would cut themselves, The
      fish jump on the s. **THO 5**
shoulders: jersey haps her shouthers **COS 5**
   Thrid part lenth in shouldris braid was he
      PER 131
show business: s.b. . . . magical world in which
   two and two can make five, but also three
   TEL 7
shower: amidst the flying s. and broken
   moonlight, the wraith of a rainbow **SWW 53**
   Through the hushed air the whitening s.
      descends **SWW 64**
   To a s. of gold, most things are penetrable
      ADV 43
showers: There'll be shoors, lang-tailed shoors,
   an' rain a' 'tween **SWW 13**

showery: In the north, on a s. day, you can *see*
   the rain **SWW 15**
showman: s. who . . . bit off their heads **ACT 4**
shrouds: I am washing the s. of the fair men
   LAM 1
shuttle: Sae nimbly as my s. flees **DAI 50**
siccar: auld ways are s. **ADV 141**
   I mak s. **MOTT 11**
sick: S. and sore I am, worn and weary **COS 40**
sickness: And to thy s. sall be na recure **CUR 18**
   Decay of language is always the symptom of a
      more serious s. **WORD 8**
   You stand convicted of s., hunger,
      wretchedness, and want **LAW 31**
Siddons, Sarah: when the great actress, Mrs S.
   first appeared in Edinburgh **REL 100**
sigh: She look'd down to blush and she look'd up
   to s. **LOVE 77**
   slumps with a world-rejecting s. **ANI 58**
sighed: S. and looked unutterable things
   MOM 50
sight: And their candillis gangis frae your sicht
   CUR 17
   Anis on a day I seemed a seemly sicht **LAM 44**
   sae accustom'd wi' the s., The view o't gies
      them little fright **DAI 9**
   saddest s. that fortune's inequality exhibits
      DAI 15
   something about me that interests most
      people at first s. **PER 51**
   then, O what a glorious s., Warm-reekin',
      rich! **FOO 29**
   Things out of s. do straight forgotten die
      ADV 9
   usewall Method . . . to get a transient S. of
      this otherwise invisible Crew **FANT 40**
   You can tell the folk at breakfast, as they
      watch the fearsome sicht **FES 11**
silence: cruellest lies are often told in s. **BAD 15**
   I can na mair my silence hald But mon put
      furth my mind **PLA 95**
   In the s. and the darkness . . . Listen to the
      little children **MOM 1**
   My words go through the smoking air,
      Changing their tune on s. **SWW 37**
   Of noise alone is born the inward sense Of s.
      THO 76
   one has music and the flying cloud, The other,
      s. and the wakeful stars **REL 114**
   paradoxically the s. was song **MOU 32**
   Poetry is a river that deepens into s. **POET 65**
   s., awful, deep, and long **MOM 41**
   S. is deep as Eternity; speech is as shallow as
      time **WORD 16**
   S. is in the air: The stars move to their places
      SWW 59
   S. is, perhaps, the greatest hallelujah
      PLEAS 14
   S. is the element in which great things fashion
      themselves together **THO 27**
   There was s. deep as death **MOM 12**
   To stand . . . receptive to the influences of . . .
      sound and s. **MOM 21**

silent: all the s. birds that sit In this snow-
travelled wood MOM 54

Ballads are a voice from . . . s. peoples
POET 36

Her s. watch the mournful mother keeps
CHI 13

S. and serene the stars move to their places
SWW 59

s. hosannas of the sun, the stars, the trees and
the flowers PLEAS 14

You have talked unsparingly of Scotland, and
had better have kept s. INS 66

silk: brave s. knickers that Mrs Colquhoun wore
COS 30

siller: I will twine thee a bow'r By the clear s.
fountain LOVE 85

Land on my luif an' bring S. tae me ANI 8

Mealie was his s. M-W 15

Na Kindness at Court Without S. ADV 93

There's gowd in the breast o' the primrose
pale, And s. in every blossom NAT 12

There's . . . the sang o' a s. bell intil't
FANT 62

silver: across the glistening lowlands Slant the
moonbeams' s. bars MOM 1

And fill it in a s. tassie FOO 21

Finn saw the flashing s. of the salmon ANG 5

s. scalit fishes ANG 3

swinging A s. slaver from each chin ANI 56

sin: Bible says the wages of s. is death and the Act
says thirty shillin's REL 24

appearance is only s.. deep ADV 106

English players . . . come down to fill up our
cup of s. ACT 14

I daurna think on Jamie, for that wad be a s.
M-W 86

I fear I have nothing original in me,
Excepting original s. REL 33

It is for our s. that . . . ruin now enters in
LAM 4

lowest and vilest alleys . . . do not present a
more dreadful record of s. LAND 22

might live in s. as much as you pleased but
were damned . . . if you hadn't a white sark
PLA 128

nane will their awin s. confess HUM 11

nicest boy who ever committed the s. of
whisky PER 234

paused . . . in the belief that I had committed
the unforgivable s. BAD 14

sinner: Detested, shunn'd by saint and s. ANI 22

yet the huge bulk of s. Said there was neither
spirit nor matter PER 38

sinners: heedless s. shall be damn'd, Unless they
mend their ways TRA 8

My children . . . loves me and fears me as s.
dread death CHI 52

sire: Be all the sons as senseless as the s. CUR 14

Quick came the reply . . . 'The breadth of this
table, S.' INS 39

Bright ran thy line, o Galloway, Thro' many a
far-fam'd s. INS 15

O hush thee, my babie, thy s. was a knight
CHI 39

s. turns o'er, wi' patriarchal grace, The big
ha'-Bible REL 28

sister: my s. gathered my banes FANT 14

Still gentler, s. woman ADV 28

sisters: two officers . . . transgressed with two
s. REL 31

we spill the beans and we swill our gin, and
discover we're S. under the Skin M-W 88

skellie: Tho' his richt e'e doth s. LOVE 16

skellum: She tauld thee weel thou wast a s.
INS 19

skelp: monie a s. o' triple-tonguit tawse EDU 18

prays to God to give him strength To s. the
bairns on Monday EDU 1

Whene'er I forgather wi' Sorrow and Care,
I gie them a s. as they're creepin alang
THO 23

sketch: When he has made a s. . . . . He then walks
about looking for a person proper to be a model
ART 12

when I did my fireman s. ACT 11

skian dhu: My claymore and my dirk and s.d.
COS 43

skies: Now skaills the skyis: The night is neir
gone SWW 48

With mystie vapouris, cluddis and skyis,
Nature all curage me denyis SWW 29

But the s. there are not island s. SWW 2

Rugby . . . a game that all the gods of Greece
might crowd the northern s. to see SPOR 45

skill: It baffles a' skill To tether his gill ANG 14

skin: blind-worm's s. about her knee FANT 59

league between us written . . . in the flesh and
s. of men HIS 12

Gin ye hae catcht a drookit s., To Luckie
Middlemist's loup in FOO 50

It is rather nice, but dampish . . . one shrinks a
trifle under one's s. LAND 35

s. of a man of letters is peculiarly sensitive
BOO 61

sticking wet and dirty to the s., is not very
easily pulled off COS 14

Value your cause above your s. ADV 71

skirt: Ladies in walking generally carried the s.
of the gown COS 17

skua: It'll be the Bonxie, that noble Scua ANI 61

sky: everything created In the bounds of earth
and s. HUM 17

eyes of a cow shine . . . like moons in a misty
s. ANI 13

He formed this gnat who built the s. ANI 78

How our . . . eyes reveled in the . . . glories of
the hills and the s. SWW 50

keen diffusive s., Breathing the soul acute
LAND 60

lark descendis from the skyis hycht SWW 26

Live ourselves and see our friends cold
beneath the s. WAR 59

'Look, the peaks of Arran,' . . . a low dark
smudge against a pale patch of s. MOU 20

Machines of death from east to west Drone through the darkened s. **WAR 88**

My tea is nearly ready and the sun has left the s. **MOM 49**

northern wind had purifyit the air, And shed the misty cloudis fra the s. **SWW 41**

rectangular blocks . . . rise . . . against the s. **UNI 10**

Sea and s. and the folk who wrought . . . lasted but as a breath **LAND 27**

sea below still as deep as the s. above **PLA 121**

Soay and Hirta and Boreray comb and rake the s. with their rugged fangs **SWW 35**

To stand . . . receptive to the influences of earth and s. **MOM 21**

travellers know How dull the shale s. is **THO 48**

Under the wide and starry s. Dig the grave, and let me lie **DEA 66**

Skye: I hae dreamed a dreary dream Beyond the Isle of S. **FANT 13**

If you are a delicate man . . . You had better not think of S. **PLA 127**

O great island, island of my love . . . great beautiful bird of S. **PLA 126**

Speed, bonnie boat, like a bird on the wing Over the sea to S. **PLA 125**

There was a snake that dwelt in S. **ANI 52**

To see Mr Samuel Johnson lying in Prince Charles's bed, in the Isle of S. **MOM 4**

slae: Its back was like the s. **FANT 53**

ye sing like the shuilfie in the s. **MUS 52**

slain: I can fecht and nae be s. **BOA 3**

'slaters': 's.', alias . . . wood-lice, were in constant request . . . to heal the scurvy **MIN 27**

slaughter: You will stand amidst the s. **CUR 6**

slave: hardest form of slavery is to serve as a s. in one's own native country **THO 46**

Sic a reptile was Wat, sic a miscreant s. **INS 18**

slaves: It is fit only for the s. who sold it **SPIR 22**

sleep: Art ye on sleip, quod she. O fye for shame! **LOVE 63**

grant us in the end the gift of s. **REL 121**

hand in hand we'll go, And s. thegither at the foot **M-W 43**

I . . . s. sounder lying on the ground than I used to do in the palaces of Rome **MIN 51**

thinking that anyone who would s. with him would s. with anybody **M-W 128**

that I in my bed could lie And s. for ever more **THO 5**

too sick tae s., too tired tae stay awake **MIN 55**

war and the pest will gar ye s. **DEA 37**

When you s. in your cloak there's no lodging to pay **ADV 140**

sleight: by some devilish cantrip s. **FANT 22**

cut you up wi' ready s. **FOO 29**

Sligachan: 'Where could I buy two pints of foaming shandy in shiny tankards?' 'S.' **MOU 46**

slogan: That day through high Dunedin's streets Had pealed the s.-cry **WAR 17**

slugs: houseless s., . . . Snails too lazy to build a shed **ANI 67**

slum: Remembering smoke and flowerless s. **FANT 52**

slumber: heavy on the s. of the moorland The hardship and poverty **LAND 41**

Red hand in the foray, How sound is thy s.! **LAM 54**

slums: I would welcome the end of . . . our history, our nationhood . . . if it could cleanse the Glasgow s. **POL 41**

Now is the yaird kail boiled and hashed While Muses feed in s. **POET 25**

sly: And gie the s. boy a surpriser **ANG 14**

small: sma' thing maks us stare **ADV 16**

states too much in trying to be s. **ADV 53**

smallpox: 'Yes, mem, I've had the sma'pox, the nirls, the blabs, the scaw' **MIN 41**

smart: This is s. stuff **FOO 75**

smeddum: He was a man of no s. in discourse **PER 111**

It needs s. to be either right coorse or right kind **ADV 69**

smell: s. of the sharn rising feuch! in her face **BOO 32**

We had some fun, haud awa' wi' the s. **PLEAS 1**

What a fine and heartsome s. has rank cow-dung **LAND 28**

what grand's the s. ye'll get Frae the neep-fields by the sea! **LAND 31**

You will not remember the salt s. of the sea **SWW 2**

smells: s. (known as the 'flowers of Edinburgh') filled the air **DAI 28**

smile: art thou sure that thou hast a right to s. at me? **MOM 13**

I saw, I saw that winsome s., The mouth that did my heart beguile **FANT 58**

nae s. was seen on Kilmeny's face **FANT 36**

they waste their toil For the vain tribute of a s. **POET 56**

when they s., I . . . guard myself against mischief **PPL 51**

With a s. on her lips and a tear in her eye **LOVE 77**

smiles: True humour . . . issues not in laughter, but in still s. **HUMO 4**

smiling: children . . . Should always have a s. face **CHI 41**

I've seen the s. of Fortune beguiling **LAM 24**

Like pensive beauty, s. in her tears **THO 25**

s. anxiety That rules a house where a child is about to be born **FAMI 25**

Smith, Adam: A.S. saying that half the people standing one day at the Cross of Edinburgh were mad **MIN 38**

Johnson no sooner saw S. than he attacked him **INS 86**

smoke: habit of regulating the time of evening worship by the appearance of the s. of Edinburgh **PLA 38**

in the depest pot of hell He smorit thame with
smuke **INS 33**

one's but smoake, the other is but wind
THO 10

Remembering s. and flowerless slum
FANT 52

s. of the village chimneys is rising into the sky
MOM 45

That awful loneliness Received our souls as
air receives the s. **MOU 42**

wilfully corrupted by this stinking s. **BAD 7**

smout: wee s. of a callant **CHI 32**

snail: Scho met thar . . . Ane ask rydand on a
s. **FANT 25**

snails: slugs . . . s. too lazy to build a shed **ANI 67**

snake: There was a s. that dwelt in Skye **ANI 52**
deathless names by this dead s. defiled **BIO 13**

snow: And climbed thy steep summit, oh
Morven of s.! **LOVE 38**

As the chill s, is friendly to the earth **MIN 36**

Frae my tap-knot to my tae, John, I'm like the
new-fa'n s. **M-W 50**

God of moorland walks abroad with . . . his
bodyguard of s. **SWW 44**

Her brow is like the snaw-drift **LOVE 42**

Her straight bare legs that whiter were than
snaw **COS 52**

Let dorty dames . . . Seem caulder than the
snaw **M-W 105**

One door shuts out the s. and storm **BUI 15**

rain may rain and the snaw may snaw **WAR 13**

she shall bloom in winter's s., Ere we two
meet again **LAM 53**

simple tune, with quiet flow, To match the
falling of the s. **SWW 38**

s. shall be their winding-sheet **LAM 23**

subtle curves of the wind-blown s. **MOU 14**

twinkling Earn, like a blade in the s. **RIV 9**

Ye're shairly no expectin' snaw? **ANI 15**

snowy: s. vesture beautiful came flowing o'er her
feet **BATH 3**

Soay: S. and Hirta and Boreray comb and rake
the sky with their rugged fangs **SWW 35**

Soays: S. do not bunch together **ANI 45**

sober: Few go away s. at any time **FOO 34**
No laws, however stringent, can make . . . the
drunken s. **LAW 30**

soccer: s. fan attending his first Rugby
international **SPOR 48**

Social Security: bus station concourse is like a
S.S. office turned inside out **TRA 49**

socialism: queer ending for the apostle of 's. in
our time' **POL 18**
S.? These days? There's the tree that never
grew **POL 34**

socialist: I am a scientific s. **BOA 9**

society: Every man proper for a member of
this S., must have a frank, honest, open heart
M-W 37
hypocrisy, in moderation is . . . a concession
to s. **ADV 22**
kings and ministers . . . greatest spendthrifts
in s. **PHIL 57**

little s. is necessary to show a man his failings
PPL 94

No s. can surely be flourishing . . . of which
the far greater part of the members are poor
and miserable **PHIL 53**

only way we can then be useful to s. **DEA 40**

persons living in a loose and unreformed state
of s. **PPL 56**

precious articles of our national belief not
to be given up without . . . sapping the
foundations of s. **HIS 27**

principle would be laid down, inconsistent
with the well-being of s. **PHIL 12**

security of every s. must always depend . . .
upon the martial spirit of . . . the people
WAR 83

so powerful a principle that it is . . . capable of
carrying on the s. to wealth and prosperity
PHIL 55

S., the mud wherein we stand Up to the eyes
PPL 30

Thus does s. normally divide itself into four
classes **M-W 59**

socks: His socks compelled one's attention
COS 53

soil: Among the Highlanders . . . to rob was
thought at least as honourable . . . as to cultivate
the s. **HIGH 23**
before the first savages set foot upon the s.
of Scotland the first urban . . . community
had been flourishing . . . for more than a
thousand years **HIS 33**
clearing her sullen s. for a richer yield **EPI 20**
Eastern religions lose their finest strains when
transplanted out of their native s. **REL 48**
how happy is . . . that state which . . . neither
lends its children to the stranger nor calls a
foreign force on to its own s. **PPL 23**

soldier: every turf beneath their feet Shall be a
s.'s sepulchre **LAM 23**
No wonder I'm fond of a sodger laddie
WAR 28
sodger frae the wars returns **LOVE 66**
such was the wisdom . . . of that old, little,
crooked souldier **PER 31**
Weep no more, my s. laddie **WAR 16**

soldiers: nothing noo in the heids o' the gyurls
but sodgers **WAR 65**
sodgers'll blow ye up like the peelins o'
onions **POL 3**

solitude: God to man doth speak in s. **HIGH 6**
grand indifference of the great city . . . gave
one s. **ART 5**
They were a delightful set . . . merry even in
s. **PER 83**
To live in s., oh! be thy luck **INS 82**
waste away my sprightly body's bloom In
spouseless s. **M-W 122**

Solomon: gave over themselves to be guided . . .
as if he had been Great Solyman **PER 31**
what S. of modern days can answer that
CHI 11

Infidelity . . . a fearful blindness of the s.
M-W 62

It makes a man baith gash and bauld, And
heaves his saul beyond the moon FOO 105

keen diffusive sky, Breathing the s. acute
LAND 60

land he loved better than his s. or God
LAND 25

Land . . . where the finer Sensations of the S.
are not felt INS 89

No s. am I, a wave am I THO 82

not a cloud my eyes hath crossed But to my s.
is gone THO 75

Say not the will of man is free Within the
limits of his s. PHIL 37

s. of man is like the rolling world REL 114

Such a s. . . . was a chosen 'vessel of hell'
POET 14

what are the bens and glens but . . .
Immeasurable complexities of s.? HIGH 38

Whether thy s. Soars Fancy's flights ADV 35

While hard and fast I held her in my grips, My
very saul came louping to my lips LOVE 71

Would you like to see a city given over S. and
body to a tyrannising game? SPOR 61

ye saft Crazed outland skalrag saul PER 227

souls: Golden Wonder has entered into their s.
NAT 1

Hallowe'en . . . when the s. of the departed
were supposed to revisit DEA 32

is it as true that I have two s., which take
possession of my bodily frame by turns
MIN 30

Listen to the little children Praying God their
s. to keep MOM 1

mannikins scrieve oot their sauls Upon its
craw-steps BUI 31

one equality . . . will strenuously be taught –
the essential equality of human s. REL 40

s. of men that pave their hellward path With
women's s. M-W 64

That awful loneliness Received our s.
MOU 42

their saulis gang fra the visage of God
CUR 17

their s. ride on the wings of the wind
BATH 10

those poor s. who claim to own a cat ANI 84

warmth of tenderness and loving s. FAMI 25

sound: blessedest s. upon earth: The merry
merry shriek of the reel ANG 1

Souness, Graham: People say that the S.
revolution was responsible INS 98

soup: Oh Lord, heap blessings on the soup
SPOR 60

wee s. drink dis unco weel To haud the heart
aboon FOO 52

souple: s. jade she was, and strang M-W 43

Souter Johnnie: S.J., his ancient, trusty, drouthy
crony FRI 9

Southron: 'Thy deid sall be to S. full dear sauld'
LAM 29

southward: troop of Border riders . . . their faces
set s. BUI 14

sovereignty: Seventeen years of warding valour
In the s. of Alban LAM 17

Spaniards: For a moment the S. seemed taken by
surprise WAR 35

sparrow: pawky wee s. will peck off your floor
ANI 16

Spartans: race that was hard as the S., shall
return again to the charge BOA 11

spawn: S. was he in the steamy mire SCI 30

speak: S. out, and never fash your thumb
ADV 29

spectacle: as a s., the judging of the horses was
supreme ANI 14

speech: 'Deil ae word . . . did the English
understand of his s.' WORD 30

Great the blindness and the sinful
darkness . . . of those who teach, write and
foster the Gaelic s. WORD 19

His ready s. flowed fair and free, In phrase of
gentlest courtesy WORD 67

I covet the mystery of our Gaelic s.
WORD 48

I will pluck the yarrow . . . That more chaste
shall be my s. CUR 5

minister made a comic s. wi' jokes in't REL 94

never again will the old s. . . . rise but with
alien efforts to our lips THO 50

Silence is deep as Eternity; s. is as shallow as
Time WORD 16

'Tis the s. used in the Garden – Adam left it to
mankind WORD 49

we pay dem fur laernin' bairns English, no fur
unlearnin' wir Shetlan' s. WORD 68

woman, better of s., said That I should be let
in FES 4

spell: dawn of legibility in his handwriting has
revealed his utter inability to s. EDU 21

There's a s. intil't, and a well intil't FANT 62

spelling: regrettable thing about Gaelic is its
hopelessly bewildering s. WORD 39

spirit: Above all, it must be remembered that the
Scottish s. is brilliantly improvisatory SPIR 34

Can s. from the tomb . . . More hateful . . . be
than man? M-W 22

Cant! . . . enough to give a s. the guts-ache
BUR 13

dust returns to earth once more, and the s. to
God who gave it DEA 50

I am of that . . . class who never knew what it
was to be a child in s. PER 129

I go up this ladder with less fear . . . of s. than
ever I entered the pulpit REL 34

Nowhere, perhaps, has God been better
worshipped in s. REL 106

Scottish s. abhors standardisation SPIR 60

security of every society must always
depend . . . upon the martial s. of . . . the
people WAR 83

small nation has always been humanity's last
bulwark . . . for the quick freedom of the s.
SPIR 26

If their own extravagance does not ruin the s., that of their subjects never will **PHIL 57**

Most happy s., that never tak'st Revenge **HOP 9**

They loved this s.; it kept them warm **ADV 70**

to come wi' the news o' your ain defeat, And leave your men in sic a s. **WAR 82**

Toleration . . . renders diseases or distempers in the s. more strong . . . than any remedies **POL 9**

While quacks of S. must each produce his plan **M-W 45**

S. is never greater than when all its superfluous hands are employed in the service of the public **PHIL 21**

statistics: He clings to s. as a drunken man clings to a lamp-post **SCI 26**

stays: trying hard to reach them gars The lassies burst their s. **MUS 6**

steal: 'Sa lang as I may get gear to s., I never will wirk' **THO 4**

stealing: preached on s., right godly-like **BAD 5**

steam: as s. was an elastic body, it would rush into a vacuum **SCI 43**

dour age o' coal and s. **BUI 29**

even s., With all its powers, will . . . a trifle seem **FANT 51**

On the pinions of s. they shall fly **TRA 22**

steamer: asked when the s. would arrive **TRA 18**

steed: If doughty deeds my lady please, Right soon I'll mount my s. **LOVE 48**

Through all the wide Border his s. was the best **PER 214**

We lighted down to bait our s. **M-W 2**

steek: S. the awmrie **ADV 115**

step: to s. aside is human **ADV 28**

Stewart, Andy: This is the land God gave to A.S. **LAND 52**

Stewart, Dugald: D.S. . . . often forgotwhi . . . to return books **BOO 68**

Stewart, Sir James: Sir J.S., thou'lt hing in a string **INS 6**

sticks: as cross as two s. **ADV 117**

sting: s. of life is in its touch **FOO 121**

stipend: I take the s. due by right **REL 8**

stirks: They gang in s., and come out asses **UNI 3**

Stirling: he flew of the castel wall of Striveling **MOM 25**

two officers . . . had transgressed with two sisters at S. **REL 31**

stoat: Said the whitrick to the s., 'I see ye've on your winter coat' **ANI 15**

stockings: aiming vicious pecks at her legs . . . encased in thin silk s. **ANI 41**

coat, breeches and s. all knitted by his wife **COS 45**

Cursed be the king who stretched our s. **COS 40**

pitiful to think of you going about with great holes in your s. **COS 37**

They had folded their s. to make the most of the muscles of their legs **COS 39**

white or quaker-grey silk stockings **COS 19**

stoic: I may say, as the s. did to the gout **ANI 83**

stomach: I heard the cuckoo, with no food in my s. **THO 1**

must be employed but not indulged, like the . . . s. **HUM 14**

s. is the distinguishing point between an animal and a vegetable **MIN 31**

With a fearful oath, Boone clapped his hands to his outraged s. **SPOR 50**

stone (*see also* **stane**): Firm as a s., but of a heart contrite **EPI 13**

He who weeps for beauty gone Stoops to pick a flower of s. **ADV 130**

I do believe in s. and lime, a manse of large dimension **REL 8**

I turned a grey s. over: a hundred forky-tails seethed **ANI 19**

It is a s. land **LAND 46**

long swings the s. **SPOR 31**

On this s. . . . . Columba crowned Aidan king of Argyll **FANT 47**

Stone Age: S.A. baby confronts the twentieth-century mother **CHI 24**

Stonehaven: S. itself, the home of the poverty toffs **PLA 128**

story of crofter life near S. **BOO 29**

stones: Near and more near the sounding s. **SPOR 31**

s. that made walls become cairns **LAND 47**

stories: we get to thinking all the s. in the traditions belong to us personally **TEL 6**

storm: Gathering her brows like gathering s. **M-W 40**

He fell as the moon in a s. **LAM 39**

old story of those who prefer . . . s. to sunshine **FOO 82**

pure ethereal calm that knows no s. **PHIL 63**

rage and s. our welter and wally seas **SWW 27**

There is a s. coming that shall try your foundations **SPIR 48**

storms: Here's to the friends we can trust, when s. of adversity blaw **FRI 15**

S. are never counted among the resources of a country **SWW 52**

Though raging stormis movis us **SWW 7**

story: diary in which he means to write one s., and writes another **BIO 2**

I refused to learn how to be poor. That's my whole s. **DAI 31**

old s. of those who prefer . . . storm to sunshine **FOO 82**

stotter: I can hardly s. but and ben **FOO 32**

stout: And trembling too, am desperately s. **BATH 4**

Stowe, Harriet Beecher: on Love's eagle pinions borne, H.B.S.'s come **BATH 6**

strange: and pathetically waggle that s. head **ANI 30**

how s. was the sadness of Scotland's singing **MUS 31**

s. . . . . feeling that something as yet unknown was also within my grasp **MOU 32**

s. that any man of sense could have
  imagined . . . that above twenty thousand
  verses . . . could have been preserved by an
  oral tradition POET 32
S. things happen to a lone fisherman ANG 4
strangers: when s. come, and there is nought to
  offer THO 2
strath: May the herding of Columba . . .
  encompass you in s. and on ridge CUR 2
  whisper that draws a hill across a s. THO 38
Strathbogie: There's cauld kail in Aberdeen,
  And custocks in S. FOO 3
Strathnaver: The fires ye lit to gut S. PER 239
Strathspey: Lightly dance the glad S. MUS 77
Strathyre: nae greater luck that the heart could
  desire, Than to herd the fine cattle in bonnie
  S. PLA 129
straw: mak a strae wisp o' him to stap the mouth
  o'Hell REL 119
  'Tis but a cot roofed in with s. BUI 115
strawberry: Be my lips the sap of the s. CUR 5
stream: Across the silent s. Where the dream-
  shadows go FANT 44
  down thy s., Unsightly brick-lanes smoke
    COM 4
  fresher gale Begins to wave the wood and stir
    the s. SWW 63
  I feel wrong . . . like a timber broadside in a
    fast s. TRA 31
  Then to the s.-side, gladly we'll hie ANG 13
streams: O River Clyde . . . Thy s. are wonder
  strang RIV 2
  Rosa . . . one of the most pellucid s. in Britain
    RIV 13
  Ourthwart clear streamis ANG 3
  Time but th' impression stronger makes, As s.
    their channels deeper wear TIM 8
street: mourners pass along the s. DEA 50
  See our s.? FAMI 36
  With lantern and with ladder he comes
    posting up the s. MOM 49
streets: Are my poems spoken . . . In the s. o' the
  toon? POET 39
  Care in the Community policies, which threw
    these unfortunates on to the s. INS 98
  Drive thro' the s. wi' unca stear, To bid some
    chiel A gude new year FES 11
  grafted the debased Scots of the Edinburgh s.
    onto their native Yiddish WORD 21
  I bless the Academy I found in Glasgow s.
    ART 5
  if a person called *Cady!* in any of the principal
    streets BIO 9
  many a Gael . . . smothers now in urban s.
    HIGH 28
  That day through high Dunedin's s. Had
    pealed the slogan-cry WAR 17
  world is a city full of s. EPI 3
strength: fierceness of its disposition, its s. . . .
  are well-known ANI 35
  In Saxon s. that abbey frowned BUI 26
  monument o' s. and grace Til the dour age o'
    coal and steam BUI 29

prays to God to give him s., To skelp the
  bairns on Monday EDU 1
stress: This has ever been my system in times
  of s. ADV 54
strike: law . . . can either say 'It's against the law
  to go on s.' . . . or it can say 'But then there will
  be no-one left to build ships' LAW 17
Stromness: S. . . . a cosmopolitan, sophisticated
  little port PLA 130
strong: s. have fainted in the race for life
  LAM 37
  Though the way be long, let your heart be s.
    ADV 82
struggle: man, in much of his s. with the
  world . . . has fought blindly LAND 24
  s. to escape being the last done with the
    shearing FANT 24
  their s. would be the central feature in the
    history books . . . for centuries POL 107
Stuart: Nor had we known a *S.* here CUR 9
  S. blood is in my veins BOA 23
students: discipline . . . not for the benefit of the
  s. UNI 12
  s. . . . have become incomparably more docile
    UNI 6
stupid: 'Dinna be sae bluidy s.,' says the king
  ADV 126
  s. way to earn a living DAI 43
  They strike me as s., dirty, ignorant and
    barbarous HIGH 4
  Ye s. auld bitch M-W 31
style: our s. smells of the lamp and we are slaves
  of the language WORD 3
  S. . . . is the immortal thing in literature
    BOO 60
  s. Of the great *Odyssey* is what Gaelic knows
    WORD 70
  They belong to no s. of art, only to a form of
    business BUI 33
subject: professors . . . admit that I am far better
  read even in their own particular s. BOA 10
sublime: good herrin . . . It's a fush that's chust
  s. FOO 99
  'sale's a s. thing' DAI 41
  Whaur hae they writ them mair s. Than on
    yon gable-ends o' time? BUI 31
success: Alban was brimful from his day . . .
  With pride, with s., with elegance PER 43
  failure, s., what is it? Whae gies a fuck
    PHIL 66
  If your programme is to achieve artistic s.
    ART 22
  secret of my s. over the four hundred
    metres . . . with God's help, I run faster
    SPOR 42
  S. the ploughman's wages crown DAI 5
succour: Gae seek you s. where ye paid blackmail
  ADV 6
suffering: S. is the professor's golden garment
  REL 107
sugar: him and his wife stayed up of a night
  sanding the s. BAD 5

If someone burst a s. bag, the lot would die of fright **POL 5**

suicide: If s. be supposed a crime **DEA 40**

he committed s. twenty-five years after his death **PER 41**

judge has sentenced himself to a s.'s grave? **LAW 21**

Suilven: frieze of mountains, filed on the blue air **MOU 23**

S. . . . a mountain huger than itself **MOU 48**

Suilven: S. is a floating extension of Ullapool's chip-strewn littoral **FOO 41**

Sultana: bonny wee S., The bully of the Clyde **TRA 4**

summer: He would return, even as the cuckoo comes, Only with s. **EPI 28**

high grasslands on a s. day have an idyllic quality **MOU 17**

It fell on a day, and a bonnie simmer day **WAR 8**

lanely I stray, in the calm simmer gloamin' **PER 242**

There is nae mair to tell. S. is by **SWW 58**

When next the s. breeze comes by **CHI 40**

you may gather garlands there Would grace a s.'s queen **PLA 19**

summit: continually hoping that the next ridge before you will be the s. **MOU 12**

When I . . . climbed thy steep s., oh Morven of snow! **LOVE 38**

summits: rocky s., split and rent, Formed turret, dome or battlement **MOU 38**

summons: I have got s. already before a Superior Judge **DEA 57**

sun: Be my speech the beams of the s. **CUR 5**

Blows the wind today, and the s. and rain are flying **LAND 58**

bonny blue sky To welcome the bride, As she gangs to the kirk Wi' the s. on her side **SWW 6**

dark cloud came suddenly over the s. **LAW 26**

dominions, on which the s. never sets **ADV 98**

glory of the s. will be dimmed **LAM 16**

Gone is the s., come are the stars **MOM 31**

he gave the s. and the whole solar system only ninety million more years to live **PER 158**

He saw neither s. nor mune, But he heard the roarin' o' the sea **FANT 10**

Her face it is the fairest That e'er the s. shone on **LOVE 42**

Hope is like the s. **HOP 20**

How easily a small inconvenience can cover the s. **THO 117**

Is there any light quite like the June s. of the North and West? **SWW 24**

on a showery day, you can *see* the rain . . . while you stand a mile off in a patch of s. **SWW 15**

'It is HE who makes the s. shine' **CHI 10**

My tea is nearly ready and the s. has left the sky **MOM 49**

Once a week the s. shines **MOU 13**

rectangular blocks . . . rise . . . against the s. **UNI 10**

saddest sight that fortune's inequality exhibits under this s. **DAI 15**

shilpit s. is thin Like an auld man deein slow **SWW 43**

sleek s. flooding The broad abundant dying sprawl of the Dee **PLA 2**

s. is bright on heaven's brow **TIM 15**

When the s. has gone to rest, That's the time that I love best **PLEAS 11**

sun-dial: s.-d. was so aged It had gathered a thoughtful grace **TIM 20**

Sunday: as much ado about its east wind as he did about the Edinburgh S. **SWW 12**

But at least to begin the week well, We can all be unhappy on S. **SPIR 45**

group of miners stood in a ring every S. morning and they all looked up at the sky **SPOR 59**

Wha daur debait religion on a S.? **REL 54**

Sunday Post: when the last minister is strangled with the last copy of the *S.P.* **JOU 14**

sunbeam: sunbeam like an angel's sword Shivers upon a spire **MOM 51**

sunlight: As step I wi' the s. for my load **LAND 43**

waters of the Tilt gold and tawny in the s. **NAT 27**

yon crystal dancer birlin i the s. **HUM 16**

sunset: like trying to paint a s. in lamp-black **BOO 23**

'Tis the s. of life gives me mystical lore **YOU 7**

sunshine: Always there is a black spot in our s. **ADV 39**

old story of those who prefer . . . storm to s. **FOO 82**

three hours' s. in Scotland is worth three months' s. in Cairo **ART 4**

Twists thro' a glen of greenest gloom, and gropes For open s. **RIV 11**

sup: singit sheep's heid, and a haggis, And scadlips to s. till ye spue **FOO 120**

superiors: advantage of conversing freely with their s., the peasantry of no other European country enjoyed **HIGH 21**

superstition: Theirs all the grossness, all the s. Of a most gross and superstitious age **REL 111**

supreme: s. moment comes, and the fowl in a lordly dish is carried in **FOO 128**

Sure: S. and stedfast **MOTT 1**

surprise: But only, lest we gang to hell, It may be no s. **COM 3**

death mask . . . features are fixed in painful s. **PER 192**

For a moment the Spaniards seemed taken by s. **WAR 35**

Pictures there are that do not please With any sweet s. **ART 21**

soothed the offended pride of the Highlanders, by attributing Lady Juliana's agitation entirely to s. **MUS 28**

Land . . . where Genius is lost, and T. . . .
extinguished INS 89

to refine our t. . . . is scarce endeavoured in
any seminary of learning ART 18

tastes: they enshrined their t. in their sayings
ADV 70

They speak of faded t. of mine BOO 44

tattie-scones: T.-s., and the mealy-dot FOO 125

tattoos: a classy girl, though, at least all her t. are
spelt right M-W 100

tavern: Many a man who thinks to found a
home . . . has merely opened a tavern FAMI 11

taverns: eavesdropper, a common butt in the t.
of London INS 57

tawse: monie a skelp of triple-tonguit t. EDU 18

tax: have we not bought the Scots and a right to
t. them? POL 61

taxi: he'd come home by instinct, the poor man's
t. TRA 30

when I find myself in the company of singing
robes . . . I phone for a t. POET 44

Tay, River: Beautiful railway bridge of the
Silv'ry T. DEA 44

Stone-rolling T. RIV 10

This was the engine that had gone down with
the T. Bridge TRA 46

tea: Buttered toast and t., The yellow licht o' the
lamp MOM 16

ceilings are so low, all you can have for t. is
kippers BUI 18

He lived on nothing but gooseberry pie, For
breakfast, dinner and t. ANI 52

High t. in Aberdeen is like no other meal on
earth FOO 59

'honestest thing I ever saw said about t.'
FOO 101

I used to be asked if I had my morning
draught yet? I am now asked if I have had
my t.! FOO 91

Lord Kelly . . . and his brother . . . were
drinking t. with James Boswell WORD 52

level spoonful of t. for each person, and one
for the pot FOO 127

My t. is nearly ready and the sun has left the
sky MOM 49

Thon new t. room wi' the comic windows
ART 24

To give us a more than ordinary treat t. was
prepared for breakfast FOO 110

You don't even get a cup Of t. before you tidy
up M-W 109

teacher: born t. is not a problem EDU 31

good t. does not draw out EDU 32

tea chest: Operations were started by the
purchase of a t.c., an old hat box, some darning
needles SCI 1

teachers: Perhaps all t. should pour fine stuff
into children's ears EDU 20

team: Shankly . . . announced: 'The better t.
drew' SPOR 73

Sure, it's a grand old t. to play for SPOR 7

t. is currently struggling in Europe SPOR 63

ultimate Scottish international t. would be
SPOR 72

Who's the best t., you'd ask us . . . twisting
harder SPOR 78

tear: May the mouse never leave our meal-pock
wi' the t. in its eye TOA 2

t. down childhood's cheek that flows CHI 40

With a smile on her lips and a t. in her eye
LOVE 77

tears: Aidan . . . grew so sad that he began to
shed t. PER 42

body in subjection shedding t. REL 1

Dry up your t. and weep no more EPI 14

feel of the bag . . . is a gaiety lost . . . to press it
is to bring laughing or t. MUS 62

Like pensive beauty, smiling in her t. THO 25

thochts o' bygane years . . . blind my een wi'
t. THO 90

Thy distant music lulls and stills, And moves
to quiet t. MOM 24

With their shawls all pulled around them and
the salt t. running down SEA 3

woe awaits a country when She sees the t. of
bearded men LAM 52

teeth: He . . . has a beautiful set of false t. INS 29

I saw by his t. he was lauchin' at me ANG 10

Jenny wi' the airn t., Come and tak' the bairn!
CHI 6

shining like a negro's t. through the black
muir BUI 11

telephone: What more lovely than to be alone
With a Teasmade, a radio and a t. THO 69

television: decrepit Presbyterianism and
imperialist thuggery, who spirit may be
savoured by . . . a few evenings watching
Scottish t. POL 84

temperance: most perfect parody conceivable of
a t. speech MOM 7

tempest: mist of the t. that gather'd below
LOVE 38

Nor glow'ring daith wi' sudden t. mocked
DEA 55

'Tis the music of the t.'s song Leads on the
lifeboat crew SEA 22

temple: in this t. by the northern sea . . . Will
surge and seethe the fire-mist of the mind
BATH 16

temptation: confronted by t., he always followed
his own favorite suggestion, 'Why not, my
dear?' PER 110

t. . . . . to imagine he is a god. This is
particularly so in medicine MIN 10

tenants: In ancient times the t. of Lord
Breadalbane TOA 14

It becomes necessary, therefore, that a
number of small t. be removed PHIL 28

You would wonder at the change the little t.
have made . . . since they knew they are not
to be removed BUI 11

tenderness: warmth of t. and loving souls
FAMI 25

Teribus: T. ye teri odin, Sons of heroes slain at
Flodden WAR 5

Thomson, James (Seasons): contrived to force
T. into bed by . . . working on his terror for
ghosts **PER 174**
> *Oh! Jamey Thomson! Jamey Thomson, oh!*
> **POET 17**

Thomson, James ('B.V.'): It is really very
generous of Mr T. to consent to live at all
PER 16

thorn: Ayont the dyke, adist the t. **ANI 5**
> my fause lover staw my rose, But oh! he left
> the t. wi' me **LOVE 34**

thorns: glories of ancient Scotland . . . rising
sheer, not from . . . thickets of t. **BUI 9**
> our a muir, with thornis thick and sharp
> **FANT 33**
> ye peip like a mouse among thornes **INS 77**

thought: a' the dour provincial thocht That
merks the Scottish breed **PPL 60**
> contrite heart, a humble t., Are mine accepted
> sacrifice **THO 106**
> Delightful task! to rear the tender t. **EDU 40**
> Excess of thocht does me mischief **THO 42**
> he has . . . gift of compressing the largest
> amount of words into the smallest amount
> of t. **PER 81**
> hinted his uneasiness at the t. of becoming
> silly . . . or squalid **PER 206**
> If he lights upon a good t., he immediately
> drops it **POET 29**
> In every t., in every part, Made is he of a
> million slain **SCI 29**
> Never did I see such apparatus got ready for
> thinking, and so little t. **PER 76**
> put quite away All heaviness of thocht
> **THO 85**
> seen it as it were dissolve in t. and assume a
> new . . . beauty **NAT 9**
> So many Scots . . . have lapsed into the
> English habit of t. **SPIR 27**
> Style, after all, rather than t., is the immortal
> thing in literature **BOO 60**
> triumph of barbarity over taste, a gloomy and
> discouraging t. **BUI 16**
> Words are well adapted for . . . emotions, but
> for many kinds of precise t., other symbols
> are much better **WORD 35**
> words . . . so often grave obstacles to full
> honesty of t. **WORD 76**

thoughts: As I enter up my t. for the day on the
day following **DEA 64**
> cow . . . has long thoughts **ANI 13**
> Dwell her thochts whaur dwalt her een?
> **LOVE 50**
> Excuse for faitherin' Genius wi' *their* thochts
> **BUR 15**
> Far frae my hame I wander, but still my t.
> return **PPL 65**
> he had book-making so much in his t. **BOO 11**
> hundred forky-tails seethed . . . like t. out of
> an evil mind **ANI 19**
> leave their memories to resurrect it when they
> find their own t. inadequate **EDU 20**

thochts o' bygane years Still fling their
shadows ower my path **THO 90**

thrapple: but she keeps her t. bare **COS 5**

thrapples: 'time to sharp the maiden for
shearing o' craigs and t.' **HUM 12**

thread: Rowan tree and red t. Gar the witches
tine their speed **CUR 4**

throat: And cuts his t. behind his back! **BATH 1**
> To drink it at the source makes the t. tingle
> **FOO 121**

throne: verse may build a princely t. **BUR 26**

Thrums: ball of Kirriemuir has smashed The
window-pane of T. **POET 25**
> To his native T. He would return, even as the
> cuckoo comes **EPI 28**

thumb: never fash your t. **ADV 29**

thumbs: more the cobbler plies his trade, The
broader grow his t. **ADV 7**

thunder: lightning and the t., They go and they
come **MOM 30**
> running round the playground striking fire
> and t. **COS 36**
> t. crack'd and flauchts did rift Frae the black
> vizard o' the lift **SWW 55**
> When Carlyle's t. had been followed by his
> wife's sparkle **INS 84**

tide: But aye the mair he cried 'Annie,' The
braider grew the t. **LOVE 8**
> I have no playmate but the t. **FANT 45**
> Love swells like the Solway, but ebbs like its
> t. **LOVE 76**
> MacCrimmon would write down a tune on
> the wet sand as the t. began to ebb **MUS 33**
> Nae man can tether Time nor T. **TIM 6**
> This mony a year I've stood the flood an' t.
> **BUI 6**
> t. was dark and heavy with the burthen that
> it bore **SEA 16**
> vague wishless seaweed floating on a t.
> **SEA 26**
> Why weep ye by the t., ladye? **LOVE 9**

Tighnabruaich: Look at T.! . . . they'll bite their
way through corrugated iron **ANI 80**

Tillicoultry: T. hills is fair **PLA 103**

Tilt, River: waters of the T. gold and tawny in
the sunlight **NAT 27**

time: always a bore being ahead of one's t.
ADV 94
> At a t. when personal peculiarity was widely
> affected by Edinburgh people **MIN 19**
> betuix Sanct Markis Day and Lammess . . . is
> the tyme of the quhelpis **ANI 12**
> By this t. there should have turned up . . .
> some voice expressing the search for
> Scottish renewal **POL 36**
> distracted subject in a distracted t. **PER 25**
> doing the will of God, leaves me no t. for
> disputing about His plans **REL 84**
> end of the world is near when the
> MacBrayne's ship will be on t. **TRA 40**
> gin they arena deid, it's t. they were **INS 42**
> Gow and t. are even now **EPI 12**

Falkland sampled it with nose and t. FOO 55

glowered, t.-tackit, at the stars That lauched
in Jeanie's face YOU 9

guid auld honest mither t.! WORD 37

He himself had obtained perfect command of
the Scottish t. WORD 4

He's a warm Scotch heart, and a braid Scotch
t. PER 34

his land – was . . . to go to a man of another
race and another t. SPIR 43

'I sall hauld my t., For an we fecht, I'll get the
waur' M-W 12

'I will promise to hold my t. if you will make
fools hold theirs' WORD 44

My sharp t. will shrivel any man M-W 87

Our loves, our native land, our mother t.
THO 32

sae saft a voice and slid a t. WORD 63

Scotish Idiom of the British T. is more fit for
Pleading WORD 51

Seven years a t. to the warnin' bell DEA 3

Since word is thrall, and thought is free, Keep
well thy t., I counsel thee WORD 40

sing to me the auld Scotch sangs, In the braid
Scottish t. MUS 1

Society's design was . . . learn the people the
English t. WORD 20

traitor t., doubtless WORD 57

My trechour tung hes tane ane heland strynd
WORD 57

western sea alone can speak in the Gaelic t.
SEA 20

wyte Why of Virgillis verse the ornate beauty
Intill our t. may not observit be WORD 23

tongues: hard t. o' grannies aa deid an gaun
THO 63

tonic: It is the finest . . . t. a man can take
MOU 14

tonight: T. is the hard night of Hogmanay FES 4

T.'s the night – if the lads are the lads WAR 63

toon: Are my poems spoken . . . In the streets o'
the t.? POET 39

Dear old Glasgow t. PLA 63

This braw, hie-heapit toun PLA 46

When Aberdeen and Ayr are baith ae toun
M-W 4

Ye daurna swear aboot the t. BAD 1

top: They that ettle to get to the t. of the ladder
ADV 110

Tories: In the old days of the T. we sould be
standing about, talking POL 68

It is lawful – to kill T. or open murderers
REL 113

Scottish T. are an extreme case of necrophilia
POL 46

T. may think they are better born POL 21

torrent: To gaze on the t. that thunder'd beneath
LOVE 38

Tory: Let Whig and T. all agree . . . To spend the
night wi' mirth and glee POL 96

political principles, whether Whig or T.
COS 12

touch: great bulls mellow to the t. ANI 63

He either fears his fate too much . . . That
puts it not unto the t. BOA 13

sting of life is in its t. FOO 121

tough: nae problem is owre teuch COS 27

tourists: bewildered crowds of t. sway up and
down TRA 14

tower: His name was a t. PER 87

towers: woods and the glens, from the t. which
we see CHI 39

town: east coast t. with a west-coast
temperament PLA 27

Ere she see the Earl o' Moray Come soundin'
thro' the toun DEA 5

fine, bright, self-confident little t. PLA 9

Great news there's come to t.; I have not got
the particulars yet BATH 15

Highland T. is composed of a few Huts BUI 7

It was a kind of cowboy t., but I liked that
aspect PLA 26

Old tales . . . Obscure this t. PLA 119

sea-gray t., the stane-grey sea PLA 120

This grey t. That pipes the morning up before
the lark PLA 74

t. is at present agog with the ploughman-poet
BUR 6

t. with guts – you see some on the pavement
PLA 69

Yon the toast of a' the t. LOVE 30

town-council: Within this Pandemonium sat
the t.-c., omnipotent, corrupt, impenetrable
POL 27

town-planning: T.-p. is not mere place-planning
PHIL 15

townspeople: questionable indeed if the t. have
any real personal identity DAI 27

toys: I will make you brooches and t. for your
delight LOVE 83

trade: He saved our country, and advanced our
t. POL 1

I am a fiddler to my t. MUS 13

I'm a piper to my t. MUS 73

more the cobbler plies his t. ADV 7

these are the Titans of toil and t. DAI 39

two enterprising ladies who, during the war
years, drove a thriving t. TRA 47

trades: Of all the t. that I do ken, The beggin' is
the best DAI 2

tradition: I see the stream of t. rapidly lessening
HIS 28

Listening to the oral t. of the wind LAND 14

People of Scotland . . . are the inheritors . . . of
an historic t. of liberty POL 6

Phantom was begotten by . . . an impudent
Highlander upon a cloud of t. POET 71

sentimentality . . . has done very little to give
us any . . . pride in t. HIS 35

strange that any man of sense could have
imagined . . . that above twenty thousand
verses . . . could have been preserved by an
oral t. POET 32

These songs had floated down on the stream
of oral t. MUS 37

James Hutton, that t. son of fire **PER 189**

me and my t. love will never meet again
  MUS 5

not t. that woman was made from man's rib
  M-W 25

she seemed in a mortal body . . . a t. goddess
  PER 55

Their hearts and swords are metal t. **WAR 30**

They are a song in the blood of all t. men
  WAR 52

Thou must be t. thyself If thou the truth
  would'st teach **PHIL 5**

t. university these days is a collection of books
  UNI 4

We will not get t. independence in a oner
  POL 67

trumpet: I'll sing thine obsequies with t. sounds
  LAM 45

  Sound, sound the t. **FAM 10**

  You shall have The Black Rock of Kiltearn
    For . . . t. of your resurrection **PLA 88**

trust: T. in God, and do the right **REL 88**

truth: both bodies have been about equally
  hostile to t. **REL 58**

  cold rage seizes one at whiles To show the
    bitter old and wrinkled t. **THO 131**

  Every person of importance ought to write
    his own memoirs, provided he has honesty
    enough to tell the t. **BOO 62**

  great t. that property changes from one to
    another **THO 18**

  he meekly enquired of us, 'Have I told the t.?'
    PER 181

  he was so much prejudiced that he took no
    pains to determine the t. **PER 148**

  I cannot tell how the t. may be; I tell the tale
    as 'twas said to me **PHIL 48**

  I was glad to hear the t., which I never
    doubted . . . that Scotland was bought and
    sold **POL 61**

  In manly words he stated solemn t. **EPI 26**

  In t., I rather take it thou hast got . . . much
    sense about thy lot **ANI 28**

  in t. well named the country of lost causes
    LAND 57

  It is of Inglis natioune The common kind
    conditioune Of Trewis the wertu to forget
    INS 100

  lie so obvious it was another way of telling the
    t. **BAD 9**

  one was always afraid of going beyond the t.
    and the other of not reaching it **SCI 38**

  open t. And fiery vehemence of youth **YOU 24**

  regard for t. formed no part of his character
    PHIL 39

  Say no Treuth **PER 8**

  They gang in stirks, and come out asses, Plain
    t. to speak **UNI 3**

  Thou must be true thyself, If thou the t.
    would'st teach **PHIL 5**

  to approximate as closely to the t. as to image
    the Prime Mover as a Levantine Semite
    PLA 40

T. in spirit, not t. to letter, is the true veracity
  THO 120

t. is, if you're to gae up Benledi, you maun
  mak up your mind to do'd **MOU 45**

t. is. my friends, you might as weel expect to
  see my red coo climb the muckle pear tree
  REL 51

T. profits none but those who use it well
  THO 15

T. will stand when a' thin's failin' **ADV 97**

unfortunate . . . that so few enthusiasts can be
  trusted to speak the t. **THO 11**

verse may build a princely throne On humble
  t. **BUR 26**

We all know that Prime Ministers are wedded
  to the t. **BAD 13**

whatever remains, however improbable, must
  be the t. **SCI 10**

truths: commonplaces are the great poetic t.
  THO 124

  Whose t. electrify the sage **BUR 3**

Tully, Charlie: T. produced a complimentary
  admission ticket **SPOR 9**

Tuath de Danann: vain and misleading tales . . .
  of the TdeD. **WORD 19**

Tummel, River: Cam' ye by Atholl . . . Down by
  the T.? **MUS 38**

tune: *fonn*, land, earth, delight, and a t. in music
  WORD 48

  MacCrimmon would write down a t. on the
    wet sand **MUS 33**

  My luve is like a melody, That's sweetly play'd
    in t. **LOVE 27**

  My words go through the smoking air,
    Changing their t. on silence **SWW 37**

  simple t., with quiet flow, To match the falling
    of the snow **SWW 38**

tunes: Must we be thirled to the past? . . . Sham t.
  and a sham feeling **SPIR 41**

  my hostess . . . began with the utmost gravity
    to play on it the most atrocious t. **MUS 24**

turd: Can ye nocht mak a Hielandman of this
  horse t.? **PPL 1**

  man does well to rid himself of a t. **INS 38**

turf: every t. beneath their feet, Shall be a
  soldier's sepulchre! **LAM 23**

turn: virtuous to do a sheep a good t. **ADV 47**

turnip: 'It was delightful to see the two of them
  rioting over a boiled t.' **PER 86**

turnips (*see also* **neeps**): In a french field of t. or
  radishes I'll lie **POET 68**

Tweed, River: Annan, T. and Clyde Rise aa oot
  o' ane hillside **RIV 1**

  bonnie T.! **RIV 15**

  majestic scene . . . where the T., Clyde and
    Annan rise in one hill **MOM 6**

  See how they press to cross the T. **PPL 5**

  that line . . . can be read on a stone at
    Coldstream bridge midway across the T.
    WAR 45

  To the westward is T.'s well . . . where the first
    fountain of silvery T. rises **RIV 12**

V

vacant: V. heart, and hand, and eye THO 105

vacuum: as steam was an elastic body, it would rush into a v. SCI 43

You can't paint from a v. ART 3

vain: generous prayer is never presented in v. REL 120

in the v. imagination that they were veritable copies from life ART 16

pray to God as though all work were in v. REL 123

V. are all things when death comes to your door DEA 45

We waste far mair now, like v. fulis ADV 92

valet: all men, except one, and he was a v. PER 194

overheard Rosebery's v. say . . . 'Your grouse is done to a turn' POL 102

valiant: Mightier was the verse of Iain . . . Than the claymore of the v. EPI 2

valour: for the art of war and the v. of his body, Robert then had no peer PER 53

Seventeen years of warding v. LAM 17

vanities: an empty balloon, to carry him off to the limbo of v. COM 12

vanity: Herein is not only a great v. BAD 7

Thy power and thy warldis pelf Is nocht but very vanitie ADV 73

poet, whose v. was at least equal to his genius POET 59

V. dies hard ADV 132

vassal: calling the King bot Goddis sillie v. MOM 33

vassalage: Thus we reel From v. to v. POL 17

vegetable: Before his arrival, Scotland's history had been purely v. HIS 37

musty v. dampness about these stairways BUI 4

vegetarians: Of course the v. have an answer, but how valid is it? FOO 9

veins: Open all my V., that I may swim To Thee HOP 13

vengeance: Rhynie loons wore tackety boots with a v. COS 36

V. to God alone belongs THO 102

Venice: sea Runnes all the streets throughout PLA 133

Silent, powerful, submissive . . . they might have been sitting in V. POL 27

venom: gathered the venome as it dropped FANT 15

Venus: V. in a green silk goun THO 70

verdict: that bastard v., *Not proven* LAW 29

When our ashes are scattered by the winds of heaven . . . future times will rejudge your v. POL 83

verse: And, spite of the insulting foe, My sympathising v. shall flow SPIR 55

he has never in v. addressed anything to the immortal part of man POET 70

I am not a poet . . . But I will sing a v. or two POET 1

I pored over them . . . v. by v. POET 6

Mightier was the v. of Iain EPI 2

Of all my v., like not a single line POET 66

of Virgillis v. the ornate beauty WORD 23

This be the v. ye grave for me EPI 30

unfortunate for the Scottish ballads that so many who collected . . . were able to write creditable v. POET 69

vessel: Such a soul . . . was a chosen 'v. of hell' POET 14

vessels: thundering on boilers of steam v. which are to bridge the Atlantic THO 84

viable: question . . . not whether an independent Scotland would be v., but whether it would be bearable POL 75

vice: Argument to the Scot is a v. more attractive than whisky BAD 3

'I've only got one v., but it's given me more pleasure' FOO 79

restriction placed on v. . . . makes its pursuit so peculiarly agreeable BAD 6

Their notions of virtue and v., are very different HIGH 3

v. and obscenity fearfully propagated BOO 75

Who, with an Inflexible Constancy . . . Persisted . . . In the Practice of Every Human V. INS 11

Whoredom her trade, and v. her end PER 103

vices: Does the man who applauds . . . all the v. of his children . . . take the best way of loving? CHI 30

Victorian: servants' bedrooms in V. villas are the only ones with bars on the windows BUI 30

victory: But och tis sair begrutten pride, And wersh the wine o' victorie! WAR 84

grave has no v., for it never fights DEA 52

I would rather be remembered by a song than by a v. PER 224

In doubtsome v. they dealt WAR 3

'Now we despair of v., since our leader is become so effeminate' BOA 4

V. belongs to those who hold out the longest WAR 40

view: sae accustom'd wi' the sight, The v. o't gies them little fright DAI 9

'Tis distance lends enchantment to the v. THO 24

vile: doubly dying, shall go down To the v. dust from whence he sprung PER 216

'We are all but v. worms' POL 53

villa: Day by day, one new v., one new object of offence BUI 33

I will . . . go to Inverness, And a small v. rent there PLA 80

village: Dunino – where no v. is PLA 34

In a Scotch v. . . . there is no sense whatsoever of obedience to authority SPIR 29

In this v. people travel only once LAND 44

smoke of the v. chimneys is rising into the sky MOM 45

villain: good triumphs and the v. bites the dust. If anyone believes this THO 47

W

wantonness: W. for evermair, W. has been my ruin M-W 52

war: Birds . . . made love and made w. ere the making of Man ANI 53

for the art of w. . . . Robert then had no peer PER 53

In peace and w. he suffered overmuch EPI 29

in their prides and lusts they have sent us to w. POL 56

On fut sould be all Scottis weir WAR 38

only war that is worth waging is the Class W. WAR 60

There is no such thing as an inevitable w. WAR 24

Though I began and took the w. on hand LAM 29

two enterprising ladies who, during the w. years, drove a thriving trade TRA 47

w. and the pest will gar ye sleep DEA 37

When was a w. not a w.? WAR 34

waresouns: All the malesouns and w. that ever gat warldlie creature CUR 17

wark: Sleep an' let me to my w. CHI 6

Thay taik delyt in nedill w. COS 3

They winna want the wark o' the weavers DAI 49

w. gangs bonnily on REL 44

warks: We cam' na here to view your w. COM 3

warld: bands and bliss o' mutual love, O! that's the chiefest w.'s treasure LOVE 37

I think the w. is a' gane wrang, When ilka wife her man wad rule M-W 14

I vow to God, that has the w. in wauld LAM 29

It . . . wrapped itsel the w. around Til ilka rock did wail FANT 53

'just a w.'s wonder wi' the sweevil' ANG 6

ne'er will be peace, till the w. again Has learned to sing . . . We're John Tamson's bairns PPL 81

poet . . . spoke of himself as one of 'the w.'s wonders' POET 59

Quo Daith, the w. is mine DEA 37

This warl's a tap-room owre and owre THO 128

this wretched w. of sorrow ADV 62

thy warldis pelf Is nocht but very vanitie ADV 73

'w.'s room – let them beg through life' FAMI 3

weel-jointed masonwark, that will stand as lang as the w. BUI 27

warlike: If the human species fails . . . it will be because of its w. qualities ADV 49

warlock: disease 'laid upon him by a westland w.' MIN 25

'He's just a . . . w. wi' the worm' ANG 6

warm: How w. the tints of Life BUR 25

I hope you have got w. drawers COS 37

Nursing her wrath to keep it w. M-W 40

'to paint well it is necessary to have w. feet' ART 7

warrior: 'A w. . . . should not care for wine or luxury' WAR 93

warriors: Prince of w., Oscur my son! LAM 38

stern joy which w. feel In foemen worthy of their steel WAR 76

wars: I am a son of mars who have been in many w. WAR 27

warst: 'Blow your w., ye wind and rain' M-W 121

w. o' them might ha' been his queen M-W 2

washing: She never fails to hang out a bonny white w. PER 151

What worship is there not in mere w.! DAI 16

waste: light of the world . . . in its dark pilgrimage through the w. of Time BOO 21

We waste far mair now ADV 92

Wat o' the Cleuch: that dark reckless Borderer, W.o't.C. PER 140

water: across a w. not so wide but that in May-time you shall hear the cuckoo from the one shore to the other PLA 51

All day long I heard the w. talk RIV 16

Bluid is thicker than w. ADV 109

He would play a tune to the seals, and they would all pop their heads out of the w. ANI 100

his eyes . . . like deep pools of clear w. PER 86

I have seen his pen gang as fast ower the paper, as ever it did ower the w. when it was in the grey goose's wing BOO 55

It lay motionless on the w., a long oval shape MONS 10

just trying to push w. uphill POL 95

King ower the W. TOA 5

little girl pointed out a black thing in the w. and asked if it was a rock MONS 7

malts are best drunk with a little w. FOO 62

moaning and pleading for w. which could not assuage his thirst WAR 72

Naething but a perfect waste o' watter RIV 5

pursued in w., they never . . . fail to make stylish triangles ANI 59

put his net into the clear fresh w. . . . and landed from it a sea-trout M-W 75

reaching far out, the w. past his knees ANG 5

Riveris ran reid on spate with w. broun SWW 27

shape of large size moving . . . at the edge of deep w. MONS 14

sustaining the shock of thunderous w. PLA 54

They drank the w. clear, Instead of wine FOO 65

To seek het w. beneith cauld ice, Surely it is a great folie LAM 9

twenty pints o' splitter-splatter, twenty pints was waur nor w. FOO 93

Wan w. from the border hills MOM 24

w. from the granite is cold FOO 121

water closet: And hear, mid reverent Nature's hush, The w.c.'s frequent flush BUI 34

water-kelpie: bonny grey mare she swat for fear, For she heard the w.-k. roaring MONS 1

Waterloo: On W.'s ensanguined plain Lie tens of thousands of the slain POET 26

Watt, James: In the Outer Islands, W.'s machine is unknown TRA 23

his characters all want soaking in . . .
disinfectant for a w. **BOO 51**
Once a w. the sun shines **MOU 13**
weeks: had ye staid hale w. awa', Your wives they
ne'er had missed ye **EPI 16**
I saw it before my eyes in the dark and in
daylight for w. **DEA 20**
weel: smirkin' up his muckle gub, Thocht, 'Man,
I'm lookin' w.' **ANI 92**
weep: Don't you weep, my bonny lasses, though
you be left behind **SEA 3**
Dry up your tears and w. mo more **EPI 4**
I weip as I were woful, but wel is me for ever
M-W 68
My Muse 'gan w. **COS 13**
W. no more, my soldier laddie **WAR 16**
Why w. ye by the tide, ladye? **LOVE 9**
weight: I' the back end o' the year, When the
clouds hang laigh wi' the weicht o' their greetin'
SWW 42
thrust a knife into the carcase, for that
keeps the fairies from laying their w. on it
FANT 27
Weir, Isabel: 'I., . . . you have got a good man,
but you will not enjoy him long' **FANT 20**
weird: having done some w. and wonderful work
to my inside **MIN 39**
'I was the youngest, And aye my w. it was the
hardest' **LAM 6**
wild geese, wi' w. uneirdly cry **ANI 89**
welcome: bonny blue sky, To welcome the bride
SWW 6
could the good-man and the good-wife deny
to the spirits of their dead the w. which they
gave to the cows? **DEA 32**
I would welcome the end of . . . our
nationhood . . . if it could cleanse the
Glasgow slums **POL 41**
If the Honourable Member would like to be
returned . . . to the Calton Jail, he is quite w.
to do so **POL 42**
W. eild, for youth is gone **YOU 1**
well: scho wanderit and yeid by to ane elriche w.
FANT 25
wench: This here was for a w., and that other in
a trench **WAR 27**
west: 'Congo's no' to be compared wi' the W. o'
Scotland when ye come to insects' **ANI 80**
From the dim blue hill of Dream I have heard
the W. Wind blow **FANT 44**
Is there any light quite the June sun of the
North and W.? **SWW 24**
Of a' the airts the wind can blow, I dearly like
the w. **SWW 16**
O young Lochinvar is come out of the W.
PER 214
Scotland is bounded . . . on the W. by Eternity
LAND 51
twining worm cam out the wast **FANT 53**
Unhook the W. Port, and let us gae free
BOA 16
w. is broken into bars Of orange, gold and
gray **MOM 31**

Where are the folk like the folk of the W.?
PPL 79
West Bow: Up the Lawnmarket And doun the
W.B. **LAW 1**
West Coast: east coast town with a w.c.
temperament **PLA 27**
I am not sure whether Scotland (especially the
W.C.) is not the finest country in the world
LAND 33
west-coaster: no-one looks so disdainfully now
on the w.-c. as the east-coaster who has lost . . .
his Gaelic **HIGH 5**
Western Isles: Except the W.I. alone, And they
are all MacBrayne's **TRA 3**
that is why some folk make pilgrimage to the
W.I. of Scotland **HIGH 30**
westerns: first w. with Greenockian-type people
TEL 15
Westray: brave lads of Westra are bound to the
Haaf **SEA 25**
'O ye people of W. . . . mony a day since
ye wad hae putten her in the parritch pot!'
REL 101
wet: Be it wind, be it weet, be it hail, be it sleet
SWW 4
Scotland was like a w. pebble **ART 4**
This ought to a warning to all Young people
to take care of W. feet **FOO 54**
'thu'll no be a wacht o' weet' **SWW 13**
was embraced in his cold, w. arms with such
affection **DEA 21**
w. sheet and a flowing sea **SEA 7**
With flashing white fetlocks all w. with the
dew **MOM 35**
whale: bonnie ship the *Diamond* Goes a-fishing
for the w. **SEA 3**
wheatear: I saw the w. on a dike of holes **THO 1**
wheel: 'jump out, clever, and put that stone under
the back w.' **TRA 39**
underneath the wheele saw I there An ugly pit
FANT 39
wheels: I watch the w. of Nature's mazy plan
TIM 11
whelps: betuix Sanct Merkis Day and
Lammess . . . is the tyme of the quhelpis
ANI 12
cow brought forth fourteen great dog w.
FANT 23
Whig: Let W. and Tory all agree . . . To spend
the night wi' mirth and glee **POL 96**
political principles, whether W. or Tory
COS 12
whigmaleeries: nane o' yere w. and
curliewurlies **BUI 27**
whin: I saw upon a lanely w., A lanely singin'
gowk! **ANI 91**
whins: Driving their ba's frae w. or tee
PLEAS 13
w. are blythesome on the knowe **NAT 21**
whisky: A little wh-wh-whisky? **FOO 13**
Burns . . . neither so nourishing as porridge,
or stimulating as w. **BUR 11**

coggie o' yill and a pickle aitmeal, And a dainty wee drappie o' w. **FOO 122**

five hundred grey parrots who were set up . . . to cry 'Drink Pattison's W.' **COM 18**

Love makes the world go round? . . . W. makes it go round twice as fast **FOO 88**

nicest boy who ever committed the sin of w. **PER 234**

old joke about the Highlander liking two things to be naked, one of them w. **FOO 62**

proper drinking of Scotch w. is more than indulgence **FOO 44**

Scots invented golf, it's said, And also good malt w. **SPOR 2**

sharp tang of so many Scottish things; of w., especially **MOM 5**

vice more attractive than w. **BAD 3**

We went to the Cottage and took some w. **BUR 13**

W. can't be a remedy **FOO 126**

w. was invented by the Irish as an embrocation for sick mules **FOO 43**

whisper: w. that draws a hill across a strath **THO 38**

whistle: Nae a blackbird nor a mavis . . . Was a marrow to the w. that the wee herd made **MUS 63**

O w. and I'll come to you, my lad **LOVE 35**

w. o'er the lave o't **ADV 36**

White : Poor W. **EPI 8**

Whitewater, River: water in bright snowflakes scatter On boulders of the dark W. **RIV 16**

whitrick: Said the w. to the stoat, 'I see ye've on your winter coat' **ANI 15**

whittle: Kilmaurs w. can cut an inch afore the point **PLA 87**

whore: Mr — , in the Kyle, Ca'd me a common — **M-W 102**

Scarlet W. indeed, they snarl at, But like right well a w. in scarlet **M-W 104**

We call her nott a hoore . . . but sche was brought up in the company of hooremongaris **PER 154**

whunstane: grand, w. sense **ADV 137**

Wick: W. is . . . meanest of men's towns **PLA 134**

wickedness: approached as nearly to the ideal standard of perfect w. **PER 176**

great men sayis that their distress Comis for the peoples w. **HUM 11**

widow: not a maid, wife or w. whose fancy any man . . . could not conquer **M-W 65**

'sair blow to the w.' **FAMI 17**

Now I am a wedow, I wise and weill am at ese **M-W 68**

wife: And he has gotten a gentle w. **DAI 3**

At supper my w. and I had a dispute **M-W 29**

auld w. sat ayont her man, But nae auld carle saw she **YOU 9**

Bischop wald not wed ane wyfe **REL 128**

crouching vassal to a tyrant w. **CUR 11**

each gentleman brought a pint of wine to be drunk by him and his w. **FOO 102**

false dissaitful dispite . . . contenit in a w. **M-W 1**

'Gif ye'll not wed a tocherless w., A w. will ne'er wed ye' **M-W 5**

good w., a good cow, and a good razor **ADV 8**

had he not good reason for stabbing a w. who was unfaithful to him? **M-W 97**

He had a w., as sweir's himsel' **FAMI 5**

he pleaded hard to be left in the house till his w. was well **LAND 13**

him and his w. stayed up . . . sanding the sugar **BAD 5**

How mony lengthen'd, sage advices The husband frae the w. despises! **M-W 41**

'I beg your pardon, mem, I mistook ye for my w.' **M-W 31**

'I couldna afford a w.,' the Tar always maintained **M-W 99**

I think the warld is a' gane wrang, When ilka w. her man wad rule **M-W 14**

I wrote to my w., 'I have seen something very promising indeed' **MIN 44**

I'll do my best a gude w. aye to be, For Auld Robin Gray he is kind unto me **M-W 86**

Lissy, I am out looking for a w. **M-W 32**

My w. lies here conveniently **EPI 5**

My w. she drinks posset and wine o' Canary **M-W 23**

next to nae w., the best thing is a gude w. **M-W 13**

not a maid, w.. or widow whose fancy any man . . . could not conquer **M-W 65**

Poetry's my second w. **POET 45**

She is a winsome wee thing . . . This dear wee w. o' mine **LOVE 25**

She's a puir auld w. wi' little to give **SPIR 10**

then to all the world he'll tell, There ne'er was such a w. **FOO 6**

When Carlyle's thunder had been followed by his w.'s sparkle **INS 84**

When you have got a w. to please **M-W 72**

w. . . . . cannot compare, except to her disadvantage **ANI 32**

w. smiles, and lets it go at that **M-W 26**

Yet it's a hartsome thing to be a w. **CHI 36**

wifie: I'm a wee, wee w. . . . but I grip on well **PER 220**

There's a wee w. waitin' In a wee but-and-ben **FOO 94**

w. wha's bakin' a pie **ADV 138**

wig: had lost his hair and wore a w. about which he was sensitive **PER 113**

wisp-headed scowler, without hat or w. **INS 65**

wight: fine fat fodgel w. **PER 63**

gin ye ca' me seelie wicht, I'll be your friend both day and nicht **FANT 16**

He was a w. of high degree And knew how many beans make five **THO 37**

little, upright, pert, tart, tripping w. **PER 60**

Thou wants the w. that never said thee nay **LAM 44**

wights: then will he see a Multitude of W., like furious hardie Men **FANT 40**

Wigtown: Content he was with portion small, Keeped shop in W., and that's all **EPI 7**

wilderness: Bird of the w., Blithesome and cumberless **ANI 50**

In God's w. lies the hope of the world **HOP 14**

we prefer . . . the howling w. to the amenities of civilisation **PPL 59**

Wilkie, Sir David: Among the Letters of Introduction that W. brought to London **ART 8**

will: comprehended at last how the whole world of w. was doomed to eternal anguish **PHIL 33**

doing the w. of God leaves me no time for disputing about His plans **REL 84**

Gi'es but the weapons, we've the will **WAR 66**

I will govern according to the common weal, but not . . . the common w. **POL 54**

It has no purpose, heart or mind or w. **THO 132**

Say not the w. of man is free **PHIL 37**

William: May W., the son of George, be as a leafless, splintered tree **CUR 25**

Williamson, Rev. David: testicles of **INS 5**

win: That puts it not unto the touch, To w., or lose it all **BOA 13**

wind: Above the reach of wild ambition's w. **PHIL 63**

And the w. blew the bonnie lassie's plaidie awa' **M-W 108**

Be it w., be it weet, be it hail, be it sleet, Our ship maun sail the faem **SWW 4**

'Blow your warst, ye w. and rain' **M-W 121**

Blows the w. today, and the sun and the rain are flying **LAND 58**

Cold is the w. over Islay, That blows upon them in Kintyre **SWW 40**

For the writer, the w. bloweth where it listeth **BOO 13**

From the dim blue Hill of Dream I have heard the West W. blow **FANT 44**

hard out steif, Afoir the w. **SEA 2**

hint o' hairst . . . When the win' blows cauld, and the burns grow bauld **SWW 9**

I hear the little children of the w. **SWW 46**

lift grew dark, and the w. blew loud, And gurly grew the sea **SWW 5**

Listening to the oral tradition of the w. **LAND 14**

Mournfully, oh mournfully, The midnight w. doth sigh **SWW 49**

naething but me an' the w. abroad **PLA 92**

northern w. had purifyit the air **SWW 41**

Of a' the airts the w. can blow, I dearly like the west **SWW 16**

O'er his white banes . . . The w. sall blaw for evermair **DEA 2**

She flowed through fences like a piece of black w. **ANI 57**

So in Scotland witches used to raise the w. **FANT 26**

their souls ride on the wings of the w. **BATH 10**

There came a w. oot of the North, A sharp w. and a snell **FANT 17**

There's . . . health in the wild w.'s bosom **NAT 12**

very w. that wafts us towards the port May dash us on the shelves **ADV 116**

West w. to the bairn When ga'an for its name **SWW 6**

wet sheet and a flowing sea, A w. that follows fast **SEA 7**

What care we for w. or weather? **SEA 21**

Who grasped at earthly fame Grasped w. **FAM 9**

win' blaws oot o' Orkney A winter month or twa **SWW 21**

w. may blaw, the cock may craw **WAR 13**

w., that grand old harper, smote His thunder-harp of pines **SWW 57**

'You will wait for me, said the w.' **SWW 1**

window: always Scotland outside the w. **TRA 19**

But it is the other w. I turn to, with a pain at my heart **MOM 2**

literary critics . . . recall . . . a couple of hedgehogs courting beneath one's w. **BOO 48**

if they . . . blooter yir windae in wi the baw **BOA 14**

It's time to take the w. to see Leerie going by **MOM 49**

no chimneys, hardly a w. **HIGH 4**

On w.-sill and door-post . . . Embroidery of hoar-frost Was sown **SWW 25**

one w. greets the day **BUI 15**

There was no chimney and often no w. **BUI 10**

Tirling at the w., crying at the lock **CHI 31**

windows: servants' bedrooms . . . are the only ones with bars on the w. **BUI 30**

Thon new tea-room wi' the comic w. **ART 24**

winds: And about and over me Winds and clouds for ever going **EPI 21**

And bleak December's w. ensuin' **SWW 19**

curlew calls me where the salt w. blow **ANI 33**

more than birds on the hill tonight, And more than w. on the plain! **WAR 69**

When our ashes are scattered by the w. of heaven . . . future times will rejudge your verdict **POL 83**

windy: These w. spaces Are surely my own **LAND 29**

wine: can still rise into some glow of brotherhood over food and w. **FOO 37**

Claret wyn is helesum til all complexioun **FOO 64**

each gentleman brought a pint of w. to be drunk by him and his wife **FOO 102**

Glass of w. is a glorious creature **FOO 116**

Go fetch to me a pint o' w. **FOO 21**

He . . . had a genial partiality for the w. of his native land **PER 113**

It was thought sottish and rude to take w. without this **TOA 13**

king sits in Dunfermline toun, Drinking the bluid-red w. **TRA 1**

My wife she drinks posset and w. o' Canary M-W 23

O are ye come to drink the w., As ye hae doon before, O? WAR 6

'warrior . . . should not care for w. or luxury' WAR 93

wines: How beit we want the spicis and the winis FOO 78

wing: he prefers to fly around on one w. PER 36

Hope springs exulting on triumphant w. HOP 4

I have seen his pen gang as fast . . . as ever it did . . in the grey goose's w. BOO 55

Speed, bonnie boat, like a bird on the w. PLA 125

wings: could only flutter piteously its little flippers of w. ANI 30

lang, lang skein o' beatin' w. ANI 51

This Abbott tuik in hand to fly with wingis MOM 25

their souls ride on the w. of the wind BATH 10

w. and eyes Stupendous in their beauty ANI 69

winsome: She is a w. wee thing LOVE 25

winter: And weary w. comin' fast SWW 20

before W. there will not be one sound Potatoe in all the Highlands FOO 7

'Gentlemen,' says he, 'you see a severe w. approaching' WAR 89

Good claret best keeps out the cauld, And drives away the w. FOO 105

in a w. campaign . . . gave orders for rolling a snowball to lay under his head BOA 4

Lourd on my hert as w. lies The state that Scotland's in the day LAM 34

no fire in w. and would sit over their books wrapped in their plaid UNI 7

Noo that cauldrife w.'s here There's a pig in ilka bed SWW 54

On the meadow and the mountains Calmly shine the w. stars MOM 1

she shall bloom in w.'s snow, Ere we two meet again LAM 53

To cut the w. nicht and mak it short I took ane quair PLEAS 8

Wha ran barefitted in ragged claes, In summer days and w. BIO 3

win' blaws oot o' Orkney, a w. month or twa SWW 21

wished . . . she lived at a school, not tramping back in the spleiter of a w. night BOO 32

winters: 'besides, the w. here aren't w. . . . . The important thing is the underwear' SWW 11

cry of *Caller Laverocks* was always heard in severe w. FOO 90

gloom and depression of our Edinburgh w. PLA 47

So madness is but one of God's pale w. MIN 36

wireless: Curse . . . his w. set CUR 19

wisdom: doubts as to the w. of rooting out one pestiferous clan in order to 'plant in another little better' HIGH 31

If war comes it will be from failure of human w. WAR 24

nor have we sufficient w. to foresee . . . those ills with which we are constantly threatened PHIL 22

pleasure . . . in establishing to myself that name in the world for w. HOP 12

Practical w. is only to be learned in the school of experience DAI 51

self-control Is W.'s root ADV 35

such was the w. and authoritie of that old, little, crooked souldier PER 31

Then wit and w. fill the chasm LOVE 23

W. hath no sex M-W 28

within that bastard land, Hath w.'s goddess never held command LAND 12

wise: 'All the w. men in Glasgow come from the East' PLA 70

I have always considered him . . . as approximating as nearly to the idea of a perfectly w. and virtuous man, as . . . human frailty will permit PER 223

It takes a w. man to handle a lie BAD 2

Some deemed him wondrous w., and some believed him mad PER 39

Some folks are w., and some are otherwise ADV 127

We cam' na here to view your warks, In hopes to be mair w. COM 3

We may be w., or rich, or great, But never can be blest HUM 4

wonder is the key Of knowledge and of worship to the w. THO 16

wish: one has not a w. without enjoyment, the other has neither w. nor fear ANI 26

wit: dungeon of w. PER 177

He quietly creates his w. and jokes as if they were an unpermitted diversion HUMO 9

How could he compose a song, lacking . . . native w.? INS 67

I rail'd at Scots to show my wrath and w. SPIR 15

If one with w. the parent brood disgrace, Believe him bastard of a brighter race CUR 14

only glegest lugs are able . . . Tae wale a modicum o' w. WORD 71

Sin a' oor w. is in oor wame INS 91

Then w. and wisdom fill the chasm LOVE 23

Their only idea of w. . . . . is laughing immoderately at stated intervals HUMO 15

'What way hae ye sic a muckle, muckle heid?' 'Muckle w,. muckle w.' MONS 2

witch: Damn her, the old w., she has lived too long LAND 42

old woman, accused of being a w., was brought before him LAW 25

Scotch witch . . . was convicted of curing a certain Robert Kers MIN 25

When ilka w. her neebour greets On their
   nocturnal rambles FANT 43
witches: Faster than fairies, faster than w.
   TRA 42
   Lest w. should obtain the power Of Hawkie's
      milk CUR 3
   Rowan tree and red thread Gar the w. tine
      their speed CUR 4
   So in Scotland w. used to raise the wind
      FANT 26
Witt, Jacob de: no native artist could be found
   ART 15
wives: had ye staid hale weeks awa', Your w. they
   ne'er had missed ye EPI 16
   high mucky-mucks, famous fatheads, old w. of
      both sexes INS 62
   I wadna gie my three-girr'd cog For a' the w.
      in Bogie FOO 3
   Searching auld w.s' barrels. Ochon, the day!
      PER 64
   with publishers as with w. BOO 26
wizard: put his left Foot under the W.'s right
   Foot FANT 40
   wondrous Michael Scott, A W., of such
      dreaded fame PER 210
woe (*see also* **wae**): Chords that vibrate sweetest
   pleasure, Thrill the deepest notes of w. MUS 12
   Few are thy days and full of w. REL 22
   No scene of mortal life but teems with mortal
      w. THO 107
   North, where . . . man savage faith works w.
      REL 43
   Truly it might be said, 'W. to the folk of
      Scotland' LAM 3
   Were you to come near the Rough Bounds, w.
      to one in your case INS 66
   w. awaits a country when She sees the tears of
      bearded men LAM 52
   W. to the realm that has owre young a king
      LAM 33
   'Wrappit in w., ane wretch full of wane'
      LAM 32
wolf: he that slayis ane w. . . . . sall haif of ilk house
   halder . . . 1d ANI 12
   Next prowls the w., the filthy jackal last
      INS 22
   'There's the w.'s head' PER 92
wolves: it is ordainit for the destruccion of wolfis
   ANI 12
woman: All my life I have loved a womanly w.
   CHI 37
   Almighty . . . left some mighty queer kinks in
      w. M-W 63
   By God, I dout afore sic love appears, Nae
      man sall kiss a w.! SPIR 50
   Few are thy days and full of woe, O man of
      w. born REL 22
   guid weel-willie pintle! . . . Tree of life
      between Man and W. M-W 53
   He considered her assertion that it was
      written by a w. as 'nonsense' BOO 40
   Here lies a man a w. rul'd – The Devil rul'd
      the w. M-W 46

His Muse was born of w. BUR 10
it's the w.'s job to make the best of them
   M-W 66
just let me mention, The Rights of W. merit
   some attention M-W 45
Man thinks more, w. feels more M-W 69
neither reason nor force can hinder a w. from
   vengeance M-W 85
No w. bore . . . A king whose rule will be
   greater over Alban PER 45
nor any man whom any w. could not subdue if
   she chose M-W 65
not true that w. was made from man's rib
   M-W 25
O w.! in our hours of ease Uncertain, coy, and
   hard to please M-W 111
old bedridden w. . . . . Damn her . . . let her
   burn LAND 42
old w., accused of being a witch, was brought
   before him LAW 25
'old w.'s gone.' JOU 13
She is a little, quiet, feminine w. PER 89
She was a little w., of mild and genteel
   appearance MOM 4
Still gentler, sister w. ADV 28
that mim-moothed snivellin' fule, A
   fushionless w. M-W 103
There was a w. there . . . called me a big dirty
   Fenian bastard SPOR 36
They didn't like the idea of a w. doctor
   MIN 12
thing about a house without a w. FAMI 22
To promote a W. to beare rule . . . is
   repugnant to Nature M-W 84
two nights did that w. sleep in a sheep-cot,
   and on the third night she gave birth
   LAND 13
Voltaire asked why no w. had 'written even a
   tolerable tragedy' POET 10
wasn't a w. that betrayed Jesus M-W 61
w., better of speech, said That I should be let
   in FES 4
W.'s faith, and w.'s trust, Write the characters
   in dust M-W 112
Wumman's beauty gies man true content
   M-W 78
womankind: Scotland has . . . womankind not of
genius, but PE *character* M-W 101
womb: seed o' a' the men that in My virgin w.
ha'e met M-W 92
women: All w. know talent when they share a
bed with it M-W 60
   curious treachery there was in w. M-W 76
   daughter of a base and brainless breed Is given
      what countless better w. sorely need POL 63
   Do I like w.'s clothes more than their bodies?
      COS 34
   dressed himself entirely in w.'s clothes
      BOO 41
   great danger in giving voting power to w.
      POL 39
   I took a particular pleasure in the company of
      modest w. M-W 81

Though hundreds worship at his w. **FAMI 7**
voice expressing the search for Scottish
renewal. Not a word! **POL 36**
We're a' sae feared to speak our mind, As if a
w. our life wad bind **PPL 82**
w. . . . is short and quick, but works a long
result **WORD 5**
W. is to the kitchen gane, And w.is to the ha'
M-W 11

words: fishermen have always had taboos on
certain w. while at sea **WORD 32**
For the prevailing weather or w. Each object
hides in a metaphor **WORD 31**
he has . . . gift of compressing the largest
amount of w. into the smallest amount of
thought **PER 81**
I am fascinated and frightened by the power
and danger of w. **WORD 76**
it sounds sae sonorous that the w. droon the
ideas **WORD 38**
Most w. descend in value **WORD 9**
no greater impediment to the advancement
of knowledge than the ambiguity of w.
WORD 65
We've w. afouth, that we can ca' our ain
WORD 66
Wha haldis . . . of wordis the properteis,
Full oft the verity of the sentence fleeis
WORD 24
'What faith can we put in this "gentleman's"
w.?' **INS 10**
w. and weather both are cutting In
Causewayend **WORD 26**
W. are well adapted for . . . emotion, but
for many kinds of precise thought, other
symbols are much better **WORD 35**
W. of affection . . . latest spoken still are
deemed the best **WORD 1**

work (*see also* **wark**): Beis weill advisit my werk or
ye reprief **POET 19**
Business – the world's w. – is the sale of lies
DAI 19
fairly mak ye w. for your ten and nine **DAI 7**
first of all problems for a man is to find out
what kind of w. he is to do in this Universe
DAI 13
having done some weird and wonderful w. to
my inside **MIN 39**
I don't think the w. ethic is very strong
DAI 25
if you're being honest it comes through in
your w. **ART 3**
man willing to w., and unable to find w.
DAI 15
men are immortal till their w. is done **ADV 83**
Nothing is really w. unless you would rather
be doing something else **DAI 6**
only apology which this w. perhaps requires
BOO 30
Sa lang as I may get gear to steal, I never will
wirk **THO 4**
then she confessed that it was her own w.
BOO 40

w. and play! The order of the universe **DAI 20**
W., and wait, a sturdy liver **BATH 9**
W. as though w. alone thy end would gain, But
pray to God as though all w. were in vain
REL 123
'W., eh. What a stupid way to earn a living'
DAI 43
W. is a grand cure **DAI 14**
W. is the appointed calling of man on earth
DAI 53

worker: idle world will not let the w. alone . . .
but must insist on turning *him* inside out
BOO 53

workers: We know that the organised w. of the
country are our friends **POL 94**
w., slaves of the ring **DAI 27**

working class: Born into the . . . w.c., the new
King's most likely fate would have been that of
a street-corner loafer **PER 130**
no sense . . . that a w.c. man who has taken a
degree has got above himself **FAMI 14**
w.-c. is now the ruling class **POL 76**
'W.-c. Tenements!' Inspiring name! **HOM 2**

workman: trades . . . where . . . a w. can only get
better with time **BOO 13**

workmanship: every object . . . must have . . .
outstanding w. **ART 22**
strong, sure in w., and at rest **ART 17**

works: better described in physiological
textbooks than in all the w. of all the novelists
BOO 12
God made me, and knows best how to take
down His own w. **DEA 56**
he and his w. very soon settled down to the
position of being names and nothing more
PER 248
One is ashamed to be pleased with the w. of
one knows not whom **BOO 49**

world (*see also* **warld**): Above those passions that
this w. deform **PHIL 63**
Anywhere in the w. where there's a dying
language, the neighbours say the people are
lazy **WORD 59**
belief of a material w. is older . . . than any
principles of philosophy **PHIL 41**
'Beyond the Wild Wood comes the wide w.'
TRA 21
Books are a finer w. within the w. **BOO 59**
comprehended at last how the whole w. of will
was doomed to eternal anguish **PHIL 33**
either I shall offend God or else that I shall
displease the w. **REL 70**
end of the w. is near when the MacBrayne's
ship will be on time **TRA 40**
evil we do – alas! that the w. should love it
so **LAM 4**
Far from the clamorous w. **THO 40**
For the harmony of the w. is made manifest in
Form and Number **SCI 42**
Good humour and generosity carry the
day . . . all the w. over **HUM 13**
great and the good do not die even in this w.
BIO 12

twining w. cam out the wast **FANT** 53
wallidrag, the w., ane auld wobat carle **INS** 34
'warlock wi' the w.' **ANG** 6

worms: crying 'We are all but vile w.'; and yet
will judge . . . their king **POL** 53
w. ev'n damned him when laid in his grave
INS 18

worry: You can't w. too much about the future
ADV 46

worship: 'Let us w. God,' he says with solemn
air **REL** 28
one of the most unsuitable places of w., in the
Empire **BUI** 25
regulating the time of evening w. by the
appearance of the smoke of Edinburgh
PLA 38
Though hundreds w. at his word, He's but a
coof **FAMI** 7
What w. . . . is there not in mere washing!
DAI 16
wonder is the key Of knowledge and of w. to
the wise **THO** 16

worst: May the best ye've ever seen Be the w. ye
ever see **TOA** 1

worth: new men of w. are always appearing
THO 17

wound: I listened Without a w., accepting the
song I was given **YOU** 23
Sour Melancholy . . . provokes Her own
eternal w. **MIN** 4
to hide the w. that the silver bullet had made
PER 215

wounds: And write thine epitaph in blood and
w. **LAM** 45
licking of w. is second only to football as a
national sport **SPOR** 62

wrang: I think the warld is a' gane w., When ilka
wife her man wad rule **M-W** 14
she never ance thinks fat he daes can be w.
CHI 20
Tho' they may gang a kennin w. **ADV** 28

wrath: 'big fire that burns on the great day of
w.' **MUS** 29
I rail'd at Scots to show my w. and wit **SPIR** 15
indignant husband explained the reason for
his w. **M-W** 97
Lord Ullin reached the fatal shore, His w. was
changed to wailing **LOVE** 39
Nursing her w. to keep it warm **M-W** 40
O thresh him tightly with the flail of thy w.
REL 119

wraith: amidst the flying shower and broken
moonlight, the w. of a rainbow hanging frost-
white **SWW** 53
Ghost, kelpie, w., And all the trumpery of
vulgar faith **MONS** 9

wren: the w. is called 'the Lady of Heaven's hen'
ANI 39

wretch: Farewell, ye dungeons dark and strong,
The w.'s destinie! **LAM** 21
miserly w. never allows himself a candle **FRI** 8
poorest w. in life, The crouching vassal to a
tyrant wife! **CUR** 11

'Wrappit in woe, ane w. full of wane' **LAM** 32
w., concentred all in self, Living, shall forfeit
fair renown **PER** 217
W.! You cannot conceive what anxiety I am in
about you **LOVE** 40

wretched: Here lies . . . the most w. of men in the
whole kingdom **EPI** 27
most w. servile, miserable, pathetic trash
INS 97
This *coquetry* . . . of so w. a being was truly
ludicrous **M-W** 30
wavering of this wretchit warld of sorrow
ADV 62
what crowds in ev'ry land, All w. and forlorn
LAM 22

wretchedness: scene of w. which we
witnessed . . . was deplorable **LAM** 38
You stand convicted of sickness, hunger, w. ,
and want **LAW** 31

wretches: But surely poor folk maun be w.!
DAI 9

wrist: chopped off his left hand at the w. and
hurled it ashore **BOA** 7

write: W. and w. And read these stupid, worn-out
books! **BOO** 72

writer: For the w., the wind bloweth where it
listeth **BOO** 13

writers: All the men were writtaris that ever took
life **M-W** 1
first of a long series of Scottish w. . . . on terms
of an informal intimacy with God **BOO** 74
not the remotest reason why the majority of
modern Scottish w. should be considered
Scots at all **BOO** 33
Our principal w. have nearly all been
fortunate in escaping regular education
BOO 47
Scots are incapable of regarding their literary
geniuses purely as w. **BOO** 69

writing: craft of w. is in many ways a sad business
BOO 13
'I have four reasons for not w.: I am too old,
too fat, too lazy, and too rich' **BOO** 39

wrong (*see also* **wrang**): Alas! How easily things
go w.! **LAM** 35
canting moralist Who measures right and w.
PHIL 11
'humanity, right or w.!' **PER** 119
I must expect to be thought . . . a fellow of one
idea, and that idea w. **SCI** 25
If thy morals make thee dreary, depend upon
it they are w. **PHIL** 61
Instinct right, reflection w. **MUS** 48
It was several years before I discovered that he
was quite w. **M-W** 79
something *terribly* w. with the present
arrangements of the universe **BUR** 23
reading of novels is probably the most
effective training for . . . distinguishing
between right and w. **BOO** 1
we watched the w. Last too long **THO** 92
We weren't necessarily w. . . . just trying to
push water uphill **POL** 95

D.Y. . . . used to maintain . . . whisky was
invented by the Irish as an embrocation for
sick mules **FOO 43**

youth: All sorts of allowances are made for the
illusions of y. **YOU 25**

False dreams, false hopes, false masks and
modes of y. **THO 131**

'Hokey,' said the y. 'When ah'm in the
business, Ah'll have the times!' **DAI 21**

I wes in yowth on nureis knee Dandely,
Bischop, dandely **YOU 10**

It was a grim experience for y. **UNI 7**

Just at the age 'twixt boy and y. **CHI 38**

Let me now bid a cheerful adieu to my y.
YOU 8

middle age . . . had not quench'd the open
truth And fiery vehemence of y. **YOU 24**

mother and nurse for the y. and younglings of
Scotland **COM 13**

swordless Scotland . . . Fosters its sober y. on
national alms **SPIR 30**

our children are conscripts, and their y. does
nothing to alter the seriousness of this fact
EDU 14

Pleasant was the y. to me **PER 44**

showed my y. How verse may build a princely
throne **BUR 26**

Welcome eild, for youth is gone **YOU 1**

years . . . of Youth, a seeming length **YOU 6**

Y. having passed, there is nothing to lose but
memory **YOU 17**

Y. is y., and time will have it so **THO 66**

youthful: Ae day gie me o' y. life At the back o'
Benachie **TIM 2**

youths: plenty of other y. there, filled with zeal
UNI 2

Yule: fire that's blawn on Beltane een May weel
be black gin Y. **LOVE 64**

When merry Y.-day comes, I trow **FES 7**

Yuletide: So that's the way o' it! Y.'s comin'
FES 5

Z

Zarathustra: If there is anything that isn't clear I
refer you to the chronicles of Z. **PHIL 65**

zeal: community, for whose general good his
heart may glow with an ardent z. **PHIL 14**

dancing the Highland Fling, with such . . .
consuming z. **PLEAS 9**

I went to the Royal Technical College . . .
filled with z. **UNI 2**

We do that in our z. our calmer moments
would be afraid to answer **THO 104**

Whenever it was possible for the Scots to
stand in their own material light, they did so
with fanatic z. **HIS 18**

Zion: Those strains that once did sweet in Z.
glide **REL 28**

zones: z. of childhood through which we pass
CHI 34